LAW AND
THE LEGAL SYSTEM

ASPEN COLLEGE SERIES

LAW AND THE LEGAL SYSTEM

An Introduction to Law and Legal Studies in the United States

THIRD EDITION

THOMAS R. VAN DERVORT
DAVID L. HUDSON, JR.

Wolters Kluwer
Law & Business

Copyright © 2012 CCH Incorporated.

Published by Wolters Kluwer Law & Business in New York.

Wolters Kluwer Law & Business serves customers worldwide with CCH, Aspen Publishers, and Kluwer Law International products. (www.wolterskluwerlb.com)

To contact Customer Service, e-mail customer.service@wolterskluwer.com, call 1-800-234-1660, fax 1-800-901-9075, or mail correspondence to:

Wolters Kluwer Law & Business
Attn: Order Department
PO Box 990
Frederick, MD 21705

Printed in the United States of America.

1 2 3 4 5 6 7 8 9 0

ISBN 978-0-7355-0870-5

Library of Congress Cataloging-in-Publication Data

Van Dervort, Thomas R.
  Law and the legal system : an introduction to law and legal studies in the United States / Thomas R. van Dervort, David L. Hudson, Jr. — 3rd ed.
    p. cm. — (Aspen college series)
  Rev. ed. of : American law and the legal system : equal justice under the law / Thomas R. Van Dervort. 2nd ed. 2000.
  Includes index.
  ISBN 978-0-7355-0870-5 — ISBN 0-7355-0870-4 1. Law—United States. 2. Justice, Administration of—United States. 3. Procedure (Law)—United States. 4. Legal assistants—United States—Handbooks, manuals, etc. I. Hudson, David L., 1969- II. Van Dervort, Thomas R. American law and the legal system. III. Title.

  KF385.V36 2012
  349.73–dc23

                                                          2011048145

About Wolters Kluwer Law & Business

Wolters Kluwer Law & Business is a leading global provider of intelligent information and digital solutions for legal and business professionals in key specialty areas, and respected educational resources for professors and law students. Wolters Kluwer Law & Business connects legal and business professionals as well as those in the education market with timely, specialized authoritative content and information-enabled solutions to support success through productivity, accuracy and mobility.

Serving customers worldwide, Wolters Kluwer Law & Business products include those under the Aspen Publishers, CCH, Kluwer Law International, Loislaw, Best Case, ftwilliam.com, and MediRegs family of products.

CCH products have been a trusted resource since 1913 and are highly regarded resources for legal, securities, antitrust and trade regulation, government contracting, banking, pension, payroll, employment and labor, and healthcare reimbursement and compliance professionals.

Aspen Publishers products provide essential information to attorneys, business professionals, and law students. Written by preeminent authorities, the product line offers analytical and practical information in a range of specialty practice areas from securities law and intellectual property to mergers and acquisitions and pension/benefits. Aspen's trusted legal education resources provide professors and students with high-quality, up-to-date, and effective resources for successful instruction and study in all areas of the law.

Kluwer Law International products provide the global business community with reliable international legal information in English. Legal practitioners, corporate counsel, and business executives around the world rely on Kluwer Law journals, looseleafs, books, and electronic products for comprehensive information in many areas of international legal practice.

Loislaw is a comprehensive online legal research product providing legal content to law firm practitioners of various specializations. Loislaw provides attorneys with the ability to quickly and efficiently find the necessary legal information they need, when and where they need it, by facilitating access to primary law as well as state-specific law, records, forms, and treatises.

Best Case Solutions is the leading bankruptcy software product to the bankruptcy industry. It provides software and workflow tools to flawlessly streamline petition preparation and the electronic filing process, while timely incorporating ever-changing court requirements.

ftwilliam.com offers employee benefits professionals the highest quality plan documents (retirement, welfare, and non-qualified) and government forms (5500/PBGC, 1099 and IRS) software at highly competitive prices.

MediRegs products provide integrated healthcare compliance content and software solutions for professionals in healthcare, higher education and life sciences, including professionals in accounting, law, and consulting.

Wolters Kluwer Law & Business, a division of Wolters Kluwer, is headquartered in New York. Wolters Kluwer is a market-leading global information services company focused on professionals.

Contents

ABOUT THE AUTHORS

Thomas R. Van Dervort is professor emeritus of political science at Middle Tennessee State University where he has taught courses in law and the legal system for the past 40 years. He holds a doctorate degree from the University of Tennessee and has a background in legal studies and international law. Dr. Van Dervort obtained a master's degree from the Fletcher School of International Law and Diplomacy as a Woodrow Wilson scholar.

He is the author of two law-related introductory textbooks for American law and international law. He has served as pre-law advisor, mock trial coach, and member of the Board of Directors of the American Mock Trial Association.

Dr. Van Dervort's teaching philosophy is that students learn mostly by personal experience with the subject matter. Therefore, developing activities in and outside of the classroom to involve the student personally with the subject matter is most productive to the learning experience. Mock trial is one of the most productive motivational activities that contribute to learning and pursuit of law-related careers.

David L. Hudson, Jr. is a First Amendment Scholar with the First Amendment Center at Vanderbilt University. He also teaches classes at Vanderbilt Law School, Nashville School of Law, and Middle Tennessee State University. At MTSU, he teaches an introduction to law class and uses Dr. Van Dervort's text. For eight years, Hudson taught at a paralegal school teaching classes in legal research, advanced legal writing, torts, ethics, and employment law.

Hudson has authored more than 30 books, including *The Handy Supreme Court Answer Book* (Visible Ink Press, 2008); *The Rehnquist Court: Understanding Its Impact and Legacy* (Praeger, 2006); and *Let the Students Speak!: A History of the Fight for Free Expression in American Schools* (Beacon, 2011). He earned his undergraduate degree from Duke University and his law degree from Vanderbilt. He is convinced that this updated and revised textbook will enhance the learning experiences of his undergraduate students, paralegal students, and many high school students.

Preface

This undergraduate introduction to law and legal studies was first published in 1994 and has enjoyed considerable success throughout the United States. It has been thoroughly revised and updated in this new edition. This third edition provides several new chapters but retains the most unique features of the original text. Part I of the revised text has been thoroughly changed to add information on legal research, tort law, contract law, family law, employment law, and equal protection law.

Part I, *Gaining Familiarity with Basic Legal Concepts,* is designed to introduce sources of law to help students do legal research and find library resources. The addition of Internet sources and research assignments throughout the text are designed to provide initial exposure to where to find the detailed provisions of the law for particular jurisdictions. Review exercises are included in each chapter to aid students in enhancing their familiarity with legal terms and concepts. Initial familiarity with basic legal terms provides an essential orientation to law because it is necessary to know the appropriate term to use to search for detailed legal rules that may vary by jurisdiction.

The text begins with discussion of the expanding legal professions in the United States, including material of great interest to most undergraduate students who are beginning to think seriously about career choices. Students who take this course are considering careers in law-related professions and want a better understanding of what is involved, including what alternatives exist if they are unsuccessful in pursuing a law degree and becoming a professional lawyer. Ethical standards in these law-related fields, including teachers, law enforcement officers, paralegals, and lawyers, are emphasized in this first chapter.

This part of the text also explains the historical background of the ideas that have shaped our law. These fundamental concepts include common law, equity, natural law, positive law, and comparative concepts of jurisprudence. It also discusses the basic structure of our federal system and the constitutional divisions of authority between the states and the national government. This chapter also explains the complex questions of jurisdiction and the hierarchy of both federal and state courts.

It introduces the student to legal research and writing and explains the basic concepts of legal reasoning that will assist the beginning student in reading and understanding case law. Six illustrative cases are included in Appendix B in this text, offering practical examples of the major concepts included in the introductory four chapters of the revised text that compose Part I.

Part II, *Understanding Substantive Civil Law,* covers an introduction to property and contract law, tort law, family law, employment law, and equal protection law. These substantive areas are discussed, and basic principles of these areas of substantive law are explained.

Part III, *Understanding Civil Law Procedure,* is devoted mainly to an elaboration of the various aspects of civil due process of law and it develops a hypothetical case involving a products liability problem from inception through trial. The four chapters devoted to civil litigation in this section introduce basic concepts and documents used in civil litigation. The materials included in Appendix C supply witness statements that may be used to allow students to conduct a mock trial as a participatory exercise to enhance understanding of courtroom procedure.

Part IV, *Understanding Criminal Law Procedure,* develops another hypothetical case in criminal prosecution from the initial facts concerning the crime through the trial. The four chapters devoted to crimes and criminal due process illustrate the fundamental concepts involved in this field, including the pretrial process, plea bargaining, and what is involved in trials for capital offenses. Again, the major emphasis is on practical illustration of the basic terms and concepts involved in criminal prosecution.

Part V, *Understanding Administrative Due Process,* is devoted to explaining basic concepts of administrative due process, or fundamental due process of law. This area of law is of increasing importance in our highly regulated modern society. The differences between civil, criminal, and administrative due process are essential elements of this introductory text.

ACKNOWLEDGMENTS

The authors would like to thank our wives for being so patient with us through this revision and all those who contributed to this endeavor. Especially Steven Silverstein, who first recognized the potential for this revision with Aspen Publishers; David Herzig, acquisitions editor with Aspen; Elizabeth Kenny, developmental editor with Aspen; and Sylvia Rebert, project manager with Progressive Publishing Alternatives, who coordinated the editing.

GAINING FAMILIARITY WITH BASIC LEGAL CONCEPTS

Part I of this introduction to U.S. law and legal procedure provides beginning undergraduate students with an understanding of the expanding legal professions and ethical responsibilities expected of these professions, the origins of our basic concepts of law, the structure of our federal legal system, and the fundamental concepts of court jurisdiction and legal reasoning. These introductory chapters are designed to provide the necessary background for understanding more detailed concepts of substantive and procedural law that will follow in the remaining parts of the text.

The entire body of law in the United States is an impressive compilation of detailed rules covering 51 legal systems. Both the federal government and the 50 states have law-making authority, and they have produced such a mass of rules and regulations that even the most learned judges cannot claim mastery of it all. This complexity is augmented by thousands upon thousands of judicial decisions or opinions issued by different federal and state court judges or justices. The approach used in this introductory text is primarily one of helping students understand the fundamental principles and concepts used in modern legal practice.

Since the complexity of law demands that even judges and lawyers look up the precise rules that govern a given situation, the beginning student must learn the terminology that is used to reference these particular concepts. In this text, we attempt to draw attention to some key legal terms and provide an understanding of their general meaning. We also inform students how to find the detailed rules applicable in different jurisdictions. These key terms and concepts are identified by **boldface** type in the body of the text and are briefly explained in the marginal notes. We provide a glossary at the end of the text that references these terms and concepts by alphabetical index.

The first chapter in this section introduces students to the study of law by dealing with concerns about potential law-related careers. Students considering careers in the teaching profession, as law enforcement officers, as paralegals, legal assistants, or as lawyers, will find that this text offers a chance to consider what is involved in these law-related professions. The general undergraduate student will find this material valuable for providing a basic understanding of law and how it is applied in modern society. This chapter also deals with some of the fundamental ethical principles associated with these professions.

Chapter 2 is designed to provide students with the origin and characteristic features of our legal ideas, which are derived from historical developments of Western civilization. An understanding of the concept of common law and Roman code law traditions is essential background for achieving a broader knowledge of our legal systems. It also deals with the sources of law in this complex system and how conflicts of law are resolved. An introduction to individual rights and due process of law is included in this chapter, along with understanding the basic division between substantive and procedural law.

The final two chapters in Part I introduce the student to legal research and writing. They attempt to bring together the material in Part I to assist the student in performing basic tasks in legal research and writing. This includes reading and briefing cases and understanding the legal reasoning of courts in deciding disputed questions of law. They also summarize the material in the first two chapters, which provide reference sources that are used to find the more precise rules of law applied in the practical administration of the law. Sources of computer-assisted legal research are introduced, and students will be expected to gain basic understanding of how to find the law for particular jurisdictions.

The Expanding Legal Professions

Everyone knows that the law affects our daily lives and individual well-being; however, most American students will admit that our law is only vaguely understood. Generally, there has been little attempt to provide guidance for the basic principles of law in our education system. This textbook provides an introduction to law for the general college student as well as the student who is thinking about going into a legal profession.

The study of law has a more specific relevance for those considering careers in law-related professions. The general expansion of litigation (bringing legal actions in courts of law) in modern society and the societal concerns generated by the current crisis in law enforcement have created new opportunities for legal careers. Many students who have become interested in law for one reason or another are concerned about the job market for lawyers and wonder whether there is a need for more of them. They may ask: is the professional lawyer the only career opportunity for those interested in law?

The litigious nature of our society has contributed to the rising demand for legal professionals and law-related occupations. Lawyers are among the highest-paid and fastest-growing occupations. Teachers, paralegals and legal assistants, police officers and detectives, social workers and correction officials, and court reporters are also included among the fast-growing law-related occupations. Most of these occupations are growing at or above the average rate for all occupations, and the number of paralegal and legal assistant jobs is growing much faster than the average for all occupations. The *Occupational Outlook Handbook* projects that job opportunities for paralegals and legal assistants are expected to expand as more employers become aware that paralegals are able to do many tasks for lower salaries than those of lawyers (Bureau of Labor Statistics 2010).

THE LITIGIOUS SOCIETY

The United States may be the most litigious society in the world. There has generally been a doubling of the amount of **litigation** each decade for both

Litigation:
A general term used to refer to matters brought before a court of law.

civil and criminal legal actions filed in state and federal courts. Civil actions are initiated by private individuals or corporations. Criminal cases are initiated by state and federal prosecutors who represent the state or national governments. These actions are often referred to as **prosecutions**. Juvenile cases involving minors have shown even higher rates of increase over the last three decades. Slower growth rates in caseloads in our courts are becoming evident, but the level of legal activity is extremely high.

Prosecution:
A criminal legal action filed by a designated government official known as a prosecutor.

Most legal actions in the United States are brought in state courts, and the federal courts handle a relatively small amount of the total (only about 1 percent). The category of traffic filings is by far the most numerous among the activities handled by low-level state and local courts whereas bankruptcies are the most numerous filings in federal courts. Domestic relations (family law) cases, including divorce, child support/custody, and noncriminal violence, are a very large portion of the state court caseload, and these cases have been rising at a faster pace than the average increase in caseloads. Juvenile cases are growing faster than other types of cases, and they are handled by state courts.

The National Center for State Courts has recently undertaken a comparative analysis of the most advanced industrial nations and concludes that "the U.S. would indeed rank on top of an international scale [of most litigious societies], if 'civil cases' are restricted to include only general civil cases (i.e. *tort* [personal injury]), contract, and real property rights." From this study, Germany is a close rival for the most litigious society and, if summary debt collection were excluded, would surpass the United States (National Center for State Courts 1997, 15).

The statistical information from the National Center for State Courts indicates the extent to which legal activity has grown in modern society. However, their figures do not include the astronomical growth of government regulatory activity and administrative legal proceedings, nor do they include the enormous costs of criminal activity and injury to crime victims. Clearly, law and legal actions affect our daily lives more than at any time in our history. This trend will continue in the future, when our society will be required to deal with profound issues related to the emerging global economy and worldwide environmental concerns.

The efficacy of any legal system depends in large part on the willingness of citizens to obey the law. There can be no effective law enforcement without the cooperation and understanding of the overwhelming majority of people in the society. Law enforcement cannot depend on the threat of punishment alone as a deterrent to illegal activity.

Most people obey the law because they believe that it is the right thing to do; that is, it is consistent with what they believe just and fair. When this consistency is not present, they are more likely to violate the law, and in these situations threat of punishment may act as a deterrent. If the punishment is not credible (i.e., not very likely to be carried out), the threat of punishment will not work as a deterrent. Likewise, lack of knowledge or understanding of the societal norms (laws) in question will produce ineffective results.

People begin to acquire a basic knowledge of right and wrong behavior at home, where parents have an obligation to help their children understand and respect societal norms and behavioral expectations. Churches and other social groups add to this accumulation of moral values, as do peer groups and playmates, in what sociologists call the socialization process. Today the educational system, the most universal socializing agent in modern society, shares a primary responsibility with parents to help children develop an understanding of law and the legal expectations required for individual behavior.

Our society demonstrates many deficiencies in regard to the general socialization process, and these deficiencies account for much of the breakdown in effective adherence to legal norms. Other societies are more effective primarily because they do a better job in the normative socialization process than we do. Japan and Germany, for example, have crime rates that are less than 5 percent of ours, and their cultures are noted for their heavy stress on rules and obedience to social norms. These societies also have the advantage of being culturally homogeneous nations.

The United States, on the other hand, is extremely heterogeneous—a "melting pot" of diverse races, cultures, and national origins. We stress liberty and individuality. Our heroes are sometimes those who break the law. Even our most sacred expression of societal values in the Declaration of Independence is a philosophical justification for the ultimate act of legal disobedience—revolution against governmental authority. The state constitutions and the U.S. Constitution are attempts to reconcile this apparent dilemma by providing stable and reasonably orderly processes for changing the law to bring it into conformity with our beliefs of what is just and fair.

The society we have developed places heavy demands and responsibilities on its citizens. The extent and complexity of these demands may mean that they are too much to expect of the average citizen. We are expected to know and understand an increasingly complex set of laws emanating from 51 separate and independent law-making authorities and augmented by 51 different court systems. As adults, we are expected to keep track of as many as 50 different elected officials and to oversee their functions by intelligently exercising our right to vote. We are supposed to participate in the identification of community problems and to petition government for redress of grievances. We are called on to serve on juries (both investigative grand juries and trial juries, called *petit juries*), and we have a legal obligation to report crimes and to be witnesses in trials involving matters of which we have personal knowledge. Above all, we have an obligation to obey the law.

LAW-RELATED CAREERS

There are many expanding careers that involve legal studies and understanding. These careers include teachers, police officers, government agency employees, court reporters, paralegals, law office managers, lawyers, and judges. These are only the most prominent of the expanding law-related careers.

Teachers

The previous summary of the citizen's obligations under law makes it clear that our society needs competent teachers who can find ways to engage students in the vital process of developing knowledge and skills that will improve the efficacy of our legal system. An introduction to American law and the legal process helps us gain a better understanding of the characteristic features of our legal system and contributes to our abilities to know what focus we need in our educational systems. Knowing what to teach and how to teach are the particular skills of the teaching profession and cannot be dealt with effectively in an introductory course, but the following discussion will help.

The widespread recognition of our deficiencies in law-related education has produced some notable developments that have been given additional emphasis through a nationwide effort to inform teachers and citizens about educational programs that work. The American Bar Association and other interested groups are promoting **law-related education** and have developed significant new curriculum materials that are being integrated into schools across the nation. Former U.S. Supreme Court Chief Justice Warren Burger resigned from his position in 1986 in part because of his commitment to educational reform. He became the chair of the Commission on the Bicentennial of the United States Constitution, which has produced exceptional teaching materials.

Law-related education: Programs developed to promote integration of legal concepts into the K-12 curriculum.

A study conducted with the support of the federal Office of Juvenile Justice and Delinquency Prevention has demonstrated that law-related education, when taught properly, results in a significant reduction in delinquent activities by students. This two-year study, which involved a comparison of control and experimental classes of senior high school students in six communities across the nation, has important implications concerning what the schools can do to help reduce delinquency and crime among youth.

The experimental classes in the study used curriculum materials developed by the Constitutional Rights Foundation, Law in a Free Society, and the National Street Law Institute—instrumental organizations in developing teaching materials and techniques for teachers in the general area of citizenship and law-related education. These techniques are designed to foster civic competence, responsibility, and commitment to the fundamental values of a free society. The methods do not attempt to impose a particular course or curriculum on the schools, and they do not attempt to teach people to become lawyers.

ASSIGNMENT: Use the Internet to look up the Constitutional Rights Foundation (www.crf-usa.org). Look over its home page and find out what it has to offer prospective teachers.

The findings of a survey of more than 2,000 professionals in 1980 and 1981 found that law-related education can improve the behavior of individuals. Contrary to the beliefs of many, schools can teach moral development. In the 1960s, this issue was debated in the educational community, where some contended that the schools could not teach moral education. The late Professor Lawrence Kohlberg of Harvard University developed a lifetime of research to demonstrate how wrong we were to think that moral development cannot be taught. Although there are still skeptics, Professor Kohlberg made a major contribution to our understanding of moral development and the educational process necessary for achieving progressive moral development (Kohlberg 1987).

Conflict resolution programs are examples of law-related education in grade schools. These programs feature peer mediation, in which pupils are taught how to resolve their conflicts through mediation. Two student mediators resolve conflicts between students by requiring the parties to adhere to a strict set of rules that are posted on the wall: (1) identify the problem; (2) focus on the problem; (3) attack the problem, not the person; (4) listen with an open mind; (5) treat a person's feelings with respect; and (6) take responsibility for your own actions. (For a discussion of alternative dispute resolution, which is used increasingly to resolve disputes out of court, see Chapter 13).

Mock trial and mediation programs are good examples of law-related education in high schools and colleges. The American Mock Trial Association is a program for college undergraduates. Student teams of six to eight members compete in local, regional, and national competition by presenting trial cases that simulate the American trial process. New case materials are provided each year by the national association. Students must learn to present both sides of the case in competition. This activity takes a great deal of preparation, but students get excited about the activity and learn more than they do from textbooks or class discussion.

Parts III and IV of this text are designed to be used to involve the entire class in mock trials. If you are interested in both Mock Trial and Mediation programs you should contact the American Mock Trial Association to start a program at your undergraduate institution. Similar high school mock trial programs and mediation programs are sponsored by state bar associations throughout the United States. College students often assist these high school teams, which compete in statewide competitions. The state associations also sponsor a variety of law-related education programs, including mock trials. Most state bar associations have home pages on the Internet that will give you the necessary information to get involved.

> **ASSIGNMENT:** Enter the name of your state and the term "bar association," and you will find the home page for your state's bar association. Find out how valuable a resource this organization is to persons interested in law-related education. What services do they perform?

Court Reporters

Court reporters usually create verbatim transcripts of speeches, conversations, legal proceedings, meetings, and other events. Written accounts of spoken words are sometimes necessary for correspondence, records, or legal proof, and court reporters provide those accounts. **Court reporters** play a critical role not only in judicial proceedings but also at every meeting where the spoken word must be preserved as a written transcript. They are responsible for ensuring a complete, accurate, and secure legal record. In addition to preparing and protecting the legal record, many court reporters assist judges and trial attorneys in a variety of ways, such as organizing and searching for information in the official record or making suggestions to judges and attorneys regarding courtroom administration and procedure. Increasingly, court reporters provide closed-captioning and real-time translating services to the hearing-impaired community.

Court reporter:
A person who transcribes by shorthand or stenographically takes down testimony during court proceedings.

The average length of time that it takes to become a real-time stenographic court reporter is about 33 months. Training is offered by about 100 postsecondary vocational and technical schools and colleges. The National Court Reporters Association (NCRA) has certified more than 60 programs, all of which offer courses in stenotype computer-aided transcription and real-time reporting. NCRA-certified programs require students to capture a minimum of 225 words per minute, which is also a requirement for federal government employment as well. Expert knowledge of legal terminology and criminal and appellate procedure is essential for this profession. (See Bureau of Labor Statistics, *Occupational Outlook Handbook, 2010–11 Edition* and later editions.)

The Law Enforcement Officer and Public Administrator

Because of increased recognition of the problems of law enforcement in today's society, careers in law enforcement have become an area of major growth in terms of employment opportunity. No longer is this profession confined to the traditional "cop on the beat." Increased specialization and professionalization of law enforcement have expanded the range of career opportunities to include some 1,400 job classifications. Many of these jobs require college degrees and have stringent entrance requirements. The overwhelming majority of law enforcement employees work at local levels in traditional patrol and traffic officer positions. Modernization of local law enforcement agencies has been extensive, and new standards are being imposed to require college degrees for law enforcement officers, who must become involved in solving community problems, preventing crime, and reducing delinquent behavior. Many of these modern police officers are public relations and educational specialists. Detectives and criminal investigators are other positions of local specialization that offer challenging opportunities for young people with motivation to serve the public in one of the most essential, though often least appreciated, areas of public service.

At the state level, the traditional highway patrol officer is generally more highly trained and more adequately rewarded than are local officers. This agency is supported by highly trained and educated investigative bureaus (similar to the Federal Bureau of Investigation [FBI]) that employ many career officers in law-related fields. The current crisis in corrections departments of state governments has resulted in a tremendous expansion of employment opportunities in this area. Many states have been under court order to reform their correctional systems. State legislatures also are being forced to develop modern, systematic correctional procedures. The result of these efforts has been a great increase in the need for probation officers who can work closely with criminal judges to conduct background studies and sentencing recommendations as well as administer alternative sentencing programs.

Law enforcement opportunities at the federal level are expanding, and many of the fields involved are generally unknown to the student thinking about career decisions. The U.S. Department of Justice employs many persons throughout the world who perform many law enforcement functions as well as legal services to the government. The department also employs summer law interns and work-study students. The Office of Justice Programs coordinates five major bureaus that assist law enforcement programs across the country with statistical information and exemplary programs: they are the Office for Victims of Crime, the Bureau of Justice Assistance, the Bureau of Justice Statistics, the National Institute of Justice, and the Office of Juvenile Justice and Delinquency Prevention.

The FBI has jurisdiction over 200 types of cases, including white-collar crime, organized crime, foreign counterintelligence, public corruption, civil rights violations, terrorism, federal drug violations, kidnapping, bank robbery, and interstate criminal activity. The bureau works with other federal, state, and local law enforcement agencies to investigate matters of joint concern. There is a growing need for special agents, lawyers, accountants, language specialists, and computer specialists within the bureau.

Another area of employment opportunity is the Federal Bureau of Prisons (FBP). The Drug Enforcement Administration (DEA) is one of the most rapidly expanding agencies and is actively seeking young people from a variety of college disciplines. The Immigration and Naturalization Service (INS) is both a law enforcement and a service-oriented agency with responsibilities ranging from admitting, excluding, investigating, and deporting aliens to guiding and assisting them in gaining entry to the United States, receiving benefits, and becoming naturalized citizens.

Finally, there is the U.S. Marshal's Service, which is the nation's oldest federal law enforcement agency. This agency is responsible for protection of federal courts, judges, jurors, and witnesses; apprehension of federal fugitives; custody and transportation of federal prisoners; execution of court orders; custody, management, and sale of property seized from criminals; administration of the National Asset Seizure and Forfeiture Program; and the operation of the Witness Security Program.

We do not have a national police force in the United States. Our federal system places the primary responsibility for law enforcement and maintenance of domestic order with the states and local communities. As the nation has grown more interdependent in modern times, the need for interagency cooperation in law enforcement has increased. Multiple and overlapping jurisdictions of local, state, and federal agencies often produce conflicts that impede effective law enforcement and ultimately produce pressure to resolve these conflicts.

The Paralegal, Legal Assistant, and Law Office Manager

The rapid expansion of legal activity in our society over the past three decades has produced a new career opportunity in law—the paralegal profession. This area of employment opportunity is rapidly becoming a more defined profession, with emerging standards and competencies that are widely recognized by the legal and academic communities.

The role of **paralegal** today is associated with a person who has been formally trained and is experienced in the field as a legal assistant to lawyers or administrative agencies. Most of these individuals have an associate's degree in paralegal studies or a bachelor's degree in another field and a certificate in paralegal studies.

The role of **legal assistant** is now more associated with a person with legal skills who works under the supervision of a lawyer. There is no general licensing procedure for legal assistants, so all it takes to become a legal assistant is to convince a lawyer, law firm, or government agency to

Paralegal:
A person formally trained and experienced as a legal assistant to lawyers or an administrative agency.

Legal assistant:
A person with legal skills who works under the supervision of a lawyer.

hire you. However, these employers are increasingly demanding more professional skills and educational training or work experience before they will hire or continue to employ paralegals or legal assistants.

There are a number of persons who might consider themselves "legal technicians" and attempt to provide legal services without attorney supervision. This is a very risky venture because most states have statutes that restrict the practice of law to attorneys. Only lawyers are privileged to provide **legal advice** and **legal representation** to clients in a court of law. Paralegals or legal assistants commit **fraud** when they hold themselves out as lawyers and attempt to give legal advice or represent clients. A lawyer must be licensed to practice law in order to give legal advice or represent clients in a court of law. Paralegals and legal assistants may not sign documents submitted to the court or sign any documents that require an attorney's signature. However, with these few exceptions, the paralegal or legal assistant may perform most of the functions usually associated with the tasks performed by lawyers. However, lawyers who employ these assistants are held accountable for the actions of their legal assistants.

Most large law firms, corporations, and government agencies employ an increasingly large number of paralegals to perform many of the tasks formerly entrusted to lawyers. Tasks, such as drafting legal documents and discovery instruments; doing legal research, investigation, and title searches; preparing briefs; and closing real estate transactions are tasks that require considerable legal competence and ability but can be performed by trained individuals who are employed by lawyers, but who are not lawyers themselves.

Beginning in the 1960s, larger law firms began to realize that they could earn more money and provide better client services at lower costs by employing legal assistants to perform many of the tasks that more highly trained and skilled courtroom lawyers used to perform. Lawyers generally work on a billing system at an hourly rate that may be four or five times the rate a client may be billed for a paralegal doing the same task. This economic discovery by law firms and clients has been the principal motivating factor contributing to the rise of this profession.

In the early 1970s, the American Bar Association (ABA) not only recognized paralegals but also took steps to encourage the development and creation of more adequate training programs in this field by establishing an ABA approval procedure. Textbooks began to be published for the training of paralegals, and many institutions of higher education began to introduce educational programs specifically for them. In the early 1980s, there were some 300 public and private educational programs for paralegals across the country, and by 1992 the number of such programs increased to over 600. Practicing paralegals, who display an increasing sense of pride in their profession, have taken steps toward the development of certification, which is usually required in a recognized profession. Most major cities

Legal representation and advice:
Only a lawyer admitted to the bar may represent a person in court, advise a client about legal rights and duties, and especially advise the proper course of action as it relates to the law.

Fraud:
Intentional false representation, which is a serious crime.

Table 1.1. **COMPARISON OF PARALEGAL CERTIFICATION REQUIREMENTS**

Association	NFPA Paralegal Advanced Competency Exam	NALA Certified Paralegal/ Certified Legal Assistant Exam	NALS Professional Paralegal Exam
Certification Established	1996	1976	2004
Eligibility to Test	Student Member: An associate degree in paralegal studies obtained from an institutionally accredited and/or an ABA-approved paralegal program and six years of substantive paralegal experience; Or Bachelor's degree in any course of study obtained from an institutionally accredited school and three years of substantive paralegal experience; Or Four years of substantive paralegal experience on or before December 31, 2000.	Graduation from a paralegal program approved by ABA or associate degree program in paralegal studies; Or Paralegal program of 60 semester hours, 15 hours of which must be substantive paralegal courses; Or Bachelor's degree in any field, plus one year's experience as paralegal (15 hours of substantive legal courses equivalent to one year of experience as a paralegal); Or High school diploma or equivalent plus seven years of experience as a paralegal under the supervision of an attorney, plus a minimum of 20 hours of continuing legal education within a two-year period prior to the exam date.	Five years of experience performing paralegal duties. *Partial waivers:* A two-year waiver for a candidate with a paralegal degree; Or A maximum of one-year waiver for post-secondary degrees, successful completion of the PLS exam or other certification, or a paralegal certificate.

now have local chapters, and there are two major national associations: the National Federation of Paralegal Associations (NFPA) and the National Association of Legal Assistants (NALA).

A comparison of the certification programs offered by these paralegal associations is provided in Table 1.1. The Professional Paralegal Exam is required by both organizations, which now require certification renewal every two to five years and continued in-service educational programs.

In the 1980s, major law firms and corporations had become so convinced that management skills were needed to coordinate the activities of firms employing as many as 100 lawyers and 20–30 paralegals that they created a new position: **paralegal administrator**. These individuals are hired for their management skills and are frequently involved in the recruitment, training, and management of the office paralegals in large law firms and government agencies.

Paralegal administrator: A person employed by large law firms for skills in recruitment, training, and management of office paralegals.

The NALA has developed a certification program that is gaining recognition and will ultimately lead to more clearly defined professional standards for paralegals. Some have estimated that the number of paralegals may eventually exceed the number of lawyers in law offices, although today many rural and small law practices have yet to recognize the need for paralegals.

An organization called the American Association of Paralegal Education (AAPE) includes professional educators and is more than an association of paralegals. It has grown significantly in recent years and is likely to play an important role in setting future standards. Any such standards will require the cooperation of the ABA. However, at present there is no specific set of standards for the paralegal teaching profession in this country. Nonetheless, the profession is growing in numbers and prestige.

Lawyers

Many students are considering their potential for successful entry into law schools. The lure of the law is great, and many are attracted to this profession even though the profession suffers from something of a bad image, created probably by a few. Lawyers usually gain respect, are thought to be bright, are secure, are positioned to secure power, and often become rich.

The number of lawyers, now estimated to be more than 800,000 nationwide, is expected to increase at a rate about as fast as the average for all occupations (about 13 percent during the next decade; Bureau of Labor Statistics 2010). There has been a significant rise in the number of those taking the law school entrance examination (LSAT) in recent years, indicating that competition for law schools and legal careers will increase. However, fears that the profession is overloaded are unfounded. The rate of increase in new law school graduates from ABA-accredited programs, and especially new admissions to the bar, has kept pace with the expansion of litigation since the 1960s.

Growth in the population and in the level of business activity is expected to create more legal transactions, civil disputes, and criminal cases. Job growth among lawyers also will result from increasing demand for legal services in such areas as health care, intellectual property, bankruptcy, corporate and security litigation, antitrust law, and environmental law. In addition, the wider availability and affordability of legal clinics should result in increased use of legal services by middle-income people. However, growth in demand for lawyers will be constrained as businesses increasingly use large accounting firms and paralegals to perform some of the same functions that lawyers do now. Also, mediation, arbitration, and other forms of alternative dispute resolution (ADR) are increasingly being used as alternatives to litigation.

Law offers challenging professional opportunities for those who are willing and able to undertake the rigors of professional education and acquire the skills needed to become successful lawyers and judges in today's highly competitive society. Graduates with superior academic records from highly regarded law schools will have the best job opportunities. Many with law degrees may find rewarding occupations in administrative, managerial, and business positions in banks, insurance firms, real estate companies, government agencies, and other organizations.

What does it take to become a lawyer? Do I have the right stuff to make it in this demanding profession? These are questions most students ask themselves. Interest in and fascination with the subject of law is an important prerequisite: however, many are called but few are chosen! If law school is not an option, there are still many challenging law-related careers.

College guidance and counseling offices can usually provide self-scoring interest inventories. These materials help students assess their interest compatibility with those who have found successful careers in the law. Once a student concludes that the field of law is where the student's interests lie, the long process of assessment and development of the student's abilities and skills begins.

Law schools do not require any particular undergraduate major, but they expect the student to have a broad liberal arts background and a transcript that indicates that the student has taken courses that involve reading, writing, and thinking. A large number of majors in political science, history, and English are usually admitted to law school, but almost as many come from other academic disciplines. Law is an extremely versatile field, and backgrounds in business, engineering, and medicine are assets because they provide the kinds of knowledge needed to deal with the increasingly technical aspects of the law. Law school is the place where the student specializes in the law.

Admission to law schools is based primarily on two criteria: a student's undergraduate grade-point average and a student's score on the **Law School Admission Test (LSAT)**. These two criteria often determine the initial screening process, but other factors are involved in later screening. The LSAT attempts to measure a student's potential for success in law school by testing verbal skills and reasoning abilities. Grade-point averages

Law School Admission Test (LSAT): A test almost universally used in the United States as a criterion for admission to law schools; an aptitude test of logic and critical thinking.

are better indicators of success than the LSAT, but the two factors combined are considered the best predictor and are relied on by most law schools across the country.

There is increasing competition for a limited number of seats in law schools today. However, a student who has innate ability and begins early in undergraduate school to develop reasoning and communications skills will be more likely to enter his or her law school of choice. An undergraduate bachelor's degree is essential before applying to law school.

Undergraduate courses that make the student read, write, and think enhance reading comprehension and logical thinking skills. Mastery of the English language, basic understanding of history (both world and American), and knowledge of how government institutions function broaden a student's vocabulary and make the student a cultured and literate person. An understanding of logic and practice in critical thinking skills, along with general understanding of economics and business practices, are other important areas a student should stress.

Persons entering law school must be confident enough in themselves and personally committed to the pursuit of a professional career in the law to undergo the intensive and rigorous training required in law school. A minimum of three years of full-time, exacting course work is required, and on completion of law school there is no assurance that the student will pass the **bar examination**, which is administered by state agencies and must be passed before the individual can practice law in that state.

Bar examination: A test of required proficiency required to obtain license to practice law, give legal advice, and represent clients.

The evolution of American legal education has been gradual and prone to resist change. Legal education initially was based on the English model and continued as a type of apprenticeship system until after the Civil War. An aspiring lawyer in the 1800s would apply to an established lawyer with whom the apprentice would "read the law," which meant observing the mentor, drafting documents, assisting in case preparation, and reading assigned cases and commentaries until the apprentice was able to open a private practice with a letter of recommendation from the mentor.

It was not until the 1870s that law schools began to emerge as formalized educational programs, although some lawyers attended the Inns of Court in England; some gained their education in law office schools like the one established by Tapping Reeve in Litchfield, Connecticut, in 1784; and some worked with individuals who had obtained the few professorships at various universities (Abadinsky 1991, 78–79). Robert Stevens attributes the rise in formal professional law schools in the period from the 1870s to the close of the nineteenth century to the prevalent "middle class urge to get ahead through structured education" and the growing dissatisfaction with the apprenticeship model (Stevens 1983, 22). The legal profession also became a booming industry during the period of the industrial revolution in the United States, and the emerging model of legal education became associated with Cristopher Columbus Langdell of

Harvard University. Langdell perfected the dreaded **Socratic method** and case study approaches that have been so prominent in American legal education. These methods still characterized formal legal education in the 1970s, when Scott Turow's bestselling autobiography *One L*, about first-year law students at Harvard University, critically described the formal legal education process (Turow 1977).

Law schools have made minor adjustments in recent years by adding practical requirements of moot court, advocacy skills, negotiations, and ethics, but the curriculum has remained surprisingly stable and uniform across the country.

The typical first-year law student has no electives and is required to take two semester courses in torts, property, civil procedure, and contracts, along with one-semester courses in constitutional law, criminal law, and legal research. The case study approach dominates, and the student is expected to come to class prepared, having read and briefed several cases, to discuss the cases in class. Typically, only one final essay examination is given each semester to determine student grades. There is fierce competition for grades, and the student's class rank at the end of the year determines status and rewards, such as being nominated to serve on the "law review," a prestigious student publication comprised of the highest-ranking students.

In the second and third years of law school, there are more electives and opportunities to specialize, but students generally are required to take courses in the ethics of the legal profession, income tax, corporations, and evidence. They also are encouraged to participate in a clinical law program, which provides some practical experience. The remainder of the second and third-year curriculum comprises a wide variety of elective course offerings, including courses in administrative law, wills, trusts, estate law, labor law, family law, environmental law, and international law.

Specialization may begin in law school but often awaits a more significant aspect of the legal education process—practical experience with the law firm. Most lawyers claim that despite formal law school education, they really learned the practice of law from experience, and many became specialized through recognition of client needs. Students may intern with law firms even before graduation, and some of the highest-ranking students are selected to be law clerks at the federal and state Supreme Court levels.

The most prestigious law firms today have national reputations, and the attorneys in these firms generally are described as "Wall Street lawyers." They hire the highest-ranking graduates from the most prestigious law schools at very high starting salaries; the "Craveth" system is the prevalent model, involving a kind of practical postgraduate induction into the world of corporate law and lawyering (Smigel 1964). New lawyers work as lawyer interns for several years, usually for a number of the firm's partners. After five to ten years, the intern is considered for a partnership or

Socratic method:
Typical method of teaching in law schools that involves engaging students in direct questioning and relies on uncertainty about answers to develop critical thinking skills.

leaves the firm. These elite law firms handle big corporate clients and practice **preventative law**; litigation generally represents failure, and "much of what these lawyers do involves planning a client's activities so that disputes are not likely to arise" (Burton 1985, 19). Such firms are no longer confined to New York City but have branched out into nearly every major metropolitan area, especially Washington, D.C. Many Washington law firms practice influence and lobbying rather than law. An increasing number of these firms are expanding into global concerns, with offices in major cities throughout the world.

Large corporations have their own in-house counsel, with major legal divisions headed by the general counsel. Beneath the general counsel are deputy, or associate, administrators who supervise staff attorneys. Staff attorneys may be distributed throughout the different divisions of a corporation, but all are responsible to their superiors in the law department. These in-house law departments, like elite firms, actively recruit the highest-ranking law students with high starting salaries. Corporate law departments do not have the prestige of the national law firm, but a position in such a department has considerably more prestige than that of the typical lawyer in a small firm. Corporate law departments also practice preventative law, or dispute anticipatory law, and are more heavily involved in corporate planning and transactional work.

The typical lawyer falls into a third category of lawyers who do not work for national law firms or in-house corporate law departments. About half of practicing attorneys-at-law are in solo practice or in a two-lawyer firm. The typical attorney may not "hang out a shingle" immediately after law school but may do so after substantial experience with a large law firm or a governmental agency (such as a prosecutor's office). Lawyers in firms of four to ten lawyers account for about 20 percent of practicing attorneys, and lawyers who are employed by government agencies make up about 10 percent.

Although most practicing lawyers are men, more than half of the students currently enrolled in law schools are female. Racial and ethnic minorities also are represented among practicing lawyers, and law schools are actively engaging minority applicants, whose numbers are increasing across the nation.

Preventative law: The practice of preventing legal actions against clients. Since a major function of the practice of law is to give legal advice, competent legal advice prevents adverse legal action against the client.

Judges

The judicial profession in the United States is not a field in which one sets out to develop a starting career. It is generally necessary to become a lawyer first and then consider opportunities for seeking a position on the bench. American judges sit on courts of widely different types, come from an assortment of backgrounds and experiences, and are selected by a variety of methods; therefore, it is difficult to generalize about them.

Our legal system has 51 separate and independent court systems and, therefore, 51 different methods of recruiting, selecting, and removing judges. However, there are four basic methods of selection, although some states combine two or more of them.

The dominant method of direct popular election makes our system unique among the world's judicial systems. We are the only country that allows politics to enter the judicial function to this formal degree. It was not the dominant method of selection during the period of formation of the union, when selection by state legislatures was used in a majority of the states. Popular election was introduced during the period of "Jacksonian Democracy" after 1830, and many state constitutions still reflect the impact of this era by requiring popular election of judges. Modern reform movements have had to deal with this reality. Removing constitutional provisions is a very difficult process in most states, and it is almost impossible when the process involves removing a popularly elected office.

With the relatively minor exception of some lay **magistrates** who serve in judicial capacities on state courts of limited jurisdiction, all American judges have studied and been licensed to practice law. The majority of trial judges have come directly from private practices, with a broad range of legal specialties being represented. Women and minorities in significantly larger numbers are graduating from law schools, and many have been selected as state and federal judges.

Magistrates: Lower court judicial authorities, including justices of the peace.

Political involvement seems to be a primary characteristic of American judges, with some studies showing as much as 70 percent of the state's judiciary describing themselves as having been politically active. Paul

Table 1.2. BASIC METHODS OF SELECTING STATE COURT JUDGES

1. The federal model of nomination by the chief executive, with confirmation by a legislative body, is used in only a handful of states.
   (Only Rhode Island extends life terms to their judges as is the federal practice.)
2. The so-called *merit plan*, or **Missouri Plan**, involves appointment by the chief executive from a short list of persons certified for the position. This method has been promoted as a reform measure to provide a buffer against pure partisan politics and gives some assurance of professional quality. A majority of states now use this method in some form and apply it to at least the selection of the intermediate appeals court judges.
3. *Direct popular election of judges for fixed terms of office* (usually longer than the terms for legislators) is the dominant method of state judicial selection. The overwhelming majority of judges are selected in this manner.
4. *Judicial selection by election in the legislature* is the fourth method of selection and is now used in only two states: Virginia and South Carolina.

Missouri Plan (or merit plan): Appointment of judges by the governor from a list of qualified applicants. The appointee must be accepted by the voters and is subject to periodic retention approval by the voters.

Wice concludes that "gaining the favorable attention of the public officials who choose judges . . . is the most common characteristic shared by all members of the bench" (Wice 1991, 57).

Judges are viewed as members of a highly respected profession in terms of occupational prestige despite the public's growing dissatisfaction with the judicial system. Most judges are positive about their positions and enjoy the responsibilities and challenges inherent in their profession, although an increasing number of them criticize the working conditions, relatively low pay (in comparison to private law practice), administrative tedium, and irritating political involvements.

Many state court judges hear only certain types of cases. A variety of titles are assigned to these judges; among the most common are municipal court judge, county court judge, magistrate, and justice of the peace. Traffic violations, misdemeanors, small-claims cases, and pretrial hearings constitute the bulk of the work of these judges, but some states allow them to handle cases involving domestic relations, probate, contracts, and other selected areas of the law.

The employment opportunity for judges in the next decade is expected to grow more slowly than the average for all employment opportunities, but this varies by judicial specialty. This trend can be explained in part because of the expected more frequent use of ADR (Alternative Dispute Resolution) techniques, such as those discussed in the next section.

Administrative Law Judges, Arbitrators, and Mediators

Administrative law judges, sometimes called *hearing officers* or *adjudicators*, are employed by government agencies to make determinations for administrative agencies. These judges make decisions on, for example, a person's eligibility for various Social Security or workers' compensation benefits, protection of the environment, the enforcement of health and safety regulations, employment discrimination, and compliance with economic regulatory requirements.

Other fields of law-related occupations include arbitrators, mediators, or conciliators instead of judges or magistrates. They assist with ADR—a collection of processes used to settle disputes out of court. All hearings are private and confidential, and the processes are less formal than a court trial. If no settlement is reached, no statements made during the proceedings are admissible as evidence in any subsequent litigation.

Arbitrators usually are attorneys or business people with expertise in a particular field. Mediators are neutral parties who help people to resolve their disputes out of court. Conciliation, or facilitation, is similar to mediation. Conciliators are individuals usually appointed for their expertise and are not necessarily lawyers.

Employment of arbitrators, mediators, and conciliators is expected to grow faster than the average for all occupations through 2018. Many individuals and businesses try to avoid litigation, which can involve lengthy delays, high costs, unwanted publicity, and ill will. Arbitration and other alternatives to litigation usually are faster, less expensive, and more conclusive, spurring demand for the services of arbitrators, mediators, and conciliators. Most jurisdictions now have some type of alternative dispute resolution program.

ASSIGNMENT: For more detailed and current information about all of the law-related professions listed in this chapter, use the Internet to find the *Occupational Outlook Handbook* online and check out the general estimates of earnings in these fields. Use the search box provided for the handbook to find out more information about individual occupations, including estimated earnings in the field.

ETHICAL STANDARDS IN LAW-RELATED PROFESSIONS

All law-related professions perform day-to-day functions that require a high degree of responsibility to the community interests they serve. Teachers, court reporters, law enforcement officers, paralegals, administrators, lawyers, prosecutors, judges, and even arbitrators, mediators, and conciliators occupy positions of public trust that impose on them ethical standards that are higher than those for persons employed in non-law-related areas. Any person may be sued for negligence (failure to exercise reasonable care), but in these professions violations of the more stringent ethical standards of personal behavior may result in greater penalties, including suspension of the right to practice in the person's profession.

Professional **ethical standards**, especially in the area of law and government, are not merely desirable virtues or expectations, but in many respects they have been elevated to the status of legally binding rules imposed by the courts of law. The ABA standards for lawyers and those for judges are very different. Since most judges are drawn from the ranks of practicing attorneys, especially prosecutors, they may have difficulty making the ethical transition from lawyer to judge. Some critics assert that this is an example of the general bias inherent in our system compared to those of most other countries in the world where judges are not drawn from the ranks of lawyers. An individual's likelihood of obtaining justice in our system may depend on scrupulous adherence to the canons of ethics by the judge and the lawyers involved.

Ethical standards: Professional standards, usually set by state bar associations, which are often legally binding and the violation of which can result in suspension or loss of license to practice law.

Lawyers are regulated by their state bar association, which in turn operates under the authority and supervision of the state's highest court. These regulations are known as the **ABA Model Rules of Professional Conduct**, and violation of these regulations can lead to sanctions such as suspension and disbarment. In cases of disciplinary action, a committee of the bar association usually conducts a hearing and makes a preliminary decision. This action can be appealed to a designated state court (usually the supreme court), which will make the final decision on whether sanctions should be imposed.

ABA Model Rules of Professional Conduct: Model statements of ethical standards drafted by the American Bar Association.

One of these canons covers the lawyer's use of paralegals. This canon requires, in essence, that the lawyer must supervise the paralegal and ensure that the paralegal does not engage in the unauthorized practice of law. A lawyer can be disciplined for what the paralegal (or other non-lawyer) does within the employ of the lawyer. Paralegals can be prosecuted under criminal statutes for the unauthorized practice of law or held legally responsible for negligence, but bar sanctions apply only to lawyers.

The **American Bar Association (ABA)** has the major role of proposing model ethical standards and issuing opinions interpreting these rules, but the standards are not binding until state and local bar associations officially adopt them. Most state and local bar associations have adopted some or all of the ABA ethical positions. For example, a judicial candidate for elective office who publicly takes a position on a political issue or on a pending case, in violation of Canon 7 of the *Model Code of Judicial Conduct*, can lose the office to another candidate and may even face disbarment in 47 states.

American Bar Association (ABA): Voluntary national association of lawyers and judges that represents the legal profession in the United States.

ASSIGNMENT: Students interested in finding out more about the work of the ABA will find a wealth of information about the legal profession and current developments in the bar's home page on the Internet. Just enter the name and search for the appropriate topic at the ABA's home page.

The **judge's role** in legal proceedings requires that the judge exercise responsibility for enforcing the rules that govern criminal and civil cases. The judge must have no personal interest in the outcome of the case. If the judge does have such a personal interest, that judge must recuse himself or herself from the case. A judge is responsible for ensuring impartial justice under law and must avoid any impropriety or appearance of impropriety in the discharge of this function. When a jury is used, the judge determines issues of law and the jury determines issues of fact in dispute. When there is no jury, the judge determines issues of both law and fact. A judge's failure to conform to the principles of ethics and law may lead to reversal of the decision by an appellate court—a blow to the professional standing of any trial judge. Other forms of disciplinary action include being voted out of

Judge's role: One of impartiality and neutrality toward the parties.

office, denial of confirmation when appointed, and impeachment followed by removal from office.

The basic canons of the ABA's *Model Code of Judicial Conduct* are as follows:

1. A judge should uphold the integrity and independence of the judiciary.
2. A judge should avoid impropriety and the appearance of impropriety in all activities.
3. A judge should perform the duties of office impartially and diligently.
4. A judge may engage in activities to improve the law, the legal system, and the administration of justice as long as they do not cast doubt on the judge's capacity to decide impartially.
5. A judge should regulate extrajudicial activities to minimize the risk of conflict with judicial duties.
6. A judge should regularly file reports of compensation received for quasi-judicial and extrajudicial activities.
7. A judge should refrain from political activity inappropriate to the judge's office.

The **lawyer's role** is that of advocate for the client, and the standards of ethics require that the lawyer serve the client to the best of his or her ability without violating the law or the lawyer's code of ethics. The essential standards imposed by the ABA's *Model Rules of Professional Conduct* indicate that the lawyer's role is to do the following:

Lawyer's role:
Acts to advocate for the client, who is entitled to vigorous and competent representation.

1. To provide competent representation to a client
2. To refrain from counseling a client, or assisting a client, to engage in conduct that the lawyer knows is criminal or fraudulent
3. To refrain from knowingly making false statements or unlawfully obstructing another party's access to evidence, and to use candor and honesty in the practice of law
4. To keep the client informed and to conform to certain standards concerning reasonable fees
5. To refrain from revealing confidential client information without the client's consent, except in cases where criminal acts are likely to result from such confidentiality
6. To avoid conflict of interest concerning the adverse effect to another client
7. To withdraw from a case if (a) the client demands that the lawyer engage in illegal or unethical activities, (b) the lawyer is physically or mentally unable to represent the client, or (c) the client fires the lawyer

8. To avoid even the appearance of professional impropriety; and to conform to other standards concerning prohibitions against knowingly filing frivolous claims, communication with the opposing party without the consent of that party's lawyer, false or misleading advertisement, unethical solicitation of legal business, and reporting of professional misconduct

The ABA's standards require that lawyers give their paralegals "appropriate instruction" on the "ethical aspects" of the practice of law. The paralegal must be careful to avoid misrepresenting himself or herself as a lawyer and may not give legal advice or represent a client in court.

The National Association of Legal Assistants (NALA) has drafted a professional code of ethics for the paralegal profession that includes the definition and a list of canons of professional responsibility listed on page 24. It must be emphasized that paralegals are not licensed, as are lawyers. Accessing the National Association of Legal Assistants' home page on the Internet will provide a valuable source of information for the student interested in this growing profession.

Law Enforcement Officers

Administrative action against law enforcement officers is generally subject to civil service rules that emanate from state authority and are applied locally. Disciplinary actions may include temporary or permanent suspension from the force, and criminal sanctions may be applied in extreme cases. Law enforcement officers are guaranteed a "fair hearing," and they can appeal decisions that they think are unfair. Civil suits against law enforcement officers are extensive and represent an increasing occupational hazard in this area of employment.

The law enforcement officer has a fundamental duty to safeguard the lives and property of all people in the society, to respect every person's legal rights, and to maintain personal honesty, self-control, and exemplary conduct. The officer must set an example through personal adherence not only to the general law but also to the department's regulations and the community's expectations. The officer must refrain from abuse of authority, enforce the law courteously and appropriately, never employ unnecessary force or violence, and never accept gifts for services.

The standards are difficult to interpret and enforce under the extremely varied conditions of modern life, but the underlying assumption of our legal system is that justice can be done in the individual case only if ethical standards and due process of law are followed.

NALA Code of Ethics and Professional Responsibility

Each NALA member agrees to follow the canons of the NALA Code of Ethics and Professional Responsibility. Violations of the code may result in cancellation of membership. First adopted by the NALA membership in May of 1975, the Code of Ethics and Professional Responsibility is the foundation of ethical practices of paralegals in the legal community.

A paralegal must adhere strictly to the accepted standards of legal ethics and to the general principles of proper conduct. The performance of the duties of the paralegal shall be governed by specific canons as defined herein so that justice will be served and goals of the profession attained. (See Model Standards and Guidelines for Utilization of Legal Assistants, Section II.)

The canons of ethics set forth hereafter are adopted by the National Association of Legal Assistants, Inc., as a general guide intended to aid paralegals and attorneys. The enumeration of these rules does not mean there are not others of equal importance although not specifically mentioned. Court rules, agency rules and statutes must be taken into consideration when interpreting the canons.

Definition: Legal assistants, also known as paralegals, are a distinguishable group of persons who assist attorneys in the delivery of legal services. Through formal education, training and experience, legal assistants have knowledge and expertise regarding the legal system and substantive and procedural law which qualify them to do work of a legal nature under the supervision of an attorney.

In 2001, NALA members also adopted the ABA definition of a legal assistant/paralegal, as follows:

A legal assistant or paralegal is a person qualified by education, training or work experience who is employed or retained by a lawyer, law office, corporation, governmental agency or other entity who performs specifically delegated substantive legal work for which a lawyer is responsible. (Adopted by the ABA in 1997.)

CANON 1
A paralegal must not perform any of the duties that attorneys only may perform nor take any actions that attorneys may not take.

CANON 2
A paralegal may perform any task which is properly delegated and supervised by an attorney, as long as the attorney is ultimately responsible to the client, maintains a direct relationship with the client, and assumes professional responsibility for the work product.

CANON 3
A paralegal must not: (a) engage in, encourage, or contribute to any act which could constitute the unauthorized practice of law; and (b) establish attorney-client relationships, set fees, give legal opinions or advice or represent a client before a court or agency unless so authorized by that court or agency; and (c) engage in conduct or take any action which would assist or involve the attorney in a violation of professional ethics or give the appearance of professional impropriety.

CANON 4
A paralegal must use discretion and professional judgment commensurate with knowledge and experience but must not render independent legal judgment in place of an attorney. The services of an attorney are essential in the public interest whenever such legal judgment is required.

CANON 5
A paralegal must disclose his or her status as a paralegal at the outset of any professional relationship with a client, attorney, a court or administrative agency or personnel thereof, or a member of the general public. A paralegal must act prudently in determining the extent to which a client may be assisted without the presence of an attorney.

continued>

CANON 6

A paralegal must strive to maintain integrity and a high degree of competency through education and training with respect to professional responsibility, local rules and practice, and through continuing education in substantive areas of law to better assist the legal profession in fulfilling its duty to provide legal service.

CANON 7

A paralegal must protect the confidences of a client and must not violate any rule or statute not in effect or hereafter enacted controlling the doctrine of privileged communications between a client and an attorney.

CANON 8

A paralegal must disclose to his or her employer or prospective employer any pre-existing client or

personal relationship that may conflict with the interests of the employer or prospective employer and/or their clients.

CANON 9

A paralegal must do all other things incidental, necessary, or expedient for the attainment of the ethics and responsibilities as defined by statute or rule of court.

CANON 10

A paralegal's conduct is guided by bar associations' codes of professional responsibility and rules of professional conduct.

CHAPTER SUMMARY

1. The expansion of legal activity in the United States over the past three decades has produced expanding opportunities for meaningful careers in law-related areas. We are perhaps the world's most litigious society. The number of disputes taken to court has doubled every ten years.
2. The efficacy of our legal system depends on the willingness of citizens to obey the law. This willingness is conditioned on the socialization process by which citizens are taught the moral and legal values of society.
3. Citizens are expected to have a general understanding of law and know the difference between right and wrong behavior, participate in selecting officials, identify community problems, serve on juries, report crimes, serve as witnesses, and obey the law.
4. Teachers who are adequately prepared to teach law-related education are needed in greater numbers to improve our educational and socialization processes. Studies demonstrate that law-related education reduces crime and promotes moral development.
5. Increased recognition of the problems of law enforcement has led to increased specialization and professionalization of law enforcement agencies at local, state, and national levels. More emphasis is being placed on crime prevention and corrections institutions.
6. Most of the new positions in law enforcement require college degrees and knowledge of basic concepts of law. The complex nature of our

federal system places primary responsibility for law enforcement with the states and local communities.

7. The expansion of litigation has created a relatively new career field for specialists called *paralegals*, who are neither lawyers nor legal secretaries. The paralegal is a person with legal skills who works under the supervision of a lawyer.

8. The number of persons who aspire to be lawyers and judges is increasing, and the competition for entry into law school has become more difficult. However, the production of new lawyers has kept pace with the expansion of litigation.

9. A student who plans an undergraduate education properly can increase the chances of successful entry into law school and can choose a more prestigious law school than one who does not plan ahead.

10. Entering the profession of law requires a personal commitment, rigorous training, three years of postgraduate course work, and the ability to pass a rigorous state bar examination. Even after completing a bar exam, lawyers must maintain their commitment by taking continuing legal education (CLE) courses on an annual basis.

11. The most prestigious law firms are large organizations, located in major metropolitan centers, that practice corporate law. Large corporations also have law departments in which staff lawyers practice corporate planning and preventive law.

12. Each state government and the federal government employ different methods of recruiting, selecting, and removing judges. Although there are four basic methods of selection, the dominant method in the states is popular election for fixed terms. In the federal government, judges are selected for life terms by presidential nomination and confirmation by the Senate.

13. Judicial independence and professional quality are important goals, but our system contains much ambiguity in regard to achieving them, especially at the state level. Compared with other legal systems, the United States is unique in that (1) judges come to the bench from the ranks of practicing lawyers, and (2) once on the bench, they usually do not follow a promotion pattern through the ranks of the judiciary.

14. All positions in law-related professions are positions of public trust that impose on those holding them ethical standards that are higher than standards for persons employed in other professions.

15. Judges are regulated by the American Bar Association's *Model Code of Judicial Conduct* and lawyers by the ABA's *Model Rules of Professional Conduct*. These standards impose ethical and legal obligations on judges and lawyers to avoid any impropriety or appearance of impropriety. The function of judges is different from that of lawyers. They must be impartial, neutral, and fair, whereas lawyers are obligated to

represent clients to the best of their ability, carefully avoiding any illegal or unethical activity.

16. The paralegal must not misrepresent himself or herself as a lawyer and may not give legal advice or represent a client in court. This would constitute the unauthorized practice of law and could lead to criminal charges.

17. Law enforcement officers must respect every person's legal rights while protecting lives and property. Officers must obey departmental regulations, refrain from abuse of authority, never employ unnecessary force, and never accept gifts for services.

REVIEW EXERCISE

Match the following terms with their most appropriate meaning.

TERMS

1. Litigation
2. Prosecution
3. Law-related education
4. Court reporter
5. Legal assistant
6. Legal representation and advice
7. Fraud
8. Paralegal
9. Paralegal administrator
10. Law School Admission Test (LSAT)
11. Bar examination
12. Socratic method
13. Preventive law
14. Missouri Plan (or merit plan)
15. Magistrates
16. Ethical standards
17. ABA Rules of Professional Conduct
18. American Bar Association (ABA)
19. Judges' role
20. Lawyers' role

MEANING

____ selection of judges by appointment subject to voter approval
____ person who transcribes legal proceedings
____ lower-court judicial authorities (e.g., justices of the peace)
____ professional standards in law-related professions
____ model ethical standards for lawyers and judges
____ national association of lawyers and judges
____ general term for actions brought before a court of law
____ person formally trained and experienced as a legal assistant to lawyers or administrative agencies
____ criminal legal action filed by the government
____ one of impartiality
____ that of advocate for the client
____ required proficiency to obtain license to practice law
____ aptitude test needed to apply for law school
____ a person with legal skills employed by a lawyer
____ intentional false representation (crime)
____ advising a client about legal rights and duties, which can only be performed by a lawyer
____ typical method of teaching in law schools
____ practice of preventing legal actions through competent legal advice
____ programs that integrate legal concepts into K-12 education
____ person employed by law firms to manage paralegals and the law firm

DISCUSSION QUESTIONS

1. How has the expansion of legal activity in the United States resulted in the expansion of law-related career opportunities?
2. What are the basic responsibilities of citizenship in our society?
3. What role do teachers and law-related education play in the process of political socialization?
4. How have the problems of our society in the areas of law enforcement and corrections expanded opportunities for law-related careers?
5. How has the expansion of the amount and cost of litigation contributed to the rise of the paralegal (or legal assistant) in the United States?
6. What qualifications are needed to enter law school and to become a lawyer?
7. What are the major characteristics of law school education in the United States?
8. How are judges selected in the United States?
9. What are the basic ethical standards for judges, lawyers, paralegals, and law enforcement officers?

ASSIGNMENT

ASSIGNMENT: Find out how to use the Internet to access the material in this course. A good place to start is with the professional agencies described in this chapter. The American Bar Association (www.abanet.org), the American Mock Trial Association (www.collegemocktrial. org), and the American Association for Paralegal Education (www.aafpe.org) are good places to start. The U.S Bureau of Labor Statistics, *Occupational Handbook*, can be found by just typing the title into any search engine, and you can check out areas of interest to you personally.

SOURCES AND SUGGESTED READING

Abadinsky, Howard. 1991. *Law and Justice: An Introduction to the American Legal System*. 2d ed. Chicago: Nelson-Hall Publishers.

American Bar Association. 1980. *Law Schools and Professional Education*. Chicago: American Bar Association.

Baum, Lawrence. 1986. *American Courts: Process and Policy*. Boston: Houghton Mifflin.

Bureau of Labor Statistics. 2010. *Occupational Outlook Handbook*. Washington, D.C.: U.S. Government Printing Office.

Bureau of Labor Statistics. 2010. *Occupational Outlook Quarterly*. Washington, D.C.: U.S. Government Printing Office.

Burton, Steven L. 1985. *An Introduction to Law and Legal Reasoning*. Boston: Little, Brown.

Kohlberg, Lawrence. 1987. *Child Psychology and Childhood Education: A Cognitive-Developmental View*. New York: Longman. (See also entire issue of *Social Education*, April 1976, devoted to practical application of Kohlberg's stages of moral development for teachers.)

Kramer, Jerome. 1989. "Scholarship and Skills." *National Law Journal* (January 9).

Lieberman, Jethro K. 1981. *The Litigous Society*. New York: Basic Books.

MacKenzie, John P. 1974. *The Appearance of Justice*. New York: Charles Scribner's Sons.

Meador, Daniel John. 1991. *American Courts*. St. Paul, Minn.: West Publishing.

Moll, Richard W. 1990. *The Lure of the Law*. New York: Penguin Books.

National Center for State Courts. 1997. *Examining the Work of State Courts, 1996: A National Perspective from the Court Statistics Project*, ed. B. Ostrom and N. Kauder. Williamsburg, Va.: National Center for State Courts.

Pashigian, A. Peter. 1978. "The Number and Earnings of Lawyers—Some Recent Findings." *American Bar Foundation Research Journal* (winter): 51–82.

Shapo, Helene, and Marshall Shapo. 1996. *Law School Without Fear*, Westbury, N.Y.: Foundation Press.

Siegel, Brian. 1974. *How to Succeed in Law School*. Woodbury, N.Y.: Barron's Educational Series, Inc.

Smigel, Erwin O. 1964. *The Wall Street Lawyer: Professional Organization Man*. Glencoe, Ill.: Free Press.

Statsky, William. 1992. *Introduction to Paralegalism: Perspectives, Problems, Skills*. 4th ed. St. Paul, Minn.: West Publishing.

Statsky, William. 1993. *Paralegal Employment: Facts and Strategies for the 1990s*. 2d ed. St. Paul, Minn.: West Publishing.

Stevens, Robert. 1983. *Law School: Legal Education in America from the 1850s to the 1980s*. Chapel Hill: University of North Carolina Press.

Stinchcomb, James D. 1976. *Opportunities in Law Enforcement and Related Careers*. Louisville, Ky.: Vocational Guidance Manuals.

Strumpf, Harry. 1988. *American Judicial Politics*. New York: Harcourt Brace Jovanovich.

Turow, Scott. 1977. *One L*. New York: Penguin Books.

Wice, Paul. 1991. *Judges and Lawyers: The Human Side of Justice*. New York: HarperCollins.

Zemans, Francis, and Vicory Rosenbloom. 1981. *The Making of a Public Profession*. Chicago: American Bar Foundation.

The Origin and Basic Structure of Our Federal Legal System

The American legal system consists of 51 separate and independent systems coordinated by the principles of law established in the U.S. Constitution. All 50 states of the federal union have their own constitutions that define and limit the powers of governmental agencies within the geographical boundaries of their territories. The powers of the states include the authority to establish their independent court systems and laws designed to regulate the social order and promote the interests of the inhabitants of those states.

The federal, or national, government was created after the 13 British colonies declared their independence. The states drafted their original constitutions and created independent legal systems during the 13 years between the signing of the Declaration of Independence (1776) and the ratification of the U.S. Constitution (1789). This federal union transferred a limited, but in many ways vague, set of powers to the national government while leaving many basic responsibilities of law and order to the state governments. The federal government is limited by the U.S. Constitution but has the authority to create its own court system and laws within its sphere of delegated powers. The state governments are also limited by the U.S. Constitution as well as their own constitutions, but retain the basic authority over their own legal systems.

In this chapter we will first explain the historical origin and sources of many of our basic legal concepts and then the fundamental structure of our federal system.

COMMON LAW AND EQUITY

The original 13 colonies of Great Britain developed their ideas of law from the distinctive practices and principles of law developed in medieval England. The first settlements in America began in 1607–1620. The colonies experienced an evolution of legal concepts derived from English law over a period of some 150 years before declaring their independence in 1776. These colonies followed the British practice of *common law*, the term given to law developed by judges in written opinions. The American colonies adopted the British common-law tradition. Since then, we added *statutory* (or code) *law* (enacted by legislatures) on top of this base, and finally we developed constitutional principles that limit and define the authority of government. Constitutions form the highest order of law, followed by statutes, and then the common law.

Common Law

The English foundation of law is called **common law**. This body of law was derived from the practices of early judges appointed by the king to settle disputes arising among the population of the early communities conquered by the French Normans in 1066. After William the Conqueror assessed the extent of his conquest, he began the arduous process of considering how to maintain it. He discovered that there was no law of England; there was only the law of the various tribes. Gradually, over a period of 200 years, English common law replaced these early tribal systems. It could be identified as judge-made law because it is derived from judicial decisions and court practices.

Common law:
The body of judge-made law that has no source other than judicial decisions. It originated in medieval England.

The idea of judges making law is somewhat alien to our thinking today. But in the formative period of the English common law there were no legislative institutions, and medieval kings were not thought of as possessing the authority to make law. To the medieval mind, law was not wholly made by human beings, but rather was an expression of what is right and just in the settlement of disputes among members of the community. After the conquest of England, the early Norman kings were at first concerned only with exacting tribute in the form of taxes from the English inhabitants. The first royal courts were created to collect taxes and maintain the king's peace. The areas involving the king's peace were limited at first, and tribal customs continued to be used to decide disputes where the king had no interest.

The Norman invaders of England gradually began to fashion the variety of local customs into a single body of general principles. This process began in 1086 when William sent commissioners throughout the realm to make a record of the names of towns and numbers of persons, cattle, and houses, as well as the customs and norms of the population. The Norman Conquest made French the language of the royal household and the royal courts. Anglo-French, or "law French," was used in pleadings before the emergent courts. Lawyers of the period had to become multilingual because they were required to draft all formal records in Latin, the language employed in the Middle Ages for formal written records. Anglo-French was a dialect from which the English legal profession first developed a precise vocabulary for the expression of legal concepts. Words such as *tort*, *plaintiff*, and *defendant* are of French origin. Many of the terms still used today, such as "last will and testament," are expressions of both English (will) and French (testament), which were originally expressed in this manner so they would be understood in both languages.

The judges were directed to decide disputes *secundum acquitatem*, that is, by general consideration of *fairness and equity* (justice).

The decisions of these early royal judges gradually began to take on a life of their own. The earliest decisions may have reflected common customs among the various tribes of the realm, but the concept of justice and fairness was the presumed basis of these decisions.

A cardinal principle that emerged was that in order to do justice the courts must follow their own rulings when disputes having analogous (similar) facts again came before the court. This court doctrine, reflecting the need for consistency in legal decisions, is called **stare decisis**, or the doctrine of following judicial precedent. It is derived from a longer phrase in Latin that means "stand by the previous decision and do not change that which has been established." This reliance on previous judgments was at first stiffly applied and meant that judges must look to past decisions for *judicial precedent* to keep the law consistent. This meant that year books would have to be developed to record these precedents.

Stare decisis:
The doctrine of following judicial precedent.

Gradually, over a period of more than 200 years, the body of law known as the *common law of England* began to be summarized and simplified in formal, systematically organized written works describing its principles. These professional guides to the classification and description of the common law are often called *treatises*. The first of these was compiled by Henry Bracton toward the middle of the thirteenth century. He prepared a huge treatise on the law as administered by actions in the king's court and recorded in year books. Since the recorded volume of these so-called year books continued to mount over the years, this attempt to simplify and describe the emerging principles of law in a form that could be understood had to be repeated periodically.

The struggle between feudal barons and the king was a characteristic feature of the period that witnessed the rise of the common law. The Magna Carta, signed in 1215, was produced as a result of the barons' dissatisfaction with King John I. Its most important accomplishment was to establish that "the king must obey the law, because it is the law that makes him king." Later documents, culminating in the Great Charter of 1225, resulted in the codification of feudal rights, chiefly the rights of great vassals against the king. The charter was, however, deliberately drafted in general terms, and its most famous section included the rights of every free person.

By the end of the thirteenth century, the process of developing a legislative body (Parliament) began to take place. General regulations intended to change or abrogate customary law and to be valid for the entire realm became recognized as statutes. Thus, statutory authority to create positive law emerged along with the common law of the realm. During the fourteenth century, it became established that a statute, in order to be valid, needed the formal agreement of the Great Council of the magistrates. The Latin term for this conference, *parliamentum*, ultimately gave rise to the name of the British legislative body known today as Parliament.

Even at the end of the fourteenth century, the common law was far from being the law of all England. The use of the king's courts increased rapidly, but the feudal courts remained important. Ecclesiastical (church) courts maintained control over such matters as marriage and divorce and other family matters, including the distribution of personal property upon death. Only after several centuries did the common law of England become dominant. However, its progress can be seen through successive treatises that were used as guides. Bracton's early treatise on court practice in the thirteenth century was replaced by one prepared by Thomas Littleton in 1470. Sir Edward Coke's *Institutes* in the sixteenth century later became the major source for understanding English law for many generations. It was Sir William Blackstone, a lecturer at Oxford on the laws of England, who produced the most influential treatise on the common law, entitled *Commentaries,* which was published in four volumes in 1756.

The Glorious Revolution, which overthrew King James II, produced the English Bill of Rights in 1689 and the Act of Settlement in 1701. The English Bill of Rights was more like the American Declaration of Independence than the U.S. Bill of Rights in that it spoke of "inalienable rights" and restoration of ancient rights rather than of legal innovation. The Crown was forbidden to suspend the laws or to levy money without the approval of Parliament. The Act of Settlement of 1701 ensured that monarchs must bow to the rule of Parliament and established an independent judiciary that could not be dismissed by the Crown. All this occurred before Blackstone's treatise on the law of England, and his treatise included the effects of these changes.

Blackstone's treatise was enormously successful, not only in England but also in the American colonies. The first book (volume) of the *Commentaries* set out the fundamental rights of individuals. It provided the promoters of the American Revolution with many of their principal arguments, and the entire set of volumes was the principal guide for colonial lawyers and judges in administering the law in colonial courts. At the time of the American Revolution, the new states rejected British rule and acts of Parliament, but local judges retained the common law practice because it was the only law they knew.

The tradition of periodically restating the principles of law derived from judicial precedent, and consistent practice gave rise to the series of treatises today referred to as the **Restatements of the Law** published by the American Law Institute. In the tradition of Bracton, Littleton, Coke, and Blackstone, these time-honored principles of the law derived from practical experience in administering justice in individual disputes are today *restated*

Restatements of the Law: Scholarly treatises that restate the common law in a form that expresses clearly the basic concepts of that body of law. They are authored by panels of judges, professors, and leading attorneys in different areas of law.

periodically by the American Law Institute. (See list of modern *Restatements of the Law* at the end of this chapter.)

Equity

The American colonies inherited another curious concept of dispute settlement from English historical development that still persists in our current legal system. This concept is known as **equity**, which refers to a remedy seeking a specific performance order of the court such as an injunction or cease and desist order. Its origin stems from a period in the common law development around the year 1300 when the common law courts became tied down by a number of wholly artificial restrictions that left them incapable of doing justice in a large number of legal matters, many of which were of common occurrence. As a result of this situation, the era witnessed an expansion of petitions to the king asking that justice be done—not as a matter of right (or law), but by grace to be extended to those who could not get justice in the other courts (Zane 1927, 234). Many states have chancery courts, which are traced back to these English courts of equity.

Equity:
Refers to a remedy seeking a specific performance order of the court such as an injunction or cease and desist order.

The king's chancellor was an office that developed to oversee the king's court. In time, these petitions to the king seeking a remedy for matters that were rejected by the courts of law were forwarded to the Lord High Chancellor. Over a period of nearly a century, the practice of granting or rejecting these petitions evolved into a real court with a procedure of its own. The *Chancery Court* became an alternative court where an equitable remedy could be found even when the common law courts had refused to provide a remedy. The decisions made by the *Chancery Court* were decrees (not judgments) that took the form of specific performance orders.

An example of how this dual system of courts of law and equity functioned in early English courts is illustrated by a situation created by a simple error on the part of a debtor who, after paying his debt in full, failed to demand a release from the debt under seal. A dishonest creditor could sue on this already paid obligation in the common law courts and obtain judgment for a second payment. The common law precedents demanded that a sealed instrument could be discharged only by another sealed instrument; hence, the justice of the matter was sacrificed to mere form. A plea of payment on the part of the debtor would be held by the common law courts to be insufficient, and the dishonest creditor would then be granted judgment against the honest debtor who had in fact paid his debt.

However, the creditor now had recourse to the chancellor, who was considered to be the keeper of the king's conscience. In Chancery Court, the judge would recognize that double payment was wrongful conduct since he had read in the Roman Digest that good faith does not suffer that the same thing should be twice exacted. Often, the chancellor was a bishop or an archbishop who knew something of the elevated spirit of the ancient

Roman law with its superiority to mere form. As the keeper of the king's conscience, he was a superior judge who had none of the rigid notions of the common law judges. The swindled debtor could then present his action in equity explaining the circumstances. The chancellor then had the power to subpoena the creditor, force his attendance, and require him to answer under oath as to the payment. If the debtor could produce two witnesses that he had paid the debt in question, the chancellor would use his powers to order a specific performance decree resolving the dispute.

The most common forms of equity actions today are injunctions and cease and desist orders. Many of the principles of equity were derived from ancient Roman law, with its comprehensive code reflecting the experience of a thousand years of law development. This earlier body of law was never re-codified in the English law, but such a process did take place in Europe and will be explained later in this chapter. Instead of using rules of law in reaching decisions, the English court of equity used *equitable maxims*. The following maxims (short statements that contain the gist of much equity law) are still used today as guides in the decision-making process in disputes in equity.

> Equity will not suffer a right (or wrong) to exist without a remedy.
> Equality is equity.
> He who comes into equity must do so with clean hands.
> He who seeks equity must do equity.
> Equity aids the vigilant.
> Delay resulting in prejudicial change defeats equity (*laches*).
> Equity regards as done that which ought to be done.
> Equity regards substance rather than form.
> Equity follows the law.
> Equity acts *in personam* (personal rights) rather than *in rem* (property rights).

This separate court for matters of equity existed in England until about the time of the American Revolution. A few states in the United States, such as Tennessee, still have separate chancery courts, but generally both in England and the United States the chancery functions have been merged into the courts of law.

The common law of England and the concept of equity took root in the American colonies. After gaining independence, the individual colonies became independent states and began developing their own variations of common law and equity. The common law concept does not mean that judicial precedent must always be followed. In the course of its historical development, the common law broke free from slavish adherence to the past and began to entertain arguments that a past precedent that was grossly unfair could not continue to be applied in a system founded on the idea of fairness and justice. Courts began occasionally to reverse these decisions and create new precedents.

Another aspect of this peculiar historical development of English law, including common law and equity, is that it continued to develop by adding new precedents when novel factual situations appeared before the court. A **case of first impression** (where no previous precedent exists) is decided by the judges, and this decision creates a new precedent that adds to existing law. This is one of the major aspects of the life of the common law in that it evolves and becomes more refined by new decisions that enable it to respond to changing circumstances.

Case of first impression: A dispute involving a new factual situation never previously before the courts that adds new precedent when decided.

MODERN COMMON LAW SOURCES

This unwritten body of law, known as common law today, is still a vital part of our legal systems. It can be found in the individual court opinions that are written by trial and appellate judges when their rulings reflect a contribution to the body of common law or clarify the application of the common law to novel and unique fact situations. These rulings are found in *Reporters*, which are books that contain judicial opinions from different courts in rough chronological order. This seems like an impossible task given the great accumulation of the body of common law, which is not identical in each of our 50 states.

Modern legal guides and *digests* have created systematic methods of finding appropriate cases. These finding tools, as well as learning how to read and understand a case in law, will be discussed in Chapter 3.

> **ASSIGNMENT:** Turn to Appendix B, on page 555 of this text, and begin by reading the first two illustrative court opinions provided in edited form. There are six illustrative cases in Appendix B, which represent examples of cases in law for your analysis. You will be asked to brief these cases in Appendix B at the end of Part I of this text. The first four chapters will be used to provide the appropriate background needed to accomplish this task.

As illustrated in the first of the cases in the appendix, *Du Pont v. Christopher*, the growth of the *common law* occurs generally by small steps in logical extension of long-established principles of law. This is a case of first impression involving aerial photography of a plant under construction to obtain a trade secret from the Du Pont Corporation. No previous decision of the Texas courts had decided such a case before, and therefore any decision made by the courts would create new precedent. Note that this case involves no statutory or constitutional law and must be decided by reference to common law. The *Restatement of Torts* (Second) is used by the court to deduce the answer to the legal question in this case along with reference to previous Texas court decisions that accept the principles of common law restated in this secondary source. Common law refers to that body of law that has no other source than judicial decisions.

The concept of equity is illustrated in the last of these six cases in the appendix—*Marvin v. Marvin*. In this case the plaintiff (party bringing the civil legal action) is seeking court action in the form of equitable relief as well as a monetary award in an action in contract (law). These are really separate legal actions. The equity action asks the court to freeze the assets of the late actor Lee Marvin so that they will not be dissipated before an award can be made by court judgment involving the claim in contract. This illustrates the modern merger of both law and equity that is typical of almost all courts today. Such specific performance orders to freeze assets of a defendant are common in damage suits.

Why has this complex and cumbersome concept of common law been retained in the modern era of positive, or code, law developed through legislative enactments? This is a very good question that deserves thoughtful consideration. Most judges and lawyers answer that the common law method of law development is superior to legislative enactment because it is a practical method of considering the law as a working hypothesis that is continually tested in the courts. The courts must continually reexamine the basis of our legal system founded on considerations of fairness and justice. Most thoughtful observers acknowledge that the ideas of common law and equity give the law its vitality and capacity to sustain change while adhering to time-honored principles that are universal in their acceptance as the basis for dispute settlement (Glendon 1994; Knight 1996).

Justice Oliver Wendell Holmes Jr., one of our most famous U.S. Supreme Court justices, took a special interest in the common law. In his critical analysis of its characteristic development, he concludes:

> The life of the law has not been logic; it has been experience. The felt necessities of the time, the prevalent moral and political theories, institutions of public policy, avowed or unconscious, even the prejudices which judges share with their fellow men, have had a good deal more to do than syllogism in determining the rules by which men should be governed. The law embodies the story of a nation's development through many centuries, and it cannot be dealt with as if it contained only the axioms and corollaries of a book of mathematics. In order to know what it is, we must know what it has been, and what it tends to become. The very considerations which judges most rarely mention, and always with an apology, are the secret root from which the law draws all the juices of life. I mean, of course, considerations of what is expedient for the community concerned.
>
> (Oliver Wendell Holmes 1881, 1–2)

NATURAL LAW AND POSITIVE LAW

As a result of the peculiar origin of our law in English (or Anglo-Saxon) development, the general legal philosophy of the American legal system is usually referred to as *Anglo-American jurisprudence*. The term **jurisprudence** refers to the philosophy of law or to the basic principles of a particular school of thought about the origin, development, and application of the law. Learned jurists assert that *jurisprudence*, properly defined, is the science that ascertains the principles upon which legal rules are based and allows us to proceed by logical deduction to proper application of these rules in new and doubtful cases.

Jurisprudence: Philosophy or study of law.

During the early colonial period of American history, Blackstone argued in his influential *Commentaries* that there was a *natural law* character to the body of common law and asserted that any human law contrary to natural law had no validity (Abadinsky 1991, 5).

The *natural law school of jurisprudence* was the basic philosophy of law in Europe during the period of Blackstone's clarification of the principles of English common law. He and many others since have praised the common law as a method of discovery of the principles of natural law through experience. Although the concept of natural law is mysterious in its precise meaning, it takes as its basic assumption that individuals have fundamental rights that must be protected by law; therefore, it is a rights-based philosophy.

This natural law concept goes back to the ancient Greeks. The earliest notions about natural law can be traced to the Greek Sophists of the fifth century B.C. The true significance of natural law lies in the function it has performed since classical antiquity as a moral standard by which to measure the actions of governments.

An appeal to a higher law than that devised by human beings alone has been a great force in the entire development of law. It is more of an idea of the limitations upon governmental authority than a prescription of how to develop specific rules of law. The most widely accepted expression of the concept of natural law in our culture is found in the Declaration of Independence written by Thomas Jefferson. Jefferson and the American colonial leaders were faced with the difficult problem of how to justify the Revolution and the act of treason involved against duly constituted governmental authority. The words of the document are a classic example of the natural law philosophy expressed by English philosopher John Locke from whom Jefferson borrowed it.

What Jefferson meant is simply that there are limits to governmental authority to create and enforce rules in society. He expressed the idea that reason and human intelligence are capable of understanding this idea and that any government that becomes systematically destructive of basic

---

The Declaration of Independence

"We hold these truths to be self-evident, that all men are created equal, that they are endowed by their Creator with certain unalienable Rights, that among these rights are Life, Liberty and the pursuit of Happiness—That to secure these Rights, Governments are instituted among Men, deriving their just Powers from the consent of the governed—That whenever any Form of Government becomes destructive of these ends, it is the Right of the People to alter or to abolish it, and to institute new Government, laying its foundation on such principles and organizing its powers in such form, as to them shall seem most likely to effect their Safety and Happiness." . . .

(July 4, 1776)

human rights should be replaced. His reference to God is not to be confused with religious doctrine.

This idea led to the development of modern constitutions that recognize the fundamental nature and purpose of government, including limitations on governmental authority. Many of the provisions of the Bill of Rights are clearly rooted in natural law thinking. However, this vague notion is very imprecise and has led to many conflicting opinions as to how such ideas could be converted into practical concepts of law.

Statutory law is the written law enacted by legislative authority and has a much clearer meaning than natural law. Generally, what is meant by the term **statutory** (or positive) **law** is reference to legislative enactments that form the basis of our written codification of the law. This source of law is also subject to interpretation by the courts that have elaborated on the meaning of these provisions by court decisions.

Statutory law:
Legislative enactments, written sources of law in the form of statutes.

MODERN STATUTORY LAW SOURCES

The enormous body of our law today has been codified by legislative enactment into written law, which can be found in the *United States Code* and the 50 state codes. These compilations of the entire body of our written law have been organized by topic to enable easy access to their provisions. The *United States Code* is the official government publication. However, there are better sources called *annotated codes* that include all of the official enactments updated every three months as well as annotations to case opinions and other legal materials that elaborate on the meaning of these statutory provisions. Legal researchers prefer annotated codes because they provide more than simply the text of statutes. They also provide citations to cases and other legal sources that cite or explain the statutes. The annotated code that is most commonly found in college libraries is the *United States Code Annotated*, published by West Publishing Company. All of the state codes are not usually available in college libraries; however, your library will probably have your own state's annotated code, for example, *Tennessee Code Annotated* (TCA). These annotated codes include constitutional law as well as all legislative enactments with case annotations and supplemental resources.

ASSIGNMENT: Read the third and fourth cases in Appendix B found on pages 562. These are criminal cases that illustrate court opinions concerning the interpretation of statutory law, or positive law. Look for the problems of interpreting the intent of the legislature in these cases.

Almost all of the specific definitions of criminal offenses are written in statutory form as illustrated by the two criminal cases in Appendix B. In *People v. Moore*, the court is required to determine the meaning of a vague provision of the Municipal Code of the State of New York. Reading the specific statutory language and attempting to ascertain its intent is illustrated in the court's procedure. Similarly, in the case entitled *People v. Braly*, the Colorado Supreme Court is asked to interpret the statute under which Mr. Braly was convicted to determine if the required specific intent of the statute was proven at trial. To answer these questions the court refers to a previous decision concerning the meaning of the statute.

Code Law and Common Law States

The states that compose our federal union today have expanded from the original 13 former colonies of Great Britain to include areas of North America that had experienced legal backgrounds that were not of common law origin. For example, the State of Louisiana is a code law state drawing its legal heritage from the ancient Roman code law tradition. Indeed, our common law has derived many of its concepts from ancient Roman law.

Texas and California had similar experiences with Spanish colonization and application of their versions of the Roman Code. This basic code remained in force in Texas until 1840. In California, a basic version of the

Table 2.1 **CODE LAW AND COMMON LAW STATES**

States with Code Law Traditions (Examples)	States with Common Law Traditions (Examples)
Arizona, California, Idaho, Louisiana, Nevada, New Mexico, Texas, Washington, and Wisconsin	Connecticut, Delaware, Georgia, Maryland, Massachusetts, New Hampshire, New Jersey, New York, North Carolina, Pennsylvania, Rhode Island, South Carolina, and Virginia

Roman Code remained for a decade longer than it did in Texas (Edmunds 1959). Other states that have been influenced by the Roman Code law tradition because of early Spanish and French colonization in America include Arizona, New Mexico, Nevada, Washington, Idaho, and Wisconsin.

The original 13 colonies and those states that derived their legal traditions from the original colonies are considered common law states.

THE BASIC STRUCTURE OF OUR FEDERAL SYSTEM

The fundamental legal document coordinating the entire American legal system is the U.S. Constitution found in its amended form in Appendix A in the back of this text. It defines and limits the powers of the federal government. It also regulates conflicts between the states and the federal government and among the states themselves. It defines the basic structure of the federal government and designates the basic individual rights to be preserved against governmental regulation.

> **ASSIGNMENT:** Read the U.S. Constitution found in Appendix A on page 543. Look for the general methods used to separate legislative, executive, and judicial functions and the method used to divide powers between the states and the national government (see powers of Congress in Article I). What rights are reserved to the states? What are the methods of ratification and amendment? Come to class prepared to discuss what you have learned from this exercise.

Federalism and Separations of Powers

The particular circumstances of the American Revolutionary period (1776–1789) provided an unprecedented opportunity to put into effect many of the ideas that have been discussed previously. The Framers of our Constitution, as well as the drafters of the state constitutions of the former colonies, were educated in the classical schools of the period, which stressed Greek, Roman, and English history and languages. Most of them were lawyers, judges, and governors and had extensive legal backgrounds. They had served in their own colonial assemblies and were experienced political leaders.

The practical effect of the Declaration of Independence was to signal the creation of 13 independent sovereign nation-states. Each of the former colonies established constitutional conventions to draft fundamental documents for the organization of their new governments. *Sovereignty* was assumed to have passed from Great Britain to these newly established state governments. The term **sovereignty** requires some clarification here because it is so fundamental to the understanding of the modern

Sovereignty: Supreme and independent political authority of the nation-state within its own territory.

nation-state. Sovereignty refers to supreme and independent political authority of the nation-state within its own territory.

Modern nation-states emerged in Western Europe out of the preceding feudal societies during the period around the time of the Peace of Westphalia in 1648. This settlement of the Thirty Years War (1618–1648), which had devastated most of Europe during the Reformation, was an agreement to respect the territorial boundaries of the various nations involved. It was recognized that each *state* (nation-state) had the right to govern its inhabitants and the responsibility to settle all disputes within its territory independent of any foreign interference. This idea became the basis of modern **international law**. International law, or the Law of Nations, is based upon mutual respect for the sovereign equality of nations. It consists of a body of law derived from the customary practices of nations, recognized as legally binding, and treaty obligations. International law governs the relationships with other nations and was specifically recognized in the U.S. Constitution (Art. I, Sect. 8, para. 9).

International law:
The law of nations that consists of customary practices, regarded by them as legally binding, and treaty obligations.

At the time of the Declaration of Independence (1776), our original 13 states assumed individual sovereignty and proceeded to reorganize their governments in a manner that reflected the will of the people. The state constitutions were drafted by conventions and approved by the assemblies that had been popularly elected during the colonial period. This expedient development of constitutional authority accepted these assemblies as representatives of the people. Eventually, all of the states developed constitutions that require approval of the voters directly. This process put into effect what many philosophers had long advocated—a government based upon popular consent.

These state governments proceeded to cooperate, through the Continental Congress, with the other state governments in taking the necessary actions to repel the British during the Revolutionary War. They also entered into a treaty obligation legally binding them to form a confederation. This document was called the *Articles of Confederation*. It was not put into effect until 1781, when it was finally ratified by all 13 of the new states. The Confederation was instrumental in bringing the Revolutionary War to an end by its representatives negotiating a peace settlement with Great Britain, known as the Treaty of Paris (1783), which recognized the independence of the former colonies. In exchange for this recognition, the Confederation agreed to compensate British citizens for their property losses during the war. However, this confederate alliance between sovereign states did not possess the power to compel the states to live up to the treaty obligations contained in the Treaty of Paris. The central government lacked other fundamental powers, including the power to tax, to regulate commerce, to exclusively coin money and regulate the currency, to create a central court system, and to make laws directly applicable upon individuals without further state action.

As James Madison, the "father of the Constitution" and future fourth president of the United States observed, "the Confederation suffered not from a want of specific powers, but of power in general." By this he meant that, although the Confederation was given considerable authority, it had no power to make laws to exercise this authority independent of the individual state governments. The Articles of Confederation gave the central government authority to make war and peace, send and receive ambassadors, enter into treaties and alliances, coin money, fix the standard of weights and measures throughout the United States, establish a post office, regulate Indian affairs, appoint officers, and make rules for military forces in the service of the United States. But the treaties it made could not be enforced because it could not tax or make laws that were necessary to carry out these treaty obligations.

The British government retaliated by closing the West Indies to American trade, Spain closed access to its port at New Orleans, and the French and Dutch were reluctant to negotiate treaties with a nation that could not meet its commitments. The commercial life of these early American states depended upon production of raw materials that were shipped to European ports and exchanged for manufactured goods. The farmers could not get their products to markets without paying excessive tariffs levied by each state. The central authority lacked power to regulate commerce and prohibit each state from charging tariffs.

These were a few of the most significant problems that ultimately brought about the convening of the Constitutional Convention of 1787. The convention's original instruction from the Continental Congress was "solely to revise the Articles of Confederation." This instruction was ignored, and the drafters proceeded to propose a wholly new document that attempted to rectify the problems plaguing the early union of independent sovereign states.

The answers to these problems are the essential elements of the national governmental structure we have today. **Federalism** refers to the division of governmental authority between the states and the national government. This concept is found by examining Article I, Section 8, granting powers to the U.S. Congress; Article IV admitting new states and guaranteeing a Republican form of government; and the Tenth Amendment to the U.S. Constitution, reserving powers to the states.

Federalism:
Divided sovereignty, or division of authority of government between the national and state governments.

The list of powers in Article I, Section 8, essentially adds to the powers of the central governmental authority to create a national court system; taxing and spending power; power to regulate commerce (among the several states and Indian tribes); power to establish uniform rules for naturalization, patents and copyrights, and bankruptcies; and control over the District of Columbia. Note that the other listed powers in Article I are virtually identical to those as defined in the Articles of Confederation. Article I, Section 8, further includes a "necessary and proper" clause at the end of this list that makes it clear that the intent of the Framers was to provide sufficient authority to carry into execution the **delegated powers** to the national government.

This is a limited set of functions, but now the central government would have the authority to create law and enforce it against individual violators without being dependent upon the states for legal action. The statement in the Tenth Amendment (of the Bill of Rights) that the "powers not delegated to the United States by the Constitution, nor prohibited by it to the States, are reserved to the States respectively, or to the people" is a clarification of the intent of the Framers to form a limited national government and to share sovereign authority with the states.

However, one must look more closely to find an even narrower set of powers that are exclusive to the national government, since they are denied to the states. Article I, Section 10, lists those powers that are denied to the states, after listing certain powers denied to both the states and the national government in Article I, Section 9. By comparing the powers granted to the national government and those denied to the states, one can discover the **exclusive national powers**. There is much vagueness here, but essentially the power to conduct foreign policy (declare war, make treaties, and set tariffs) would be included in this list of exclusive national powers. The power to coin money is clearly intended to be an exclusive national power denied to the states. The intent of the Framers to prevent the states from erecting tariffs on goods transported between the various states is also an exclusive national power. Regulation of patents and copyrights, bankruptcies, Indian affairs, and naturalization of citizens are others.

The other powers going to the national government may be shared with the states. A good example is the taxing power, which is not denied to the states. The creation of courts, laws, and regulations to promote the public health and safety are other significant shared powers. These powers are called shared or **concurrent powers**.

Courts have had to interpret many ambiguous provisions of the U.S. Constitution through the years. But with the ratification of the U.S. Constitution in 1789, a new form of government was established. European countries that had just emerged from feudal societies to form nation-states believed that in order to have a nation-state there must be one central authority with the ultimate power to decide all disputes arising within the nation. That is what sovereignty meant to European nations. Now, the United States proposed to divide sovereignty. Many thought such a scheme unworkable, but it is the basis of our legal system today.

Separation of powers is another concept that permeates the U.S. Constitution and is fundamental to the understanding of our governmental order. The Framers conscientiously endeavored to protect us from abuse of power by constructing the basic institutions of national government in such a manner so as to require them to exercise checks and balances over

Delegated powers:
Those powers given to the national government in Article I, Section 8, of the U.S. Constitution (and in several amendments).

Exclusive national powers:
Those powers given to the national government but denied to the states (e.g., foreign policy, coining money, and regulation of interstate and foreign commerce).

Concurrent powers:
Shared powers, or those powers given to the national government but *not* denied to the states (i.e., taxing power, creation of courts, laws, and regulations to promote public health and safety are a few of these shared powers).

Separation of powers:
The division of authority within a governmental structure to prevent abuse of power by a system of checks and balances between the legislative, executive, and judicial branches.

each other. This division of authority within the governmental structure can be seen in the division of the articles of the U.S. Constitution. The first three of these articles deal respectively with the legislative, executive, and judicial branches of government. Each of these institutions is given separate and different methods of selection so that each would have an independent source of power. Each branch is given independent powers, but these are shared with the other branches to enable them to check each other.

The concept of separation of powers was considered to be a particular attribute of British government that had evolved through governmental practice. Charles-Louis de Secondat, Baron de Montesquieu, a French writer, had clearly explained this concept attributed to British government in *The Spirit of the Laws*, and the state constitutional conventions had employed it. But the particular genius of the Framers of our national Constitution brought the concept to a highly refined level of achievement. If one compares these three articles describing the branches of national government carefully, one will find checks and balances everywhere. The Framers truly believed that tyranny was the result of concentration of power, and they did everything they could to prevent it by providing a check upon each grant of authority. Part of the reason for their intense effort was that they had experienced tyranny and knew what it was. The other reason was that they would have to persuade the states to give up significant powers, and they knew that this would be accomplished only if they could devise a scheme that would ensure responsible government.

Separation of powers and checks and balances are central to the ideal of fostering the rule of law that gained universal acceptance among the Framers of the Constitution. They had been warned by the future second president of the United States, John Adams (then ambassador to Great Britain), that an attempt to create a purely democratic form of government was doomed to failure and that such a government would end up destroying itself. The *Federalist Papers* were written by James Madison, Alexander Hamilton, and John Jay under the pen name of *Publius* to explain the new proposal and to promote ratification by the states. Madison argued, in *Federalist Number 10*, that the system of government proposed by the Constitution was actually a republic, rather than a democracy. What he meant by a *republic* was a representative government limited by constitutional checks that prohibited simple majority popular will from violating the principles of rule of law. The Framers drew upon ideas of Greek and Roman legal philosophy, including Aristotle's concept of "mixed government," upon Roman experience, as well as upon the newer ideas of Montesquieu and Locke.

Madison and the other Framers of the Constitution argued that the proposed Constitution would set up separate legislative, executive, and judicial institutions that would have balanced powers and authority in their separate functional spheres. "Ambition must be made to control ambition" in this new government characterized by separation of powers. If one branch got too far out of line, the independent powers of the others would be able to check abuses of power.

The extent to which powers are checked is illustrated by the **legislative process**, or law-making process. The law-making, or legislative, power is basically granted to the Congress. However, Congress is divided into the House of Representatives and the Senate (the principle of *bicameralism*); each must pass proposed legislation by a majority vote, and the bills passed must be in identical form. This gives each house an absolute veto over the other house. Each house is selected by a different constituency. The House is selected by popular vote in districts devised by the states, with a national allocation of the number of representatives to each state based upon that state's proportion of the entire population of the United States.

Legislative process: The law-making process defined in the U.S. Constitution, which has become similar in most of the states.

The original Constitution designated that the state legislatures would select two senators for six-year terms to represent the state interests in the legislative process (now amended to provide for direct popular election in each state, Amendment XVII adopted in 1913). Moreover, the senators' terms would be staggered so that only one-third of them would be selected in any one election period, whereas the House members would be subject to reelection every two years.

Assuming a bill emerged from this process in identical form and was passed by both houses, it still has to be presented to the president, who could veto or approve it. The president's approval would enable it to become law; however, a presidential veto would require it to be passed by a two-thirds majority of both houses, and it could still become law without the president's approval. The president is chosen independently of the House or Senate and has a different constituency, derived from the states acting through their power to select an electoral college, which would in turn select the president. This process has been altered by the states, which have acted to allow direct popular election of the members of the electoral college from each state.

However, this is not the end of the checks and balances that are included in the U.S. Constitution. Even after the bill becomes law, the law may be tested in the courts, and if found contrary to the Constitution, it can be rendered null and void and cannot be enforced through the courts. This final check, known as **judicial review**, is subject to some controversy, but it has been broadly accepted today and is an established principle of law. This concept refers to the power of the courts to hold acts of all branches and levels of government unconstitutional and therefore null and void. It is rooted in the supremacy clause found in Article VI, paragraph 2, of the U.S. Constitution.

Judicial review: The power of the courts to hold acts of all branches and levels of government unconstitutional, null and void, and non-enforceable.

While the Congress is given the vast legislative powers, shared with the other branches, the president is given relatively few constitutional powers in the form of executive functions. These presidential powers include the clear authority to command the military forces of the United States and power to grant pardons and reprieves; to make treaties (with the advice and consent of a two-thirds majority of the Senate); to appoint, send, and receive ambassadors (recognition of foreign governments); to appoint other judges of the federal courts and other officers (with the approval of the Senate); and to convene Congress on extraordinary occasions; but above all, the president is to see that the laws are faithfully executed. Note that all of these powers are appropriately checked. Congress is given the power to declare war and the Senate to consent to treaties and appointments. The vast powers associated with the presidency today are given to that office by the Congress. These powers can be withdrawn by Congress also.

The impeachment and removal power is another example of checks and balances. The House is given the sole power of impeachment (bringing of charges), and only after such charges are brought by the House can the Senate remove the president, vice president, or other officer of the U.S. government. In the Senate trial presided over by the Chief Justice of the Supreme Court, there is a two-thirds majority required to remove an officer, upon "Impeachment for and Conviction of, Treason, Bribery, or other high Crimes and Misdemeanors." Furthermore, "Judgment in Cases of Impeachment shall not extend further than to removal from office. . . ." However, once removed from office, that person may be charged with crime and punished under the normal legal procedures by a court of law.

The Supremacy Clause and Judicial Review

The central issue concerning the Framers of the U.S. Constitution was how to ensure that the national government would have the authority to make laws with supreme authority over the states, although they agreed to limit that authority and place it within bounds defined by the Constitution.

The **supremacy clause** is the heart of the division of authority between the states and the national government and the core concept that enables us to understand and make sense out of the incredible variety of sources of law in the United States today. For this reason it is useful for us to quote it here because it provides the starting point for our understanding of the general principles of conflict of laws. The complexity of our U.S. legal system can be simplified by starting with a clear understanding of the supremacy clause. It provides the following wording:

Supremacy clause: Defines the U.S. Constitution, acts of Congress, and all treaties as the supreme law of the land, making them superior to all other forms of law (Art. VI, para. 2).

> This Constitution, and the Laws of the United States which shall be made in Pursuance thereof; and all Treaties made, or which shall be made, under the authority of the United States shall be the supreme Law of the Land; and the Judges in every State shall be bound thereby, any Thing in the Constitution or Laws of any State to the Contrary notwithstanding.
>
> (Art. VI, para. 2)

Alexander Hamilton, in *Federalist Number 78*, asserted that the federal judiciary would be given life tenure (good behavior) because it must have independence in this system of separation of powers. It would be given the power to negate violations of the other branches of government, he argued, because it was the "least dangerous branch" and would be adequately checked by the "power of the purse" given to Congress and the "power of the sword" given to the presidency.

This power of the courts to negate constitutional violations of the other branches of government is called *judicial review*. This term is somewhat ambiguous in that it may be used sometimes to refer to an appeal from a lower court. However, it is a broader concept that refers to the power of the courts to hold acts of all other branches and levels of government null and void and non-enforceable in the courts if they are found to be in violation of the Constitution.

The state courts have also assumed this role and have the authority to refuse to enforce any act of a governmental agency that is contrary to the U.S. Constitution or to their own state constitutions. This power is exercised not merely by the U.S. Supreme Court, but by all courts, state and federal, and it is merely an extension of the function of the courts to determine the applicable law in specific cases before them. However, the U.S. Supreme Court has the final authority over interpretations of the U.S. Constitution.

The U.S. Supreme Court opinion in *Marbury v. Madison,* 5 U.S. 137, 2 L. Ed. 60 (1803), was the famous decision authored by Chief Justice John Marshall that established the power of the courts to review the constitutionality of actions by the legislative and executive branches. The issue identified by the Court in this case was whether or not an act of Congress (the Judiciary Act of 1789, creating the federal court system) could require the Supreme Court to take cases in original jurisdiction. Normally, cases must be filed first in trial courts of original jurisdiction; however, the Constitution provides for original jurisdiction of the Supreme Court in cases involving disputes between states, between states and the federal government, and in international matters (see Art. III, Sect. 2). The Court held that portion of the Judiciary Act of 1789, which purported to change the original jurisdiction of the Supreme Court, unconstitutional, and therefore it could not be enforced by the Supreme Court. The reasoning of the Court was that in cases of conflict between a U.S. constitutional provision and an act of Congress, the constitutional provision must prevail because it is the more fundamental law that the courts are sworn to uphold. A constitutional amendment would be required to make such changes. This was the first exercise of judicial review against an act of Congress.

It is clear that the Framers intended for the federal courts to have the authority to negate state laws by the U.S. Supreme Court from the wording of the supremacy clause: ". . . and the Judges in every State shall be bound thereby, any Thing in the Constitution or Laws of any State to the Contrary notwithstanding." This means that federal law is superior to all state law when a conflict arises.

Another example of judicial review is provided in Appendix B in the case of *People v. Moore.* Here the court must decide whether an act of the New York state legislature (Art. 18, Sect. 805A of Municipal Law of the State of New York) is unconstitutionally vague and non-enforceable. The court must look to previous federal court opinions to determine the answer. Both the U.S. Constitution and the New York Constitution (due process clauses) are invoked as being in conflict with the state statute.

The Sources of Law and Conflict of Laws

The wording of the U.S. Constitution in the supremacy clause expressly indicates that an act of Congress must be "pursuant to the Constitution," in other words, a valid exercise of its authority under the most fundamental source of law. This power of the courts to hold acts, not only of the Congress but also of the president and the states, unconstitutional is inherent in the judicial function, which must decide which law is to prevail in cases of conflict. The Constitution creates a hierarchy of laws that enables us to understand how the various sources of law discussed in the evolution of law can be rationally ordered. The sources of law in order of their priority are displayed in Table 2.2.

Conflict of Laws

The problem of **conflict of laws** is especially significant in the U.S. legal system, which has so many sources of law that may be applicable. When different sources of law come into conflict with each other, the courts must decide which law prevails. Much of the common law deals with this problem, and a series of volumes entitled *The Restatement of the Law: Conflict of Laws* covers this subject in greater detail. (See list of *Restatements* at the end of this chapter.)

Conflict of laws:
When different sources of law come into conflict with each other, the courts must decide which law prevails. The general principle of determination is that the more fundamental law prevails. (See *Restatement of the Law: Conflict of Laws.*)

Table 2.2 **THE BASIC ORDER OF PRIORITY AMONG SOURCES OF LAW IN THE U.S. LEGAL SYSTEM**

Federal Sources of Law	State Sources of Law
1. U.S. Constitution	1. Constitutional law
2. Acts of Congress and treaties	2. Statutory law
3. Federal common law and equity	3. Common law and equity (except in Louisiana)
4. Entire state hierarchy of laws (all other laws)	4. Contracts

Although there are a total of 51 separate legal systems in our entire federal order, there is a practical way to understand how conflict of laws, which frequently occur, can be resolved. The basic principle for deciding which law prevails is that *the most fundamental law takes priority* over the less fundamental law, as indicated in the ordering of these sources in Table 2.2.

When there is no provision of the U.S. Constitution, act of Congress, or treaty involved, the state constitution prevails over state statutory law and common law prevails over contracts.

Contracts are private agreements that create legally binding obligations between the parties, and they can be enforced in the courts if they meet the legal requirements provided in the common law or statutory law. Note, however, that the U.S. Constitution prohibits the states from "making laws impairing the Obligation of Contracts" in Article I, Section 10.

Contracts:
Private agreements that create legally binding obligations between the parties.

When federal sources of law are involved, the hierarchy is somewhat different. Here, the U.S. Constitution prevails over all other forms of law in the United States. Acts of Congress and treaties are given an equal status in the wording of the document, and they have been treated on a level of equality with each other by decisions of the Supreme Court. When they are deemed by the courts to be in conflict with the U.S. Constitution itself, they are non-enforceable and the constitutional provision prevails. There are areas of federal common law and equity as well as administrative regulations that are a part of the body of federal law (see Art. III, Sect. 2). All other state sources of law are subordinate to the U.S. Constitution, acts of Congress, and treaties, as the supremacy clause dictates.

Individual Rights and Due Process of Law

At the Constitutional Convention of 1787, the Framers of our national Constitution thought that the limited set of prohibitions on governmental authority in Article I, Section 9, would be sufficient to provide protection for individual rights. They also argued that the state bills of rights in the newly formulated state constitutions would be sufficient. However, during the ratification struggle it became clear that a federal Bill of Rights was needed to obtain popular support for the Constitution. Several states ratified the Constitution with the understanding that a Bill of Rights would be added by the amending process provided in the original U.S. Constitution. The initial ratification process required nine states to ratify by special conventions elected by the voters in each state before the union would be consummated. By 1789, when the Constitution was put into effect and the first national elections held, 12 states had ratified. Rhode Island finally ratified in 1790 when all original 13 states entered the union.

The subsequent amending process described in Article V requires *proposal* of amendments by a two-thirds majority of both houses of Congress and *ratification* by three-fourths of the states. There is another method of proposal by a national constitutional convention that may be convened by a two-thirds majority of the states. This convention could then make proposals that would have to be ratified by three-fourths of the states. However, this second method of proposal has never been used.

There are also two methods of ratification depending upon the designation of the proposing agency. The states may be required to act through special constitutional conventions or their own state legislatures. In 1791, the first ten amendments were ratified by the states through their state representatives, and they form what is referred to as our national Bill of Rights.

The states have their own amending processes for their own constitutions that vary widely. However, all of them today require the ultimate approval of state constitutional changes by direct popular vote. Many states today even allow the voters to initiate changes through the *initiative* and *referendum* process, requiring the approval by a certain percentage of the voters to place a specific issue on the ballot and allowing the voters to bypass the state assemblies (legislatures).

The National Bill of Rights

The national Bill of Rights is an example of the practical consequence of the idea of natural law insofar as the congressional drafters of this concept could devise. They knew that this was an imperfect list as illustrated in the language of the Ninth Amendment: "The enumeration in the Constitution of certain rights shall not be construed to deny or disparage others retained by the people."

Many of the rights found in these first ten amendments go back to the English Magna Carta (1215), when King John of England was forced to acknowledge that the king must obey the law, because that law made him king. Others went back to the English Bill of Rights in 1689 and the Act of Settlement in 1701. However, there are unique American contributions in the wording and content of these provisions.

According to the First Amendment of the Bill of Rights, "Congress shall make no law respecting an establishment of religion, or prohibiting the free exercise thereof; or abridging the freedom of speech, or of the press, or the right of the people peaceably to assemble, and to petition the Government for a redress of grievances." These First Amendment freedoms of religion, speech, press, assembly, and petition serve as our blueprint for personal liberty. They provide that individuals have the freedom to think and believe what they will without governmental interference, to communicate beliefs to others, to participate in peaceful collective action, and to express grievances. Although the First Amendment provides that "Congress shall make no law" limiting speech, there are certain types of speech that receive no protection. These include obscenity, child pornography, libel, fighting words, true threats, and incitement to imminent lawless action.

The Second Amendment's right to "keep and bear arms" has been subject to recent decisions by the U.S. Supreme Court. For many years, this provision was interpreted to protect only a collective right on the part of a "well-regulated militia" to bear arms. In *District of Columbia v. Heller*, 554 U.S. 570 (2008), the Supreme Court ruled that the Second Amendment protects an individual's right to possess a firearm as opposed merely to a collective right. The Court later ruled that this freedom was extended to state and local government prohibitions in *McDonald v. Chicago*, 561 U.S. 3025 (2010).

The Third Amendment's protection against the quartering of troops in private homes has never presented much of a problem.

The Fourth, Fifth, Sixth, and Eighth Amendments all pertain to criminal matters, including an extensive list of fundamental concepts that will be elaborated in Part IV of this text. They include such significant concepts as protection of privacy in the criminal investigative process, limitations upon formal accusation of crime, limitations upon criminal prosecutions (including the right to trial by jury, confrontation of witness, access to compulsory process for obtaining witnesses, and the right to counsel), and finally limitations upon punishments in the Eighth Amendment.

The Seventh Amendment deals with civil litigation and guarantees the right to trial by jury in "suits at common law" where the amount exceeds $20. Here the phrase "Suits at common law" excludes cases brought in equity. As will be explained more fully later, this provision applies only in federal courts.

The Eighth, Ninth, and Tenth Amendments have already been explained. However, it is important to note here the vagueness of the Tenth Amendment's wording when compared with the wording of the Second Article of the Articles of Confederation. The previous document used the following wording in Article II: "Each State retains its sovereignty, freedom, and independence, and every power, jurisdiction, and right, which is not by this Confederation expressly delegated to the United States in Congress assembled." The wording of the Tenth Amendment simply says, "The powers not delegated to the United States by the Constitution, nor prohibited by it to the States, are reserved to the States respectively, or to the people."

The Due Process Clauses

The opening statement in the national Bill of Rights colors the entire ten amendments that were ratified in 1791. This introduction cannot discuss all of the amendments; however, it is important to explain that the original ten amendments were intended to limit the national government alone. Each state had its own bill of rights, but the provisions of each differed significantly in content and state court interpretation. Until the end of the Civil War and the adoption of the "Civil War Amendments"—the Thirteenth, Fourteenth, and Fifteenth Amendments, the Supreme Court was only willing to enforce the provisions of the national Bill of Rights against the federal government (*Barron v. Mayor of Baltimore*, 32 US 243, 1833).

Originally, James Madison had proposed an amendment in the Bill of Rights. His original Fifth Amendment provided that "[n]o State shall violate the equal rights of conscience, or the freedom of the press, or the trial by jury in criminal cases." Madison considered this his most important amendment because he foresaw that states would often violate individual rights more than the federal government. But, the Senate did not ratify this proposed amendment, so it never made it into the Bill of Rights.

This meant that for many years the Bill of Rights limited only the federal government, not state and local government officials. It was only through the due process clause of the Fourteenth Amendment that the freedoms in the Bill of Rights became extended to the states. This process was known as *selective incorporation*. This idea in criminal cases will be dealt with more fully in Part IV explaining the criminal justice process, but the "due process" clauses of both the Fifth Amendment and the Fourteenth Amendment are so important that they must be mentioned here.

The Fifth Amendment prohibits the national government from depriving any person of "life, liberty, or property, without due process of law." This same phrase is used in the Fourteenth Amendment, but with the clear intention of application against state action: ". . . nor shall any State deprive any person of life, liberty, or property, without due process of law; nor deny to any person within its jurisdiction the equal protection of the laws." Much of our recent history in the United States is involved with implementing these provisions.

There is an enormous body of constitutional law surrounding the national Bill of Rights that results from decisions of the Supreme Court interpreting these provisions in controversies that have arisen over their specific meaning. This body of law may be accessed by reference to the state or federal codes, which include case annotations associated with each provision of the Constitution. Note here that judicial opinions interpreting the meaning of constitutional provisions have the rank of constitutional law in the previously explained hierarchy of sources of law because they have their source in the Constitution. These precedents are not part of common law, which has no other source than judicial decision.

The other amendments to the U.S. Constitution are far less controversial; however, their wording may be puzzling and require some clarification. The Eleventh and Twelfth Amendments are perhaps the most difficult to comprehend. The Eleventh Amendment simply prohibits damage suits against a state in federal courts. This was an attempt on the part of the states to preserve sovereign immunity from civil liability. It has had very little effect in practice since suits against governmental officials may be brought, and equity actions seeking enforcement of the Constitution, acts of Congress, and treaties are not prohibited. The Twelfth Amendment simply rewrites the provision of the original Constitution concerning the electoral college to provide for separate selection of the president and vice president. This was to prevent the tie situation between Thomas Jefferson and Aaron Burr that existed in the election of 1800, causing the outcome to be decided in the House of Representatives where each state gets only one vote.

The other amendments are far less obscure for the modern reader and require little explanation. The Thirteenth through Fifteenth Amendments were all adopted after the Civil War. The most important of these provisions basically prohibits slavery, defines U.S. citizenship, and prohibits the denial or abridgment by either the national government or the states of the right of citizens of the United States to vote on account of race, color, or previous condition of servitude. Note that these Civil War amendments all carry the right of Congress to enforce by appropriate legislation.

The rest of the amendments allow Congress to lay and collect income taxes, provide for the direct election of senators, extend the right to vote to women, allow citizens of the District of Columbia to select presidential electors, prohibit the poll tax, provide for Congress to select a vice president when the office is vacant, extend the voting rights to 18-year-olds, and prohibit the Congress from increasing their salaries during a single two-year term. This Twenty-seventh Amendment is notable in that it was one of the original 12 proposed amendments that did not pass by three-fourths of the states in 1791 when the national Bill of Rights was ratified. Since there was no congressional instruction that it could not be revived after all these years, the proposed amendment was revived and finally received enough state ratifications to become law in 1992. Members of Congress must now wait for a new election of the House before completing the process of increasing their own salaries.

The due process clause of the Fourteenth Amendment is by far the most significant provision of these amendments in terms of stimulating legal actions alleging violations of the U.S. Constitution originating in the states. The meaning of this clause will occupy us throughout this textbook, because it has produced, through court interpretation, a set of minimal standards for civil due process and criminal due process, as well as administrative due process. The states have their own bills of rights and may extend these procedural rights within their own state; however, the U.S. Constitution provides a set of minimal standards.

Substantive Law and Procedural Law

In our legal system, which stresses procedural rights of the individual, there is a great body of law that restricts governmental procedure when applying the law. In order to understand the basic sources of law described in this chapter, it is important to make a distinction between *substantive* law, such as crimes, and *procedural* law, such as the right to a fair trial. It is not always easy to distinguish the difference between them, but courts are required to make these distinctions in the course of administering the law.

Substantive law refers to the rules of law that have been developed to govern the behavior of individuals in our society. These rules may be criminal, civil, or regulatory rules of individual behavior. They form the great body of laws that we normally associate with the function of law.

Substantive law:
Rules of law that restrict individual behavior (e.g., crimes and torts).

However, there is another body of law that has been developed to regulate the government itself in its administration of the law. This body of laws is called **procedural law** and restricts the governmental authorities that administer the law as well as the legislative and executive institutions that create positive law. These rules are mainly constitutional in character but may include statutory and common law sources. Table 2.3 compares the substantive and procedural areas of law.

Procedural law:
Rules that restrict governmental authorities in administering the substantive law (e.g., fair trial, jury procedure in criminal cases, fair hearing in administrative cases).

The substantive areas of law are listed in the first column of Table 2.3. They can be found in the state and federal codes, for the most part, and define individual violations, governmental regulations restricting business interests, civil wrongs of a personal injury nature, rules concerning property rights, and contract provisions (which are substantive rules enforced by courts between the parties when valid).

The procedural areas of law are essentially those listed and found in the national and state bills of rights. There is, however, a great body of procedural rules of courts that is much more complex; these rules will be discussed throughout the rest of this textbook. The basic concepts of due process of law and equal protection of the laws are central to the development of this very important body of law. The ability of courts to do justice involves adherence to these principles of law, which are fundamental to our sense of justice.

There is a curious term in the list of procedural rules that may cause difficulty for beginning students—**substantive due process**. This term is used to describe an even more fundamental concept in our constitutional law that restricts even the political branches of government that make our laws. Describing these rules has been the major objective of this chapter. While this term may be associated with an era of *economic substantive due process* concerning contract rights, which has been subsequently overturned by the New Deal court, the modern Supreme Court has invoked *substantive due process* to protect personal liberty values ranging from reproductive autonomy, to the right to marry, to the right of families to live together. When the courts hold acts of the legislative authority unconstitutional, they are exercising substantive due process of law because they

Substantive due process:
Term used to describe the power of the courts to hold acts of the legislative authority nonenforceable when in violation of constitutional powers granted to the legislature.

Table 2.3 **COMPARING SUBSTANTIVE LAW AND PROCEDURAL LAW EXAMPLES**

Substantive Law Examples	Procedural Law Examples
CRIMINAL OFFENSES AGAINST THE STATE Felonies (serious crime) Misdemeanors (lesser crimes) Summary violations (traffic violations)	**DUE PROCESS AND EQUAL PROTECTION OF LAW** The rules of civil, criminal, and administrative procedure and evidence: The right to a fair trial The right to demand a jury trial in felony cases The right to consult a lawyer when accused of a crime The right to be informed of the charges The right to a fair hearing in administrative cases The right to access to the courts The right to enforce contracts
CIVIL DUTIES AND RESPONSIBILITIES Administrative regulations Torts (personal injury wrongs) Property rights (real, personal, and intellectual) Contracts	**SUBSTANTIVE DUE PROCESS** Unconstitutional acts

are prohibiting a substantive law that is in violation of the constitutional authority granted to the legislature from being enforced.

An example of substantive due process is provided in the cases you have been assigned to read and is found in Appendix B. *People v. Moore* involves a *conflict of laws* situation in which even a trial court holds an act of the state legislature unconstitutionally vague and non-enforceable. This is an exercise of substantive due process because it invalidates a portion of a substantive rule. The legislative statute was not specific enough to meet the constitutional due process standards.

The case of *Marvin v. Marvin* in Appendix B illustrates a contract dispute. The plaintiff seeks to enforce an expressed contract in the California courts. She is denied the right to bring her case to trial by a preliminary ruling of the trial court of original jurisdiction. She then appeals her case to the California Supreme Court. Find out how this court decides her claim to a right to bring her case to trial.

American jurisprudence places great emphasis on procedural fairness. The meaning of the constitutional phrase *due process of law* is vague, and

I. CIVIL ACTIONS IN LAW AND EQUITY

Substantive duties owed by one individual to another which include torts, contracts, property, or other constitutional or statutory rights.

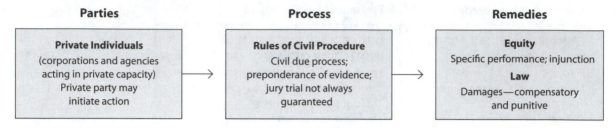

Parties	Process	Remedies
Private Individuals (corporations and agencies acting in private capacity) Private party may initiate action	**Rules of Civil Procedure** Civil due process; preponderance of evidence; jury trial not always guaranteed	**Equity** Specific performance; injunction **Law** Damages—compensatory and punitive

II. CRIMINAL ACTIONS

Substantive duty involves conduct that is offensive to society as generally defined by legislative authority.

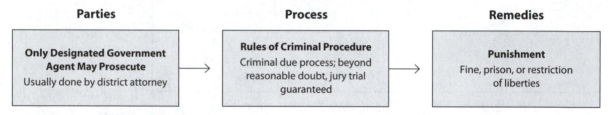

Parties	Process	Remedies
Only Designated Government Agent May Prosecute Usually done by district attorney	**Rules of Criminal Procedure** Criminal due process; beyond reasonable doubt, jury trial guaranteed	**Punishment** Fine, prison, or restriction of liberties

III. ADMINISTRATIVE ACTIONS

Substantive duty involves conduct regulated by government in its capacity to enforce administrative rules and regulations authorized by legislative authority.

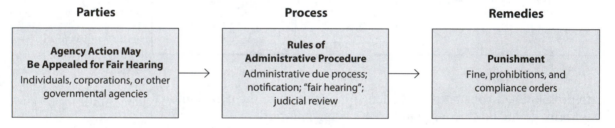

Parties	Process	Remedies
Agency Action May Be Appealed for Fair Hearing Individuals, corporations, or other governmental agencies	**Rules of Administrative Procedure** Administrative due process; notification; "fair hearing"; judicial review	**Punishment** Fine, prohibitions, and compliance orders

there is no comprehensive definition of due process that applies to all situations. However, the central core of the idea of procedural due process centers on fundamental fairness. "A person should always have notice and a real chance to present his or her side in a legal dispute, and no law or governmental procedure should be arbitrary or unfair" (Neubauer 1991, 40).

Although all legal actions must be essentially fair and are limited by procedural rules recognized by law, they differ considerably in form and substance. Civil, criminal, and administrative procedures require separate legal actions, although a real-life situation may involve all these dimensions. Each legal action has to conform to the rules of procedure in a specific area and must be filed with the appropriate court (or agency) having the authority to decide such matters. The following overview of the three basic divisions of legal procedure (see Figure 2.1) will provide an initial orientation to the fundamental differences among civil, criminal, and administrative actions. Parts III, IV, and V of this text contain extended hypothetical examples of the various stages involved in these forms of legal actions.

Civil Legal Actions

Private (or civil) law is the area of legal process that allows individuals to bring their disputes into the courts for authoritative settlement. Civil legal actions enable individuals to file suit before the courts against another individual, group of individuals, or corporations. Corporations generally have the right to sue and be sued in civil jurisdiction, and even governmental agencies can be sued (or bring suit) where governmental authority has been granted to do so. The fundamental principle of sovereign immunity prevents government from being sued without its consent; however, in modern times, such authority has been extensively granted by legislative enactment.

The *plaintiff* is the party bringing suit, and the *defendant* is the party being sued. Civil actions may be taken in both law and equity in areas involving substantive duties owed by one individual to another, including torts, contracts, property, and other constitutional or statutory rights. Civil due process involves a less stringent standard of proof than criminal due process; the standard is known as "preponderance of the evidence." A jury trial is not always guaranteed in civil actions.

Criminal Legal Actions

Crimes are defined as conduct deemed offensive to society. Criminal legal actions are brought only by a designated agent of either the state or federal government, known as a *prosecutor*. A crime is defined by the legislative authority as a wrong against society, so the governmental entity that has been wronged must bring suit.

The rules of criminal procedure are quite extensive and subject to all the constitutional guarantees because they involve the most severe penalties. Criminal due process involves the more stringent standard of proof "beyond a reasonable doubt," and a trial by jury is guaranteed.

Administrative Legal Actions

Administrative law governs administrative agencies and courts in actions not covered by civil or criminal procedures. These governmental actions include court decrees, summary fines for violations of governmental regulations, and court orders. Governmental agencies must exercise their authority within the limits of fundamental rules of fairness. They must not be arbitrary or capricious, and they must follow *fundamental due process of law*.

Administrative standards vary considerably and, in many instances, depend upon statutory authority as well as common law court decisions. Due notification of an action by a governmental agency, the right to a *fair hearing*, and the right to confront witnesses are considered minimal guarantees to ensure that the fundamental principles of fairness are met. A fair hearing does not mean a trial, but it does mean that the private party has a right to be heard.

> **ASSIGNMENT:** Read all of the cases in Appendix B before we proceed to the next chapter. They will provide further examples of the concepts we will introduce. These cases illustrate most of the basic concepts that are introduced in Part I of this text. In the next chapter, we will discuss legal reasoning and how to brief a case in law. By the end of the next chapter you should be able to go back over these cases and brief them properly.

The case illustrations in the appendix demonstrate the extent to which the actions, even of a private university, are required to meet fundamental due process standards. *Ryan v. Hofstra University* is a civil legal action brought in the New York state courts in equity to nullify an administrative action by Hofstra University that expelled Robert Ryan from the university, fined him and his parents over $1,000, and prohibited him from obtaining his records to transfer to another school for alleged vandalism. Read this case to discover how the court ruled.

Katko v. Briney is a civil legal action to recover damages sustained when the plaintiff entered an abandoned, boarded-up farmhouse looking for fruit jars (a tort—see Chapter 1). The defendant had set a spring-loaded shotgun to deter intruders, and the plaintiff sustained permanent damage to his leg when he was shot by this device. Does he have a right to recover the damages awarded by a trial court in Iowa?

It should be noted that all three of the forms of legal action listed above could be undertaken at the same time, before different courts and administrative agencies, concerning the same events or circumstances. The next chapter will discuss the organization of the state and federal courts and their authority to administer the law in specific cases. We will elaborate on the meaning of the due process clause throughout this text.

CHAPTER SUMMARY

1. The U.S. legal system consists of 51 legal systems that are coordinated by the U.S. Constitution. The overwhelming majority of the states derived their basic legal concepts from English common law, which

was practiced in the American colonies for 150 years before they declared their independence.

2. *Common law* is judge-made law that has no other source than judicial decision. It originated as the practice of judges who were instructed by the king to go out and do justice.

3. The principle of *stare decisis* generally requires that previous decisions (*precedent*) be followed in cases involving similar fact situations. The recording of these cases began to accumulate a body of law with general principles that are found today in the *Restatements of the Law*.

4. This body of common law was supplemented by the concept of *equity* (fairness) administered by the Chancery Court to grant exceptions to the law. *Equity* today is a form of remedy used when one is asking the court for a specific performance order to prevent unfair injury, such as an injunction.

5. Common law evolves through *cases of first impression* (where new fact situations extend the common law) and the overturning of past precedents that are found no longer to be fair. *Stare decisis* is not a rule of law but a general guiding principle for courts. Natural law is an ancient concept that provides a moral standard by which governments and laws have been judged. It has been associated with common law and constitutional law and *asserts that* law must be consistent with the fundamental rights of individuals in society. Statutory law refers to legislative enactments, or written positive law.

6. The schools of jurisprudence (philosophy of law) include the rights-based school of natural law, the positivist school of law emanating from sovereign authority, and the historical school. Modern democratic theory accepts the idea that law arises from the popular consent of the people who form themselves into a legal community.

7. Louisiana is a *code law state* that does not share the common law heritage of English law development. This state's basic concepts of law are derived from the ancient Roman code law tradition.

8. The U.S. Constitution creates a federal structure by dividing *sovereignty* (governmental authority) between the national government and the states. This is done by listing the *delegated powers* going to the national government and reserving those not given up to the states or to the people.

9. *Separation of powers* is another principle of dividing powers within a governmental structure to prevent the abuse of power. It employs a system of checks and balances to achieve this result. The *legislative process*, for example, ultimately requires the approval and cooperation of all three branches.

10. The *supremacy clause* makes the U.S. Constitution, acts of Congress, and treaties the supreme law of the land and instructs the judges in

every state to give these federal instruments of law priority over all state laws.

11. *Judicial review* is the power of the courts to hold acts of other branches and levels of government unconstitutional and non-enforceable when they are in conflict with the Constitution. Both state and federal courts exercise this power in relationship to both the U.S. and state constitutions, but the U.S. Constitution has the highest priority.

12. The general hierarchy of laws used to decide *conflict of laws* gives highest priority to constitutions (with the U.S. Constitution, acts of Congress, and treaties given priority over all state laws). Statutory law is given priority over common law and equity, and contracts are inferior to common law in that order.

13. *Substantive laws* are those rules that have been developed to govern the behavior of individuals in our society. They include crimes, torts (personal injury wrongs), and government regulations.

14. *Procedural laws* are those rules that restrict the governmental authorities that administer the law as well as the legislative and executive institutions that create positive law. They include many of our most fundamental rights as individuals, such as due process of law, equal protection of the laws, and a fair trial.

15. The U.S. Constitution was originally ratified by each state joining the union. It can be amended by the ultimate requirement that three-fourths of the states approve. State constitutions today require the ultimate approval of the voters directly.

REVIEW EXERCISE

Match the following terms with their most appropriate meaning.

TERMS
1. Common law
2. Stare decisis
3. Restatements of the Law
4. Equity
5. Case of first impression
6. Jurisprudence
7. Statutory law
8. Sovereignty
9. International law
10. Federalism
11. Delegated powers
12. Exclusive national powers

MEANING
____ judge-made law
____ body of law created by legislative authority
____ philosophy, or study of law
____ general principles of common law
____ doctrine of following judicial precedent
____ remedy seeking a specific performance order from court
____ new factual situation never decided by court previously
____ different sources of law in conflict
____ law that restricts individual behavior, for example, crimes
____ power of courts to hold any governmental act unconstitutional
____ supreme and independent political authority
____ the law of nations
____ the law making process
____ divided sovereignty
____ powers given to national government alone

13. Concurrent powers
14. Separation of
    powers
15. Legislative process
16. Judicial review
17. Supremacy clause
18. Conflict of laws
19. Contracts
20. Substantive law
21. Procedural law
22. Substantive due
    process

____ powers shared by the national and state governments
____ division of authority within a governmental structure
____ private agreements which make law for parties
____ defines the U.S. Constitution, acts of Congress, and treaties as supreme law of the land
____ the power of the courts to hold acts of all branches and levels of government unconstitutional, null, and non-enforceable when in violation of the Constitution
____ powers given to the legislature
____ rules that restrict governmental authorities in administering the law

DISCUSSION QUESTIONS

1. What is common law? Why does it form the base of most of our state legal systems?
2. What is equity? How is it used in our legal systems today?
3. Compare natural law philosophy with positive law.
4. How does the U.S. Constitution divide sovereignty between the national government and the states? What is meant by delegated powers, exclusive national powers, and concurrent powers?
5. How was separation of powers employed to control the legislative process in the U.S. Constitution?
6. How does the supremacy clause provide a means of resolving conflict of laws that are bound to occur frequently in our federal legal system?
7. What is the basic order of priority of state sources of laws?
8. What is the difference between substantive laws and procedural laws?
9. Do you think federal judges should be given life tenure? What are the advantages and disadvantages of life tenure for federal judges?
10. How can the U.S. and state constitutions be changed?
11. What is the importance of the national Bill of Rights?
12. How have the Civil War Amendments altered the application of the national Bill of Rights?

ASSIGNMENTS

ASSIGNMENT: Turn to Appendix B, on page 555 of this text and begin by reading the first two illustrative court opinions provided in edited form. There are six illustrative cases in Appendix B that represent examples of cases in law for your analysis. You will be asked to brief these cases from Appendix B by the end of Part I of this text.

The first four chapters will be used to provide the appropriate background needed to accomplish this task.

ASSIGNMENT: Read the third and fourth cases in Appendix B found on pages 562. These are criminal cases that illustrate court opinions concerning the interpretation of statutory law, or

positive law. Look for the problems of interpreting the intent of the legislature in these cases.
ASSIGNMENT: Read the U.S. Constitution found in Appendix A on page 543. Look for the general methods used to separate legislative, executive, and judicial functions and the method used to

divide powers between the states and the national government (see powers of Congress in Article I). What rights are reserved to the states? What are the methods of ratification and amendment? Come to class prepared to discuss what you have learned from this exercise.

SOURCES AND SUGGESTED READING

Abadinsky, Howard. 1991. *Law and Justice: An Introduction to the American Legal System*. 2d ed. Chicago: Nelson-Hall Publishers.

Damaska, Mirjam R. 1986. *The Faces of Justice and State Authority: A Comparative Approach to the Legal Process*. New Haven, Conn.: Yale University Press.

Edmonds, Palmer D. 1959 (originally published in 1788). *Law and Civilization*. Washington, D.C.: Public Affairs Press.

The Federalist. 1937. New York: New Modern Library.

*Garraty, John A. 1987. *Quarrels that Have Shaped the Constitution*. New York: Harper & Row Publishers.

*Glendon, Mary Ann. 1994. *A Nation Under Lawyers*. Cambridge, Mass.: Harvard University Press.

Holmes, Oliver Wendell Jr. 1881. *The Common Law*. Boston: Little, Brown and Co.

*Knight, Alfred H. 1996. *The Life of the Law*. New York: Crown Publishers, Inc.

Maine, Henry S. 1961. *Ancient Law: Its Connection with the Early History of Society, and Its Relation to Modern Ideas*. New York: Cockcroft & Co.

Murphy, Walter E., and C. Herman Pritchett. 1986. *Courts, Judges, and Politics*. New York: Random House.

Neubauer, David W. 1991. *Judicial Process*. Pacific Grove, Calif.: Brooks/Cole Publishing Co.

U.S. Constitution, reprinted in Appendix B in this text.

*Vile, John R. 1997. *A Companion to the United States Constitution and Its Amendments*. 2d ed. Westport, Conn.: Praeger Publishers.

Zane, John Maxcy. 1927 (republished 1998). *The Story of the Law*. 2d ed. Indianapolis: Liberty Fund.
(*Recommended reading)

LEGAL LIBRARY RESOURCES
See Federal Practice Digest and appropriate state digests. See also American Law Institute (publisher) *Restatements of the Law:*
Agency (Second) (1954)
Conflicts (Second) (1969)
Contracts (Second) (1880)
Foreign Relations Law of the United States (Third) (1987)
Judgments (Second) (1942)
Property (1936-44)
Landlord and Tenant (Second) (1976)
Restitution (1936)
Security (1941)
Torts (Second) (1964–77)
Torts: Products Liability (Third) (1998)
Trusts (Second) (1957)
United States Code Annotated and the appropriate annotated code for your state. (See *constitutions* and *annotations*: your state code will have a volume devoted to constitutions and will provide annotations to both the U.S. Constitution and your state's constitution. Case citations will include a paragraph describing the court interpretations of particular provisions.) Note that many libraries now have these codes on CD-ROM, which provides electronic access.

Court Jurisdiction

This chapter will explain the practical aspects of administration of the law in our federal legal system. In a practical sense, the law develops from court decisions that resolve disputed legal issues in society. These disputes take the form of civil, criminal, and administrative legal actions. It is the central function of the courts to decide in each case before them what the law means as applied to a particular set of facts. Juries decide disputed questions of fact, such as the credibility of a witness or whether a certain event took place. However, judges decide questions of law.

As we have explained in Chapter 1, the state courts handle the overwhelming majority of actions filed in U.S. courts. Even if one considers all cases handled by both the state and federal courts, the state courts handle nearly 30 times the number of cases than do federal courts.

In our system of federalism, the 50 states and the federal government have their own court systems, each of which include a hierarchy of courts. This court hierarchy includes an ordering of courts from those of the lowest legal authority to the courts of last resort, or final authority. (Note that the nomenclature of the courts varies from jurisdiction to jurisdiction. For example, in most states the supreme court is the highest court, but in New York the supreme court is a trial court.)

This chapter will explain the complex dual hierarchy of our state and federal courts and the ways in which they interact. We will begin with the federal courts because their jurisdiction (authority to decide disputes) is granted in the U.S. Constitution, and the jurisdiction of the state courts is residual, meaning that they have ultimate authority over all other disputes. State courts are created by state constitutions.

THE JURISDICTION AND HIERARCHY OF FEDERAL COURTS

The federal courts have what is called **limited jurisdiction**, that is, the authority to hear only those types of cases that are authorized by the U.S. Constitution. Article III, Section 2, specifically lists the extent of

Limited jurisdiction: Authority to decide subject matter disputes in a limited number of types of cases.

the judicial power of the federal courts. It states clearly, "The judicial Power shall extend to all Cases, in Law and Equity, arising under this Constitution, the Laws of the United States, and Treaties made, or which shall be made, under their Authority . . . ." This general principle is referred to as **federal question jurisdiction**. We will first discuss federal question jurisdiction of the federal courts because it is the most fundamental principle.

Federal question jurisdiction:
The basic jurisdiction of the federal courts to hear and decide all cases in law and equity arising under the U.S. Constitution, the laws of the United States, and treaties.

Federal Question Jurisdiction

The language of the U.S. Constitution quoted above has no clear and precise definition. Inventive lawyers have found many ways to argue successfully that their case "arises under" the federal question jurisdiction of the federal courts and have had their cases heard. In fact, none of the various definitions provided by the courts seems to encompass all the different cases. Perhaps the best definition is that the federal courts will entertain cases that involve *a substantial claim founded directly upon federal law*. Notwithstanding the controversial nature of this distinction, some examples of federal question cases are disputes involving federal crimes, federal income tax laws, the federal securities laws, bankruptcy laws, or federal constitutional claims.

The U.S. Constitution contains a number of very specific grants of jurisdiction that have been interpreted to be "exclusive." A case over which the federal courts have **exclusive jurisdiction** is one that is denied to the states. This relates to subject matter jurisdiction where these topics are the "item" or the "object" of the legal action. Among these very narrow grants of exclusive jurisdiction are

Exclusive jurisdiction:
Areas of federal court jurisdiction that are denied to the states.

- all cases of admiralty or maritime jurisdiction,
- all cases affecting ambassadors and other public ministers and consuls,
- all cases in which the United States is a party, and
- all cases of disputes between states or states and the national government (sovereign entities).

There are many other types of cases over which the federal courts have exclusive jurisdiction derived from grants of federal authority found elsewhere in the Constitution. These areas of exclusive jurisdiction are implied by the wording of the Constitution and practice of the courts. They include

- bankruptcy proceedings,
- cases arising under patent or copyright laws,
- cases involving customs duties and regulation of imports and exports,

- cases involving some sort of penalty under a federal law, and
- cases involving interstate commerce and antitrust actions.

An important part of federal question jurisdiction involves federal crimes. Federal crimes are included within the broad jurisdiction of the federal courts over all offenses that are against the laws of the United States. A person accused of a federal crime must be brought before the federal courts, and states cannot prosecute for a violation of a federal statute. The U.S. Supreme Court has ruled that there are no federal "common law crimes" (*U.S. v. Hudson*, 11 U.S. (7 Cranch) 32, 1812). This means that all federal crimes must be clearly defined by an act of Congress. The *federal criminal code* refers to Title 18 of the *United States Code* (18 U.S.C.), which defines a broad variety of federal crimes. The same title of the *U.S. Code Annotated* (18 U.S.C.A) is a better source in that it provides reference to the court interpretations and background resources related to these statutory provisions in so-called *annotations*. Many legal researchers prefer annotated codes for this very reason, as we explain in more detail in Chapter 4.

Diversity of Citizenship and Pendent Jurisdiction

There are areas of overlapping, or **concurrent jurisdiction**, where both the federal courts and the state courts may have authority to decide the dispute. This overlapping occurs in only two types of cases, referred to as *diversity of citizenship* actions and *pendent jurisdiction* cases.

> **Concurrent jurisdiction:** Areas where both state and federal courts have jurisdiction to hear the same types of disputes.

Civil cases involving disputes between citizens of different states, or between a state government and a citizen of another state, or between a citizen of a state and foreign government or foreign individual, are legal actions that may be brought either in state court or federal court. This is referred to as **diversity jurisdiction**, and very strict rules apply to their acceptance in federal courts. The party bringing the legal action has the opportunity to decide where the case will be filed in diversity actions. As we will explain more fully in Chapter 10, there may be various opportunities for choice of court in civil actions. To meet the federal court's criteria for diversity of citizenship jurisdiction (see 28 U.S.C. §1332) there must be genuine diversity of citizenship and each party bringing the action must have a claim that is greater than $75,000. Examples of diversity of citizenship jurisdiction are as follows:

> **Diversity jurisdiction:** Civil legal actions involving disputes between citizens of different states where the sum in question is greater than $75,000.

- Disputes between citizens of different states. Example: A citizen (or corporation) of Maryland sues a citizen (or corporation) of Texas.
- Disputes between citizens of a state within the United States and a citizen of a foreign state. Example: A citizen of Tennessee sues a citizen of Germany.

• Disputes between citizens of one state, or several states, and a foreign state. Example: Citizens of New York and New Jersey sue France.

These examples are not exhaustive in that it may be possible for a citizen of one state to sue another state. However, the Eleventh Amendment may bar such suits. Disputes between two states may also qualify under diversity jurisdiction, and the parties bringing the action may elect to file their dispute in the federal district court (trial level). However, they may also take advantage of the constitutional provision that gives the Supreme Court original jurisdiction in such cases.

The Judiciary Act of 1789, the federal law that established the federal court system, provided for diversity jurisdiction of the federal courts. The historical reason for giving this area of overlapping jurisdiction to the federal trial courts was fear that the state courts in which these cases might be tried would be biased against noncitizens. Thus, to avoid any hint of bias or prejudice, a neutral forum (court) for diversity of citizenship cases is provided in the federal courts.

The first case in the appendix of this textbook, *Du Pont v. Christopher*, is a case that involves diversity of citizenship between the parties. The federal Fifth Circuit Court of Appeals is a neutral forum to which the appellant (the party bringing the appeal) has elected to bring the case. As explained in the introduction to this case, there is also an appeal from a *preliminary judgment* (before trial) of the Texas trial courts. The Du Pont Corporation had the initial option of filing its case in the state of Texas or in a federal district court in that state. It chose the state trial court; however, the defendants now have the choice on appeal.

Pendent jurisdiction refers to another type of overlap that occurs between state courts and federal courts. It allows the federal district court (trial court in the federal court system) to make decisions on matters that otherwise would be exclusively within the jurisdiction of a state court. If a federal court already has jurisdiction over a case, it may extend its jurisdiction to other matters raised in that case, even though the court otherwise would not have jurisdiction over those matters had they been presented independently. A federal question claim extends to any nonfederal claim against the same defendant. The federal question claim must be substantial, and the nonfederal claims must constitute a single cause of action. The test is whether substantially the same evidence will prove both the federal and nonfederal claim.

Pendent jurisdiction: Discretionary authority allowing an exclusive state matter to be decided in federal courts.

For example, a plaintiff might bring suit claiming injury as a result of the defendant's violation of certain federal antitrust laws. Such a case raises a "federal question" and is properly within the jurisdiction of the federal court. That same plaintiff might claim that the defendant committed common law fraud. The common law fraud claim is normally a state claim over which the federal court has no jurisdiction. Because the plaintiff raised it in the federal case, however, the federal court has the power to hear it.

Access to the Federal Courts

Since the federal courts are all courts of limited jurisdiction, both the trial courts and the appellate (appeals) courts have developed certain criteria that are used to screen out cases they will not hear. This set of criteria is often collectively referred to as the *doctrine of judicial self-restraint*. There must be a "case or controversy," and the party bringing the suit must have standing, or a personal stake in the litigation. The federal courts will not issue advisory opinions nor decide "political," hypothetical, or moot questions that no longer present a controversy because the matter has been settled.

"Case or controversy," is the most significant of these criteria, since the others are merely variations on the same concept. A **justiciable controversy** is one that may properly come before the court. The courts will only consider a "justiciable" controversy, as distinguished from a hypothetical difference of opinion or one that is academic or moot. Article III, Section 2, refers to judicial power over *cases* and *controversies*; these words have been interpreted by the Supreme Court to mean that a case must be between bona fide adversaries and must involve the protection or enforcement of valuable legal rights, or the punishment, prevention, or redress of wrongs that directly concern the party or parties bringing suit.

Justiciable controversy:
A controversy that the court may properly entertain. It must be between bona fide adversaries and assert a claim of legal right by one who has a personal interest at stake.

The matter must be definite, and the remedy requested must be capable of being granted through specific relief, such as a specific amount of damages or an injunction. A person bringing suit must have a personal stake in the litigation of a sufficient nature to justify the federal court accepting jurisdiction. This element is called the **standing to sue doctrine**. Standing to sue is measured by determining whether the litigant can establish a sufficient personal economic interest in the controversy or whether the litigant claims that his or her own rights are being violated.

Standing to sue doctrine:
A jurisdictional requirement that the person bringing suit must have a personal stake in the litigation.

The types of potential matters that are not cases or controversies in federal court practice include *advisory opinions* and *hypothetical questions*. The U.S. Supreme Court's refusal to answer some 29 questions proposed by the U.S. Secretary of State Thomas Jefferson in 1793 provided the precedent for a practice that the courts will not answer such questions because they do not present a bona fide case or controversy. Similarly, Congress cannot ask the courts for an opinion as to whether, if passed, a law they are considering would be unconstitutional. This issue must be tested after legislative enactment with parties that have *standing* before the court. However, since 1934 the federal courts are empowered to render so-called *declaratory judgments*. Declaratory judgments differ from advisory opinions in that there exists an actual controversy; however, the courts may decide respective rights under a law, contract, will, or any other official document (Abraham 1996, 9).

Mootness is a similar situation that occurs when, after filing a justiciable controversy before the court, a subsequent event resolves the issue. For example, if Robert Ryan, in the case in the appendix (*Ryan v. Hofstra University*), had been granted his request by the university nullifying its own decisions before the court acted, there would no longer be a case or controversy. The court would dismiss the case because it is moot, and nothing remains for the court to decide.

Another jurisdictional matter that may stop the progress of a dispute in the courts is the **political question doctrine**. This doctrine asserts that the issue is one that has been given to the political branches of government— the legislative or executive authorities—by the Constitution. In declining jurisdiction over such matters, the courts have relied upon the doctrine of separation of powers and judicial self-restraint. This is done out of deference to the other coequal branches of government, and a matter that can be handled more appropriately by another branch of the government is not a "justiciable" matter for the courts.

Political question doctrine:
In court practice, matters left to the discretionary authority of the political branches of government and therefore non-justiciable.

The courts can change their mind about some of these rulings as the U.S. Supreme Court did in *Baker v. Carr*, 369 U.S. 186, 82 S. Ct. 691, 7 L. Ed. 2d 663 (1962). In this case, the Court overturned a previous decision that state reapportionment laws defining the legislative districts were political questions. Since *Baker v. Carr*, the federal courts have opened the gates to a vast number of such similar legal actions that are now considered justiciable.

The Federal Hierarchy of Courts

The U.S. Constitution, in Article III, Section 1, states "The judicial Power of the United States, shall be vested in one supreme Court, and in such inferior Courts as the Congress may from time to time ordain and establish." The Constitution designates the existence of "one supreme Court" and defines its original and appellate jurisdiction. It has *original jurisdiction* (meaning trial functions) "in all Cases affecting Ambassadors, other public Ministers and Consuls, and those in which a State shall be a Party. . . ." In all other cases, the Supreme Court has *appellate jurisdiction*.

The U.S. Constitution does not provide for the number of Supreme Court justices. Congress sets the number of justices. At its inception in 1790, the Supreme Court had six justices. The number has remained constant at nine for more than 140 years, ever since the Judiciary Act of 1869. Congress set the number at nine at that time because there were nine federal circuit courts of appeals.

The Constitution gives the power to Congress to determine the structure of lower federal courts. Congress promptly acted with the Judiciary Act of 1789, setting up the federal judicial system with trial courts

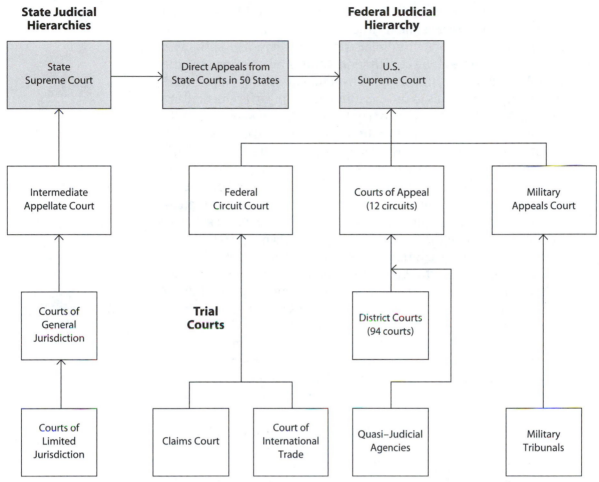

Figure 3.1
**The Dual Hierarchy
of Federal and
State Courts**

in every state. In 1891, Congress created the first set of intermediate courts with purely appellate jurisdiction. These acts put in place the federal court structure that essentially exists today. Figure 3.1 outlines the basic structure of the state and federal courts in the United States.

The federal judicial hierarchy includes a number of **administrative courts**, some of which are listed in the boxes at the base of the federal pyramid in Figure 3.1. They include the *U.S. Claims Court*, the *Court of International Trade*, quasi-judicial tribunals of the federal regulatory agencies, and military tribunals. These courts were created by Congress under their authority in Article I, Section 8, of the Constitution, which defines the regulatory powers of the national government, and Clause 9, which specifically grants Congress the power "[t]o constitute Tribunals inferior to the Supreme Court." These *legislative* courts, as they are sometimes called, also include the *U.S. Tax Court*, and the newest of these lesser tribunals, called the *U.S. Court of Veterans Appeals,* which was created in 1988.

Administrative courts:
Those courts created under the grant of legislative authority in Article I, Section 8, of the U.S. Constitution. They perform administrative and quasi-legislative roles as well as serve as quasi-judicial bodies.

The legislative courts are in many ways distinctively different from the *constitutional* courts created under Article III. The administrative character of these courts involves them in administrative and quasi-legislative as well as judicial tasks, whereas the constitutional courts are confined to strictly judicial roles. They are, unlike the constitutional courts, empowered to render advisory opinions as to the constitutionality of governmental action in the absence of a bona fide case or controversy. The *magistrates* of these inferior tribunals are not subject to the same tenure, salary, and independence that characterize the constitutional courts (Abraham 1996, 8-9). The independence of the legislative courts has been strengthened in recent years, but these judges do not serve for life as do all the constitutional judges. These legislative courts and administrative agencies are answerable to the constitutional courts for their actions on appeal. This avenue of appeal is generally to the intermediate U.S. courts of appeal.

These administrative courts will be discussed in Chapter 18 of this textbook along with an introduction to administrative due process. They are certainly important parts of our entire federal court structure; however, our focus in this chapter is on the original courts created under Article III and often referred to as the *constitutional* courts. They are the *U.S. district courts*, the *U.S. courts of appeals*, and the *U.S. Supreme Court*. These courts are the central components of the hierarchy of the federal courts.

The basic trial courts in the federal judicial system are called **federal district courts**. The trial courts of the federal system are referred to as the courts of original jurisdiction, where "cases or controversies" are filed for the first time. Congress has created 94 districts that serve as the base of the federal judicial structure. There is at least one district court in each state and in all territories of the United States.

Federal district courts: The basic trial courts in the federal system.

Federal district court judges, like all other federal judges, are appointed by the president with the approval of the Senate. They serve for life and can be removed only by impeachment in the House and conviction in the Senate. They are required to reside in the district in which they sit. There are more than 600 of these judges who are assisted by a number of federal officers and agencies, which include a U.S. district clerk's office, a U.S. marshal's office, and a U.S. attorney's office. Preliminary matters in both civil and criminal cases are usually performed by *U.S. magistrate judges* who are appointed by a majority of the judges of the district court for a term of eight years, and they may be removed by a majority of the judges for incompetence, neglect of duty, or physical or mental disability.

With the exception of the Supreme Court's very limited area of original jurisdiction, these district courts conduct the trials of all cases in the federal judicial system. In these cases, the district court judge supervises pre-trial matters, conducts the trial, and enters the judgment. Trials are fact-finding procedures that usually involve only one judge, and they may include juries. Juries decide questions of fact, and the judges decide questions of

Figure 3.2
**The Federal Judicial
Circuits**

law. In Parts III and IV of this text the trial process will be examined in more detail.

The district judge may decide to write an opinion on the issues of law or fact in a particular case. Such opinions often are published to provide guidance for other courts faced with similar issues. They appear in the reporter called the *Federal Supplement*, which contains select opinions of the federal district courts.

Congress has established 13 federal judicial circuits and one military court of appeals that provide the federal intermediate court structure. The **U.S. courts of appeals** were established to hear appeals from district court decisions, thereby facilitating the prompt disposition of cases and easing the caseload of the Supreme Court. These courts consider only questions of law in dispute and do not conduct trials. Eleven of these circuits are numbered (first to eleventh), each embracing several states and territories of the United States (see map, Figure 3.2). The remaining two circuit courts are both located in Washington, D.C. and are known as the *District of Columbia Circuit* and the *Federal Circuit*. The Federal Circuit has jurisdiction to hear appeals from all 94 district courts in cases arising under the patent laws and in certain damage suits against the federal government. It also has jurisdiction over appeals from several administrative agencies and from decisions of two special trial courts: the *U.S. Claims Court* and the *Court of International Trade*.

U.S. courts of appeals:
The intermediate appeals courts in the federal system.

There is a proposal in Congress to divide the current Ninth Circuit into two circuits, thus creating a Twelfth Circuit Court of Appeals. This process is what led to the creation of the Eleventh Circuit in 1981, as members of Congress and other members of the legal community believed that the Fifth Circuit had become too large. Currently, there are proposals to create a new federal appeals court because the Ninth Circuit is thought to be too large.

The newest federal appeals court was established in 1983 and is called the *Military Court of Appeals*. The 1983 Military Justice Act conferred jurisdiction on the Supreme Court to review designated categories of appeals from the Military Court of Appeals. This marked the first time in the history of the United States that any court established under Article III of the Constitution was authorized to review the decisions of military courts (Grilliot and Schubert 1992, 92).

There are over 200 judges serving on the intermediate U.S. courts of appeals in the 13 circuits. Each court is composed of active and senior judges and include up to 28 total judges. The court is located in a particular city within its district, which encompasses three or more states or territories (except for the D.C. Circuit). The chief judge of a particular circuit is the judge with the longest active service who has not yet reached 70 years of age. They are all appointed by the president with the approval of the Senate and cannot be removed except through the impeachment and removal process.

These courts do not conduct trials but perform the function of oversight and review of the trial courts and administrative agencies. The U.S. courts of appeals hear appeals in both civil and criminal cases. Generally, they hear appeals from a **final judgment** (after trial), but they may hear **interlocutory appeals** (before trial). Interlocutory orders are rulings of the court that do not finally dispose of the case but require some further action of the court before a final decision can be rendered. Two of our illustrative cases in the appendix are examples of interlocutory appeals in state courts: *Du Pont v. Christopher* and *Marvin v. Marvin*.

Most cases are heard by three-judge panels at this level. There must be at least two judges present, and at least two must agree before there is a valid decision. Sometimes all the judges in a particular circuit sit *en banc* (together) to hear a case. The decision to hear the case *en banc* is made by a majority vote of the judges in regular active service on that circuit. The final decision, after hearing the case, is made by at least a majority of the active judges sitting *en banc* who constitute a quorum, and a majority has the authority to render a decision. These decisions on questions of law either uphold the lower court's judgment, reverse it, or reverse and remand (refer) it back to the trial court for further action with instructions. They may also certify cases on to the U.S. Supreme Court on rare occasions. Federal appeals court judges often grant *en banc* review when there are two conflicting three-judge panel decisions in the circuit.

Final judgment: Action of the trial court concluding the trial process and ending the litigation on the merits, where nothing more remains to do but to execute the judgment.

Interlocutory appeal: From interlocutory (preliminary) orders of a trial court before a trial takes place.

The appeals process will be illustrated in civil, criminal, and administrative cases in later chapters of this text. However, here it is important to note that decisions of the U.S. courts of appeals are required to be in writing, stating facts and making conclusions of law. The courts of appeals have a duty to follow majority opinions of the Supreme Court, just as U.S. district courts are bound by the law established by the appeals court in the circuit in which they are located. Many decisions of the federal courts of appeals (not all because some are unpublished) are reported in the *Federal Reporter* series published by West Publishing Company.

The **U.S. Supreme Court** occupies a unique position in the U.S. judicial system because it has jurisdiction to review all decisions of the federal appellate courts and also has jurisdiction over decisions of the highest state courts when those courts have decided a question of federal law. It is, therefore, the court of last resort in all cases involving federal law arising in both state and federal courts.

U.S. Supreme Court: The court of last resort in all cases involving federal law.

The Supreme Court has come far in stature and prestige as the final authority of the entire U.S. legal system. It is the chief institution that coordinates the entire legal system, although it is the final authority in state cases only when the state court's decision involves a controlling question of federal law that triggers federal question jurisdiction. "The Supreme Court has no jurisdiction to decide state law questions in cases coming from the state courts; in each state, the state supreme court [court of last resort] is the final and authoritative expositor of that state's law." (Meador 1991, 29)

The U.S. Supreme Court is the original constitutional court of appeals created by the Judiciary Act of 1789. The Constitution does not specify the number of judges on the Supreme Court, and Congress has authorized various numbers of members of the court since 1789 when six justices served in this capacity. The composition of the Court has remained nine members since 1869, and this idea has become permanently fixed, although Congress could change it. The Chief Justice and the eight Associate Justices are appointed by the president with the advice and consent of the Senate, and they serve for life. They can be removed by impeachment in the House and conviction in the Senate; however, no Supreme Court justice has ever been removed in this manner, although impeaching proceedings were brought against Associate Justice Samuel Chase in 1804. The House voted to impeach him, but he was not convicted in the Senate.

The presence of six justices constitutes a quorum, and five justices must agree before a decision of the Supreme Court becomes official and binding. The regular term of the Court always commences on the first Monday in October of each year and continues until the latter part of June. On rare occasions, the Court will convene in special session during the summer to hear important cases.

The Chief Justice of the United States has several important functions in addition to those of presiding over the sessions and deliberations of the

Court. The Constitution requires the Chief Justice to preside over impeachment trials of the president in the Senate, a duty that a Chief Justice has had to exercise only twice during the history of the nation—the impeachments of Andrew Johnson and William Jefferson Clinton, administered by Chief Justices Salmon P. Chase and William H. Rehnquist, respectively.

Congress has given the Chief Justice other administrative duties as chairperson of the Federal Judicial Center and the Judicial Conference of the United States. The Federal Judicial Center is the research and development arm of the federal judiciary and plays an important role in the training of new federal judges. The Judicial Conference of the United States considers such problems as proposed legislation in new areas of law, the need for increased efficiency of the courts, and more efficient use of jurors' time. These activities occupy as much as one-third of the time of the Chief Justice.

The Chief Justice—if he or she is in the majority—also has the important power to assign which Justice will write an opinion in a case. If the Chief Justice is not in the majority, the power moves to the senior Associate Justice on the Court. The opinion-assignment power is a vital power of the Chief Justice that has been handled differently through the years.

The specific jurisdiction of the U.S. Supreme Court is really quite complex and often confusing because it performs a variety of functions as the federal court of last resort: (1) It has direct review of certain decisions of the federal district courts; (2) it reviews decisions of the federal courts of appeals; (3) it reviews certain decisions of the state courts of last resort; and (4) it has original jurisdiction in certain matters dealing with disputes between sovereign entities—the states, the federal government, and foreign states.

Therefore, the Supreme Court exercises both a limited original jurisdiction and an extensive appellate jurisdiction. Jurisdiction of the Supreme Court extends to criminal and civil matters. The Court's jurisdiction may be *exclusive* (denied to any other court) or *concurrent* (shared with other federal and/or state courts). Table 3.1, gives a few examples in each of these areas to help clarify this complex jurisdiction.

This detailed and complex court jurisdiction can be simplified by the recognition that, with minor exceptions, the Supreme Court's jurisdiction is discretionary. Litigants must petition the Court for a *writ of certiorari* in all cases except those of *original jurisdiction*, where there is a *right of appeal*, and where the case has reached the Court by *certification* from the U.S. courts of appeals.

The Supreme Court receives more than 8,000 petitions each term and is able to narrow these to less than 300 that it actually acts upon in some way other than denial of the **writ of certiorari**. This form of petition is an appeal to the discretionary authority of the Supreme Court to hear the appeal from a lower court. A decision on the petition coming from the state courts of last resort, the federal district courts, or the U.S. courts of appeal is made by the "rule of four." The "rule of four," which the Court has followed since at

Writ of certiorari: Order by the appellate court that is used when the court has discretion regarding whether or not to hear the appeal. An order to have lower court records sent to higher court for review. It requires the approval of four Justices to be reviewed by the Court.

Table 3.1 **JURISDICTION OF THE U.S. SUPREME COURT**

1. Direct Review of Federal District Courts:	**3. Review from Courts of Appeals Decisions:**
When the district court stipulates its immediate importance involving: Equitable relief in antitrust laws, Enforcement of the interstate Commerce Act or, Recovery under the common carriers section of the Communications Act. Actions required to be heard by a three-judge federal district court. Actions of any federal court holding an act of Congress unconstitutional.	By *writ of certiorari* (most frequently used) By right of appeal where: The appellate court has held an act of Congress unconstitutional or A court of appeals has held a state statute unconstitutional. By certificate, asking for instructions in either criminal or civil cases (rarely used).
2. Direct Review of State Court Decisions:	**4. Original Jurisdiction:**
When the highest court in the state has rendered a final judgment and the validity of a treaty or statute of the United States is involved; or The validity of a state statute is alleged to conflict with the Constitution, treaties, or laws of the United States; or Any title, right, privilege, or immunity is specifically claimed under the U.S. Constitution or federal law.	Exclusive jurisdiction: Actions by one state against another state or by a state against citizens of another state or against aliens. Actions by ambassadors or other public ministers of foreign states Concurrent jurisdiction: Actions by the United States against a state or against aliens. Actions by ambassadors or other public ministers of foreign states or to which consuls or vice consuls of foreign states are parties.

least 1924, requires that any four of the nine justices may decide to grant a writ of certiorari and the case will be taken up for decision; otherwise, certiorari is denied and the decision of the lower court stands. "Cert. Denied" is often taken to be a sign of approval for the precedent created by the lower decision; however, all it means is that the court decided not to review the case. The Roberts Court, led by Chief Justice John G. Roberts Jr., only hears about 75-80 cases per term.

A petition that asserts a *right of appeal* is very infrequent, but when a lower court in either the states or the federal government has held an act of Congress or a state law unconstitutional for the first time there is statutory authority requiring the court to hear the case. Thus the Court is bound to review the petition.

Certification from the U.S. courts of appeals is even rarer, but does exist. Occasionally, the appeals courts will ask the Supreme Court for instructions in a particularly difficult matter where they do not wish to second guess the court of last resort.

The written opinions of the U.S. Supreme Court are the most authoritative judicial decisions concerning questions of law and must be followed

Certification: A request from a U.S. court of appeals asking the Supreme Court for instructions.

by both state and federal courts. These opinions are reported in the series of volumes called the *United States Reports*. This is the official reporter for the U.S. Supreme Court, and all citations to Supreme Court cases must use this official citation. However, there are other reporters—the *Supreme Court Reporter* and the *Lawyers Edition*—that provide head notes and other supplementary material for research purposes. Note that in previous citations we have used three parallel citations to these reporters. These are three different reporters where the same case may be found. The other reporters include the *Supreme Court Reporter* (abbreviated S.Ct.) published by West Publishing Company and *Lawyers Edition* (abbreviated L. Ed.) published by Bancroft-Whitney.

THE JURISDICTION AND HIERARCHY OF STATE COURTS

State courts are the more prevalent courts where the overwhelming volume of legal action is initiated. The state courts handle more than 30 times as many legal actions as the federal courts, and as a practical matter they are of greatest interest to everyday practice of the law. Most legal actions do not involve federal questions and do not involve cases where there is diversity of citizenship. These cases must be filed in state courts. Each of the 50 states has its own written constitution that creates the court system in some states and authorizes the state legislature to establish the judicial structure in others. The structure of state courts can vary quite a bit from state to state. They are defined by state constitutional and legislative authority. They differ in detail, but resemble each other in broad outline. The key components of state courts, which provide a general pattern, are described in the following paragraphs and illustrated in the diagram in Figure 3.1 above. The reader may wish to supplement this discussion with details that are current and applicable in the reader's own state. (The National Center for State Courts provides an excellent overview of every state's court system. See nesconline.org.)

The state courts have **general jurisdiction** as opposed to the limited jurisdiction of the federal courts. This means that they can handle all types of cases involving both state and federal law that are not specifically designated as within the *exclusive* jurisdiction of the federal courts. State judges are bound by the supremacy clause of the U.S. Constitution to apply federal law as the "supreme law of the land." These state judges also take an oath to enforce both the U.S. Constitution and the constitution of their own state. In this respect they serve two sovereigns.

However, within the state courts hierarchy there are limitations upon the various courts that have been created by the state constitutions or legislative authority. The courts of *limited jurisdiction* are lower courts that handle specific matters that may be more related to administrative

General jurisdiction: Authority to decide questions of both state and federal law in the course of litigation and not limited to a restricted list of delegated authority. The state courts are restricted only by the very narrow range of cases that fall within the exclusive jurisdiction of the federal courts.

functions. Local courts such as traffic courts, municipal courts (night court), juvenile courts, probate courts, small claims courts, justice of the peace courts, general session courts, and landlord-tenant courts are some of the names associated with these magistrate courts in the state systems.

State Trial Courts

The courts of *general jurisdiction* are the trial level courts that handle all contested cases and are the fundamental courts of original jurisdiction in significant lawsuits and criminal actions. There is usually a restriction in terms of the amount of the claim that may be filed in these courts. However, all contested cases are overseen by these courts of general jurisdiction. Typical names for these trial courts are criminal court, circuit court, superior court, district court, court of common pleas, and chancery court. In New York, the confusing title of *supreme court* is given to some courts of general jurisdiction. Judges are typically elected directly by the voters at this level and serve for fixed terms (usually eight years). The *trial courts* and *appellate courts* are the most important distinctions in all these classifications of state courts. Understanding how to recognize which of these two types of courts are delivering an opinion is important to assess the relative weight one should give to their legal opinions.

Trial courts of general jurisdiction often conduct jury trials in which witnesses are called to testify and contested facts are resolved. A trial is a fact-finding procedure in which issues of both fact and law are *adjudicated* (authoritatively decided). These judges decide all questions of law in dispute, and when they decide a question of first impression, or add to the body of case law, they may write judicial opinions for the record. These decisions become a part of the body of law that may be cited in future cases until they are overruled by a higher court. Judgments of trial courts are subject to review and possible reversal by courts above them in the judicial hierarchy. For some courts of limited jurisdiction, the first review is in the upper level trial court of general jurisdiction. For the trial courts of general jurisdiction, and sometimes for lower trial courts, review is in the appellate courts.

Trial courts: Decide cases or controversies involving facts in dispute or questions of law in dispute. Juries are frequently given the capacity to decide questions of fact in dispute. The judge decides all questions of law in dispute.

State Appellate Courts

In most states, there are intermediate **appellate courts** that have been established to relieve the workload of the courts of last resort in their appellate functions. A few less-populated states may rely upon the state supreme court, or court of last resort, to handle all appeals. Some states have a single intermediate appellate court, whereas most have multiple courts organized into geographic districts or divided by subject matter jurisdiction. Regardless of how they are divided, these intermediate-level appellate courts sit in

Appellate courts: Courts that do not conduct fact-finding procedures as trial courts do. They consider only questions of law in dispute and exercise review over trial courts performing the functions of error correction and law development. There are both intermediate appellate courts and courts of last resort.

three-judge panels for purposes of hearing and deciding appeals. Many of these courts have more than three judges, but at least three judges are involved in the appeals process in a particular case.

The intermediate appeals courts are primarily involved in error correction functions, and the appeals courts of last resort are primarily involved in the law development role inherited from the English common law tradition. However, these roles of the appeals courts are not clearly separable, and both levels are involved with the two basic functions of error correction and law development. The appeals courts are not fact-finding bodies and do not conduct trials. The court of appeals will *remand* (refer) the case back to the court of original jurisdiction if a further fact-finding process is deemed necessary.

The appeals courts at the intermediate level are typically selected by some form of the Missouri Plan (described in Chapter 1). They usually sit in panels of three judges, and a majority of the judges is necessary to make a final decision. These courts frequently publish their opinions to serve as guidance for the lower courts.

Further appeals may be taken to the state court of last resort. This court is usually called the supreme court. However, in New York and Maryland, the highest tribunal is called the *court of appeals*; in Massachusetts and Maine, it is called the *supreme judicial court*; and in Texas and Oklahoma, there are two courts of last resort: the *supreme court* (for civil cases) and the *court of criminal appeals* (for criminal cases). Most state courts of last resort have seven judges called "justices." The smallest court has five justices, and the largest nine. In a few states these courts function in panels of fewer than all their members; however, in most states, all justices sit together so that the court functions as a unit when hearing and deciding appeals (Meador 1991, 13-14).

Like the U.S. Supreme Court, these courts of last resort in the states perform functions related to the general oversight of the administration of justice in their respective states. The opinions of the appellate courts are given greater weight than trial court opinions, and, when in conflict, the court of last resort prevails. The opinions of the state courts can be found in regional reporters, which will be discussed in Chapter 4. These reporters include written opinions coming from all three levels of courts (trial, appeals, and courts of last resort). The regional reporters are published by West Publishing Company and include several states in each region. There are individual state series that may provide parallel reports for each state individually.

The dual hierarchies of state and federal courts depicted in Figure 3.1 illustrate that cases may go directly from the state court of last resort to the U.S. Supreme Court. However, they must involve a controlling federal question issue and usually require the approval of at least four Supreme Court Justices before the *writ of certiorari* will be granted. This dual hierarchy provides exceptionally thorough protection against arbitrary or abusive actions among the individual judges of our legal system. It is a major extension of the checks and balance system of our federal structure. There are many opportunities for appeal to a higher authority to correct errors made by trial judges. Violations, misinterpretations, misapplications, and even violations of the ethical standards of judges may be corrected through this process. Many states have even supplemented this appellate review process with a *court of the judiciary* that investigates complaints against judges and exercises disciplinary authority over them, including removal from office in extreme cases.

For review purposes, Table 3.2 has been included to help the student remember the basic concepts discussed in this chapter. It was prepared by the Administrative Office of the U.S. Courts on behalf of the Federal Judiciary.

Table 3.2 **COMPARING FEDERAL AND STATE COURTS**

The Federal Court System	The State Court System
STRUCTURE	
Article III of the Constitution invests the judicial power of the United States in the federal court system. Article II, Section 1, specifically creates the U.S. Supreme Court and gives Congress the authority to create the lower federal courts.	The Constitution and laws of each state establish the state courts. A court of last resort, often known as a supreme court, is usually the highest court. Some states also have an intermediate court of appeals. Below these appeals courts are the state trial courts. Some are referred to as circuit or district courts.
Congress has used this power to establish the 13 U.S. courts of appeals, the 94 U.S. district courts, the U.S. Court of Claims, and the U.S. Court of International Trade. U.S. bankruptcy courts handle bankruptcy cases. Magistrate judges handle some district court matters.	States also usually have courts that handle specific legal matters, for example, probate court (wills and estates), juvenile court, family court, etc.
Parties dissatisfied with a decision of a U.S. district court, the U.S. Court of Claims, and/or the U.S. Court of International Trade may appeal to a U.S. court of appeals.	Parties dissatisfied with the decision of the trial court may take their case to the intermediate court of appeals.
A party may ask the U.S. Supreme Court to review a decision of the U.S. court of appeals, but the Supreme Court usually is under no obligation to do so. The U.S. Supreme Court is the final arbiter of federal constitutional questions.	Parties have the option to ask the highest state court to hear the case.
	Only certain cases are eligible for review by the U.S. Supreme Court.

continued >

The Federal Court System	The State Court System
TYPES OF CASES HEARD	
Cases that deal with the constitutionality of a law. Cases involving the laws and treaties of the United States. Ambassadors and public ministers. Disputes between two or more states. Admiralty law. Bankruptcy.	Most criminal cases, probate (involving wills and estates). Most contract cases, tort cases (personal injuries), family law (marriages, divorces, adoptions), etc. State courts are the final arbiters of state laws and constitutions. Their interpretation of federal law or the U.S. Constitution may be appealed to the U.S. Supreme Court. The Supreme Court may choose to hear or not to hear such cases.
Congress has created several Article I, or legislative, courts that do not have full judicial power. Judicial power is the authority to be the final decider in all questions of Constitutional law, all questions of federal law, and to hear claims at the core of habeas corpus issues. Article I courts are the U.S. Court of Veterans' Appeals, the U.S. Court of Military Appeals, and the U.S. Tax Court.	

CHAPTER SUMMARY

1. The federal courts have limited subject matter jurisdiction in those areas delegated by the U.S. Constitution. These areas are referred to as *federal question jurisdiction* and include matters directly related to the U.S. Constitution, the laws of the United States, and treaties.

2. There are few areas of *exclusive federal question jurisdiction.* They include disputes involving admiralty or maritime jurisdiction, ambassadors and other foreign public ministers and consuls, cases in which the United States is a party, disputes between states as sovereign entities, bankruptcy, patent or copyright, customs, penalties under federal law, and interstate commerce and antitrust actions. All federal crimes must be prosecuted in federal courts.

3. Areas of overlapping or current jurisdiction shared by the state and federal courts include civil cases involving *diversity of citizenship* and *pendent jurisdiction* involving matters of state law that may arise in the consideration of a federal question claim. Diversity jurisdiction is limited to actions involving parties that are citizens of different states (including foreign states) and the sum in question is greater than $75,000.

4. Access to the federal courts requires a *justiciable dispute*; that is, that a case or controversy exists between bona fide adversaries and there must be a claim of right asserted by a party that has standing to sue. *Non-justiciable disputes* include hypothetical, moot, or political questions that are more appropriately decided by the political branches of the government.

5. The structure of the federal courts forms a hierarchy of oversight of lower courts by higher courts. Administrative courts have been created under Article I, Section 9, and are not subject to the same rules as the constitutional courts created under Article III. The Article I courts are subject to review by the constitutional appeals courts.

6. The district courts are the basic trial courts in the federal system. They are the courts of original jurisdiction for contested cases, with the exception of disputes between sovereign entities (states) where the Supreme Court has original jurisdiction.

7. The federal courts of appeals are intermediary appellate courts in that they decide only questions of law in dispute and review actions by the trial courts. They hear appeals from both final judgments (after trial) and may hear interlocutory appeals (before trial). Three-judge panels usually review these cases and decide by majority vote of the judges.

8. The U.S. Supreme Court has a unique position as the court of last resort for any matter that constitutes a federal question. They review such cases coming directly from the state courts of last resort, certain decisions of the federal district courts, decisions of the federal courts of appeals, and they have a very limited original jurisdiction over disputes between states.

9. In general, the U.S. Supreme Court has discretionary authority to refuse to grant a *writ of certiorari* in most cases. Granting of this petition to have the case heard requires four votes out of the nine justices on the court. There is a very limited *right of appeal* in cases involving lower courts holding acts of legislative authority unconstitutional for the first time, and federal appeals courts may *certify* matters directly to the court of last resort.

10. The state courts have general subject matter jurisdiction in our legal system, except for the very limited areas of exclusive federal jurisdiction, and they process the overwhelming majority of legal actions. The lowest tribunals are called courts of limited jurisdiction, and contested cases may be appealed to the trial courts of general jurisdiction, to intermediate appeals courts, and finally to the state courts of last resort.

11. The trial courts of original jurisdiction conduct fact-finding procedures that may involve juries to determine questions of fact in dispute. All questions of law in dispute are determined by the judge. These

decisions may be appealed to the appellate courts for review and possible reversal.

12. The appellate courts usually include two tiers of appeals courts that function to hear issues of law in dispute. They hear cases in panels of at least three judges and refer cases back to the trial level, if additional fact-finding procedures are required. The courts of last resort are the final authority in all matters of state law. Federal questions may be appealed directly to the U.S. Supreme Court.

REVIEW EXERCISE

Match the following terms with their most appropriate meaning.

TERMS	MEANING
1. Limited jurisdiction	____ action of the trial court concluding the trial process and ending the litigation on the merits
2. Federal question jurisdiction	____ the court of last resort in all cases involving federal law
3. Exclusive jurisdiction	____ discretionary order to have lower court records sent to higher court for review (S.C. 4 votes)
4. Concurrent jurisdiction	____ request from a U.S. court of appeals asking the Supreme Court for instructions
5. Diversity jurisdiction	____ authority to decide disputes using state and federal law, except for exclusive federal cases
6. Pendent jurisdiction	____ consider only questions of law in dispute and exercise review over trial courts
7. Justiciable controversy	____ intermediate appeals court in the federal system
8. Standing to sue doctrine	____ limited authority to decide subject matter disputes in a limited number of types of cases
9. Political question doctrine	____ courts created under Article I of the U.S. Constitution
10. Administrative courts	____ basic subject matter jurisdiction of the federal courts
11. Federal district courts	____ federal court jurisdiction denied to the states
12. U.S. courts of appeal	____ areas where both state and federal courts have jurisdiction to hear the same types of disputes
13. Final judgment	____ appeals from a preliminary decision of a trial court before a trial takes place
14. Interlocutory appeal	____ decide cases or controversies involving facts in dispute and conduct fact-finding procedures
15. U.S. Supreme Court	____ civil legal actions between citizens of different states involving a sum greater than $75,000
16. *Writ of certiorari*	____ discretionary authority allowing federal courts to decide state questions of law when jurisdiction under federal law exists
17. Certification	____ a controversy the court may properly entertain
18. General jurisdiction	____ a person with a personal stake in the litigation
19. Trial courts	____ the basic trial courts in the federal system
20. Appellate courts	____ a matter left to the political discretion of government and therefore nonjusticiable

DISCUSSION QUESTIONS

1. What are the basic differences between federal and state subject matter jurisdiction?
2. What are the basic areas of exclusive federal court jurisdiction?
3. What are the basic areas of federal and state concurrent jurisdiction?
4. How do cases reach the U.S. Supreme Court?
5. What is meant by the dual hierarchy of the U.S. court system?
6. What area of sovereignty remains with the states?

ASSIGNMENTS

ASSIGNMENT: As you read this chapter go back to the six cases in Appendix B of this textbook. By the end of the next chapter, you will be expected to draft brief summaries of these cases using the format included in this chapter. We will explain the aspects of each case that will require your focus in completing this assignment

SOURCES AND SUGGESTED READING

Abraham, Henry J. 1996. *The Judiciary*. 10th ed. New York: New York University Press.

Aldisert, Ruggero J. 1989. *Logic for Lawyers: A Guide to Clear Legal Thinking*. New York: Clark Boardman.

Grilliot, Harlod J., and Frank A. Schubert. 1992. *Introduction to Law and the Legal System*. 5th ed. Boston: Houghton Mifflin.

*Lewis, Alfred J. 1985. *Using American Law Books*. 2d ed. Dubuque, Iowa: Kendall/Hunt.

Livi, Edward H. 1948. *An Introduction to Legal Reasoning*. Chicago: University of Chicago Press. (This is a classic and concise explanation of the evolution of law through the process of legal reasoning.)

*Meador, Daniel John. 1991. *American Courts*. St. Paul, Minn.: West Publishing Company.

Murphy, Walter F., and C. Herman Pritchett. 1986. *Courts, Judges, and Politics: An Introduction to the Judicial Process*. 4th ed. New York: Random House.

National Center for State Courts. 1997. *Examining the Work of State Courts, 1996: A National Perspective from the Court Statistics Project*, ed. B. Ostrom and N. Kauder. Williamsburg, Va.: National Center for State Courts.

*Schulze, P., Michael Jung, and Rebecca P. Adams. 1994. *Introduction to the American Legal System*. 3rd ed. Dallas, Texas: Pearson Publications Company.

(*Recommended reading)

Introduction to Legal Research and Writing

Can a tenant sublet an apartment if the lease is silent on the matter? Can a landlord evict a tenant on only seven days' notice? Can an employer terminate an employee for off-duty behavior unrelated to the job? Can a parent lose custody of her child after being arrested for drunk driving? Can spouses obtain a greater share of the marital estate if they can show that their partner committed adultery? Can a public university consider race in its admissions policy without violating the Equal Protection Clause of the Fourteenth Amendment? Can the police pull over a car because it has very tinted windows and the driver appears nervous? These are just some of millions upon millions of legal questions that people have on a daily basis. The process of finding applicable law that governs a particular situation is called **legal research**. It can be frustrating but also rewarding—particularly when one finds an answer to a difficult problem.

> **Legal research:** Answering questions about application of legal rules governing particular situations.

Legal research also involves the ability to read and brief cases that serve as guiding precedent to answer questions arising from specific fact situations. We will begin this chapter with a discussion of legal reasoning and how to read and brief a case.

ASSIGNMENT: As you read this chapter, go back to the six cases in the appendix that we are using for illustrations. By the end of this chapter, you will be expected to draft brief summaries of these cases using the format included in this chapter. We will explain the aspects of each case that will require your focus in completing this assignment.

LEGAL REASONING AND READING CASE LAW

The most important aspect of traditional legal education in the United States, as practiced in law schools across the nation, involves the development of legal reasoning skills. Some undergraduates find it difficult to grasp the basic concepts involved in legal reasoning. They typically enter the area of law with the idea that rules of law are to be memorized, and rarely do they think about the problems of rule application in the diverse factual situations of real life.

Statutory and case law cannot answer all legal questions. This is true because no one can anticipate all future circumstances that might be described plausibly in the language of a rule of law from a statute or a case. We are human beings with imperfect knowledge; even if a person stating a rule had perfect knowledge at the time, circumstances change and the future brings new situations.

The English common law tradition has been preserved, and even extended, because of the realization of the imperfect nature of our rule-making capacity. Lawyers and judges must analyze and interpret established rules in light of possible cases, and specific factual situations may present new possibilities.

"Thinking like a lawyer" involves understanding this concept of flexibility in the law, and the student wishing to achieve the skills of a lawyer must understand the developmental nature of the law. The "spirit" of the law is more important than the "letter" in achieving this state of awareness. Consequently, a lawyer must go beyond the rules themselves to predict what a court would rule, or could be persuaded to rule, in a case involving a particular set of facts.

Different Forms of Legal Reasoning

The two basic forms of legal reasoning are *deductive reasoning* and *inductive reasoning*. They are not much different from commonsense reasoning; however, they have been given more formal, and consequently more self-conscious, rigorous, and uniform expressions in law than in everyday life. As U.S. Supreme Court Justice Oliver Wendell Holmes indicated, formalism must be tempered with the understanding that the life of the law is experience, not logic. He also wrote that a "page of history is worth a volume of logic."

Logicians call the form of reasoning involved in deductive logic a **syllogism**. The conclusion of a valid syllogism follows necessarily from the premises. The classical syllogism was used by the ancient Greeks to develop an understanding of deductive reasoning. Its simplest form is illustrated below.

Syllogism:
The full logical form of a single argument in deductive logic.

- Major premise: All men are mortal.
- Minor premise: Socrates is a man.
- Conclusion: Socrates is mortal.

The syllogism is valid only if all the premises are true and if the conclusion must follow. This form of reasoning is very powerful and is used extensively in legal reasoning. Finding premises that all agree with can be difficult, but when they are present and result in an irrefutable conclusion, it is a very strong and persuasive argument. The form of the syllogism is not infallible, and an argument is not correct simply because it takes the form of a syllogism. It can be demonstrated to be in error. See how many errors you can find in the following syllogism.

- Major premise: A foot has 39 inches.
- Minor premise: Susan has a foot.
- Conclusion: Susan has 39 inches.

(See Steven J. Burton, *An Introduction to Law and Legal Reasoning*, for a more thorough discussion of legal reasoning.)

Inductive logic in the scientific community refers to reasoning by reference to empirical facts, that is, the formulation of conclusions to explain the observed facts through systematic analysis. This method is not quite the one the legal community uses in inductive reasoning; it is more properly called the **analogist form of reasoning**, since it basically proceeds by analogy. The common law tradition of *stare decisis* means that like cases should be decided alike. It is often expressed as the doctrine of following precedent, or the principle of equal treatment under the law. The Latin phrase from which the term is derived is *stare decisis et non quieta movere*: "stand by the decision and do not disturb what is settled." The spirit of this doctrine is that it would be unfair to change rules that have been previously applied to others. An even more fundamental principle, however, is that the rules must be essentially fair, and a previously applied rule that does injustice in light of changed circumstances must be altered. Thus, a more essential principle than *stare decisis* is that experience must teach us to do justice in the individual case.

> **Analogistic form of reasoning:**
> By analogy; analysis of comparative likeness and differences.

One method of altering the previous rule is to *distinguish* the facts of a particular case as different from those of the precedent-setting case by applying a new rule or a different rule. A judge may not in good conscience, however, ignore a relevant authoritative precedent without incurring much criticism. The principle that like cases should be decided alike implies that *unalike* cases should be decided differently if the differences are more important than the similarities.

A more drastic method of dealing with problem cases is for the highest court to *overrule* its own precedents. A case that overrules earlier case law becomes the proper base point for future cases and represents a change in the law. Courts do not often make such decisions because they tend to undermine the credibility and authority of the court. Courts will take great pains to construe the law, if at all possible, in a manner that will not overturn precedent.

Finally, all the factors mentioned by Justice Holmes—"necessities of the times," "prevalent moral and political theories," "institutions of public policy," "even the prejudice of judges"—influence judicial decision making. In the final analysis, the law is what the judges say it is. The legitimacy of the court, however, is determined by the court's ability to exercise its function within the general parameters of reason and fairness. The court ultimately will fail if it cannot explain its decisions on these grounds. Courts neither command armies nor appropriate funds to enforce their decisions. They depend upon the moral conscience and sense of legitimacy that reason and logic dictate.

The Case Method of Legal Training

The skills of legal reasoning involve habits of mind that develop over a person's lifetime. No one is born with these skills; however, the propensity to acquire them may be innate. Legal training involves exposure to the written forms of legal reasoning of the courts that are relied upon as evidence of what the law is, as applied to specific factual situations.

What Is a Case in Law?

Burton describes a case in law or a judicial opinion as "a short story of an incident in which the state acted or may act to settle a particular dispute. Decided cases tell a story with a beginning, a middle, and an end—a story that occurred once and resulted in the settlement of a particular dispute by the coercive dispute settlement machinery of the state." (Burton 2007) Another definition of a judicial opinion is that it is a judicially written resolution of disputed legal issues. These specific sets of factual situations press lawyers and judges to think hard about justice, the limits of proper governmental power, and the scope of individual freedom.

Very few legal matters that are adjudicated involve problems of rule development. Most legal issues fall into clearly defined categories of established law. These typical fact situations are settled by reference to already recorded norms of judicial behavior and allow lawyers to give clients reasonably accurate legal advice about what the law will allow. However, in those court cases in which the rules are unclear or doubtful in their application to a particular set of facts, the courts may find it necessary to render a written opinion that expresses the court's reasoning in applying a new rule or clarifying an older rule. These court opinions, in more difficult cases, accumulate and provide the voluminous body of case law that creates and builds the common law tradition.

How to Analyze a Case in Law

Legal training usually begins by learning how to read a case in law. The student must develop the ability to identify the most significant elements of the opinion because some cases get quite complicated. Following a careful procedure will help the student focus on essential legal issues. Understanding the legal issues will help the student to identify the narrow kernel of law being developed in the opinion. Case law is not a record of individual litigation; its central purpose is to explain the rules of law.

Judges differ in the way they write their opinions. They often discuss material that helps to clarify the ruling but is not necessary in deciding the fact situation that is a part of the kernel of law being defined. The beginning student who is used to underlining the most important statements in a text may be confused by this approach, but the list of basic elements provided below will help the student find the significant elements of the case in law and avoid this confusion. Once the advice given has been practiced and applied to the cases illustrated in Appendix B, the student will know what to look for in reading other cases. Noting the important elements of a case becomes easier with practice.

The method of note taking, often referred to as the "case brief," is simply reformulating the written opinion to conform to a systematic scheme of analysis. The most difficult task for the beginning student is formulating the **holding**, which represents the narrow kernel of law that may be used as precedent in future cases. "The holding is a statement that captures in a sentence or two the probable significance of a single precedent as a basic point for reasoning by analogy in future cases." (Burton 2007) It is said that Anglo-American jurisprudence grinds out law (the mill analogy): It grinds ever so slowly, but it grinds exceedingly fine.

Holding:
Legal precedent drawn from the opinion of the court on a specific legal question.

Many opinions make statements that are not **on point**, that is, relevant directly to the specific facts of the case. These statements are often confused with the holding. They are called **dicta (or obiter dicta)** and are not considered binding in future cases. Lawyers often disagree whether language from a court opinion constitutes a controlling holding or mere dicta. The student must avoid confusing such statements with the specific holdings in the case. These extraneous statements are useful and help the reader understand the essential spirit of the underlying concepts of law that are being expounded in the case. The legal reasoning behind the rule laid down in the case is called the *ratio decedendi* and should be noted as the "court's reasoning."

On point:
Directly related to the legal question at issue in the case and analogous with the basic facts of the case.

Dicta (or obiter dicta):
Statements in opinions that go beyond the facts and specific legal issues before the court. Generalizations that may not accurately reflect the narrow kernel of law decided in the case.

The end of the opinion is always signaled by the court's disposition of the case. This end statement lets the reader know what specific action the court took in the case, but it should not be confused with the holding, which refers to the precedent the case establishes for future cases.

Ratio decedendi:
The grounds for or reasoning behind the decision; the point in the case that determines the judgment.

A *majority opinion* is usually written by one judge and represents the principles of law that a majority on the court deem operative in a given decision. At the Supreme Court level, a majority opinion would have five justices that subscribe to it. A *concurring opinion* is an opinion that agrees with the final result of a majority opinion but not necessarily the reasoning. A *dissenting opinion* disagrees with the result of the majority opinion and thus disagrees with the reasoning and/or the principles of law used by the majority in deciding the case. Dissenting and concurring opinions may ultimately influence later opinions in future cases.

BASIC ELEMENTS OF A CASE IN LAW

The six illustrative cases in the appendix that you have already read now need to be analyzed in a written brief presenting your notes to these cases. Each must be analyzed individually using this format and following the illustration in this chapter.

1. *Title and citation* Note who the parties are, whether the case is civil or criminal, which court is deciding the case (trial or appeals), and where to find the case in the law books. It is important to note the date the opinion was issued. The citation of a case is the legal abbreviation for where a case is located. A citation for a U.S. Supreme Court case includes the name of the case, the volume number of the reporter where a case is located, the abbreviation for the reporter (i.e., *United States Reports*), the beginning page of the opinion, and the year the case was decided.

2. *Background* Note what type and form of litigation is involved. Is it a trial court judgment, an appeal from a preliminary trial court decision (interlocutory appeal), or an appeal from a final trial court judgment? What basic facts are relevant to the decision?

3. *Sources of law* Note relevant constitutional, statutory, or common law sources and whether a question of conflict of law is involved. If case law is the only source, then specify the state where the common law principle applies (e.g., common law of Texas). Don't list underlying case precedents here; they should be used in the reasoning.

4. *Legal issues* Note the specific legal question, as framed by the judge, in terms that can be answered with a yes or no. Some law professors want these questions drawn very specifically and use the answer as the holding. There may be many legal issues in a single case, and these issues form separate precedents.

5. *Holdings* Note the answer to each of the legal issues (see above), and follow the yes or no answer with a clear, concise statement that includes the basic salient facts that will identify this holding as a precedent in future cases. (Draft a clear statement of the rule of law created by this decision.)

6. *Reasoning* Note how the court supported its decision; include the most important statutory and case citations, as well as the logical arguments used to apply these rules. Follow the court's reasoning step by step to get the *ratio decedendi* of the opinion on the specific

legal question. This explanation should be the longest part of the brief.

7. *Questions* Note comments or questions about the case. These should be discussed in class. Dissenting opinions by minority judges and concurring opinions by majority judges are good sources of questions, and they indicate that even learned judges can disagree. The majority opinion states the law, but dissenters often become persuasive and may prevail in the future. Do you agree with the majority opinion or that of the dissenter? Why, or why not?(The student may wish to add a conclusion section.)

An example of a case brief using this format is illustrated in the case of *Erie Railroad Company v. Tompkins*, which follows

Erie Railroad Company v. Tompkins

304 U.S. 64 (1938)

Title and citation: This is a civil case decided by the U.S. Supreme Court in 1938.

Background: The case was originally filed in federal district court in New York, where the railroad company was a citizen, under the diversity of citizenship jurisdiction of the court in civil matters. It is an appeal from a final judgment after a trial by jury that awarded Tompkins $30,000 in damages. The judgment was affirmed by the Circuit Court of Appeals. Tompkins, a citizen of Pennsylvania, had been injured in a railroad accident while he was trespassing on the railroad company's right of way. The trial judge refused to apply the common law of the state of Pennsylvania, as pronounced by that state's highest court, that "persons who use the pathway along a railroad are trespassers; and that the railroad is not liable for injuries to undiscovered trespassers resulting from its negligence, unless it be wanton or willful."

Sources of law: The Judiciary Act of 1789 provides that "The laws of the several States, except where the Constitution, treaties, or statutes of the United States otherwise require or provide, shall be regarded as rules of decision in trials at common law, in the courts of the United States, in cases where they apply." Common law of the State of Pennsylvania and the U.S. Constitution are used in the court's decision.

Legal issue: Whether the doctrine of the federal courts, established by the U.S. Supreme Court in *Swift v. Tyson* in 1842 applying general (federal) common law in cases where a statute or constitutional provision of the states is not available, should be overturned.

Holding: Yes, this case specifically overruled *Swift v. Tyson* and established a new precedent that the federal courts must apply the *common law* as established by the state court of last resort in diversity cases. This initiated the "Erie Doctrine" in diversity cases, which states that federal courts must apply the substantive law of the state where the case is filed. The substantive law includes the state's common law as well as its statutory law.

Reasoning: In overturning this long-established precedent in *Swift v. Tyson* (16 Pet. 1, 1842), the Supreme Court begins its reasoning from the congressional statute itself, which appears to support the new precedent (see wording above). Justice Louis Brandeis, writing for the majority in *Erie*, criticizes the majority opinion in *Swift v. Tyson* as a fallacy based upon the assumption of the existence of a general common law. The common law of the state is the only common law that the federal courts can apply under the U.S. Constitution in diversity cases. The majority reasons that the *Swift v. Tyson* doctrine is "an unconstitutional assumption of powers by the Courts of the United States . . . ." Section 34 of the Federal Judiciary Act of 1789 (quoted above) is not held unconstitutional, but is clarified by declaring that in applying the doctrine of *Swift v. Tyson* the federal courts have invaded rights that are reserved by the Constitution to the states.

Questions: Does this decision mean that state procedural as well as substantive law must be applied in federal diversity cases? Justice Pierce Butler writes a dissenting opinion joined by Justice James R. McReynolds, arguing essentially that long precedent and "general common law" should be applied. The dissenters agree with *Swift v. Tyson*, which treated decisions of courts alone as "at most, only evidence of what the laws are, and are not, of themselves, laws."

LEGAL RESEARCH SOURCES

Legal research is a required skill for attorneys. State rules of professional conduct—attorney ethical codes—require that attorneys have the requisite degree of competence to research and handle a client's case. Inadequate legal research can lead not only to punishment of attorneys for ethical violations but also to legal malpractice actions—charges that the attorney committed professional negligence. The American Bar Association has issued the Model Rules of Professional Conduct, which nearly every state has used as a model for its own attorney disciplinary codes. Rule 1.1 requires attorneys to be competent. The comments to the rule indicate that a lawyer must be able to adequately identify the relevant law and be able to research the matter to provide competent representation.

ABA Model Rule of Professional Conduct, Rule 1.1.—Competence

THE RULE

"A lawyer shall provide competent representation to a client. Competent representation requires the legal knowledge, skill, thoroughness and preparation reasonably necessary for the representation."

COMMENTS

Legal Knowledge and Skill

[1] In determining whether a lawyer employs the requisite knowledge and skill in a particular matter, relevant factors include the relative complexity and specialized nature of the matter, the lawyer's general experience, the lawyer's training and experience in the field in question, the preparation and study the lawyer is able to give the matter and whether it is feasible to refer the matter to, an associate or consult with, a lawyer of established competence in the field in question. In many instances, the required proficiency is that of a general practitioner. Expertise in a particular field of law may be required in some circumstances.

[2] A lawyer need not necessarily have special training or prior experience to handle legal problems of a type with which the lawyer is unfamiliar. A newly admitted lawyer can be as competent as a practitioner with long experience. Some important legal skills, such as the analysis of precedent, the evaluation of evidence and legal drafting, are required in all legal problems. Perhaps the most fundamental legal skill consists of determining what kind of legal problems a situation may involve, a skill that necessarily transcends any particular specialized knowledge. A lawyer can provide adequate representation in a wholly novel field through necessary study. Competent representation can also be provided through the association of a lawyer of established competence in the field in question.

[3] In an emergency a lawyer may give advice or assistance in a matter in which the lawyer does not have the skill ordinarily required where referral to or consultation or association with another lawyer would be impractical. Even in an emergency, however, assistance should be limited to that reasonably necessary in the circumstances, for ill-considered action under emergency conditions can jeopardize the client's interest.

[4] A lawyer may accept representation where the requisite level of competence can be achieved by reasonable preparation. This applies as well to a lawyer who is appointed as counsel for an unrepresented person. See also Rule 6.2.

Thoroughness and Preparation

[5] Competent handling of a particular matter includes inquiry into and analysis of the factual and legal elements of the problem, and use of methods and procedures meeting the standards of competent practitioners. It also

continued >

includes adequate preparation. The required attention and preparation are determined in part by what is at stake; major litigation and complex transactions ordinarily require more extensive treatment than matters of lesser complexity and consequence. An agreement between the lawyer and the client regarding the scope of the representation may limit the matters for which the lawyer is responsible. See Rule 1.2(c).

Maintaining Competence

[6] To maintain the requisite knowledge and skill, a lawyer should keep abreast of changes in the law and its practice, engage in continuing study and education and comply with all continuing legal education requirements to which the lawyer is subject.

Mandatory and Persuasive Legal Authority

The ultimate goal for a legal researcher is to locate *mandatory, primary authority* that provides an answer to a legal question. Both of these adjectives—mandatory and primary—are important in legal research circles. **Mandatory authority** refers to legal precedent that a court must follow. For example, U.S. Supreme Court decisions are mandatory authority for lower courts. Because it is the court of last resort, these decisions have ramifications for all lower courts, both state and federal. A Tennessee statute or law is mandatory authority for a court in Tennessee. A decision by the Tennessee Supreme Court would be mandatory authority for any state trial court judge in Tennessee.

> **Mandatory authority:** Legal precedent that a court must follow.

Many times in law we encounter **persuasive authority**. Persuasive authority refers to legal authority that a court may—but does not have to—follow. Persuasive authority is nonmandatory authority. For example, a Kentucky Supreme Court decision is persuasive, not mandatory, authority for a court in Tennessee. A Colorado law is persuasive authority for a court in Utah. Persuasive authority is still important, however, as oftentimes a legal researcher may not find any mandatory authority bearing on a question. For example, a lawyer in Tennessee may find that the Tennessee courts have not addressed a particular question, but the question has been addressed by the Kentucky courts. The lawyer's job then is to convince the judge to adopt the reasoning of a court from another jurisdiction—to persuade the court that the persuasive authority really is persuasive.

> **Persuasive authority:** Legal authority that a court may, but does not have to, follow.

Secondary Sources: What Are They and Why Use Them?

Primary authorities, or primary sources, refer to law itself in whatever form. Court opinions, statutes or laws, ordinances, and regulations are all examples of law and primary authority. Contrast that with **secondary authority**. Secondary authority refers to legal materials that help to explain, clarify, or inform about the law, but are not law.

> **Secondary authority:** Legal materials that help to explain, clarify, or inform about the law, but are not law.

These sources, or tools, often aid attorneys and other legal professionals, such as paralegals or law clerks, in their quest to find mandatory, primary authority. Sometimes attorneys need help in interpreting, understanding, or finding the law.

Secondary sources include legal encyclopedias, law journals, treatises, and books about law. Researchers may consult secondary sources for several reasons. First, secondary sources explain or clarify the law. If an attorney is not familiar with an area of law, he or she may consult a secondary source in order to understand the legal landscape better. Other times, there may not be primary authority directly on point, and the researcher is left with trying to find some legal authority to support his or her point. On other occasions, researchers use secondary sources as a way to find citations to primary authority.

There are numerous types of secondary sources. **Legal encyclopedias** are a popular secondary source that provide short overviews on nearly every legal topic imaginable. There are two main national legal encyclopedias: *Corpus Juris Secundum* (C.J.S.) and *American Jurisprudence* (Am. Jur.). Both of these encyclopedias now are published by Thomson Reuters Corporation, which purchased West Publishing, the giant of legal publishing. The encyclopedias provide a good starting point for researchers but rarely serve as an ending point.

Legal encyclopedias: Secondary sources that provide short overviews on legal topics, such as *Corpus Juris Secundum* (C.J.S.) and *American Jurisprudence* (Am. Jur.).

Many attorneys will want to be careful in relying on a national legal encyclopedia because state laws can be quite different. If you are a Tennessee attorney, you do not want to rely on an encyclopedia article that quotes California and Utah cases. For this reason, many attorneys prefer to begin their research in a state-specific legal encyclopedia. An example is *Tennessee Jurisprudence* published by Michie. *Tennessee Jurisprudence* provides its readers with numerous citations to primary authority from Tennessee.

Another good secondary source is ***American Law Reports***, known by its acronym A.L.R. *American Law Reports* is divided into two parts: A.L.R. and A.L.R. Fed. The regular A.L.R. examines state law issues, whereas A.L.R. Fed examines federal law issues. Volumes of the A.L.R. contain detailed overview articles of specific points of law called annotations that cite to case law all across the United States. If a researcher can find an A.L.R. article on point, it can be a treasure trove. A.L.R. annotations tend to be specific.

American Law Reports (A.L.R.): Contain detailed overview articles called annotations that cite cases all across the United States.

For example, let's say that a potential client comes to a lawyer's office saying that he had been injured by a foul ball at a baseball game. The potential client believes that either the owner of the stadium or the baseball team or the player in question that hit the ball should pay him for the injuries he suffered when hit by the foul ball. The attorney likely will not know off the top of her head a case citation or what the law exactly is in her jurisdiction. She may start by looking for an applicable A.L.R. annotation. Consider the following A.L.R. titles: "Liability to spectator at baseball game who is hit by ball or injured as result of other hazards of the game"; "Liability of spectator at basketball game due to hazards of the game"; and "Liability for injury or death on or near golf course." Obviously, the first quoted A.L.R. title would be applicable. It contains cases from all around the country. This is a classic example of an attorney finding a relevant secondary source that provides numerous citations to primary authority.

Another common type of secondary source is **law review** or **law journal articles**. These journals are published at different law schools around the country. A group of students—often some of the best-performing students academically—serve as the group that solicits articles from law professors and others around the country on different legal topics. The students then work with the professor on editing the article and then arranging for publication. A common feature of a law review article is the literally hundreds of footnotes found in these articles, which sometimes can be quite theoretical and not as practical as other secondary sources. But, a relevant law review article can provide a researcher with a mother lode of citations to primary authority. Historically, some law review articles have changed the legal landscape. For example, two Boston-based attorneys and former law school classmates, Samuel Warren and Louis Brandeis, published an article in the *Harvard Law Review* in 1890 that called for the creation of a new cause of action in tort law: the invasion of the right of privacy.

Law review or law journal articles: Secondary sources that provide researchers with citations to primary authority.

Another leading secondary source is the ***Restatements of the Law***, published by the American Law Institute. The *Restatements* take an area of the law and seek to restate the basic black-letter principles of law in that subject. For example, there are *Restatements* for the core legal subjects of torts, contracts, and property. The *Restatements* consist of the black-letter law rules, comments, and illustrations. The black-letter law rules give the reader the core information as to what the law is. The comments explain the reasoning or purpose or policy behind the rule. The illustrations provide sample examples of the principles.

Restatements of the law: Authoritative restatements of common law in basic black-letter principles of law on that subject.

For example, take a look at the following example from the *Restatement of Torts,* Second Edition. The following excerpt is from the restatement section on a particular branch of common law tort privacy called "public disclosure of private facts." The *Restatement* again consists of three parts: (1) the black-letter law rule, (2) comments, and (3) illustrations.

Restatement of Torts (2d)

§652D Publicity Given to Private Life

One who gives publicity to a matter concerning the private life of another is subject to liability to the other for invasion of his privacy, if the matter publicized is of a kind that

     (a) would be highly offensive to a reasonable person, and

     (b) is not of legitimate concern to the public.

   . . .

---

continued >

COMMENTS & ILLUSTRATIONS:

Comments:

a. Publicity. The form of invasion of the right of privacy covered in this Section depends upon publicity given to the private life of the individual. "Publicity," as it is used in this Section, differs from "publication," as that term is used in §577 in connection with liability for defamation. "Publication," in that sense, is a word of art, which includes any communication by the defendant to a third person. "Publicity," on the other hand, means that the matter is made public, by communicating it to the public at large, or to so many persons that the matter must be regarded as substantially certain to become one of public knowledge. The difference is not one of the means of communication, which may be oral, written or by any other means. It is one of a communication that reaches, or is sure to reach, the public.

Thus it is not an invasion of the right of privacy, within the rule stated in this Section, to communicate a fact concerning the plaintiff's private life to a single person or even to a small group of persons. On the other hand, any publication in a newspaper or a magazine, even of small circulation, or in a handbill distributed to a large number of persons, or any broadcast over the radio, or statement made in an address to a large audience, is sufficient to give publicity within the meaning of the term as it is used in this Section. The distinction, in other words, is one between private and public communication.

Illustrations:

1. A, a creditor, writes a letter to the employer of B, his debtor, informing him that B owes the debt and will not pay it. This is not an invasion of B's privacy under this Section.

2. A, a creditor, posts in the window of his shop, where it is read by those passing by on the street, a statement that B owes a debt to him and has not paid it. This is an invasion of B's privacy.

3. A, a motion picture exhibitor, wishing to advertise a picture to be exhibited, writes letters to a thousand men in which he makes unprivileged and objectionable statements concerning the private life of B, an actress. This is an invasion of B's privacy.

Restatements are considered a very persuasive secondary source in part because they are written by panels of judges, law professors, and practicing attorneys. Perhaps because some judges participate in the American Law Institute and the drafting of certain restatement sections, courts tend to view them with a healthy dose of respect.

Still other important secondary sources are treatises, and books written on a particular legal subject by leading scholars. For example, lawyers who practice criminal law dealing with drug cases and constitutional law issues, might often consult a six-volume treatise by Professor Wayne LaFave of Indiana Law School. This is considered the leading source on search and seizure law. If an attorney had a question about workers' compensation, he or she might consult Worker's Compensation Law by Lex Larson.

This 12-volume set actually began in the 1950s as a two-volume set by Lex's father, Arthur Larson, a Cornell law professor.

Still other leading secondary sources are various **form books**. Legal work involves the creation of many documents: letters, complaints, answers, motions, contracts, memoranda, and partnership agreements to name a few. Many times lawyers need some guidance in creating these documents. Form books are useful for lawyers to be able to see an example of the type of work they have to create for a client. For example, let's say that an attorney regularly practices employment law on behalf of plaintiffs, employees or ex-employees who believe they have been the victim of discrimination in the workplace. This attorney normally handles race and sex discrimination claims. But, a potential client has come to her office, asking for legal representation on an age-discrimination case. The attorney fervently believes that the client has a good case and has been wronged by her employer. But, the attorney has never handled an age discrimination case. This attorney may want to look at a sample complaint—the initial charging document in which one party sues another—in an age discrimination case. An attorney may be able to find such a complaint in a form book. A commonly used set of national legal form books are called *American Jurisprudence Legal Forms* or *AmJur Legal Forms*. Attorneys must be careful when using national form books, however, as state laws can differ. In other words, a national form book may not reflect individual state law differences.

Form books:
Sources that provide model forms in various legal fields such as *American Jurisprudence Legal Forms* (or *AmJur Legal Forms*).

Determining What Law Applies

In order to provide the answer to a problem, a researcher must first identify and then find the relevant body of law. The initial question for a legal researcher is determining what type of law applies. This question is more difficult than it sounds. Recall ABA Model Rule 1.1., the duty of competence. The comments to that rule state that "perhaps the most fundamental legal skill consists of determining what kind of legal problems a situation may involve, a skill that necessarily transcends any particular specialized knowledge." The researcher must determine what legal subject matter the question involves and then determine whether it is governed by federal law, state law, or both. For example, the researcher has to determine whether a question concerns contract law, family law, employment law, personal injury (tort) law, constitutional law, bankruptcy law, or some other type of law. Sometimes a legal problem involves multiple areas of law.

For example, let's say that a woman comes to a lawyer's office wanting to file for a divorce. She informs the attorney that before she got married, she signed a prenuptial agreement. She also knows that one of her husband's property businesses on which she is listed as a partner is failing. This scenario potentially involves at least three general areas of law: *family* (also called domestic relations) *law, contract law,* and *bankruptcy law.*

The attorney may have to research all three areas of law to give the woman competent legal representation.

Another issue for legal researchers is determining whether federal law applies, state law applies, or both. Some areas of law are predominately matters of state law. Personal injury, tort law, and family law are governed mainly by state law. Bankruptcy is largely a matter of federal law. But, other areas of law, such as employment law, are a mixture of both.

Types of Research

Fortunately, there are many avenues for the legal researcher to explore in finding applicable legal sources. Many materials are available in print from law libraries and other locations. A law library in your hometown should contain most of the core information you will need. If there is no law school, a regular university library or general library may well contain the needed materials. Fortunately, there are easier ways to research law than through books. More and more legal materials are available free of charge on the Internet. The largest concentration of legal sources is found in subscription-based online legal databases. The two largest and most popular are LEXIS and Westlaw. Nearly all printed legal research materials are found on LEXIS or Westlaw. Later in this chapter we will focus specifically on researching in these databases.

STATUTORY LAW SOURCES

Many legal problems are governed by laws passed by federal, state, or local governing bodies. These laws are called *statutes* (at the federal or state level) or *ordinances* (at the local level). A statute is simply another name for a law. Federal and state laws are found in sets of books known as **annotated codes**. When laws are passed, they are later placed topically into the official code or collection of laws. Federal laws are found in the *United States Code*, the *United States Code Annotated*, or the *United States Code Service*.

Annotated codes: Statutory law placed topically into the official code or collection of statutory law.

Federal laws are arranged into 50 different titles. For example, Title 11 deals with bankruptcy; Title 17 deals with copyrights; Title 18 with crimes and criminal procedure; and Title 42 with public health and welfare. Codes contain general indexes that allow researchers to formulate search terms. From the index, a researcher hopes to obtain a **citation** for a statute. A citation is a shorthand reference to a legal authority. Citations are vitally important in legal research and in the legal system itself. Without a valid citation, a researcher may not be able to find legal authority. Without a valid citation, an attorney cannot present a believable argument to a court. Judges care very deeply about whether legal documents contain adequate citations. Citations for federal statutes include a title number, the abbreviation of the code, and a section number.

Citation: Shorthand reference to legal authority.

Titles of the *United States Code*

Title 1: General Provisions	Title 28: Judiciary and Judicial Procedure
Title 2: Congress	Title 29: Labor
Title 3: The President	Title 30: Mineral Lands and Mining
Title 4: Flag and Seal, Seat of Government, and the States	Title 31: Money and Finance
Title 5: Government Organization and Employees	Title 32: National Guard
	Title 33: Navigation and Navigable Waters
Title 6: Domestic Security	Title 34: Navy (this title has been repealed and moved into Title 10 in the 1950s)
Title 7: Agriculture	
Title 8: Aliens and Nationality	Title 35: Patents
Title 9: Arbitration	Title 36: Patriotic and National Observances
Title 10: Armed Forces	
Title 11: Bankruptcy	Title 37: Pay and Allowances of the Uniformed Services
Title 12: Banks and Banking	
Title 13: Census	Title 38: Veterans' Benefits
Title 14: Coast Guard	Title 39: Postal Service
Title 15: Commerce and Trade	Title 40: Public Buildings, Property and Works
Title 16: Conservation	
Title 17: Copyright	Title 41: Public Contracts
Title 18: Crimes and Criminal Procedure	Title 42: Public Health and Welfare
Title 19: Customs Duties	Title 43: Public Lands
Title 20: Education	Title 44: Public Printing and Documents
Title 21: Food and Drugs	Title 45: Railroads
Title 22: Foreign Relations	Title 46: Shipping
Title 23: Highways	Title 47: Telegraphs, Telephones, and Radio-telegraphs
Title 24: Hospitals and Asylums	
Title 25: Indians	Title 48: Territories and Insular Possessions
Title 26: Internal Revenue Code	
Title 27: Intoxicating Liquors	Title 49: Transportation
	Title 50: War and National Defense

For example, the beginning statute in the Americans with Disabilities Act (ADA), the major federal disability discrimination law, is cited as 42 U.S.C. §12101. This means that in Title 42 of the *U.S. Code* at section 12101 one will find the text of that provision of the ADA.

Text of a Statute in the Americans with Disabilities Act

42 U.S.C. §12101

(a) Findings

The Congress finds that—

(1) physical or mental disabilities in no way diminish a person's right to fully participate in all aspects of society, yet many people with physical or

---

continued >

mental disabilities have been precluded from doing so because of discrimination; others who have a record of a disability or are regarded as having a disability also have been subjected to discrimination;

(2) historically, society has tended to isolate and segregate individuals with disabilities, and, despite some improvements, such forms of discrimination against individuals with disabilities continue to be a serious and pervasive social problem;

(3) discrimination against individuals with disabilities persists in such critical areas as employment, housing, public accommodations, education, transportation, communication, recreation, institutionalization, health services, voting, and access to public services;

(4) unlike individuals who have experienced discrimination on the basis of race, color, sex, national origin, religion, or age, individuals who have experienced discrimination on the basis of disability have often had no legal recourse to redress such discrimination;

(5) individuals with disabilities continually encounter various forms of discrimination, including outright intentional exclusion, the discriminatory effects of architectural, transportation, and communication barriers, overprotective rules and policies, failure to make modifications to existing facilities and practices, exclusionary qualification standards and criteria, segregation, and relegation to lesser services, programs, activities, benefits, jobs, or other opportunities;

(6) census data, national polls, and other studies have documented that people with disabilities, as a group, occupy an inferior status in our society, and are severely disadvantaged socially, vocationally, economically, and educationally;

(7) the Nation's proper goals regarding individuals with disabilities are to assure equality of opportunity, full participation, independent living, and economic self-sufficiency for such individuals; and

(8) the continuing existence of unfair and unnecessary discrimination and prejudice denies people with disabilities the opportunity to compete on an equal basis and to pursue those opportunities for which our free society is justifiably famous, and costs the United States billions of dollars in unnecessary expenses resulting from dependency and nonproductivity.

(b) Purpose

It is the purpose of this chapter—

(1) to provide a clear and comprehensive national mandate for the elimination of discrimination against individuals with disabilities;

(2) to provide clear, strong, consistent, enforceable standards addressing discrimination against individuals with disabilities;

(3) to ensure that the Federal Government plays a central role in enforcing the standards established in this chapter on behalf of individuals with disabilities; and

(4) to invoke the sweep of congressional authority, including the power to enforce the fourteenth amendment and to regulate commerce, in order to address the major areas of discrimination faced day-to-day by people with disabilities.

The most important facet of a code is that it contains the text of statutes. But, annotated codes contain more than just the text of a statute. They contain more detailed information in the notes or annotations portion after the text of the statute, such as summaries of court opinions that mention the statute in question, secondary sources that cite the statute, and a little bit of legislative history, such as when the statute was passed and amended. What this means is that if a researcher finds an applicable statute, he or she will find citations for much more legal authority. The researcher will find citations to court cases, secondary sources, attorney general opinions and a bevy of other information.

RESEARCHING CASE LAW

Many times statutory law will not govern a particular situation. The United States, as you will recall from Chapter 1, has a legal system of both code law (statutory law) and common law (another word for case law). Much of the U.S. legal system descended from the English system of common law, or judge-made law. This means that oftentimes a legal researcher will have to find out whether there is a controlling U.S. Supreme Court case, state high court case, or some other judicial decision that provides the key to answering a question.

Published judicial opinions are found in sets of books called *reporters*. All published decisions are placed in these reporters. Unpublished decisions are not placed in a reporter and must be accessed electronically or from the court itself. The difference is key because published decisions have much more persuasive power to a court than unpublished decisions. U.S. Supreme Court decisions are found in the *United States Reports*, the *Supreme Court Reporter*, and the *Lawyer's Edition*. Federal appeals court decisions are found in the *Federal Reporter*, and federal district court decisions are found in the *Federal Supplement*. The *U.S. Reports* is published by the federal government, and the *Supreme Court Reporter* and the *Lawyer's Edition* are published by private publishing companies. State appellate court decisions are found in state reporters, regional reporters, or both. Recall, however, that reporters are chronological compilations of cases. They do not allow a researcher to research a subject topically. Reporters are useful if a researcher has a case citation. With such a citation, a researcher can simply go to the applicable reporter and find the judicial opinion, but without a citation, the researcher is helpless without a topical guide to case law.

Citation for a Case

Citation is important in the world of legal research. One reason citation is so important is that attorneys have to provide legal support or precedent for the points that they make. In other words, attorneys have to provide a court with some legal authority to bolster their arguments. They need to provide correct citations so the judges—and the judges' law clerks—can evaluate the merits of the citation.

The citation for a judicial opinion consists of several things, including the following:

- The name of the case
- The volume number of the reporter in which the case appears
- The abbreviation for the reporter in which the case appears
- The beginning page number of the case in the reporter
- The abbreviation for the court that decided the case and the year of the decision in parenthesis

Let's look at an example: *Bethel School District v. Fraser*, 478 U.S. 675 (1986). This was a 1986 decision by the U.S. Supreme Court dealing with a high school student's free-speech rights. Notice that the case name is italicized. This is customary in legal circles: all case names are italicized or underlined. This citation means that if you go to volume 478 of the *United States Reports* and turn to page 675 you will find the Court's opinion in *Fraser*. Notice that in the parenthesis only the year is given. That is because the only court whose opinions are found in the *United States Reports* is the U.S. Supreme Court. However, if there was a judicial opinion found in the *Federal Reporter,* that could be a decision from any 1 of 13 federal appeals courts, as you learned in Chapter 3. Thus, you would need to include in the parenthesis either (1st Cir. Year) or (6th Cir. Year) or another circuit.

Let's take another example: *Boroff v. Van Wert Board of Education*, 220 F.3d 465 (6th Cir. 2000). This is another student speech case from the Sixth Circuit. In this case, the rule of citation is that you must include the name of the lower court (the Sixth Circuit) because the *Federal Reporter* contains judicial opinions from different courts.

Another concept important in the legal world is that of the **pinpoint citation**. A pinpoint citation refers to a point of law found on a specific page of a case. Some judicial opinions are very, very long. *Furman v. Georgia* (1972) is a death penalty decision decided by the U.S. Supreme Court that is more than 230 pages long. Lawyers have to be able to point to the specific location in the case that provides support for the point that they are arguing. Thus, the attorney must include the pinpoint citation when citing a judicial opinion.

Pinpoint citation:
A point of law found on a specific page of a case.

For more information about legal citations, consult the premier book on legal citations, *The Bluebook: A Uniform System of Citation,* better known as "the Bluebook." See http://www.legalbluebook.com/ for more information. The book is now in its 19th edition.

FINDING TOOLS

Fortunately, there are sets of books that are tools for finding cases. They are called **digests**. The entire body of published case law is indexed in these digests. The initial step for the legal researcher is to identify the appropriate digest. U.S. Supreme Court decisions are located in the *Supreme Court Digest*. Federal appeals court decisions and federal district court decisions are found in the *Federal Practice Digest*. State court decisions may be found in a state digest, a regional digest, or both. For example, Tennessee state appellate court decisions are indexed in the *Tennessee Digest*. Georgia state appellate court decisions are indexed in both the *Georgia Digest* and the *Southeastern Digest* (the digest used for the *Southeastern Reporter*, the regional reporter that includes Georgia decisions).

    Digests are arranged by *topic* and *key numbers*. There are more than 470 digest topics arranged alphabetically from abandoned and lost property to zoning. Examples of other digest topics include torts, negligence, products liability, contracts, landlord and tenant, civil rights, and constitutional law. Each digest topic is then arranged even more into hundreds, if not thousands of key numbers. Each key number addresses a particular point of law in a digest topic.

    Sometimes, a researcher will know that a certain digest topic will contain the applicable area of law. But many times there are multiple digest topics that might cover a particular situation. For example, there are separate digest topics titled Search & Seizure and Arrest. One or both of these may apply in a given situation. Thus, a researcher must often start from scratch when using a set of digest books.

    For example, let's say that a lawyer is asked to research the question of injuries caused by lawnmowers. The person may not know what digest topic applies. The researcher must go to a set of books at the end of the digest series, called indexes or **descriptive word indexes**. Using a descriptive word index enables a researcher to find the appropriate search terms. The researcher might use the index, which is arranged alphabetically, to look up the terms mower, lawnmower, and power mowers. Eventually, the researcher will find PROD LIAB 56. PROD LIAB refers to the digest topic, Products Liability, and 56 refers to the key number associated with injuries caused by lawnmowers.

Digests:
The entire body of published case law is indexed in these publications.

Descriptive word indexes:
Indexes that enable a researcher to find the appropriate terms used by the publication.

ASSIGNMENT: Using the descriptive word index of your state digest, see if you can find a case that provides an example of conduct that constitutes "intentional infliction of emotional distress." What is the case name? Describe the nature of the conduct.

Steps for Researching Cases by the Traditional Book Method

1. Locate the appropriate digest set.
2. If there is a case citation, look in the table of cases volume of the digest.
3. If there is no case citation, look in the index or descriptive word index and think of search terms.
4. Locate an applicable digest topic and key number.
5. Pull the appropriate volume of the digest and see if there are any case blurbs listed under that topic and key number.
6. If so, then write down the citation and pull the opinion from the applicable reporter.

With the digest topic and key number, the researcher can pull the applicable volume of the digest, which is arranged alphabetically by topics. The reader then turns to Products Liability and key number 56 to see if there are any cases cited. If there is a case citation, the reader can then go to the reporter. This system works because all the judicial opinions found in the West reporter system contain certain editorial enhancements at the beginning of the judicial opinion. These enhancements include several **headnotes**, which are the main points of law found in the body of the judicial opinion. Each headnote is labeled with an appropriate digest topic and key number. These headnotes, topics, and key numbers form the essence of the book method of legal research. What makes the West system so useful is that the same digest topics and key numbers are used for the entire system. That means that the same digest topic and key number are used in all the different digests in the West system.

Headnotes:
The main points of law found in the body of the judicial opinion.

Case law research by the traditional book method is harder than statutory research because statutory research requires the use of only one set of books, the applicable annotated code. On the other hand, case law research generally requires the use of two sets of books: digests and reporters.

USING LEXIS AND WESTLAW

If research using books seems challenging, that's because it is. Some attorneys are not very good at legal research and either make subordinate attorneys, called associates or clerks, do the work, or they hire legal research specialists to do the job. Fortunately, there are much easier ways to do legal research than through the tedious and time-consuming book method of research. Many lawyers use a subscription-based online legal research database to serve their needs. The two most common are **LEXIS** and **Westlaw**.

LEXIS and Westlaw:
Subscription-based online legal research databases.

Before using either database, the attorney must provide an ID and password. Once this routine step is completed, the attorney has a range of options. The initial step in using either one of these products is to identify the appropriate database. For example, in LEXIS the attorney might research directly in the "CASES" area. The attorney can choose from several databases: Federal and State Cases, Federal Court Cases, or State Court Cases. An attorney would use a general database like this if he or she were looking for case law on a national basis. But oftentimes an attorney will want to research only in a specific state database. For example, a Tennessee attorney may want to research only Tennessee state cases, or federal and state cases in Tennessee. The databases in Westlaw are similar; Westlaw just uses different names for its databases. For example, its database of federal court cases is called "ALLFEDS."

Once an attorney selects the appropriate database, he or she then must search for cases using one of two methods: (1) a **terms and connectors search** or (2) a **natural language search**. Under a terms and connectors search, the user types in certain words that should be found in the judicial opinions. For example, let's say an attorney wishes to search for "slip and fall cases in Tennessee" to determine the appropriate standard of care for a store owner. The user may type in the words "slip and fall," "negligence," and "store." This search will pull up all the cases in the database containing all three of these words. If an opinion does not contain all three of these search terms, it will not appear in the search results.

Terms and connectors search:
Search using certain user-supplied words that should be found in the judicial opinions.

Natural language search:
Search using natural language terms to find judicial opinions.

ASSIGNMENT: Using LEXIS or Westlaw, go to the database that covers U.S. Supreme Court opinions. Using either a terms and connectors or natural language search, find a U.S. Supreme Court case that deals with freedom of speech and whether individuals have a right to protest near a funeral. How did the Court decide the case?

Researchers can narrow their searches by using different connectors to be more precise in their findings. For example, a researcher can type in the terms "speech/obscenity" in the search box. This means that all opinions listed will have the word *speech* appear in the same sentence as the word *obscenity*.

Terms and connectors searches are good for those users who are familiar with an area of law. For example, the coauthor of this textbook, David L. Hudson Jr., is a First Amendment expert. Because of his day-to-day work on free speech and other First Amendment issues, he knows the applicable judicial terminology that judges use in free-speech cases. Thus, he usually uses terms and connectors searches when researching free-speech questions.

However, if Hudson had to research an area of law in which he is not as familiar, say domestic relations law, he might choose the other method of searching: natural language. In a natural language search, a researcher simply types in the information in natural, everyday language—even in colloquial, natural language. Beginning researchers often prefer natural language searching until they become more familiar with an area of law. Some users simply have personal preferences for one method over the other. There is no one-size-fits-all method for every user. A researcher should use whatever method he or she is more comfortable with and the method leads to better results.

Whatever method is chosen, a researcher can narrow the results through several methods. First, a user can restrict the findings by date. An attorney may wish to search for certain decisions over the past year, month, or even week. Similarly, a researcher may wish to search only for opinions by a specific judge; this can be done as well.

A common use of the online databases by lawyers and other legal researchers is that of updating legal authority. An attorney may find a case that looks great on paper: It is on point, it examines the issues well, and it has a ruling in favor of a person like the attorney's client. However, a later court decision may negatively impact that decision. Sometimes, courts will overrule their past decisions in later court decisions. For example, in the equal protection chapter (see Chapter 9), students will learn that the U.S. Supreme Court overruled its decision in *Plessy v. Ferguson* (1896) 58 years later in *Brown v. Board of Education* (1954). It is a very bad practice for attorneys to cite a case or statute to a court that has been overruled or limited by later case law. Thus, after attorneys find a law that they deem relevant, they must "update" that legal authority to make sure it is still valid.

The traditional book method for updating legal research is quite tedious and requires the researcher to navigate through a separate set of books called *citators*. Fortunately, on LEXIS and Westlaw the process of updating legal authority consists of clicking on a button and reading the resulting entries. In LEXIS, the process of validating legal authorities is called **Shepardizing** and in Westlaw it is called **KeyCiting.** If the attorney has to validate legal authorities through the traditional book method, one key method is looking at the back of many legal research books for a paper insert called a **pocket part**. A seminal rule of legal research using paper books is to always check the pocket part. For example, many annotated codes will have an annual paper insert in the back of the book, containing recent legislative updates that may change certain statutes. A legal researcher must check the pocket part to make sure he or she is reading the most current version of the law.

Online Legal Research

There are many other research materials on the Internet aside from the subscription fee online databases of LEXIS and Westlaw. Another valuable

Shepardizing:
Validating legal case authority by the LEXIS process.

KeyCiting:
Validating legal case authority by the Westlaw process.

Pocket part:
The method of validation of case law authority when using the traditional book method whereby annual paper inserts are found in the back of the volume used.

research tool is provided by the federal judiciary. It is known as PACER, which stands for Public Access to Court Electronic Records. PACER's Web site is http://www.pacer.gov. Its mission is stated as follows: "Public Access to Court Electronic Records (PACER) is an electronic public access service that allows users to obtain case and docket information from federal appellate, district and bankruptcy courts, and the PACER Case Locator via the Internet. PACER is provided by the federal Judiciary in keeping with its commitment to providing public access to court information via a central-ized service."

Researchers love PACER because they can access not only judicial opinions but also nearly every document filed in a case. It costs about eight cents a page to download different documents from PACER. From this site, attorneys can download complaints, answers, summary judgment motions, and other legal filings (known as *pleadings*) from a case. Recall that earlier the text mentioned form books as a way for attorneys to learn from existing work product. PACER is another avenue attorneys can use to see examples of court filings. For example, an attorney might want to look at documents filed in a particularly high-profile employment law case because he or she is working on a similar type case.

Unlike PACER, many online research sites are free. An excellent start-ing point for free online legal research is FindLaw at http://www.findlaw. com. Using FindLaw, researchers can access a great majority of the free sources of law on the Internet. For example, on FindLaw one can access the U.S. Constitution, the *Code of Federal Regulations* (federal regulations from executive branch administrative agencies), and the *United States Code*. There also is a "State Laws" collection that provides links to every state's legal code or statutory law. In another section, entitled "Research the Law," one can find decisions from a host of federal and state courts. FindLaw also offers a section of legal commentary articles written by lead-ing professors, attorneys, and other authors called FindLaw's Writ. The authors distill complex legal subjects into understandable articles.

Courts' individual Web sites provide an excellent source for recent case law. A prime example is the U.S. Supreme Court's own Web site at http://www.supremecourt.gov. From the Court's site, you can access recent opin-ions from the current term as well as the Court's docket to see if the Court has granted or denied review in a particular case. Researchers can also access the rules of the Supreme Court, the legal briefs filed in pending cases, and much more material. Nearly every court in the country has its own Web site, most of which contain the court's individual rules and many contain its recent judicial decisions. For example, on the Sixth U.S. Circuit Court of Appeals' Web site, one can access Sixth Circuit's published decisions since 1999 and unpublished decisions since 2004.

Individuals can also track federal and state legislation online for free. The best place to search the work product of the U.S. Congress is the

Thomas site at http://thomas.loc.gov. As the Web site reads at the top of the home page, the Library of Congress's THOMAS site is "In the spirit of Thomas Jefferson, legislative information from the Library of Congress." Researchers can access bills pending in the U.S. House of Representatives and the U.S. Senate. They also can search the *Congressional Record* and individual committees and subcommittees for hearings, reports, and other pertinent information. From Thomas, a researcher can access the Web pages of individual members of Congress. Individual state legislatures also have Web sites where one can track the work product of the state legislature during the current session. Many of these sites contain numerous links to other important sources of state governing bodies and law.

The executive branch also has work product available to access on the Internet free of charge, just as the judicial and legislative branches of government do. For example, many federal administrative agencies post relevant material on their Web sites. The Equal Employment Opportunity Commission (EEOC), the administrative agency in charge of enforcing many federal antidiscrimination laws, has a host of important information on its Web site (http://www.eeoc.gov), including the texts of federal laws, information on how to file a complaint with the EEOC, and the EEOC's interpretative guidelines, which often are given strong credence by courts in employment law cases. Another example is the Federal Trade Commission. Its Web site contains relevant federal law and regulations and an assortment of publications about issues such as medical theft, identity theft, telemarketing, the National Do Not Call Registry, and others.

Other growing research sources for attorneys and researchers are legal blogs—Web blogs devoted to legal topics. Many attorneys write or blog about legal issues, judicial decisions, and other legal news. A good example is SCOTUSblog, which many consider as the number one source for following the U.S. Supreme Court. This blog features veteran U.S. Supreme Court reporter Lyle Denniston, who provides commentary on Supreme Court decisions and activities and analysis from experts such as the blog's founder, leading U.S. Supreme Court litigator Tom Goldstein. Another popular legal blog is called How Appealing, a blog created by Pennsylvania-based appellate attorney Howard Bashman. It contains links to various court decisions and media articles on leading legal developments.

CHAPTER SUMMARY

1. Legal reasoning involves both deductive and inductive logic, which can be observed in case law analysis. Deductive logic takes the form of the syllogism involving premises that must be valid and conclusions that must logically follow from valid premises. Inductive logic takes

the form of analogy, or analysis of likeness and differences of case precedents.

2. The case method of analysis involves clear understanding of the basic elements of a case in law and determination of the narrow kernel of law defined in the holding, or answer to specific legal questions that provide precedents for future cases.

3. Legal research is a required skill for attorneys. It is an ethical violation for attorneys to provide inadequate, sloppy, or incorrect legal research. Such conduct would violate Rule 1.1 of the *ABA Model Code of Professional Conduct*, a standard that has been adopted by various states in their ethical codes.

4. The ultimate goal for a legal researcher is to locate mandatory, primary legal authority bearing on a legal problem. Mandatory authority refers to authority that a court must follow. For example, a decision by the Tennessee Supreme Court is mandatory authority for a trial court judge in Tennessee. Primary authority refers to law itself, whether it be a constitution, statute, regulation, or judicial opinion.

5. Persuasive authority refers to authority that a court may, but does not have to, follow. For example, a Kentucky Supreme Court decision would be persuasive authority for a trial court in Tennessee. Many times researchers have to rely on persuasive authority because there is no mandatory legal authority available.

6. Secondary authority refers to the vast array of legal materials that are not the law itself but that explain the law. Common secondary sources include legal encyclopedias, law review articles, treatises, and *American Law Report* annotations. Particularly persuasive secondary sources are *Restatements*, which are published by the American Law Institute. They attempt to provide a comprehensive overview of the substantive principles of an area of law.

7. Cases are published in sets of books called reporters. Decisions found in reporters are published decisions, and decisions not found in reporters are called unpublished decisions. Published decisions have more precedential value than unpublished decisions; however, unpublished decisions can still be important if they are factually on point with an attorney's case.

8. To find cases in a reporter, one needs to know the citation of the case. Sometimes a researcher will not know the citation of a case, so he or she will have to use another set of books other than reporters. These sets of books are called digests. Digests are finding tools and topical compilations of cases. The West digest system works on a system of digest topics and key numbers.

9. Citation is very important in legal research. Without a proper citation, an attorney may lose his or her case for the client. Generally, when an

attorney argues a point of law, he or she needs to be able to provide some authority for that point. In other words, the attorneys must cite some law to the court. Attorneys often must use pinpoint citations to provide the exact page number in a judicial opinion on which they are relying.

10. Much legal research is now done online. The two leading online sub-scription-based services are LEXIS and Westlaw. These services pro-vide attorneys with a dizzying array of legal and other information. Attorneys can find a bevy of both primary and secondary legal author-ities using these services. The two methods of searching for legal authorities are natural language searching and terms and connectors searching. Natural language searching is often favored by attorneys and researchers when they are new to an area of law or do not know all the typical terminology in an area of law. Terms and connec-tors allow researchers to search for sources that contain specific words and phrases. This method of searching is sometimes favored by researchers familiar with a particular area of law and its nomenclature.

11. A powerful use of the online subscription services is the ease with which they enable attorneys to update their legal authorities. Updating legal authorities is a vital process because attorneys do not want to cite or rely on bad law or law that is no longer valid or that has been under-mined by later legal authorities. Westlaw's version of updating is called KeyCite, and LEXIS's version is called Shepardizing.

12. Another powerful online research tool for attorneys is PACER, which stands for Public Access to Court Electronic Records. PACER enables attorneys to search for pleadings or documents in federal court cases across the country. There is a charge to print out pages of these docu-ments, but the cost is relatively small.

13. Another powerful online research tool is the Thomas Web site, named after Thomas Jefferson. It enables researchers to follow the work prod-uct of the U.S. Congress. One can access the *Congressional Record*, committee hearings, and committee reports and find the Web sites of individual members of Congress.

14. The Web sites of federal administrative agencies also are an excellent research source because those agencies have much legal information on their sites. For example, the Web site of the Equal Employment Opportunity Commission (EEOC) has a plethora of information for those who practice employment law.

15. Blogs are the wave of the future, perhaps both in journalism and in law. There are numerous legal blogs that carry significant influence in the legal world and culture. Two of the most popular are the SCOTUSblog, which monitors the U.S. Supreme Court, and How Appealing, which monitors legal developments from the appellate courts nationwide.

REVIEW EXERCISE

Match the following term with their most appropriate meaning.

TERMS	MEANING

TERMS
1. Syllogism
2. Analogistic form of reasoning
3. Holding
4. On point
5. Dicta (or obiter dicta)
6. *Ratio decedendi*
7. Legal research
8. Mandatory authority
9. Persuasive authority
10. Secondary authority
11. Legal encyclopedias
12. *American Law Reports* (A.L.R.)
13. Law review or law journal articles
14. Restatements of the law
15. Form books
16. Annotated codes
17. Citation
18. Pinpoint citation
19. Digests
20. Descriptive word indexes
21. Headnotes
22. LEXIS and Westlaw
23. Terms and connectors search
24. Natural language search
25. Shepardizing
26. KeyCiting
27. Pocket part

MEANING
____ legal materials that help to explain, clarify, or inform about the law, but are not law
____ secondary sources that provide short overviews, such as *Corpus Juris Secundum* and *American Jurisprudence*
____ validating legal case authority by the LEXIS process
____ user types in certain words that should be found in the judicial opinion
____ the full logical form of a single argument in deductive logic.
____ user types in natural language terms for a search
____ method of validating case law authority using traditional book method
____ reasoning by analogy
____ the main points of law found in the body of the judicial opinion
____ legal precedent that a court must follow
____ validating legal case authority by the Westlaw process
____ legal precedent used to decide future cases
____ subscription-based online legal research database
____ the entire body of published case law indexed in these publications
____ directly related to the legal question at issue
____ refers to a point of law found on a specific page of a case
____ can provide researchers with citations to primary authority
____ opinions that go beyond the facts and specific legal issues before the court
____ statutory law placed topically into the official code or collection of statutory law
____ enable a researcher to find the appropriate terms used by the publication
____ reasoning behind the decision of the court.
____ sources that provide model forms in various legal fields, such as American Jurisprudence Legal Forms
____ contains detailed overview articles called annotations that cite decisions all across the nation
____ shorthand reference to legal authority
____ authoritative statements of common law in basic black-letter principles of law on that subject
____ legal authority that a court may, but does not have to, follow
____ answering questions about applicable legal rules governing particular situations

DISCUSSION QUESTIONS

1. How are both inductive and deductive logic involved in legal reasoning?
2. Must the principle of *stare decisis* always prevail, or is there an even more fundamental standard of fairness?
3. How does legal research impact the duty of attorneys to provide competent representation? Find your state attorney ethical code and compare it to the ABA's Model Code. Are there any differences with regard to the duty to provide competent representation?
4. What is the importance in legal research between mandatory and persuasive authority? What is the importance of the difference between primary and secondary authority?
5. What are the two types of searching that one can do on LEXIS and Westlaw? Why would one prefer a *terms and connectors search* over a *natural language search*?
6. Find your state high court's Web site. How far back does the site go in terms of the court's opinions? Find the state high court's rules. Why are these important for attorneys?
7. Why is FindLaw such a useful site for legal researchers? Give several examples of the legal materials one can access on FindLaw.

ASSIGNMENTS

ASSIGNMENT: As you read this chapter, go back to the six cases in the appendix that we are using for illustrations. By the end of this chapter, you will be expected to draft brief summaries of these cases using the format included in this chapter. We will explain the aspects of each case that will require your focus in completing this assignment.

ASSIGNMENT: Using the descriptive word index of your state digest, see if you can find a case that provides an example of conduct that constitutes "intentional infliction of emotional distress." What is the case name? Describe the nature of the conduct.

ASSIGNMENT: Using LEXIS or Westlaw, go to the database that covers U.S. Supreme Court opinions. Using either a *terms and connectors* or *natural language search*, find a U.S. Supreme Court case that deals with freedom of speech and whether individuals have a right to protest near a funeral. How did the Court decide the case?

SOURCES AND SUGGESTED READINGS

Bouchoux, Deborah. 2011. *Legal Research and Writing for Paralegals*. 6th ed. New York: Aspen Publishers.

Burton, Steven J. 2007. *An Introduction to Law and Legal Reasoning*. 3rd ed. New York: Aspen Publishers.

Cohen, Morris L., and Kent Olson. 2010. *Legal Research in a Nutshell*. 10th ed. Tampa, Fla.: Thomson West, 2010.

Putman, William H. 2010. *Legal Research*. 2d ed. Florence, Kan.: Cengage Learning.

Sloan, Amy E. 2009. *Basic Legal Research: Tools and Strategies*. 4th ed. New York: Aspen Publishers.

WEBSITES
American Law Institute
    http://www.ali.org
Equal Employment Opportunity Commission
    http://www.eeoc.gov
FindLaw
    http://www.findlaw.com

How Appealing
  http://howappealing.law.com
Law Reviews
  http://www.lawreview.org/LEXIS
  http://www.lexis.com
PACER
  http://www.pacer.gov/
SCOTUSblog
  http://www.scotusblog.com

Thomas
  http://thomas.loc.gov
U.S. Supreme Court
  http://supremecourtus.gov
Westlaw
  http://www.westlaw.com

UNDERSTANDING SUBSTANTIVE CIVIL LAW

Part II provides readers with an introduction to various substantive areas of civil law. It conveys a general understanding of what these areas of law involve. These are complex areas of civil law and cannot be dealt with in any degree of completeness in this introductory textbook. However, the authors have attempted to include the most common concepts related to property and contract law, tort law, family law, employment law, and equal protection law. The general area of contract law is also included as aspects of the other areas of substantive civil law.

A Brief Introduction to Property and Contract Law

Property and contract law are two of the most fundamental areas of law. They both have ancient origins traced to English common law and Roman civil law. The terminology of these areas is essential for an introductory law text. We will discuss these concepts briefly to provide a general understanding of the basic terms. There is, however, no attempt to treat these areas of law in an exhaustive manner in this textbook. The case law and codes of a respective jurisdiction should be consulted, as well as valuable secondary sources (the *Restatement of Property Law* and *Restatement of Contract Law*).

BASIC PROPERTY LAW

Property rights are considered among the most fundamental concepts in our law. The basic principles and terms used to describe these rights are derived from our English common-law heritage. These common-law rules concerning property rights have been altered, modified, and in some cases abolished by later court decisions or statutes. However, the common-law concept of *property* still refers to a person's ownership rights to things and to a person's interests in things owned by someone else. It includes rights to possess, use, and dispose of things.

Property rights may be held in tangible objects, such as a car, a book, or an item of clothing, or they may be intangible things, such as the property interest in an invention, a copyright, or a trademark. We often refer to the objects as property; however, property refers only to ownership rights and interests in land.

The two grand divisions of property rights are referred to as personal property (*personalty*) and real property (*realty*). The basic difference between these two types of property is that personal property is movable and not fixed to land or to permanent structures on land. Personal property consists of physical objects that are not *realty* (or fixtures) and all intangible rights, duties, and obligations arising out of the ownership of physical objects. **Personalty** also includes intangible property, such as money,

Personalty:
Personal property; movable property; chattels. Things that are movable and not attached to land or real property interests. Also includes intangible property, such as intellectual property interests, money, and other paper substitutes for ownership rights.

119

stocks and bonds, and *promissory notes*, which are paper substitutes for certain ownership rights.

Realty refers to real property rights in land and things attached to the land that are immovable or fixed. This generally includes buildings and improvements to the land as well as the rights in the land itself. However, there are many different rights that may or may not be owned by an individual in real property. An *easement*, for example, is an encumbrance to real property rights including land and anything that restricts the owner of the property rights. A tenant also has property rights fixed to the land as well as in real property, but they are not the full bundle of rights that a property owner would have who is free from all other encumbrances on that property. The **tenant** has minimal property rights, and the owner has maximal property rights. These maximal rights include the right to lease, rent, use, and exclude others from the property; mineral rights; and the right to convey the property by sale or inheritance to others. Note that landlord-tenant law is a special area of property law generally covered comprehensively in state codes.

A **fixture** is a classification of objects that may be either *personalty* or *realty*, depending on whether they are fixed to real property in such a way that they cannot be easily moved. Examples include lighting fixtures, bathroom fixtures, and other items that have been physically incorporated into the structure but that are removable. Generally, a dishwasher is not considered a fixture until it is built into the kitchen cabinets of a dwelling. Washing machines, dryers, and refrigerators are generally not considered fixtures but are classified as *personalty*, unless they are built into the residence and cannot easily be removed. A mobile home may be quite difficult to classify, depending on whether it is fixed to the land and cannot be easily moved. A modular home that is transported to the site and then fixed to the site by a foundation is considered *realty*, but a trailer with wheels attached, even if lacking tires, could be considered *personalty*.

The two basic divisions of property into personal property and real property have many important practical considerations, including rules concerning resolution of conflicts that arise over property rights. The common-law rules of each state are the basis of real property rights, whereas the **Uniform Commercial Code (UCC),** which has been adopted by all state legislatures in some form, often governs personal property rights. The discussion that follows attempts to describe these major distinctions between the various ownership rights in personal property and real property. We will begin with personal property, then the basic concepts of real property, and finally the basic concepts involving limitations on property rights imposed by government regulation.

Personal Property Rights

The acquisition of personal property can occur in many ways. These include purchase, creation, capture, accretion, finding, confusion, gift,

Realty:
Brief term for real property or real estate; also anything that partakes of the nature of real property, including land and anything fixed to the land as well as interests attached to the land. Also includes easements and tenant rights.

Tenant:
One who has minimal property rights, whereas an owner has maximal property rights.

Fixture:
An object in the nature of personal property that has been so annexed to the realty that it is regarded as a part of the land.

Uniform Commercial Code (UCC):
An attempt to codify the common law of commercial transactions that is now adopted in some form by all states in the United States.

and inheritance. Another way to acquire personal property of another is through bailment. *Bailment* refers to the temporary transfer of personal property to another without transference of title to that property. Examples include when a person borrows, loans, or rents personal property or leaves one's truck for repairs with a mechanic.

Purchases involve an exchange of money for the ownership rights to goods, which is a contractual relationship governed by the *Uniform Commercial Code*. A person who manufactures products out of raw materials through physical or mental labor has title to the property created and may sell or convey that title by sale. A person who builds a boat, writes a book, makes a sweater, or develops a software program will have property rights in this creation. However, a person who is employed to produce something will not have title to ownership rights, which belong to the employer.

Capture is another form of acquisition of personal property, such as the catching of fish or taking of wild fowl when done in accordance with the government and private property regulations of the state and federal authorities. Another method of acquiring ownership rights is by accretion. *Accretion* refers to natural increase and would include the accretion of the value of a savings account by accruing interest or the increase in livestock because of offspring produced by reproduction.

Lost property is a frequent occurrence, and the fundamental rules governing the finding of lost property need to be explained. A **finder of lost property** has title that is good against everyone except the true owner. Some states have legal requirements that a finder of a lost item with a value that exceeds a designated amount has a duty to turn the item over to the police for a period of time. If the true owner fails to claim the item, the finder takes title, and the ownership rights are passed to the finder. A finder has a duty to make reasonable efforts to locate the true owner.

Lost property differs from mislaid and abandoned property. **Mislaid property** is intentionally left in a place and later forgotten. The owner of the premises where mislaid property is found has a claim superior to that of all others except the true owner.

Abandoned property requires demonstrating that the owner gave up possession with the intent to relinquish dominion, control, and title to the property. The finder's right to this personal property is superior to all others when these conditions are met.

Confusion involves the mixing of items of property in such a manner that the items belonging to one person are confused with those belonging to another in such a manner that the property of each can no longer be distinguished. This can happen when several farmers store their grain in the same bin or several persons keep their money in a common place. Disputes are settled by reference to the common-law rules on this subject, which provide that when the contributions are known, the parties become *tenants in common* of the mass *in proportion* to their respective interests regardless

Finder of lost property:
One who has good title against everyone except the true owner. The finder has a duty to make reasonable efforts to locate the true owner.

Mislaid property:
Items of value that are intentionally left in a place and later forgotten. Mislaid property belongs to the owner of the premises where it is located if unclaimed by the true owner.

of how the confusion took place. When the contributions are unknown and the confusion was innocent (e.g., by an act of God or an act of a third party), the parties share equally. When the confusion was caused wrongfully by one of the owners (or his or her agent, *bailee*, or trustee), the burden is on the wrongdoer to identify his or her own portion. If this party cannot do so, the entire mass belongs to the innocent owner.

Gifts are voluntary transfers of all rights in an item to another. The person making the gift is called a *donor*, and the recipient a *donee*. In common law, the claimant has the burden of proof that the donor intended to make a present, effective, and gratuitous transfer of ownership. The evidence must be clear and convincing and must consist of something more than merely the testimony of the *donee*. The law requires that a *donor* make an actual or constructive delivery of the item. Where possible, the *donor* must physically deliver the item to the *donee*, such as bringing a fishing boat that is a gift to the *donee*. When this is not possible, a constructive delivery is accepted by delivery of the keys to the boat. Most courts will accept a written document evidencing a gift, which is called "symbolical" delivery. Finally, the *donee* must accept the item for a valid gift to have taken place.

Inheritance is another method of acquiring good title to property rights. This is done through the courts in distributing a deceased person's estate. This may be done according to a will or without a will (intestate) when the property distribution is done according to statutory plan rather than the expressed wishes of the deceased.

A **bailment** is a relationship arising out of delivery of personal property by one person, called the *bailor*, to another person, called the *bailee*, for the accomplishment of a certain purpose and subject to a duty to return the property. There is no transfer of title in this relationship. An example is leaving an automobile with a mechanic for repairs. However, there are several different forms of bailment. *Gratuitous bailments* benefit only one person—either the *bailor* or the *bailee*—such as when one asks a neighbor to keep his or her car in the neighbor's barn. This bailment primarily benefits the *bailor*, and the common law imposes on the *bailee* a duty only of slight care as to the bailed article. However, liability will result if the *bailee* acted in bad faith or was grossly negligent. When the bailment primarily benefits the bailee, such as when a neighbor borrows your lawn mower, the law imposes on the *bailee* a duty to exercise a *high degree of care* as to the bailed article. Liability will result from slight negligence.

A *bailment for hire* is one for the mutual benefit of the parties and requires the *bailee* to exercise due care as to the property. **Due care** is that degree of care that persons of ordinary prudence exercise under similar circumstances with respect to their own property or the property of others placed in their custody. For example, these *bailments for hire* include taking an automobile for repairs to a mechanic who is for hire, shoes to a shoe

Gifts:
A voluntary transfer of property to another made gratuitously and without consideration, requiring capacity, intention, and completed delivery by donor and acceptance by donee.

Inheritance:
Property that is distributed according to a will or by the court intestate.

Bailment:
A delivery of goods or personal property by one person to another in trust for the execution of a special service beneficial either to the *bailor* or to the *bailee* or both. Includes express or implied contractual obligation.

Due care:
That degree of care that persons of ordinary prudence would exercise under similar circumstances with respect to their own property or the property of others placed in their custody.

repair shop, or clothes to the dry cleaners. The *bailee* is not allowed to use the bailed object for his or her benefit but may work on the object for the benefit of the *bailor*. The *bailor's* duties include paying the *bailee* and warning the *bailee* of any hidden dangers associated with the bailed object.

Legal Actions to Recover Personal Property

Many legal disputes arise over property rights from disagreement over the rights of possession and ownership of property. If the property in question was stolen, then criminal laws apply, and recovery of property that can be identified will be facilitated by law enforcement authorities. If a contract (expressed or implied) existed between the original and subsequent possessor regarding the property, then an action for breach of contract may exist. The contract action may be possible when there is unauthorized use of property by the opposing party. There is also a remedy in law known as *conversion*, which is the civil law version of the criminal offense of theft. Another possibility is an action in equity known as *replevin*, which is used to recover property.

Conversion is the basis for a civil (not criminal) legal action when one receives possession of personal property belonging to another and permanently deprives the owner of the rightful use of the property. This may occur when one seizes control of property without permission or when a party refuses to return property that was previously bailed. In the case of *bailment*, there may also be a cause of action for the tort of negligence or breach of contract. The plaintiff must show that another person is in wrongful possession of the property and intends to exercise control to the exclusion of the owner from rightful possession and ownership of the property. In a *conversion* action, the owner may recover the property, or if it has been altered or disposed of in some way, the value of the property may be recovered. The owner may also recover the fair market value of the use of the property during the time the owner was deprived of the property. In these circumstances, a criminal action also may exist to punish the party responsible. Another option in less serious cases may be taken in what is called *trespass to chattels*. This type of action for return of property and damages exists when a party substantially interferes with another person's possession and/or ownership of property, including less serious damage, alteration, use, etc., of the other person's property.

A **replevin** is an equitable remedy that results in the return of the property or a specific performance order. When livestock wander onto another person's property and the owner seeks only to recover his livestock, the traditional remedy is to get a court order to have the property returned. This remedy in equity is sought when money damages are insufficient to remedy the wrong. This form of action applies only to personal property.

Conversion: When one receives possession of personal property belonging to another and permanently deprives the owner of the rightful use of the property.

Replevin: An equitable remedy that results only in the return of the property or a specific performance order.

Real Property

In order to understand our laws concerning real property, one must go back to their origin in the medieval common law of England. Under the feudal law of this period, all land was derived from the king. People could own estates in land but not actual land. Estates are classified according to their duration and the bundle of real property rights and types of interests involved. Even today, this fundamental concept of land ownership rights is the basis of our law. However, the role of the king has passed to the government, which has regulatory rights that involve the use of the land and potential taking of the real property under **eminent domain**, which requires just compensation under the Fifth Amendment of the U.S. Constitution and similar provisions in state constitutions.

An estate in land is the amount of interest (or rights) that a person has in the land and all things attached to the land. A person who holds an **estate in fee simple** has the maximum rights allowed by law to the estate. This form of ownership rights in real property is the most frequent form of transfer of title today, and a deed of title to property is understood to take this form unless other encumbrances are stipulated in the deed. It entitles the real property rights owner to use of the land and its attachments (*quiet enjoyment*), alteration and improvement of the land (as long as it does not interfere with the rights of others), and the right to dispose or transfer title to the land rights by sale, gift, or inheritance.

Other types of estate are classified according to the type of limitation placed upon the owner of the property rights. A person who has an estate in land for the duration of his or her life has a *life estate* in land. *Life estates* cannot be passed on to heirs. A person who leases real property has only a possessory interest in land called a **leasehold**. Leaseholds allow tenants to obtain possessory interests in real property by contract for a specified duration (for specific problems, consult the *Restatement of Property, Land-Lord and Tenant Law*, and the case law digest of the particular state jurisdiction).

The landowner of an *estate in fee simple* has all rights to the property above and below the ground and to airspace above the land. However, these rights may be subject of government regulation and control when the public interest is involved. With respect to moving waters on the property, the landowner possesses the streambed when the water flow constitutes a non-navigable stream but cannot substantially alter the flow of water across another person's property. Navigable streams are a part of the public domain, and the possessor of real property generally has rights that extend only to the shore.

The bundle of rights that constitute the maximum rights of the landowner in a *fee simple estate* may be altered by the conveyance of a deed or by the agreement to relinquish some or all of these rights in the land, either

Eminent domain:
The power to take private property for public use by a government entity; authorized to exercise functions of a public character. (See Fifth Amendment.)

Estate in fee simple:
Maximum real property rights to which an owner is entitled, including all rights to sell, transfer, and pass on to heirs.

Leasehold:
An estate in *realty* held under lease. Rights and privileges that the lessor of property has by virtue of the nature of his or her lease.

through sale, gift, or inheritance. Therefore, real property may have restrictions on the future conveyance of property, for example, where the mineral rights have been sold to another party. In addition to these forms of restrictions, there may be *easements* and *covenants* where others have certain rights and interests that provide further restrictions on the use of the property.

An **easement** is the limited right of someone other than the owner to use the property of the owner. An example would be a provision in a property deed giving access through the property to a neighboring property owner. Local governments have easements along public roads that enable utility lines to be laid in the interest of access to serve the entire community. This may be considered an easement of necessity. Another example is a property owner who is prevented access to the property without traveling through the property of another. If the only reasonable way to access the property is through another person's property, the court will grant an easement limited to travel across a specific portion of that land. An *easement* may be created by necessity without the consent of the owner, but unless the owner agrees to the easement, it must first be recognized by a court before it can be enforced. An affirmative easement would be involved if owner A conveys to B the right to lay a pipeline across A's land. A *negative easement* also may exist when A conveys part of his land to B and retains an *easement* that forbids B to burn trash on the land.

A **license** is a temporary grant of authority, such as when a landowner grants permission to hunt or fish on the land. Such a license can be oral and can generally be revoked at will since it is not an actual estate in land and therefore not subject to the *Statute of Frauds*.

Covenants, on the other hand, are attached in writing to the deed and may restrict the use of the land in various ways. Some covenants may be placed in the deed by the purchaser of land to require the seller to make certain promises in the deed, called *grantor's covenants*, to ensure that the title is free and clear of encumbrances. *Restrictive covenants* that discriminate against people because of race, religion, and national origin are no longer enforceable in the courts. Covenants that run with the land must be intended to pass on to future landowners, and they must "touch and concern" the land. That is, they cannot be personal promises unrelated to the land.

Buyers' and Sellers' Rights

One of the most important traditional functions of local governments is the registering of deeds. In every county or parish, there is an office called the registry of deeds that maintains an index of documents relating to all real property transactions. These documents include deeds, easements, options, and mortgages.

Easement:
A right to use over the property of another, including rights of way, rights concerning flowing waters, and other interests.

License:
A temporary grant of authority, such as when a landowner grants permission to hunt or fish on the land.

Covenant:
An agreement, convention, or promise of two or more parties, by deed in writing, signed, and delivered, by which either of the parties pledges himself or herself to do something or not do something or stipulates as the truth of certain facts concerning the estate.

A title search and title abstract are essential elements of the process of sale of real property. The abstract summarizes all the recorded claims that affect the seller's title. When disputes arise between competing claimants, the recorded documents help the courts resolve such disputes. Modern procedures used in the sale of real property involve a very thorough review of the history of the property that is double-checked by various participants in this process.

Closing a **real estate transaction** may take from two to six months to complete. This process begins with a *purchase agreement*, which involves the seller agreeing to sell to another and requires the buyer to pay earnest money as a deposit. Under the *Statute of Frauds*, conveyances of title to real property must be in writing. Professional legal assistance is needed in these transactions, which also usually include the services of a lawyer, broker, *mortgagor*, financier, and others who play important roles in completing the transaction. (A mortgagor is the person who gives legal title or a lien to the mortgagee to secure the mortgage loan.)

The documents associated with such transactions include the purchase agreement, mortgage, financing agreement, deed (recording the transfer of title), required inspections, an escrow agreement (specifying who will hold the earnest money deposit), and title policy (insurance policy from a title company that guarantees the title search and that the property is free and clear of other claims).

Usually, the purchase agreement specifies who bears the risk of loss during the period of preparation of the real estate transaction. However, this is an important aspect of the transaction, and the buyer should be aware that, if not specified in the agreement, the buyer might be required to bear the cost of damage to the property during this process. All sellers have a general duty to care for the property and protect it from damage during the transaction period, and the purchase agreement should enable the buyer to be released from the purchase when defects are discovered or financial arrangements cannot be completed. Buyers have a general duty to make reasonable investigations and discover defects in the property (*caveat emptor*—let the buyer beware).

There are general rights and duties of property ownership that affect both the true owner of the property and any leaseholder. The right of quiet enjoyment of the property includes the obligation not to use the property in such a way that it becomes a public or private **nuisance** to surrounding areas, affecting the rights of others. A *private nuisance* refers to a use that has a direct adverse effect on certain private parties. Unreasonable noise, noxious fumes, or even unsightly appearance of a residential dwelling may be considered a *private nuisance*. Persons damaged by such private nuisances may have a cause of action in equity to have the court order the conduct to cease, and they may sue in law for damages resulting from the nuisance. There is also the concept of *public nuisance*, which involves

Real estate transaction: Conveyances of title to real property by sale that must be in writing under the Statute of Frauds. Such transactions usually involve the services of a lawyer, broker, mortgagor, financier, and others who assist in the transaction process.

Nuisance: Activity that arises from unreasonable, unwarranted, or unlawful use of a person's own property, working obstruction, or injury to the right of another, or to the public producing such material annoyance, inconvenience, and discomfort that the law will presume resulting damage.

use of property that has a continuing adverse effect on the public good, welfare, or safety. When the effect of the nuisance extends over a broad area, the public authorities may bring legal actions against the party creating the nuisance.

Property owners and leaseholders may exclude *trespassers*, but there are certain obligations owed even to those who enter on the land without permission. Duties to a **trespasser** are minimal and include the duty to correct conditions that would cause injury that a *trespasser* could not expect. A *licensee*, who has been given permission to be on the property, not connected with business purposes, is owed a greater duty, which includes the duty to warn of any dangers by giving notice of such conditions.

Trespasser:
One who without permission enters on the property of another without any right, lawful authority, or an express or implied invitation or license.

An **invitee**, who is on the property for business purposes that benefit the owner or leaseholder, is due a duty of care that is the most extensive. The home owner or leaseholder has a duty to protect these persons from unreasonable harm.

Invitee:
Person who enters another's property by invitation, expressed or implied, or in connection with business invitation where there is benefit to the owner.

Remedies for breaches of real property rights and duties include actions in *contract*, *trespass*, and *equitable relief* in the form of nuisance abatement and eviction actions that result in specific performance orders.

INTELLECTUAL PROPERTY RIGHTS

Under intellectual property law, owners are granted certain exclusive rights to a variety of intangible assets, such as musical, literary, and artistic works; discoveries and inventions; and words, phrases, symbols, and designs. Common types of intellectual property include copyrights, trademarks, patents, industrial design rights, and trade secrets in some jurisdictions.

These legal principles governing intellectual property have evolved over the centuries. However, it was not until the nineteenth century that the term *intellectual property* began to be used, and not until the late twentieth century that it became commonplace in the United States. The modern *World Intellectual Property Organization* (WIPO) was established by treaty convention in 1967 as an agency of the United Nations. The United States had not been a party to the earlier European treaty on this subject, known as the *Berne Convention*, but became a party to WIPO with the passage of the *Bayh-Dole Act* in 1980.

We have long recognized patents and copyrights, but with modern technology other forms of intellectual property such as music, recordings, films, Internet publications, and artistic works have proliferated. International problems of enforcing these legal protections have greatly expanded. Economists estimate that two-thirds of the value of large businesses in the United States can be traced to intangible assets or intellectual property.

U.S. copyright law governs the legally enforceable rights of creative and artistic works under the laws of the United States. It is part of federal law authorized by the U.S. Constitution in Article I, Section 8.

> *The Congress shall have Power [8] to promote the Progress of Science and useful Arts, by securing for limited Times to Authors and inventors the exclusive Right to their respective Writings and Discoveries.*

The detailed provisions concerning the vast array of protected intellectual property rights in the United States can be found by consulting the *U.S. Code Annotated*. Copyright law arguably has become even more important in the Internet age, where it has become easier to infringe on others' copyrighted material. We will briefly comment on the topics of *patents* and *copyrights* in this introductory chapter.

Patents

The term **patent** usually refers to an exclusive right granted to anyone who invents any new, useful, and non-obvious process, machine, article of manufacture, or composition of matter, or any new and useful improvement thereof, and claims that right in a formal patent application. The additional qualification, *utility patent*, is used in the United States to distinguish it from other types of patents (e.g., design patents) but should not be confused with utility models granted by other countries. Examples of particular species of patents for inventions include biological patents, business method patents, chemical patents, and software patents.

Patent:
An exclusive right granted to anyone who invents a new, useful, and nonobvious process, machine, article of manufacture, or composition of matter, or any new and useful improvement thereof, and claims that right in a formal patent application.

A patent is not a right to practice or use the invention. Rather, a patent provides the right to exclude others from making, using, selling, offering for sale, or importing the patented invention for the term of the patent, which is usually 20 years from the filing date subject to the payment of maintenance fees. Therefore, a patent is a limited property right. Like other property rights, it may be sold, licensed, mortgaged, assigned or transferred, given away, or abandoned.

In the United States, an infringement may occur when the defendant has made, used, sold, offered to sell, or imported an infringing invention or its equivalent. Indirect infringement occurs when one actively and knowingly induces another to infringe and thus is liable for that infringement. Types of *indirect infringement* include *contributory infringement* and *induced infringement*.

No infringement action may be started until the patent is issued. However, pre-grant protection is available under 35 U.S.C. §154(d), which allows a patent owner to obtain reasonable royalty damages for certain infringing activities that occurred before the patent's date of issuance. This right to obtain provisional damages requires a patent holder to show that (1) the infringing activities occurred after the publication of the patent application, (2) the patented claims are substantially identical to the claims in the published application, and (3) the infringer had *actual notice* of the published patent application.

Copyrights and Authors' Rights

Copyright is literally, the right to copy, though in legal terms *the right to control copying* is more accurate. Copyrights are exclusive statutory rights to exercise control over copying and other exploitation of the works for a specific period of time. The copyright owner is given two sets of rights: an exclusive, positive right to copy and exploit the copyrighted work, or license others to do so, and a negative right to prevent anyone else from doing so without consent, with the possibility of legal remedies if they do.

Copyright initially only granted the exclusive right to copy a book, allowing anybody to use the book to, for example, make a translation, adaptation, or public performance. The exclusive rights granted by copyright law to copyright owners have been gradually expanded over time and now accepts *dramatization, translations,* and *derivative works* as *adaptations* and *transformations*, that fall within the scope of copyright.

In the United States, works created in or after 1979 are extended copyright protection for a term defined in 17 U.S.C. §302. These works are granted copyright protection for a term ending 70 years after the death of the author. However, if the work was a work for hire (e.g., those created by a corporation), then copyright persists for 120 years after creation or 95 years after publication, whichever is shorter.

There are defenses to copyright actions. One of the most important from an educational standpoint is **fair use**. Federal copyright law recognizes the fair use defense for the reproduction of particular works for certain uses, such as criticism, news reporting, teaching, scholarship, and research.

Copyright:
Exclusive statutory rights to exercise control over copying and other exploitation of works for a specific period of time.

Fair use:
Defense in copyright law for the reproduction of particular works such as criticism, news reporting, teaching, scholarship, and research.

BASIC CONTRACT LAW

As may have already become abundantly clear, modern society would not function without the extensive reliance on contractual obligations. Contracts are the basis of nearly all commercial and business activity, and they are indispensable in the regulation of private relationships between individuals. The modern legal action in contract originated in medieval English common law as a variety of legal actions relevant to various aspects of the modern consolidated concept of contract. *Debt* (involving money contracts), *detinue* (involving personal property), and *covenant* (involving real property) were each subject to different actions in the early English courts. The action of *assumpsit* was later used to recover damages for the nonperformance of a *parol*, or simple contract for services. The advance of modern commercial activity in the 1800s produced a consolidation of the complex forms of legal action into the one general action, today referred to as a **contract action**, to recover damages or to enforce legal obligations resulting from contracts.

Contract action:
Legal action to recover damages or to enforce legal obligations resulting from a contract.

The modern legal definition of a *contract* is an agreement between two or more persons that creates an obligation to do or not to do a particular thing. Its essentials are competent parties, an offer, an acceptance, and mutuality of obligation.

Most states have adopted a version of the *Uniform Commercial Code* (UCC), which governs the sale of goods. Under the *Uniform Commercial Code*, the term "contract" refers to the total legal obligation which results from parties' agreement as affected by the code. This includes sales contracts for goods and services as well as "contract for sale," which includes both a present sale of goods and a contract to sell goods at a future time. (See *UCC* Section 1-201.)

Enforceable Contracts

Most of the law of contracts today is still based in the common-law decisions of the courts. However, this area of law has been altered by statutory law, such as the *Statute of Frauds* (adopted by most states), requiring certain types of contract to be in writing, and other state versions of the *Uniform Commercial Code*.

The *Uniform Commercial Code* is an attempt to codify the common law of contracts related to commercial transactions. This code has now been adopted in some form by legislative authority in all states. It covers commercial sales, commercial paper, bank collection processes, letters of credit, bulk transfers, warehouse receipts, bills of lading, other documents of title, investment securities, and secured transactions. However, it does not cover private sales of, and private contracts to sell, goods, defined as *movables*, or personal property having tangible form. It does not cover transactions involving realty, services, or the sale of intangibles.

A legally enforceable contract is an agreement involving a promise or promises, for the breach of which the law provides a remedy or for the performance of which the law recognizes a duty. Therefore, legal obligations may be created by these agreements when they are enforceable in the courts. The contract may be an express, implied, or written agreement and may take the form of a promise by one party to another based on the conditions stipulated in the promise. The **standard elements of an enforceable contract** are the following legal requirements. There must be (1) an *offer and acceptance*, (2) between *competent parties*, (3) based on genuine assent of the parties (*agreement*), (4) supported by *consideration*, (5) that is not a violation of law or public policy. Each of these requirements is briefly discussed in the following paragraphs.

Standard elements of an enforceable contract:
Offer and acceptance, competent parties, agreement, consideration, and not in violation of law or public policy.

All contracts involve at least two parties. In order for a contract to be formed, there must be mutual agreement between two or more competent parties who must demonstrate their intent to be bound to definite terms of the agreement. Bargaining to arrive at agreement usually takes the form of one party making an offer and the other party—in an expressed or implied manner—accepting the terms of the offer. There must be some evidence of agreement that would convince a reasonable person to think that an offer and acceptance had taken place by words, conduct, or actions by the parties.

There are many examples of non-contractual obligations, such as agreement to attend a social event where there is no expectation of intent to be legally bound by an offer and acceptance. Expressions of offer and acceptance made in anger, excitement, or jest would also lack the necessary intent. Therefore, the surrounding circumstances and context of the expressions would have to be examined to determine what a reasonably prudent person would believe. A legally effective offer must be a definite proposal made with the intent to contract and communicated to the *offeree*. The offer may be withdrawn by the *offeror* at any time before there is an acceptance by the offeree. However, there may be an option, which is an enforceable contract, when there is consideration given in return for the promise to hold the offer open. An acceptance is the agreement of the offeree to be bound by the terms of the offer, and there must be a meeting of minds between the contracting parties. In common law, the acceptance must be a "mirror image" of the offer. If it changes the terms of the offer in any way, it is merely a *counteroffer* that must be accepted by the other party. Consent obtained through duress, undue influence, fraud, or misrepresentation are defenses against enforceability and usually void the contract.

Consideration can take many forms and is simply that which is bargained for and given in exchange between the parties as fulfillment of the agreement. A promise to make a gift by itself is not an enforceable contract because there is no consideration. Therefore, nominal consideration is usually used to ensure that there is evidence of a contractual obligation. However, consideration does not have to involve money; it can take the form of doing something that has value or of not doing something that is considered valuable. A contract to pay for services is an enforceable contract involving consideration.

The full contractual capacity is met when a person is of legal age and without mental disability or incapacity. These defects do not automatically void the contract since it is presumed that all parties to an agreement have full legal capacity to contract. Therefore, any party using incapacity as a defense has the burden of proving the incapacity. The particular classes given some degree of special protection under the rules of incapacity are minors, insane people, and intoxicated people.

Contracts with minors are today generally considered voidable, but only by the minor or minors engaged in such a contract. An adult who engaged in a contract with a minor is still required to complete the contract, but the minor has a defense against enforcement. Parents are not generally held liable for contracts entered into by their minor children.

An *emancipated minor* (who is married or living independently) may still be held to most forms of contract.

Insanity or mental incompetence is also a defense against enforcement of contract when this condition exists at the time the agreement was reached. Intoxicated persons who can show that they were so intoxicated that they did not know at the time they were executing a contract have a defense. The party possessing capacity to contract has no right to unilaterally void the contract.

A contractual obligation is *illegal* when either its formation or performance is criminal, a civil *tortious* act, or opposed to public policy. Therefore, a contract for murder is evidence of a crime, not an enforceable contract. A contract for prostitution is another example. Such contracts are not enforceable by either party, with few exceptions. These exceptions include circumstances in which the law involved is intended to protect one of the parties, such as a person who purchases securities from a corporation that is not in compliance with the law. Under such conditions, the purchaser may obtain a refund, if demanded. Another exception is when the parties to the contract are not equally at fault, that is, when duress, undue influence, or fraud is involved. A contract provision is against public policy when it is injurious to the interest of the public, violates a statute, or tends to interfere with the public health, safety, or general welfare.

The **Statute of Frauds** was one of the earliest acts of the English Parliament in 1677. It provides for certain contracts to be in writing. In modern times, all state and federal jurisdictions have enacted such statutes of frauds. Each state's statute should be consulted for specific provisions. However, there are basically six kinds of contracts that are governed by the statute of frauds and must be in writing. They include the following types of agreements: (1) promises by an executor of an estate to pay out of pocket to answer for the debt of a decedent, (2) promises made to a prospective spouse or third party with marriage as the consideration, (3) promises to answer for the debt or default of another, (4) promises that cannot be expected to be performed in one year, (5) sale of real property, and (6) sale of goods above a certain dollar amount (Schubert 1996, pp. 422-424).

Statute of Frauds: Provides for certain contracts to be in writing, which in modern times has been enacted in some form by every jurisdiction.

The Statute of Frauds leaves many areas of contractual obligation that may be enforceable when *not in writing*. Of course, it is more difficult to prove an express or implied contractual obligation.

The remedies for breach of contract include civil legal actions in contract for damages, which are usually limited to *expectation damages*. Other forms of damages are *restitution interest* and *detrimental reliance*. *Punitive* or exemplary damages are traditionally not awarded in contract cases.

Relief in *equity* is also a remedy when a specific performance order is desired to compel an opposing party to fulfill the obligations of the contract.

Expectation damages place the non-breaching party in the position in which he or she would have been if the contract had been performed. *Expectation damages* generally mean that the non-breaching party is given damages or placed in the position in which he or she would have been if the contract was performed properly. *Restitution damages* apply when the non-breaching party has already performed his or her obligations, but the other side does not perform. At other times, the non-breaching party has not yet performed his or her contractual duties when the other party breaches the contract. The non-breaching party may have detrimentally relied on the contractual promises and incurred some expenses, which are recoverable.

THE UNIFORM ELECTRONIC TRANSACTION ACT

The communications revolution has produced a corresponding need for changes in statutory law surrounding the expansion of digital or electronic transactions in commercial and banking activity. These activities are contractual in nature and require the expansion of legal definitions and evidence of transactions involving the fulfillment of contractual obligations.

The **Uniform Electronic Transaction Act (UETA)** was drafted by the *Conference of Commissioners on Uniform State Law* in 1999 in an attempt to validate commercial electronic transactions, concretely, those involving electronic records and signatures. Its goal is not to establish contractual rules for *e-transactions*; instead, it is designed to complement state statutes dealing with digital signatures and electronic records. This codification has been adopted into statutory law by all states, with the exception of New York, Illinois, and Washington, as of 2011.

Uniform Electronic Transaction Act (UETA): Model legislation adopted by most states to validate commercial electronic transactions concerning records and signatures.

In the United States, commercial contracts are regulated by state law. Also, most states have enacted digital signature statutes to be applied to commercial dealings. Thus, UETA was not enacted to supersede state law, but rather to complement and bring them into accord. UETA §3 limits its scope: It states that UETA applies to electronic records and electronic signatures related to a "transaction." It does not apply to (1) the creation and execution of wills, codicils, or testamentary trusts and (2) to transactions subject to other substantive state law. *Transaction* is defined as "an action or set of actions occurring between two or more persons relating to the conduct of business, commercial, or governmental affairs." For instance, UETA applies to electronic signatures and records held by the banking and insurance industry. In sum, UETA influences the way commercial information, records, and signatures may be presented and retained under current legal standards.

UETA Applies to the Following Transactions

(1) Commercial trusts or trusts other than testamentary trusts. Following UETA's definition of transaction, business and commercial trusts are covered by the act. Since commercial trusts may be agreed on orally, the Legislative Commission did not see a reason why commercial trusts should be excluded from UETA's application scope;

(2) Power of attorney. The commission noted that, usually, no formal requirements for paper or execution were found to be applicable to the validity of power of attorneys. Thus, UETA's rules are applicable to these powers unless excluded by specific substantive state law. For instance, special health power of attorneys may be ruled by specific state laws; in this case, UETA may not apply according to §3;

(3) Real estate transactions. The Legislative Commission distinguished between the efficacy of paper involving real estate between the parties as opposed to their effects on third parties. UETA may apply to the commercial transactions between the parties if they so agree. Yet, for these transactions to be effective against third parties, state law usually requires specific filings with state government offices. If the state has not yet validated electronic filings and electronic notarizations, physical paper requirements and signatures may still apply in those cases. Hence, in those states allowing real estate electronic filings, UETA's rules apply;

(4) Consumer protection transactions. The Legislative Commission was concerned with those state consumer protection statutes that require paper and actual signatures; the paper requirement leaves them outside UETA's scope. It is precisely in these consumer/government transactions where electronic means prove to be efficient. Thus, the Legislative Commission stated UETA's rules could coexist with those consumer statutes requiring writings, specific forms, and formatting (letter size, type, etc.). UETA, the commission noted, would not eliminate those requirements but make them accessible through electronic means, together with an opt-out feature for consumers.

ASSIGNMENT: Use the Internet to look up provisions in the *Uniform Commercial Code* adopted in your state that are of interest to you concerning property law or contract law. Just type in the name of your state and "Code Annotated" and go to the provisions that interest you.

.Then find out what contracts must be in writing in your state by selecting the term *Statute of Limitations*, and then go to the provisions that interest you.

Look up the Uniform Electronic Transaction Act (UETA) in your state's code, or find out whether and when your state has enacted the UETA.

This chapter has attempted to provide the reader with the most fundamental concepts involved in the complex detail associated with the terms *property law* and *contract law*. The next four chapters will include discussion of these basic topics in connection with modern tort law, family law, employment law, and equal protection law. Each of these chapters will include more information about various aspects of property and contract law.

CHAPTER SUMMARY

1. Property rights include ownership rights to things and to interests in things owned by others. They include tangible and intangible objects, or things, and are divided into *personalty* (personal property) and *realty* (real property).

2. *Personalty* consists of physical objects that are not realty and all intangible rights, duties, and obligations arising out of the ownership of physical objects. *Realty* consists of land and all things attached to the land and immovable or fixed to the land. Fixtures are things that become real property when they are fixed to the land (or structures) in such a way that they cannot be easily moved.

3. Methods of legal acquisition of personal property include purchase, creation, capture, accretion, finding, confusion, gift, and inheritance. *Bailment* refers to the temporary transfer of personal property to another without transference of title to that property. A finder of lost property has a duty to make reasonable efforts to locate the true owner, but has good title against everyone except the true owner. Mislaid property is intentionally left in a place and later forgotten, and it becomes the property of the owner of the property where it was mislaid when unclaimed. A trespasser has no rights to lost or mislaid property.

4. Bailments create a variety of obligations, depending on who benefits from the relationship. Bailments benefiting only the *bailor* impose a duty of only slight care for the object of personal property. However, when it benefits only the *bailee*, such as borrowing a lawn mower, there is a duty to exercise a high degree of care, and liability will result from slight negligence. A *bailment for hire* is mutually beneficial to both parties and imposes a duty to exercise due care as to the property.

5. Legal actions to recover personal property include an action in contract when there is an express, implied, or written agreement, such as in a bailment for hire and unauthorized use of the property in question. *Conversion* is the basis for a civil legal action when one receives possession of personal property belonging to another and permanently deprives a person of rightful use of the property. An action in *trespass to chattels* may be possible for damages to property that are less serious than conversion, including damage, alteration, and use. *Replevin* is an equitable remedy resulting in the return of the property by specific performance order of the court.

6. Real property ownership consists of the bundle of rights and interests involved in possession, use, and capacity to convey real property. A person who holds an *estate in fee simple* has the maximum allowable rights, which are restricted only by the duties imposed by government regulation and taxes. Other types of estate are classified according to the limitations placed on the owner of property rights. A *life estate*

cannot be passed on to heirs or sold. *Leaseholds* allow tenants to obtain possessory interests in real property by contract for a specific period of time. An *easement* is the limited right of someone other than the owner to use the property of the owner. *Restrictive covenants* are attached in writing to the deed of title and may restrict the use of the land in various ways that are not prohibited by law.

7. Conveyance of real property by sale involves a complex process that includes many documents and the professional assistance of a lawyer, broker, mortgagor, financier, and others. The documents associated with such transactions include the purchase agreement, mortgage or financing agreement, deed, required inspections, escrow agreement, buyer and seller agreements, and title search. Such transfers are recorded by the local government office of registry of deeds.

8. Property owners and leaseholders have the right to quiet enjoyment of the property, but they also have the duty to prevent both private and public nuisances that interfere with the rights of others. They owe minimal duties even to trespassers to correct conditions that would cause injury a trespasser could not expect. *A licensee* is owed an even greater duty to be warned of any dangers by being given notice of such conditions. An *invitee*, who is on the property for business purposes that benefit the owner or leaseholder, is due a duty to protect the invitee from unreasonable harm.

9. Intellectual property rights result from grants of certain exclusive rights to a variety of intangible assets, such as music, literary, and artistic works; discoveries and inventions; and words, phrases, symbols, and designs. These intellectual properties include patents, copyrights, trademarks, industrial design rights, and trade secrets in some jurisdictions. *Fair use* is an important defense in copyright law.

10. The modern legal action in contract originated in medieval English common law as a variety of legal actions relevant to various aspects of the modern concept of contract. Most of the law of contracts is still based on the common-law decisions of the courts; however, the *Statute of Frauds* require certain types of contract to be in writing, and the *Uniform Commercial Code* (U.C.C.), which applies to the sale of goods, codifies extensive areas of contract law concerning commercial transactions.

11. An enforceable contract is an agreement between competent parties on the basis of genuine assent of the parties, supported by consideration, which does not contravene principles of law or public policy and does not always have to be in writing. Defects in these requirements may make the contract voidable only when there is a legally recognized defense against court enforcement. The Statute of Frauds requires only certain contracts to be in writing.

12. Remedies for breach of contract include civil legal actions in contract for damages that are usually limited to compensatory damages.

Punitive damages are not allowed. Relief in equity is also available when specific performance is desired to compel an opposing party to fulfill the obligations of contract.

13. The U.S. *Uniform Electronic Transaction Act of 1999* is a model act of the *Conference of Commissioners on Uniform State Law* that attempts to validate commercial electronic transactions involving electronic records and signatures. It has been adopted by all states except New York, Illinois, and Washington, as of early 2011.

REVIEW EXERCISE

Match the following terms with their most appropriate meaning.

TERMS	MEANING
1. Personalty	____ renter of property who has minimal rights to real property
2. Realty	____ exclusive control over copying and other exploitation of works for a specific period
3. Tenant	
4. Fixture	____ ordinary prudence a person would exercise under similar circumstances
5. *Uniform Commercial Code (UCC)*	____ exclusive right granted to one who invents a new, useful, and non-obvious process, or object
6. Finder of lost property	____ when a person receives possession of personal property belonging to another and deprives owner of use of the property
7. Mislaid property	____ equitable remedy that results only in the return of the property or a specific performance order
8. Gifts	____ temporary grant of authority, such as when a landowner grants permission to hunt or fish on the land
9. Inheritance	
10. Bailment	____ model legislation adopted by most states to validate commercial electronic transactions
11. Due care	
12. Conversion	____ one who without permission enters the property of another without right, lawful authority, or invitation
13. Replevin	
14. Eminent domain	____ legal action to recover damages or to enforce legal obligations resulting from a contract
15. Estate in fee simple	____ power to take private property for public use by a government entity
16. Leasehold	____ relinquishing possession of personal property to another in trust without transfer of title
17. Easement	
18. License	____ person who enters another's property by invitation, expressed or implied
19. Covenant	____ offer and acceptance, competent parties, agreement, consideration, and not in violation of law
20. Real estate transaction	
21. Nuisance	____ the maximum real property rights to which an owner may be entitled (sell, transfer, or pass on)
22. Trespasser	
23. Invitee	____ a right to use over the property of another, such as a right-of-way
24. Contract action	____ a restriction on real property limiting use of the property or stipulating the truth of certain facts
25. Standard elements of an enforceable contract	____ conveyance of title to real property by sale involving written contract and transfer of title
26. *Statute of Frauds*	____ an estate held under lease

27. Patent
28. Copyright
29. Fair use
30. Uniform Electronic Transaction Act (UETA)

____ codification of common law of contract related to commercial transactions

____ activity involving use of real property that is unreasonable and injurious to others

____ codification providing for certain contracts to be in writing

____ voluntary transfer of property to another gratuitously and without consideration

____ has good title against everyone except the true owner but must make reasonable effort to find owner

____ property distributed according to a will or by the court intestate

____ personal property, movable property, chattels

____ rights and interests in land and things attached to land

____ an object so annexed to realty that it is regarded as part of the land and cannot easily be removed

____ that which is intentionally left in a place and later forgotten

____ defense for reproduction of particular works such as criticism, news reporting, teaching, scholarship, and research

DISCUSSION QUESTIONS

1. How is property ownership classified between personal property, real property, and fixtures?
2. What are the basic rights and duties of personal property owners and real property owners?
3. When you park your car in a parking lot, the ticket may say "no bailment is created." Why does the ticket say there has been no bailment?
4. What is involved in real property transactions by sale?
5. What is an enforceable contract?
6. What are the remedies for breach of contract?
7. Do you believe that contracts should be in writing? How do you imagine someone proves that there was an oral contract?
8. Shouldn't minors be held to contracts that they entered into willingly? Do you agree with current law regarding minors and contracts?

ASSIGNMENTS

ASSIGNMENT: Use the Internet to look up provisions in the *Uniform Commercial Code* adopted in your state that interest you concerning property law or contract law. Just type in the name of your state and "Code Annotated" and go to the provisions you find interesting. Then find out what contracts must be in writing in your state by selecting the term "Statute of Limitations," and go to the provisions that interest you.

ASSIGNMENT: Look up the Uniform Electronic Transaction Act (UETA) in your state's code, or find out whether and when your state has enacted the UETA.

SOURCES AND SUGGESTED READING

American Law Institute. 1980. *Restatement of the Law Second, Contracts*. Philadelphia: American Law Institute.

American Law Institute. 1976. *Restatement of the Law Second, Property (Landlord and Tenant)*. Philadelphia: American Law Institute, 1936-1944.

American Law Institute. *Uniform Commercial Code*. 2007. Philadelphia: American Law Institute. (Official text with comments.) See also your state's code for the provisions applicable to your state (except Louisiana).

Conference of Commissioners on Uniform State Law. 1999. *Uniform Electronic Transaction Act (UETA)*. Uniform Law Commission: Chicago. See also your state's code for the provisions applicable to your state.

Schubert, Frank A. 1996. *Grilliot's Introduction to Law and the Legal System*. 6th ed. Boston: Houghton Mifflin.

Statute of Limitations. (See your state's provisions in that state's code.)

Walston-Dunham, Beth. 1990. *Introduction to Law*. St. Paul, Minn.: West Publishing Company.

World Trade Organization. 1994. *Agreement on Trade-Related Aspects of Intellectual Property Rights*. Geneva: World Trade Organization.

Introduction to Tort Law

Take a moment and think of lawsuits that you've read or heard about in the news. A woman sues McDonald's for burn injuries suffered from scalding hot coffee she ordered at the drive-through window. A group of people sue restaurants for selling fatty foods. Families sue an airline company after a plane crashes due to pilot or mechanical error, tragically killing all passengers. A family sues a neighbor after the neighbor's dog—a dog with vicious propensities—maims their young child. Two automobile drivers sue each other after a frightening collision in which one driver was texting on the phone and the other was exceeding the speed limit. A woman sues a store after slipping and falling while shopping. A man sues a manufacturing company due to a product defect in his lawn mower that caused severe injuries to his arms and legs.

These are all tort actions, civil causes of action in which one party (or litigant) sues another for injuries he or she has suffered from socially unreasonable conduct. A *tort* is a civil cause of action in which a victim generally sues a defendant, called a *tortfeasor*, for monetary damages. A **tortfeasor** is the person who allegedly committed a tort and engaged in socially unreasonable conduct that harmed another. Automobile accidents, dog bites, malpractice claims, and slip and falls are all potential tort suits.

Tortfeasor:
Person who allegedly committed a tort or engaged in socially unreasonable conduct that harmed another.

Consider the typical slip and fall case. A customer enters a store and falls on her back because of a very slick floor. She suffers injuries from her fall. She may file a lawsuit against the store, alleging that the store engaged in socially unreasonable conduct in having unsafe, slick floors for customers. Her lawsuit is a tort suit. The woman is the plaintiff, and the store is the defendant and the alleged tortfeasor (the person or entity who allegedly committed a tortious act).

The genesis of the word *tort* is subject to some dispute. Some trace it to the Latin word *tortus*, which means twisted. This makes sense, as tort law deals with unreasonable, or twisted, conduct.

Tort law is a form of civil law, as opposed to criminal law. In criminal law, the government—federal, state, or local—brings legal action against a defendant for wrongful conduct. The government seeks to fine and often imprison the defendant for violating societal norms and laws. The purpose of criminal law is to protect society by punishing the person or persons who committed crimes. Tort law is different in that most tort suits involve one private party suing another for monetary damages.

The purpose of tort law is to compensate a victim for the harm he or she has suffered due to the socially unreasonable conduct of a defendant. There are several other differences between tort law and criminal law. A major difference is purpose. The purpose of criminal law is to punish those who commit crimes, whereas the purpose of tort law is to compensate victims.

Criminal law serves the interests of society at large, whereas tort law generally serves individual interests. Another key difference is the standard of proof. The typical standard of proof in a tort suit is *preponderance of the evidence,* which means "more likely than not." A plaintiff must simply show that his or her version of the case was more likely than not to be what happened. By contrast, the standard of proof in a criminal case is *beyond a reasonable doubt,* a much more onerous standard. Finally, criminal cases are governed by different procedural rules—the Rules of Criminal Procedure—and tort cases are governed by the Rules of Civil Procedure.

Even though there are differences between tort and criminal law, the same conduct can constitute both a tort and a crime. If A shoots and kills B with a gun, the state may prosecute A for a homicide offense. However, the family of B may file a wrongful death tort lawsuit against A for killing their loved one. Another example involves fisticuffs at a local bar. Two men are drinking beer at a local bar when they argue about an upcoming football game. C punches D in the face after D insulted C's favorite team. The police and local district attorney's office could prosecute C for assault and battery, and D could sue C for monetary damages under a tort suit for assault and battery.

Tort law also differs from contract law even though both are areas of civil law. In contract law, the persons who sign a contract owe obligations to the other parties to the contract. In tort law, people owe a duty to everyone in society. When a person operates an automobile, that person owes everyone a duty to operate that motor vehicle in a reasonably safe fashion.

BASIC TYPES OF TORTS

There are three basic types of torts: (1) intentional torts, (2) torts of negligence, and (3) strict liability torts. They differ based on the intent or mindset of the tortfeasor. **Intentional torts** occur when a tortfeasor acts knowing that a certain result will occur or acts with substantial certainty that a harmful result will occur. If you get mad at your best friend, take your car and then ram it into his car, you have committed an intentional tort (battery). You intended to cause damage to his vehicle. Likewise, if you are in a small room and start swinging a golf club recklessly, the golf club could fly out of

Intentional torts: Tortfeasor intends a certain result or acts with substantial certainty that his or her conduct will result in harm.

your hands and strike another. That may constitute an intentional tort if a judge or jury determines that it was *substantially certain* that the club would strike another.

Negligence refers to failure of a person to exercise due care or acting carelessly or recklessly causing harm to another. For example, if a person texts while driving and then rear-ends a car, that person acted carelessly or negligently. The driver did not intend to strike another car, but he or she was at fault—or negligent—because the driver did not drive the car as a reasonable person would under the circumstances. It is not a valid defense to say, "Your honor, it was an accident. I didn't mean to hit the other car." The driver committed a tort because he or she had a duty to operate his vehicle in a safe manner.

Strict liability is applied by the courts in product liability cases in which a seller is liable for any and all defective or hazardous products that unduly threaten a consumer's personal safety. It applies in just a few special circumstances, such as injuries caused by a wild animal kept in captivity, injuries resulting from highly dangerous activities, or injuries from some product-liability cases. For example, if a defendant transports toxic materials in his or her truck and then gets into an accident, the driver and the driver's company will be strictly liable for the harm caused. Furthermore, if a person owns a wild animal and the animal somehow gets away and harms someone, the owner is strictly liable in tort for those damages.

Negligence:
Failure to exercise due care or acting carelessly or recklessly in a way that causes harm to others.

Strict liability:
Does not require proof of intent or even fault but is strictly liable for harmful results, as in a defective product unreasonably dangerous to the user.

GENERAL TYPES OF TORTS

Intentional Torts Against a Person

There are four major intentional torts against a person: (1) assault, (2) battery, (3) false imprisonment, and (4) intentional infliction of emotional distress. **Assault** refers to the intentional causing of an apprehension of harmful or offensive contact. Assault often goes hand in hand with the related tort of **battery**. Battery refers to the causing of a harmful or offensive contact.

Assault:
Intentional causing of an apprehension or appreciation of harmful contact.

Battery:
Consummation of an unlawful assault by making contact with the other person or the causing of a harmful or offensive contact upon another. (You can have a battery without an assault or contact without apprehension.)

Assault and Battery

The key difference between assault and battery is that assault requires the victim to apprehend, or appreciate, an impending contact, whereas battery simply involves contact. Take the following three examples:

Example 1. A and B get into a verbal argument at a local bar. A throws a punch at B, who manages to elude the punch. A has committed assault, because there was an apprehension of harmful contact by B.

However, A has not committed battery, because A did not connect with his punch on B.

Example 2. A and B get into a verbal argument that gets physical. A throws a punch at B and connects. In this case, A has committed assault and battery. He is liable for assault because B apprehended the contact. A is liable for battery, too, because he made contact with B.

Example 3. A and B get into a verbal argument. Later, when B's back is turned, A throws a punch. A, who is inebriated, fails to connect with the punch and actually falls down. A has committed neither assault nor battery. He is not liable for assault, because B did not apprehend the contact. He also is not liable for battery, because there was no contact. (Note that he may be prosecuted for disorderly conduct or some other criminal law.)

There is a split in the courts as to whether mere words can constitute an assault. Generally, threatening words can constitute an assault ("I am going to kill you") if the victim reasonably believes that the speaker can carry out his or her threat. Remember that unlike assault, battery requires contact. The contact needs to be either harmful or offensive. Kissing a stranger while he or she is sleeping constitutes a battery. Throwing and hitting someone with a water balloon can constitute a battery. Spitting on someone is a battery.

Years ago in Texas, an African-American man successfully sued a local restaurant after an employee snatched a plate out of his hand and refused to serve him because of his race. The incident occurred years before Texas had a state anti-discrimination law, which would prohibit discrimination in places of public accommodation. Instead, the man and his attorney sued for battery, alleging that the snatching of the plate was an offensive contact. The Texas Supreme Court agreed in *Fisher v. Carrousel Motor Hotel, Inc.,* 424 S.W.2d 627 (Tex. 1967), writing:

> *Under the facts of this case, we have no difficulty in holding that the intentional grabbing of plaintiff's plate constituted a battery. The intentional snatching of an object from one's hand is as clearly an offensive invasion of his person as would be an actual contact with the body. . . .*
>
> *Personal indignity is the essence of an action for battery; and consequently, the defendant is liable not only for the contacts which do actual physical harm, but also for those which are offensive and insulting. We hold, therefore, that plaintiff was entitled to actual damages for mental suffering due to the willful battery, even in the absence of any physical injury.*

False Imprisonment

False imprisonment refers to the unjustifiable intentional confinement of another against his or her will. In a sense, it is a civil law analog to the

False imprisonment:
Unjustifiable intentional confinement of another against his or her will.

criminal concept of kidnapping. For example, consider that A owes B money. In order to recover his money, B takes A, locks him in a room for two hours until A agrees to return the money he borrowed. B has committed the tort of false imprisonment.

False imprisonment tort suits often arise after a customer is detained at a store on suspicion of shoplifting. If store personnel detain a customer for an unreasonable period of time and do not have good reason to believe that the customer stole store property, they may be liable for false imprisonment. Many states have what is called a "shopkeepers' privilege" statute that provides immunity for merchants if they act reasonably under the circumstances.

Tennessee's Shopkeepers' Privilege Statute

T.C.A. §40-7-116. Shoplifting; Detention of Suspect

(a) A merchant, a merchant's employee, or agent or a peace officer who has probable cause to believe that a person has committed or is attempting to commit the offense of theft, as defined in §39-14-103, may detain that person on or off the premises of the mercantile establishment if the detention is done for any or all of the following purposes:

(1) To question the person, investigate the surrounding circumstances, obtain a statement, or any combination thereof;

(2) To request or verify identification, or both;

(3) To inform a peace officer of the detention of that person, or surrender that person to the custody of a peace officer, or both;

(4) To inform a peace officer, the parent or parents, guardian or other private person interested in the welfare of a minor of the detention and to surrender the minor to the custody of that person; or

(5) To institute criminal proceedings against the person.

(b) Probable cause to suspect that a person has committed or is attempting to commit the offense of theft may be based on, but not limited to:

(1) Personal observation, including observation via closed circuit television or other visual device;

(2) Report of personal observation from another merchant;

(3) Activation of an electronic or other type of mechanical device designed to detect theft; or

(4) Personal observation of dressing rooms, including observation via closed circuit television, two-way mirrors, or other visual devices, shall be limited to observation by a person of the same sex as the person being observed. No observation shall be lawful unless notices are posted in the dressing rooms that monitoring may occur.

(c) A merchant, merchant's employee or agent, or a peace officer who detains, questions, or causes the arrest of any person suspected of theft shall not be criminally or civilly liable for any legal action relating to the

continued >

detention, questioning or arrest if the merchant, merchant's employee or agent, or peace officer:

(1) Has reasonable grounds to suspect that the person has committed or is attempting to commit theft;

(2) Acts in a reasonable manner under the circumstances; and

(3) Detains the suspected person for a reasonable period of time.

(d) The merchant may use a reasonable amount of force necessary to protect the merchant, to prevent the escape of the person detained, or to prevent the loss or destruction of property.

(e) A reasonable period of time, for the purposes of this section, is a period of time long enough to accomplish the purpose set forth in this section and shall include any time spent awaiting the arrival of a law enforcement officer or the parents or guardian of a juvenile suspect, if the merchant or the merchant's employee or agent has summoned a law enforcement officer, the parents or a guardian of a juvenile suspect, if the merchant or the merchant's employee or agent has summoned a law enforcement officer, the parents or a guardian.

Intentional Infliction of Emotional Distress

Intentional infliction of emotional distress refers to intentional or reckless conduct of an extreme and outrageous nature that causes another person to suffer severe emotional distress. In some states, this tort is called *outrageous conduct*. The conduct complained of must be beyond the pale of decency such that it would cause a reasonable person to exclaim "That's an outrage!" or "That's outrageous!" Another key requirement is that the conduct must cause *severe* emotional distress—much more than mere annoyance or negative feelings.

Some examples of conduct held to constitute intentional infliction of emotional distress by courts are falsely telling someone that his or her spouse had passed away as a cruel joke, subjecting an employee to sexual harassment over a long period of time, detaining a potential car buyer for four hours of extreme pressure accompanied by misrepresentations, humiliating an employee by demoting him or her from company vice president to janitor, planting company checks on an employee to make it appear falsely that the person was stealing from the company, refusing to release the body of a widow's husband because she decided to seek services from another funeral home, and accusing a customer of shoplifting and then pummeling the person.

In some jurisdictions, it is difficult to recover under this tort. In *Hassing v. Wortman* (Neb. 1983), the Nebraska Supreme Court reversed a jury's award of more than $18,000 for intentional infliction of emotional distress. The case involved a couple that had been married for 30 years.

After the woman named Hassing remarried, her ex-husband, Mr. Wortman, allegedly drove by her house 10–15 times a month, crawled around in a bush outside her home, nearly drove her and her new husband off the road, revealed personal information about his ex-wife in Christmas cards sent to relatives, and other bad behavior. Still, the Nebraska Supreme Court determined by a 5-2 vote that this admittedly "repugnant" conduct was not enough to cause severe distress. "The absence of any medical testimony in this case and the absence of any evidence that the plaintiff's job performance was adversely affected is of some significance," the Nebraska high court wrote. "The plaintiff failed to prove that she had suffered emotional distress so severe that no reasonable person could have been expected to endure it."

Two justices dissented, finding that Wortman's pattern of harassment caused severe emotional distress. "The deliberate harassing intrusions, repeated frequently and for a continued period, are savage, uncivilized, and outrageous," wrote the dissent. "I reject outright the conclusion that the conduct here is not sufficiently horrid to be classified as outrageous. The law must and should provide protection from this absurd conduct and not be seen to stand helplessly by, wringing its hands. Often the most effective method of teaching good manners is the money judgment." The dissent also questioned the ruling that medical testimony is needed to show and prove that a plaintiff suffered severe emotional distress.

Cases are all over the map concerning whether certain conduct crosses the line and is considered outrageous enough to be actionable. Opinions in different states also differ on whether medical testimony is needed to prove severe emotional distress. It certainly helps a plaintiff's case for emotional distress to have medical testimony that documents and details the harmful impact of the defendant's conduct.

Other Intentional Torts Against a Person

There are other intentional torts against a person. One is *malicious prosecution*, a tort designed to give people redress who have been unreasonably prosecuted for a crime he or she did not commit. If a tortfeasor files false criminal charges, has no probable cause, and acted out an improper motive, then the tortfeasor has committed the tort of malicious prosecution.

In order to prove malicious prosecution, the plaintiff must show that the defendant caused criminal proceedings to be instituted against the plaintiff without probable cause and with a bad motive. The plaintiff must also show that the criminal proceedings were dismissed or rejected. In other words, the plaintiff must be found not guilty of the criminal charges, the prosecutor must have decided not to prosecute, or the grand jury refused to indict the plaintiff.

Two related torts are wrongful institution of civil proceedings and abuse of process. *Wrongful institution of civil proceedings* applies when a defendant institutes a civil lawsuit against the plaintiff for a bad motive and has no probable cause. Abuse of process refers to when a defendant uses litigation devices for improper purposes. The *Restatement of Torts (Second)* gives the example of a party using a subpoena to harass the opposing party to settle the case rather than for the proper reason to force someone to testify in a case. *Abuse of process* usually involves one party using litigation tactics to place undue pressure on the other party.

Intentional Torts Against Property

Tort law also provides causes of action for those who have suffered injury to their property. The most common intentional torts against property are conversion, trespass to chattels, and trespass to land. *Conversion* is the civil law equivalent of the criminal law concept of theft. It applies when a person takes another's property and converts it to his or her own. *Trespass to chattels* is similar to conversion but not quite the same degree of dispossession. *Trespass to land* occurs when a person intentionally enters the land of another or remains on the land after being asked to leave. All that is required to commit the tort of trespass is intent to enter the land of another. A person can be liable for trespass even if he or she did not intend to trespass on the land of another.

A related cause of action is the tort of **nuisance**, which refers to activity that substantially and unreasonably interferes with plaintiff's use and enjoyment of his or her land. The key difference between trespass to land and nuisance is that trespass impacts someone's exclusive possession of land, whereas nuisance impacts someone's use and enjoyment of the land.

Nuisance: Activity that substantially and unreasonably interferes with plaintiff's use and enjoyment of his or her land.

Consider these two examples:

Example 1. Person A lives directly above B in an apartment complex. One day A believes that he has the right to enter B's apartment to borrow a coat. A enters B's apartment without asking permission and takes B's coat. A has committed trespass (trespass to chattels and maybe conversion).

Example 2. On another day, A plays his music at a very high decibel level, which bothers B in his apartment. A has committed the tort of nuisance by creating the excessive noise, which impacts B's right to enjoy his apartment.

Defenses to Intentional Torts

Some applicable defenses to intentional torts are consent, self-defense, necessity, and statute of limitations.

Consent is a common defense in torts alleged during the commission of athletic competitions. For example, a defense tackle pounds an opposing quarterback into the turf with a very hard hit. The quarterback suffers a concussion from the vicious sack. However, it would be difficult for the quarterback to sue the defensive tackle because he consented to the physical contact—even violent contact—when he agreed to play competitive football. If the defensive tackle hits the quarterback after the whistle had been blown with an illegal helmet-to-helmet hit, then the quarterback might have a valid claim. That's because the actions of the defensive tackle went well beyond the rules of the game. The quarterback consented to playing the game but did not consent to violent, harmful conduct committed far outside the confines of the rules of the game. The quarterback might be able to sue for the tort of battery.

Self-defense could be used by someone who allegedly committed an assault and battery. If the alleged victim was the aggressor in the confrontation, the alleged tortfeasor might have a good case for self-defense, as long as he did not use unreasonable force to subdue the "victim." For example, A is drinking in a local restaurant when he sees B approach him. A believes that B is going to strike him. B confirms this by saying, "I'm going to pound you into submission." A has a right to tackle B and protect himself. The key is whether the person used *reasonable force* under the circumstances. A person has a right to use deadly force if he reasonably believes that his life is in imminent danger.

One cannot use *deadly force* or *unreasonable force* to protect property. The Iowa Supreme Court explained this principle in the famous case of *Katko v. Briney* (1971), which is included in this text (see Appendix B). Marvin Katko trespassed on the land of Edward Briney for the purpose of stealing property. Katko sought to break into an unoccupied building on Briney's property. Briney, who had been victimized by thieves in the past, had installed a spring gun that would go off when the door was opened. When Katko broke into the building, the spring gun went off, causing Katko serious injuries. Katko later sued Briney for the injuries caused by the spring gun. A jury awarded Katko $30,000 in damages. The Iowa Supreme Court upheld the award, reasoning that Briney's installation of the spring gun was excessive force and that Katko could recover in his tort suit. The Iowa Supreme Court explained that "the law has always placed a higher value upon human safety than upon mere rights in property." Briney could not use the spring gun in this instance because it was clearly capable of causing death or serious bodily injury, and Briney's life was not in danger by someone breaking into his shed.

There are two types of *necessity*: public necessity and private necessity. *Public necessity* refers to otherwise tortious conduct being excused because it was done to avoid an imminent public disaster. For example, if public officials come onto A's land and destroy his two pit bulls who have mauled other dogs and are infected with a contagious disease, the officials are not liable for trespass and other torts. They are not liable because the presence of A's dogs presented a viable threat to the community at large.

Private necessity refers to conduct that saves the life of an individual, rather than the community at large.

Statutes of limitations are laws that place a time limit on when a plaintiff in a tort suit has to file a lawsuit for damages. A key for legal researchers is that the term used to describe statutes of limitations is *"limitations of actions."* In many states, would-be plaintiffs have a one-year statute of limitations for most tort suits. This means that if the plaintiff does not sue until 366 days (a year and a day) after the injury-causing accident, the defense has a valid defense because the lawsuit is time-barred. This is not uniform. In many states, the statutes of limitations are different. For example, in Tennessee the statute of limitation for a personal injury tort action is one year, in Texas the applicable statute of limitations is two years, and in North Carolina the statute of limitations for a personal injury tort suit is three years. Attorneys and their clients must pay particular attention to the applicable statute of limitation to determine the deadline for filing a tort suit.

Statutes of limitations: Laws that place a limit on when a plaintiff has to bring suit or legal action for damages.

NEGLIGENCE

Most tort suits involve claims of negligence, defined as conduct that fails to conform to a reasonable standard of care and leads to harm to another. Negligence refers to socially unreasonable conduct even though the tortfeasor did not intend to cause the harm. When you drive your car down the road, you have a responsibility to everyone else on the road to operate your vehicle in a safe fashion. If you drive too closely behind the car in front of you and rear-end that car, you likely were negligent or at fault. It is not a valid defense to say, "I did not intend or mean to hit the car in front of me; it was an accident." Yes, it was an accident, but it was an accident caused by your failing to operate your motor vehicle in a reasonably safe manner.

The elements of a *negligence claim* are (1) duty of care, (2) breach of duty of care, (3) causation, and (4) damages. *Duty of care* refers to a legal duty to conform your conduct to a required (and reasonable) standard of care. **Breach of duty of care** refers to a failure on the part of the tortfeasor to adhere to a reasonable standard of care. *Causation* means that the defendant's negligent action (or inaction) caused the harm to the victim. The term *damages* means that the victim suffered actual, compensable harm.

Breach of duty of care: Failure on the part of the tortfeasor to adhere to a reasonable standard of care.

Duty of care is often the easiest prong of a negligence case. If you operate a motor vehicle, you have a duty to drive that vehicle safely. If you walk your dog in the neighborhood, you have a duty to protect your neighbors and others from your dog. If you operate a business, you have a duty to make sure that the business is in a safe condition for customers. Sometimes in tort law there are special relationships that create an elevated duty. For example, innkeepers have a special relationship with their guests. When you check into a hotel or motel, their employees are supposed to keep you safe. There is no absolute guarantee of safety, but there is a duty of care involved. Sometimes, professionals have a special duty imposed on them by reason of their special skill and knowledge.

For example, if you need legal assistance and seek out an attorney, that attorney has a *fiduciary duty*—a duty in which one party reposes special trust in another—to give you competent legal advice.

In some cases, duty may be a stumbling block in negligence cases. What if you go to a shopping mall and an unknown assailant mugs you in the parking lot. Does the shopping mall owner owe you a duty to keep you safe in the parking lot? The general rule is that property owners do have a duty to protect their patrons from reasonably foreseeable third-party criminal attacks. The key question is whether similar criminal incidents have happened in the past. If they have, that puts the business owner on notice to take further precautions to provide a reasonably safe environment.

Breach of Duty

Breach of duty is one of the most difficult elements of a negligence suit to prove. It often is *the most contentious* part of a litigated tort case. The plaintiff asserts that the defendant breached a duty of care by not acting reasonably, and the defendant counters that he or she acted reasonably and sometimes bad things just happen without any fault.

The reasonable person standard becomes important in determining whether there has been a breach of duty. The *reasonable person standard* refers to the standard of care that a reasonable person in the position of the defendant should follow under the circumstances.

Take note of the hotel-guest relationship in the following hypothetical case. A woman named Mrs. Smith checks into a hotel because the hotel is hosting a convention she needs to attend for her job. After attending a session at the convention, the woman goes into a restaurant located inside the hotel. A man notices the woman wearing her name tag from the convention in the restaurant and observes her for an insidious purpose. The woman then leaves and goes to her hotel room. The man—a sexual predator—goes to the hotel front desk. He tells the hotel desk clerk that he is Mr. Smith, the husband of Mrs. Smith the patron. He says he wants to surprise his wife with a special gift to support her working so hard for the family. The desk clerk fails to ask for photo identification of Mr. Smith and simply gives him a room key. The man posing as Mr. Smith then goes up to the hotel room and commits a sexual offense upon Mrs. Smith, the hotel patron.

The hotel clerk breached a duty of care by failing to act reasonably by not asking for photo identification of "Mr. Smith." A reasonable person in the position of the clerk would have made sure that the man was Mr. Smith and might have called the room of Mrs. Smith to make sure that the couple were on good terms and she was amenable to her husband having a key to the room. Instead, the desk clerk breached a duty of care by compromising the patron's safety.

Vicarious Liability and Deep Pockets

The hotel desk clerk example introduces two other important concepts in tort law: vicarious liability and deep pockets. Mrs. Smith could sue not only the negligent desk clerk but also the hotel. An employer is *vicariously liable* for torts committed by an employee during the scope and course of employment. This is important in many negligence suits, because a plaintiff needs to seek compensation from a tortfeasor with wealth, or as called in tort law, with *deep pockets*. Thus, in negligence suits the plaintiff will sue not only the offending employee but also the employer. In the hotel example, the plaintiff will sue the hotel in part because the hotel has very deep pockets, and the desk clerk may not have any money to pay a court judgment.

Two key doctrines apply to determine whether a defendant has breached a duty of care to a plaintiff: negligence per se and *res ipsa loquitur*. **Negligence per se** means the unexcused violation of a law or regulation by a defendant that leads to harm suffered by the victim. For example, a local regulation establishes the applicable speed limits on the roads. The defendant drives his car 50 miles per hour in a 30 mile per hour zone. The defendant then loses control of the vehicle and hits a nearby pedestrian. The defendant driver was negligent per se because that driver violated the speed limit, leading to injuries suffered by the pedestrian.

Negligence per se: The unexcused violation of a law or regulation by a defendant that leads to harm suffered by the victim.

Another regulation requires school employees to ensure the identity of anyone coming to pick up a child from school. A woman walks into the school building and says she needs to pick up her child to attend a family funeral. The school employee fails to follow the rules and allows the child to leave with the woman. The woman turns out to be a kidnapper. The child's real parents may be able to rely on negligence per se in their lawsuit against the school.

Res ipsa loquitur is a concept developed through the common law (case law) whereby the defendant's negligence can be inferred through circumstantial evidence. This concept applies when the event ordinarily does not occur without negligence, and other causes are eliminated by the evidence. Most jurisdictions require that the defendant have exclusive control over the instrumentality or object that causes the harm. For example, the Washington Supreme Court ruled in *Curtis v. Lein* (2010) that a plaintiff injured when a dock she was walking on gave way beneath

Res ipsa loquitur: Common law principle that the defendant's negligence can be inferred through circumstantial evidence.

her could rely on the doctrine of *res ipsa loquitur* as evidence of negligence. The state high court reasoned: "A plaintiff may rely upon res ipsa loquitur's inference of negligence if (1) the accident or occurrence that caused the plaintiff's injury would not ordinarily happen in the absence of negligence, (2) the instrumentality or agency that caused the plaintiff's injury was in the exclusive control of the defendant, and (3) the plaintiff did not contribute to the accident or occurrence."

A mother drops off her young child at a neighbor's house. The neighbor allows the young child to enter her swimming pool. The neighbor goes into the house to answer a phone call, leaving the child in the pool. The child then drowns. The doctrine of *res ipsa loquitur* may be available in some jurisdictions to show negligence on the part of the neighbor.

Good Samaritan Statutes

Nearly every state has a **Good Samaritan statute** that generally provides a degree of protection to rescuers, those who attempt to help people in harm. Unfortunately, sometimes some Good Samaritans render aid incompetently and actually cause the injured people more harm than good. However, the legal system wants to reward, not punish, people who do good deeds. Therefore, most Good Samaritan statutes provide that a person is not liable for rendering emergency aid unless he was grossly negligent, which means extremely negligent.

> **Good Samaritan statute:**
> Law that generally provides some protection for rescuers who attempt to help people in harm except for instances of extreme negligence.

Causation

Causation means that the defendant's action (or inaction) caused the plaintiff's harm. Two types of causation exist in the legal system: factual cause and legal cause. Another term for *factual cause* is "cause in fact"; another term for *legal cause* is "proximate cause." Factual cause means that the defendant's conduct actually caused the plaintiff's harm.

Persons A and B get into an argument, and A pushes B down. If B suffers a broken bone from the fall, then A is liable in tort because A's physical act of pushing B down caused B's injuries. Person A's physical aggression was the actual, factual cause of B's injuries. One way to determine factual cause is through the use of the so-called *but-for test*. Applying the *but-for test* would lead to the following rationale: *but for* A's actions, B would not have suffered injuries.

Another test used to determine factual cause is the *substantial factor* test. This test is most useful when there are two independent causes of plaintiff's harm. For example, a plaintiff alleges that he suffered cancer because of exposure to toxic substances from a nearby industrial plant. The plaintiff contends that these toxic fumes from the plant were the actual cause of his harm. However, the defendant company introduces evidence that the plaintiff's disease was caused by his smoking habit. In this case, the question is whether the actual cause of the plaintiff's harm is the toxic substances from the plant or the cigarettes that the plaintiff smoked. Each side may present expert testimony to try to make its case to the jury.

The plaintiff has to prove actual cause by a *preponderance of the evidence*, an evidentiary standard that means more likely than not. This is far less onerous than the criminal law standard of beyond a reasonable doubt. Still, many torts cases are challenging because there are multiple possible explanations for the harm suffered by the plaintiff.

Legal or Proximate Cause

Legal or proximate cause is different from actual cause. **Proximate cause** limits a defendant's liability to the reasonably foreseeable injuries caused by his or her tortious conduct. In other words, let's say a man gets into a fight at a local bar. The man suffers a broken nose and a lacerated arm. An ambulance comes to transport him to a local hospital. However, a driver who is texting on his phone pulls out in front of the ambulance driver, leading to a head-on collision. The injured man in the ambulance dies from the crash. It is not reasonably foreseeable that minor injuries in a bar would lead to a death in the ambulance. The family of the injured man in the bar could not successfully sue the person who punched him in the bar for wrongful death, because there is no *proximate cause*. The family could sue the driver of the car who was texting while driving, as that was the epitome of negligent conduct.

Proximate (or legal) cause:
That which, in a natural and continuous sequence, unbroken by any superseding cause, produces injury and without which the result would not have occurred.

The classic case on proximate cause is *Palsgraf v. Long Island Railroad* (N.Y. 1928). The case involved a man who tried to jump onto a train from a platform with a package in his arm. The man fell. Two guards attempted to pick the man up and help him onto the train. The guard's actions dislodged the package, which contained fireworks. The fireworks exploded and knocked down some scales on the other side of the railway platform, striking a woman named Helen Palsgraf. Mrs. Palsgraf sued the railway company for negligence based on the conduct of the guards. A trial court ruled in her favor, but the New York Court of Appeals (that state's highest court) reversed by a 4-3 vote in a majority opinion by Justice Benjamin Cardozo (who later served on the U.S. Supreme Court). Cardozo reasoned that the railroad company was not liable because the injuries to Mrs. Palsgraf were not reasonably foreseeable. "Nothing in the situation gave notice the falling package had in it the potency of peril to persons thus removed," Cardozo wrote. "Here, by concession, there was nothing in the situation to suggest to the most cautious mind that the parcel wrapped in the newspaper would spread wreckage through the station. If the guard had thrown it down knowingly and willfully, he would not have threatened the plaintiff's safety, so far as appearances would warn him." To Cardozo, it simply was not reasonably foreseeable that the guard's actions in helping a man on a train would lead to an injury of the sort that Mrs. Palsgraf suffered. If the guards had run to the man and knocked Mrs. Palgraf to the ground, this would have been a different case.

Sometimes there are intervening, superseding causes that break the chain of causation. In the bar fight example, the person who punched the victim at the bar is liable for the damages he caused to the victim's face. However, the texting driver who rammed into the ambulance was a superseding cause that broke the chain of causation. Other superseding causes are acts of God, the gross medical malpractice of a doctor after injuries caused by the defendant, and unforeseeable criminal acts by third parties.

Damages

There are three types of damages in tort law: nominal damages, compensatory damages, and punitive damages. *Nominal damages* refer to very minimal damages—damages in name only. Nominal damages occur when a judge or jury recognizes that a plaintiff is correct in theory but believes there is little merit to the lawsuit because there has been little if any damage suffered.

Compensatory damages are those damages designed to compensate a plaintiff for the harm he or she suffered as a result of the defendant's negligent conduct. Compensatory damages can include property damage, lost wages, medical bills, pain and suffering, and loss of future earning capacity. Some types of compensatory damages are more acceptable than others. If liability is established, it is clear that the responsible defendants will be liable for property damage, lost wages, and medical bills. However, pain and suffering can be an illusory concept, with the litigants disagreeing mightily over the proper amount of damages.

Compensatory damages or actual damages: Those damages that compensate the plaintiff for the harm suffered as a result of the defendant's negligent conduct, as opposed to punitive damages.

In many tort cases, liability is not questioned or disputed. In other words, the parties agree that the defendant committed a tort. Rather, the parties disagree mightily over the proper amount of damages. Sometimes parties will ask for a *bench trial*—(a trial before a judge only and not a jury) to have the judge determine the proper amount of damages in the case.

Punitive damages are those damages that are designed to punish the tortfeasor as opposed to compensate the plaintiff; of course, they also compensate the plaintiff. Punitive damages are reserved for the most egregious conduct and occur when the judge or jury determines that a clear message needs to be sent that such socially unreasonable behavior cannot occur again. Some criticize punitive damages because they believe that they are a windfall for the plaintiff. Punitive damages also provide an interesting bridge between tort law and criminal law, as the primary purpose of criminal law is to punish the offender.

Punitive damages: Those damages designed to punish the tortfeasor as opposed to compensate the plaintiff.

Comparative Negligence and Contributory Negligence

Often a plaintiff who sues for injuries in tort is not always blameless. Plaintiffs may have contributed to their own injuries. Defendants can plead that their liability should be reduced by the relative fault of the plaintiffs. This forms the essence of **comparative negligence** in which a judge or jury compares the negligence of the plaintiff and defendant to determine the appropriate measure of fault.

Forty-six states have adopted a version of comparative negligence. Under a pure comparative negligence system, a plaintiff can recover even if a jury determines he or she is more at fault than the defendant(s). In a *modified comparative negligence* system, a plaintiff can recover as long as he or she is not more negligent than the plaintiffs. In most of these modified comparative negligence states a plaintiff can recover as long as he or she was less negligent than the defendant. For example, many states provide that a plaintiff can recover in tort if he or she is less than 50 percent at fault. Four states, Alabama, Maryland, North Carolina, and Virginia, and the District of Columbia still adhere to a system of contributory negligence.

Under a system of **contributory negligence**, a plaintiff cannot recover if he or she contributed to his or her injuries. Most states have moved away from contributory negligence because of its all-or-nothing harshness, allowing some culpable defendants to escape liability for their negligent conduct. Many states have enacted laws that specifically provide for comparative fault.

Comparative negligence: Measures in terms of percentages of fault on each side so that the trier of fact compares the negligence of the plaintiff and defendant to determine the appropriate degree of fault.

Contributory negligence: Plaintiff cannot recover if he or she contributed to their own injuries.

Massachusetts' Law on Comparative Negligence

§85. Comparative Negligence; Limited Effect of Contributory Negligence as Defense.

Contributory negligence shall not bar recovery in any action by any person or legal representative to recover damages for negligence resulting in death or in injury to person or property, if such negligence was not greater than the total amount of negligence attributable to the person or persons against whom recovery is sought, but any damages allowed shall be diminished in proportion to the amount of negligence attributable to the person for whose injury, damage or death recovery is made. In determining by what amount the plaintiff's damages shall be diminished in such a case, the negligence of each plaintiff shall be compared to the total negligence of all persons against whom recovery is sought. The combined total of the plaintiff's negligence taken together with all of the negligence of all defendants shall equal one hundred per cent.

The violation of a criminal statute, ordinance or regulation by a plaintiff which contributed to said injury, death or damage, shall be considered as evidence of negligence of that plaintiff, but the violation of said statute, ordinance or regulation shall not as a matter of law and for that reason alone, serve to bar a plaintiff from recovery.

---

continued >

The defense of assumption of risk is hereby abolished in all actions hereunder.

The burden of alleging and proving negligence which serves to diminish a plaintiff's damages or bar recovery under this section shall be upon the person who seeks to establish such negligence, and the plaintiff shall be presumed to have been in the exercise of due care.

Other states have moved to comparative negligence through the common law, a judicial decision by the state's highest court. For example, the Tennessee Supreme Court changed from a system of contributory negligence to a system of comparative negligence in its 1992 decision *McIntyre v. Ballentine.*

McIntyre v. Ballentine

833 S.W. 2d 52 (Tenn. 1992)

After exhaustive deliberation that was facilitated by extensive briefing and argument by the parties, amicus curiae, and Tennessee's scholastic community, we conclude that it is time to abandon the outmoded and unjust common law doctrine of contributory negligence and adopt in its place a system of comparative fault. Justice simply will not permit our continued adherence to a rule that, in the face of a judicial determination that others bear primary responsibility, nevertheless completely denies injured litigants recompense for their damages.

We recognize that this action could be taken by our General Assembly. However, legislative inaction has never prevented judicial abolition of obsolete common law doctrines, especially those, such as contributory negligence, conceived in the judicial womb. Indeed, our abstinence would sanction "a mutual state of inaction in which the court awaits action by the legislature and the legislature awaits guidance from the court," thereby prejudicing the equitable resolution of legal conflicts.

Nor do we today abandon our commitment to *stare decisis.* While "confidence in our courts is to a great extent dependent on the uniformity and consistency engendered by allegiance to *stare decisis,* . . . mindless obedience to this precept can confound the truth and foster an attitude of contempt."

Two basic forms of comparative fault are utilized by 45 of our sister jurisdictions, these variants being commonly referred to as either "pure" or "modified." In the "pure" form, a plaintiff's damages are reduced in proportion to the percentage negligence attributed to him; for example, a plaintiff responsible for 90 percent of the negligence that caused his injuries nevertheless may recover 10 percent of his damages. In the "modified" form, plaintiffs recover as in pure jurisdictions, but only if the plaintiff's negligence

continued >

either (1) does not exceed ("50 percent" jurisdictions) or (2) is less than ("49 percent" jurisdictions) the defendant's negligence.

Although we conclude that the all-or-nothing rule of contributory negligence must be replaced, we nevertheless decline to abandon totally our fault-based tort system. We do not agree that a party should necessarily be able to recover in tort even though he may be 80, 90, or 95 percent at fault. We therefore reject the pure form of comparative fault.

We recognize that modified comparative fault systems have been criticized as merely shifting the arbitrary contributory negligence bar to a new ground. However, we feel the "49 percent rule" ameliorates the harshness of the common law rule while remaining compatible with a fault-based tort system. We therefore hold that so long as a plaintiff's negligence remains less than the defendant's negligence the plaintiff may recover; in such a case, plaintiff's damages are to be reduced in proportion to the percentage of the total negligence attributable to the plaintiff.

In all trials where the issue of comparative fault is before a jury, the trial court shall instruct the jury on the effect of the jury's finding as to the percentage of negligence as between the plaintiff or plaintiffs and the defendant or defendants. The attorneys for each party shall be allowed to argue how this instruction affects a plaintiff's ability to recover.

Under a comparative negligence system, a plaintiff's recovery is reduced by the percentage of the plaintiff's own negligence. Consider the following example. In a state with comparative negligence, A plaintiff sues B defendant over injuries from a car accident. The jury determines that A suffered $40,000 in damages, A was 20 percent negligent, and B was 80 percent negligent. How much can A recover?

(a) Nothing
(b) $40,000
(c) $30,000
(d) $32,000

The correct answer is (d) $32,000. A suffered $40,000 in damages but was 20 percent at fault. This means that A's recovery is reduced by 20 percent of $40,000, or $8,000, leading to a final result of $32,000.

Let's take another example. In a modified comparative (less than 50 percent) negligence system, A sues B defendant for injuries from a car accident. A jury determines that A suffered $100,000 in damages, A was 50 percent at fault, and B was 50 percent at fault. How much does A recover?

(a) $100,000
(b) Nothing
(c) $50,000
(d) $51,000

The correct answer is (b) nothing. Remember that the problem said that the accident took place in a state of modified comparative negligence, which generally means that the plaintiff can recover damages for negligence if his or her negligence was less than that of the defendant. Here, since the jury determined that both litigants were equally at fault, the plaintiff recovers nothing.

Tort of Negligent Hiring or Negligent Retention

Some states recognize the tort of negligent hiring or negligent retention. *Negligent hiring* means that an employer negligently hired an employee that it knew, or should have known through reasonable diligence, presented a risk to the public. *Negligent retention* means that an employer knew, or should have known, that retaining an employee presented unreasonable risk to others.

The Georgia Court of Appeals recognized both of these related torts in *TGM Ashley Lakes v. Jennings* (2003). An apartment complex and its manager hired a maintenance worker who then strangled to death a female tenant. The maintenance worker had a lengthy criminal history, including convictions for rape and armed robbery. The worker had even told one of the managers that he had a criminal history, but the apartment complex management did not conduct their normal criminal background check. Furthermore, after the worker's hiring, numerous residents had complained of break-ins and robberies in their apartments. Still, the apartment complex failed to investigate and terminate the maintenance worker.

The Georgia appeals court explained:

The causation element requires showing that, given the employee's dangerous propensities, the victim's injuries should have been foreseen as the natural and probable consequence of hiring the employee. . . . With regard to negligent hiring, the manager who recommended Oliver [the maintenance worker] for employment as a maintenance worker knew that Oliver had been in trouble with the law, including time spent in jail. This simple fact raises a jury issue of whether TGM should have further inquired into Oliver's past criminal record prior to hiring him. . . .

The case is stronger for negligent retention. TGM learned that a series of unforced entries and burglaries had occurred at the premises since Oliver had been hired; that some residents suspected an employee; and that Oliver had been discovered in one apartment without authorization. Also, one resident had even suggested that criminal background checks be performed because she was positive that an employee was the culprit. These facts raised an issue for the jury of whether TGM, acting reasonably, should have taken additional steps to investigate the criminal background of their employees, including Oliver.

For example, let's say that a trucking company hires a new driver who then drives drunk and injuries some motorists. If a reasonable investigation by the employer would have revealed past convictions for drunk driving, the injured motorists would have a good case against the trucking company for *negligent hiring*.

Similarly, let's say that the trucking company hires another employee who did not have a similarly poor background with respect to drunk driving. However, while on the job, the driver has two alcohol-related crashes. The trucking company retains the employee even though he has shown a pattern of drinking and driving. If that driver then gets involved in another alcohol-related accident, the trucking company would be liable for *negligent retention*. The theory behind negligent retention is that the employee should have known that this particular employee presented a risk to the public and should have terminated his employment earlier.

MALPRACTICE

Malpractice refers to negligence committed by professionals, those who have a special duty to provide expertise to others. Professionals have a *fiduciary duty*, a duty in which one party reposes trust in another, to provide competent service to the people they help. Physicians, dentists, attorneys, and accountants are types of professionals subject to malpractice laws.

Malpractice:
Negligence committed by professionals.

Many states have specific statutes dealing with professional negligence. Some states have laws pertaining to medical malpractice, and others have laws related to accountant malpractice. In many states, plaintiffs in malpractice cases must present *expert testimony* providing that the defendant-professional failed to adhere to the requisite standard of care. For example, Tennessee has a statute that provides that a plaintiff must present expert testimony in medical malpractice cases and that expert must be licensed in Tennessee or in a state that borders Tennessee. Thus, a plaintiff suing for medical malpractice in Tennessee could not rely on an expert who is licensed in Florida.

The theory behind the so-called contiguous state rule is that an expert from a state not close to Tennessee would have little familiarity with the prevailing local standard of care in the specific community in Tennessee. Others criticize such a rule and say that there should be a national standard of care for medical and other professionals.

Experts are not unique to malpractice cases, as expert testimony is used in a wide variety of cases. Often, particularly in malpractice cases that go to trial, each side will present an expert witness. Juries decide the outcome of cases based on which side's expert witness is more credible.

Professionals must ensure that they maintain competence in their chosen fields by keeping abreast of recent changes and developments. For example, attorneys in nearly every state have to take continuing legal education courses. Physicians have to take continuing medical education courses. Accountants must be aware of the ever-changing tax laws.

In malpractice cases, professionals are often held to the standard of care of a practitioner in their particular specialty. For example, a neurosurgeon will be held to the standard of care of a competent neurosurgeon as opposed to the standard of care and knowledge of a general surgeon. Likewise, a criminal trial attorney charged with malpractice will be judged according to the standard of care that a reasonably competent criminal law attorney should provide.

Defamation and Invasion of Privacy

Two other torts deserve special mention, particularly in modern society with the media of mass communication available to so many people. These torts are defamation and invasion of privacy. **Defamation** refers to the communication of a false statement of fact that harms someone's reputation. *Invasion of privacy* refers to conduct that infringes on someone's right to be let alone.

Defamation: Communication of a false statement of fact that harms someone's reputation.

The hallmark of a defamation claim is a false statement that creates reputational harm. There are two general types of defamation: (1) libel and (2) slander. *Libel* refers to written defamation, and *slander* refers to oral defamation. Note that most cases are considered libel cases, as many spoken defamation cases have a written transcript. For example, a talk radio host's comments would be evaluated as a libel case, as there is a transcript of what the host said on the radio.

Identification is a necessary element of a defamation claim. The defamatory comment must identify the plaintiff or, at least, let a reasonable reader know who the article or comment is addressing. In most cases, this is a routine requirement, as people refer to individuals by name. The more difficult question arises when the statement refers to someone but does not explicitly name them. For example, writing that a professor at the local university beats his spouse would not be specific enough to identify a particular person. However, writing that a professor in the political science department who teaches Introduction to Law beats his spouse would be sufficient identification.

Falsity is a required element of a defamation claim. Truth is generally the best defense for any person accused of defaming another. For example, if someone said, "the authors of this textbook are convicted sex offenders," the person would be uttering false statements. However, if someone called a person listed on a sex offender registry "a convicted sex offender," that would be a true statement. Many states also recognize a defense called the *substantial truth doctrine*, which holds that a defendant is not liable for defamation as long as the gist or essence of the story is true. A newspaper crime reporter inaccurately writes that police arrested a defendant for possession of marijuana, cocaine, and meth. It turns out that the police charged the defendant only with possession of marijuana and cocaine. Even though the reporter made a mistake, the gist of the story was true.

Another required element of a defamation claim is that the statement must be capable of having a defamatory meaning. One federal court explained that calling a personal-injury attorney an "ambulance chaser" could be defamatory because attorneys are forbidden by their lawyer ethics rules from directly soliciting clients. Context also can be important in determining whether certain comments are defamatory. If an editorial writer pens that a school board chairperson is a "Nazi," that may sound defamatory, but it may be permissible as an example of rhetorical hyperbole. Sportswriters sometimes have been able to defend against libel claims by relying on this defense.

Another required element of a defamation claim is some level of fault, as it is not a strict liability tort. This may be the most difficult aspect of defamation law. The level of fault depends upon the status of the plaintiff. A public official (e.g., politician) or a public figure (celebrity) must show that the defendant made the defamatory statement with **actual malice**, which is defined as acting with knowing falsity or reckless disregard of the truth. Meanwhile, a private person must only show fault or negligence.

Actual (or express) malice: Acting with knowing or deliberate falsity or reckless disregard of the truth.

This may seem like a strange rule, but the U.S. Supreme Court articulated the "actual malice" standard in its 1964 decision *New York Times Co. v. Sullivan*. The *New York Times* had printed an editorial advertisement by a group called "the Committee to Defend Dr. Martin Luther King Jr." The ad spoke about civil rights violations committed in Montgomery, Alabama, and at a university campus in the city. Even though the city did not name him, L.B. Sullivan, a city commissioner with authority over the police, sued the *Times* for libel in Alabama state court. The Alabama state court jury found for the defendant and in Sullivan's favor, mainly because the editorial advertisement contained inaccurate statements.

However, the U.S. Supreme Court reversed that decision because of its concern that punishing the press for every false statement would inhibit reporting on important public issues. Justice William J. Brennan wrote that the case must be understood "against the background of a profound national commitment to the principle that debate on public issues should be uninhibited, robust, and wide-open, and that it may well include vehement, caustic, and sometimes unpleasantly sharp attacks on government and public officials." Brennan reasoned that a defamation plaintiff who was a public official (like city commissioner Sullivan) could not recover unless he showed by clear and convincing evidence that *The New York Times* knowingly printed the false statements or acted very recklessly in printing them. Brennan explained the rule: "The constitutional guarantees require, we think, a federal rule that prohibits a public official from recovering damages for a defamatory falsehood relating to his official conduct unless he proves that the statement was made with 'actual malice'—that is, with knowledge that it was false or with reckless disregard of whether it was false or not."

The U.S. Supreme Court later extended this "actual malice" standard to public figures and limited-purpose public figures—individuals who are considered public figures for purposes of a particular controversy. Two rationales support the creation of a higher burden of proof on public officials than on private persons in defamation cases. The first is that public officials and public figures have greater access to the media to counter allegedly false and defamatory statements. The U.S. Supreme Court explained this rationale in *Gertz v. Robert Welch* (1974): "Public officials and public figures usually enjoy significantly greater access to the channels of effective communication and hence have a more realistic opportunity to counteract false statements than private individuals normally enjoy. Private individuals are therefore more vulnerable to injury, and the state interest in protecting them is correspondingly greater."

If a tabloid defames a major movie star, that movie star can use his public relations team to issue a press release and counter the false statement. However, a private person, which includes most people, would have trouble having the access to reach enough people to undo the damage of the defamatory statement.

The other reason for the differential treatment is that there is a willing price to fame and public attention. People know if they become a public official or a celebrity that there will be enhanced attention. The Court explained in its *Gertz* decision: "An individual who decides to seek governmental office must accept certain necessary consequences of that involvement in public affairs."

The question of whether someone is a public figure or a limited public figure is difficult. State courts differ in such determinations. For example, it is obvious that a mayor is subject to the *Times v. Sullivan* rule, but what about a public school teacher, a high school athlete, or a patrolling police officer? The U.S. Supreme Court in its *Gertz* decision ruled that Elmer Gertz, a well-known Chicago attorney, was a private person, not a public figure, when he sued a publication for falsely stating that he was a Communist.

Invasion of Privacy

A growing tort in the U.S. legal system is *invasion of privacy*, a tort that owes its existence to an 1890 *Harvard Law Review* article titled "The Right of Privacy." Two Boston-based attorneys, Samuel Warren and Louis

Brandeis (who later became a U.S. Supreme Court Justice), wrote the article to argue that the press should be liable when they printed material about the private affairs of others. The story, which some scholars say is dubious, is that Warren was quite upset at local press coverage of his wife and daughter at exclusive Beacon Hill parties. He wanted to support a legal theory that could silence the invasive actions of the press.

The authors talked about the "right to be let alone" and warned about two dangerous developments: (1) "numerous mechanical devices" such as "instantaneous photographs" and (2) the overreaching conduct of the press. Warren and Brandeis wrote that "the press is overstepping in every direction the obvious bounds of propriety and decency." Ironically, more than 120 years later, these remain two of the chief complaints against modern media.

The Warren-Brandeis article caused many in the legal world to think seriously about recognizing a new tort called invasion of privacy. The Georgia Supreme Court recognized a type of privacy claim in the early 1900s. Others followed suit slowly.

In the 1960s, an influential scholar named William Prosser wrote that invasion of privacy really consists of four distinct subtorts, or types of privacy: (1) intrusion, (2) public disclosure of private facts, (3) false light, and (4) appropriation.

Intrusion represents the core type of privacy, as it refers to invasive conduct that would be highly offensive to a reasonable person. Following a person around and invading his or her private space constitutes *intrusion*. Installing a hidden camera in a bathroom to spy on employees or members of the public is intrusion. If a "paparazzo" harasses a movie star, tailgates her in his car, peeps in her apartment windows, and similar conduct, then the paparazzo might be liable for intrusion. Famed paparazzo Ron Galella ran into trouble when he maintained a consistent pattern of following former First Lady Jacqueline Onassis (formerly Jackie Kennedy) and her young children. He followed the children when they rode their bicycle, romanced a servant in the Onassis home to keep tabs on the family's movements, invaded the children's private schools, and constantly photographed Jackie O. and her children in public and private places.

In *Galella v. Onassis* (2d. Cir. 1973), a federal appeals court modified but upheld an injunction that required Galella to maintain some distance between him and the Onassis family. The appeals court noted: "Galella's action went far beyond the reasonable bounds of news gathering. When weighed against the *de minimis* public importance of the daily activities of the defendant, Galella's constant surveillance, his obtrusive and intruding presence, was unwarranted and unreasonable."

Public disclosure of private facts refers to revealing very personal, highly sensitive information about a person that is not of legitimate concern to the public. Revealing someone's medical history or medical records would be public disclosure of private facts. Revealing someone's sexual orientation might form the basis of such a claim. This tort is different from defamation, because a public disclosure of private facts claim involves punishing someone for revealing truthful information.

False light invasion of privacy is the tort closest to defamation. It involves publishing information that places a person in a false light in a way that would be highly offensive to a reasonable person. A false light case requires that the defendant made false statements or falsely portrayed the plaintiff. Consider the following example. A newspaper writes a story about the prevalence of juvenile delinquency in single-parent homes. In the story, the editors run stock footage of a single mother and her teenage son. It turns out that the teenager in the picture is an honor-roll student, not a juvenile delinquent. The mother sues on behalf of her son, alleging that he was placed in a false light. False light is similar to defamation. Some states do not recognize the false-light tort because they consider it duplicative of defamation.

Appropriation prohibits someone from using someone else's name, likeness, or personality for advertising, a commercial purpose, or similar use. The *Restatement (Second) of Torts*, §652C defines the tort:

> One who appropriates to his own use or benefit the name or likeness of another is subject to liability to the other for invasion of privacy.

Appropriation or misappropriation: Using another's name, likeness, or personality for advertising, a commercial purpose, or similar use without the permission of the person.

A business owner tries to drum up business for this fledgling operation. He attaches photographs of a famous athlete, hoping that the attachment of the athlete's photo will increase his customer flow. The problem is that the business owner did not seek permission from the athlete or the athlete's agent to use his photo. Instead, the business owner appropriated the image of the athlete for commercial use.

PRODUCTS LIABILITY

Products liability is a branch of tort law concerned with injuries caused by defective products that harm consumers or users. *Products liability* often is governed by statute more than the common law in many states. This body of law is based on three different theories of recovery: (1) strict liability, (2) negligence, or (3) warranty.

Strict liability forms the primary basis of liability for manufacturers of products. It may seem harsh to hold manufacturers liable if they did not intend to cause harm and even used reasonable care in creating the product, but manufacturers are in a better position to defray the costs of harm than the consumer who has been injured by the product. Strict liability is justified on the basis that manufacturers are economically better able to deal with the damages caused by defective products.

Restatement of Torts

Section 402A

Special liability of seller of product for physical harm to user or consumer.

(1) One who sells any product in a defective condition unreasonably dangerous to the user or consumer or to his property is subject to liability for physical harm thereby caused to the ultimate user or consumer, or to his property, if

    (a) the seller is engaged in the business of selling such a product, and

    (b) it is expected to and does reach the user or consumer without substantial change in the condition in which it is sold.

(2) The rule stated in subsection (1) applies although

    (a) the seller has exercised all possible care in the preparation and sale of his product; and

    (b) the user or consumer has not bought the product from or entered into any contractual relation with the seller.

Another reason for strict liability is that modern products are complicated and intricate. It may be very difficult for the average consumer or the consumer's lawyer to prove that the product was designed or manufactured negligently. Strict liability will allow more consumers to recover damages and be made whole.

Products liability lawsuits result from different problems. Sometimes a product is produced properly the vast majority of the time, but every now and then one product is produced poorly. This is called a manufacturing defect. If a manufacturer produces 100 go-carts, 98 or 99 of them will run properly and are not unreasonably dangerous. However, the 1 or 2 problem go-carts may have manufacturing defects.

Design defects are different. These refer to an inherent flaw in the construction of the product. An example of a design defect might be a swimming pool that is not deep enough near the diving board. This could lead to tragic consequences, as individuals could suffer severe head injuries because the pool was too shallow near the diving board.

A classic example of a design defect was the Ford Pinto. Ford Motor Company introduced the Pinto as an affordable, subcompact car. The Pintos seemed fine, but several people died from rear-end vehicle accidents. It was discovered that a defect in the fuel delivery system made it more likely that the car would explode when in rear-end accidents. Evidence showed that Ford executives knew of the design defect, but decided that economically it would be too burdensome and expensive to fix the problem. This resulted in juries imposing some large damage awards, including punitive damage awards, in some cases.

Another area ripe for product liability actions includes *failure to warn* cases. The theory behind this type of a case is that the manufacturer should warn the consumer of certain dangers associated with the product even if the dangers come from misuse by the consumer. A court could look at whether the warning would lead to a reduction in the number of accidents or injuries.

Some product liability cases are tried under a *breach of warranty* theory. This is a hybrid of tort and contract law in which a seller or manufacturer claims or warranties that a product is of a certain level or quality. There are two types of warranties: express warranties and implied warranties. In an express warranty, a seller expressly represents that a product is of a certain quality. For example, if a seller proclaims that a window is "shatterproof," that is an express warranty that the product will not shatter in most circumstances. An implied warranty, which is based more on contract law, means that the product will meet a certain standard.

TORT REFORM

Many groups believe that the tort system in the United States is broken, that too many frivolous lawsuits are filed, that punitive damage awards are excessive, and that too many people simply want to get rich off other's hard work and entrepreneurship. This forms the basis for many complaints about the tort system generally included under the "tort reform" movement.

The American Tort Reform Association seeks to reform the civil justice system, believing that the current $246 billion civil justice system is too expensive and financially burdensome for doctors, businesses, and others.

Certainly, there are frivolous lawsuits. A couple sued an airline company for millions of dollars for insufficient legroom. A man sued an adult entertainment establishment because an exotic dancer's breasts hit him too hard on his head during a lap dance. A man sued because at a concert he saw two women in the men's bathroom.

Mission of the American Tort Reform Association (ATRA)	
ATRA supports an aggressive civil justice reform agenda that includes the following: • Health care liability reform • Class action reform • Promotion of jury service • Abolition of the rule of joint and several liability	• Abolition of the collateral source rule • Limits on punitive damages • Limits on noneconomic damages • Production liability reform • Appeal bond reform • Sound science in the courtroom • Stopping regulation through litigation.

Source: http://www.atra.org/about/

Critics of tort reform counter that there are adequate ways to deal with frivolous lawsuits. Defendants can file motions to dismiss for failure to state a claim under Rule 12 of the Rules of Civil Procedure. Courts can issue sanctions against attorneys and parties who file frivolous lawsuits.

Another major area of contention in tort reform is punitive damages, those damages reserved for the most egregious of actions by tortfeasors. The U.S. Supreme Court has provided that some punitive damage awards are so excessive that they can violate the Due Process Clause of the Fourteenth Amendment. A case in point was the Court's 1996 decision in *BMW of North America v. Gore*. In this decision, a doctor named Ira Gore Jr. purchased a black BMW for more than $40,000. He took the car to a detail shop to make it look snazzier. He then discovered that the car had been repainted. BMW had a policy that if repairing a car cost 3 percent or less of the suggested retail price of the car, it would not disclose that the car had some repairs and it would be sold as a new car.

Feeling cheated, Gore sued BMW for compensatory and punitive damages. A jury awarded him $4,000 in compensatory damages and $4 million in punitive damages, reduced by the trial judge to $2 million. The rationale for the high punitive damage award was that BMW had sold 1,000 cars without disclosing that they had suffered some form of minor damage.

Writing for the majority, Justice John Paul Stevens reasoned: "Elementary notions of fairness enshrined in our constitutional jurisprudence dictate that a person receive fair notice not only of the conduct that will subject him to punishment but also of the severity of the penalty that a State may impose." Stevens identified three main criteria for reviewing punitive damage awards: the "degree of reprehensibility" of the tortfeasor's conduct, the ratio between compensatory and punitive damages, and "sanctions for comparable misconduct." Because the ratio of compensatory damages ($4,000) to punitive damages ($2 million) was 500 to 1, the Court rejected the jury's award, even as reduced by the judge from $4 million to $2 million.

Tort reform has become a hot-button political topic in recent years. For many years, it was a divisive political issue, with Republicans generally favoring tort reform limits more than Democrats. Recently, however, President Barack Obama may have signaled a change by saying that he was not opposed to setting some limits on medical malpractice suits in order to reduce health costs.

CHAPTER SUMMARY

1. Tort law is designed to provide compensation or another remedy for individuals who have been harmed by socially unreasonable conduct.

There are three main types of torts: (1) intentional torts, (2) torts of negligence, and (3) strict liability torts.

2. Tort law differs from criminal law. Unlike criminal law, tort law is a form of civil law. The main purpose of tort law is compensation, whereas the main purpose of criminal law is punishment. The standard used in tort cases most of the time is preponderance of the evidence, and the standard used in criminal cases is beyond a reasonable doubt.

3. Assault, battery, false imprisonment, and intentional infliction of emotional distress are the main intentional torts against a person. Assault and battery often go hand-in-hand, with the key differences being that assault requires apprehension of contact, and battery requires an actual offensive or harmful contact. False imprisonment involves confining someone against his or her will. Intentional infliction of emotional distress involves outrageous conduct that causes severe emotional distress.

4. Tort suits, like other causes of actions, have discrete statutes of limitations. These are laws that provide for a specific period of time in which a plaintiff has to file suit. If a plaintiff fails to file a lawsuit within the appropriate statute of limitations, he or she loses the right to sue.

5. Negligence refers to socially unreasonably conduct caused by failing to use reasonable care. The requisite elements of negligence claims are duty, breach of duty, causation, and damages.

6. *Res ipsa loquitur* and *negligence per se* are important doctrines that often apply in determining whether there was negligence and, specifically, breach of duty. *Res ipsa loquitur* applies when the only explanation of plaintiff's injury is negligence and the defendant has exclusive control over the instrumentality that caused the harm. Negligence per se applies when the defendant violates a statute or regulation that was designed to protect a class of persons such as the plaintiff.

7. In tort law, there are three main types of damages: (1) nominal damages, (2) compensatory damages, and (3) punitive damages. Nominal damages are damages in name only. Compensatory damages are damages designed to compensate the plaintiff for the harm he or she has suffered. Punitive damages are damages designed to punish the tortfeasor.

8. Comparative negligence and contributory negligence are the two basic systems of negligence in U.S. law. Most jurisdictions employ some form of comparative negligence, which means that the negligence of the plaintiff and defendant are compared, and the plaintiff's recovery is limited by the percentage of the plaintiff's own negligence. Contributory negligence, used only in a few states, provides that a plaintiff cannot recover damages for negligence if he or she contributed to his or her injuries.

9. Malpractice refers to professional negligence: failure of professionals such as lawyers and doctors to adhere to applicable standards of care. In many malpractice cases, plaintiffs must present expert testimony showing a breach of duty.

10. Negligent hiring and negligent retention are torts that apply when an employer hires or retains an employee whom they knew or should have known presented a risk to the public. Some employers commission criminal background checks to avoid such claims.

11. Defamation is a tort that consists of libel and slander. Libel is written defamation and slander is oral defamation. Libel law depends in part on the status of the plaintiff. Public officials and public figures who sue for defamation must show evidence of actual malice, whereas private persons usually must show negligence.

12. Invasion of privacy is a growing tort that involves invasive or harmful conduct that is highly offensive to a reasonable person. The four types of invasion of privacy in tort law are (1) intrusion, (2) public disclosure of private facts, (3) false light, and (4) appropriation.

13. Products liability is the area of tort law that holds manufacturers, sellers, and suppliers of products liable for unreasonably dangerous products that harm consumers or users. Products liability actions are sometimes based in strict liability but in other jurisdictions are based also in negligence and warranty.

14. Tort reform is a movement designed to reform the civil justice system. Many believe there are too many frivolous laws suits, that punitive damage awards are excessive, and that too many people simply want to get rich off others' hard work and entrepreneurship.

REVIEW EXERCISE

Match the following terms with their most appropriate meaning.

TERMS	MEANING
1. Tortfeasor	____ failure to exercise due care or acting carelessly or recklessly in a way that causes harm to others
2. Intentional torts	
3. Negligence	____ liability not requiring intent or proof of fault, such as defective product
4. Strict liability	____ activity that substantially and unreasonably interferes with plaintiff's use and enjoyment of property or land
5. Assault	
6. Battery	____ harmful or offensive contact
7. False imprisonment	____ apprehension of harmful or offensive contact
8. Nuisance	____ unjustifiable intentional confinement of another against his or her will
9. Statute of limitations	____ failure on the part of the tortfeasor to adhere to a reasonable standard of care
10. Breach of duty of care	____ the unexcused violation of a law or regulation by a defendant that leads to harm suffered by the victim

11. Negligence per se
12. *Res ipsa loquitur*
13. Good Samaritan statute
14. Compensatory damages
15. Proximate or legal cause
16. Punitive damages
17. Comparative negligence
18. Contributory negligence
19. Malpractice
20. Defamation
21. Actual malice
22. Appropriation

____ damages designed to compensate plaintiff for harm

____ system where plaintiff's recovery is reduced by percentage of his or her own fault

____ tortfeasor intends a certain result or acts with substantial certainty that his conduct will result in harm to another

____ acting with knowing or deliberate falsity or reckless disregard of the truth

____ damages awarded to punish the tortfeasor

____ common-law principle that the defendant's negligence can be inferred through circumstantial evidence

____ time period in which to file a lawsuit

____ individual who commits a tort

____ law providing some protection for rescuers who attempt to help people in harm, except for extreme negligence

____ that which, in a natural and continuous sequence, unbroken by any intervening cause, produces injury and without which the result would not have occurred

____ communication of a false statement of fact that harms someone's reputation

____ system in which plaintiff is denied recovery because he was also negligent

____ use of someone's likeness for commercial use without permission

____ negligence by a professional

DISCUSSION QUESTIONS

1. How can tort law differ from state to state? Do you think there should be that much variation?
2. Does your state have a system of comparative or contributory negligence? If it is a system of comparative negligence, is it controlled by statute or by a court decision?
3. Do you believe that punitive damages represent a windfall for plaintiffs? Should there be tort reform that limits the amount of punitive damages in certain types of tort cases?
4. Find an example of a court decision in your state that deals with intentional infliction of emotional distress. What type of conduct was involved in that case? Do you agree with the result of the decision? Do you think that medical testimony should be

required to prove severe emotional distress?
5. Does your state have a shopkeepers' privilege statute? If so, read the statute and determine whether you think it provides a fair, workable standard for merchants. How long is a reasonable amount of time to detain a suspected shoplifter? Why should merchants receive any immunity if they wrongly suspect someone of shoplifting?
6. Do you believe that plaintiffs in professional negligence (malpractice) cases should be required to submit expert testimony to prove their cases?
7. Does your state have a Good Samaritan law? Do you believe that there should be any type of immunity for those who attempt to rescue others?

8. Do you believe that public officials and public figures should have to meet a higher standard to sue for defamation than do private persons? Do you think the actual malice standard gives too much, too little, or just the right amount of protection for media defendants?

9. Does your state recognize all four privacy subtorts: intrusion, public disclosure of private facts, false light, and appropriation? If it does not recognize one of them, what is the rationale? Should there ever be a viable intrusion claim when the person is in public places?

10. Do you believe that employers should be held liable for hiring individuals who commit crimes? Should a detailed background check be mandatory for all employers?

11. Should the U.S. Congress pass legislation that limits liability in medical malpractice cases? Would it reduce health care costs or just sanction more negligence?

12. Should strict liability be the proper standard to use in tort lawsuits based on defective products? Is it fair to manufacturers or sellers or should a system of negligence be used?

ASSIGNMENTS

ASSIGNMENT: Remember what you learned about statutes of limitations, a very important concept in law. Find out the statute of limitations for intentional torts against a person in your state and the statute of limitations for intentional torts against property in your state.

ASSIGNMENT: This chapter also talked about punitive damages. Are there any limitations in your state, in either the state code or in the state's common law (case law), that provide for a ceiling on punitive damages?

SOURCES AND SUGGESTED READING

Helland, Eric, and Alexander Tabarrok. 2006. *Judge and Jury: American Tort Law on Trial*. Oakland, Calif.: Independent Institute.

Levmore, Saul, and Catherine M. Sharkey. 2009. *Foundations of Tort Law*. New York: Foundation Press.

White, G. Edward. 2003. *Tort Law in America: An Intellectual History*. 2d. ed. New York: Oxford University Press.

COURT CASES

BMW of North America v. Gore, 517 U.S. 559 (1996)

Curtis v. Lein, 239 P.3d 1078 (Wash. 2010)

Fisher v. Carrousel Motor Hotel, 424 S.W.2d 627 (Tex. 1967).

Galella v. Onassis, 487 F.2d 986 (2d. Cir. 1973)

Gertz v. Robert Welch, 418 U.S. 323 (1974)

Hassing v. Wortman, 333 N.W.2d 765 (Neb. 1983)

Katko v. Briney, 183 N.W.2d 657 (Iowa 1971)

McIntyre v. Ballentine, 833 S.W.2d 52 (Tenn. 1992)

Palsgraf v. Long Island Railroad, 162 N.E. 99 (N.Y. 1928)

WEB SITES

American Association for Justice (formerly Association of Trial Lawyers of America) http://www.justice.org/cps/rde/xchg/justice/hs.xsl/default.htm

American Tort Reform Association
  http://www.atra.org/
Findlaw on Torts
  http://www.findlaw.com/01topics/22tort/
  index.html
Lawyers for Civil Justice
  http://www.lfcj.com/

Media Law Resource Center
  http://www.medialaw.org
Personal Injury Center
  http://injury.findlaw.com/

Introduction to Family Law

A young couple in love with each other wishes to enter into a formal acknowledgement of their relationship by marrying. Two people of the same sex also wish to have their relationship recognized by the state as a formal marriage. Still another couple has tired of continual fighting and disagreements, and they wish to terminate their marriage by seeking a divorce. An already-divorced couple continues to battle over custody and visitation rights. Still another couple realizes they can't have children through the traditional method and wish to adopt a child.

A young man believes that he is the father of a child borne by his former girlfriend. He wishes to establish paternity to obtain his rights as a parent. A young woman rearing her young child on her own believes that she should obtain help from the young man with whom she conceived the child. She sues to establish child support.

All of these subjects—marriage, divorce, child custody and visitation, paternity, child support, and adoption—comprise an area of law known as family law or domestic relations. Most state law codes contain a separate section or sections, called a title or titles, that deal exclusively with family law. For example, Tennessee has a separate title (Title 36) in its collection of laws known as the *Tennessee Code Annotated* called "Domestic Relations." Attorneys often specialize in a particular area of family law given its complexity.

Family law interacts with many other areas of law, including contracts, torts, crimes, and other areas. Marriage represents a civil contract between two parties, usually a man and a woman. Both parties must consent to the marriage just as with any other type of contract. Sometimes parties will enter into contractual arrangements before marriage, referred to as prenuptial agreements. Sometimes parties to a marriage will allege criminal and/or tortious conduct committed by their partner. For example, one parent may accuse the other party of kidnapping the children by acting contrary to a visitation agreement. Or one parent may accuse another party of intentional infliction of emotional distress—a tort action—for withholding the children from the other parent.

MARRIAGE

Marriage is a civil contract or union between two persons (in nearly all U.S. jurisdictions between one man and one woman) who live together and share their lives. Marriage ideally involves two people sharing emotional and physical bonds till "death due us part," typically part of a marriage vow.

Unfortunately, we know that a large number of marriages dissolve and end up in divorce, the formal process by which a marriage is legally terminated. Most marriages occur in a ceremony, often a religious-based ceremony performed by a minister or preacher. Many other people are married through a ceremony performed by a secular figure such as a judge or a justice of the peace.

Marriage:
Civil contract between a man and a woman (in most jurisdictions) to live together and share their lives.

State Marriage Laws

Michigan: MCLS §551.2 Marriage As Civil Contract; Consent; License; Solemnization

So far as its validity in law is concerned, marriage is a civil contract between a man and a woman, to which the consent of parties capable in law of contracting is essential. Consent alone is not enough to effectuate a legal marriage on and after January 1, 1957. Consent shall be followed by obtaining a license as required by . . . law.

A few states recognize a **common-law marriage**, meaning that these states recognize a couple as legally married even though they have not performed a ceremonial marriage. In common-law marriages, if the parties reside together for a certain number of years (often seven) and hold themselves out as a married couple, then they will have a valid, *common-law* marriage. The states of Alabama, Colorado, Idaho, Iowa, Kansas, Montana, Rhode Island, South Carolina, Texas, and Utah still recognize common-law marriages. The District of Columbia also recognizes common-law marriages. Georgia recognizes existing common-law marriages that were entered into before January 1, 1997.

Common-law marriage:
Some states recognize that couples living together for a period of years (usually seven) and that hold themselves out as married, are regarded as having marriage rights and duties.

Generally, a party must show three things in order to establish a common-law marriage: (1) capacity to enter into a marriage-type relationship; (2) present, mutual agreement to permanently enter the marriage relationship to the exclusion of all other relationships; and (3) public recognition of the relationship as a marriage and public assumption of marital duties and cohabitation. If the parties don't own property together, share bank accounts, or take the same last name, a court might find that there is no common-law marriage.

People must provide certain information to the government to obtain a marriage license. They must provide their names, addresses, ages, and social security numbers to obtain the license from the local county clerk. Sometimes more information is required, such as place of birth, current job, and previous marriages. The individuals must swear that the information they provide is true. The parties obtain the marriage license, which they give to the person performing the marriage ceremony. As with any license, applicants also must pay a fee for the license that varies in amount from state to state. In the past, marriage applicants used to have to take blood tests before marriage. This requirement has been eliminated in nearly all states. Montana still has a requirement for a blood test.

Some states recognize a new type of marriage called a **covenant marriage** in which the parties agree that marriage is a lifelong bond between them. These individuals willingly enter authorized premarital counseling and agree that grounds for divorce for them will be more limited. A party can obtain a divorce in a covenant marriage only when there has been a complete breach of the marriage agreement, such as adultery or the commission of a felony. This means that parties who enter into a covenant marriage will not be able to be divorced simply on the basis of "irreconcilable differences," the most common ground for divorce where the parties simply can't get along with each other. Arkansas law defines a covenant marriage as "a marriage entered into by one male and one female who understand and agree that the marriage between them is a lifelong relationship." Only a few states recognize covenant marriages, including Louisiana, Arizona, and Arkansas.

Covenant marriage:
A couple freely enters into authorized premarital counseling and agree that grounds for divorce will be more limiting for them.

"Covenant Marriage" Law

ARIZONA

A.R.S. §25-901 (2011)
§25-901. Covenant Marriage; Declaration of Intent; Filing Requirements

A. Persons who have the legal capacity to marry pursuant to this title may enter into a covenant marriage by declaring their intent to do so on their application for a license obtained pursuant to section 25-121 and by complying with the requirements of this chapter. The returned marriage license shall be recorded as provided by section 25-123 with an indication that the marriage is a covenant marriage, and the declaration shall be filed by the clerk.

B. A declaration of intent to enter into a covenant marriage shall contain all of the following:

1. The following written statement:

Covenant Marriage

We solemnly declare that marriage is a covenant between a man and a woman who agree to live together as husband and wife for as long as they both live. We have chosen each other carefully and have received

continued >

premarital counseling on the nature, purposes and responsibilities of marriage. We understand that a *covenant marriage* is for life. If we experience marital difficulties, we commit ourselves to take all reasonable efforts to preserve our marriage, including marital counseling.

With full knowledge of what this commitment means, we do declare that our marriage will be bound by Arizona law on covenant marriages and we promise to love, honor and care for one another as husband and wife for the rest of our lives.

2. An affidavit by the parties that they have received premarital counseling from a member of the clergy or from a marriage counselor. Premarital counseling shall include a discussion of the seriousness of covenant marriage, communication of the fact that a covenant marriage is a commitment for life, a discussion of the obligation to seek marital counseling in times of marital difficulties and a discussion of the exclusive grounds for legally terminating a covenant marriage by dissolution of marriage or legal separation.

3. The signatures of both parties witnessed by a court clerk.

C. A notarized attestation that is signed by the clergy or counselor must be submitted with the application for a license and shall confirm that the parties were counseled as to the nature and purpose of the marriage and the grounds for its termination and that the counselor provided to the parties the informational pamphlet developed by the supreme court pursuant to this chapter. The clerk shall document that the attestation was submitted.

Forbidden Marriages

The law does not recognize certain types of marriages. For example, states have different laws limiting the right of people to marry certain family members. Marrying a family member who is too closely related is called **incest**. Connecticut law provides: "No person may marry such person's parent, grandparent, child, grandchild, sibling, parent's sibling, sibling's child, stepparent or stepchild. Any marriage within these degrees is void." Such a marriage can be annulled, or viewed as if it never took place. There is no need to file a formal divorce decree.

Incest:
Marrying a family member who is too closely related in blood line.

Georgia's Incest Law
Limiting Marriages to Certain Family Members

§19-3-3. Degrees of Relationship Within Which Intermarriage Prohibited; Penalty; Effect Of Prohibited Marriage

(a) Any person who marries a person to whom he knows he is related, either by blood or by marriage, as follows:

(1) Father and daughter or stepdaughter;

(2) Mother and son or stepson;

continued >

> (3) Brother and sister of the whole blood or the half blood;
>
> (4) Grandparent and grandchild;
>
> (5) Aunt and nephew; or
>
> (6) Uncle and niece shall be punished by imprisonment for not less than one nor more than three years.
>
> (b) Marriages declared to be unlawful under subsection (a) of this Code section shall be void from their inception.

Not all family-related marriages are void in all states, as first cousins can marry in several states. For example, Tennessee allows first cousins to marry.

Every state prohibits individuals from having multiple spouses. If a person marries more than one person, that person has committed the crime of **bigamy**. In the late nineteenth century, an individual filed a religious freedom-based challenge to a bigamy law, but the Supreme Court ruled in *Reynolds v. United States*, 98 U.S. 145 (1879) that states had legitimate reasons to prohibit multiple marriages by one person.

Bigamy:
Having multiple spouses, which is prohibited in all U.S. jurisdictions.

Most states have age limitations for marriages. In Ohio a male must be 18 and a female must be at least 16. In many states a minor (person under the age of majority) must obtain the consent of a parent or guardian before marriage.

California Laws on Marriage Age

Cal. Family Code §301. Capacity of Adult to Consent to and Consummate Marriage

An unmarried male of the age of 18 years or older, and an unmarried female of the age of 18 years or older, and not otherwise disqualified, are capable of consenting to and consummating marriage.

§302. Capacity of Minor to Consent to and Consummate Marriage

(a) An unmarried male or female under the age of 18 years is capable of consenting to and consummating marriage upon obtaining a court order granting permission to the underage person or persons to marry.

(b) The court order and written consent of the parents of each underage person, or of one of the parents or the guardian of each underage person shall be filed with the clerk of the court, and a certified copy of the order shall be presented to the county clerk at the time the marriage license is issued.

Same-Sex Marriage

In the vast majority of states, parties of the same sex are legally forbidden to marry each other. Many states have a specific law or constitutional amendment proscribing such marriages. Consider the following Alabama law.

Alabama Law Forbidding Same-Sex Marriages

Code of Ala. §30-1-19 (2011)

§30-1-19. Alabama Marriage Protection Act; Marriage Defined; Marriage Between Individuals of Same Sex Invalid

(a) This section shall be known and may be cited as the "Alabama Marriage Protection Act."

(b) Marriage is inherently a unique relationship between a man and a woman. As a matter of public policy, this state has a special interest in encouraging, supporting, and protecting the unique relationship in order to promote, among other goals, the stability and welfare of society and its children. A marriage contracted between individuals of the same sex is invalid in this state.

(c) Marriage is a sacred covenant, solemnized between a man and a woman, which, when the legal capacity and consent of both parties is present, establishes their relationship as husband and wife, and which is recognized by the state as a civil contract.

(d) No marriage license shall be issued in the State of Alabama to parties of the same sex.

(e) The State of Alabama shall not recognize as valid any marriage of parties of the same sex that occurred or was alleged to have occurred as a result of the law of any jurisdiction regardless of whether a marriage license was issued.

In many states, the state constitution—in addition to a statute or law—prohibits same-sex marriage. Opponents of same-sex marriage felt so strongly against the idea of gay marriage that they amended the state constitution. Consider the following examples.

State Constitutional Provisions Prohibiting Same-Sex Marriages

Arkansas Constitution, Amendment 83, §1: "Marriage consists only of the union of one man and one woman."

Georgia: Georgia Constitution, Art. I, §4: "(a) This state shall recognize as marriage only the union of man and woman. Marriages between persons of the same sex are prohibited in this state.

(b) No union between persons of the same sex shall be recognized by this state as entitled to the benefits of marriage. This state shall not give effect to any public act, record, or judicial proceeding of any other state or jurisdiction respecting a relationship between persons of the same sex that is treated as a marriage under the laws of such other state or jurisdiction. The courts of this state shall have no jurisdiction to grant a divorce or separate maintenance

---

continued >

with respect to any such relationship or otherwise to consider or rule on any of the parties' respective rights arising as a result of or in connection with such relationship."

Michigan: Michigan Constitution, Art. I, §25: "To secure and preserve the benefits of marriage for our society and for future generations of children, the union of one man and one woman in marriage shall be the only agreement recognized as a marriage or similar union for any purpose."

Missouri: Missouri Constitution, Art. I, §33: "That to be valid and recognized in this state, a marriage shall exist only between a man and a woman."

South Dakota: South Dakota Constitution, Art. 21, §9: "Only marriage between a man and a woman shall be valid or recognized in South Dakota. The uniting of two or more persons in a civil union, domestic partnership, or other quasi-marital relationship shall not be valid or recognized in South Dakota."

However, same-sex persons can marry in the states of Connecticut, Maine, Massachusetts, New Hampshire, Vermont, and Iowa. In 2009, the Iowa Supreme Court legalized gay marriage.

Iowa Supreme Court in *Varnum v. Brien* 763 N.W.2d 862 (2009)

So, today, this court again faces an important issue that hinges on our definition of equal protection. This issue comes to us with the same importance as our landmark cases of the past. The same-sex-marriage debate waged in this case is part of a strong national dialogue centered on a fundamental, deep-seated, traditional institution that has excluded, by state action, a particular class of Iowans. This class of people asks a simple and direct question: How can a state premised on the constitutional principle of equal protection justify exclusion of a class of Iowans from civil marriage? . . .

Therefore, with respect to the subject and purposes of Iowa's marriage laws, we find that the plaintiffs are similarly situated compared to heterosexual persons. Plaintiffs are in committed and loving relationships, many raising families, just like heterosexual couples. Moreover, official recognition of their status provides an institutional basis for defining their fundamental relational rights and responsibilities, just as it does for heterosexual couples. Society benefits, for example, from providing same-sex couples a stable framework within which to raise their children and the power to make health care and end-of-life decisions for loved ones, just as it does when that framework is provided for opposite-sex couples.

continued >

In short, for purposes of Iowa's marriage laws, which are designed to bring a sense of order to the legal relationships of committed couples and their families in myriad ways, plaintiffs are similarly situated in every important respect, but for their sexual orientation. As indicated above, this distinction cannot defeat the application of equal protection analysis through the application of the similarly situated concept because, under this circular approach, all distinctions would evade equal protection review. Therefore, with respect to the government's purpose of "providing an institutional basis for defining the fundamental relational rights and responsibilities of persons," same-sex couples are similarly situated to opposite-sex couples.

A few states do not recognize gay marriages, but they do recognize an intermediate step called **civil unions**. These are a recognized category of relationship between two persons that provides many of the benefits of marriage. It represents a separate legal category that allows persons of the same sex to enter into a protected and recognized legal relationship that accords benefits to its parties. Vermont became the first state to pass a civil union law in 2000. In November 2008, Connecticut passed a law allowing civil unions between members of the same sex. While not marriages, civil unions do provide benefits to the people in the union, but those benefits may not be recognized in other states.

Civil union: Relationship between two persons providing many of the benefits of marriage (recognized in a few states).

LawSpeak—Vermont Civil Union Statute

§1201. Definitions
As used in this chapter:
(1) "Certificate of civil union" means a document that certifies that the persons named on the certificate have established a civil union in this state in compliance with this chapter and 18 V.S.A. chapter 106.
(2) "Civil union" means that two eligible persons have established a relationship pursuant to this chapter, and may receive the benefits and protections and be subject to the responsibilities of spouses.
(3) "Commissioner" means the commissioner of health.
(4) "Marriage" means the legally recognized union of one man and one woman.
(5) "Party to a civil union" means a person who has established a civil union pursuant to this chapter and 18 V.S.A. chapter 106. (Added 1999, No. 91 (Adj. Sess.), §3.)

§1202. Requisites of a Valid Civil Union
For a civil union to be established in Vermont, it shall be necessary that the parties to a civil union satisfy all of the following criteria:
(1) Not be a party to another civil union or a marriage.
(2) Be of the same sex and therefore excluded from the marriage laws of this state.

continued >

(3) Meet the criteria and obligations set forth in 18 V.S.A. chapter 106.

§1204. Benefits, Protections and Responsibilities of Parties to a Civil Union

(a) Parties to a civil union shall have all the same benefits, protections and responsibilities under law, whether they derive from statute, administrative or court rule, policy, common law or any other source of civil law, as are granted to spouses in a marriage.

(b) A party to a civil union shall be included in any definition or use of the terms "spouse," "family," "immediate family," "dependent," "next of kin," and other terms that denote the spousal relationship, as those terms are used throughout the law.

(c) Parties to a civil union shall be responsible for the support of one another to the same degree and in the same manner as prescribed under law for married persons.

(d) The law of domestic relations, including annulment, separation and divorce, child custody and support, and property division and maintenance shall apply to parties to a civil union.

(e) The following is a nonexclusive list of legal benefits, protections and responsibilities of spouses, which shall apply in like manner to parties to a civil union:

(1) laws relating to title, tenure, descent and distribution, intestate succession, waiver of will, survivorship, or other incidents of the acquisition, ownership, or transfer, inter vivos or at death, of real or personal property, including eligibility to hold real and personal property as tenants by the entirety (parties to a civil union meet the common law unity of person qualification for purposes of a tenancy by the entirety);

(2) causes of action related to or dependent upon spousal status, including an action for wrongful death, emotional distress, loss of consortium, dramshop, or other torts or actions under contracts reciting, related to, or dependent upon spousal status;

(3) probate law and procedure, including nonprobate transfer;

(4) adoption law and procedure;

(5) group insurance for state employees under 3 V.S.A. §631, and continuing care contracts under 8 V.S.A. §8005;

(6) spouse abuse programs under 3 V.S.A. §18;

(7) prohibitions against discrimination based upon marital status;

(8) victim's compensation rights under 13 V.S.A. §5351;

(9) workers' compensation benefits;

(10) laws relating to emergency and nonemergency medical care and treatment, hospital visitation and notification, including the Patient's Bill of Rights under 18 V.S.A. chapter 42 and the Nursing Home Residents' Bill of Rights under 33 V.S.A. chapter 73;

(11) advance directives under 18 V.S.A. chapter 111;

(12) family leave benefits under 21 V.S.A. chapter 5, subchapter 4A;

continued >

(13) public assistance benefits under state law;

(14) laws relating to taxes imposed by the state or a municipality;

(15) laws relating to immunity from compelled testimony and the marital communication privilege;

(16) the homestead rights of a surviving spouse under 27 V.S.A. §105 and homestead property tax allowance under 32 V.S.A. §6062;

(17) laws relating to loans to veterans under 8 V.S.A. §1849;

(18) the definition of family farmer under 10 V.S.A. §272;

(19) laws relating to the making, revoking and objecting to anatomical gifts by others under 18 V.S.A. §5240;

(20) state pay for military service under 20 V.S.A. §1544;

(21) application for early voter absentee ballot under 17 V.S.A. §2532;

(22) family landowner rights to fish and hunt under 10 V.S.A. §4253;

(23) legal requirements for assignment of wages under 8 V.S.A. §2235; and

(24) affirmance of relationship under 15 V.S.A. §7.

(f) The rights of parties to a civil union, with respect to a child of whom either becomes the natural parent during the term of the civil union, shall be the same as those of a married couple, with respect to a child of whom either spouse becomes the natural parent during the marriage. (Added 1999, No. 91 (Adj. Sess.), §3; amended 2001, No. 6, §12(a), eff. April 10, 2001; 2001, No. 140 (Adj. Sess.), §19, eff. June 21, 2002.)

Gay marriage proponents point to the law's evolution with regard to interracial marriages, which used to be forbidden in many states. The first state supreme court to recognize such marriages was the California high court in *Perez v. Sharp*, 198 P.2d 17 (Cal. 1948). It took the U.S. Supreme Court nearly 20 years in *Loving v. Virginia*, 388 U.S. 1 (1967), to strike down a state law banning such marriages. The Court ruled that a Virginia law banning such marriages violated the equal protection clause of the Fourteenth Amendment. This clause often prohibits the government from discriminating against individuals based on race. (See Chapter 9.) At the time of the *Loving* decision, more than a dozen states still had laws banning interracial marriages.

Chief Justice Earl Warren in *Loving v. Virginia* (1967)

There is patently no legitimate overriding purpose independent of invidious racial discrimination which justifies this classification. The fact that Virginia prohibits only interracial marriages involving white persons

continued >

demonstrates that the racial classifications must stand on their own justification, as measures designed to maintain White Supremacy. We have consistently denied the constitutionality of measures which restrict the rights of citizens on account of race. There can be no doubt that restricting the freedom to marry solely because of racial classifications violates the central meaning of the Equal Protection Clause.

Premarital Agreements

Premarital agreements, or **prenuptial agreements**, are enforceable contracts that the parties to an impending marriage enter into to protect their individual assets. Usually, a wealthy person might wish to enter into such an agreement in order to ensure that his or her money does not become part of a marital estate and become divided if there is a divorce. These agreements are valid as long as each party willingly entered into the agreement and there was no fraud committed during the process. For example, a party might be able to contest a prenuptial agreement if he or she did not receive full knowledge of the available assets. A party could also contest such an agreement if it is too one-sided or *unconscionable* under state law.

Prenuptial agreements:
Enforceable contracts that the parties enter into to protect their individual assets before marriage.

More than half the states have adopted the Uniform Premarital Agreement Act, which describes when prenuptial agreements are valid and enforceable. Under this law, agreements are not enforceable if one party did not enter into the agreement voluntarily or did not receive full and fair disclosure of the other party's assets. These states have adopted a version of this uniform law: Arizona, Arkansas, California, Connecticut, Delaware, Hawaii, Idaho, Illinois, Indiana, Iowa, Kansas, Maine, Montana, Nebraska, Nevada, New Jersey, New Mexico, North Carolina, North Dakota, Oregon, Rhode Island, South Dakota, Texas, Utah, Virginia, and Wisconsin.

Prenuptial agreements can cover the gamut of family law, including rights and obligations, disposition of property, spousal support or alimony, life insurance policies, and other financial arrangements. However, the parties cannot contract away the right to child support. For example, Arkansas law states, "The right of a child to support may not be adversely affected by a pre-marital agreement."

DIVORCE

Divorce refers to the process of formally ending a marriage. The legal document that a court approves to end a marriage is called a **divorce decree**. In many states, a party files for divorce, specifying a ground for the action.

Divorce:
Process of formally ending a marriage.

Divorce decree:
The formal legal document in which a marriage is dissolved and the parties' legal responsibilities are explained

Grounds for divorce vary from state to state. Common grounds for divorce include the failure of either party to consummate the marriage, imprisonment of one party, abandonment (desertion), bigamy, adultery, desertion, cruel and inhumane treatment, conviction of a felony or infamous crime, insanity, incurable mental illness, drug addiction, and attempted murder.

Many states allow divorces under the catch-all category **irreconcilable differences**. This means that the marriage relationship has broken down and the parties agree that they cannot live in a harmonious marriage any longer. Not every state uses the same language, as Maine uses the term "irreconcilable marital differences."

Mississippi law provides that "no divorce shall be granted on the ground of irreconcilable differences where there has been a contest or denial." North Dakota law defines irreconcilable differences as "those grounds which are determined by the court to be substantial reasons for not continuing the marriage and which make it appear that the marriage should be dissolved."

Abandonment is another recognized ground for divorce. This occurs when one spouse simply leaves or abandons the family unit for a certain period of time. In some states, that period of time is one year or longer. Connecticut law provides that grounds for divorce exist if there has been "willful desertion for one year with total neglect of duty."

Another valid reason for divorce is if a spouse commits certain crimes. It depends on individual state laws as to what types of crimes provide grounds for divorce. Tennessee law provides that legal grounds for divorce exist if a spouse is convicted of a felony and has to spend time in the penitentiary. In Georgia, any crime of moral turpitude in which a party is sentenced to prison terms two years or longer suffices as grounds for divorce. West Virginia law provides that any felony conviction can constitute a valid ground for divorce.

> **Irreconcilable differences:**
> When parties agree that the marriage has broken down and they cannot live in harmony.

> **Abandonment:**
> Recognized ground for divorce when a spouse leaves the family for a certain period of time.

Tennessee Law on Grounds for Divorce

T.C.A. 36-4-101

  (a) The following are causes of *divorce* from the bonds of matrimony:

  (1) Either party, at the time of the contract, was and still is naturally impotent and incapable of procreation;

  (2) Either party has knowingly entered into a second marriage, in violation of a previous marriage, still subsisting;

  (3) Either party has committed adultery;

  (4) Willful or malicious desertion or absence of either party, without a reasonable cause, for one (1) whole year;

  (5) Being convicted of any crime that, by the laws of the state, renders the party infamous;

continued >

(6) Being convicted of a crime that, by the laws of the state, is declared to be a felony, and sentenced to confinement in the penitentiary;

(7) Either party has attempted the life of the other, by poison or any other means showing malice;

(8) Refusal, on the part of a spouse, to remove with that person's spouse to this state, without a reasonable cause, and being willfully absent from the spouse residing in Tennessee for two (2) years;

(9) The woman was pregnant at the time of the marriage, by another person, without the knowledge of the husband;

(10) Habitual drunkenness or abuse of narcotic drugs of either party, when the spouse has contracted either such habit after marriage;

(11) The husband or wife is guilty of such cruel and inhuman treatment or conduct towards the spouse as renders cohabitation unsafe and improper, which may also be referred to in pleadings as inappropriate marital conduct;

(12) The husband or wife has offered such indignities to the spouse's person as to render the spouse's position intolerable, and thereby forced the spouse to withdraw;

(13) The husband or wife has abandoned the spouse or turned the spouse out of doors for no just cause, and has refused or neglected to provide for the spouse while having the ability to so provide;

(14) Irreconcilable differences between the parties; and

(15) For a continuous period of two (2) or more years that commenced prior to or after April 18, 1985, both parties have lived in separate residences, have not cohabited as man and wife during such period, and there are no minor children of the parties.

(b) A complaint or petition for divorce on any ground for divorce listed in this section must have been on file for sixty (60) days before being heard if the parties have no unmarried child under eighteen (18) years of age, and must have been on file at least ninety (90) days before being heard if the parties have an unmarried child under eighteen (18) years of age. The sixty-day or ninety-day period shall commence on the date the complaint or petition is filed.

Some states have both **fault divorce** and **no-fault divorce**. In other words, a party may petition for divorce, alleging fault on their spouse—such as that the spouse committed adultery. If one party committed adultery, the other party can petition for a divorce on fault grounds. However, "irreconcilable differences" is a typical ground for no-fault divorce.

A key issue is whether a party's marital fault can limit his or her recovery of the marital estate. State laws vary on this important issue. Some states allow fault-based divorces, in which one party's recovery of marital property may be limited by his or her own culpable conduct. Other states, such as Tennessee, are no-fault states, meaning that the distribution of marital property generally is done without attribution of fault by either party.

Fault divorce:
Petition for divorce alleging fault on a spouse.

No-fault divorce:
Petition for divorce without alleging fault, such as irreconcilable differences.

In many divorces, the most important or contentious part of the divorce is dividing up the parties' assets and debts. In other words, the parties often vigorously fight over how much each party gets from the marital estate, assets called **marital property**. Generally speaking, property acquired during the course of a party's marriage is considered marital property, meaning that it is subject to an equitable division by the courts. Property that a party had before entering into marriage may well be considered separate, or nonmarital, property. **Separate property** remains the property of the individual spouse and does not have to be divided up with the former partner. Most assets acquired during the marriage are marital property, even pension benefits earned by one spouse. For example, Illinois law provides that "all pension benefits acquired by either spouse after the marriage and before a judgment of dissolution of marriage or declaration of invalidity of the marriage are presumed to be marital property, regardless of which spouse participates in the pension plan."

Courts do not divide separate, nonmarital property; that remains the property of the separate individual. In many states, if one party inherits money from parents, that property also would be considered separate property.

Marital property: Generally property acquired during the course of a party's marriage subject to equitable division by the court.

Separate property: Belonging to the individual spouse and does not have to be divided in the divorce.

Tennessee Law on Distribution of Marital Property

T.C.A. §36-4-121 Distribution of Martial Property

(a) (1) In all actions for divorce or legal separation, the court having jurisdiction thereof may, upon request of either party, and prior to any determination as to whether it is appropriate to order the support and maintenance of one (1) party by the other, equitably divide, distribute or assign the marital property between the parties without regard to marital fault in proportions as the court deems just.

Sometimes, separate property can be converted into marital property. Wisconsin law provides that "mixing marital property with property other than marital property reclassifies the other property to marital property unless the component of the mixed property which is not marital property can be traced."

Courts vary in how they divide marital property. Laws in many states provide a great deal of discretion to trial courts to apportion marital property. Many states provide a list of factors for courts to consider. For example, Missouri law (Mo. Rev. Stat. §452.330.1 (2008)) provides that courts should consider the following five factors in apportioning marital property:

1. The economic circumstances of each spouse at the time the division of property is to become effective, including the desirability of awarding the family home or the right to live therein for reasonable periods to the spouse having custody of any children;
2. The contribution of each spouse to the acquisition of the marital property, including the contribution of a spouse as homemaker;
3. The value of the nonmarital property set apart to each spouse;
4. The conduct of the parties during the marriage; and
5. Custodial arrangements for minor children.

In some states, courts start with a presumption that the marital property should be distributed equally, but the parties can rebut that presumption by presenting evidence of marital fault or substantial contributions by one spouse.

ALIMONY

Alimony, or spousal support, refers to the support of one spouse by the other while the parties are going through divorce proceedings and after the parties are divorced. Traditionally, courts may require the spouse that makes more money to provide alimony to the spouse that makes less money. Often, a party will file a motion, seeking interim, or *pendente lite* (Latin for while the litigation is pending), support. The main goal of alimony is to give the supported spouse relatively the same level of maintenance or support that she or he enjoyed during the marriage.

There are different types of alimony, and states use different terminology to describe types of alimony. These include permanent alimony, limited duration alimony, reimbursement alimony, rehabilitative alimony, alimony *in solido*, alimony *in gross*, alimony in future, periodic alimony, and transitional alimony. New Jersey recognizes rehabilitative, reimbursement, limited duration, and permanent alimony. Often courts will award *pendente lite* or temporary support to maintain a spouse between the time of separation and eventual divorce. The other types of alimony are for a given period of time ranging from a couple of years to virtually permanent support.

Most states recognize the categories of permanent and rehabilitative alimony. **Permanent alimony** means that a party will receive alimony for the rest of his or her life. **Rehabilitative alimony** is a form of financial support from an ex-spouse that is given for a set number of years to allow the receiving ex-spouse to rehabilitate himself or herself and establish themselves by education or job training.

Courts consider numerous factors before awarding alimony. Consider the following Maryland law.

Alimony:
Support of one spouse by the other while the parties are going through divorce proceedings or for a defined period.

Permanent alimony:
A party will receive alimony for the rest of that person's life.

Rehabilitative alimony:
Form of financial support for a set period of time after divorce.

Maryland Law on Alimony

Md. Family Law Code Ann. §11-106 (2011)

(a) Court to make determination.—

(1) The court shall determine the amount of and the period for an award of alimony.

(2) The court may award alimony for a period beginning from the filing of the pleading that requests alimony.

(3) At the conclusion of the period of the award of alimony, no further alimony shall accrue.

(b) Required considerations.—In making the determination, the court shall consider all the factors necessary for a fair and equitable award, including:

(1) the ability of the party seeking alimony to be wholly or partly self-supporting;

(2) the time necessary for the party seeking alimony to gain sufficient education or training to enable that party to find suitable employment;

(3) the standard of living that the parties established during their marriage;

(4) the duration of the marriage;

(5) the contributions, monetary and nonmonetary, of each party to the well-being of the family;

(6) the circumstances that contributed to the estrangement of the parties;

(7) the age of each party;

(8) the physical and mental condition of each party;

(9) the ability of the party from whom alimony is sought to meet that party's needs while meeting the needs of the party seeking alimony;

(10) any agreement between the parties;

(11) the financial needs and financial resources of each party . . .

(12) whether the award would cause a spouse who is a resident of a related institution . . . and from whom alimony is sought to become eligible for medical assistance earlier than would otherwise occur.

(c) Award for indefinite period.—The court may award alimony for an indefinite period, if the court finds that:

(1) due to age, illness, infirmity, or disability, the party seeking alimony cannot reasonably be expected to make substantial progress toward becoming self-supporting; or

(2) even after the party seeking alimony will have made as much progress toward becoming self-supporting as can reasonably be expected, the respective standards of living of the parties will be unconscionably disparate.

Most states provide that if a person receiving alimony remarries, then the obligation to pay alimony terminates. For example, Alabama law provides that a decree for alimony "shall be modified by the court to provide for the termination of such alimony upon petition of a party to the decree and proof that the spouse receiving such alimony has remarried or that such spouse is living openly or cohabiting with a member of the opposite sex."

CHILD CUSTODY

Child custody refers to the legal process of determining what parent or legal guardian assumes custody or control over a minor child. Generally, a party to a marriage who has filed for a legal separation or divorce will file a petition for custody. Courts determine the parent or guardian to whom to award custody.

There are two basic types of custody: **sole custody** and **joint custody**. Sole custody means that one parent has legal custody of the child. Joint custody means that the parents share legal custody of the child. Some state laws, such as Arizona, divide joint custody into "joint legal custody" and "joint physical custody."

Child custody:
Legal process of determining what parent or legal guardian assumes custody over a minor.

Sole custody:
One parent has legal custody of the child.

Joint custody:
The parents share in legal custody of the child.

Alabama Law on Different Forms of Child Custody

Code of Ala. §30-3-151 (2011)
§30-3-151. Definitions.

For the purposes of this article the following words shall have the following meanings:

(1) **Joint custody.** Joint legal custody and joint physical custody.

(2) **Joint legal custody.** Both parents have equal rights and responsibilities for major decisions concerning the child, including, but not limited to, the education of the child, health care, and religious training. The court may designate one parent to have sole power to make certain decisions while both parents retain equal rights and responsibilities for other decisions.

(3) **Joint physical custody.** Physical custody is shared by the parents in a way that assures the child frequent and substantial contact with each parent. Joint physical **custody** does not necessarily mean physical custody of equal durations of time.

(4) **Sole legal custody.** One parent has sole rights and responsibilities to make major decisions concerning the child, including, but not limited to, the education of the child, health care, and religious training.

---

continued >

> **(5) Sole physical custody.** One parent has sole physical custody and the other parent has rights of visitation except as otherwise provided by the court.

Other states use different names for custody, such as legal custody, partial custody, and shared custody. For example, Pennsylvania law defines legal custody as "[t]he legal right to make major decisions affecting the best interest of a minor child, including, but not limited to, medical, religious and educational decisions."

Courts in most states employ a flexible, multifactor test known as **the best interest of the child** to determine custody for the parties' children. Many state laws presume that it is best for the child to maintain contact of some sort with each parent. Common factors in determining the best interest of the child include the reasonable preference of a child, particularly if he or she is over 12 years of age, the emotional bonds the child has with each parent, where the child currently lives, the economic ability of each parent to provide for the child, and whether either parent has been convicted of a sex crime or a domestic violence offense. Indiana law provides that a relevant factor is the mental and physical health of each parent.

Best interest of the child:
A flexible, multifactor test to determine custody for the parties' children.

Illinois and Tennessee Laws on Best Interest of the Child

Illinois Law: §750 ILCS 5/602. Best Interest of Child

Sec. 602. Best Interest of Child. (a) The court shall determine custody in accordance with the best interest of the child. The court shall consider all relevant factors including:

(1) the wishes of the child's parent or parents as to his custody;

(2) the wishes of the child as to his custodian;

(3) the interaction and interrelationship of the child with his parent or parents, his siblings and any other person who may significantly affect the child's best interest;

(4) the child's adjustment to his home, school and community;

(5) the mental and physical health of all individuals involved;

(6) the physical violence or threat of physical violence by the child's potential custodian, whether directed against the child or directed against another person;

(7) the occurrence of ongoing or repeated abuse as defined in Section 103 of the Illinois Domestic Violence Act of 1986] whether directed against the child or directed against another person;

(8) the willingness and ability of each parent to facilitate and encourage a close and continuing relationship between the other parent and the child;

continued >

(9) whether one of the parents is a sex offender; and

(10) the terms of a parent's military family-care plan that a parent must complete before deployment if a parent is a member of the United States Armed Forces who is being deployed.

In the case of a custody proceeding in which a stepparent has standing under Section 601, it is presumed to be in the best interest of the minor child that the natural parent have the custody of the minor child unless the presumption is rebutted by the stepparent.

(b) The court shall not consider conduct of a present or proposed custodian that does not affect his relationship to the child.

(c) Unless the court finds the occurrence of ongoing abuse as defined in Section 103 of the Illinois Domestic Violence Act of 1986, the court shall presume that the maximum involvement and cooperation of both parents regarding the physical, mental, moral, and emotional well-being of their child is in the best interest of the child. There shall be no presumption in favor of or against joint custody.

Tennessee Law: T.C.A. 36-6-106. Child custody

(a) In a suit for annulment, divorce, separate maintenance, or in any other proceeding requiring the court to make a custody determination regarding a minor child, the determination shall be made on the basis of the best interest of the child. The court shall consider all relevant factors, including the following, where applicable:

(1) The love, affection and emotional ties existing between the parents or caregivers and the child;

(2) The disposition of the parents or caregivers to provide the child with food, clothing, medical care, education and other necessary care and the degree to which a parent or caregiver has been the primary caregiver;

(3) The importance of continuity in the child's life and the length of time the child has lived in a stable, satisfactory environment; provided, that, where there is a finding, under subdivision (a)(8), of child abuse, as defined in §39-15-401 or §39-15-402, or child sexual abuse, as defined in §37-1-602, by one (1) parent, and that a nonperpetrating parent or caregiver has relocated in order to flee the perpetrating parent, that the relocation shall not weigh against an award of custody;

(4) The stability of the family unit of the parents or caregivers;

(5) The mental and physical health of the parents or caregivers;

(6) The home, school and community record of the child;

(7) (A) The reasonable preference of the child, if twelve (12) years of age or older;

(B) The court may hear the preference of a younger child on request. The preferences of older children should normally be given greater weight than those of younger children;

(8) Evidence of physical or emotional abuse to the child, to the other parent or to any other person; provided, that, where there are allegations that one (1) parent has committed child abuse, as defined in

continued >

§39-15-401 or §39-15-402, or child sexual abuse, as defined in §37-1-602, against a family member, the court shall consider all evidence relevant to the physical and emotional safety of the child, and determine, by a clear preponderance of the evidence, whether such abuse has occurred. The court shall include in its decision a written finding of all evidence, and all findings of facts connected to the evidence. In addition, the court shall, where appropriate, refer any issues of abuse to the juvenile court for further proceedings;

(9) The character and behavior of any other person who resides in or frequents the home of a parent or caregiver and the person's interactions with the child; and

(10) Each parent or caregiver's past and potential for future performance of parenting responsibilities, including the willingness and ability of each of the parents and caregivers to facilitate and encourage a close and continuing parent-child relationship between the child and both of the child's parents, consistent with the best interest of the child.

(b) Notwithstanding the provisions of any law to the contrary, the court has jurisdiction to make an initial custody determination regarding a minor child or may modify a prior order of child custody upon finding that the custodial parent has been convicted of or found civilly liable for the intentional and wrongful death of the child's other parent or legal guardian.

The best-interest standard has been both praised and criticized by family law practitioners and others. Proponents emphasize that the standard does focus on the child and provides courts with needed flexibility to evaluate situations on a case-by-case basis. It provides a wide range of factors for courts to consider in determining what really is best for children under specific circumstances. They contend that courts need to examine what the child wants, what emotional bonds are established with each parent, and the moral and economic fitness of each parent. They argue that the best-interest standard, while not perfect, is far superior to any other standard the law has developed in this area. Rather than try to tear down the standard, they argue that people in the family law system should work to improve the standard.

Opponents counter that the test provides too much flexibility and judicial discretion, leading to inconsistent results and stirring up more litigation. They contend that best-interest laws have too many factors, giving judges far too much discretion. For example, some state laws allow judges to consider any other factor deemed necessary. Critics say that this creates the opportunity for judges to use their personal preference and biases in selecting the primary custodial parent.

The parent who does not receive legal or primary custody usually will have reasonable **visitation rights**. This may include every other weekend, some holidays, and time in the summer. A relevant factor in many states as to

Visitation rights:
The parent who does not receive legal or primary custody usually will receive reasonable opportunity to these rights.

whether a parent can receive any type of custody or even any type of visitation is whether a parent has committed a violent crime or a sex crime.

Certainly a parent with a child-abuse or domestic violence conviction faces an uphill battle in a custody dispute. Some states prohibit or limit parents' custody if they have committed certain sex or violent crimes. For example, Arizona prohibits a parent from having custody or even unsupervised parental time if they are a convicted sex offender or a murderer of their former spouse unless the court makes written findings that the parent poses no significant risk to the child.

Pennsylvania law requires courts to give consideration to the fact that any parent seeking custody or visitation has been convicted of homicide, kidnapping, rape, unlawful restraint, prostitution, sexual abuse, indecent exposure, or indecent assault. Thus, criminal conduct can have a negative impact on a parent's future custody.

If a parent has a criminal past or abuse issues, that parent may not get visitation, or they may get a limited type of visitation called **supervised visitation.** This means that a parent can have visitation, but it has to be supervised by a person appointed by the court to monitor the situation to ensure the child's safety.

Supervised visitation: A person may have visitation, but it must be supervised by someone appointed by the court to ensure the child's safety.

Usually, supervised visitation is required for a parent when there is a concern of abuse, neglect, or past criminal behavior that would caution against the awarding of unsupervised visitation. For example, Maryland law provides: "If it is in the best interest of the child, the court may approve a supervised visitation arrangement that assures the safety and the physiological, psychological, and emotional well-being of the child."

One factor that courts generally may not consider—at least as a determinative factor—is race. However, a few courts have determined that race cannot be considered in a child custody determination. In *Palmore v. Sidoti* (1984), the U.S. Supreme Court reversed a lower court decision that had removed primary custody from a mother to a father because the Caucasian mother had married an African-American man. The trial court determined that the mother's interracial cohabitation would subject her child to peer pressures and stigma at school. The U.S. Supreme Court determined that the trial court's fixation on race as the determinative factor violated the Equal Protection Clause of the Fourteenth Amendment. "Private biases may be outside the reach of the law, but the law cannot, directly or indirectly, give them effect," the Court wrote.

Other courts have determined that race can play a factor in racial classifications. *In Re Marriage of Gambla*, 853 N.E.2d 847 (Ill. App. 2006), an Illinois appeals court allowed race to be a determinative factor in awarding custody of a couple's biracial child to the African-American mother instead of the Caucasian father. "Indeed, it appears that so long as race is not the sole consideration for custody decisions, it is not an unconstitutional consideration," the state court wrote.

Palmore v. Sidoti, 466 U.S. 429 (1984)

It would ignore reality to suggest that racial and ethnic prejudices do not exist or that all manifestations of those prejudices have been eliminated. There is a risk that a child living with a stepparent of a different race may be subject to a variety of pressures and stresses not present if the child were living with parents of the same racial or ethnic origin.

The question, however, is whether the reality of private biases and the possible injury they might inflict are permissible considerations for removal of an infant child from the custody of its natural mother. We have little difficulty concluding that they are not. The Constitution cannot control such prejudices but neither can it tolerate them. Private biases may be outside the reach of the law, but the law cannot, directly or indirectly, give them effect. . . .

This is by no means the first time that acknowledged racial prejudice has been invoked to justify racial classifications. . . .

Whatever problems racially mixed households may pose for children in 1984 can no more support a denial of constitutional rights than could the stresses that residential integration was thought to entail in 1917. The effects of racial prejudice, however real, cannot justify a racial classification removing an infant child from the custody of its natural mother found to be an appropriate person to have such custody.

Some parties to a marriage have a change in circumstances. For example, the noncustodial parent may have obtained a better-paying job and quit drinking. That noncustodial parent seeks either enhanced visitation rights or a change in custody. Most state laws provide that a party seeking a change in custody can obtain such only upon showing a **material change in circumstances**. In reality, this often means that the noncustodial parent has to show that the custodial parent has committed some wrongdoing or is putting the child at risk with his or her lifestyle. For example, if a custodial parent, the mother, begins living with a man with a drug problem, that exposes the children to harm, and the noncustodial parent well might be able to obtain a change in custody because there has been a material change in circumstances.

Another pressing issue in child-custody cases is what happens when the custodial parent wishes to move to another part of the state or even to another state. Can the noncustodial parent who has visitation rights block the custodial parent from moving? The issue is extremely tough and presents stark, competing interests of the custodial and noncustodial parent. The custodial parent sometimes needs to relocate to provide better financial and other opportunities for the child by moving to another location for a superior job. However, the noncustodial parent may have established

Material change in circumstances:
Usually means that the noncustodial parent must show that the custodial parent has committed some wrongdoing or has put the child at risk.

strong emotional bonds with the child that could be severed or harmed by the move to another, faraway location.

States differ in how they handle these thorny relocation problems. Most states have laws that deal with the relocation of custodial parents. In many states, the custodial parent must provide a certain notice to the noncustodial parent, and then the noncustodial parent has a right to object to the move.

Nevada law provides that the custodial parent must give notice to the noncustodial parent and that failure to give proper notice can be a factor in the court's ultimate custody determination. Tennessee law provides a much more detailed road map of how to handle parental relocation problems. Contrast the differences between the two state approaches.

Nevada Law on Relocation of Custodial Parents

N.R.S. 125C.200

If custody has been established and the custodial parent intends to move his residence to a place outside of this State and to take the child with him, he must, as soon as possible and before the planned move, attempt to obtain the written consent of the noncustodial parent to move the child from this State. If the noncustodial parent refuses to give that consent, the custodial parent shall, before he leaves this State with the child, petition the court for permission to move the child. The failure of a parent to comply with the provisions of this section may be considered as a factor if a change of custody is requested by the noncustodial parent.

Tennessee Law on Parental Relocation

T.C.A. 36-1-108

(1) If the parents are not actually spending substantially equal intervals of time with the child and the parent spending the greater amount of time with the child proposes to relocate with the child, the other parent may, within thirty (30) days of receipt of the notice, file a petition in opposition to removal of the child. The other parent may not attempt to relocate with the child unless expressly authorized to do so by the court pursuant to a change of custody or primary custodial responsibility. The parent spending the greater amount of time with the child shall be permitted to relocate with the child unless the court finds:

The relocation would pose a threat of specific and serious harm to the child that outweighs the threat of harm to the child of a change of custody; or

continued >

(2) Specific and serious harm to the child includes, but is not limited to, the following:

(A) If a parent wishes to take a child with a serious medical problem to an area where no adequate treatment is readily available;

(B) If a parent wishes to take a child with specific educational requirements to an area with no acceptable education facilities;

(C) If a parent wishes to relocate and take up residence with a person with a history of child or domestic abuse or who is currently abusing alcohol or other drugs;

(D) If the child relies on the parent not relocating who provides emotional support, nurturing and development such that removal would result in severe emotional detriment to the child;

(E) If the custodial parent is emotionally disturbed or dependent such that the custodial parent is not capable of adequately parenting the child in the absence of support systems currently in place in this state, and such support system is not available at the proposed relocation site; or

(F) If the proposed relocation is to a foreign country whose public policy does not normally enforce the visitation rights of non-custodial parents, that does not have an adequately functioning legal system or that otherwise presents a substantial risk of specific and serious harm to the child.

(e) If the court finds one (1) or more of the grounds designated in subsection (d), the court shall determine whether or not to permit relocation of the child based on the best interest of the child. If the court finds it is not in the best interests of the child to relocate as defined herein, but the parent with whom the child resides the majority of the time elects to relocate, the court shall make a custody determination and shall consider all relevant factors including the following where applicable:

(1) The extent to which visitation rights have been allowed and exercised;

(2) Whether the primary residential parent, once out of the jurisdiction, is likely to comply with any new visitation arrangement;

(3) The love, affection and emotional ties existing between the parents and child;

(4) The disposition of the parents to provide the child with food, clothing, medical care, education and other necessary care and the degree to which a parent has been the primary caregiver;

(5) The importance of continuity in the child's life and the length of time the child has lived in a stable, satisfactory environment;

(6) The stability of the family unit of the parents;

(7) The mental and physical health of the parents;

(8) The home, school and community record of the child;

continued >

> (9) (A) The reasonable preference of the child if twelve (12) years of age or older;
>
> (B) The court may hear the preference of a younger child upon request. The preferences of older children should normally be given greater weight than those of younger children;
>
> (10) Evidence of physical or emotional abuse to the child, to the other parent or to any other person; and
>
> (11) The character and behavior of any other person who resides in or frequents the home of a parent and such person's interactions with the child.
>
> (g) Nothing in this section shall prohibit either parent from petitioning the court at any time to address issues, such as, but not limited to, visitation, other than a change of custody related to the move. In the event no petition in opposition to a proposed relocation is filed within thirty (30) days of receipt of the notice, the parent proposing to relocate with the child shall be permitted to do so.
>
> (h) It is the legislative intent that the gender of the parent who seeks to relocate for the reason of career, educational, professional, or job opportunity, or otherwise, shall not be a factor in favor or against the relocation of such parent with the child.

Another hotly contested issue in child custody is the denial of visitation rights. Sometimes the acrimony between the parents may cause the parents to take it out on each other with respect to custody and visitation. This is not a wise option as most courts take very seriously allegations of denial of visitation rights. If one parent denies another parent's visitation rights, a court can require additional visitation time, impose further conditions to prevent future violations, and assess costs and attorney fees against the parent who thwarts reasonable visitation rights.

Many states also have statutes that provide for grandparent visitation. These are called **grandparent visitation statutes**. These laws recognize that grandparents often play a key role in the rearing and upbringing of children. However, parents who are considered fit—able parents who have not been found neglectful—have the ultimate power to determine the level of visitation by nonparents, even grandparents.

Grandparent visitation statutes:
Many states have statutes that recognize grandparent visitation rights, but parents have the ultimate power to determine the level of visitation by nonparents.

The U.S. Supreme Court in *Troxel v. Granville*, 530 U.S. 57 (2000) ruled that a Washington state grandparent visitation law intruded upon the constitutional rights of parents to rear their children as they saw fit. The Court reasoned that "so long as a parent adequately cares for his or her children (*i.e.*, is fit), there will normally be no reason for the State to inject itself into the private realm of the family to further question the ability of that parent to make the best decisions concerning the rearing of that parent's children." This means that fit parents can determine whether or not their children can visit their grandparents. If the parents are not fit, then those parents probably cannot limit grandparent visitation.

CHILD SUPPORT

Another pressing issue in family law concerns **child support**. This refers to money provided by the noncustodial parent to the custodial parent to provide economic help, including a sharing of medical expenses. Many times this involves a situation in which the mother of a child seeks to obtain financial support from the father of the child, many times in situations where there was no marriage. In those instances, the mother must establish the paternity of the father—that the father actually is the father of the child. If **paternity** is established, then the court can award child support, usually based upon the income of the party and the number of children that the noncustodial parent has to pay.

Once paternity is established, the mother can seek child support from the father. Once notice is provided, a court may order the father to contribute to the child's well-being. There are child-support agencies that exist to help mothers obtain child-support payments from fathers. These agencies will work with the parents to help establish paternity through a paternity test. These agencies can initiate legal action to help the person obtain child support.

Parties often contest the amount of child support in litigation. States have guidelines, called child support guidelines, that provide a reference point for the amount that parents should pay. Under the Maryland child-support guidelines, if a noncustodial parent (who has been ordered to pay child support) makes $5,000 a month and has one child, he or she must pay $670 a month in child support.

If a person refuses to pay child support or is continually late in making child support payments, that person risks going to jail. If a parent continues to not make child-support payments, a court may find that person in criminal contempt and order him or her to serve jail time. Many parents have substantial **arrearages**, or significant amounts of child support owed to the custodial parent. Some states have a crime called back criminal nonsupport of children, which is a felony.

Just as with custody, courts sometimes modify child-support payments under a material change in circumstances standard. This can result in either an increase or decrease of child-support payments. For example, if the noncustodial parent suddenly receives a new job with a much larger salary, the custodial parent can file a motion for increased child support. The idea is that if the noncustodial parent brings in more money, some of that money should go to support his or her children. Likewise, if a person ordered to pay child support makes less money and the court determines

Child support: Money provided by the noncustodial parent to the custodial parent to provide economic help in that support.

Paternity: When the actual father of the child is established, then the court can award child support.

Arrearages: Significant amounts of child support owed to the custodial parent by the noncustodial parent.

such a loss in income is not his or her fault, the court might order a reduction in child support.

ADOPTION

Adoption is a legal process in which a person or persons become the legal parents or guardians of a child who is not their birth child. Once the adoption process is complete, the adoptive parents are the full and legal parents of that child—just as if they were the birth parents. There are **agency adoptions** and **private adoptions**. Agency adoptions involve either a public or private adoption that is licensed by the state. A private adoption involves the parties themselves handling the adoption process. People wishing to adopt contact a lawyer who then facilitates the adoption process. Court approval is needed for private adoptions as well as agency adoptions. Many states require a minor mother to have a guardian *ad litem* appointed by the court before she can give proper consent to an adoption.

In most states, birth mothers can withdraw their consent to an adoption, although there are fairly strict time limits. For example, in Alaska a birth mother cannot withdraw her consent after there has been a court decree authorizing the adoption. A birth mother can withdraw her consent up to 10 days after giving it.

Adopting a child is a complicated process made even more complicated by extensive background checks on the prospective adoptive parents. The agencies will conduct an investigation of the prospective adoptive parents, which can include a background check for past criminal history and possible past child abuse. In most states, the agency will prepare a report and study for approval by the court that will determine whether the adoption is in the best interest of the child and that placement with the prospective adoptive parents is in the best interest of the child.

A judge approves an adoption. The judge has to determine whether the adoption will further the best interests of a child. Some states have laws specifically authorizing judges to interview adoptees to determine their attitudes about the pending adoption.

Adoption:
Legal process in which persons become the legal parents or guardians of a child who is not their birth child.

Agency adoptions:
Either a public or private adoption that is licensed by the state.

Private adoptions:
The parties themselves handle the adoption process.

CHAPTER SUMMARY

1. Family law, or domestic relations, is an intricate body of law that deals with marriage, divorce, child custody and visitation, paternity, child support, and adoption. It often intersects with other areas of law, including tort law, contract law, and employment law.

2. Marriage is a civil contract by two people who live together as a family unit. There are limitations on who can marry. For example, minors

often have to obtain special permission before legally marrying. Many marriages are conducted through a ceremonial process after the parties have obtained a marriage license. A few states allow common-law marriage—a relationship in which the parties hold themselves as married but have not been formally married.

3. Most states specifically provide that marriages are between one man and one woman. There is a growing move to allow same-sex marriages, but most states have laws that still forbid them. Many states not only have laws that prohibit such marriages but also have amended their state constitutions to prohibit them.

4. Parties may enter into prenuptial agreements. These are agreements in which those entering a marriage contractually agree to a certain dispersal of assets should the marriage end in divorce. Most states recognize these agreements as long as they are not too one-sided or no fraud was used to obtain a person's signature.

5. Divorce is the process by which parties formally end a marriage. A court will approve of a divorce decree that spells out the rights and obligations of the respective parties. Common grounds for divorce include adultery, crimes committed by a spouse, abandonment, abuse or cruelty, and a catch-all category known as *irreconcilable differences*.

6. A major issue in divorces is how to handle the parties' assets and liabilities. The courts ultimately must decide how to disperse property in the marital estate, known as marital property. Often, parties argue over whether certain assets are marital property subject to division or separate property. If property is considered marital property, the courts will divide it between the parties. If property is considered separate property, it remains with the individual party.

7. Another issue in divorces concerns spousal support, called alimony. There are different types of alimony, including permanent alimony and rehabilitative alimony. Permanent alimony lasts for the rest of a person's life unless that person remarries. Rehabilitative alimony lasts only for a period of time to allow the supported spouse an opportunity to gain an economic foothold.

8. Still another major issue in divorce is child custody and visitation. Courts make custody awards based on a best interest of the child standard. This is a multifactor analysis that focuses on the parties' relationships with the child, the ability to provide economically, the wishes of the child, and other factors. There are different types of custody arrangements, including sole custody and joint custody.

9. Courts can modify child custody and visitation rights based on a material change in circumstances. Generally, a change in custody requires a party to show a material change in circumstances.

10. Courts also often order noncustodial parents to provide child support payments to help the custodial parent rear the child and provide for

expenses. Child support is based on the income of the providing person and the number of children he or she has. Parties can seek a change in child support based on a material change of circumstances standard.

11. Before receiving child support, a party must show that the other parent is indeed the parent of the child. Generally, this involves a mother trying to establish the paternity of her child, namely, that her former mate is the father of the child. Once paternity is established, child support can be awarded.

12. Adoption is a complicated process in which persons become the legal parents and guardians of a child who was born to someone else. There are agency adoptions and private adoptions. Birth mothers retain rights and in some states can revoke consent to an adoption rather late in the process.

REVIEW EXERCISE

Match the following term with their most appropriate meaning.

TERMS
1. Marriage
2. Common-law marriage
3. Covenant marriage
4. Incest
5. Bigamy
6. Civil union
7. Prenuptial agreements
8. Divorce
9. Irreconcilable differences
10. Abandonment
11. Fault divorce
12. No-fault divorce
13. Marital property
14. Separate property
15. Alimony
16. Permanent alimony
17. Rehabilitative alimony
18. Child custody
19. Sole custody
20. Joint custody
21. Best interest of the child

MEANING
____ when established who is the actual father of the child, then the court can award child support
____ statutes that recognize grandparent visitation, but the parents have ultimate power to determine the level of visitation
____ a flexible, multifactor test to determine custody for the parties' children
____ legal process in which persons become the legal parents or guardians of a child who is not their birth child
____ when the parties themselves handle the adoption process
____ legal process of determining what parent or legal guardian assumes custody over a minor
____ petition for divorce alleging fault on the part of the spouse
____ enforceable contracts that the parties enter into to protect their individual assets before marriage
____ recognized ground for divorce when a spouse leaves the family for a certain period of time
____ a person may have visitation but it must be supervised by a person appointed by the court
____ belonging to the individual spouse, thus does not have to be divided in the divorce
____ money provided by the noncustodial parent to the custodial parent to provide economic support
____ exists when a couple freely enter into authorized premarital counseling and agree on more limiting grounds for divorce
____ involves a private adoption that is licensed by the state
____ significant amounts of child support owed to the custodial parent by the noncustodial parent

22. Visitation rights
23. Supervised visitation
24. Material change in circumstances
25. Grandparent visitation statutes
26. Child support
27. Paternity
28. Arrearages
29. Adoption
30. Agency adoption
31. Private adoptions
32. Divorce decree

____ civil contract between a man and a woman in most jurisdictions who agree to live together and share their lives together

____ when parties agree that the marriage has broken down and they cannot live in harmony

____ the formal legal document in which a marriage is dissolved and the parties' legal responsibilities are explained

____ means that a party will receive alimony for the rest of that person's life

____ usually means that the noncustodial parent must show that the custodial parent has committed some wrongdoing or has put the child at risk

____ relationship between two persons providing many of the benefits of marriage in some states

____ the parent who does not receive legal or primary custody usually will receive reasonable opportunity to these rights

____ having multiple spouses

____ petition for divorce without alleging fault, such as irreconcilable differences

____ means that one parent has legal custody of the child

____ couples living together for a period of years and hold themselves as married in some states

____ form of financial support for a set period of time after divorce

____ marrying a family member who is too closely related in blood line

____ process of formally ending a marriage

____ generally property acquired during the course of a party's marriage subject to equitable division by the court

____ support of one spouse by the other while the parties are going through divorce proceedings or for a defined period

____ means that the parents share in legal custody of the child

DISCUSSION QUESTIONS

1. What is the fee for a marriage license in your state? Do you believe that states should require individuals to engage in counseling before entering into marriage? What should the age limit be for marriage?

2. Does your state allow common-law marriages? Do you believe that two people must undergo a ceremony before being legally married?

3. Does your state recognize same-sex marriage? Do you think it violates equal protection to prohibit people of the same sex from marrying?

4. Covenant marriages are those that are more difficult to end. Given the high rate of divorce, do you think this is a positive development in the law?

5. What can courts do to ensure that parties adhere to custody and visitation agreements? Should the law favor joint custody arrangements? Why or why not?

6. If a married person has a pension from his or her job, should his or her spouse be able to obtain some of those monies if the parties end up getting divorced?

7. If one party commits adultery, do you think that fault should impact what they receive in the divorce settlement?

8. What are the positives of the best interest of the child standard in child-custody law? What are the negatives for such an approach? Should the preference of the child be a predominant factor?

9. Should people go to jail for refusing to pay child support? What if the person loses his or her job, is that person still obligated to pay child support?
10. What can be done to ensure that more people pay their child support on a timely basis?
11. Should laws be changed to make it easier to adopt children?
12. Do you think adoption records should be kept private? Why or why not?

ASSIGNMENTS

ASSIGNMENT: Find and read your state law on divorce. How many different grounds are there for a divorce?

ASSIGNMENT: Look up your state law on child custody and visitation. What factors are judges allowed to consider in making the important determination as to who is the primary custodial parent?

ASSIGNMENT: Research whether the issue of same-sex marriage has come up in your state court or state legislature.

SOURCES AND SUGGESTED READING

Jasper, Margaret C. 2008. *Marriage and Divorce.* New York: Oxford University Press.

Lind, Goran. 2008. *Common Law Marriage: A Legal Institution for Cohabitation.* New York: Oxford University Press.

Meyer, David D. "Palmore comes of age: The place of race in the placement of children," 18 *University of Florida Journal of Law & Policy* 183 (2007).

Savard, Susan W. "Through the eyes of a child: Impact and measures to protect children in high-conflict family law litigation," 84 *Florida Bar Journal* 57 (2010).

Sullivan, Andrew. 2004. *Same Sex Marriage: Pro and Con.* New York: Vintage Press.

COURT CASES
In Re Marriage of Gambla, 853 N.E.2d 847 (Ill.App. 2006)
Loving v. Virginia, 388 U.S. 1 (1967)
Palmore v. Sidoti, 466 U.S. 429 (1984)
Perez v. Sharp, 198 P.2d 17 (Cal. 1948)
Reynolds v. United States, 98 U.S. 145 (1879)
Troxel v. Granville, 530 U.S. 57 (2000)
Varnum v. Brien, 763 N.W.2d 862 (Iowa 2009)

WEBSITES
ABA Center on Children and the Law
http://www.abanet.org/child/home.html
Adoption Resources
http://www.adoptionresources.org/
Child Custody Law Firms
http://www.childcustodylawfirms.com/
Child Custody Resource
http://www.custodysource.com/
Divorce and Family Law Blog (Cavers)
http://divorce.caverslaw.com/
Divorce Source
http://www.divorcesource.com/
Divorce Support
http://www.divorcesupport.com/
Family Law Center (Findlaw)
http://family.findlaw.com/
Family Law Prof Blog
http://lawprofessors.typepad.com/family_law/
Support Guidelines
http://www.supportguidelines.com/

Introduction to Employment Law

Employment law affects nearly everyone. Many people get up early daily and commute to work. Most of these people work for a corporation, a business, a limited liability company, or some other type of business organization. These people are employees working for employers. An employer is the person or entity that controls the way that employees carry out their duties during the working day. The employer is the boss, in modern parlance, meaning that the employer dictates most of the terms and conditions of the workplace. This level of power disparity is reflected in the term "master-servant" relationship. For all practical purposes—for most employees—the employer is the master and the employee is the servant.

THE EMPLOYMENT-AT-WILL DOCTRINE

In the United States, the baseline rule governing the employment relationship in the private sector is the **employment-at-will doctrine**. This rule means that either the employer or the employee can terminate the employment relationship at will. The reasoning is that just as an employee may decide to leave his or her job at a moment's notice to pursue another job, an employer can decide to terminate an employee, eliminate a job, or hire another worker for the job.

Employment-at-will doctrine: Either the employer or the employee can terminate the employment relationship at will.

The "at-will" doctrine strongly favors employers because many employees live paycheck to paycheck and cannot easily find another job, particularly in tough economic times. The "at-will" doctrine seems to imply a balance of power between the employer and the employee when reality commands that the employer wields much more power for the vast number of workers.

The Tennessee Supreme Court expressed the concept of employment-at-will doctrine in its 1884 decision *Payne v. Western & Atlantic Railroad*, 81 Tenn. 507, when it wrote that the employer could end the employment relationship for good cause, bad cause, or no cause at all. In other words, the employer could fire an employee for virtually any reason. The Tennessee high court explained:

> Men must be left without interference to buy and sell where they please and to discharge or retain employees at will for good cause or for no cause, or even for bad cause, without thereby being guilty of an unlawful act per se. It is a right which an employee may exercise in the same way, to the same extent, for the same cause or want of cause, as the employer.

For this reason, much of employment law centers on whether the employment-at-will doctrine applies or whether exceptions to the doctrine provide protection to the employee. Many employees are not covered by the doctrine because their employment relationship is governed by a **collective bargaining agreement** (CBA), a contract between management (the employer) and a union that provides protection for the union members who are employees. Many collective bargaining agreements contain a **just-cause clause**, which means that an employee may only be terminated for a good reason. A collective bargaining agreement serves as a specialized contract in the management-union setting. The terms and conditions of the CBA control the relationship.

Collective bargaining agreement (CBA): Contract between management and employee's union that regulates terms and conditions of employment.

Just-cause clause: An employee may only be terminated for good reason.

Other employees—even those not covered by a CBA—may have signed an employment contract. If they have, this contract forms the baseline of the employment relationship and often (though not always) supersedes the employment-at-will doctrine. Many professional or high-level executives sign such contracts with their employers. Most employees do not sign such contracts for a specific term. Instead, they are governed by the employment-at-will doctrine.

Even if an employee is not part of a union or governed by a CBA, an employee could sign a contract with an employer. Employment contracts must contain the standard elements of a contract: *offer*, *acceptance*, *consideration*, and *a meeting of the minds*. An employer may make an offer of employment in the form of a written contract. If the employer agrees to the conditions, the employee has accepted the agreement.

Consideration refers to the fact that each party agrees to provide something of value to make the contract work. In the employment setting, the employee agrees to provide his or her services, and the employer agrees to compensate the employee for such services. Finally, a meeting of the minds means that both parties come to a mutual understanding as to the terms and conditions of the contractual agreement.

An employment contract should specify a description of the employee's job and particular duties. Explaining an employee's job duties can often ward off disagreements later in the relationship and provide the employee with guidance as to the expectations of the employer. Obviously, an employment contract should explain the compensation package provided by the employer, including salary, benefits, base pay and bonus pay, and severance packages.

The benefit package should include insurance, vacation days, sick days, a 401(k) retirement plan, and perhaps parking privileges.

An employment contract should also contain a **termination clause**. Preferably, the employer can terminate an employee only for good cause, rather than for a bad or unfair reason. Examples of good cause for termination often include disloyalty, the failure to perform the essential functions of the job, breach of a fiduciary duty, disclosure of work secrets, fraud or embezzlement, and illegal drug use in the workplace. Many employment contracts may have a good behavior clause that may cover a wider variety of conduct.

Termination clause:
Provision in contract for termination of the employee.

Such a contract includes an agreement that the employee will work for a specified amount of time for a certain amount of compensation. Such employment contracts exist for a number of professional or executive employees. If such a contract exists, the contract controls the parameters of the employment relationship. The at-will doctrine does not apply. These contracts usually must be written. However, sometimes courts will enforce oral contracts if express promises were made.

Still another contractual-based exception to the at-will doctrine applies with certain **employee handbooks or manuals**. An employee handbook or manual can create a legally binding contract if the employer agrees to be bound by its provisions. The handbook exception can create an implied contract with respect to the amount of an employee's probationary period, a progressive discipline policy, and merit or pay raises. Keep in mind that the general rule in most states is that an employee handbook does not create a contract and constitutes nothing more than general statements of policy. Many employers expressly include a **reservation-of-rights clause**, which gives employers discretion to modify the terms and conditions in the handbook.

Employee handbooks or manuals:
Documents that may create a legally binding contract if the employer agrees to be bound by its provisions.

Reservation-of-rights clause:
Gives employers discretion to modify the terms and conditions in the handbook.

PUBLIC EMPLOYMENT

The employment at-will doctrine governs many employees in the private sector, but does not entirely do so for the more than 22 million people that work for the government. Public employees—those who work for the federal, state, or local government—have at least some constitutional or statutory protections that give them a degree of job security. Public employees possess some First Amendment protections, meaning that a public employer may not terminate them for speaking as a citizen on matters of public importance. In *Pickering v. Board of Education*, 391 U.S. 563 (1968), the U.S. Supreme Court ruled that Illinois school district officials violated the free-speech rights of high school science teacher Marvin Pickering when they terminated him for writing a letter to the editor to his local newspaper.

The Court wrote that "the problem in any case is to arrive at a balance between the interests of the teacher, as a citizen, in commenting upon matters of public concern and the interest of the State, as an employer, in promoting the efficiency of the public services it performs through its employees." In a more recent decision—*Garcetti v. Ceballos*, 547 U.S. 410 (2006)—the Court ruled that public employees have no free-speech rights when they "make statements pursuant to their official duties" as employees. Today, courts analyze the core functions of a public employee to determine whether he or she was speaking more as a citizen or as an employee.

The due process clause sometimes limits public employers in how they treat their employees. Some public employees have property interests in their jobs, meaning that a public employer cannot take away their jobs without giving them the **procedural due process** protections of notice and a hearing to contest the adverse employment action. Procedural due process means that before a governmental entity can infringe on a person's life, liberty, or property interests, they must do so pursuant to a fair process or procedure. The touchstone of procedural due process is notice and a hearing.

Procedural due process: Protection of notice and hearing to contest adverse action by a governmental agency pursuant to a fair process or procedure.

Government employees may have the protection of various civil service statutes that give a degree of job security. These laws may provide workers for different government agencies protections that employees in the private sector simply do not possess.

Public Policy Exceptions

In most states, there are public policy exceptions to the employment-at-will doctrine even for workers in the private sector. Public policy is evidenced by the actions of the state legislature, creating legislative exceptions to employment at will. Courts also can create judicial exceptions to employment at will. For example, in many states an employer cannot fire an employee who serves on a jury, blows the whistle on illegality in the workplace, or files a workers' compensation claim. Tennessee's Public Protection Act of 1990 prohibits employers from terminating employees for refusing to remain silent about illegal activities in the workplace.

Selected State Whistleblower Laws

Minnesota's Law, Minn. Stat. §§181.931-181.935

An employer shall not discharge or otherwise discriminate against an employee for reporting a violation of any federal or state law, or for participating in an investigation. An employee shall not be discharged for refusing to perform an action that violates state or federal law.

---

continued >

Oregon Whistleblower Law, Or. Rev. Stat. §659.550

An employer shall not take any retaliatory action against an employee because the employee has in good faith reported criminal activity, assisted or cooperated in a criminal or civil investigation, hearing, proceeding or trial.

Tennessee's Public Protection Act, T.C.A. §50-1-304

No employee shall be discharged or terminated *solely* for refusing to participate in, or for refusing to remain silent about, illegal activities.

The theory behind public policy exceptions is that there is a larger societal interest in certain actions, such as having citizens fulfill their civic duty and serve on juries, that trump the employer's interests. In many states, if an employer takes adverse action against an employee for serving on a jury, the employer will be liable for both compensatory and punitive damages (see Chapter 6).

Consider the case of Cathy Jackson, who worked as a circulation manager for a newspaper in Nebraska. The newspaper promoted her twice during her tenure. However, she suffered an injury to her left wrist while working a labeling machine at work. She had to have surgery and filed a workers' compensation claim. Her physical therapist contacted her employer and said that she needed relief from manual repetitive labor. The newspaper terminated her employment. She sued for retaliatory discharge, claiming that the paper fired her in retaliation for filing a workers' compensation claim and for suffering an injury. The newspaper relied on the employment-at-will doctrine as its defense.

The Nebraska Supreme Court ruled in favor of the employee in *Jackson v. Morris Communications Corporation*, 657 N.W.2d 634 (2003). The Nebraska high court reasoned that the workers' compensation laws in the state recognized the strong interest in protecting injured workers. The court explained: "We are convinced that the unique and beneficent nature of the Nebraska Workers' Compensation Act presents a clear mandate of public policy which warrants application of the public policy exception. Thus, we recognize a public policy exception to the at-will employment doctrine and allow an action for retaliatory discharge when an employee has been discharged for filing a workers' compensation claim."

The Washington Supreme Court ruled in its 2008 decision *Danny v. Laidlaw Transit Services, Inc.*, 193 P.2d 128, that the state had a strong public policy against employers terminating employees who take time off from work to protect their families from the threat of domestic violence. The state high court explained: "The legislature's consistent pronouncements over the last 30 years provides evidence of a clear public policy to prevent domestic violence—a policy the legislature has sought to further by taking clear, concrete actions to encourage domestic violence victims to end abuse, leave their abusers, protect their children, and cooperate with law enforcement and prosecution efforts to hold the abuser accountable."

However, the employment-at-will doctrine still applies in many situations and often seemingly leads to unfair results. Consider the case of *Bammert v. Don's Super Value*, 646 N.W.2d 365 (Wis. 2002). Karen Bammert worked at Don's Super Value store for owner Don Williams. The problem began when Williams's wife was arrested on suspicion of drunk driving. One of the arresting officers was Karen Bammert's husband. Williams retaliated by firing Karen Bammert, presumably for her husband's participation in his wife's arrest.

The Wisconsin Supreme Court reasoned that to create a public policy exception to the employment-at-will doctrine requires "a constitutional, statutory or administrative provision that clearly articulates a fundamental and well-defined public policy." Bammert argued that the public policy exceptions were enforcement of drunk-driving laws and marriage laws, but, the Wisconsin Supreme Court found that these valid laws and interests were not sufficiently related to the employment context. "Of course, a natural sense of outrage over the facts alleged in this case brings on a desire to see the law provide a remedy, but it does not," the Wisconsin Supreme Court wrote.

Wisconsin Supreme Court Decision in *Bammert v. Don's Super Value* 646 N.W.2d 365 (Wis. 2002)

Bammert was not fired for *her* participation in the enforcement of the laws against drunk driving; she was fired for *her husband's* participation in the enforcement of those laws. Discharges for conduct outside of the employment relationship by someone other than the discharged employee are not actionable under present law. The public policy generally favoring the stability of marriage, while unquestionably strong, provides an insufficient basis upon which to enlarge what was meant to be, and has always been, an extremely narrow exception to employment-at-will.

Bammert advocates an expansion of the public policy exception far beyond that contemplated by our case law, and she cites no authority for it. Up to now, where the exception has been applied, the public policy at issue has always been vindicated by the employee himself or herself, within the context of the employment relationship. . . .

Bammert's claim identifies a public policy completely unrelated to her employment, being enforced by someone else, who is employed elsewhere. That the "someone else" is her husband makes her discharge obviously retaliatory, and reminds us of the sometimes harsh reality of employment-at-will, but it does not provide acceptable grounds for expansion of the public policy exception beyond its present boundaries. . . .

continued >

Public policy comes in many variations, is implicated in many contexts, and is carried out by many people, both publicly and privately. Once expanded in the manner argued here, the public policy exception would no longer be subject to any discernable limiting principles. It would arguably apply to retaliatory discharges based upon the conduct of *any* non-employee relative, for the fulfillment of or refusal to violate public policy in a wide variety of ways and in a manner completely unconnected to the employment relationship.

The public policy exception cannot be stretched that far and still be recognizable under Brockmeyer's limited formulation. Accordingly, we decline to recognize a cause of action for wrongful discharge under the public policy exception to the at-will employment doctrine for terminations in retaliation for the conduct of a non-employee spouse.

In 2007, the Oklahoma Supreme Court refused to find an exception to the employment-at-will doctrine, ruling that a bank could terminate one of its employees for the employee's refusal to drop an open records counterclaim against the city government. Even though the employee ultimately prevailed in his open-record dispute against the city, the reviewing courts sided with the bank and upheld its termination decision.

The Oklahoma high court explained in *Shero v. Grand Savings Bank*, 161 P.3d 298 (Ok. 2007): "We hold that because the Open Records Act is silent regarding any aspect of the employment relationship, the Open Records Act does not contain a clear mandate of public policy and therefore, the Employer/Bank did not violate any public policy when it terminated Employee's employment for his refusal to dismiss his claims against a third party pursuant to the Open Records Act."

States vary in their allegiance to the at-will doctrine. Some states are called "at-will" states because they recognize fewer exceptions to employment at will. Montana legislatively abrogated employment at will with a 1987 law: the Wrongful Discharge from Employment Act. In Montana, an employer can fire an employee only if the employer has just cause.

Another exception to the employment-at-will doctrine is the **duty of good faith and fair dealing**. Courts in a few states provide that certain bad conduct by an employer may cross the line and become so unfair that it violates the basic principles of good faith and fair dealing. Many states do not recognize this exception.

Duty of good faith and fair dealing: Courts in a few states apply an exception to the employment-at-will doctrine based on this standard of good faith, but most states do not allow this exception.

EMPLOYMENT DISCRIMINATION

Perhaps the largest exception to employment at will is employment discrimination. Employers over a certain size cannot fire or discriminate against an employee because of that employee's race, sex, religion, color, or national origin. Other federal laws prohibit discrimination based on age and disability. There are a litany of federal and state laws that prohibit such conduct by employers. These laws do not cover all employers. Make sure to check the definition of "employer" in the different laws to ensure that they cover smaller employers.

Title VII of the Civil Rights Act of 1964

The largest federal antidiscrimination law is **Title VII of the Civil Rights Act of 1964**. Passed during the civil rights movement, the law makes it an "unlawful employment practice for an employer . . . to discriminate against any individual with respect to his compensation, terms, conditions, or privileges of employment, because of such individual's race, color, religion, sex, or national origin." The law also prohibits employers from retaliating against employees who participate in employment discrimination proceedings or oppose unlawful employment practices.

Title VII of the Civil Rights Act of 1964: Makes it unlawful to discriminate against employees on the basis of race, color, religion, sex, or national origin.

Title VII applies to all public and private employers who employ 15 or more full-time employees for 20 weeks during that year or the previous year. This means that some smaller employers are not subject to Title VII. However, state laws might provide protection. For example, the Tennessee Human Rights Act of 1978 (the THRA) applies to all those employers with eight or more full-time employees.

Congress passed Title VII largely to prohibit rampant discrimination against African Americans, who still faced discrimination in employment even though the U.S. Supreme Court had ruled segregation laws unconstitutional. Congress believed that the law was necessary to ensure equal opportunity for African Americans and others. Even though Congress passed Title VII because of discrimination against racial minorities, it is clear that Title VII provides protections to persons of all races. If an employee of one race is treated worse than a similarly situated employee of another race, then that might constitute unlawful employment discrimination. For example, if two employees, an African-American employee and a Caucasian employee, both come to work late, the employer should treat them generally the same. If the employer terminates the African-American employee and only gives a slap on the wrist to the Caucasian employee, the employer may have engaged in unlawful racial discrimination against the African-American employee.

Often, it is very difficult for plaintiffs to prove employment discrimination. Rarely do employers admit that they terminated someone because of their race. It also is difficult to find so-called "smoking gun" evidence that clearly shows direct evidence of discrimination. Rather, employment discrimination plaintiffs must rely on circumstantial evidence to prove that an employer treated an employee differently. This theory of discrimination is called **disparate treatment**. This theory applies when an employer treats an employee worse than other similarly situated employees not in the employee's protected class or category. For example, if an employer treats white employees better than Latino employees, the employer is engaging in unlawful disparate treatment based on race.

The U.S. Supreme Court created a standard for evaluating employment discrimination claims when there is circumstantial evidence in *McDonnell Douglas Corp. v. Green*, 411 U.S. 792 (1973). Percy Green, an African American involved in civil rights activities, worked as a mechanic at McDonnell Douglas from 1956 until he was laid off in 1964. He believed that his layoff was racially motivated, as several white employees with less seniority were retained by the employer.

Green then protested his layoff in various ways, including picketing the home of James F. McDonnell, chairman of McDonnell Douglas. In October 1964, he and others organized a "stall-in," where they stalled their cars on the main roads leading to the McDonnell Douglas plant. In July 1965, Green applied for work at McDonnell Douglas, who was hiring workers again. Although qualified for the job, Green was not hired. He believed this is because of his civil rights activity and because of his race. He filed a claim for race discrimination under Title VII.

The federal district court ruled against Green in 1970, finding that McDonnell Douglas did not rehire him because of his participation in the "stall-in." The district court reasoned that the "stall-in" was illegal activity and that it was not protected activity.

Green appealed to the Eighth U.S. Circuit Court of Appeals, which reversed and found that the district court was too quick to dismiss Green's racial discrimination claim. "McDonnell has not demonstrated . . . that Green's participation in the 'stall-in' would impede his ability to perform the job for which he applied," the appeals court wrote. "There is no evidence that Green's conduct would cause fellow employees or supervisors to refuse to cooperate with Green, thereby disrupting plant operations."

McDonnell Douglas appealed to the U.S. Supreme Court, which set forth a three-step standard of proof for employers and employees in Title VII discrimination cases. The three steps are as follows: (1) the employee must make out a prima facie, or basic case, of discrimination; (2) the employer must counter with a legitimate, nondiscriminatory reason for its action against the employee; and (3) the employee must then show that the defendant's stated reason was *pretexual* (invalid reason) or false.

The first step is that the plaintiff must present enough evidence to survive early dismissal by a court. A prima facie case means that a plaintiff has initially shown that the employer may have acted unlawfully, or in a discriminatory manner. In other words, the prima facie prong establishes a presumption that the employer committed unlawful discrimination. The

Disparate treatment: When an employer intentionally treats an employee substantially worse than other similarly situated employees not in the protected class or category.

Supreme Court explained this prima facie prong in its *McDonnell Douglas* decision:

> *The complainant in a Title VII trial must carry the initial burden under the statute of establishing a* prima facie *case of racial discrimination. This may be done by showing (i) that he belongs to a racial minority; (ii) that he applied and was qualified for a job for which the employer was seeking applicants; (iii) that, despite his qualifications, he was rejected; and (iv) that, after his rejection, the position remained open and the employer continued to seek applicants from persons of complainant's qualifications.*

If the plaintiff-employee establishes a prima facie, or basic, case of discrimination, the burden shifts to the employer to establish a **legitimate nondiscriminatory reason** for the discharge. For example, an employer might argue that the employee could not get along well with co-employees or showed insubordination on the job.

Legitimate nondiscriminatory reason: A legally acceptable employer defense where there is evidence of discharge for reasonable cause.

If the employer asserts a legitimate, nondiscriminatory reason for its adverse action against the plaintiff, then the burden shifts back to the plaintiff to establish that the defendant's stated reason was false, or *pretexual*. This is called the **pretext stage**.

Pretext stage: When burden of proof shifts back to the plaintiff after employer asserts a legitimate nondiscriminatory reason.

Applying this standard, the Supreme Court then sent the case back down to the trial court, saying that the trial court must determine whether McDonnell Douglas failed to rehire Green because of his civil rights activities or because he participated in the stall-in. On remand, the district court found that Percy Green was not rehired at McDonnell Douglas, because of his illegal activities, not because of his race. He appealed, and the Eighth U.S. Circuit Court of Appeals affirmed the lower court.

Percy Green's discrimination case involved an alleged failure to rehire. But, the so-called McDonnell-Douglas formula applies to many different types of cases, including discharges, failure to promote, and virtually any other type of adverse employment action taken against an employee.

In order to establish a race discrimination claim, a plaintiff must show that he or she is a (1) member of a protected class; (2) was qualified for the position or meeting the legitimate business expectations of the job; (3) suffered an adverse employment action; and (4) was treated worse than a similarly situated person outside of the protected class.

The first prong is relatively easy to establish, as every employee is a member of a specific racial group. The second prong focuses on whether the employee is qualified or is meeting the minimum threshold requirements of the job. An employer should be able to discipline a person who is clearly not meeting even the basic threshold duties of the job.

The third prong is that the plaintiff must show that he or she suffered an adverse employment action—or a tangible loss in the workplace.

Discharges, demotions, and suspensions without pay clearly are adverse employment actions, but other employer actions are not as clear. What if an employer transfers an employee to a less-desirable job but does not reduce the employee's pay? The employer will contend there is no adverse employment action because the employee did not suffer any loss in pay. The employee will counter that the transfer led to a less desirable position.

What if an employer gives an employee a negative job evaluation? The employer will say that a job evaluation, in and of itself, has not led to an ultimate employment decision. The employee will counter that a negative job evaluation is often the first step toward a later adverse action taken by an employer.

The final prong often focuses on whether the employee can point to some evidence that he or she was treated worse than employees of another race, sex, or religion. Take the example of an African-American manager at a restaurant who is fired for making a nighttime deposit one day late. Because of a family emergency, the manager made the deposit in the morning instead of the evening. The employer says that the employee has been terminated for failing to adhere to a generally applicable rule, that managerial employees must make daily deposits in a timely fashion. This would appear to be a solid defense for the employer.

But let's say the evidence shows that a Caucasian manager made a deposit two days late and received only a verbal warning. That difference in treatment could be strong circumstantial evidence of race discrimination—that the employer treats Caucasian managers better than African-American managers.

These cases often boil down to whether a judge or jury believes that the stated reason for the employee's fate was a discriminatory reason or a legitimate reason. Often, the employee must try to disprove the employer's supposedly legitimate reason at the pretext phase. The employee can try to do so in three different ways. These include showing that (1) the employer's stated reason has no basis in fact—that it didn't happen; (2) the employer's stated reason did not actually motivate the employer; or (3) the employer's stated reason was insufficient to motivate the employer, as other employees were not fired or treated the same way for similar conduct.

Disparate Impact Claims

Most discrimination claims are disparate treatment suits where an individual alleges that he has suffered disparate, or differential, treatment. These are intentional discrimination claims. There is another type of discrimination case: disparate impact cases. **Disparate impact claims** refer

Disparate impact claims: Apparently neutral employment practices that have an adverse impact on a particular group of individuals based on race or sex.

to what appear to be neutral employment policies that have an adverse impact on a particular group of individuals based on race or sex.

If a police department adopts a general height and weight requirement for its officers, that may work an adverse impact on women. If the department mandates that all officers must stand at least 5 feet 7 inches tall and weigh at least 140 pounds, many more women will be excluded than men. This works a disparate impact based on sex.

The U.S. Supreme Court first recognized the disparate impact theory in the race-discrimination case of *Griggs v. Duke Power*, 401 U.S. 424 (1971). Thirteen black employees of Duke Power, including lead plaintiff Willie Griggs, sued Duke Power after the company adopted a requirement that employees have a high school education and pass two intelligence tests before transferring to certain classes of jobs in the plant. Prior to July 2, 1965, the company openly discriminated against African-American employees, hiring them only for the lowest paid manual labor jobs. The company had discriminated on the basis of race and refused to hire African Americans until the U.S. Supreme Court began striking down segregation laws in the 1950s and 1960s.

The company then adopted the high school test and intelligence tests, which resulted in African Americans being unable to transfer to the more desirable divisions because they had often received inferior educational opportunities due to segregated educational systems. These new requirements had an adverse impact on black workers and the district court found that while the company previously followed a policy of overt racial discrimination in a period prior to the act, such conduct had ceased. The district court also concluded that Title VII was intended to be prospective only, and consequently, the impact of prior inequities was beyond the reach of corrective action authorized by the act.

The U.S. Supreme Court reversed, finding that the plaintiffs could pursue a claim of disparate impact discrimination. The Court reasoned:

> The objective of Congress in the enactment of Title VII is plain from the language of the statute. It was to achieve equality of employment opportunities and remove barriers that have operated in the past to favor an identifiable group of white employees over other employees. Under the Act, practices, procedures, or tests neutral on their face, and even neutral in terms of intent, cannot be maintained if they operate to "freeze" the status quo of prior discriminatory employment practices.

The Court reasoned that Duke Power had failed to show that the high school diploma and performance on the intelligence tests were related to good job performance. The Court added that "history is filled with examples of men and women who rendered highly effective performance without the conventional badges of accomplishment in terms of certificates, diplomas, or degrees."

> ## Chief Justice Warren Burger in *Griggs v. Duke Power* (1971)
>
> The Act proscribes not only overt discrimination but also practices that are fair in form, but discriminatory in operation. The touchstone is business necessity. If an employment which operates to exclude Negroes cannot be shown to be related to job performance, the practice is prohibited. . . .
>
> In short, the Act does not command that any person be hired simply because he was formerly the subject of discrimination, or because he is a member of a minority group. Discriminatory preference for any group, minority or majority, is precisely and only what Congress has proscribed. What is required by Congress is the removal of artificial, arbitrary, and unnecessary barriers to employment when the barriers operate invidiously to discriminate on the basis of racial or other impermissible classification.

The *Griggs* decision did not prohibit employers from using professionally developed tests to determine future employees. What it required was that such tests have a connection to actual job performance. The tests cannot be used as a guise to discriminate against particular groups.

In disparate impact cases, once a plaintiff shows that an employment practice does have an adverse impact on a particular group, then the employer must show that the practice is "job related for the position in question and consistent with business necessity." This means that the testing requirement or other rule actually has a close connection with effective job performance. The **Equal Employment Opportunity Commission (EEOC)**, the federal agency that enforces Title VII and other antidiscrimination laws, requires that employers only use job-related tests. The EEOC uses a *four-fifths or 80% rule* to determine whether an employment practice has a disparate impact on a protected group. Under this rule, if the protected group is selected at less than 80% for the preferred group, then the employment practice is questionable. If the EEOC finds that a practice meets this four-fifths standard, then it assumes that the practice has a disparate impact on a protected group

Equal Employment Opportunity Commission (EEOC): The federal agency that enforces Title VII and other antidiscrimination laws.

Administrative Requirements

Before filing a Title VII claim, a person must file a **charge of discrimination** before the EEOC. A charge of discrimination is a complaint that an employee has suffered some type of discrimination in the workplace. There are time limits that a person must adhere to or lose the claim forever. In most states, an individual must file an EEOC charge within 180 days after the allegedly discriminatory act. In other states, individuals have 300 days to file a complaint. In the charge, the individual explains his or her allegation. The EEOC then conducts an investigation to determine whether or not the complaint has substance.

Charge of discrimination: Complaint filed with EEOC that an employee has suffered some type of discrimination in the workplace.

Sometimes, the EEOC will pursue the claim itself on behalf of the aggrieved individual. But many times, the EEOC will issue the individual a **"right to sue" letter**. Once the individual receives a right to sue letter, that person has 90 days to file suit in court.

Right to sue letter:
EEOC informs the individual of the right to sue and must file suit in court within 90 days.

Section 1981 of the *United States Code*

There are other laws that prohibit race discrimination in employment. An older civil rights law dating back to 1866 (42 U.S.C. §1981) also prohibits intentional race discrimination.

Text of Section 1981 of the *United States Code*

§1981 Equal Rights Under the Law

(a) Statement of equal rights: All persons within the jurisdiction of the United States *shall have the same right in every State and Territory to make and enforce contracts*, to sue, be parties, give evidence, and to the full and equal benefit of all laws and proceedings for the security of persons and property *as is enjoyed by white citizens*, and shall be subject to like punishment, pains, penalties, taxes, licenses, and exactions of every kind, and to no other.

(b) "Make and enforce contracts" defined: For purposes of this section, the term "make and enforce contracts" includes the making, performance, modification, and termination of contracts, and the enjoyment of all benefits, privileges, terms, and conditions of the contractual relationship.

(c) Protection against impairment: The rights protected by this section are protected against impairment *by nongovernmental discrimination* and impairment under color of State law.

Section 1981 applies to disparate treatment race discrimination cases, not disparate impact claims. In other words, Section 1981 applies to cases of intentional racial discrimination. In general, the proof scheme in Section 1981 cases is the same as for Title VII race cases.

There are key differences between Section 1981 and Title VII; for instance, an employee does not have to first file with the EEOC before making a Section 1981 claim. There are no administrative exhaustion requirements under Section 1981. Therefore, the statute can be an important tool for a plaintiff who has failed to file a charge with the EEOC or failed to file a lawsuit within 90 days of receiving a notice of right to sue.

Section 1981 provides two distinct advantages over Title VII when it comes to seeking damages from state defendants. First, unlike Title VII, Section 1981 provides for punitive damages against state officials acting in their individual capacity. Second, unlike Title VII, Section 1981 does not impose any caps on the amount of compensatory or punitive damages that can be awarded to the plaintiff.

Section 1981 also covers retaliation claims advanced by those who alleged their employer retaliated against them for race-based reasons. In *CBOCS West Inc. v. Humphries,* 553 U.S. 442 (2008), the Supreme Court held that Section 1981 of the Civil Rights Act, guaranteeing equality in the right to make a contract without regard to race, encompasses claims of retaliation.

SEX DISCRIMINATION AND HARASSMENT

The United States has a long and sordid history of gender discrimination. Much of this discrimination has surfaced in employment law. In 1873, the U.S. Supreme Court ruled that the state of Illinois could refuse Myra Bradwell, a female attorney from Vermont, a license to practice law. Justice Joseph Bradley wrote in *Bradwell v. Illinois,* 83 U.S. 130: "The paramount mission and destiny of women are to fulfill the noble and benign offices of wife and mother."

Consider also that when U.S. Supreme Court Justices Sandra Day O'Connor and Ruth Bader Ginsburg, the first two women to serve on the Court, graduated near the top of their law school classes, they had trouble finding employment with law firms. Title VII prohibits discrimination based on sex in the employment arena.

When originally drafted, Title VII did not prohibit sex discrimination in employment. Rather, the purpose of the bill, passed during the civil rights movement, was to prohibit racial discrimination, arguably the most pressing domestic issue in the United States at that time. Rep. Howard Smith inserted a one-word amendment, "sex," to the bill. Some historians and political scientists suggest that the initial motivation for adding "sex" to Title VII was to drive opposition to the measure to ensure that it didn't pass. However, the strategy failed, and the measure passed.

Sex discrimination claims vary, but the basis is that a person is treated worse because of his or her gender. A special type of sex discrimination claim is **sexual harassment**, a form of sex discrimination in which an employee has to endure severe and pervasive harassment based on sex. There are different types of sexual harassment claims, including *quid pro quo* and *hostile work environment* claims. **Quid pro quo claims** occur when an employer or supervisory employee engages in conduct that seeks sexual benefits in exchange for job benefits. A classic example is where a supervisory employee tells a worker "sleep with me or lose your job."

Hostile workplace environment claims apply to situations in which an employee has to endure severe and pervasive harassment that negatively impacts the employee's working environment. Forcing an employee to endure a series of sexually laced jokes and comments could rise to the level of hostile environment harassment. In a hostile environment claim, a plaintiff does not have to show a loss of a job or other tangible benefit to recover. In some courts, there used to be a restrictive rule that a sexual

Sexual harassment: Discrimination in the form of severe and pervasive harassment based on sex.

Quid pro quo claims: When an employer or supervisor engages in conduct seeking sexual favors in exchange for job benefits.

Hostile workplace environment claims: Situations in which an employee has to endure severe and pervasive sexual harassment that negatively impacts the employee's working environment.

harassment plaintiff had to show evidence of severe psychological injury or harm to recover damages. Courts adopted this rule in order to reduce the likelihood of frivolous claims. But in *Harris v. Forklift Systems*, 510 U.S. 17 (1993), the U.S. Supreme Court ruled that a sexual harassment plaintiff did not have to show severe psychological harm, but show that the harassment is severe and pervasive enough to alter the working conditions of the employee.

U.S. Supreme Court in *Harris v. Forklift Systems* 510 U.S 17 (1993)

This standard, which we reaffirm today, takes a middle path between making actionable any conduct that is merely offensive and requiring the conduct to cause a tangible psychological injury. As we pointed out in Meritor, "mere utterance of an . . . epithet which engenders offensive feelings in a employee," ibid. (internal quotation marks omitted) does not sufficiently affect the conditions of employment to implicate Title VII. Conduct that is not severe or pervasive enough to create an objectively hostile or abusive work environment—an environment that a reasonable person would find hostile or abusive—is beyond Title VII's purview. Likewise, if the victim does not subjectively perceive the environment to be abusive, the conduct has not actually altered the conditions of the victim's employment, and there is no Title VII violation.

But Title VII comes into play before the harassing conduct leads to a nervous breakdown. A discriminatorily abusive work environment, even one that does not seriously affect employees' psychological wellbeing, can and often will detract from employees' job performance, discourage employees from remaining on the job, or keep them from advancing in their careers. Moreover, even without regard to these tangible effects, the very fact that the discriminatory conduct was so severe or pervasive that it created a work environment abusive to employees because of their race, gender, religion, or national origin offends Title VII's broad rule of workplace equality. The appalling conduct alleged in Meritor, and the reference in that case to environments "so heavily polluted with discrimination as to destroy completely the emotional and psychological stability of minority group workers," merely present some especially egregious examples of harassment. They do not mark the boundary of what is actionable.

We therefore believe the District Court erred in relying on whether the conduct "seriously affect [ed] plaintiff's psychological wellbeing" or led her to "suffe[r] injury." Such an inquiry may needlessly focus the factfinder's attention on concrete psychological harm, an element Title VII does not require. Certainly Title VII bars conduct that would seriously affect a reasonable person's psychological wellbeing, but the statute is not limited to such conduct. So long as the environment would reasonably be perceived, and is perceived, as hostile or abusive, there is no need for it also to be psychologically injurious.

In 1998, the U.S. Supreme Court explained in *Burlington Industries v. Ellerth*, 524 U.S. 742, that the key differences in harassment cases focused on whether the harasser was a supervisor or co-employee of the plaintiff and whether the harassment led to a tangible employment action against the plaintiff, such as a discharge or demotion. In supervisory harassment cases that lead to tangible employment actions (dismissal, demotion, etc.), the employer is strictly liable.

If the employee is not fired or demoted, the employer has a chance to offer an affirmative defense (1) that the employer had a sexual harassment policy in place and exercised reasonable care to prevent and promptly correct any improper sexually harassing behavior and (2) that the plaintiff-employee unreasonably failed to file a claim or seek redress under the employer's sexual harassment policy. In cases of coworker harassment, an employer is liable if the employer knew or should have known of the harassment.

Burlington Industries v. Ellerth
524 U.S 742 (1998)

An employer is subject to vicarious liability to a victimized employee for an actionable hostile environment created by a supervisor with immediate (or successively higher) authority over the employee. When no tangible employment action is taken, a defending employer may raise an affirmative defense to liability or damages, subject to proof by a preponderance of the evidence, see Fed. Rule Civ. Proc. 8(c). The defense comprises two necessary elements: (a) that the employer exercised reasonable care to prevent and correct promptly any sexually harassing behavior, and (b) that the plaintiff employee unreasonably failed to take advantage of any preventive or corrective opportunities provided by the employer or to avoid harm otherwise. While proof that an employer had promulgated an anti-harassment policy with complaint procedure is not necessary in every instance as a matter of law, the need for a stated policy suitable to the employment circumstances may appropriately be addressed in any case when litigating the first element of the defense. And while proof that an employee failed to fulfill the corresponding obligation of reasonable care to avoid harm is not limited to showing any unreasonable failure to use any complaint procedure provided by the employer, a demonstration of such failure will normally suffice to satisfy the employer's burden under the second element of the defense. No affirmative defense is available, however, when the supervisor's harassment culminates in a tangible employment action, such as discharge, demotion, or undesirable reassignment.

Another example of impermissible sex discrimination in employment is taking negative action against an employee simply because she is pregnant. In 1978, Congress amended Title VII by adding the **Pregnancy**

Discrimination Act of 1978, known as the PDA. Under this law, employees cannot refuse to hire workers because they are pregnant. The EEOC explains that "pregnant employees must be permitted to work as long as they are able to perform their jobs" and that "employers must hold open a job for a pregnancy-related absence the same length of time jobs are held open for employees on sick or disability leave."

Pregnancy Discrimination Act of 1978 (PDA): Prohibits employers from not hiring or firing employees because they are pregnant.

Title VII does not currently provide a remedy for those employees who are terminated because they are gay or lesbian. Sexual orientation discrimination is not a protected category under Title VII, like race or sex. However, many states have laws that do safeguard employees from discrimination based on sexual orientation. California, Colorado, Connecticut, Hawaii, Illinois, Maine, Maryland, Massachusetts, Minnesota, Nevada, New Hampshire, New Jersey, New Mexico, New York, Oregon, Rhode Island, Vermont, Washington, and Wisconsin all have state laws that prohibit such discrimination in both the public and private sector.

Nearly every year since 1994, legislators have introduced into Congress a bill known as the *Employment Non-Discrimination Act*. This measure would amend Title VII to prohibit employers from discriminating against employees based on their sexual orientation. The measure has never passed both houses of Congress.

THEORIES OF DISCRIMINATION

Most of the examples in this text have examined cases in which an employee of one race was clearly treated differently from an employee of another race. In other words, these are cases of intentional discrimination or *disparate treatment* discrimination. Title VII applies to more than just disparate treatment. It also applies to cases of *disparate impact*: when an apparently neutral employment policy has an adverse impact upon a particular protected class.

United States Code
Title VII Provision on Disparate Impact
42 U.S.C. 2000e-k

(k) Burden of proof in disparate impact cases:

(1) (A) An unlawful employment practice based on disparate impact is established under this subchapter only if—

(i) a complaining party demonstrates that a respondent uses a particular employment practice that causes a *disparate impact* on the basis of race, color, religion, sex, or national origin and the respondent

---

continued >

> fails to demonstrate that the challenged practice is job related for the position in question and consistent with business necessity; or
>
> (ii) the complaining party makes the demonstration described in subparagraph (C) with respect to an alternative employment practice and the respondent refuses to adopt such alternative employment practice.

MIXED MOTIVE CASES

Sometimes it is not always easy to determine whether an employer acted for an illegitimate or a legitimate reason when taking action adverse to an employee. Sometimes, there might be multiple or mixed motives on the part of the employer. In employment discrimination law, these are called "mixed motive" cases. The U.S. Supreme Court first addressed mixed motive in the famous case of *Price Waterhouse v. Hopkins*, 490 U.S. 228 (1989).

Ann Hopkins found out that discrimination in the workplace continued when she worked at Price Waterhouse. Hopkins attended a women's college in Virginia and then went to graduate school for mathematics. She later worked at IBM and then for a big accounting firm Touche Ross. She met her husband there. He made partner and she was informed that under the company's anti-nepotism policy, neither could be a partner if both were at the firm.

Ann Hopkins left and landed a job at Price Waterhouse. She had three kids, a demanding job, and an unfaithful husband. Still, she helped land a $25 million dollar contract from the State Department for her employer. After five years at Price Waterhouse, several partners in her department proposed her for partnership consideration. She was denied advancement and instead placed on hold. Several senior partners focused on her abrasive, aggressive style.

One of Hopkins's partners informed her that she should "walk more femininely, talk more femininely, dress more femininely, wear make-up and jewelry, have my hair styled." Other comments attributed to various partners at the accounting firm were "too macho," "suggest a charm school before she is considered for admission," "arrogant and self-centered," and "great intellectual capacity but very abrasive in her dealings with staff."

Hopkins soldiered back to work and tried to make the best of a bad situation, but many of the partners in her own firm withdrew their support for her. She was not happy and eventually filed a complaint with the Equal Employment Opportunity Commission. She held on at the firm for several more months but then resigned in December 1983. The case went all the way to the U.S. Supreme Court. The U.S. Supreme Court ruled that if an employee can show that gender was a factor in the employment decision, it shifts the burden of proof to the employer to show that the same decision would have been made absent the discrimination. An employer who makes this showing can avoid liability. According to the court, "a defendant may avoid liability by proving by a preponderance of the evidence that it would have made the same decision had it not taken the plaintiff's [gender] into account."

But, the Court also recognized that Title VII provided a remedy for those employees who were the victim of sex stereotyping. "An employer who objects to aggressiveness in women but whose positions require this trait places women in an intolerable and impermissible Catch-22: out of a job if they behave aggressively and out of a job if they do not. Title VII lifts women out of this bind."

The Supreme Court remanded Hopkins's suit back down to the lower court. She eventually won her case and went back to work at Price Water-house, finishing out her career at the job.

Later, Congress addressed the mixed-motive type of case by amending Title VII in 1991. The law now provides "An unlawful employment practice is established when the complaining party demonstrates that race, color, religion, sex or national origin was a motivating factor for any employment practice, even though other factors also motivated the practice." Employers can still argue that they would have made the same decision in spite of the illegitimate factor and reduce their exposure under the law.

Retaliation

Title VII and state antidiscrimination laws also prohibit unlawful retaliation by employers against employees who oppose discriminatory actions or who participate in a discrimination case. Section 704(e) of Title VII provides:

> It shall be an unlawful employment practice for an employer to discriminate against any of his employees . . . because he has opposed any practice made an unlawful employment practice by this subchapter, or because he has made a charge, testified, assisted, or participated in any manner in an investigation, proceeding or hearing under this subchapter.

Title VII's anti-retaliation provision, 42 U.S.C. Section 2000e-3(a), has two parts: (1) an opposition clause and (2) a participation clause. The opposition clause protects those employees who oppose unlawful employment discrimination. The participation clause protects those employees who testify, assist, or participate in any manner in a Title VII proceeding.

Take the example of an employee who is subpoenaed to give a deposition in a co-employee's discrimination suit. The employer cannot take adverse action against that employee simply because he or she participated in the lawsuit.

Title VII contains both a *participation clause* and an *opposition clause*. If an employee complains to management about what that employee perceives as a sexually harassing environment and the employee is demoted two weeks later, the employer has committed unlawful retaliation. If an employee gives testimony to an investigator about the harassing conduct of the employee's supervisor and the employer demotes that employee, the employer has committed unlawful retaliation.

Retaliation claims can survive even when the underlying discrimination claim does not. In *Thompson v. North American Stainless*, 131 S.Ct. 863 (2011), the U.S. Supreme Court ruled that Eric Thompson could sue for retaliation when his employer fired him after his fiancée filed a sex discrimination claim against the employer. Even though Thompson was not engaged in protected activity himself, the Court reasoned that it still constitutes retaliation to take adverse action against an employee simply because his spouse or significant other complained of discrimination.

In fiscal year 2010, the EEOC reported that there were more retaliation claims filed under Title VII than any other type of claim, even more than race and sex discrimination claims.

AGE DISCRIMINATION

Another leading federal antidiscrimination law is the **Age Discrimination in Employment Act of 1967**, known by its acronym the ADEA. The ADEA provides that employers may not discharge or otherwise discriminate against employees who are 40 years of age or older. For example, if a 47-year-old man is fired by his employer and replaced by a 26-year-old, the employer may be liable for unlawful age discrimination. An employer can violate the act even if it replaces an older worker with someone who is older than 40, as long as the replacement is substantially younger than the original worker. For example, the U.S. Supreme Court ruled in *O'Connor v. Consolidated Coin Caterers Corp.*, 517 U.S. 308 (1996) that an employer violated the ADEA by replacing a 56-year-old worker with a 40-year-old.

Employers who impose different standards of performance on older workers violate the ADEA. Such standards must be applied to all workers regardless of age. Even when an employer conducts a general reduction in force, the employer may not use the employer's age as a negative factor. In other words, an employer cannot use a reduction in force as a way to get rid of its older workers.

Just as with race and sex claims, workers can sue an employer for creating a hostile workplace environment based on age. If an older worker can show that he or she was subjected to severe and pervasive age-based harassment, the employee may have a good age discrimination claim. The ADEA applies to all employers—public and private—that employ 20 or more employees.

Age Discrimination in Employment Act of 1967 (ADEA):
Provides that employers may not discharge or otherwise discriminate against employees who are 40 years of age or older.

DISABILITY DISCRIMINATION

In 1973, Congress passed a law called the Rehabilitation Act, which provided protection to those federal employees who were "handicapped," but the vast majority of workers in the private sector were left without federal protection. That changed in 1990 when a bipartisan Congress passed the **Americans with Disabilities Act of 1990 (ADA)**. Title I of the ADA prohibited discrimination against those qualified individuals with a disability in the workplace.

Americans with Disabilities Act of 1990 (ADA): Prohibits discrimination against qualified individuals with a disability in the workplace.

Congress recognized in its findings that "unlike individuals who have experienced discrimination on the basis of race, color, sex, national origin, religion, or age, individuals who have experienced discrimination on the basis of disability have often had no legal recourse to redress such discrimination."

The ADA provides: "No covered entity shall discriminate against a *qualified individual on the basis of disability* in regard to job application procedures, the hiring, advancement, or discharge of employees, employee compensation, job training, and other terms, conditions, and privileges of employment." Under the ADA, disability has three definitions:

The term "disability" means, with respect to an individual

(A) *a physical or mental* impairment *that* substantially limits *one or more* major life activities *of such individual;*
(B) *a record of such an impairment; or*
(C) *being regarded as having such an impairment.*

Disabilities can include physical impairments or even mental impairments, such as depression. Dreaded disease such as cancer or heart problems are disabilities within the meaning of the ADA. Importantly, the illegal use of drugs is not a disability and is not covered by the ADA. However, an employer may not discriminate against an employee who has undergone drug rehabilitation through an employee assistance program (an EAP).

**Employee Assistance Program
Provision of the Americans with Disabilities Act of 1990
(42 U.S.C. 12114 (b))**

Nothing in subsection (a) of this section shall be construed to exclude as a qualified individual with a disability an individual who:

(1) has successfully completed a supervised drug rehabilitation program and is no longer engaging in the illegal use of drugs, or has otherwise been rehabilitated successfully and is no longer engaging in such use;

---

continued >

> (2) is participating in a supervised rehabilitation program and is no longer engaging in such use; or
>
> (3) is erroneously regarded as engaging in such use, but is not engaging in such use; . . .

The term "qualified individual" means an individual who, with or without **reasonable accommodation**, can perform the essential functions of the employment position that such individual holds or desires. A reasonable accommodation might mean a transfer to a less physically strenuous job, the restructuring of work hours, the use of an interpreter or reader, and modification of equipment. Employers must offer a reasonable accommodation to an employee who is a qualified individual with a disability unless granting such an accommodation would work an undue hardship—a severe economic burden—upon the employer.

Reasonable accommodation: Employers must offer such accommodation to an employee who is a qualified individual with a disability unless granting such an accommodation would work an undue hardship.

To establish a prima facie case under the ADA, a plaintiff must be able to show that he or she

1. has a "disability,"
2. is a "qualified individual," and
3. has suffered an adverse employment action because of that disability.

Similar to sexual harassment claims under Title VII, the courts recognize claims of disability harassment under the ADA if they meet the following criteria:

1. the employee belongs to a protected group;
2. the employee was subjected to unwelcome harassment;
3. that the harassment complained of was based on disability or disabilities;
4. that the harassment complained of affected a term, condition, or privilege of employment; and
5. that the employer knew or should have known of the harassment and failed to take prompt, remedial action.

Importantly, the ADA also prohibits discriminating against an employee because that employee has a disabled spouse or close family member.

Federal Regulation Against Associational Disability Discrimination

It is unlawful for a covered entity to exclude or deny equal jobs or benefits to, or otherwise discriminate against, a qualified individual because of the known disability of an individual with whom the qualified individual is known to have a family, business, social or other relationship or association.

The ADA applies, like Title VII, to all public or private employers with 15 or more full-time employees.

Privacy Rights of Employees

Employees fear that employers have become like Big Brother, monitoring their private lives and infringing on their privacy rights. Some employers read e-mail, monitor voice-mail communications, and drug test their employees. When speaking of the right of privacy, one must distinguish between privacy rights under the federal or state constitution, laws, state common law, or contract. In the private sector, the most common privacy disputes center on whether an employer violated an employee's privacy rights under a specific statute or the common law (a privacy tort claim).

A common claim of privacy from employees concerns drug testing. In 1988, Congress passed the Drug-Free Workplace Act, which is designed to help small businesses move toward drug-free workplaces. Many states have laws that allow employers to drug test their employees. There are different types of drug testing: pre-employment testing, reasonable suspicion testing, post-accident testing, and random drug testing. Pre-employment testing occurs before a prospective employee is officially offered a job. If the person fails the drug test, he or she will not get the job or the job offer may be rescinded. The next two types of tests involve drug testing those employees who either raise legitimate suspicions of drug use or who have been involved in a motor vehicle or other accident. These types of drug tests usually are not considered to be an invasion of privacy.

However, random drug testing more directly implicates privacy concerns. Here, an employer initiates drug testing on an employee without any individualized suspicion that the employee is engaging in any illegal activity. The case law varies from state to state as to the legitimacy of random drug testing.

Polygraph Testing

The **Employee Polygraph Protection Act (1988)** places restrictions on employer's use of lie-detector tests on employees. This law prohibits an employer from taking adverse action against an employee for refusing to take a polygraph test, for negative results on a lie-detector test, or for challenging the employer's use of such tests under this federal law.

The law does allow some limited testing of employees when the employer is engaged in an ongoing investigation of theft at the employer's place of business. If the employee in question had access to the missing property and the employer has a reasonable suspicion that the employee may have been involved in the theft, the law allows the use of a polygraph.

Employee Polygraph Protection Act of 1988: Places restrictions on employer's use of lie detector tests on employees but allows some testing when employer is engaged in ongoing investigation of theft.

Employee Polygraph Protection Act
(1988) 29 U.S.C. 2001

Except as provided in sections 2006 and 2007 of this title, it shall be unlawful for any employer engaged in or affecting commerce or in the production of goods for commerce:

(1) directly or indirectly, to require, request, suggest, or cause any employee or prospective employee to take or submit to any lie detector test;

(2) to use, accept, refer to, or inquire concerning the results of any lie detector test of any employee or prospective employee;

(3) to discharge, discipline, discriminate against in any manner, or deny employment or promotion to, or threaten to take any such action against:

(A) any employee or prospective employee who refuses, declines, or fails to take or submit to any lie detector test; or

(B) any employee or prospective employee on the basis of the results of any lie detector test; or

(4) to discharge, discipline, discriminate against in any manner, or deny employment or promotion to, or threaten to take any such action against, any employee or prospective employee because:

(A) such employee or prospective employee has filed any complaint or instituted or caused to be instituted any proceeding under or related to this chapter;

(B) such employee or prospective employee has testified or is about to testify in any such proceeding; or

(C) of the exercise by such employee or prospective employee, on behalf of such employee or another person, of any right afforded by this chapter.

CHAPTER SUMMARY

1. The doctrine that governs the employment relationship in the private sector is the employment-at-will doctrine. Under this doctrine, an employer or employee can terminate the employment relationship at any time. The doctrine favors employers who usually can find replacements for employees far more quickly than most employees can find jobs.

2. There are many exceptions to the employment-at-will doctrine. One of the most common exceptions is the contract exception. Employees who sign an employment contract have whatever rights are mentioned in the contract. Many employees in the labor union setting are protected by a contract called a *collective bargaining agreement*.

3. A common exception to the employment-at-will doctrine is the public policy exception. Many states have public policy exceptions providing that employers cannot fire employees for filing a workers' compensation claim, serving on a jury, or blowing the whistle on illegal activity in the workplace.

4. Employment discrimination laws also serve as a prominent exception to the employment-at-will doctrine. The most expansive federal anti-discrimination law is Title VII of the Civil Rights Act of 1964, which covers employers, both public and private, that have 15 or more employees. Title VII prohibits discrimination against employees on the basis of race, color, sex, national origin, or religion.

5. An employee who files a Title VII claim must first show a prima facie or basic case of discrimination. This requires that the employee show that he or she is (1) in the protected class, (2) is qualified or meeting the legitimate business expectations of the employer, (3) suffers an adverse employment action, and (4) is treated worse than a similarly situated person outside of the protected class. The employer then has the obligation to provide a legally acceptable justification, called a legitimate non-discriminatory reason, for the adverse action. The employee then must show that the employer's stated reason is *pretextual*.

6. There are two basic theories of discrimination (1) disparate treatment and (2) disparate impact. Disparate treatment refers to employer actions that intentionally treat employees differently based on race, sex, or another protected activity. Disparate impact refers to an apparently neutral employment practice that has an adverse impact on one group.

7. Before filing a lawsuit in court for a Title VII violation, an individual must file a charge of discrimination with the Equal Employment Opportunity Commission (EEOC). In many states, this charge must be filed within either 180 days or 300 days of the alleged discriminatory event. The EEOC will then issue to the complaining party a notice of a right to sue, called a *right to sue letter*. The individual then has 90 days to file suit in court.

8. Title VII is not the only federal law that prohibits racial discrimination. Another statute is an older nineteenth-century statute, 42 U.S.C. Section 1981, known as Section 1981. This law prohibits intentional racial discrimination and does not require the individual to first file administratively before the EEOC.

9. Title VII also prohibits sex discrimination in employment. A special form of sex discrimination is sexual harassment, when a worker suffers severe and pervasive harassment based on sex that alters the terms and

conditions of the workplace or makes the workplace much more difficult to endure. A common type of sexual harassment claim is the hostile workplace environment claim. Different legal standards apply to harassment claims depending upon whether the harassing employee was a supervisor or coemployee of the victim.

10. Title VII does not prohibit discrimination based on sexual orientation. The Employment Non-Discrimination Act, which has been introduced in Congress nearly every session of Congress since 1994, has not been passed into law. It would prohibit such discrimination. Several states have laws that do prohibit discrimination in employment based on sexual orientation.

11. Sometimes an employer has multiple reasons for taking adverse action against an employee—a discriminatory reason and a non-discriminatory reason. These are called mixed-motive cases. A plaintiff can still prevail in a mixed-motive case, although the employer might be able to reduce damages by showing that they would have made the same decision.

12. Title VII not only prohibits unlawful employment discrimination but it also prohibits employers from retaliating against employees who either oppose unlawful employment practices or who participate in Title VII proceedings. A retaliation claim can survive even if an underlying discrimination claim fails.

13. The Age Discrimination in Employment Act, or ADEA, was a federal law passed in 1967 to prohibit unlawful age discrimination. Modeled after Title VII, this law provides protection to those workers who are 40 years of age or older. If a 55-year-old employee is fired and replaced by someone significantly younger, he or she has a claim for age discrimination.

14. The Americans with Disabilities Act of 1990 is a federal law designed to prohibit employment discrimination against those employees who have a physical or mental impairment that significantly limits a major life activity. The law protects those employees who have a disability, have a record of a disability, or who are regarded as disabled. Employers often have a duty under this law to provide a reasonable accommodation to disabled workers.

15. Workers sometimes argue that employer practices infringe on their privacy rights. Employers often monitor employees in the workplace, including reading their e-mails and listening to their phone calls. Workers also often object to drug testing in the workplace, particularly random drug testing. Employers are limited in the use of polygraph tests on employees.

REVIEW EXERCISES

Match the following terms with their most appropriate meaning.

TERMS

1. Employment-at-will doctrine
2. Collective bargaining agreement
3. Just-cause clause
4. Termination clause
5. Employee handbooks or manuals
6. Reservation-of-rights clause
7. Procedural due process
8. Duty of good faith and fair dealing
9. Title VII of the Civil Rights Act of 1964
10. Disparate treatment
11. Legitimate non discriminatory reason
12. Pretext stage
13. Disparate impact claims
14. Equal Employment Opportunity Commission (EEOC)
15 Charge of discrimination
16. Right to sue letter
17. Sexual harassment
18. Quid pro quo claims
19. Hostile work environment claims
20. Pregnancy Discrimination Act of 1978 (PDA)

MEANING

____ makes it unlawful to discriminate against employees on the basis of race, color, religion, sex, or national origin

____ may be legally terminated when there is evidence of reasonable cause

____ contract between management and employee's union that regulates terms and conditions of employment

____ means that either the employer or the employee can terminate the employment relationship

____ may create a legally binding contract if employer agrees to be bound by its provisions

____ gives employers discretion to modify the terms and conditions in the handbook

____ federal agency that enforces discrimination laws

____ notice and hearing to contest adverse employment action by a government agency

____ a few states use this exception to the employment-at-will doctrine, but most do not

____ letter from EEOC giving person right to sue

____ provision in contract for termination of the employee

____ evidence of discharge for reasonable cause

____ discrimination in the form of severe and pervasive harassment based on sex

____ prohibits employers from not hiring or firing employees because they are pregnant

____ prohibits discrimination against qualified individuals with a disability in the workplace

____ places restrictions on employer's use of lie detector tests on employees

____ treatment of employee worse than other employees not in the protected class

____ when burden of proof shifts back to the plaintiff after employer asserts a legitimate nondiscriminatory reason

____ apparently neutral employment practices that work an adverse impact on a particular group of individuals based on race or sex

____ complaint filed with EEOC that an employee has suffered some type of discrimination in the workplace

____ when employer engages in conduct seeking sexual favors in exchange for job benefits

____ situations where employee has to endure severe and pervasive sexual harassment that negatively impacts employee's working environment

21. Age Discrimination in Employment Act of 1967 (ADEA)
22. Americans with Disabilities Act of 1990 (ADA)
23. Reasonable accommodation
24. Employee Polygraph Protection Act

____ provides that employers may not discharge or otherwise discriminate against employees who are 40 years of age or older

____ employer must offer such accommodations to a qualified employee unless granting such accommodation would work an undue hardship

DISCUSSION QUESTIONS

1. Do you think the employment-at-will doctrine is fair and provides enough protection to employees? What are some exceptions to the employment-at-will doctrine in your state? Should employers only be able to discharge employees for just cause?

2. How should public policy be determined in your state? Do you think that legislative action is the only evidence of public policy? What could be other examples of public policy in your state or community?

3. Examine the EEOC's web site and their statistics of discrimination in the last year. There are thousands upon thousands of discrimination charges filed with the agency every year. Why do you think this is?

4. Do you believe that sexual harassment plaintiffs should have to show "severe and pervasive" harassment in order to recover? Why was this standard adopted? Is it superior to a standard that would require a plaintiff to show evidence of severe psychological injury?

5. Do you think that Congress should amend Title VII—pass the Employment Non Discrimination Act—and prohibit employers from discriminating against employees based on sexual orientation? Does your state have a law that prohibits such actions?

6. Title VII applies to employers with 15 or more workers. Is that enough coverage? What can employees do who work for smaller employers? Is it fair that workers for smaller employees receive no federal protection?

7. Examine your state antidiscrimination in employment law and compare it to Title VII. What are some similarities and what are some differences between the two?

8. Recall the story of Ann Hopkins. Do you think that her "mixed motive" case of employment discrimination was rightly decided by the U.S. Supreme Court? Why are mixed motive cases so hard to decide?

9. Can you think of some other employment policies that might work an adverse or disparate impact on a protected group? Should the Court recognize disparate impact claims when they don't involve any type of intentional discrimination?

10. The Age Discrimination in Employment Act prohibits employment discrimination against workers who are 40 years of age or older. Do you think this is the appropriate age? Should there be a law that provides protection to younger workers

who face discrimination vis-à-vis older workers?

11. The Americans with Disabilities Act sometimes requires employers to provide disabled workers with reasonable accommodations. Read the text of the ADA and provide some common examples of reasonable accommodations. What are some other reasonable accommodations not listed in the law?

12. Does your state allow for the random drug testing of employees under your state constitution or state law? Do you believe that drug tests invade the privacy rights of employees?

ASSIGNMENTS

ASSIGNMENT: Use the home page of the EEOC to find any of the following major acts or agencies related to this chapter. Choose one or more acts that you are particularly interested in and discover where you can obtain additional information about modern employment law.

ASSIGNMENT: Type in "Americans with Disabilities Act" (or EDA), "Equal Employment Opportunity Commission" (or EEOC), "Age Discrimination in Employment," and "Title VII of the Civil Rights Act of 1964" and you will find these categories at the EEOC official home page.

SOURCES AND SUGGESTED READING

Covington, Robert N. 2009. *Employment Law in a Nutshell*. 3rd ed. New York: West Publishing.

Friedman, Joel William (ed.). 2005. *Employment Discrimination Stories*. New York: Foundation Press, 2005.

Hopkins, Ann Branigar. 1996. *So Ordered: Making Partner the Hard Way*. Boston, Mass: University of Massachusetts Press.

Hudson, David L. Jr. 2010. *The Handy Law Answer Book*. Canton, Mich: Visible Ink Press.

Smith, Robert Samuel. 2008. *Race, Labor & Civil Rights: Griggs v. Duke Power and the Struggle for Equal Employment Opportunity*. Baton Rouge, La: Louisiana University Press.

COURT CASES

Bammert v. Don's Super Value, Inc., 646 N.W.2d 365 (Wis. 2002)

Burlington Industries v. Ellerth, 525 U.S. 742 (1998)

CBOCS West Inc. v. Humphries, 553 U.S. 442 (2008)

Danny v. Laidlaw Transit Services, Inc., 193 P.3d 128 (Wash. 2008)

Garcetti v. Ceballos, 547 U.S. 410 (2006)

Griggs v. Duke Power, 401 U.S. 424 (1971)

Jackson v. Morris Communications Corp., 657 N.W.2d 634 (Neb. 2003)

McDonnell Douglas Corp. v. Green, 411 U.S. 792 (1973)

O'Connor v. Consolidated Coin Caterers Corp., 517 U.S. 308 (1996)

Payne v. Western & Atlantic Railroad, 81 Tenn. 507 (1884)

Pickering v. Board of Education, 391 U.S. 563 (1968)

Price Waterhouse v. Hopkins, 490 U.S. 228 (1989)

Shero v. Grand Savings Bank, 161 P.3d 298 (Ok. 2007)

*Thompson v. North American Stainless,—U.S.—(2011)

WEBSITES

ADAResources.htm

Age Discrimination Lawyers
http://www.agediscriminationlawyers.com/

Americans with Disabilities Act
http://www.ada.gov/pubs/ada.htm

Americans with Disabilities Act Resource Center
http://www.ncsconline.org/D_KIS/

EEOC on Age Discrimination in Employment Act
http://www.eeoc.gov/policy/adea.html

EEOC Regulations
   http://www.eeoc.gov/policy/regs/index.html
EEOC's Facts about Sexual Harassment
   http://www.eeoc.gov/facts/fs-sex.html
Equal Employment Advisory Council
   http://www.eeac.org
Equal Employment Opportunity Commission
   (EEOC)
   http://www.eeoc.gov/
National Employment Lawyers Association
   http://www.nela.org/NELA/

Title VII of the Civil Rights Act of 1964
   http://www4.law.cornell.edu/uscode/42/
   2000e.html
U.S. Department of Labor
   http://www.dol.gov/
U.S. Department of Labor on Age Discrimination
   http://www.dol.gov/dol/topic/discrimination/
   agedisc.htm
Workplace Prof Blog
   http://lawprofessors.typepad.com/laborprof_
   blog/

Introduction to Equal Protection Law

A defining feature of the U.S. legal system is its ideal of fairness, of giving people the right of equal treatment under the law. The part of the U.S. Constitution that embodies this principle is the *Equal Protection Clause* of the Fourteenth Amendment. It reads: "nor shall any state . . . deny to any person the equal protection of the laws." Legal scholars John Nowak and Ronald Rotunda write in their constitutional law treatise that "the equal protection guarantee has become the single most important concept in the Constitution for the protection of individual rights."

This was not always the case. The Equal Protection Clause used to be, as Justice Oliver Wendell Holmes once wrote, "a constitutional argument of last resort." Now, the clause has taken center stage whenever any person or group contends that they have been treated worse under the law than other persons or groups. The essence of the Equal Protection Clause is that similarly situated persons or groups should be treated the same or in a similar fashion. A classic violation of the Equal Protection Clause occurs when people are treated differently based on race.

A MATTER OF RACE

The 39th Congress passed the *Fourteenth Amendment* in the late 1860s during the period of Reconstruction, along with the *Thirteenth Amendment*, which outlawed slavery and involuntary servitude, and the *Fifteenth Amendment*, which dealt with the right to vote. The Fourteenth Amendment was passed largely to ensure that the recently freed black slaves would have essential rights necessary to become full citizens of the country. The promise did not match reality, as stark discrimination continued. It was litigation under the Equal Protection Clause that eventually forced great change in the legal system.

An early example of the Equal Protection Clause in action involved the case of *Strauder v. West Virginia* (1880). The state had a law that provided: "all white male persons who are twenty-one years of age who are citizens of this State shall be eligible to serve as jurors." The case involved an African

American charged and convicted of murder. His attorneys argued that his conviction should be overturned because he was tried by an all-white jury with a jury system that prevented any blacks from serving on a jury.

The Court explained that the purpose of the Equal Protection Clause was to ensure that African Americans were treated equally to whites. The Court determined that the law clearly violated the equal protection rights by denying blacks the right to jury service: "The very fact that colored people are singled out and expressly denied by a statute all right to participate in the administration of the law, as jurors, because of their color, though they are citizens, and may be in other respects fully qualified, is practically a brand upon them, affixed by the law, an assertion of their inferiority, and a stimulant to that race prejudice which is an impediment to securing to individuals of the race that equal justice which the law aims to secure to all others."

Strauder v. West Virginia
100 U.S. 303 (1880)

This is one of a series of constitutional provisions having a common purpose; namely, securing to a race recently emancipated, a race that through many generations had been held in slavery, all the civil rights that the superior race enjoy. The true spirit and meaning of the amendments, as we said in the Slaughter-House Cases, cannot be understood without keeping in view the history of the times when they were adopted, and the general objects they plainly sought to accomplish. At the time when they were incorporated into the Constitution, it required little knowledge of human nature to anticipate that those who had long been regarded as an inferior and subject race would, when suddenly raised to the rank of citizenship, be looked upon with jealousy and positive dislike, and that State laws might be enacted or enforced to perpetuate the distinctions that had before existed. Discriminations against them had been habitual. It was well known that in some States laws making such discriminations then existed, and others might well be expected. The colored race, as a race, was abject and ignorant, and in that condition was unfitted to command the respect of those who had superior intelligence. Their training had left them mere children, and as such they needed the protection which a wise government extends to those who are unable to protect themselves. They especially needed protection against unfriendly action in the States where they were resident. It was in view of these considerations the Fourteenth Amendment was framed and adopted. It was designed to assure to the colored race the enjoyment of all the civil rights that under the law are enjoyed by white persons, and to give to that race the protection of the general government, in that enjoyment, whenever it should

continued >

be denied by the States. It not only gave citizenship and the privileges of citizenship to persons of color, but it denied to any State the power to with-hold from them the equal protection of the laws, and authorized Congress to enforce its provisions by appropriate legislation.

While the Court showed promise in interpreting the Equal Protection Clause broadly, that changed in some subsequent decisions in the late nine-teenth century. In 1883, the Court decided a series of cases from Kansas, Missouri, California, New York, and Tennessee known as the *Civil Rights Cases*. All the cases involved African Americans who sued after being denied admission to various forms of public transportation or accommoda-tions. Private property owners denied African Americans access to thea-ters, hotel rooms, and other buildings. The plaintiffs sued under a law known as the Civil Rights Act of 1875, which prohibited discrimination in areas of public accommodation and transportation. Congress passed the law based on its powers under the Fourteenth Amendment.

The plaintiffs in these cases contended that the actions of these parties violated their rights to equal protection under the law. However, the U.S. Supreme Court ruled that the Fourteenth Amendment only protected per-sons from discrimination by state or governmental actors, not private busi-ness owners or private persons. The Court described the incidents as "private wrongs" beyond the reach of the Fourteenth Amendment or the Civil Rights Act of 1875, which the Court declared unconstitutional.

"It would be running the slavery argument into the ground to make it apply to every act of discrimination," Justice Joseph Bradley wrote for the Court. "When a man has emerged from slavery, and by the aid of benefi-cent legislation has shaken off the inseparable concomitants of that state, there must be some stage in the progress of his elevation when he takes the rank of a mere citizen, and ceases to be the special favorite of the laws."

Only one justice dissented, Justice John Marshall Harlan of Kentucky from a slave-owning family. Harlan earned the moniker "the Great Dissen-ter" for his lone dissents in this case and another decision that upheld seg-regation practices, *Plessy v. Ferguson* (1896). In the *Civil Rights Cases*, Harlan wrote that "the substance and spirit of the recent amendments of the constitution have been sacrificed by a subtle and ingenious verbal crit-icism" and that "the rights which congress, by the act of 1875, endeavored to secure and protect are legal, not social, rights."

The effect of the *Civil Rights Cases* was that the Supreme Court inter-preted the Equal Protection Clause to apply only to state-sanctioned acts of discrimination, not purely private acts of discrimination. This means that the Equal Protection Clause, like other constitutional provisions, only pro-tects individuals from actions by government officials. Just as private indi-viduals cannot violate a person's First Amendment free-speech rights or a person's Fourth Amendment right to be free from unreasonable searches and seizures, only the government can invade someone's equal protection rights. The legal system does protect people from discrimination by private actors, but that is done by statutes or laws, not the Constitution.

The U.S. Supreme Court once again took a crabbed view of the Equal Protection Clause in the infamous decision of *Plessy v. Ferguson* (1896). The case involved a constitutional challenge to an 1890 Louisiana law that provided for separate accommodations on railway cars based on race. Many other states also provided separate railroad accommodations based on race. Homer Plessy, an *octoroon* (term for someone who was one-eighth black), challenged the law on equal protection grounds.

The U.S. Supreme Court upheld the law based on the **separate but equal doctrine**. The Court reasoned that as long as each race had substantially equal public facilities, there was no violation of the Equal Protection Clause. "If the two races are to meet upon terms of social equality, it must be the result of natural affinities, a mutual appreciation of each other's merits and a voluntary consent of individuals," wrote Justice Henry Billings Brown for the majority. "If one race be inferior to the other socially, the Constitution of the United States cannot put them upon the same plane."

Justice Harlan once again filed a solitary dissent. In impassioned language, he railed against the unfairness of the separate but equal doctrine. He wrote in an oft-cited passage:

> In view of the Constitution, in the eye of the law, there is in this country no superior, dominant, ruling class of citizens. There is no caste here. Our Constitution is color-blind, and neither knows nor tolerates classes among citizens. In respect of civil rights, the humblest is the peer of the most powerful.

Harlan added: "The arbitrary separation of citizens, on the basis of race, while they are on a public highway, is a badge of servitude wholly inconsistent with the civil freedom and the equality before the law established by the Constitution."

The decision in *Plessy* led to an expansion of segregation laws called **Jim Crow laws**. Jim Crow was the name of a character in a minstrel show that placed African Americans in a subordinate and derogatory position. The term *Jim Crow law* refers to any law that segregated the races. Jim Crow laws permeated all aspects of American society, including separation in places of public accommodation, restrooms, swimming pools, athletic contests, and even things as innocuous as checkers. An Alabama law actually prohibited whites and blacks from playing the game of checkers together.

The National Association for the Advancement of Colored People (NAACP) was formed in the early twentieth century. One of its early

Separate but equal doctrine: Early Court reasoning that as long as each race had substantially equal facilities there was no violation of the Equal Protection Clause.

Jim Crow laws: Laws that segregate the races.

missions was to attack segregation laws. Early on, the NAACP attacked segregation laws based on the separate but equal doctrine, arguing that laws were unconstitutional under the Equal Protection Clause because they failed to provide substantially equal facilities. The NAACP decided to attack segregation laws in education, first at the postgraduate level. The thinking was that white opposition to segregation in elementary and other secondary schools would simply be too overwhelming.

The NAACP faced serious opposition in its efforts not just from Southern whites but from the federal government, which investigated it for allegedly subversive activities. World War II and the noble efforts of many African-American soldiers changed the views of at least some in the country. The U.S. Supreme Court also gradually became filled with some more progressive justices who were more sensitive to charges of racial discrimination.

Scholar Michael Klarman writes in his book *From Jim Crow to Civil Rights*: "The NAACP initially hoped that higher education litigation would pressure Southern states to appropriate sufficiently large sums for equalizing black opportunities that they would eventually capitulate by integrating." (Klarman, 204)

The U.S. Supreme Court ruled in *Sipuel v. Oklahoma* (1948) that the state of Oklahoma needed to provide a legal education for an African-American woman named Ada Lois Sipuel. A few years later, the Court ruled in *Sweatt v. Painter* that the all-white University of Texas had to admit African-American mail carrier Heman Sweatt. Initially, when Sweatt filed his lawsuit on equal protection grounds, the state of Texas quickly appropriated funds to create a black law school—what later became known as Texas Southern University. But the NAACP successfully argued that the quickly created black law school was not sufficiently equal to the all-white law school. The U.S. Supreme Court unanimously ruled that the University of Texas had to admit Mr. Sweatt to the University of Texas.

These higher education cases set the stage for the U.S. Supreme Court to examine segregation in secondary education. The NAACP now decided not to litigate under the separate but equal doctrine but to challenge that doctrine on its face to achieve *integration* of public elementary schools. The NAACP filed lawsuits in four states (Kansas, Delaware, Virginia, and South Carolina) and the District of Columbia. These lawsuits made their way through lower courts and eventually were consolidated into *Brown v. Board of Education* (the four state cases) and *Bolling v. Sharpe* (the District of Columbia case).

Brown v. Board of Education was originated in Topeka, Kansas. The lead plaintiff was Reverend Oliver Brown, a 32-year-old minister who sought to enroll his eight-year-old daughter Linda in a neighboring all-white Sumner Elementary School. Brown and 12 other families sued, challenging segregation in Kansas.

On May 17, 1954, the U.S. Supreme Court issued its historic decision in *Brown v. Board of Education*. The Court unanimously ruled that segregated educational facilities violated the Equal Protection Clause. Chief Justice Earl Warren, newly appointed by President Dwight D. Eisenhower, wrote the opinion for the Court: "Separate educational facilities are inherently unequal."

The Court initially was not unanimous in its decision. The Court first heard arguments in the cases in 1952 when Fred Vinson still served as Chief Justice. Vinson and Justice Stanley Reed initially voted against striking down segregation. But when Vinson died unexpectedly, Eisenhower chose a former political rival, Earl Warren, the governor of California, to become the next Chief Justice.

It was somewhat ironic that Warren later became the man who invalidated segregation and breathed life into many areas of constitutional law. It is ironic because Warren, as governor of California during World War II, had supported the internment of more than 100,000 persons of Japanese descent throughout the war. The U.S. Supreme Court had rejected constitutional challenges to the internment process in *Korematsu v. United States* (1944).

But Warren believed strongly that *Plessy v. Ferguson* should be overruled. He accepted as legitimate the social science evidence put forth by the NAACP lawyers. They cited a study by Dr. Kenneth Carter showing that African-American children consistently picked white dolls over black dolls when given the choice. The evidence showed that black children were made to feel that white was superior and that black was inferior. Chief Justice Warren viewed segregated education as a culprit in creating these feelings of inferiority: "To separate them from others of similar age and qualifications solely because of their race generates a feeling of inferiority as to their status in the community that may affect their hearts and minds in a way unlikely ever to be undone."

Supreme Court: *Brown v. Board of Education*
347 U.S. 483 (1954)

Today, education is perhaps the most important function of state and local governments. Compulsory school attendance laws and the great expenditures for education both demonstrate our recognition of the importance of education to our democratic society. It is required in the performance of our most basic public responsibilities, even service in the armed forces. It is the very foundation of good citizenship. Today it is a principal instrument in awakening the child to cultural values, in preparing him for later professional training, and in helping him to adjust normally to his environment. In these days, it is

---

continued >

> doubtful that any child may reasonably be expected to succeed in life if he is denied the opportunity of an education. Such an opportunity, where the state has undertaken to provide it, is a right which must be made available to all on equal terms.
>
> We come then to the question presented: Does segregation of children in public schools solely on the basis of race, even though the physical facilities and other "tangible" factors may be equal, deprive the children of the minority group of equal educational opportunities? We believe that it does. . . .
>
> We conclude that in the field of public education the doctrine of "separate but equal" has no place. Separate educational facilities are inherently unequal. Therefore, we hold that the plaintiffs and others similarly situated for whom the actions have been brought are, by reason of the segregation complained of, deprived of the equal protection of the laws guaranteed by the Fourteenth Amendment.

The Court later issued another decision in the Brown litigation, *Brown v. Board of Education* (1955), often referred to as *Brown II*. In this decision, the Court said that public schools should desegregate with "all deliberate speed." Unfortunately, school districts across the country—and many lower courts—focused more on the word "deliberate" than the word "speed." This meant that it took until the 1960s and even 1970s before many school systems were integrated.

The Court's decision in *Brown* did lead to a series of rulings striking down various segregation laws in many aspects of American life. Courts invalidated segregation laws at restaurants, public swimming pools, sporting matches, and prisons.

MARRIAGE AND EQUAL PROTECTION

In 1967, the Supreme Court unanimously struck down a ban on interracial marriage in *Loving v. Virginia*. In 1958, Richard Loving, a white man, married Mildred Jeter, a black woman, in the District of Columbia where interracial marriages were legal. However, when they moved back to their home state of Virginia in Caroline County, they were charged with violating the state law banning interracial marriages. The Lovings challenged the ban on interracial marriages under the Equal Protection Clause.

A trial judge sentenced the Lovings to one year in prison, but suspended the sentence if the Lovings would leave the state and not return for 25 years. "Almighty God created the races white, black, yellow, malay and red, and he placed them on separate continents," the judge wrote. "And but for the interference with his arrangement there would be no cause for such marriages. The fact that he separated the races shows that he did not intend for the races to mix."

Virginia Statutes in the *Loving* Case

Leaving State to evade law. If any white person and colored person shall go out of this State, for the purpose of being married, and with the intention of returning, and be married out of it, and afterwards return to and reside in it, cohabiting as man and wife, they shall be punished as provided in 20-59, and the marriage shall be governed by the same law as if it had been solemnized in this State. The fact of their cohabitation here as man and wife shall be evidence of their marriage.

Punishment for marriage. If any white person intermarry with a colored person, or any colored person intermarry with a white person, he shall be guilty of a felony and shall be punished by confinement in the penitentiary for not less than one nor more than five years.

Unfortunately, this type of thinking led to much discrimination in American life. At the time of the *Loving* case, 16 states had antimiscegenation laws that forbade interracial marriages. The California Supreme Court had rejected a ban on interracial marriages in 1948, but many states, particularly in the South, still officially forbade such marriages.

The Lovings appealed their case all the way to the U.S. Supreme Court. The state of Virginia had argued that the Court's decision in *Pace v. Alabama* (1883) supported its position. In *Pace*, the Court had upheld an Alabama law that imposed greater penalties on those who committed adultery with someone outside of their race than with someone of their own racial group.

Chief Justice Warren once again wrote for a unanimous Court in striking down this racially discriminatory law: "There can be no doubt that restricting the freedom to marry solely because of racial classifications violates the central meaning of the Equal Protection Clause."

Loving v. Virginia
388 U.S. 1 (1967)

There can be no question but that Virginia's miscegenation statutes rest solely upon distinctions drawn according to race. The statutes proscribe generally accepted conduct if engaged in by members of different races. Over the years, this Court has consistently repudiated "[d]istinctions between citizens solely because of their ancestry" as being "odious to a free people whose institutions are founded upon the doctrine of equality." . . .

There is patently no legitimate overriding purpose independent of invidious racial discrimination which justifies this classification. The fact that Virginia prohibits only interracial marriages involving white persons demonstrates that the racial classifications must stand on their own justification, as

continued >

> measures designed to maintain White Supremacy. We have consistently denied the constitutionality of measures which restrict the rights of citizens on account of race. There can be no doubt that restricting the freedom to marry solely because of racial classifications violates the central meaning of the Equal Protection Clause.

The looming question regarding marriage and equal protection concerns *same-sex marriage*. As indicated in Chapter 7, many states have laws and/or constitutional provisions that limit marriage to between one man and one woman. Gays and lesbians contend that this ban on same-sex marriage violates their equal protection rights. They have found some success in the courts. For example, the Iowa Supreme Court ruled in *Varnum v. Brien* (2009) that a state law prohibiting same-sex marriages violated the equal protection guarantee of the state constitution. The Iowa Supreme Court noted that it was the first state to admit women to practice law and had a long history of interpreting equal protection principles to prohibit discrimination against classes of people.

Varnum v. Brien
763 N.W.2d 862 (Iowa 2009)

So, today, this court again faces an important issue that hinges on our definition of equal protection. This issue comes to us with the same importance as our landmark cases of the past. The same-sex-marriage debate waged in this case is part of a strong national dialogue centered on a fundamental, deep-seated, traditional institution that has excluded, by state action, a particular class of Iowans. This class of people asks a simple and direct question: How can a state premised on the constitutional principle of equal protection justify exclusion of a class of Iowans from civil marriage? . . .

Therefore, with respect to the subject and purposes of Iowa's marriage laws, we find that the plaintiffs are similarly situated compared to heterosexual persons. Plaintiffs are in committed and loving relationships, many raising families, just like heterosexual couples. Moreover, official recognition of their status provides an institutional basis for defining their fundamental relational rights and responsibilities, just as it does for heterosexual couples. Society benefits, for example, from providing same-sex couples a stable framework within which to raise their children and the power to make health care and end-of-life decisions for loved ones, just as it does when that framework is provided for opposite-sex couples.

The U.S. Supreme Court has not decided the question of whether bans on same-sex marriage violated the Equal Protection Clause. In *Lawrence v. Texas* (2003), the Court did strike down a criminal law that prohibited same-sex sodomy. The Court reasoned that the state violated the Due Process Clause. However, Justice Sandra Day O'Connor in her concurring opinion noted that the law violated the Equal Protection Clause because it prohibited only private sex acts among members of the same sex. In its decision, the Court specifically avoided deciding the gay marriage question, writing: "It does not involve whether the government must give formal recognition to any relationship that homosexual persons seek to enter."

It remains to be seen how the law will evolve with regard to same-sex marriage and equal protection.

EQUAL PROTECTION TERMINOLOGY

The U.S. Supreme Court continues to look with great skepticism at laws that draw racial classifications. The Court has said that racial classifications are inherently suspect and are subject to the highest form of judicial review, known as **strict scrutiny**. Strict scrutiny requires that the government show that its policy or regulation advances a compelling, or extremely strong, interest in a very narrowly tailored manner. The strict scrutiny test or compelling interest test means that most racial classifications are invalidated.

Strict scrutiny applies in the equal protection context when a practice impacts a **suspect class**: a class that by history has been saddled with iniquities or injustices. Suspect classes in constitutional law include classifications based on race, national origin, and alienage.

There are two other standards of review in constitutional law that apply in the area of equal protection. They are **intermediate scrutiny** and **rational basis** (see Table 9.1). Intermediate, or midlevel, scrutiny provides that the governmental regulation must advance a substantial governmental

Strict scrutiny:
Requires that the government show that its policy or regulation advances a compelling or extremely strong interest in a very narrowly tailored manner.

Suspect class:
A class that historically has been saddled with inequities or injustices.

Intermediate scrutiny:
A government regulation must advance a substantial government interest.

Rational basis:
Government must only show that it has a legitimate reason that is not arbitrary.

Table 9.1 **U.S. SUPREME COURT STANDARDS USED IN JUDICIAL REVIEW REGARDING EQUAL PROTECTION OF THE LAW**

Standard of Review	Governmental Interest	Classifications
Strict scrutiny	Compelling	Race, national origin, alienage
Intermediate scrutiny	Substantial	Gender, illegitimacy
Rational basis	Legitimate (rational)	Social and economic

interest. This standard applies to classifications based on gender and illegitimacy.

Rational basis is a much more government-friendly standard. Under this level of review, the government must only show that it has a legitimate reason for its regulation that is not arbitrary. Laws evaluated under rational basis are almost always upheld.

AFFIRMATIVE ACTION

A controversial area of equal protection law remains: **affirmative action**, which refers to policies designed to create greater diversity for historically underrepresented groups of people. Affirmative action was the alliterative label coined by Hobart Taylor, an African-American man appointed by then-President John F. Kennedy to serve as special counsel to the President's Commission on Equal Employment Opportunity.

President Lyndon Baines Johnson in a 1965 speech delivered at Howard University famously described the need for affirmative action: "You do not take a man who for years has been hobbled by chains, liberate him, bring him to the starting line of a race, saying 'you are free to compete with all the others.'"

Affirmative action became controversial in education circles, as universities used race as a controlling factor in their admission policies. This issue reached the U.S. Supreme Court in *Regents of the University of California v. Bakke* (1978). The case involved a white applicant to University of California Davis's medical school, Allan Bakke, who scored very high on his medical admissions test and had excellent grades.

The school denied Bakke admission to the school. The school had a set-aside program for minority applicants under which 16 of 100 seats were reserved for historically under-represented groups. Bakke contended that the school violated his equal protection rights as a white person by treating him worse in the admission process than other racial groups. In other words, Bakke alleged that the school's admission policy constituted a form of *reverse discrimination*.

The U.S. Supreme Court ruled in Bakke's favor by a 5-4 vote. The justices sparred mightily over whether there was a difference in racial classifications designed to help certain groups and racial classifications designed to harm or subjugate groups. "The guarantee of equal protection cannot mean one thing when applied to one individual and something else when applied to a person of another color," wrote Justice Lewis Powell in his opinion. Several justices believed that any racial classification is "inherently suspect" whatever the purpose behind the measure.

Other justices would have voted against Allan Bakke and upheld the admissions program. "In order to get beyond racism, we must first take

Affirmative action:
Policies designed to create greater diversity for historically underrepresented groups.

account of race," wrote Harry Blackmun. "There is no other way. And in order to treat some persons equally, we must treat them differently. We cannot—we dare not—let the Equal Protection Clause perpetuate racial supremacy."

Even though he wrote that racial classifications were "inherently suspect," Powell also ruled that a university has a compelling interest in achieving a diverse class and that race can be an important factor in that calculus. He wrote that diversity "clearly is a constitutionally permissible goal for an institution of higher learning." He reasoned that a university can institute an admissions policy where "race or ethnic background is simply one element in the selection process."

The decision established that universities could not establish set-asides based on race, but they could use race as a factor in the admissions decision. Controversy continued over the practice. Twenty-five years later, the Court returned to the affirmative action in education debate by examining the admission policies of the undergraduate school and the law school at the University of Michigan.

The undergraduate program specifically assigned extra points to applicants of certain racial groups, whereas the law school program considered race as a plus factor, and one of many factors in the admissions decision. The U.S. Supreme Court split the difference in divided rulings, striking down the undergraduate program in *Gratz v. Bollinger* (2003) and upholding the law school admission program in *Grutter v. Bollinger* (2003). The undergraduate admissions policy was too close to the set-aside program in Bakke, and the law school program simply used race as one of many factors, rather than the determinative factor.

In her opinion in *Grutter v. Bollinger*, Justice Sandra Day O'Connor wrote about the government's compelling interest in achieving diversity. However, she also warned: "We expect that 25 years from now, the use of racial preferences will no longer be necessary to further the interest approved today."

GENDER DISCRIMINATION

The United States has a long history of discrimination against women, who did not receive the right to vote until the passage of the Nineteenth Amendment in 1920. In 1873, the U.S. Supreme Court ruled in *Bradwell v. Illinois* that the state of Illinois could prohibit female Myra Bradwell from practicing law as an attorney, even though she had previously practiced as a lawyer in Vermont.

Even though women now can practice law, they have had significant barriers in the legal professional. U.S. Supreme Court Justices Sandra Day O'Connor and Ruth Bader Ginsburg, the first two women to serve on the

U.S. Supreme Court, had trouble landing legal employment after graduating law school, even though they finished near the top of their classes.

Another example of the legal system's second-class treatment of women occurred in Michigan involving sisters Valerie and Margaret Goesart. Michigan law prohibited women from serving as bartenders unless their father or husband owned the bar. The Goesart sisters contended that their equal protection rights were violated because they were treated worse than women whose fathers or husbands owned bars.

The U.S. Supreme Court upheld the law and rejected the equal protection claim. The Court concluded that the Michigan legislature could rationally conclude that allowing women to tend bar without a male relative could present "moral and societal problems."

Goesart v. Cleary
335 U.S. 464 (1948)

Since bartending by women may, in the allowable legislative judgment, give rise to moral and social problems against which it may devise preventive measures, the legislature need not go to the full length of prohibition if it believes that as to a defined group of females other factors are operating which either eliminate or reduce the moral and social problems otherwise calling for prohibition. Michigan evidently believes that the oversight assured through ownership of a bar by a barmaid's husband or father minimizes hazards that may confront a barmaid without such protecting oversight. This Court is certainly not in a position to gainsay such belief by the Michigan legislature.

Three justices dissented, contending that the law violated the equal protection rights of women bar owners, treating them worse than male bar owners. "The statute arbitrarily discriminates between male and female owners of liquor establishments," Justice Wiley Rutledge wrote. "A male owner, although he himself is always absent from his bar, may employ his wife and daughter as barmaids. A female owner may neither work as a barmaid herself nor employ her daughter in that position, even if a man is always present in the establishment to keep order."

The Court in the *Goesart* case analyzed the law only under the lenient rational basis standard. In the 1970s, the U.S. Supreme Court applied the Equal Protection Clause with more vigor in gender cases. In *Reed v. Reed* (1971), the Court invalidated an Idaho law that preferred males over females in handling estates.

The Reed case arose after divorced parents' minor son died. The mother applied to be the administrator of the estate and so did the father. The Court gave preference to the father based on the Idaho statute.

The state argued that the statute furthered the rational goal of making the administration of estates easier. However, the Court reasoned that administrative ease did not satisfy the rational basis test: "To give a mandatory preference to members of either sex over members of the other, merely to accomplish the elimination of hearings on the merits, is to make the very kind of arbitrary legislative choice forbidden by the Equal Protection Clause of the Fourteenth Amendment."

In 1976, the U.S. Supreme Court for the first time examined a gender-classification law with more scrutiny than rational basis. Ironically, the Court's heightened examination of such a law occurred when a law disfavored males rather than females. In *Craig v. Boren*, the Court examined the constitutionality of a law that allowed the sale of 3.2 percent beer to females 18 and older and to males 21 and older.

Several men challenged the law, contending that the law violated their equal protection rights as 18- to 20-year-old men. The state argued that statistics provided a valid reason for the gender-based distinction. There were many more arrests for driving while under the influence of alcohol (DUI) offenses for men 18-20 than for women 18-20 and more males involved in traffic accidents involving alcohol. There was a statistical difference based on gender, as .18 percent of females and 2 percent of males were arrested from the 18-20 age group.

"Certainly if maleness is to serve as a proxy for drinking and driving, a correlation of 2 percent must be considered an unduly tenuous fit," the Court reasoned in applying heightened scrutiny. The Court approved of the use of intermediate scrutiny: "[C]lassifications by gender must serve important governmental objectives and must be substantially related to achievement of those objectives."

Craig v. Boren
429 U.S. 190 (1976)

Even if this statistical evidence was accepted as accurate, it nevertheless offers only a weak answer to the equal protection question presented here. The most focused and relevant of the statistical surveys, arrests of 18- to 20-year-olds for alcohol-related driving offenses, exemplifies the ultimate unpersuasiveness of this evidentiary record. Viewed in terms of the correlation between sex and the actual activity that Oklahoma seeks to regulate—driving while under the influence of alcohol—the statistics broadly establish that .18% of females and 2% of males in that age group were arrested for that offense. While such a disparity is not trivial in a statistical sense, it hardly can form the basis for employment of a gender line as a classifying device. . . .

---

continued >

There is no reason to belabor this line of analysis. It is unrealistic to expect either members of the judiciary or state officials to be well versed in the rigors of experimental or statistical technique. But this merely illustrates that proving broad sociological propositions by statistics is a dubious business, and one that inevitably is in tension with the normative philosophy that underlies the Equal Protection Clause. Suffice to say that the showing offered by the appellees does not satisfy us that sex represents a legitimate, accurate proxy for the regulation of drinking and driving. In fact, when it is further recognized that Oklahoma's statute prohibits only the selling of 3.2% beer to young males and not their drinking the beverage once acquired (even after purchase by their 18-20-year-old female companions), the relationship between gender and traffic safety becomes far too tenuous. . . .

In the 1990s, the Court examined the constitutionality of an all-male admissions policy at Virginia Military Institute. Several women contended that their equal protection rights were violated by their denial. The State of Virginia argued that a single-sex education system offered educational benefits to the male students. After the denied female applicants sued, the State of Virginia then said that it would create a similar, separate school for women called the Virginia Women's Institute for Leadership (VWIL). The state claimed that this school would provide a "parallel program" giving women equal opportunities.

The U.S. Supreme Court ruled in favor of the female applicants, saying that the state's reasons were based on stereotypes. Justice Ruth Bader Ginsburg, who litigated gender equality cases as a lawyer and law professor before the Court, wrote the Court's majority opinion. She wrote that the proposed all-female school was no match for VMI in terms of "student body, faculty, course offerings and facilities." She compared the State of Virginia's response to what Texas tried to do more than 50 years before in the Heman Sweatt case.

United States v. Virginia
518 U.S. 515 (1996)

Single-sex education affords pedagogical benefits to at least some students, Virginia emphasizes, and that reality is uncontested in this litigation. Similarly, it is not disputed that diversity among public educational institutions can serve the public good. But Virginia has not shown that VMI was established, or has been maintained, with a view to diversifying, by its categorical exclusion of women, educational opportunities within the State. In cases of this genre, our precedent instructs that "benign" justifications proffered in

continued >

defense of categorical exclusions will not be accepted automatically; a tenable justification must describe actual state purposes, not rationalizations for actions in fact differently grounded. . . .

Mississippi Univ. for Women is immediately in point. There the State asserted, in justification of its exclusion of men from a nursing school, that it was engaging in "educational affirmative action" by "compensat[ing] for discrimination against women." Undertaking a "searching analysis," the Court found no close resemblance between "the alleged objective" and "the actual purpose underlying the discriminatory classification." Pursuing a similar inquiry here, we reach the same conclusion. . . .

Virginia's VWIL solution is reminiscent of the remedy Texas proposed 50 years ago, in response to a state trial court's 1946 ruling that, given the equal protection guarantee, African Americans could not be denied a legal education at a state facility.

EQUAL PROTECTION IN THE CRIMINAL JUSTICE SYSTEM

Sometimes criminal laws have treated people differently based on the crimes they have committed, their race, or some other distinction that triggers the application of the Equal Protection Clause. In *Skinner v. Oklahoma* (1942), the U.S. Supreme Court examined an Oklahoma law called the Oklahoma Criminal Sterilization Act of 1935 that provided for the sterilization of habitual criminals. The law defined habitual criminals as those who had committed three or more felonies. The law was to be applied to defendant Jack Skinner, who had been convicted of one offense of stealing chickens and convicted twice for armed robbery.

However, the law had an exception for embezzlement and other white-collar crimes. This presented an equal protection problem for the Court, specifically the difference in treatment of those convicted of larceny and those convicted of embezzlement. Those convicted of larceny could be sterilized, whereas those convicted of embezzlement—even if it involved the taking of a lot more money—would not be subject to the same punishment. The Court viewed this as a pristine equal protection violation.

Skinner v. Oklahoma
316 U.S. 535 (1942)

Larceny is grand larceny when the property taken exceeds $20 in value. Embezzlement is punishable "in the manner prescribed for feloniously stealing property of the value of that embezzled." Hence, he who embezzles

continued >

property worth more than $20 is guilty of a felony. A clerk who appropriates over $20 from his employer's till and a stranger who steals the same amount are thus both guilty of felonies. If the latter repeats his act and is convicted three times, he may be sterilized. But the clerk is not subject to the pains and penalties of the Act no matter how large his embezzlements nor how frequent his convictions. A person who enters a chicken coop and steals chickens commits a felony; and he may be sterilized if he is thrice convicted. If, however, he is a bailee of the property and fraudulently appropriates it, he is an embezzler. Hence, no matter how habitual his proclivities for embezzlement are and no matter how often his conviction, he may not be sterilized.

Oklahoma makes no attempt to say that he who commits larceny by trespass or trick or fraud has biologically inheritable traits which he who commits embezzlement lacks. We have not the slightest basis for inferring that that line has any significance in eugenics, nor that the inheritability of criminal traits follows the neat legal distinctions which the law has marked between those two offenses. In terms of fines and imprisonment, the crimes of larceny and embezzlement rate the same under the Oklahoma code. Only when it comes to sterilization are the pains and penalties of the law different. The equal protection clause would indeed be a formula of empty words if such conspicuously artificial lines could be drawn. . . .

The power to sterilize, if exercised, may have subtle, far-reaching and devastating effects. In evil or reckless hands it can cause races or types which are inimical to the dominant group to wither and disappear. There is no redemption for the individual whom the law touches. Any experiment which the State conducts is to his irreparable injury. He is forever deprived of a basic liberty. We mention these matters not to reexamine the scope of the police power of the States. We advert to them merely in emphasis of our view that strict scrutiny of the classification which a State makes in a sterilization law is essential, lest unwittingly, or otherwise, invidious discriminations are made against groups or types of individuals in violation of the constitutional guaranty of just and equal laws.

Peremptory Challenges

The Court addressed another important equal protection issue in the criminal justice system: the use of **peremptory challenges** in trials. In cases, attorneys select a trial jury from a larger panel (or pool) through a process known as **voir dire**. During this process, attorneys ask a series of questions of the prospective jurors to determine whether or not attorneys wish them to serve on the jury. Attorneys can challenge jurors for cause if they can convince the court that the juror is obviously biased. For example, in a case that involves testimony by a police officer, a juror who says that he

Peremptory challenges:
In jury selection, the parties may be given a limited number of challenges to eliminate jurors without cause.

Voir dire:
The jury selection process.

or she doesn't trust police officers would be biased and subject to a for-cause challenge. But, the legal system also allows attorneys to strike jurors without showing obvious bias; these are the peremptory challenges.

In *Swain v. Alabama* (1965), the U.S. Supreme Court ruled that striking jurors based on race could constitute an equal protection violation if the criminal defendant was able to show a clear pattern of discrimination. But the Court placed a heavy evidentiary burden on defendants attempting to make out such a claim of discrimination. Defendants had to show a pattern of discrimination on the part of the prosecutor in case after case. Defendants could not make out a cognizable claim based on discrimination in their own individual case.

The U.S. Supreme Court changed that requirement in *Batson v. Kentucky* (1986) in which the U.S. Supreme Court ruled that attorneys may not use peremptory challenges in a racially discriminatory manner in an individual case. The case involved the prosecution of defendant James Batson, an African-American man, for burglary. The prosecutor in Batson's case struck all four African-American jurors from the jury pool, leaving Batson before an all-white jury. After his conviction, Batson's attorneys appealed, alleging an equal protection violation. The U.S. Supreme Court agreed that Batson should be entitled to a new trial because of the prosecutor's race-based use of the peremptory challenges.

The Court established a three-step process for defendants asserting an equal-protection claim against the use of *peremptories*. The first step is that a defendant must show a "pattern of strikes" in his or her case. Batson met this prong, as the prosecutor struck all four of the African-Americans on the jury panel.

If a defendant passes the first step, then the burden shifts to the prosecution to show that it had *race-neutral reasons* for striking the jurors. Race-neutral reasons could include that prospective jurors were inattentive, had previous experience with the criminal justice system as a defendant, or were simply too young. If the prosecution establishes a race-neutral reason, then a defendant must establish that the prosecutor's allegedly race-neutral reasons were false or pretextual. In other words, the reviewing court has to analyze whether the prosecution's neutral reasons are reasonable or more likely a guise for discrimination.

The Court in *Batson* reasoned that removing jurors based on race harms more than just the individual defendant. Rather, it harms the entire criminal justice system. "The harm from discriminatory jury selection extends beyond that inflicted on the defendant and the excluded juror to touch the entire community," wrote Justice Lewis Powell in his majority opinion. "Selection procedures that purposefully exclude black persons from juries undermine public confidence in the fairness of our system of justice."

Batson v. Kentucky
476 U.S. 79 (1986)

In deciding whether the defendant has made the requisite showing, the trial court should consider all relevant circumstances. For example, a "pattern" of strikes against black jurors included in the particular venire might give rise to an inference of discrimination. Similarly, the prosecutor's questions and statements during voir dire examination and in exercising his challenges may support or refute an inference of discriminatory purpose. These examples are merely illustrative. We have confidence that trial judges, experienced in supervising voir dire, will be able to decide if the circumstances concerning the prosecutor's use of peremptory challenges creates a prima facie case of discrimination against black jurors.

Once the defendant makes a prima facie showing, the burden shifts to the State to come forward with a neutral explanation for challenging black jurors. Though this requirement imposes a limitation in some cases on the full peremptory character of the historic challenge, we emphasize that the prosecutor's explanation need not rise to the level justifying exercise of a challenge for cause. . . .

Just as the Equal Protection Clause forbids the States to exclude black persons from the venire on the assumption that blacks as a group are unqualified to serve as jurors, so it forbids the States to strike black veniremen on the assumption that they will be biased in a particular case simply because the defendant is black. The core guarantee of equal protection, ensuring citizens that their State will not discriminate on account of race, would be meaningless were we to approve the exclusion of jurors on the basis of such assumptions, which arise solely from the jurors' race. Nor may the prosecutor rebut the defendant's case merely by denying that he had a discriminatory motive or "affirm[ing] [his] good faith in making individual selections." If these general assertions were accepted as rebutting a defendant's prima facie case, the Equal Protection Clause "would be but a vain and illusory requirement." The prosecutor therefore must articulate a neutral explanation related to the particular case to be tried. The trial court then will have the duty to determine if the defendant has established purposeful discrimination. . . .

While we recognize, of course, that the peremptory challenge occupies an important position in our trial procedures, we do not agree that our decision today will undermine the contribution the challenge generally makes to the administration of justice. The reality of practice, amply reflected in many state- and federal-court opinions, shows that the challenge may be, and unfortunately at times has been, used to discriminate against black jurors. By requiring trial courts to be sensitive to the racially discriminatory use of peremptory challenges, our decision enforces the mandate of equal protection and furthers the ends of justice. In view of the heterogeneous population of

continued >

> our Nation, public respect for our criminal justice system and the rule of law will be strengthened if we ensure that no citizen is disqualified from jury service because of his race.

Justice Thurgood Marshall, the Court's first African-American jurist, sided with Batson in a concurring opinion but reasoned that the Court should eliminate peremptory challenges entirely. "The decision today will not end the racial discrimination that peremptories inject into the jury-selection process," he wrote. "That goal can be accomplished only by eliminating peremptory challenges entirely. . . . Misuse of the peremptory challenge to exclude black jurors has become both common and flagrant."

Chief Justice Warren Burger and Associate Justice William Rehnquist each wrote dissenting opinions. Burger emphasized that peremptory challenges had been a part of the judicial system for more than 200 years and had become "part of the fabric of our jury system." Rehnquist believed that there was no equal protection violation as long as prosecutors can use peremptory challenges to strike jurors of any race. He wrote: "In my view, there is nothing unequal about the State's using its peremptory challenges to strike blacks from the jury in cases involving black defendants so long as such challenges are also used to exclude whites in cases involving white defendants, Hispanics in cases involving Hispanics, Asians in cases involving Asian defendants and so on."

The Court has extended the Batson rationale in different contexts. In *Hernandez v. New York* (1991), the Court ruled that the principle from Batson applied to prohibit prosecutors from striking Latino jurors in a case involving a Latino defendant. The Court later extended Batson to prohibit the race-based use of peremptory challenges even when the defendant and the jurors in question do not share the same race. In *Powers v. Ohio* (1991), the Court ruled that a white defendant could object to the striking of African-American jurors in his case. Justice Anthony Kennedy wrote for the Court's seven-member majority: "Invoking the Equal Protection Clause and federal statutory law, and relying upon well-established principles of standing, we hold that a criminal defendant may object to race-based exclusions of jurors effected through peremptory challenges whether or not the defendant and the excluded juror share the same race."

In *Georgia v. McCollum* (1992), the Court ruled that criminal defense attorneys, just like prosecutors, could not exercise peremptory challenges in a racially discriminatory manner. The case involved two white defendants charged with assaulting African-American victims. The defense team argued that it should be allowed to exclude African-American jurors because of the very racially charged nature of the case. The U.S. Supreme

Court disagreed, writing: "Just as public confidence in criminal justice is undermined where racial discrimination has occurred in jury selection, so is public confidence undermined where a defendant, assisted by racially discriminatory peremptory strikes, obtains an acquittal."

The Court later extended the Batson principle to gender in its 1994 decision *J.E.B. v. Alabama ex. rel. T.B.* In this paternity and child support action, the state used nine of its ten peremptory challenges to strike male jurors, meaning that J.E.B., the person against whom the paternity proceedings had been filed, was tried before an all-female jury. "Discrimination in jury selection, whether based on race or on gender, causes harm to the litigants, the community, and the individual jurors who are wrongfully excluded from participation in the judicial process," wrote Justice Blackmun for the Court majority. "The litigants are harmed by the risk that the prejudice which motivated the discriminatory selection of the jury will infect the entire proceedings."

J.E.B. v. Alabama ex. rel. T.B
511 U.S. 127 (1994)

Discrimination in jury selection, whether based on race or on gender, causes harm to the litigants, the community, and the individual jurors who are wrongfully excluded from participation in the judicial process. The litigants are harmed by the risk that the prejudice which motivated the discriminatory selection of the jury will infect the entire proceedings. The community is harmed by the State's participation in the perpetuation of invidious group stereotypes and the inevitable loss of confidence in our judicial system that state-sanctioned discrimination in the courtroom engenders.

When state actors exercise peremptory challenges in reliance on gender stereotypes, they ratify and reinforce prejudicial views of the relative abilities of men and women. Because these stereotypes have wreaked injustice in so many other spheres of our country's public life, active discrimination by litigants on the basis of gender during jury selection "invites cynicism respecting the jury's neutrality and its obligation to adhere to the law." The potential for cynicism is particularly acute in cases where gender-related issues are prominent, such as cases involving rape, sexual harassment, or paternity. Discriminatory use of peremptory challenges may create the impression that the judicial system has acquiesced in suppressing full participation by one gender or that the "deck has been stacked" in favor of one side. See id., at 413 ("The verdict will not be accepted or understood [as fair] if the jury is chosen by unlawful means at the outset").

In recent cases, we have emphasized that individual jurors themselves have a right to nondiscriminatory jury selection procedures. Contrary to respondent's suggestion, this right extends to both men and women. See *Mississippi University for Women v. Hogan*, (that a state practice

continued >

"discriminates against males, rather than against females, does not exempt it from scrutiny or reduce the standard of review"); cf. Brief for Respondent 9 (arguing that men deserve no protection from gender discrimination in jury selection because they are not victims of historical discrimination). All persons, when granted the opportunity to serve on a jury, have the right not to be excluded summarily because of discriminatory and stereotypical presumptions that reflect and reinforce patterns of historical discrimination. Striking individual jurors on the assumption that they hold particular views simply because of their gender is "practically a brand upon them, affixed by law, an assertion of their inferiority." It denigrates the dignity of the excluded juror, and, for a woman, reinvokes a history of exclusion from political participation. The message it sends to all those in the courtroom, and all those who may later learn of the discriminatory act, is that certain individuals, for no reason other than gender, are presumed unqualified by state actors to decide important questions upon which reasonable persons could disagree.

The U.S. Supreme Court and lower courts continue to hear challenges about the improper use of peremptory challenges. In *Miller-El v. Dretke* (2005), the U.S. Supreme Court ruled that the prosecution's use of peremptory challenges to remove 10 of 11 African Americans from a jury pool entitled a criminal defendant to a new trial.

Crack Cocaine and Sentencing Disparities

In the 1980s, crack cocaine became the scourge of the inner city, wreaking havoc on lives and leading to great devastation. Crack cocaine was cheaper than powder cocaine and, according to some experts, more addictive. Though essentially the same substance, crack cocaine was viewed as a greater problem than powder cocaine. As a result of this, Congress in the 1980s approved of the Anti-Drug Abuse Act, which increased penalties for those trafficking in crack cocaine. Under the new criminal laws, there was a 100-to-1 ratio on criminal sentencing for crack versus powder cocaine offenses. In other words, a defendant with 5 grams of crack cocaine could receive the same sentence as someone with 500 grams of powder cocaine.

This great sentencing disparity implicates the Equal Protection Clause, because the vast majority of crack-cocaine defendants are African American, whereas the majority of those with powder cocaine are white. Some African-American defendants argued that the severe disparities in punishment for crack cocaine offenses as compared to powder cocaine offenses violated the Equal Protection Clause because it had such a disproportionate impact based on race.

A few courts have accepted such equal protection claims. For example the Supreme Court of Minnesota in *State v. Russell* (1991) ruled that the harsh crack-powder cocaine sentencing disparities violated the equal protection provision of the Minnesota Constitution. "There comes a time when we cannot and must not close our eyes when presented with evidence that certain laws, regardless of the purpose for which they were enacted, discriminate unfairly, on the basis of race," the court wrote. "That, in Minnesota, the predominately black possessors of three grams of crack cocaine face a long term imprisonment with presumptive execution of sentence while the predominately white possessors of three grams of powder cocaine face a lesser term of imprisonment with presumptive probation and stay of sentence."

However, most courts rejected such challenges. These courts reasoned that the U.S. Congress had valid reasons for increasing the sentences of crack cocaine defendants, including that crack cocaine was more addictive, cheaper, more potent, and was used at an increasing rate. This showed that Congress did not have a discriminatory purpose when it created the enhanced sentences for crack cocaine defendants. For example, the Eighth U.S. Circuit Court of Appeals in *United States v. Clary* (1992) reasoned that "the evidence of the haste with which Congress acted and the action it took is as easily explained by the seriousness of the perceived problem as by racial animus."

Congress finally acted to restore a measure of fairness in the crack cocaine sentencing area. The legislature passed the Fair Sentencing Act of 2010, which lowered the 100-to-1 ratio between crack and powder cocaine offenses to an 18-to-1 ratio. Still, there are those who believe that more reform is necessary and the ratio should be dropped to 1-to-1.

Selective Prosecution

A related equal protection issue in the criminal justice system concerns charges of **selective prosecution**. A selective prosecution charge alleges that the government has selectively singled out a particular group of people for criminal prosecution. For example, today many believe that there is selective prosecution in the enforcement of immigration laws, as government officials seemingly target persons of Hispanic appearance.

Selective prosecution: Allegation that the government has selectively singled out a particular group for criminal prosecution.

In the late nineteenth century, the Court did address a selective prosecution claim, although it did not use the term at that time. In *Yick Wo v. Hopkins* (1886), the Court ruled that a San Francisco ordinance prohibiting Chinese laundry businesses from operating in wooden structures violated the Equal Protection Clause. The ordinance allowed city officials to grant a permit to a laundry business owner in a wooden structure. City officials routinely allowed whites such permits, but denied permits to Chinese applicants. The Court ruled this way in the face of overwhelming evidence that the ordinance was applied to Chinese defendants who operated the majority of laundries in the city. City officials routinely granted permits to persons of non-Chinese descent, but denied permits to those who were Chinese. The Court unanimously ruled that the ordinance was applied "with a mind so unequal and oppressive as to amount to a practical denial by the State of that equal protection of the laws which is secured to the petitioners."

The U.S. Supreme Court addressed a selective prosecution claim in *United States v. Armstrong* (1996). The defendants in the case were charged with distributing crack cocaine. They alleged that the government selectively prosecuted them because they were African American. They submitted evidence showing that every major drug case involving crack cocaine in the prosecutor's office in 1991—all 24 cases—were against African-American defendants.

However, the Supreme Court rejected the selective prosecution claim, finding that the defendants must show both that the law had a discriminatory effect and a discriminatory purpose. The Court reasoned that the defendants failed to show a discriminatory effect based on race because they failed to show that there were similarly situated individuals of a different race who could have been prosecuted. "The vast majority of the Courts of Appeals require the defendant to produce some evidence that similarly situated defendants of other races could have been prosecuted, but were not, and this requirement is consistent with our equal protection case law," wrote Chief Justice William Rehnquist for the majority. "The study (submitted by the defendants) failed to identify individuals who were not black and could have been prosecuted for the offenses for which respondents were charged, but were not so prosecuted."

Justice John Paul Stevens, in part because of the reality that most crack cocaine defendants are African American and that most of them are prosecuted in federal court, noted the "troubling patterns of enforcement."

John Paul Stevens Dissenting in *U.S. v. Armstrong* 517 U.S. 456 (1996)

The extraordinary severity of the imposed penalties and the troubling racial patterns of enforcement give rise to a special concern about the fairness of charging practices for crack offenses. Evidence tending to prove that black defendants charged with distribution of crack in the Central District of California are prosecuted in federal court, whereas members of other races charged with similar offenses are prosecuted in state court, warrants close scrutiny by the federal judges in that district. In my view, the District Judge, who has sat on both the federal and the state benches in Los Angeles,

continued >

> acted well within her discretion to call for the development of facts that
> would demonstrate what standards, if any, governed the choice of forum
> where similarly situated offenders are prosecuted.

Race of the Victim Discrimination

Perhaps the most troubling equal protection issue in the criminal justice
arena involves the ultimate punishment—death. Early in American history,
discrimination in the application of the death penalty was focused on the
skin color of the defendant. States that had slavery had many crimes for
which slaves could be executed, but not whites. Virginia, for example, had
more than 70 death-eligible crimes for slaves but only one—murder—for
whites.

Even in recent times, racial issues in the death penalty continue.
Numerous studies have shown that black defendants who kill white victims are more likely to be sentenced to death than those who kill nonwhite
persons. The most famous study was the 1977 Baldus Study, named after
Professor David C. Baldus who, along with two others, examined thousands of murder cases in Georgia in the 1970s. The study showed that
those who killed whites were more than four times likely to be prosecuted
for capital murder (death) than those who killed nonwhites.

In *McCleskey v. Kemp* (1987), the U.S. Supreme Court decided the case
of an African-American man, Warren McCleskey, accused and convicted of
killing a white police officer. McCleskey argued that this death sentence
should be overturned because Georgia's criminal justice system was
racially biased in violation of the Equal Protection Clause. The U.S.
Supreme Court did not refute the Baldus Study, but said that it does indicate
a "discrepancy that appears to correlate with race." However, the Court
added that "apparent disparities in sentencing are an inevitable part of
our criminal justice system" and that McCleskey failed to show that the
individual prosecutors in his own individual case acted with impermissible
racial bias. Several justices dissented, including William Brennan, who
wrote: "Considering the race of a defendant or victim in deciding if the
death penalty should be imposed is completely at odds with this concern
that an individual be evaluated as a unique human being."

Sadly, more recent studies also have found race of the victim discrimination in the death penalty. For example, a 2003 study conducted at the
University of Maryland determined: "Offenders who kill white victims,
especially if the offender is black, are significantly and substantially
more likely to be charged with a capital crime." Because of such findings,
some members in Congress continue to introduce legislation to attempt to

address problems of racial disparities in the criminal justice system. For example, Rep. Steve Cohen (D.-Tenn.) has introduced in several sessions the Justice Integrity Act, which would create a five-year pilot program to examine the causes and incidents of racial disparities in the criminal justice arena.

CHAPTER SUMMARY

1. The Equal Protection Clause of the Fourteenth Amendment is designed to ensure that similarly situated persons are treated similarly. It was a key part of the Fourteenth Amendment, a Reconstruction era provision designed to prohibit rampant discrimination against African Americans. Originally, "a constitutional argument of last resort," the Equal Protection Clause has become one of the most important sources of protection for individual rights.

2. The Equal Protection Clause limits only government conduct. It does not reach private conduct. Today, there are statutes or laws that limit discriminatory action by employers and owners of businesses, but the Constitution does not do so. The U.S. Supreme Court established this principle in the *Civil Rights Cases* (1883).

3. In the late nineteenth century, the U.S. Supreme Court upheld a Louisiana segregation law that provided for separate railway accommodations based on race. The Court ruled in *Plessy v. Ferguson* (1896) that segregation laws were constitutional as long as the government provided substantially equal facilities to all races. This was known as the separate but equal doctrine.

4. The U.S. Supreme Court finally cracked the walls of segregation first in higher education cases, ruling that public universities needed to provide African Americans with a school of their own or admit the applicants to the all-white universities. Eventually, the NAACP challenged the separate but equal doctrine head-on. In *Brown v. Board of Education* (1954), the U.S. Supreme Court ruled that separate educational facilities are inherently unequal. This decision led to the dismantling of many segregation laws, although it took longer than it should have.

5. Laws that draw distinctions among people based on a suspect class such as race are subject to the highest form of judicial review, known as *strict scrutiny*. Racial classifications are inherently suspect. Other classifications, such as those based on gender or on quasi-suspect classes, are subject to *intermediate scrutiny* or *midlevel scrutiny*. Finally, most classifications, such as economic classifications, are subject only to *rational basis*. The difference in terminology is often outcome determinative, as most laws subject to strict scrutiny are invalidated and most laws subject to rational basis are upheld.

6. Many years ago, the U.S. Supreme Court struck down a ban on interracial marriage as a stark violation of the Equal Protection Clause. The current issue facing some courts now is whether a ban on same-sex marriage also violates the Equal Protection Clause. The U.S. Supreme Court has avoided deciding that question.

7. Affirmative action refers to a policy that seeks to increase representation among groups that have historically been disadvantaged. Affirmative action is controversial because to many it constitutes a form of reverse discrimination. The U.S. Supreme Court has upheld narrowly crafted affirmative action policies in the education setting. Many employers also have affirmative action programs. Affirmative action programs often are subject to strict scrutiny.

8. The United States has a long history of gender discrimination, just as it does racial discrimination. Women were not allowed to vote until the early twentieth century with the passage of the Nineteenth Amendment. In the twentieth century, women were denied certain jobs and not allowed to sit on juries in some jurisdictions. Gender classifications are subject to intermediate scrutiny, and over the last 30 years, courts have viewed such classifications with greater skepticism.

9. Equal protection issues often arise in the criminal justice system. A classic example is the use of peremptory challenges, a longstanding practice in which attorneys dismiss jurors because they have a hunch that they would not be good for their client. In *Batson v. Kentucky* (1986), the U.S. Supreme Court ruled that prosecutors may not use peremptory challenges in a racially discriminatory fashion. The Court later extended this principle to defense attorneys and also later ruled that attorneys could not use peremptory challenges to discriminate on the basis of gender.

10. Many believed that the stark difference (100-to-1 ratio) in sentencing for defendants charged with crack cocaine offenses and those charged with powder cocaine offenses constituted an equal protection violation. This was because most of the crack cocaine defendants were African American. However, most courts ruled that Congress had legitimate reasons to believe there should be enhanced sentences for crack cocaine defendants.

11. Selective prosecution claims also trigger the protections of the Equal Protection Clause. To make out a claim of selective prosecution, a defendant must show that a law had a discriminatory effect based on race or another protected characteristic and that the law was pursued with a discriminatory purpose. These claims are very difficult to prove.

12. Many studies have found that those who kill white victims are far more likely to be charged with the death penalty than those who kill nonwhite victims. Such studies seem to show a disturbing racial

correlation in the implementation of the death penalty. However, that is not enough to end the practice of the death penalty, according to the U.S. Supreme Court.

REVIEW EXERCISES

Match the following terms with their most appropriate meaning.

TERMS	MEANING
1. Separate but equal doctrine	____ requires that the government show that its policy or regulation advances a compelling or extremely strong interest in a very narrowly tailored manner
2. Jim Crow laws	
3. Strict scrutiny	____ policies designed to create greater diversity for historically under-represented groups
4. Suspect class	
5. Intermediate scrutiny	____ government must only show that it has a legitimate reason that is not arbitrary
6. Rational basis	____ in jury selection, the parties may be given limited challenges to eliminate potential jurors without cause
7. Affirmative action	
8. Peremptory challenges	____ early court reasoning that as long as each race had substantially equal facilities there was no violation of the Equal Protection Clause
9. Voir dire	____ class historically saddled with iniquities or injustices
10. Selective prosecution	____ the jury selection process
	____ any law that segregates the races
	____ means that government regulation must advance a substantial government interest
	____ alleges that the government has selectively singled out a particular group for criminal prosecution

DISCUSSION QUESTIONS

1. Do you believe that the Equal Protection Clause should be limited to actions by government officials? Does this give private persons a license to discriminate? What state laws can limit the discriminatory actions of private persons?
2. Why did the NAACP first try to integrate institutions of higher learning before public secondary schools?
3. Why did the U.S. Supreme Court take two decisions to decide *Brown v. Board of Education*? What were the troubling implications of the Court's order in *Brown II* for schools to integrate with "all deliberate speed."
4. When were local secondary schools in your city first integrated?
5. Should the Equal Protection Clause treat racial classifications differently from gender classifications? Given that there is a long history of both race and gender discrimination, why should there be any difference?
6. Do you believe there is still discrimination against women or groups of women in society? When were women first allowed to practice law in your state?
7. Do you believe that affirmative action positively promotes diversity or does it constitute a form of reverse discrimination?

8. Do you believe that the race-based use of peremptory challenges violates the Equal Protection Clause? Do you agree with Justice Thurgood Marshall's view that the judicial system should eliminate peremptory challenges entirely or with Chief Justice Warren Burger's view that peremptory challenges are a "fabric" of our judicial system?

9. Do you think the sentencing disparities for crack and powder cocaine offenses are justifiable, or were they perhaps enacted for a racially discriminatory purpose?

10. What are the troubling implications of selective prosecution claims? Do you think it is too hard to prove such claims?

11. What are the disturbing implications if there really is "race of the victim" discrimination in the implementation of the death penalty? What can be done to stop this?

ASSIGNMENTS

ASSIGNMENT: Find out when high schools in your city and county were integrated. See if you can locate and interview some of the first African-American students who integrated the school. Ask them their perspectives on what was a challenging time in American history.

ASSIGNMENT: Call up the prosecutors and public defender's office in your hometown. Ask them about the practice of peremptory challenges in criminal cases. Do they support such practices? Are there any reforms that you would suggest as to how our legal system deals with peremptory challenges?

SOURCES AND SUGGESTED READING

Ball, Howard. 2000. *The Bakke Case: Education & Affirmative Action*. Lawrence, Kan.: University Press of Kansas.

Foner, Eric. 1998. *The Story of American Freedom*. New York: W.W. Norton & Company.

Higginbotham, A. Leon Jr. 1996. *Shades of Freedom: Racial Politics and Presumptions of the American Legal Process*. New York: Oxford University Press.

Hudson, David L. Jr. 2002. *The Fourteenth Amendment: Equal Protection Under the Law*. Berkeley Heights, N.J.: Enslow Press.

Hudson, David L. Jr. 2005. *Race, Ethnicity, and the American Criminal Justice System: A Resource Guide for Teachers*. Chicago: American Bar Association.

Klarman, Michael J. 2004. *From Jim Crow to Civil Liberties*. New York: Oxford University Press.

Nowak, John E., and Ronald D. Rotunda. 2009. *Constitutional Law*. 8th ed. St. Paul, Minn: Thomson Reuters.

COURT CASES

Batson v. Kentucky, 476 U.S. 479 (1986)
Bradwell v. Illinois, 83 U.S. 138 (1873)
Civil Rights Cases, 109 U.S. 3 (1883)
Goesart v. Cleary, 335 U.S. 464 (1948)
Gratz v. Bollinger, 539 U.S. 244 (2003)
Grutter v. Bollinger, 539 U.S. 306 (2003)
Lawrence v. Texas, 539 U.S. 558 (2003)
Plessy v. Ferguson, 163 U.S. 537 (1896)
Powers v. Ohio, 499 U.S. 400 (1991)
Regents of the University of California v. Bakke, 438 U.S. 265 (1978)
Skinner v. Oklahoma, 316 U.S. 535 (1942)
State v. Russell, 477 N.W.2d 886 (Minn. 1991)
Strauder v. West Virginia, 100 U.S. 303 (1880)

Swain v. Alabama, 380 U.S. 202 (1965)
United States v. Armstrong, 517 U.S. 456 (1996)
United States v. Clary, 34 F.3d 709 (8th Cir. 1994)

ONLINE SOURCES
Brown v. Board of Education National Historic Site
    http://www.nps.gov/brvb/index.htm
Charles Hamilton Houston Institute for
    Race & Justice
    http://www.charleshamiltonhouston.org/
    Home.aspx

Institute on Race and Justice
    http://www.irj.neu.edu/
National Association for the Advancement
    of Colored People
    http://www.naacp.org
National Organization for Women
    http://www.now.org/

UNDERSTANDING CIVIL LAW PROCEDURE

The next four chapters of this text illustrate the major procedural stages of a civil legal action involving a products liability claim for injuries and damage, including wrongful death, resulting from an automobile accident. It illustrates the diversity of the jurisdiction of the federal courts in civil legal actions and the use of state law in civil cases.

The first chapter in this section introduces a hypothetical civil action originating from an automobile accident. The case is followed through the stages of finding a lawyer, initiating a civil legal action in federal court, the pretrial discovery process, jury trial, and appeal.

Initiating Civil Legal Process

CHAPTER 10

The Centerville News Journal September 9, 2010

The Centerville area witnessed a severe rainstorm last night. Power lines were reported out of operation for as long as two hours in some areas of Rural County. Seven accidents were reported in the area ranging from minor fender benders to a severe accident on Interstate 24 about three miles from Centerville.

William P. Consumer, a professor at Middle State University, was reported dead on arrival at the hospital after his automobile collided with a tractor-trailer. He is survived by his wife, Jane Consumer, who was also injured in the accident. Jane Consumer was reported in serious condition by the Mid-State Medical Center this morning. Details of the accident are not known at this time, but it appears that the Consumer vehicle was traveling south on I-24 and crossed over the median, hitting a tractor-trailer traveling north on the opposite side of the highway.

The storm lasted only about 30 minutes and began around 10:30 P.M. The News Journal rain gauge recorded 1.5 inches of precipitation. Heavy flooding was reported in some low-lying areas, which caused damage to homes and automobiles.

There has not yet been an assessment of the damage caused by the storm in the area.

Automobile accidents are one type of personal and property damage that frequently lead to disputes of a civil nature involving private parties. The accident described above may seem somewhat unusual, but such events appear in the media quite often. In the example, Bill Consumer was killed, and his wife, Jane Consumer, was severely injured in an accident that occurred during a rainstorm. Such a personal tragedy has several important legal implications, and this example will be used to illustrate many aspects of private, or civil, law.

Jane Consumer found that her life had been drastically altered by a sudden and completely unexpected event. She suffered a broken back in the accident and the loss of her husband. Bill Consumer was an associate professor of psychology at Middle State University. He was the sole support for the Consumer family, which included three children. The oldest child was a sophomore in college, and there were two younger children, aged 15 and 11. The Consumers were a typical middle-class family who considered themselves fortunate to enjoy a decent standard of living and thought they would be able to provide for the education of their children and a secure future.

After the accident, Jane Consumer realized she was confronted with a number of significant problems that required the assistance of a lawyer. Bill Consumer's employer was helpful in providing information about the benefits Jane would receive from an insurance policy carried by the university, but after a few months, she would no longer have the benefit of group insurance rates. The automobile insurance company indicated that the family car could not be repaired and offered to settle Jane's claims under the family's liability and casualty insurance policies. Jane was not sure whether the insurance company was offering a fair value to compensate for the "totaled" automobile. Jane also knew she would have to file legal papers concerning her husband's estate but knew nothing about the process.

Above all, Jane Consumer was concerned about why the accident happened in the first place. The car just suddenly went out of control on the way home from a shopping trip. Bill was trying to pass a van on the interstate highway when he looked at her in panic and said, "The wheel won't turn." The car went out of control and crossed the median, hitting a truck on the other side of the interstate highway. Jane had heard a strange noise just before the car went out of control and thought there was something wrong with the vehicle. Bill had complained about the car leaning to the left for some time and had even taken it to the dealer to be fixed, but the mechanics there said they found nothing wrong with it. After going through Bill's papers, Jane found a letter from the manufacturer of their car that indicated the car should be taken to the dealer for repairs.

Jane began to suspect that she might have cause for legal action against the manufacturer or the dealer for failing to repair the car. At any rate, she needed legal advice about the probate matters concerning her husband's estate. She was uncertain and confused about her financial affairs and thought it would be helpful to have professional advice about them.

FINDING A LAWYER

There is no simple answer to the question of how to choose a good lawyer. Complaints against lawyers and stories of malpractice suits and of lawyers who have taken advantage of their clients are common, but the majority of lawyers are honest professionals dedicated to client service. The American Bar Association created the Model Rules of Professional Conduct for lawyers, who require high ethical standards. States then model their ethical rules after the ABA's Model Rules. Attorneys can be disbarred for violations of these state ethics rules. Even though lawyers can help people in many situations, many people are reluctant to seek legal advice because of the fear that a lawyer's services will be very expensive and the feeling that even though a lawyer is needed, it is difficult to know whom to trust.

Choosing a lawyer is a lot like choosing a doctor. Professional services such as legal aid societies, local bar associations, better business bureaus, and even private lawyer referral services can be contacted for advice. The best lawyers achieve reputations for various types of practice within their communities, so asking friends and relatives is another method of locating a lawyer. However, it is important to know more about the area of expertise that you may need before committing to a particular lawyer.

The Internet is very helpful for finding out what lawyers in your community specialize in the area of law that you need. *LexisNexis* has a search instrument available to all that will provide a list of lawyers in your community with the specialty you select. This Web site is entitled Find a Lawyer, and typing in the name is all that is needed to find it on the Web. The Martindale Hubbell directory for locating lawyers is found at Martindale.com and is also supported by LexisNexis. This source will give you a peer review rating for the lawyers of interest in your community or other areas of interest. If you enter the lawyer's name, the Web site will provide information about the lawyer's reputation.

In many communities, reputable lawyers do not charge a fee for an initial consultation, or they charge only a nominal fee. It is even possible to consult with a lawyer online about your concerns (see the same lists of sources from Find a Lawyer). Jane Consumer knew that her husband had employed a lawyer to draft their separate wills. His name was John Gaither. Jane did not know him very well and had met him only once when she and her husband Bill signed the wills.

It was logical for her to contact Mr. Gaither for an initial consultation concerning her problems. The secretary indicated that since Mr. Gaither had drafted wills for the Consumers, he would not charge for an initial consultation. Jane and the secretary agreed on an appointment date.

Jane brought Bill's will, her auto insurance policy, the letter from the manufacturer, and other papers to the appointment. At the law firm, she was anxiously waiting for the secretary to show her into Mr. Gaither's office. Mr. Gaither greeted her with a friendly handshake and expressed his regrets about Bill's death.

She told him what she knew concerning Bill's **estate** and **probate** matters. Mr. Gaither also had a copy of the will and proceeded to explain that the simple will he had drawn up made her the executrix of the estate of her late husband, William P. Consumer; that is, she would be responsible for seeing that the provisions of the will were effectively executed.

Jane would have to file the petition she had received from the clerk's office to open the estate and then appear before the probate judge to open the estate and admit the estate to probate. The assets of the estate would be frozen for six months to allow creditors to file claims. She would have to

Estate:
The degree, quantity, nature, and extent of interest a person has in real and personal property.

Probate:
The court procedure by which a will is proved. The term includes all matters and proceedings concerning administration of estates of deceased persons.

announce the opening of the estate in the newspaper and prepare an accounting of the assets and liabilities. At the end of the six-month period, the estate would be placed on the probate court docket, and Jane would have to show that the estate was free and clear of all obligations, including inheritance taxes due to the state. She would then receive an order from the judge closing the estate.

Mr. Gaither said Bill wisely had drafted the will three years before the accident. He explained to Jane, "Most people your age don't think it's important to have a will, but when someone dies *intestate*—that is, without a will—it can be a very complex matter to close an estate. Even a self-drafted, handwritten document, witnessed properly, can prevent many costly problems. But in your case, the matter is quite simple; you don't have any complex problems."

Jane told the attorney how concerned she was about her finances and that she wondered how she would keep her daughter Kim in college. She asked Mr. Gaither how much he would charge for his services. He indicated that his normal fee for probate work, when a will existed, was $200 an hour. However, the *testate procedure* involving a simple will would require very little of his time, and his legal assistant, Chris Martin, would be able to do most of the work. The firm would bill only $40 an hour for Mr. Martin's services. "I will, of course, oversee his work and make sure it is complete," said Mr. Gaither, "but as long as we don't run into any complications, a minimal fee of $400 would be a reasonable estimate from what you have told me."

Jane was relieved. She thought lawyers charged more for their services. She then told Mr. Gaither that she had a number of other questions that troubled her. The first had to do with the car they were driving—a 2009 Supreme Brougham Executive. The insurance company said it was totaled and wanted to settle for a $15,000 payment on the collision insurance. Jane pointed out, "We paid $20,000 for it, and it's only two years old."

The attorney looked up the book value in a small paperback on his desk and asked a few questions about extras on the vehicle. He concluded that the agent had quoted the correct amount according to the information normally used to calculate replacement value. "It would be difficult to get more from them under your contract," he replied.

Jane then explained her suspicion that there may have been something wrong with the car that could have caused the accident. The attorney listened attentively as she explained about the noise she heard just before the car went out of control, and he asked questions as she told her story. He said he would have to investigate to determine whether she had a legal cause of action against the dealer or manufacturer of the automobile. He asked where the car was located and whether her husband had any receipts for the inspection of the car by the dealer. Jane thought they might still be in the glove compartment of the car, which was located at a local wrecker services impoundment lot. Mr. Gaither was also very interested in the factory-recall letter that Jane gave him during their consultation.

Mr. Gaither explained he needed a list of various documents, records of assets, and liabilities that could be attributed to Bill Consumer's estate to probate the will. He would put his legal assistant to work on probating the will right away.

Attorney Gaither would also need to begin an investigation of the possible cause of the accident and would need the factory recall letter. He had her sign a request to examine the accident vehicle, and would take steps to find out more about her suspicion that there was something wrong with the car. He would let Jane know what he found out.

TYPES OF LEGAL ACTION

Civil actions cover a vast array of issues and include all noncriminal actions within the jurisdiction of the courts. The overwhelming majority of legal actions filed in court are civil actions. These include actions in both law and equity. The distinction between law and equity here relates primarily to the remedy sought. Suits for money damages must be brought in law, as opposed to equity actions, which are sought to secure specific performance orders, such as injunctions (although in equity actions the judge may exercise punitive money damages as punishment for malicious acts).

Money Damages

The law strives to afford a suitable remedy to every person who has suffered an actual loss caused by the unlawful conduct of another. The general area of civil law that the attorney considered regarding Jane Consumer's concern about something being wrong with the accident vehicle was **tort law,** discussed in Chapter 6 of this text. The key word *unlawful* is used to describe conduct that is in violation of statutory or common-law standards. The fact that Jane Consumer has suffered an actual loss does not mean that she has a remedy for that loss. Attorney Gaither needs to conduct a preliminary investigation to determine the potential for establishing a **cause of action**.

Tort law:
The area of civil law involving personal injury or property damages, excluding contracts.

Cause of action:
The fact or facts that give a person a right to judicial relief.

PRELIMINARY INVESTIGATION

John Gaither had another appointment that afternoon and could not begin research into Jane's questions, but he kept thinking about the accident and the recall letter. At the end of the day, he gave his legal assistant, Chris Martin, instructions to begin work on Jane Consumer's petition to open the estate. He asked Chris to meet with him in the morning at 9:00 A.M. to discuss the questions raised by Jane about the cause of the accident that killed her husband.

Chris Martin had been employed by the law firm of Smith and Gaither for about two years as a legal assistant and had worked with Attorney Gaither on several cases. He had done a lot of title searches and preliminary investigations for the firm. At their meeting the next morning, Attorney Gaither explained the situation concerning Mrs. Consumer's case. "The letter from the factory concerning the recall on Bill's car needs to be checked out with the factory and dealer," he told Chris. "And go down to the garage and see if you can find any maintenance receipts in the glove compartment of Bill's car. We are looking for some comment on checking the suspension (left side) or coils."

That afternoon, Chris had some interesting facts to report. The factory confirmed that there was a problem with the coil spring suspension on the left side of that particular model automobile with serial numbers within the range of those for Bill's car. Chris also found two maintenance receipts that indicated an order to check the rear suspension because the "car leans to the left." Both receipts had dealer's notations that said, "Checked, OK." The receipts were dated March, 7, 2010, and August, 15, 2010. "The factory wouldn't tell me what was wrong with the coil spring," Chris explained.

"Who's the best mechanic in town, Chris?" asked Gaither. Chris had no answer, but the attorney said, "Mack Racer. He owns the Speed Shop in town and works on championship race cars—everybody knows he's the best. I'll call him and see if we can get him to look at Bill's car."

Mack Racer took a couple of days to get to it, but he reported to Attorney Gaither that he had removed the rear coils from Bill's car and found the left coil broken in half. He also found that the right coil was obviously made of thicker stronger material and was undamaged. "Why would they be different?" asked the attorney. "Could this difference have caused the accident?"

Mack responded, "I'll stake my reputation on it. These coils are made for two different cars, and the left coil was too weak to support that heavy car. If it broke when Bill was passing that van, it would have caused the accident. I'll testify to that in court."

After receiving this preliminary information, Attorney Gaither began to prepare an *investigation plan* (Table 10.1) to efficiently organize the tasks that had to be researched.

John Gaither had an engineer from the National Safety Research Institute examine the coils that Mack Racer recovered from the accident vehicle. The engineer's report to the firm was consistent with that of the expert mechanic who had removed the coils for the accident vehicle. He stated that the coils were definitely not matched and that the right coil was of different gauge and thickness from that of the left coil. He could not say that this caused the accident, but he verified that the coils should not have

Table 10.1 **INVESTIGATION PLAN TO DETERMINE IF THERE IS A CAUSE OF LEGAL ACTION**

For Jane Consumer	
We have some preliminary evidence that there is a potential cause of legal action concerning products liability in regard to Bill Consumer's accidental death and destruction of his automobile. 1. Chris Martin needs to follow up on his phone call to the manufacturer, the Factory Motor Company. Get all the written evidence available on the recall of Bill Consumer's car. 2. Attorney Gaither will contact the City Auto Company who sold and serviced this vehicle and get as much documented evidence as possible concerning liability for the improper coil found on the left rear of the vehicle. 3. Call Mack Racer back to the office to take a deposition and have him bring the two removed rear coils from Bill Consumer's vehicle with him.	4. Have the secretary contact the Safety Research Institute to inquire into the safety standards about the different coils on Bill Consumer's vehicle to see if their engineer can confirm Mack Racer's opinion that the two incompatible coils could have caused the accident. 5. Attorney Gaither will prepare a preliminary legal research report on the potential for a products liability suit in this case. 6. Prepare a report for Jane Consumer concerning our findings at the conclusion of these assignments. We also need an analysis of our options and chances of winning this case, if filed, and an analysis of the costs. We need to provide Jane with a contractual agreement if we undertake this case.

been used on the same vehicle and could have caused the accident if the left coil broke before the accident took place.

The attorney then contacted the manager of City Auto Company, which had sold the vehicle to the Consumers and whose service department had reportedly done regular maintenance on the car. He explained the situation to the manager over the phone and asked whether he could retrieve the service records on the Consumers' car. The manager indicated that he would examine the service records and check on the manufacturer's recall concerning the vehicle in question. They agreed to meet in the manager's office.

This meeting confirmed that the Consumer vehicle had been serviced properly at regular intervals. The attorney was convinced that even a reasonable mechanic could not have detected the fact that the rear suspension coils were not matched, and it was clear that City Auto Company had not replaced any of the original equipment on the vehicle. The service manager, Jody Courteous, met with them and agreed to sign an **affidavit** (see Form 10.1), which is a sworn statement regarding factual evidence from a potential witness.

Affidavit: Written statement of facts made voluntarily under oath.

John Gaither was convinced that he had a products liability action against Factory Motor Company, the manufacturer of the accident vehicle. He concluded that he had enough preliminary evidence to discuss the terms of a contractual agreement with his client, Jane Consumer.

Form 10.1 **AFFIDAVIT**

This affidavit was given by Jody Courteous, Service Manager of City Auto Company, Centerville, Middle State, on December 2, 2010, before a Notary Public in the presence of Attorney William Green.

1
2
3
4
5
6
7
8
9
10
11
12
13
14
15
16
17
18
19
20
21
22
23
24

My name is Jody Courteous. I am forty-two years old, and I have been employed by the City Auto Company as service manager for the past three years. I was employed by the same company as a mechanic for five years before being promoted to service manager. I was certified by the Factory Motor Company as a qualified mechanic in 2002 and attended more recent training sessions in Lake State.

We try to keep thorough records on the vehicles we sell. I can confirm that the vehicle owned by William P. Consumer was purchased from us on October 20, 2008, and that regular service maintenance was done on the car. I recall when Mr. Consumer brought the car in for the last maintenance check, he asked me to examine the suspension and complained of the car leaning to the left. My mechanic asked me to look at the car after he had it jacked up in the shop. I looked at both coils and checked their attachment, making sure they were secure. Neither the mechanic nor I could conclude from this visual inspection that there was anything wrong with the coils. We did not remove the coils or alter them in any way. I made a note on the work order that the coils checked out OK.

We did get a factory recall on this vehicle, which I discovered when Mr. Sellers, the owner of City Auto Company, asked me to check on it. The recall instructed us to replace the left coil on 2009 models that matched Mr. Consumer's vehicle serial number. This order to us was dated September 1, 2010, and was received six months after our inspection of the car in March.

Had we been given any indication from the factory that these coils were a problem, we might have been able to detect the differences in the coils. But when we inspected Mr. Consumer's vehicle in March, it was impossible to detect the differences without pulling both coils and looking at them side by side.

THE UNDERSIGNED HEREBY CERTIFIES THAT THIS IS A TRUE AND ACCURATE STATEMENT:

Sworn to and subscribed before on
this_____day of_____, _____.

SEAL OF NOTARY PUBLIC

Jody Courteous, Service Manager
City Auto Company

A Contractual Agreement

Attorney Gaither had his secretary set up an appointment with Jane Consumer the next day. After telling her what he had discovered in his preliminary investigation, he indicated that he thought she had a case worth pursuing. "If all this checks out, I believe we have grounds to sue the Factory Motor Company for damages caused in the accident. Since you are the executrix of your husband's estate, you may be able to recover damages both for your injuries and for those suffered to his estate."

Jane wanted to know whether a lawsuit would be very costly to pursue and what the risks were if the court did not award her damages. Gaither explained that he would work on her case on a contingency fee basis and that she would not owe him anything for his services if he was unable to recover damages on her behalf. She would, however, be required to pay court costs if the case got that far. He would keep track of the expenses in the case, and if an award were made, the expenses and court costs would be deducted from the award.

"If we do recover damages, my fee would be a percentage of the award after court costs and expenses are deducted—25 percent if settled out of court, one-third if we have to file suit, and 40 percent if we have to go to appeal with the case," explained the attorney. "I'll give you my standard **contingency fee contract** that explains this in writing so you can think it over."

"Can I get out of this contract if I'm dissatisfied with your progress?" Jane asked. "Yes, all you have to do is tell me I'm fired. Lawyers are employed by the clients and represent them only on their request. You would owe me only for the court costs and expenses in the case, including a reasonable hourly fee for my services up to that point."

Jane also asked if there were other alternatives to the contingency fee contract. Gaither explained that there are different methods of paying for the professional services of a lawyer: a fixed fee, which was offered in the legal work concerning the probating of Bill's will, with the agreement that there would be no complications that developed, and the hourly fee that he had explained was $200 per hour. These alternative methods would be more risky for Jane, he explained.

Jane took the contract (see Form 10.2) home and consulted her daughter and father-in-law about it. They agreed that she should sign the contract and proceed with the case. Bill's father indicated that Attorney Gaither had a good reputation. He asked some of his friends whether the contract was a good one and was told that other lawyers charge more for settlement out of court, which might induce the lawyer to bargain for a lower settlement, so Mr. Gaither's offer appeared satisfactory. Jane was gratified with Gaither's interest in the case. Maybe there was a chance that she could recover some of the monetary loss she knew would adversely affect the family, and she hoped the recovery would allow her to keep Kim in school.

Contingency fee contract: Agreement to pay for attorney services contingent on recovery in damage suit.

Form 10.2 **AGREEMENT WITH LAWYER**

The Law Firm of
Smith and Gaither, Attorneys
57 Courthouse Square
Centerville, Middle State

John Gaither
Attorney-at-Law

I, the undersigned client, hereby retain and employ John Gaither as my attorney to represent me in my claim for damages against the seller and/or manufacturer of the 2009 Supreme Brougham Executive, involved in an accident that occurred on September 8, 2010, in which William P. Consumer, my late husband, was killed and I was severely injured.

As compensation for said services, I agree to pay for the court costs, if necessary, and to pay my attorney from the proceeds of recovery, after the deduction of court costs and expenses, the following fees:

25% if settled without suit;
33% if suit is filed;
40% if an appeal is taken by either side.

It is agreed that this employment is on a contingent-fee basis, so that if no recovery is made, I will not owe my attorney any amount for attorneys' fees.

Dated this_____day of_____20_____.

_____
                              Client

I hereby accept the above employment,

_____
John Gaither, Attorney

ASSIGNMENT: Students should follow the attorney's legal research and look up the terms discussed in the following portion of this chapter. These terms will be found in your state's annotated code (e.g., *Tennessee Code Annotated*) and the *U.S. Code Annotated*. You should also find the *Restatement of Torts (Second)* in your library or on the Internet.

LEGAL RESEARCH

After receiving the contract from Jane Consumer, Gaither began his legal research in the firm's law library. He knew from his legal training and experience practicing law in Middle State that he had a potential cause of action in three areas of law. These areas are known as negligence, products liability, and contract. He also knew that he could bring suit in either federal district court or in state court because of the diversity of citizenship of the two parties involved.

This area of overlapping (federal and state) jurisdiction in civil cases exists because of the complicated structure of our federal government. Historically, diversity jurisdiction has served an important purpose by enabling disputes that might not be admitted in state court jurisdiction to enter the courts through the federal structure.

Federal Jurisdiction

Civil cases involving diversity of citizenship of the parties to the dispute were first granted federal jurisdiction in the Judiciary Act of 1789. Therefore, **diversity jurisdiction** has been a significant feature of the federal courts for over 200 years and has been the subject of debate over the entire period. It was first granted because of the fear that state courts would be biased against out-of-state litigants. However, modern state courts are improved, and many argue that parochial state prejudices have been altered to the point where diversity jurisdiction is no longer needed. This area of overlapping jurisdiction could be eliminated without changing the Constitution, and jurisdiction could be left to the states only; however, many lawyers remain concerned about local favoritism in state courts and fight to retain the option of filing their cases in either state or federal court.

Since 1938, the U.S. Supreme Court has tried to reduce the potential for conflict of law arising out of this situation of overlapping jurisdiction by adopting a curious rule known as the **Erie doctrine**. In the case of *Erie Railroad Co. v. Tompkins*, 304 U.S. 64 (1938), the Court held that the substantive law of the state where the case is filed will be applied in federal diversity cases when no federal question is involved. This decision means that whether the case is filed in the state or federal court, the law of the state

Diversity jurisdiction: Jurisdiction of the federal courts when the two parties are citizens of different states or foreign countries and the sum in question exceeds $75,000.

Erie doctrine: Federal practice in civil diversity cases applying the substantive law in the state where the case is filed.

where the court sits will be applied; however, the procedural rules of the federal courts will be applied when the case is filed in federal court.

Diversity of citizenship of the opposing parties must be complete; no two parties on opposing sides may be citizens of the same state. As mentioned in Chapter 3, the sum in question must be greater than $75,000 to meet federal diversity jurisdiction requirements. Federal case law has also established that the parties must have "minimum contact" with the state where jurisdiction is sought. In *World-Wide Volkswagen Corp. v. Woodson*, 444 U.S. 286 (1980), the Supreme Court held that a corporation that conducts no business in the state and has no "contracts, ties, or relations" with the state cannot be expected to answer to legal actions in that state under diversity jurisdiction.

John Gaither was confident that Jane Consumer's case met all the qualifications for diversity jurisdiction since the Factory Motor Company was both incorporated in and had its headquarters in Lake State, and Jane Consumer, the plaintiff, was a citizen of Middle State. Factory Motor Company had dealerships in Middle State and did business in the state on a regular basis, therefore establishing the minimum contacts required by the federal courts.

State Jurisdiction

Both Middle State and Lake State had jurisdiction over civil matters as well; indeed, states have jurisdiction over all matters that are not specifically designated in the U.S. Constitution, in valid federal statutes, or in treaties. These supreme laws of the land confer exclusive federal jurisdiction over certain matters, and these are not a part of state court jurisdiction. This rule leaves a vast residual area of jurisdiction to the states, and much of it is shared between the state and federal governments, as in diversity cases.

Therefore, Gaither knew that he could file his legal action in either Middle State's or Lake State's federal district court since there is a federal district court in every state and territory of the United States. The choices were fairly easy to make in this case, but these options can have important implications for the lawyer making such a decision. In some cases, the lawyer's choice may have an influence on the outcome of the case.

Choice of Law and Court

Gaither knew from his legal research that Middle State's substantive law recognized the principle of products liability in tort law described in section 402A of the *Restatement of Torts (Second)*. This concept, often referred to as strict liability, defines a special liability that deviates from the specific elements of **negligence**. Gaither's focus was on **products liability** law from the beginning because he knew that this special tort does not require proof

Negligence: Failure to exercise due care.

Products liability: Legal liability of manufacturers and sellers to compensate buyers, users, and even bystanders for damages or injuries suffered because of defects in goods purchased.

of a duty of care, as is required in negligence actions. It requires proof of a "dangerously defective product." (See Table 10.1.)

The strict liability concept was originally developed through the process of common law but was elevated to statutory law in Middle State in 1978. Middle State's code specifically recognizes the elements of the law described in the *Restatement of Torts* (*Second*) below.

Topic 5. Strict Liability
Restatement of Torts (Second)

402 A, Special Liability of Seller of Product for Physical Harm to User or Consumer

(1) One who sells any product in a defective condition unreasonably dangerous to the user or consumer or to his property is subject to liability for physical harm thereby caused to the ultimate user or consumer, or to his property, if

    (a) the seller is engaged in the business of selling such a product, and

    (b) it is expected to and does reach the user or consumer without substantial change in the condition in which it was sold.

(2) The rule stated in Subsection (1) applies although

    (a) the seller has exercised all possible care in the preparation and sale of his product, and

    (b) the user or consumer has not bought the product from or entered into any contractual relation with the seller.

Comparing Affirmative Defense Elements

The affirmative defense in regard to products liability (defective product) had more advantages in the Consumer case than that of the traditional law of negligence. The basic affirmative defense in negligence actions is **contributory negligence**; that is, a plaintiff's negligence with regard to the injuries sustained would negate recovery for damages in many jurisdictions. This rule was the law in Middle State at the time this case was conceived, although later Middle State followed the lead of many other jurisdictions and altered this concept to allow for what has become known as **comparative negligence**. Here the plaintiff's claim may be reduced by the percentage of negligence attributable to the party bringing suit. For example, if the plaintiff's negligence is 20 percent of the fault, the court may reduce the damage claim by 20 percent. The claim is negated if the degree of fault reaches 50 percent.

John Gaither found the basic affirmative defense in the products liability law of Middle State more advantageous to his case than that of

Contributory negligence: Act or omission amounting to lack of ordinary care on the part of the complaining party, that, along with defendant's negligence, is the proximate cause of injury.

Comparative negligence: Liability measured in terms of percentages; any damages allowed are reduced by the proportion of the amount of the plaintiff's negligence.

negligence law. The products liability law stipulated an affirmative defense of **voluntary assumption of a known risk**. This defense requires proof that the plaintiff knew the risk involved in use of a defective product and voluntarily assumed the risk. This defense is more difficult to prove than contributory negligence.

Voluntary assumption of a known risk: In which the plaintiff voluntarily assumed a know risk.

Statute of Limitations

Another question that concerned Attorney Gaither in his legal research was the time limitation provided in law for the initiation of a cause of legal action. This limitation is generally known as the **statute of limitations**. These statutes are provided by state and federal legislatures. The time limitation for tort actions in many jurisdictions is one year, but the time limitation for contract is usually longer. In Middle State, contract actions had a time limitation of three years, but the time began to run at the time of consummation of the contract, in this case, when the automobile was purchased two years before the accident. Tort time limitations begin at the time the injury is detected. If Jane Consumer delayed filing suit beyond one year, she would have no cause of action that the courts would recognize. Jane has consulted her lawyer within three months of the accident, however, so Gaither had ample time to file before the 12-month deadline.

Statute of limitations: Statutes that prescribe the periods within which actions may be brought on certain claims or within which certain rights may be enforced.

Standing to Sue

Another consideration by the attorney was standing to sue. Jane Consumer had **standing to sue** for recovery of damages she sustained in the accident, but the larger amount of potential claim would be to the estate of William P. Consumer. Under ancient common-law concepts, the right to legal action ended with an individual's death. However, modern legislative enactments known as **wrongful death and survival statutes** specifically provide for status to sue on behalf of the estate of the deceased person. These statutes specify and limit recoverable damages on behalf of the estate.

Middle State statutes used the survival statute concept limiting some otherwise recoverable damages, such as pain and suffering and mental suffering of the family resulting from loss of spouse's affection or loss of spouse or parent. However, the estate could recover damages for lost earnings that would have benefited the family and for necessary expenses to the estate resulting from the deceased's injuries, although the deceased's potential earnings had to be reduced by the probable living expenses for the deceased had he lived. These exceptions to the recovery of damages are in keeping with the theory of survival benefits, which are benefits that would have accrued to the deceased had he survived the injuries sustained.

Standing to sue: Requirement that is satisfied if plaintiff has a legally protected and tangible interest in the litigation.

Wrongful death and survival statutes: A cause of action in favor of decedent's personal representative for the benefit of certain beneficiaries.

Damages Estimated

Gaither calculated the estimated damages that Jane Consumer individually and as executrix of the estate of William P. Consumer could reasonably expect to recover to be about $500,000. William P. Consumer was only 48 years of age when he died and could have earned much more than this amount during his lifetime. According to life expectancy tables, he would have 27 years of reasonable life remaining had he not been killed in the accident. Middle State law required that William P. Consumer's potential earnings be reduced by the amount he would have spent had he lived.

A more significant reduction would be the adjustment of his potential earnings to **present value**. This calculation involves a sort of reverse compounding of interest to arrive at a sum of money that could earn the expected amount over the 27 years of life expectancy. There was no question about whether his case would meet the $75,000 limitation for filing a federal diversity action. Jane Consumer's individual injuries and medical expenses were estimated to be about $90,000 and would also meet the minimal requirements.

Present value: Adjustment to account for investment earnings of a specific sum of money over time.

Choice of Federal District Court

The attorney had given considerable thought to whether he should file his case in Middle State's circuit court or in the federal district court located in Capital City, only 30 miles away. Because of the Erie doctrine, he knew that both courts would apply the substantive law of Middle State. The Federal Rules of Civil Procedure would be used in the federal district court, however, and Gaither preferred them to the rules applied in Middle State. They were more flexible and gave him advantages in service of process and procedure that might make a difference in the outcome of the case. With so much at stake in the case, he also preferred the quality of the judges in federal court; he felt that both the quality and efficiency of the federal court were greater than those of the state court. He also checked the dockets in both courts and found that his case would be handled much faster in federal court.

Gaither was now confident that he could report to his client that she had cause for legal action against Factory Motor Company.

REQUEST TO SETTLE OUT OF COURT

Gaither mailed Jane Consumer a report of his preliminary investigation, outlining what he had uncovered so far in the case. He asked her to contact his secretary for an appointment so they could discuss the progress of her case against Factory Motor Company and make some decisions about how to proceed. He included an estimate of the damages he could claim under the laws of Middle State.

At the meeting with his client, Gaither reviewed his findings orally and explained that the facts indicated that she had a possibility of recovering damages through a products liability, or defective products, suit. There were a number of negative factors in the case, including the rainstorm and wet highway, which would be used by Factory Motor Company in their defense. But the faulty manufacture of the vehicle with unsafe equipment was evident from the factory recall letter and had been confirmed by City Auto Company. Gaither told Jane, "We have two experts, one an expert mechanic and the other an engineer, who will verify that the coil on the left side was broken and was not the proper coil for the vehicle. This indicates that we have reasonable grounds to proceed with the case. However, it is far from certain that you will be able to recover the amount of our initial estimate."

The law provides a standard for the private settlement of disputes, and well over 90 percent of civil cases are settled out of court based on the requirements of the law. "We can try for an out-of-court settlement at this point, but don't get your hopes up," the attorney warned Jane. "This is a complicated case, and the Factory Motor Company will more than likely want to take it at least through the discovery process, where we will both have the power of the court to compel evidence, which will enable us to conduct a much more thorough investigation into the facts in the case."

Gaither informed his client that he would draft a letter to Factory Motor Company informing them of the intent to file legal action and asking for a conference to negotiate settlement. Jane Consumer agreed and asked about the amount he would be requesting in the settlement.

"I will send them our initial estimate of the damages," said Gaither. "If they intend to settle we will set up a conference, and you, the client, would have to approve any offer of settlement. I will let them know that you are intent upon filing suit for the amount in our estimate. If they do intend to settle, it will be for considerably less than the amount of our estimate. We will just have to consider the offer and the alternative consequences of going to court. My decision will depend on your determination. My job is to provide competent legal advice."

Gaither sent a letter to Factory Motor Company requesting damages in the amount of $597,200 for the injuries caused by the defective coil, which he asserted was the proximate cause of the accident.

CHAPTER SUMMARY

1. The material described in this chapter illustrates several areas of law that are of concern to the average person. The subjects of wills, estates, torts, and contracts may all be involved in the services that are most

commonly sought from lawyers. They illustrate that individuals may have multiple purposes for seeking legal advice and services.

2. Competent legal advice is needed in crisis situations, and it is a good idea to have a lawyer with whom you feel comfortable before a crisis arises. Lawyers provide initial consultation at no cost or on a nominal fee basis. They will state their fee for a particular problem to the client so that the client can seek a second opinion and compare the differences.

3. Preliminary investigation is needed to determine whether there is a legal cause of action based on the specific facts in the case. Civil legal actions cover all noncriminal actions within the jurisdiction of the courts. They include actions in law and equity, with equity providing a remedy in the form of a specific court action and law providing a means by which to seek money damages.

4. Some of the most significant civil legal actions of a constitutional nature are brought as actions to secure specific performance, but the typical civil lawsuit involves an action to recover money damages in the areas of torts and contract.

5. The law strives to afford a suitable remedy when parties suffer actual loss caused by the unlawful conduct of another. However, there must be a cause of action in law to establish a legitimate claim.

6. The general elements of tort law include breach of a legal duty, damage, and proof of proximate cause. Breach of contract requires competence to contract, offer and acceptance, exchange of legal consideration, breach of contract, and actual loss suffered because of the breach. Each specific area of tort and contract law may involve more detailed elements that must all be proved in order to recover damages. Each tort has certain affirmative defenses that may provide a means by which the defendant can negate a claim or reduce the amount of the award. These elements of state law may be found in the appropriate state code (e.g., *Tennessee Code Annotated*).

7. Clients enter into contractual relations with lawyers in both oral and written form. Contingency fee contracts are used frequently in tort cases. Hourly rates are used in other cases, and some lawyers can be kept on retainer to secure their services. These contracts do not bind the client to keep the lawyer if the client becomes dissatisfied, but they do require the client to provide reasonable compensation to the lawyer for services rendered.

8. Legal research in tort cases usually starts with a preliminary review of the areas of law that are relevant to the known facts in the case. Each type of tort has specific elements that must be proved. The specific elements of negligence and products liability law were examined in this chapter as the attorney in the example chose an appropriate legal basis for the action.

9. Given the facts developed in this illustrative case there is a choice of court option that includes filing this case in state court or in federal district court in the same state. This option results from the diversity of citizenship of the two parties.

10. The Erie doctrine requires the federal courts in diversity cases to use the substantive law of the state in which the case is filed along with federal procedure. No two parties on opposing sides can be citizens of the same state, and the sum in question must be greater than $75,000.

11. Complicated issues of jurisdiction, time limitations, status to sue, recoverable damages, and choice of courts must be considered before the decision to file a formal action is made.

REVIEW EXERCISES

Match the following terms with their most appropriate meaning.

TERMS	MEANING
1. Estate	____ failure to exercise due care
2. Probate	____ prescribed time limitations within which actions may be brought
3. Cause of action	
4. Tort law	____ lack of ordinary care on part of plaintiff that negates recovery of damages in many states
5. Affidavit	
6. Contingency fee contract	____ plaintiff must have a legally protected and tangible interest in the litigation
7. Diversity jurisdiction	____ negligence of both plaintiff and defendant measured in terms of percentages of fault
8. Erie doctrine	____ agreement to pay attorney contingent upon recovery in damage suit
9. Negligence	
10. Products liability	____ adjustment to account for investment earnings of a specific sum of money over time
11. Contributory negligence	____ provided standing to sue on behalf of the estate of a deceased person
12. Comparative negligence	____ strict liability of manufacturer or seller of products for injury caused by defective product
13. Voluntary assumption of a known risk	____ when plaintiff knowingly accepted the risk of injury
14. Statute of limitations	____ federal practice in diversity cases of applying substantive law of the state where case is filed
15. Standing to sue	____ the extent of interest a person has in both real and personal property
16. Wrongful death and survival statutes	____ the fact or facts that give a person a right to judicial relief
17. Present value	____ civil law involving personal injury
	____ federal jurisdiction when parties are citizens of different states and sum is above specified amount
	____ written statement of facts made under oath
	____ court procedure by which a will is proved

DISCUSSION QUESTIONS _____

1. How would one go about finding a lawyer if one needed legal assistance?
2. What is meant by a legal cause of action, and why is it important to consult a lawyer as soon as possible after a legal question arises?
3. What are the major types of civil legal actions?
4. What are the general elements of tort and contract law?
5. How does products liability law differ from negligence law?
6. What are the basic affirmative defenses in negligence and products liability actions?
7. What choices of courts did Jane Consumer have in her case against the auto manufacturer?
8. Why was the federal district court chosen?

ASSIGNMENT _____

ASSIGNMENT: Students should follow the attorney's legal research and look up the terms discussed in this chapter. These terms will be found in your state's annotated code (e.g., *Tennessee Code Annotated*) and the *U.S. Code Annotated*. You should also find the *Restatement of Torts (Second)* in your library or on the Internet.

SOURCES AND SUGGESTED READING _____

Ball, Howard. 1987. *Courts and Politics: The Federal Judicial System*. 2d ed. Englewood Cliffs, N.J.: Prentice-Hall.

Blanchard, Roderick D. 1990. *Litigation and Trial Practice for the Legal Assistant*. 3d ed. St. Paul: West Publishing.

Bumiller, Kristin. 1980-1981. "Choices of forum in diversity cases: Analysis of a survey and implications for reform." *Law and Society* 15:749-774.

Neubauer, David W. 1991. *Judicial Process*. Pacific Grove, Calif.: Brooks/Cole Publishing.

Restatement (Second) of Law: Torts. 1965. Vol. 2, 281-503. Washington, D.C.: American Law Institute.

Restatement (Third) of Law: Torts. 1998 Washington, D.C: American Law Institute.

Schuk, Peter H., ed. 1991. *Tort Law and the Public Interest: Competition, Innovation, and Consumer Welfare*. New York: W.W. Norton. (See especially *The Evolution of Products Liability as a Federal Policy Issue*, by Linda Lipsen.)

Tennessee Code Annotated (T.C.A.). (Each state has a similar code of statutory law arranged by topic for specific reference. These codes contain a wealth of information, including case law citations, scholarly publications, cross-references, and tables to find life expectancy and compound accumulation for damage estimates.)

Uniform Commercial Code (U.C.C.). (This uniform legislation has been enacted by most states and attempts to codify the general principles of common law to facilitate commercial transactions.)

United States Code (U.S.C.). (This series of volumes contains all federal law arranged by topic, like the state codes, for handy reference.)

Weaver, Jefferson Hane. 1990. *The Compact Guide to Tort Law: A Civilized Approach to the Law*. St. Paul: West Publishing.

_____. 1990. *The Compact Guide to Contract Law: A Civilized Approach to the Law*. St. Paul: West Publishing.

Pretrial Process in Civil Cases

This chapter discusses the pleading and discovery process used in modern civil procedure to prepare the evidence for settlement or trial. During this process, parties have access to the power of the court to compel the production of evidence relevant to the legal action. Attorney John Gaither intended to file his case in federal district court and, therefore, was required to use the **Federal Rules of Civil Procedure (FRCP)**, a detailed set of rules that define the steps of legal procedure in federal courts. The rules are somewhat complex because of the wide variety of circumstances that can arise, but they also are flexible. Great effort has been made to simplify the rules and remove the technicalities that once characterized Anglo-American common-law practice.

Federal Rules of Civil Procedure (FRCP): Detailed rules of federal civil procedure that must be followed in federal court litigation. Most states have similar statutory rules.

ASSIGNMENT: Use the Internet to find the Federal Rules of Civil Procedure. Just type in "Federal Rules of Civil Procedure" and select a source that will provide the latest rules without cost. A good source is federalrulesofcivilprocedure.net. Read the current description of the rules mentioned in this chapter and check out any areas of interest as we proceed through this text.

When we left Attorney Gaither in the last chapter, he had just sent a letter informing the Factory Motor Company of Jane Consumer's intent to file a lawsuit for damages in the amount of $597,200 for the injuries caused by the defective coil, which he asserted was the proximate (legal) cause of the accident.

DEFENSE CONSIDERATIONS

When the letter arrived at Factory Motor Company, it was sent to the firm's general counsel, Herman Hardnose. Mr. Hardnose called in his staff attorney, Maria Farmer, who had eight years of experience dealing with defective products suits against the firm. Mr. Hardnose explained that this situation needed to be looked into and dealt with effectively: The particular defect involved in the recall was not considered dangerous, and the company had not received any previous reports of accidents resulting from the problem. He wanted her to work closely with City Auto Company and their legal counsel on the matter. He indicated that she should not settle out of court unless there was no possibility of winning the suit.

Maria Farmer understood her instructions and proceeded to check out the information in Attorney Gaither's letter. Factory Motor Company contended that the coil in question was not dangerously defective and that it would have held up under normal use. There was a problem with a particular run on the assembly line that affected 250 vehicles: a mix-up had resulted in the installation of the wrong coil on the left side of these vehicles, and the mistake was not detected until after the automobiles were sold. The factory engineers tested the equipment and determined that the unmatched coils did not present a safety hazard. Factory simulation indicated that the equipment would take normal wear and tear for at least 100,000 miles. The firm issued a recall order only because the coils in question affected the appearance of the car, not the safety of the vehicle. Maria Farmer, therefore, concluded that Factory Motor Company would not attempt to settle out of court.

When Gaither received this reply, he again let Factory Motor Company know that his client was resolute in filing a formal legal claim. Farmer confirmed that she would not consider settling before the conclusion of the discovery process.

Attorney Gaither informed his client that the defendant had refused to settle out of court. He asked whether she wished to proceed to file suit and indicated that she would risk only court costs and expenses if he were unsuccessful in winning an award. Jane Consumer agreed that he should file suit. Gaither then asked his paralegal, Chris Martin, to prepare a formal complaint. The various aspects of filing a complaint and discovery are discussed below.

THE PLEADINGS

The English common-law tradition initially provided the stiff, technical set of rules of pleading, often referred to as **fact pleading**. The common-law courts placed great emphasis on pleadings, which proceeded through a set of rigid stages and could continue almost indefinitely. The object was to reach a single issue of law or fact that would dispose of the case. The common-law emphasis on developing the facts of the case through pleadings represented a perilous course for lawyers and litigants alike (Neubauer

Fact pleading: Common-law emphasis on detail in pleadings that was rigid and cumbersome.

1991, 279). This practice was transferred to the United States during the colonial period, at which time it took on a more relaxed, but still cumbersome, character.

The English common law was ill-suited to the frontier conditions of the New World. Reformers who opposed the cumbersome methods of common-law pleadings were first successful in New York in 1848, when statutory enactment of a complete code of civil procedure took place under the leadership of New York lawyer David Dudley Field. This reform movement spread to other states and has even influenced modern practices in England. However, the process of reform has been gradual, and many states have retained the old common-law rules of pleading with certain modifications. The rules of pleading that resulted from this first wave of reform were called *code pleadings* because the statutory enactment of a set of written rules was an innovation.

Modern federal civil procedure began in 1938 with the adoption of the Federal Rules of Procedure in statutory form, abolishing fact pleading in favor of **notice pleading**. Notice pleading emphasizes the need for notification to the opposing party, and the court does not require verification of the allegations during the pleading stage of civil procedure. The rules initially adopted by statute in 1938 have not remained static, and the effort to remove technical barriers to the efficient development of evidence in preparation for a lawsuit has continued through a series of revisions.

Notice pleading: Simplified rules of modern pleading that emphasize notification and response and leave the narrowing of facts to discovery.

The Judicial Conference of the United States and its extensive committee system composed of judges at all levels (as well as practicing attorneys) proposed and secured adoption of numerous changes designed to improve the efficiency of the process of handling legal actions in the federal courts. The Judicial Conference is presided over by the Chief Justice of the U.S. Supreme Court. When committee recommendations are passed by a majority of the members of the Judicial Conference, they are then submitted to the Supreme Court. After passage by a majority on the Supreme Court, they are transmitted to Congress, where they automatically become law in 90 days unless Congress acts adversely.

The states also have altered their cumbersome procedures and have tended to follow the federal leadership. About 35 states have adopted the basic federal rules for local use, and the others have revised their rules to reflect at least partially the federal innovations (Neubauer 1991, 280).

Modern notice pleading is much more flexible and able to accommodate reasonable changes that do not inject a bias against one party or the other as the legal process develops. A **complaint** and **answer** are the basic pleadings. Under the common law, each type of case had a separate form for pleading. Modern pleadings do not attempt to prove facts but merely provide a short, plain statement of the basic elements of the complaint or answer.

Complaint: Initial pleading by which a legal action is commenced.

Answer: Formal written statement setting forth the grounds of defense.

The Complaint

Rule 8 (FRCP) defines the general rules of pleading to include a short and plain statement of the grounds on which the court's jurisdiction depends, a claim showing that the pleader is entitled to relief, and a demand for judgment for the relief the pleader seeks.

Rule 10 (FRCP) outlines the form of pleadings. Every pleading must contain a caption setting forth the name of the court, title of the action, and file number (added by the clerk). The complaint must include the names of all parties, but other pleadings may name the first party on each side with appropriate indication of other parties. The basic elements must be asserted in separate numbered paragraphs, each limited, as far as practical, to a single set of circumstances.

The complaint must be signed by the lawyer preparing it or by the party entering the plea. This requirement carries penalties for violation. A responsible agent must file the complaint, and the signature certifies that the person who has signed the pleading has read it and believes there are grounds to support the allegations in the pleading. If the pleading has been filed for purposes of an ulterior or malicious motive, the court may award the opposing party retribution in the form of reasonable expenses and attorneys' fees caused by the action. Paralegals may prepare a pleading, but the signature certifies that it has been read by an attorney or by the party acting as his or her own attorney. The person who signs the pleading must assume responsibility for the legal action.

A complaint was prepared in the *Consumer* case by Chris Martin and presented to Attorney Gaither for his approval (see Form 11.1). Gaither had Jane Consumer come into the office to discuss the complaint. He asked her whether she had any questions about the complaint and whether she agreed with the statements in it. Jane Consumer agreed with all the factual information in the complaint and thought that it expressed the essential elements of the legal action. Gaither then asked her whether she agreed that a **jury trial** should be demanded.

Jane said she had not given it any thought. "What are the alternatives?" she asked.

"You have a choice, as the plaintiff in a civil suit of this nature, to demand a jury trial," replied the attorney. "If a jury trial is not demanded, the court will conduct what is known as a **bench trial**, without a jury. In a jury trial, the jury is the 'trier of fact' in the case and is called on to answer questions of fact in dispute. In a bench trial, the judge decides all questions of fact and law in the case."

Failure to demand a jury trial in the manner prescribed by Rule 38(b) (FRCP) results in a waiver of the right to a jury trial, and all issues of fact and law are tried by a judge without a jury. The plaintiff can demand a jury trial by a statement in a conspicuous place on the complaint that a jury trial

Jury trial:
Trial of issues of fact in dispute by an impartial and qualified jury.

Bench trial:
Trial conducted without a jury in which the judge decides issues of both fact and law in dispute.

Form 11.1 **COMPLAINT**

IN THE UNITED STATES DISTRICT COURT
FOR THE MIDDLE DISTRICT OF MIDDLE STATE

JANE CONSUMER	)	
Executrix of the	)	
ESTATE OF	)	
WILLIAM P. CONSUMER	)	
and JANE CONSUMER,	)	
individually	)	Civil Action
Plaintiffs	)	No. _____
	)	
v.	)	
	)	
FACTORY MOTOR COMPANY,	)	JURY DEMAND
a manufacturing corporation	)	
Defendant	)	

COMPLAINT

Comes now Jane Consumer, executrix of the estate of William P. Consumer, deceased, on behalf of William P. Consumer and Jane Consumer, individually, and states unto the court the following:

1. The plaintiff Jane Consumer resides at 140 Consumer Lane, Centerville, Middle State. Jane Consumer is also the executrix of the estate of William P. Consumer, deceased, who was killed on September 9, 2010, in the accident referred to herein.

2. The defendant, Factory Motor Company, 200 Factory Boulevard, Lake State, is a corporation having its principal place of business and organized under the laws of Lake State. Factory Motor Company is engaged in the manufacture of automobiles and does substantial business in Middle State.

3. On or about October 20, 2008, the plaintiffs purchased a 2009 model Supreme Brougham Executive (serial number: 1FMCB14T9KUA14073) from City Auto Company, Centerville, Middle State. This model was manufactured by the defendant, Factory Motor Company.

4. On or about September 9, 2010, around 10:30 P.M., the plaintiff and her decedent, William P. Consumer, were traveling south on Interstate 24 approximately three miles from Centerville, Middle State. Upon passing a van on this interstate

continued >

highway, the aforementioned automobile, manufactured by the defendant, would not respond to the steering wheel, and the plaintiff's decedent was unable to maintain control of the automobile. William P. Consumer was killed and the plaintiff Jane Consumer was seriously injured when the automobile collided with a tractor-trailer on the opposite side of the interstate highway.

5. At the time of the accident, the plaintiff's decedent was a user of the automobile in question and was using it in the manner and for the purpose expected and intended by the defendant.

6. At the time of the accident, the automobile existed without substantial change from the condition in which it was manufactured and sold. The automobile was less than two years old and had been driven only 22,000 miles. It was in a defective condition in that the left rear coil was defectively manufactured and unreasonably dangerous to users. Defendant knew or should have expected that the automobile would reach users without substantial change in the condition in which it was manufactured and sold.

7. Death of plaintiff's decedent and resulting injury to the plaintiff Jane Consumer, a passenger in the vehicle, were caused by the conduct of the defendant in defectively manufacturing such automobile and selling it in a defective or unreasonably dangerous condition to intended users as well as to persons reasonably expected to be within the orbit of such use. Defendant is strictly liable for the death and injuries set forth herein.

8. By reason of the aforesaid wrongful acts of the defendant that directly and proximately caused the death of William P. Consumer, and for bodily and mental injury to his spouse, plaintiff-executrix claims damages of the defendant on behalf of the wife and children of the deceased as follows;

   a) To the estate for loss of established earnings and earning power of the deceased for a period of time beginning September 10, 2010, and continuing to the termination of his natural life, which earnings and earning power would have continued but for his death on September 9, 2010; and for medical and funeral expenses under the Abatement and Survival Act (T.C.A. 20-5-106) in the amount of $507,200.

   b) To plaintiff for loss due to bodily and mental injuries sustained in the accident in the amount of $90,000.

For further relief the plaintiff forever prays.

A JURY TRIAL IS DEMANDED

JOHN GAITHER

By: _____
    Attorney for Plaintiffs
    57 Courthouse Square
    Centerville, Middle State

is demanded. If the plaintiff waives this right, the defendant has an opportunity to demand a jury trial in the answer. The Seventh Amendment to the U.S. Constitution grants a fundamental right to a jury trial in federal civil cases "at common law" as opposed to equity. Some states restrict the use of jury trials in civil actions, in which case this federal amendment applies only to the federal courts.

Jane thought a jury was essential to what she considered a fair trial. "I would stand a better chance of winning with a jury, wouldn't I?" she asked.

"Yes I think you would," Gaither agreed, "although jurors can become confused about their instructions from the judge regarding the legal standards they must apply, particularly in strict liability cases. But jurors are likely to be more sympathetic with your situation and less sympathetic with that of the manufacturer."

Court Filing and Service of Process

Attorney Gaither took two copies of the complaint to the office of the clerk of the court for the U.S. District Court in Capital City. One copy was for the court and the other for service of process on the defendant. The court was located in the Federal Building only about 30 miles from Gaither's office, so the forum would be as convenient for witnesses as the state court located in Centerville.

The clerk received the complaint and summons prepared for the defendant to be notified of the court suit. She received payment of the filing fee and then assigned a number (10-547) to the case and entered it on the court's docket. The first two numbers of the case number indicate the year, and the remaining numbers the order of filing during the year. The **docket** is the formal record of the court's activities; all action taken in each case must be recorded.

Docket:
List of important acts done in court in the process of each case; sometimes used to refer to the calendar of cases set to be tried in a specific term.

The clerk then signed the summons prepared by the plaintiff's attorney and applied the court's seal to the document.

Federal courts usually have several judges and use a rotation system of assigning cases. In state court, the lawyer filing the case may have some choice concerning the particular judge who will handle the case. In federal court, the clerk assigns a judge to the case at the time of filing. This system evens the caseload among the judges and prevents "judge shopping." Judge Stern was assigned to the *Consumer* case.

Judge Stern would follow all aspects of the case through trial in accordance with the local procedure of that district court. Other district courts use a master calendar system by which different aspects of the same case are handled by different judges assigned to specific functions. The clerk's office is responsible for the record-keeping function. The case number and the judge's name were stamped on the *Consumer* case's file jacket, and notice of assignment was sent to Judge Stern. All actions and documents would be kept in the office of the clerk until needed by the judge.

The clerk then signed the **summons** prepared by the plaintiff to be served on the defendant, Factory Motor Company (see Form 11.2). **Service of process** refers to the important task of notifying the defendant that a lawsuit has been filed against the individual or corporation. The consequences of failure to respond to a summons are severe; therefore, assurance that proper notification has been received is important. The defendant must answer the complaint within a specified period of time after service is perfected (usually 20 days) or risk judgment by default.

Had Attorney Gaither filed his suit in state court, the process would have been more complicated. Most states have long-arm statutes that enable courts of one state to exercise jurisdiction over nonresidents whose actions produce a wrong within that state. Various forms of substitute service of process may be used that involve processing the complaint through secretaries of state for the states involved. Local sheriff's offices usually serve a state's processes—a method that is less flexible than the new methods provided by federal district courts in Rule 4 (FRCP).

The 1980 amendment to Rule 4 (FRCP) authorizes service of process to be made by any person who is not a party to the lawsuit and is at least 18 years of age. The current provision of Rule 4(a) instructs the clerk to issue a summons and deliver it and a copy of the complaint to the plaintiff or the plaintiff's attorney who shall be responsible for proper service of the summons.

Filing the complaint commences a civil lawsuit; however, the time limitation in the summons (20 days) does not begin to run until the day after service of process. If the action is not perfected by service within 120 days after filing the complaint, the action is subject to dismissal.

The default provision in the summons (20 days) is subject to the defendant's motion for reasonable delay, but if the defendant does not respond within the 20-day period and has been verifiably served, the default may be executed, and the court will award reasonable uncontested damages to the plaintiff.

The summons and complaint may be served on an adult defendant by mailing copies to the defendant or legal representative along with two copies of a notice and acknowledgment of service. The acknowledgement is to be returned if the defendant accepts service, and it is customary for the plaintiff to provide a self-addressed envelope with postage prepaid. If the defendant fails to acknowledge receipt of the summons and complaint, service is not perfected; the plaintiff then has to use the services of a U.S. marshal or process server to consummate service. The cost of the service of process may be charged to the defendant if the defendant loses the case.

Summons:
Instrument used as a means of acquiring jurisdiction over a party and to commence a civil action.

Service of process:
Reasonable notice to the defendant of legal proceedings to afford the defendant an opportunity to appear and be heard.

Form 11.2 **SUMMONS**

IN THE UNITED STATES DISTRICT COURT FOR THE
MIDDLE DISTRICT OF MIDDLE STATE

JANE CONSUMER,	)	
Executrix of the ESTATE OF	)	
WILLIAM P. CONSUMER	)	
and JANE CONSUMER,	)	
individually,	)	Civil Action
Plaintiffs	)	No. 10-547
v.	)	
	)	
	)	
FACTORY MOTOR COMPANY,	)	SUMMONS
A manufacturing corporation	)	
Defendant	)	

To the above-named defendant:

You are hereby summoned and required to serve upon John Gaither, plaintiff's attorney, whose address is 57 Courthouse Square, Centerville, Middle State, an answer to the complaint that is herewith served upon you, within 20 days after service of this summons upon you, exclusive of the day of service. If you fail to do so, judgment by default will be taken against you for the relief demanded in the complaint.

SEAL OF THE COURT

_____
Clerk of the court

Dated: _____
Note: This summons is issued pursuant
To Rule 4 of the Federal Rules of Civil Procedure.

Rule 4 of the Federal Rules of Civil Procedure

Serving Notice

1. According to Rule 4, a summons is a document that informs a defendant in a civil law suit that he or she must appear in court. The summons must include the complaint.

2. The summons must also inform the defendant that failure to answer the summons and complaint will result in the court ordering a judgment in favor of the plaintiff. It must have been filed with the court and, therefore, must be signed by the court clerk and have the court's seal on the document.

3. Anyone over the age of 18 can serve the summons and complaint on the defendant. Once the process server has delivered the summons and complaint to a defendant, he or she completes an affidavit of service, which provides proof to the court that the defendant was properly served with Notice under Rule 4.

4. There are three options to serve notice on a defendant. A) Rule 4 requires personal service, meaning that the defendant must be given a copy of the summons and complaint. B) Should the defendant not be available to receive personal service, the law allows the person serving notice to leave a copy of the summons and complaint at the defendant's residence, with a person above the age of consent who resides there. That person, other than the defendant, can accept service and is most often a spouse or one of the defendant's children who is over the age of 18. C) Under Rule 4 a copy of the summons and complaint can be served on an agent of the defendant, who was previously authorized to accept service. This usually happens when a defendant is already aware of a pending lawsuit and has an attorney who will accept service of the summons and complaint.

5. Under Rule 4(m), once a summons and complaint has been filed with the court, the plaintiff then has 120 days to serve the defendant with notice. If that time has expired, the court may either dismiss the lawsuit against the defendant or order that the plaintiff provide service within a time period specified by the court.

Defendant's Response

In the *Consumer* case, service of the summons and complaint was made by regular mail: They were delivered to Factory Motor Company's general legal council, Herman Hardnose. Mr. Hardnose called Maria Farmer into his office to discuss the complaint and again indicated that she should prepare to go to trial with the case.

Farmer told Hardnose that she would need local assistance in Middle State. She had been in contact with Bill Green of the Capital City law firm of Green, Wagnor, and Johns. He represented City Auto Company, which sold and serviced the vehicle in question, and he was familiar with local court rules. His office would be needed during the discovery process and trial. Mr. Hardnose approved, stating, "You will have whatever resources you need to prepare our defense in this case."

Farmer then contacted Bill Green in Capital City and asked whether he would assist in Factory Motor Company's defense of the lawsuit filed in federal district court in Capital City. Bill was concerned about the interests of his client, City Auto Company, and he wanted assurance that he would not be placing himself in a **conflict of interest** situation. He asked Farmer, "Is there any chance that my client will be drawn in as a party to the suit that has been filed?"

Conflict of interest: Ethical conflict involving violation of trust in matters of private interest and gain. A lawyer may not serve two clients with opposing interests.

Farmer assured Bill that the complaint named Factory Motor Company as the sole defendant. Bill again emphasized, "I can accept your offer only under the condition that my first obligation is to defend my existing client as required by professional ethics."

Farmer understood this professional obligation and agreed that Bill should withdraw from the case if a conflict of interest became evident. She asked him to begin immediately gathering preliminary information from local sources that would be needed in the case. Farmer said she would work on gathering information relevant to the case from sources in Lake State. The complaint and summons would be faxed to Bill's firm so he could get started right a way. Farmer indicated that they would stay in touch by telephone and Internet to coordinate their activities.

Farmer then called the research department of Factory Motor Company and set up a meeting with the chief engineer in charge of testing, Mr. Superior Tester. She had a written report on the assembly line mix-up concerning the original coils on the cars manufactured in 2008, and the serial number in the complaint matched the range of serial numbers involved in the incident. The report indicated that the coils mounted on the left side of these vehicles were tested to see whether they would hold up. Mr. Tester brought his lab report on the testing of the coils in question to their meeting.

"Did the coils that were installed on the left side of these vehicles violate any of the governmental standards prescribed by the Department of Transportation's safety specifications?" asked Farmer.

"No," replied Mr. Tester. "There are no particular safety standards for these coils. They are installed primarily for comfort to guarantee a smooth ride for the passengers."

"What were the results of your testing in the lab on these coils?" Farmer queried.

Mr. Tester explained, "We put three of these coils on a simulation machine and let them run under stress until they broke. They all broke after 1,700 hours on the machine. The first one broke at 1,726 hours, and the other two at 1,824 and 1,891 hours. The 1,700 hours of testing simulated 154,000 miles of normal wear. We therefore concluded that the coils would be safe for the normal life of the vehicle."

Farmer kept copies of the report for her files. She explained that a lawsuit had been filed concerning these coils and that an allegation had been made that one of the coils caused an accident. "Do you think this is possible, Mr. Tester?"

Mr. Tester said he could not say for certain, but he doubted that even a broken coil could affect the safety of the vehicle. "It would most likely cause some noise, and perhaps discomfort," he noted. "It might tip the vehicle to the left, but it would not cause it to go out of control."

"We may have to prove that in court," Farmer responded.

After the meeting with Mr. Tester, Farmer called an independent expert, Professor Drivesafe from Lake State University. She explained the complaint and the factory testing done on the coils to the professor and asked whether driving conditions could be a potential cause of the accident. He had no details concerning the accident, but he agreed to look into the matter once the case was far enough along that detailed information about the accident would be available. He had served as consultant concerning the cause of accidents in many cases and would be willing to so serve in this case.

Farmer examined 50 complaints that had been forwarded to the factory from owners of the 250 vehicles involved in the production mix-up. All the owners had complained of the vehicles leaning to the left. The decision to recall these automobiles was made on the basis that the problem was a cosmetic one that should be eliminated. The records indicated that 200 of these cars had received coil replacements since the recall notice was mailed and that no other accidents had been reported.

The Answer

The defendant may appear in the case by serving a motion to challenge jurisdiction, a motion for an order to strike the complaint, a motion for a judgment on the pleadings, or a motion for an order to compel a more definite statement of the allegations in the complaint (Rule 12[a]; FRCP). The defendant does not need to serve an answer while a Rule 12 motion is pending because such a motion suspends the 20-day time period for the answer. After the court rules on the motion, an answer is due within 10 days of the ruling, unless the court dismisses the complaint or sets a different time limit within which to answer (Rule 12[a], FRCP).

Maria Farmer concluded that no reasonable grounds for Rule 12 motions existed at the time, although a motion to rule on the pleadings can be made at any time after the answer is filed and before the trial (but may not be used to delay the trial).

The defendant's answer must admit the truth of those allegations in the complaint that are known to be true. Formal admissions in the answer remove these allegations from controversy, and the plaintiff does not have to prove these admitted facts. Since the jury ultimately will be informed about the admissions, it is advantageous to the plaintiff to frame the complaint in such a way as to encourage the defendant to admit as many facts as possible.

The defendant's answer must specifically deny those allegations in the complaint that are not true. Any allegation in the complaint that is not denied is presumed to be admitted (Rule 8[d], FRCP). If the defendant does not have sufficient knowledge on which to form a belief concerning an allegation, a statement to that effect is interpreted as a denial.

The defendant's answer uses numbered paragraphs, as does the complaint, to separate each set of circumstances and each admission or denial. The answer must allege all of the defendant's affirmative defenses (Rule 8[c], FRCP) because any affirmative defense not asserted in the answer is waived. An **affirmative defense** is a fact or set of circumstances that defeats the plaintiff's claim even though the plaintiff is able to prove a cause of action. Defendants who raise affirmative defenses have the burden of proof to establish such defenses.

Affirmative defense:
In pleading it raises new matter that constitutes a defense. It must be raised in the answer in response to the pleading (Rule 8(c), FRCP).

Maria Farmer mailed the answer to the complaint in the *Consumer* case to the court, and she sent copies of the answer to the plaintiff's attorney, John Gaither (see Form 11.3).

DISCOVERY

The stage in the legal process during which each party has access to the court's power to compel testimony and factual materials relevant to the case is known as **discovery**. This period can be quite lengthy and generally exists from the time the complaint is filed until the time of trial. Power to compel information may be granted even before the complaint is filed if warranted by the circumstances.

Discovery:
The legal process in which each party to a lawsuit has access to the court's power to compel testimony and factual materials relevant to the case (FRCP Rules 26-37).

In civil cases, the discovery process is broad and allows each party to gain access to information relevant to the legal action. The concept of "relevancy" is interpreted broadly by the courts, and even material that might not be admitted as evidence at trial can be within the definition of relevant information. The parties generally have access to any information if it is even remotely relevant to the subject matter of the action or if there is a possibility that the information will lead to other evidence that will be admissible at trial.

Nonetheless, there is some information that is privileged and immune from the court's power to compel testimony. The most important privilege is the individual's protection from being compelled to testify against

Form 11.3 **ANSWER FROM FACTORY MOTOR COMPANY**

IN THE UNITED STATES DISTRICT COURT FOR THE
MIDDLE DISTRICT OF MIDDLE STATE

JANE CONSUMER	)	
Executrix of the ESTATE OF	)	
WILLIAM P. CONSUMER	)	
And JANE CONSUMER,	)	
individually	)	Civil Action
Plaintiffs	)	No. 10-547
v.	)	
	)	
FACTORY MOTOR COMPANY	)	ANSWER
A manufacturing corporation	)	
Defendant	)	
	)	

Now comes the defendant FACTORY MOTOR COMPANY, USA, A CORPORATION, and by its attorneys file the following answer to the plaintiff's complaint:

1. The Factory Motor Company admits the averments in paragraph 1 of the Complaint.
2. The Defendant admits the averments in paragraph 2 of the Complaint.
3. Admitted in part, denied in part. Defendant admits that it manufactured a 2009 Supreme Brougham Executive (serial number IFMCB14T9KUA14073). However, defendant is without sufficient knowledge to form a belief as to the remaining allegations in paragraph 3.
4. Denied. Defendant is without sufficient knowledge to form a belief as to the allegations in paragraph 4.
5. Denied. Defendant is without sufficient knowledge to form a belief as to the allegations in paragraph 5.
6. Denied. Defendant denies the allegation that the automobile was in a defective condition at the time of sale and that the left rear coil was unreasonably dangerous to users. Defendant is without sufficient knowledge to form a belief as to the remaining allegations in paragraph 6.
7. Denied. Defendant denies the allegations in paragraph 7 of plaintiff's complaint that injury to plaintiff's decedent and injury to plaintiff Jane Consumer was caused by the conduct of the defendant.

continued >

8. Denied. Defendant, after reasonable investigation, lacks sufficient knowledge to form a belief regarding the truth of Plaintiff's injuries, and therefore denies same.

Each and every other allegation of the Complaint not heretofore admitted, explained or denied specifically is now denied generally.

AFFIRMATIVE DEFENSE

The Defendant avers that if William P. Consumer's death was caused by defendant's acts as alleged in Plaintiff's Complaint, William P. Consumer voluntarily assumed the risk.

Respectfully submitted,
Factory Motor Company

_____

MARIA FARMER
Attorney for Defendant

himself or herself in a criminal matter. In civil cases, this privilege may operate when there is a potential for criminal action. Protective orders may be obtained from the judge that limit or bar discovery of material in privileged areas. Other privileges include the lawyer-client privilege, protection of the attorney's work product, and protection from unreasonable use of the discovery process as a means of harassment.

PRIVILEGES AND WORK PRODUCT IMMUNITY IN FEDERAL COURT

Rule 501 (FRCP)
Except as otherwise required by the Constitution of the United States or provided by Act of Congress or in rules prescribed by the Supreme Court pursuant to statutory authority, the privilege of a witness, person, government, State, or political subdivision thereof shall be governed by the principles of the common law as they may be interpreted by the courts of the United States in the light of reason and experience. However, in civil actions and proceedings, with respect to an element of a claim or defense as to which State law supplies the rule of decision, the privilege of a witness, person, government, State or political subdivision thereof shall be determined in accordance with State law.

The discovery rules are enforced by the judge who can hold an unresponsive party in contempt of court. In extreme cases, the contempt may involve incarceration. The purpose of discovery is to prevent surprises at trial, to encourage settlement, and to facilitate a just result. Competent attorneys use the discovery process to reveal all the knowable facts in the case and do not conclude the process until that objective has been reached.

The rules of discovery, found in Rules 26-37 (FRCP), are extensive. There may also be local rules that must be followed. The instruments of discovery include interrogatories, depositions, and requests to produce documents or material evidence. Other forms include requests for admissions (specific questions requiring answers) and requests for mental or physical examinations. The date by which discovery must be concluded is usually established in federal court by agreement, and a formal discovery schedule must be filed with the court fairly early in the process.

Interrogatories

The plaintiff's attorney and the two attorneys for the defendant in the *Consumer* case wanted more specific information in order to be prepared for trial. They knew that much of the information was already known to the opposing attorneys. Bill Green and Maria Farmer communicated frequently about what information they would need. Bill understood that his law firm would be called on to provide much of the legal work because of their location in Middle State and that it would be unproductive to have both lawyers for the defense duplicating their efforts.

Bill Green's paralegal, Jan Professional, received a briefing on the *Consumer* case. Bill gave her access to his file on the case and outlined her responsibilities. He told her that she could get a copy of the accident report from the highway safety department down the street from the law office. This document would give them valuable information and identify the patrol officer who filed the accident report. "In addition, we will need to construct interrogatories to John Gaither to find out what witnesses he has identified," Green instructed.

Jan had prepared many interrogatories in similar cases and knew that they represented an inexpensive method by which to gain preliminary information about potential witnesses. **Interrogatories** are sent by mail and contain written questions that must be answered under oath by the party served. They may be sent only to the parties to the lawsuit. Local rules often stipulate that the court clerk receive copies as well as all parties concerned. Jan was familiar with these rules.

Interrogatories: Written questions about the case submitted by one party to the other party.

While Bill Green and Jan Professional were discussing the case and preparing their interrogatories (see Form 11.4) in Capital City, John Gaither and Chris Martin were engaged in similar discussions concerning the information they needed to prepare for trial. Martin also was instructed to

Form 11.4 **INTERROGATORIES**

IN THE UNITED STATES DISTRICT COURT
FOR THE MIDDLE DISTRICT OF MIDDLE STATE

JANE CONSUMER,   )
Plaintiff   )   Civil Action
            v.   )   No. 10-547
)
FACTORY MOTOR COMPANY,   )
Defendant   )
)
)

Defendants respectfully submit to the plaintiffs for answer by them under oath as provided for by the Federal Rules of Civil Procedure the following interrogatories:

1. State decedent's date and place of birth.
2. Describe fully the extent of decedent's formal education, including the schools attended, degrees obtained, and dates of completion.
3. State the amount decedent reported as income in the United States federal tax returns for each of the years 2007, 2008, and 2009, respectively.
4. Describe decedent's employments during the five years preceding his death, including the name of each employer, period of time for each employment, his job title, and a description of the work he performed in each job.
5. As to each personal injury accident the decedent had, state:
   a. the date of the accident;
   b. the location of the accident;
   c. the type of accident;
   d. the nature and extent of the injuries sustained;
   e. the names and addresses of physicians who attended him;
   f. the names and addresses of hospitals at which he received treatment;
   g. the nature and extent of any consequential disability; and
   h. the name and address of all persons against whom claims were made due to the accident.
6. State the name, address, age, and relationship to decedent of each next of kin for whom claim is being made in this action.
7. Describe in detail the occurrence of the accident referred to in the complaint.
8. State the medical cause of decedent's death.

continued >

9. If decedent was ever convicted of a crime, identify the court where judgment was entered and the date of conviction and describe the nature of the offense for which he was convicted.
10. State the names and addresses of all witnesses who have any knowledge or information about the alleged accident.
11. Identify by names and addresses of all witnesses who have any knowledge or information about the alleged accident.
12. State the names and addresses of all persons from whom statements have been obtained and indicate the date on which each statement was made.
13. State the names and addresses of all other persons who have any knowledge or information about the accident referred to in the complaint, including expert witnesses.

(Note: Adequate space should be allowed where appropriate answers can be typed in spaces provided.)

June 1, 2011

_____
Attorney for Defendant

prepare interrogatories for service on the defendant. Gaither wanted to make sure the following items were included in these interrogatories:

1. The existence of any documents explaining the cause of the recall of automobiles relevant to the plaintiff's recall letter
2. The existence of any documents involving testing of the coils in question
3. The names and addresses of any expert witnesses that have been or are likely to be called in regard to this case

Once the interrogatories were answered, the lawyers on both sides of the *Consumer* case would be able to assess the need for more precise methods of discovery. The answers to the interrogatories would identify the witnesses to be called in the more expensive face-to-face questioning process known as a deposition.

Depositions

The **deposition** is a formal stage in the discovery process that can amount to a possible rehearsal of what will more than likely take place at trial.

Deposition:
Testimony of a witness taken outside of court, where both parties may question the witness and a transcript of the statement is made.

Potential witnesses are called to an appropriate location (usually within 40 miles of the place of service) to answer questions under oath. A court reporter records every question and answer, and a transcript of the entire session is prepared.

The deponents are allowed to read the transcript before signing it and attesting that it is a true and accurate copy of the facts known to the deponent. There is no judge present at these sessions, but the answers given are important. Depositions can be introduced at the trial and used for such purposes as contradicting testimony, known as impeaching the witness.

Notice to all parties is required prior to deposition and is served upon the parties' attorneys as well as the parties themselves. The direct parties to the lawsuit do not require subpoenas but must be notified. Potential witnesses that are not parties must be served in person by **subpoena** requested through the court clerk's office. The subpoena commands the person to whom it is directed to appear and give testimony at the time and place specified, and a **subpoena duces tecum** commands that the person bring along relevant documents or materials in his/her possession.

After several months of difficulties with scheduling and notifications, the potential witnesses were all questioned by the attorneys involved in the case. John Gaither had to travel to Lake State to participate in the deposition session held there. Maria Farmer and Bill Green also had to travel to meet in places that were convenient to the witnesses. Ambulance driver, Jackie Lifesaver, was identified and subpoenaed for a deposition session. Professor Drivesafe was sent to Middle State to investigate the site of the accident and the condition of the vehicle that was still located at the garage because Maria Farmer had requested an impoundment of the vehicle by the judge. The professor's deposition was taken in Lake State during the same week as that of Superior Tester. The transcripts resulting from these sessions were quite lengthy since they included direct and cross-examination of witnesses and follow-up questions by all attorneys.

Depositions were taken for some of the potential witnesses at trial, but some potential witnesses were not subjected to this process since they would not be principal witnesses. The defense deposed Jane Consumer, Jim Trucker (an eyewitness whose tractor-trailer was hit by the *Consumer* vehicle), George Goodcop (the patrol officer who responded to the scene of the accident), and Mack Racer (the expert mechanic who discovered the broken coil)—all of whom were considered principal witnesses for the plaintiff and would be likely to testify for the plaintiff's side at the trial. The plaintiffs deposed Dr. Jan Intern (the attending physician at the hospital), Superior Tester (Factory Motor Company laboratory technician), Jackie Lifesaver (the attending paramedic at the scene of the accident), and Professor Drivesafe (an engineer whose special field was accident research).

Subpoena:
A command by a judge to appear at a certain time and place to give testimony on a certain matter.

Subpoena duces tecum:
Adds to the personal subpoena a command that the person bring along relevant documents or materials in their possession.

The full transcripts from these deposition sessions were made available to all parties, and copies were placed in the court's record by the court clerk. For purposes of convenience, the transcripts were reduced to short summaries containing the essential facts revealed during these sessions. (See Appendix C for these summary statements.) The statements illustrate what was discovered through the deposition process. The lawyers would base their decisions during the next stages on what they learned, and the statements made at deposition helped define the issues of controversy in the case.

Production of Documents

Another discovery method used by both sides in the *Consumer* case was a **request to produce**. This request may be served on any party having relevant documents or material evidence and can be used to gain entry to the premises of the other party for purposes of inspection, photographing, sampling, copying, and other means of obtaining relevant evidence (see Form 11.5). The request is backed by the court's authority to order compliance and can be executed by law enforcement officers if necessary.

Request to produce: Discovery method used to secure relevant documents or material evidence.

This type of request was also used in the discovery process to enable Professor Drivesafe to conduct his investigation and to enable John Gaither to obtain information from the factory concerning their decision to recall the passenger car involved in the accident. Factory Motor Company allowed John to make copies of the relevant documents when he attended Superior Tester's deposition session in Big City, Lake State.

PRETRIAL CONFERENCES

The attorneys on both sides of the *Consumer* case gradually worked through their lists of leads to be followed and information to be obtained through discovery. John Gaither and Chris Martin sat down to review the information they had obtained. Cora Smith, the senior partner in the firm, was asked to review all the materials in the *Consumer* file, which had now grown to fill a small file cabinet. They were aware that their opponents had every fact that they obtained in the case and began to grow confident that there were no surprises to be uncovered.

John Gaither said, "What the case really boils down to is a contest between expert witnesses."

Chris Martin commented that the defense had two witnesses that they would attempt to qualify as experts. "Does this hurt our chances?" he asked.

Cora Smith cautioned, "It depends on the jury. We have material evidence on our side, but we'll have to make some convincing arguments at trial."

Form 11.5 **REQUEST TO PRODUCE**

IN THE UNITED STATES DISTRICT COURT FOR THE
MIDDLE DISTRICT OF MIDDLE STATE

JANE CONSUMER,	)	
Executrix of the	)	
ESTATE OF	)	
WILLIAM P. CONSUMER	)	
and JANE CONSUMER,	)	
individually	)	Civil Action
Plaintiff	)	No. 10-547
v.	)	
	)	
	)	
FACTORY MOTOR COMPANY	)	REQUEST TO PRODUCE
Defendant	)	
	)	

Plaintiff above named hereby requests pursuant to Rule 34 of the Federal Rules of Civil Procedure that defendant, Factory Motor Company, Inc., a corporation, produce and permit plaintiff to inspect and to copy each of the following documents:

    a. reports of tests conducted by defendant on the coils installed in the 2009 Supreme Brougham Executive sold to plaintiff, serial number 1FMCB14 T9KUA14073; and

    b. reports of causes for recall of such automobiles within the serial number range of plaintiff's vehicle.

It is requested that the aforesaid production be made on the day of July 10, 2011, when plaintiff's attorney will be present for a deposition session at the Law Department of the Factory Motor Company, Big City, Lake State.

By_____
    Attorney for Plaintiff
    57 Courthouse Square
    Centerville, Middle State

"Are we agreed then that we are ready to talk with the defense attorneys?" asked Gaither. Cora agreed but thought they should consult with the client first.

When they consulted with Jane Consumer about what they had discovered during the months of fact-finding in the case, Jane agreed that she could think of no further questions, but she was concerned about what would be discussed at the lawyers' conference.

Attorney Gaither explained that the attorneys for both sides would be involved in a complicated process of negotiations concerning the strength of their respective cases. This process is often crucial to successful settlement out of court.

"Cora and I will attempt to convince the Factory Motor Company lawyers that our case is so strong that they should settle," explained the attorney. Both sides would assess the probability of the trial outcome. If they agreed on all the issues of fact, the law would decide the outcome. The lawyers would assess the results of the discovery process and determine what facts remain in contention. This process narrows the issues that will be argued at trial and enables the parties to decide what witnesses to call and to plan the trial. Any issues of law in dispute also would be discussed to alert the opponent that these issues will be raised at trial.

Jane was puzzled. "This sounds like you will be trying to make a deal and I'm not involved," she commented.

Gaither indicated that if the defendant made an offer, Jane would be informed of it and could make the decision at that time. Both Gaither and Jane agreed that a settlement would be preferable to trial since the trial outcome was uncertain.

Gaither then drafted a letter to Maria Farmer asking if the defense was ready for a pretrial conference.

Maria Farmer then set up a telephone conference to include the firms General counsel, Herman Hardnose; Bill Green; Maria Farmer; and Jan Professional, Bill Green's paralegal. As they discussed the status of the case, Herman Hardnose asked, "Do we have all the knowable facts in this case?"

Farmer and Jan believed that they had all the knowable facts of the case. Bill answered that he did not know of any potential evidence that could be obtained or documents that needed to be produced. They all agreed that the files were complete and that there would be no surprises.

Herman Hardnose then asked, "Should we file a **motion to dismiss**?"

Maria Farmer concluded that the defense had no grounds for a motion to dismiss and found no reason to attempt to delay the inevitable. Herman Hardnose warned that they should be prepared to fight this case and he would not authorize a settlement out of court. Hence, she and Herman Hardnose agreed to reply to John Gaither that they were ready for a pretrial conference. They also agreed that a conference should be set up with John Gaither and that Maria Farmer and Bill Green would attend.

Motion to dismiss:
A motion that is generally filed before trial to attack the action on the basis of insufficiency of the pleading, of process, venue, etc. (Rule 12(b), FRCP).

Jan Professional asked about stipulations and whether there was agreement on what witnesses to call. Defense attorneys Farmer and Green agreed to work on the matter before the conference with the plaintiff's attorney.

Attorneys' Conference

After checking with his client, Bill Green set up the **attorneys' conference** with John Gaither. John indicated that he wanted his senior partner at the meeting, which would be held at the law firm of Smith and Gaither in Centerville in two weeks.

At the meeting, it quickly became evident that the defendant was not interested in an out-of-court settlement, and the business turned to the construction of a pretrial memorandum that must be submitted to the court by each side in preparation for the pretrial conference with the judge. The discussion followed the format that would be needed to prepare the memoranda: questions of jurisdiction, contentions of liability, discussion of damages, witnesses to be called by each side and identification of those who would serve as experts, review of pleadings to determine whether amendments were in order, matters to be stipulated, and estimated length of trial. Issues concerning exhibits were explored, with each side letting the other know about any exhibits they intended to bring to trial.

A **stipulation** is an agreement to admit the truth of those matters no longer at issue. The lists in Table 11.1 illustrate the matters that were stipulated and the matters that would be contested at trial before the jury in the *Consumer* case:

Attorneys' conference: Meeting of lawyers for both sides in a civil legal action to discuss the results of the discovery process and reach settlement or prepare for trial.

Stipulation: Agreement, admission, or confession made in a judicial proceeding by the parties or their attorneys.

Table 11.1 **MATTERS STIPULATED AND THOSE STILL AT ISSUE IN THE *CONSUMER* CASE**

MATTERS STIPULATED
1. Questions of jurisdiction
2. Defendant manufactured automobile in question
3. City Auto Company did not replace coil in question
4. Coil reached user in substantially unaltered condition
5. Left coil was not identical to right coil
6. No federal standards existed for suspension coils
7. Automobile was properly serviced and maintained

MATTERS STILL AT ISSUE
1. Whether coil was dangerously defective
2. Whether accident was caused by coil breaking
3. Whether accident was caused by wet road conditions
4. Whether driver was under influence of intoxicants
5. Whether coil was broken before or after the accident
6. Whether damages were fairly assessed

Judge's Conference

A final conference with Judge Stern was scheduled in three weeks. The attorneys would meet briefly with the judge to submit their drafted pretrial order that would include all the matters discussed at the attorneys' conference. Most judges are very active in their efforts to try to settle cases out of court because of the caseload, but Judge Stern was favorably impressed with the thorough preparation of the parties' attorneys and agreed that the lists of witnesses were not excessive. He did not attempt to convince them to settle out of court. He asked, "I suppose you have considered settlement of this case, haven't you?" Both parties indicated agreement. The judge then asked each party's attorney to prepare and submit to him a brief of the legal issues involved in the case, copies of which would have to be sent to the opposing parties as well before the trial date.

The judge can render a **summary judgment** at this stage if there is no dispute on relevant questions of fact and if the only questions in dispute are issues of law. Either party can file a motion for summary judgment. Since there were plenty of facts in dispute in this case, the issue was not raised.

The two parties in the *Consumer* case were notified in February that their trial date would be August 9, 2011. Although it was more than one year after the accident, Jane Consumer would finally get her "day in court." The next chapter illustrates and discusses the trial process.

Summary judgment: A dispositive motion filed by a party that argues the judge should dismiss the case before trial because there are no genuine issues of material fact and the moving party is entitled to prevail as a matter of law.

CHAPTER SUMMARY

1. This chapter illustrates the initiation of a civil legal action involving the filing of a complaint, service of process, and answer. Successful completion of this process subjects both parties to the court's jurisdiction. The discovery process enables both sides to gain access to the court's power to compel relevant evidence in preparation for trial.

2. The complaint serves to initiate legal action and to inform the court and defendants of the nature of the allegations and the basis in law for settlement. It need not present proof of these allegations, but it must include enough information to assert a claim that a legally protected interest of the plaintiff has been violated by the parties named as defendants.

3. The complaint and summons must be served on the defendants in a legally acceptable manner to allow them to answer the complaint within a reasonable period of time (usually 20 days). Failure to answer the complaint can result in an award to the plaintiff by default; therefore, proper service of these documents is important to a fair process.

4. An answer to the complaint by the defendant informs the plaintiff and the court whether facts will be contested and whether other forms of relief will be sought. A motion to dismiss for lack of jurisdiction indicates

a contention that the plaintiff failed to meet the court's jurisdictional requirements. Agreement to the allegations indicates no contest and allows the judge to rule on issues of law. An answer that poses questions of fact in dispute indicates the beginning of the discovery process.

5. The discovery process generally exists from the time the complaint is filed until trial. The discovery period allows both parties access to the court's power to compel evidence and witness testimony. This power covers all relevant information in civil actions and is applied broadly by the courts. The courts have power to issue compliance orders and to impose contempt penalties for noncompliance with these orders.

6. Interrogatories are mailed requests for specific information that can be served on the opposing parties to the complaint. The questions in the interrogatories must be answered under oath, but there is no opportunity for cross-examination. This method of discovery is used to obtain general information in an inexpensive manner.

7. Depositions, which are also part of the fact-gathering process, are more formal than interrogatories. Subpoenas may be issued through the court to compel the presence of potential witnesses. Both parties' attorneys must be notified and given ample opportunity to question potential witnesses under oath. A transcript of all relevant statements made is prepared by a court reporter, and the potential witnesses must verify the accuracy of the transcript. These transcripts may be used to impeach witnesses at trial and expose inconsistencies in their statements.

8. Requests to produce relevant documents or material evidence are another form of discovery. These requests are backed by the court's power to compel evidence, which includes the power to gain entrance to premises where such evidence may be located. Admissions and medical examinations (physical and mental) are additional forms of discovery backed by the court's authority.

9. The discovery process is supervised by the judge and usually ends once both parties have concluded that all available evidence and testimony concerning the facts of the case have been revealed. Discovery ensures that there will be no surprises at trial and therefore that the process is fair. If the parties are unable to come to agreement on termination of discovery, the judge may be asked to rule on the issue.

10. An attorneys' conference is usually required in order for the attorneys for both sides to discuss the findings of the discovery process and to explore the possibility of out-of-court settlement on the basis of these findings. When factual issues remain in contention, the attorneys must prepare pretrial memoranda describing the factual issues still in contention, the witnesses they will call, and the estimated length of trial time needed.

11. A pretrial conference with the judge has become common practice to facilitate more efficient use of the court's time. The judge becomes

more familiar with the case, and the parties are encouraged to refrain from calling an excessive number of witnesses. At this time, settlement out of court may be achieved by agreement of the parties, or a summary judgment is possible if the only questions in dispute are issues of law.

REVIEW EXERCISES

Match the following terms with their most appropriate meaning.

TERMS

1. Federal Rules of Civil Procedure (FRCP)
2. Fact pleading
3. Notice pleading
4. Complaint
5. Answer
6. Jury trial
7. Bench trial
8. Docket
9. Summons
10. Service of process
11. Conflict of interest
12. Affirmative defense
13. Discovery
14. Interrogatories
15. Deposition
16. Subpoena
17. Subpoena duces tecum
18. Request to produce
19. Motion to dismiss
20. Attorneys' conference
21. Stipulation
22. Summary judgment

MEANING

____ pretrial meeting of lawyers (both sides) to discuss results of discovery and possible settlement

____ discovery method used to secure relevant documents or material evidence

____ written questions about the case submitted by the parties to each other in preparation for trial

____ ethical conflict involving violation of trust in matters of private interest and gain

____ legal materials collected by the court in trial preparation or a list of court cases set for the court

____ trial of issues of fact in dispute by a group of lay citizens

____ initial pleading by which a legal action is commenced

____ common-law emphasis on detail pleading

____ agreement, admission, or confession made prior to trial by both sides as to facts in the case

____ a command to appear at a certain time and place to give testimony on a certain matter

____ pretrial period when court's authority exists to obtain information relevant to the case

____ instrument used as means of gaining jurisdiction over a party commencing a civil legal action

____ conducted without jury where judge decides questions of law and fact in dispute

____ formal written statement setting forth the grounds of defense in civil legal action

____ simplified rules of modern pleading

____ reasonable notice to the defendant of legal proceeding against that party

____ motion to rule on a challenge to the pleadings challenging court's jurisdiction

____ detailed rules of federal civil procedure that must be followed in federal cases

____ pretrial judgment that no genuine issues of fact are in dispute and awards decision as matter of law

____ testimony of witness outside of court where both parties may question a witness producing a witness statement

____ a command that the person bring along relevant documents or materials in his or her possession

____ motion that is generally filed before trial to attack the action on the basis of insufficiency of the pleading, of process, venue, etc. (Rule 12(b), FRCP).

DISCUSSION QUESTIONS

1. How is a civil legal action initiated?
2. Why are these pleadings necessary in order for the court to have jurisdiction over the parties involved in the lawsuit?
3. What is meant by a ruling on the pleadings?
4. What are the basic purposes of discovery?
5. How could the discovery process be abused by those filing frivolous or malicious complaints?
6. Is settlement more likely to occur before or after discovery? Why?
7. Are the lawyers' conferences with the judge necessary stages in the pretrial process?
8. If more than 90 percent of the cases filed are settled out of court, what types of cases proceed to trial?

ASSIGNMENT

ASSIGNMENT: Use the Internet to find the Federal Rules of Civil Procedure. Just type in "Federal Rules of Civil Procedure" and select a source that will provide the latest rules without cost. A good source is federalrulesofcivilprocedure.net. Read the current description of the rules mentioned in this chapter and check out any areas of interest in these rules.

SOURCES AND SUGGESTED READING

Blanchard, Rodrick D. 1990. *Litigation and Trial Practice for the Legal Assistant*. 3d ed. St. Paul: West Publishing.

Kane, Mary Kay. 1991. *Civil Procedure in a Nutshell*. 3d ed. St. Paul: West Publishing.

Neubauer, David W. 1991. *Judicial Process*. Pacific Grove Calif.: Brooks/Cole Publishing.

Federal Rules of Civil Procedure (FRCP) (*U.S. Code Annotated* and various other publications.)

United States Code. Washington, D.C.: U.S. Government Printing Office.

United States Code Annotated. St. Paul: West Publishing.

Federal Civil Judicial Procedure and Rules. St. Paul: West Publishing.

(State rules of civil procedure can be found in the state's annotated code or in paperbacks published by West Publishing Company that have the state's name and *Rules of Court*. These publications contain both federal rules of court and those of the particular state. It is important to check the most recent edition of these publications.)

Civil Trial: Argument and Adjudication

On the morning of August 9, 2011, the date set by Judge Stern for the *Consumer* trial to begin, Jane Consumer was very nervous. She did not know what to expect as she had never been involved in a trial. She met John Gaither and Cora Smith at their office, and together they drove to Capital City in Attorney Gaither's car.

The two lawyers reassured Jane on the trip to the federal building that they were well prepared to handle her case effectively. They explained that the jury selection process would allow all the participants at trial to become familiar with each other. This process would last through at least the first day of the trial and might last longer, depending on the complexity of the problems involved.

They arrived at the courthouse early and found their way to the assigned courtroom before anyone else had arrived. This gave the lawyers a chance to explain the physical dimensions of the courtroom.

The judge's bench, in the center of the room, occupied the immediate focus of attention in the courtroom. From this lofty perch, the judge would have a clear view of all participants and would symbolize authority over the court proceedings. The witness stand was to the judge's right beyond the witness box but within the clear view of the judge, which meant that the jury box was somewhat tilted toward the judge's bench and the witness box. The bailiff (or tipstaff), who maintains order in the courtroom, would be seated to the right of the judge, and the court reporter, who makes a complete transcript of the court's proceedings, would be seated in the same area. Modern courtroom arrangements feature a semicircular design to facilitate closeness, permitting the major participants to hear and see each other.

Most court buildings have multiple courtrooms and often the adjoining courtrooms are side-by-side. This arrangement requires an adjoining jury deliberation room and this may reverse the position of the jury box and other positions in the courtroom. So depending on which courtroom is assigned, the jury box may be located either to the left or to the right of the judge.

THE JURY SELECTION PROCESS

The jury selection process is known as **voir dire**, which is a term meaning "to speak the truth." This phrase denotes the preliminary examination of potential jurors during which their competence and objectivity to serve as jurors in a specific case may be questioned. The trial court clerk generally uses the voter registration lists in the judicial district to select a jury venire, or panel of potential jurors, large enough to serve the needs of the court. These potential jurors are notified for jury duty well in advance of the court date and are warned that failure to appear can result in contempt of court charges.

Usually there is some form of screening device used, such as a questionnaire, to eliminate those who are obviously incompetent, who may belong to certain occupational groups considered vital to the community, or whose government employment may present a conflict of interest. This practice excludes a large number of persons on a systematic basis. Physically or mentally handicapped persons, those who have been convicted of a felony, and law enforcement officers, teachers, nurses, and members of the clergy are frequently excused or not even considered in the pool of potential jurors. However, some states have laws on the books that specifically allow individuals with certain disabilities to serve on juries. For example, Tennessee law generally prohibits discrimination against a prospective juror who is blind.

Form 12.1 is an example of the typical jury personal history questionnaire used to screen potential jurors, and filled out by jurors before trial.

The court clerk had assembled the potential jurors in the *Consumer* case in an adjoining room. A jury wheel was used to select 20 persons for the trial panel designated for Judge Stern's courtroom. These individuals were then escorted into the courtroom and asked to be seated in the audience section.

As Judge Stern entered the courtroom, the bailiff announced the court was now in session with, "All rise! Oyez, Oyez the Federal District Court for the Middle State District is now open to oral statement, the Honorable Judge Stern presiding, all persons having business before this Honorable Court draw near, give attention, and you shall be heard. God save the United States and this Honorable Court."

Judge Stern took his place at the bench and invited the audience to be seated. He called the case of *Consumer v. Factory Motor Company* and checked to see that the lawyers for both sides were present and ready for trial. He then addressed the jury panel and explained the purposes and procedures of the voir dire process.

Voir dire:
Preliminary examination of jurors, or witnesses, to challenge their qualifications to serve in such capacities.

Form 12.1 **UNITED STATES DISTRICT COURT FOR THE MIDDLE DISTRICT OF MIDDLE STATE**

JUROR PERSONAL HISTORY QUESTIONNAIRE

TO THE JUROR: In order for us to determine your qualifications to serve as a juror you must answer the following questions:

The questions asked in this questionnaire are questions which could be asked of you in open court. You are therefore given more privacy by having to answer them in this questionnaire.

You are required by the rules of this Court to answer the questions truthfully. Refusal to answer, or the giving of a false answer, subjects you to fine or imprisonment, or both, for contempt of court. As you answer the questions it will become obvious to you why such questions must be asked.

ANSWERS MUST BE LEGIBLY WRITTEN OR PRINTED
BY THE JUROR HIMSELF

1. Print name plainly: _____

              LAST NAME   FIRST NAME   MIDDLE NAME

2. Address: _____

                        CITY   STATE   ZIP

    (A)   How many miles will you travel from your home to the Courthouse?_____

    (B)   Are you a U.S. citizen?   ☐ Yes   ☐ No

3. Date of Birth: _____ Place: _____

   Telephone Number: Home _____ Office: _____

4. Sex _____

5. Are you a freeholder (owner of real estate)?_____

6. State briefly the extent of your business or professional experience or other employment:

   _____

7. What is your present occupation? _____

8. Employed by: _____

9. If not employed, state your present means of livelihood (for example, housewife; pension; etc.) _____

10. What duties do you perform in your present job?_____

continued >

11. State what other occupations you have been in during the past 10 years and what duties you perfomed:_____

12. Marital status (check one):
    ☐ Single   ☐ Married   ☐ Divorced   ☐ Separated   ☐ Widow or Widower

13. Name of spouse: _____

14. Occupation of spouse: _____

15. Spouse employed by: _____

16. Number of children at home and ages: _____
    _____

17. Have you any defects in your hearing? _____

18. Have you any defects in your vision? _____

19. Is your general health good? _____

20. Have you any physical disability? (Explain) _____
    _____

21. Are you, or have you ever been, an officeholder for any state, county, or municipality? (Specify) _____
    _____

22. Are you, or have you ever been, a law enforcement officer? (Specify) _____
    _____

23. Are you a landlord, or tenant? (Specify) _____
    _____

24. How long have you lived in this county? _____

25. Have you ever studied law? (Explain) _____

26. Have you ever studied medicine? (Explain) _____

27. How far did you go in school? (Indicate highest grade completed or degrees received): _____

28. Have you ever served as a juror? _____

29. If so, when and in what courts? _____

30. Have you ever been disqualified (not excused) for jury service? _____

31. If so, for what cause? _____

32. Do you drive a car? _____

33. Do you (or your spouse) own a car? _____

continued >

34. Have you ever been in an accident? (Explain) _____
_____

35. Has any member of your family or a close friend ever been in an accident? If so, explain: _____
_____

36. Are you an officer, director of, or do you own stock in, any insurance companies?
_____

37. Have you ever been employed as a claims adjuster? _____

38. What companies? _____

39. Were you ever an inmate in an institution? (Explain): _____

40. Have you ever been convicted of a crime or misdemeanor other than a traffic violation? _____

41. If so, explain: _____

42. Have you ever been arrested and charged with any crime? _____
_____

43. If so, is that charge pending? _____

44. Have you ever been a party to any suit, either civil or criminal? _____

45. If so, state the nature of each suit and in what court: _____

46. Has any of your property or the property of your family been taken for public improvement? _____
If yes, explain. _____
_____

I certify that I have answered the above questions fully and truthfully. I realize that a false answer subjects me to the penalties for contempt of court.

OATH OF ALLEGIANCE

I do also solemnly swear (or affirm) that I will support the Constitution of the United States and that I will faithfully discharge the duties of my position as a juror with the Federal District Court for the Middle District to the best of my ability.

(Sign Here) _____

**Do not mail this form.
Bring it with you to orientation**

Voir Dire Challenges

There is considerable variation in local practice regarding the conduct of the jury selection process. The judge has to explain the manner in which he or she will proceed. The judge is aware of the responsibility for conducting a fair process and is also aware that the lawyers on both sides may ultimately challenge the manner in which the process was conducted on appeal. Therefore, the judge generally seeks to establish the concerns of the opposing lawyers and to identify the potential issues.

Challenges for Cause

The judge may ask the questions or may also allow the lawyers to address the jury panel and pose their own questions. The lawyers are allowed to move that the court disqualify a juror "for cause," but the decision to remove that juror must be made by the judge. The judge will allow both parties to present opposing arguments concerning **challenges for cause**.

Challenges for cause: Requests from parties to the judge to remove potential jurors for specified reasons.

Peremptory Challenges

When arguments concerning elimination of potential jurors for cause have been exhausted, the judge allows both parties an opportunity to exercise their **peremptory challenges**. These challenges enable attorneys to strike jurors for virtually any reason—in other words, peremptorily. However, the Equal Protection Clause prohibits lawyers from using peremptory challenges in a racially (or based on gender) discriminatory manner. The number of peremptory challenges is fixed by the rules of civil procedure for that jurisdiction and may vary from state to state. Three peremptory challenges per party in the selection of a jury of six would be typical. Parties do not have to use all their peremptory challenges.

Peremptory challenges: Requests from parties to remove jurors without cause. Each party is allowed a fixed number of these challenges.

It is good strategy for the lawyer to approach potential jurors in a courteous manner, taking care not to arouse their animosity. Many lawyers try to ingratiate themselves to the jurors and win their sympathy from the start. One strategy is to display confidence by not asking too many questions and being very cooperative with all jurors, making them feel good about themselves and sympathetic toward the lawyer. For this reason, the judges in federal courts usually conduct the voir dire themselves, and the lawyers are required to formulate questions through them. This practice attempts to reduce the skillful attorney's ability to win the jury before the facts are established.

The voir dire process is quite diverse in U.S. courts, and the procedures used in practice are about as varied as the number of judges who hold trials. In the *Consumer* case, Judge Stern used a combination of methods in conducting the voir dire. He first asked the trial panel to stand and raise their right hands. "Do you solemnly swear to make true answers to all questions that shall be asked of you touching your competency as jurors?" he asked. The entire trial panel responded affirmatively.

The judge then identified the parties to the lawsuit, their respective legal counsel, and the witnesses who would appear in the case. He asked the jurors whether any of them were related to or had any personal dealings with any of these persons or whether the jurors knew of any reason that they might be disqualified from serving on the jury in this case. A secretary employed at Middle State University knew the deceased plaintiff, a nephew of Jim Trucker had talked with him about the accident, a salesman was employed at City Auto Company, and one potential juror was a former client of Bill Green's law firm. The judge asked several questions of these potential jurors and allowed the opposing lawyers to comment or pose questions of their own, then thanked them and asked them to rejoin the general jury panel in the assembly room.

Both parties to the dispute made use of their peremptory challenges. The judge allowed each party to name any three potential jurors for elimination without cause. John Gaither and Cora Smith agreed to eliminate the owner of a small factory, the manager of a small airport, and a salesperson for an auto parts firm. Bill Green and Maria Farmer chose a college student, a union steward, and a widowed housewife for their arbitrary eliminations.

Once Judge Stern was satisfied that an impartial jury had been selected, he thanked the remaining members of the jury panel who had not been selected as trial jurors or alternates in the *Consumer* case, and they were escorted back to the jury assembly room to await consideration for selection on other juries.

Federal practice now uses 6 jurors in civil cases, but several states still use 12 jurors. Most states at least have the option of using 6 jurors in civil trials today. The jury finally selected by Judge Stern for the *Consumer* trial included 6 jurors and 1 alternate, who would replace any of the original 6 jurors if circumstances arose during the trial to make it impossible for an original juror to continue. The principal jurors were Tina Spencer, age 24, married to a construction worker, two children; John Hollis, age 35, a computer programmer employed by an advertising firm, married, no children; Nancy Blast, age 26, secretary for a real estate firm, single; William Johnson, age 54, salesman for a local supermarket, married with two children. The alternate juror was Betty Moore, age 42, factory worker, single parent of one child.

When the selection process had been completed, the judge asked the jury to take a second oath "to judge this case fairly, according to law." The jurors all agreed to the oath.

TRIAL ARGUMENTS

The next day, Judge Stern opened the session with the following preliminary instructions to the jury.

"Ladies and gentlemen of the jury: now that you have been sworn as jurors in this case, I will briefly tell you something about your duties as jurors and give you some instructions. At the end of the trial, I will give you more detailed instructions, and those instructions will control your deliberations.

"It will be your duty to decide from the evidence what the facts are. You, and you alone, are the judges of the facts. You will hear the evidence, decide what the facts are, and then apply those facts to the law that I will give you. That is how you will reach your verdict. In doing so, you must follow the law whether you agree with it or not.

"You must not take anything I say or do during the trial as an indication of what your verdict should be. Don't be influenced by my taking notes at times. What I write down may have nothing to do with what you will be concerned with at this trial.

"You will not be allowed to take notes so that you can devote your full attention to the witnesses and evidence presented. You will be given written evidence and exhibits that have been admitted during the trial to assist you in your deliberations, but you will need to listen carefully to the personal testimony of the witnesses.

"The **opening statements** and **closing arguments** of the attorneys are not evidence but are provided to the court for the purpose of clarification and understanding of the facts that will be presented through the witnesses and material evidence. In like manner, the lawyers' questions are not evidence.

"We will begin with opening statements for the plaintiff. Is counsel ready to begin?"

John Gaither took the lawyer's position at the podium in front of the judge's bench and looked at the judge as he asked, "May it please the court, your honor?" Getting a nod from the judge, Attorney Gaither began his opening statement.

Opening statements: Opposing lawyers' formulations of the nature of the case and anticipated proof to be presented.

Closing arguments: Opposing lawyers' summaries of the evidence they think has been established or refutations of opposing evidence.

Plaintiff's Opening Statement

"Ladies and gentlemen of the jury, I am John Gaither, and this is my co-counsel Cora Smith (pointing toward plaintiff's table). We will be representing Jane Consumer at this trial against the Factory Motor Company.

"This case is about negligence and strict liability on the part of Factory Motor Company.

"Bill Consumer and his wife had been shopping and had dinner in Capital City. They were driving home at about 10:30 in the evening of September 9, 2010. About halfway home, it began to rain, and Bill slowed down to about 60 mph. They were traveling on Interstate 24 and were almost home—just three miles from the Centerville turnoff. The car approached a van from the rear that was traveling at a slower speed, and Bill pulled into the left passing lane in a normal passing maneuver. Jane Consumer, who was sitting beside Bill in the passenger seat, will tell you she heard a loud 'popping noise' coming from the rear of the car. She looked at Bill, whose face revealed sheer panic as he shouted, 'The wheel won't turn!'

"He was pumping the brakes as the car sped across the grassy median separating the two lanes of directional traffic. The car collided with a tractor-trailer headed in the opposite direction, spun around, and ended up on the far side of the interstate. Bill was killed and Jane severely injured in the accident.

"An expert mechanic will testify that on examination of the wrecked automobile, after the accident, he found a broken suspension coil on the left side of the vehicle that did not match the coil on the right side. A factory mix-up on the assembly line resulted in the improper installation of this defective coil in the Consumers' car. The defective coil was shorter and weaker than the coil on the right side. It broke at the moment when Jane Consumer will testify it made a loud 'popping noise' just before the accident.

"The broken coil dropped the left rear side of the vehicle down at least three inches, causing the weight of the car to shift to the left rear axle. This shift of weight lifted the front of the car, causing the tires to hydroplane on the wet pavement and resulted in Bill's inability to control the vehicle.

"The Factory Motor Company, who manufactured this car, knew that it was improperly assembled and waited more than two years before issuing a recall letter. The letter they issued did not warn of the danger or even identify the defective condition of the coil in question but merely asked that the car be taken to a certified dealer for replacement repairs. Bill had received this letter the day before the accident and had intended to take the car to the dealer the next day. Unfortunately, Bill was killed in the accident on Wednesday, September 9, 2010.

"The defendant's lawyers in this case will tell you that they tested the mistaken coils and concluded that they were safe. But the coils they tested were only like the one mounted in the Consumer's car by mistake. They did not test the defective coil in the car that caused the accident. Their testing is a lame excuse for not doing what they should have done in the first place—to immediately issue a factory recall when they discovered their mistake. Instead, they waited for testing and complaints, allowing Bill Consumer and his wife to drive an unsafe vehicle for two years and 22,000 miles before making any effort to contact them. The Factory Motor Company put money ahead of safety in their corporate philosophy, and it cost Bill Consumer his life!

"The Consumer family has suffered irreparable damage from this accident in the form of loss of a loved one who cannot be replaced. Jane Consumer has suffered needless physical and mental injuries, and their three children cannot be made to suffer further injury from the loss of the income their father would have provided.

"The witnesses and evidence we will present will prove these facts to you the members of the jury. You will decide this matter on the legal basis of a special liability standard that requires merely the existence of a defective condition that was the proximate cause of the injuries sustained. The legal standard of proof is a preponderance of the evidence . . . and ladies and gentlemen when you have heard all the evidence, I am confident you will conclude that the weight of the evidence supports the plaintiff's right to recover damages."

Judge Stern then asked the defense team whether they were ready for their opening statement, and Maria Farmer approached the lawyers' podium. "May it please the court, your honor?" she asked. She then introduced her co-counsel, Bill Green, and began her statement.

Defense Opening Statement

"Ladies and gentlemen of the jury, the tragic accident involved in this case was caused by unavoidable weather conditions and driver error, not by any alleged defective condition of the automobile in question.

"On the night of the accident, the section of Interstate 24 where the car left the road was soaked by a drenching rainstorm—one and one-half inches of rain fell within half an hour. This sudden downpour caused water to stream down the gentle slope there, collecting in a pocket at the bottom of the slope where Bill Consumer's car left the road.

"When the front tires of the car hit this pool of water at 60 mph, they began to ski across the surface of the water, preventing the driver from controlling the vehicle because the tires were not in contact with the road surface. One of the foremost experts in the country on the causes of accidents has carefully examined these road conditions and the condition of the wrecked vehicle involved. He will testify that the weight of the scientific evidence proves vehicle hydroplaning to be the cause of this accident and not an alleged faulty coil.

"Bill Consumer had been drinking beer on the night of the accident, and his reaction time had been affected. He also had failed to slow his vehicle to a speed appropriate for the heavy rain he encountered before the accident. These were factors contributing to the accident that would not have happened had he been more cautious.

"The suspension coil in question was not defective, unsafe, or dangerous, as we will demonstrate from the results of our extensive testing using 'state of the art' scientific equipment. The specific coil in question did not break before the accident, as the plaintiff alleges, but that damage was caused by the impact of the collision itself. The car hit a tractor-trailer on the opposite side of the Interstate. Both vehicles were traveling in excess of 60 mph, and the combined speed generated a force equivalent to that of hitting a stationary object at more than 120 mph. The tremendous force of this collision caused the car to spin around. It made a complete circle and ended up facing in the opposite direction from that of the initial impact.

Needless to say, the coils on this vehicle were not designed to withstand that kind of impact.

"The testimony of expert witnesses and the evidence we will produce during the trial will prove these facts. The Factory Motor Company acted responsibly in manufacturing this vehicle to meet all government safety standards. This company is proud of the record it has achieved by using existing technology to prevent accidents caused by defective products—but the factory cannot be held responsible for the weather, for road conditions, or for driver error.

"Just because a tragic accident occurred, that fact does not prove that it was caused by a defective product, and it would be grossly unfair to assume so. I have faith in the good sense of this jury not to be fooled by sympathy or prejudice. I know you will listen carefully to the scientific facts in this case and arrive at a just verdict."

Examination of Witnesses

The examination of each witness called to testify at trial is conducted in accordance with the following steps:

1. **Direct examination** consists of questioning by the attorney for the party who calls the witness. The objective is to establish the facts or claim of that party.

2. **Cross-examination** involves questioning by opposing counsel and is optional. It offers counsel for the opposing party opportunity to attack both the credibility and the testimony of the witness.

3. Redirect examination, or re-questioning by the attorney who conducted the direct examination, is optional and is generally used to "rehabilitate" a witness following cross-examination, that is, to recapture the witness's lost credibility. The subject matter is generally limited to that which was brought out on cross-examination.

4. Recross examination, or requestioning by the opposing counsel, is an option following the redirect examination. The questioning is generally limited to new matters brought out on redirect. Further exchange is limited by the recross-examination, if used, and the judge will not allow testimony to proceed beyond this point with this witness.

Direct examination: Initial questioning by the attorney who calls the witness.

Cross-examination: Questioning done by opposing counsel of the party who called the witness.

Rules of Evidence and Objections

The **rules of evidence** are a detailed set of standards governing the admissibility of evidence at trial and must be carefully followed by lawyers. The opposing lawyer has the responsibility of raising objections to any infraction of these rules during the conduct of the trial. The judge will allow opposing lawyers to comment, but ultimately the judge will decide whether the material in question is admissible or inadmissible.

Rules of evidence: Detailed rules that govern the admissibility of evidence at trials and hearings.

The complexity of the rules of evidence prohibits full explanation of them in this chapter. However, a few of the basic topics that may cause concern are leading questions, relevancy, asked and answered, beyond the scope, excessive narration, hearsay, and best evidence. (The Federal Rules of Evidence is available on the Internet and should be consulted for these details.)

Leading Questions

In the direct examination of a witness, **leading questions** are not usually permitted. These are questions that instruct the witness how to answer or imply an answer, that is, put words into the mouth of the witness. They are not permitted because the attorney, rather than the witness, may actually be testifying by the way the lawyer frames the questions. The object on direct examination is to allow the witnesses to testify to their firsthand knowledge that is relevant to the case, in their own words.

On cross-examination, the leading questions rule does not apply. The lawyer for the party who did not call the witness can ask leading questions to probe the credibility of the witness.

Leading questions: Questions framed in such a way that they instruct the witness how to answer or put words into the witness's mouth to be echoed back.

Hearsay and Best Evidence Rules

One of the most complex rules of evidence is the **hearsay rule**, which excludes evidence that consists of what another person has said or written outside the court when that evidence is offered for purposes of establishing the truth of what was said or written. The very nature of hearsay evidence suggests its weakness since the competence and credibility of the originator of the statement cannot be tested.

The purpose of the hearsay rule is related to that of the **best evidence rule**, which prevents secondhand information from being presented as evidence unless the court is satisfied that there is no better source from which the evidence can be obtained. Rules 803 and 804 of the Federal Rules of Evidence list at least 29 specific exceptions to the hearsay rule, including statements of a deceased person who can no longer testify and statements made in a moment of excitement.

Hearsay rule: Testimony in court of a statement made out of court, offered to show the truth of matters asserted, is not permitted.

Best evidence rule: Requires primary evidence as opposed to secondary evidence, in other words, the best evidence available.

ASSIGNMENT: Using the information that follows and the appendix information about this case, prepare and enact the trial, in class, using students to play the roles of judge, plaintiffs/defense attorneys, witnesses, and jurors. If this assignment is too time consuming, then witness the jury deliberations by students assigned to the task of being jurors for this case.

THE PLAINTIFF'S CASE IN CHIEF

Judge Stern asked whether the plaintiff's attorneys were ready to call their first witness. Cora Smith called Jane Consumer as her first witness, and the bailiff administered the oath to "tell the truth, the whole truth, and noting but the truth" before she was seated in the witness box.

Direct Examination

Jane Consumer was a little nervous being on the witness stand for the first time. Smith tried to put her at ease by asking questions that prompted her to explain her answers. After the preliminary questions dealing with identification of the witness were answered, Jane related her experiences on the night of the accident. She began by telling about the shopping trip and dinner that evening. Smith prompted her with pointed questions. "What did Bill have to drink with dinner?" Smith asked.

"He had one glass of beer with his meal," replied Jane.

Jane continued relating the events that occurred during the trip home that evening, with prompting from Smith's questions. When she reached the point of stating that she heard a loud "popping noise" after Bill started his passing maneuver, Smith asked, "What did this noise sound like, to you?"

"It sounded metallic—like a 'pong'—as though a spring snapped under pressure," Jane replied.

"What did you do then, after you heard the noise?" Smith continued to prompt Jane.

"I looked at Bill and he was frantic," Jane said. "He shouted, 'My God, the wheel won't turn.'"

"What do you think he meant by that statement?" Smith queried.

"He must have meant that the steering wheel would not turn the car because he was turning the steering wheel in panic at the time," answered Jane.

Smith asked, "What else did you observe him doing at this time?"

"He was pumping the brakes," replied Jane. "I could see his knee going up and down."

Smith introduced the bill of sale for the car and the affidavit from the service manager at City Auto Company attesting to the fact that the vehicle in question had not been altered by the dealer. These documents provided proof of purchase, date of purchase, that the car had been properly maintained, that complaints had been made concerning the leaning of the vehicle prior to the accident, and that the coil had not been altered by the dealer.

The procedure for introducing documents is first to show the document to the judge to mark as a plaintiff or defense exhibit and give it an identifying mark, then to show the document to the opposing counsel for their

Court Protocol for Introducing Documents or Material Evidence

This material would have been discussed and any objections raised in the judge's conference before trial. However, the procedure involves additional measures to avoid surprises. At trial, the attorney needs an appropriate witness to use to introduce this type of evidence and will proceed in the following manner:

1. "Your honor may I approach the bench?" After receiving a nod, the attorney approaches the bench with the appropriate document or material evidence and shows it to the judge.

2. The attorney then asks the judge for permission to approach opposing counsel. And after receiving an affirmative response, the attorney shows the evidence to opposing counsel.

3. Opposing counsel is then asked by the judge if there are any objections. If objections are offered, they are heard by the judge and both sides have an opportunity to respond.

4. The judge makes a ruling as to whether the witness may respond to the document.

5. Assuming that the judge does not stop the examination of the document by the witness, the initiating attorney begins questioning the witness concerning the document or material evidence.

6. Once the evidence or document is appropriately established as introduced by a witness who can substantiate the credibility of this evidence, the initiating attorney asks the court to admit the evidence for consideration by the jury.

---

examination. At this point, the lawyer introducing the document asks the judge to admit it as evidence. The judge asks opposing counsel whether there are any objections. The judge may consider any objections in making the ruling to admit the document as evidence or to exclude it.

A letter from the manufacturer (see Form 12.2) was then introduced in the manner described and was accepted as evidence.

"What is this document, Mrs. Consumer?" Smith asked.

"It is the letter I found on Bill's desk after the accident," explained Jane.

"What does it say?" Smith prompted.

"It asks Bill to bring the car in for recall repairs at the Factory's expense." Jane said. "But," she noted, "it doesn't say anything about any danger involved, and it doesn't say anything about coils being improperly installed."

Smith continued her questioning. "Did Bill mention this letter to you?"

"Yes, he said he thought it was important and that he would have our daughter take him down to the City Auto Company on Thursday morning," replied Jane.

"What Thursday morning was that?" Smith queried.

"The day after the accident; that would be on September 10, 2010."

Smith shifted the topic to damages and introduced the death certificate, the hospital bills, the doctor bills, and the funeral expenses. She asked Jane about her husband's employment and salary, including what she knew about his expectations for promotions and fringe benefits. Attorney Cora

Form 12.2 **LETTER FROM FACTORY MOTOR COMPANY TO WILLIAM P. CONSUMER**

(PLAINTIFF'S EXHIBIT C)

THE FACTORY MOTOR COMPANY, INC., U.S.A.
200 FACTORY BOULIVARD
BIG CITY, LAKE STATE

September 1, 2010

Mr. William P. Consumer
140 Consumer Lane
Centerville, Middle State

Dear Mr. Consumer,

Our records indicate that you purchased a 2009 Supreme Brougham Executive manufactured by the Factory Motor Company with serial number 1FMCB14T9KUA14073.

If you are still in possession of this vehicle, please bring it in to the dealer where you purchased it, or any certified Factory Motor Company dealer, as soon as possible for recall repairs at our expense.

Bring this letter with you to your preferred dealer and present it to the service manager.

We hope you are satisfied with the automobile you have purchased and want to assure you that our company is dedicated to consumer satisfaction. At the Factory Motor Company, quality is our most important priority.

Sincerely yours,

A.B. Johnson
Production Director

Smith also asked a line of questions concerning Jane's personal injuries sustained from the accident. This exchange produced no new information but had to be entered for the record. Smith then indicated that she had finished her direct examination.

Cross-Examination

Bill Green slowly approached the lawyer's podium after Smith had finished her direct examination. He was obviously thinking of some penetrating questions to ask Jane on cross-examination.

"I'd like to ask you a few questions about your shopping trip at that new mall, before you had dinner on the night of the accident," Green began. "Were you with your husband all the time during this shopping period?"

"No," Jane replied. "We were separated for about an hour during this period."

"Did your husband like to shop, Mrs. Consumer?" asked Green.

"No, not very much," admitted Jane.

"Is there a place that sells beer at the mall, Mrs. Consumer?" Green queried.

"I don't know . . . I suppose so," Jane replied uncertainly.

"Did Bill often have a beer at the mall?" the attorney asked.

"Not to my knowledge," answered Jane.

"But he could have had a beer, or two, during that hour you were separated, couldn't he?" Green persisted.

"Yes, I suppose so," Jane replied.

After several other questions, Attorney Green got to the point of asking Jane about the moments just prior to the accident. "When did it start raining on the trip back home, Mrs. Consumer?" He queried.

"I don't know exactly." Jane hesitated, then said, "About 10 minutes before the accident, I guess."

"Was it raining hard enough to affect visibility?" Attorney Green asked.

"Yes, I suppose so, but Bill slowed down and had the windshield wipers on," replied Jane.

Green then asked about the speed at which the vehicle was traveling. "You said that Bill slowed down from 65 to 60 mph. How could you tell us that so precisely?"

"I looked at the speedometer," answered Jane.

"Wasn't it dark in the vehicle and hard to see the speedometer?" Green wondered.

"No," Jane replied. "I could see from the dash lights and I was sitting close to Bill."

The defense attorney said pointedly, "I thought you said you had your seat belt on, Mrs. Consumer. Could you get close to your husband under these conditions?"

"I could see the speed indicator," Jane reiterated.

"Could you smell beer on Bill's breath?" the attorney asked.

"No," replied Jane.

Redirect Examination

Smith chose the option of redirect examination. "How much alcohol did your husband normally consume, Mrs. Consumer?"

"He only drank beer with his meals, sometimes," Jane replied. "He was not a heavy drinker."

"What is the condition of your eyesight and hearing?" Smith asked.

Jane answered, "I have never worn glasses. My vision is 20/20, and I have never had any trouble with my hearing. I could see the speedometer clearly and I heard the 'popping noise' distinctly."

There was no recross-examination and the next witness was called for the plaintiff.

Direct Examination

Judge Stern called for the next witness, and John Gaither called Jim Trucker to the stand. Gaither began with the same prompting questions that Smith had used to aid the witness through the known testimony without putting words in his mouth. Jim Trucker was a good witness who confirmed many aspects of the accident, but he had little to add to the facts that Jane had provided.

Cross-Examination

The defense attorney, Maria Farmer, asked a few questions about the amount of rain on the night of the accident and the road conditions, but Jim Trucker's answers did not add any significant information. There was no redirect examination and therefore no recross-examination of this witness.

Then Cora Smith called George Goodcop to the witness stand.

Direct Examination

After establishing the officer's identity and his relationship to the accident, the attorney introduced the officer's accident report and asked for permission to show the jury an enlarged version of the sketch in the officer's report (see Figure 12.1). The judge and the opposing party had no objections.

Smith asked the officer, "Where did you start your investigation of the path of the Consumer vehicle?"

"I walked across the median, and my feet got pretty wet on the way, as I recall," George answered. "There were tire marks on the southbound

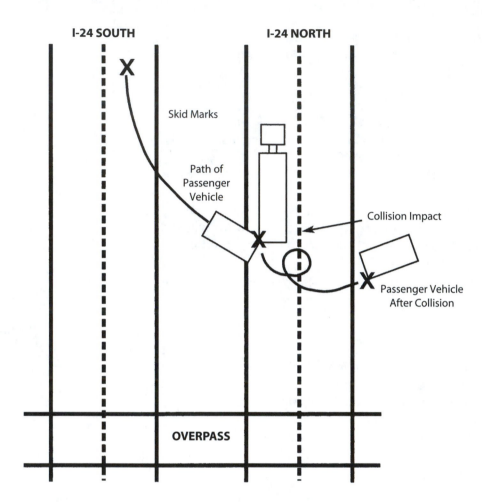

I-24 SOUTH

I-24 NORTH

Skid Marks

Path of
Passenger
Vehicle

Collision Impact

Passenger Vehicle
After Collision

OVERPASS

Figure 12.1
**Officer's Accident
Sketch**

traffic lane starting at the point I have indicated on my sketch." He went to the exhibit and pointed to the start of the skid marks. "This indicates that the driver had applied the brakes before he left the asphalt roadbed."

"How wet was the roadbed where you found the skid marks?" queried Smith.

"There was no standing water on the highway at that time," George replied. "But," he noted, "I made this investigation more than half an hour after the accident took place and it had stopped raining."

Cross-Examination

Bill Green proceeded to cross-examine the witness. "Did you investigate the interior of the accident vehicle after the medics had removed the passengers?" he asked.

"Yes, I did," answered the officer.

"Did you find any evidence related to alcohol consumption in the vehicle?" the attorney asked.

"I did find an empty beer can in the floorboard under the passengers seat," Officer Goodcop said.

"You said the driver was not wearing a seat belt," the attorney continued. "Does the law in Middle State require seat belts?"

"Yes, it does," confirmed the officer.

"Therefore, the driver was in violation of the law, wasn't he?" persisted the attorney.

"Yes sir," the officer replied.

"How many accidents have occurred at this location, to your knowledge?" questioned Green.

"I have been patrolling this section of the highway for four years," answered Officer Goodcop, "and to my knowledge, there have been two other accidents at this particular location. We have had several complaints about poor drainage in this area."

Redirect Examination

Attorney Smith tried on redirect examination to reduce the impact of George's testimony. "Whose beer can did you find in the car, Officer?"

"I have no idea," George replied. "Single beer cans are often stored under seats and they fly out in accidents."

Following this exchange, there were no further questions for Officer Goodcop.

Direct Examination

John Gaither called Mack Racer as the next witness and began the final direct examination for the plaintiff. John was careful to lay a foundation for qualifying this witness as an expert mechanic. He asked a number of detailed questions about Mack's qualifications and experience. Most witnesses cannot be asked hypothetical questions that call for opinions. But if a proper foundation is laid showing the witness is qualified by reason of special knowledge, skill, experience, training, or education to arrive at conclusions concerning a given set of facts, the rules of evidence allow an exception for such an **expert witness**.

After aiding the witness to explain his extensive experience and qualification, John Gaither asked the judge to qualify Mack Racer as an expert mechanic who could be asked opinion questions in his area of expertise. Maria Farmer objected, stating that the witness lacked the proper educational and theoretical knowledge and training to be qualified as an expert. Judge Stern overruled the objection but cautioned that he might

Expert witness:
One who has specialized knowledge in a particular field, obtained from either education or personal experience, which qualifies the person to answer opinion questions.

sustain an objection at the time that the specific hypothetical questions were posed.

Attorney Gaither focused on the coils that the mechanic removed from the vehicle and asked, "What was the condition of the shock absorbers when you removed the coils from the accident vehicle?"

"Both rear shock absorbers were broken loose from their mountings," answered Mack Racer.

Attorney Gaither introduced as evidence, without objection by defense counsel, the actual coils that had been removed from the Consumers' car by the mechanic. "Are these the coils you removed?"

"Yes, they are." Taking them in his hands, Mack held up the obviously thicker and longer coil. "This is the right coil that is undamaged, and the left coil, as you can see, is broken off at the base. The left coil is made of thinner and weaker material and is about one inch shorter than the right coil," explained the mechanic.

The coil parts were passed around to the jury members for their inspection, then Gaither resumed questioning Mack. "In your opinion, would the shorter coil on the left side have caused any change in the vehicle's performance?"

Maria Farmer stood. "Objection, your honor. It is beyond the scope of the witness's qualifications to answer a hypothetical engineering question."

The judge looked at Gaither. "Attorney Gaither, do you have a reply to this objection?"

"Yes, your honor," Gaither answered. "As was established earlier, this witness has been an engineering consultant for several nationally prominent race car teams and is fully qualified to answer this question."

"Objection overruled," the judge declared. He told Mack, "You may answer the question."

"In my opinion," said Mack, "it would have caused the weight of the vehicle to be unevenly distributed. More specifically, it would have transferred the weight of the vehicle to the rear axle, thus reducing the weight on the right front axle. This weight shift would cause the vehicle to have reduced traction on the right front tires. This would, in turn, affect the steering capabilities under adverse conditions, such as driving through snow, ice, or water. We put heavy-duty coils on our racing stock cars to increase the traction on the front tires specifically for the purpose of increasing handling capabilities."

The attorney continued his line of questioning. "In your opinion, what would be the effect if the coil broke under the conditions you have just described?"

"Objection, your honor," Farmer interjected. "This witness is not an engineer and is not qualified to answer this question."

"Overruled," declared the judge, and turning to Mack, said, "You may answer."

"If the left coil had broken under wet driving conditions," Mack explained, "the weight of the vehicle would have dropped five or six inches to the axle. This sudden force would have caused the front end of the vehicle to be lifted in corresponding fashion. The reduced traction of the front tires would have caused the vehicle to hydroplane, even if there was only soaked pavement under the front tires."

Cross-Examination

Maria Farmer was obviously irritated when she took the podium for cross-examination, but she regained her composure and managed to smile as she began. "You're a good mechanic aren't you, Mr. Racer?"

"I try to be," Mack agreed.

"Do you have an engineering degree, Mr. Racer?" the attorney queried.

"No," he replied, "but I have more than 20 years of experience working on Factory Motor Company vehicles and advising race car drivers."

"Can you prove that the left coil broke before the accident?" Farmer asked.

"No, I can't say for certain that the coil broke before or after the accident," replied Mack.

"Could the coil break from an impact at a speed equal to 120 miles per hour?" Farmer asked, and added, "Just answer yes or no."

"Yes," answered the mechanic.

Redirect Examination

Attorney Gaither used his opportunity to recover his witness on redirect by asking, "What area of the accident vehicle took the initial impact of the collision, Mr. Racer?"

Mack answered, "The left driver's side of the vehicle was collapsed, indicating that the hood of the car had passed underneath the tractor-trailer and the driver's cab had taken the initial impact on the corner where the driver sits."

"Where would the corresponding stress have taken place?" the attorney asked.

"On the right coil," the mechanic answered, "because the initial impact would have transferred the stress to that location. The right coil should have broken, not the left one."

Maria Farmer declined to recross-examine the witness.

Direct Examination

John Gaither then called Professor Walter Rogers, an economist specializing in questions concerning economic values. Gaither was careful to establish how many times the witness had given expert testimony in the past and had the economist list his professional publications. Rogers was therefore accepted as an expert in the field of economic value estimates. Gaither asked that the professor's report (see Form12.3) be read into the record, and, as there were no objections, the judge so ordered. Then, after questioning the expert concerning his assumptions, Gaither indicated that he had finished his direct examination.

Cross-Examination

Bill Green attempted to challenge the expert witness by implying that there was only one standard method for calculating present value and that the usual period for calculating earnings stops at age 65 when social security benefits begin. The professor took issue with these assumptions and denied Bill's inference.

There were no further questions for this witness, and John Gaither indicated that the plaintiff had no other witnesses to call at this time.

Conclusion of the Plaintiff's Case in Chief

Bill Green moved for a **directed verdict** in favor of the defense. The plaintiff has the initial **burden of proof** and must establish evidence that, if not refuted, will meet all the required elements of the law. The judge could have ended the *Consumer* trial at this point if he believed that the plaintiffs had failed to meet their initial burden of proof of a *prima facie* case.

There was no question in this case that the plaintiffs had met their burden of demonstrating sufficient evidence for a **prima facie case**. Judge Stern overruled the motion for a directed verdict and declared a recess until the following Monday morning, when the jury would begin hearing the defendant's case in chief. He cautioned the jurors not to discuss this case with anyone and not to seek any advice about matters involving this case. The jury would be required to make a decision solely on the basis of what they heard and observed in the courtroom.

Directed verdict:
When the party with the burden of proof has failed to present a prima facie case for jury consideration, the trial judge may enter a verdict as a matter of law.

Burden of proof:
Obligation of a party to establish by evidence a requisite degree of belief concerning a fact in the mind of the court.

Prima facie case:
A case that will prevail until contradicted and overcome by other evidence.

THE DEFENDANT'S CASE IN CHIEF

After Judge Stern reconvened the trial on Monday morning, Maria Farmer called Mr. Superior Tester as her first witness. Farmer was careful to lay a proper foundation to qualify Mr. Tester as an expert witness. He had a master's degree from the Massachusetts Institute of Technology and eight years of experience as a laboratory technician. He also had been qualified as an expert witness on numerous occasions in federal court, and the plaintiffs raised no objections to his qualifying as an expert.

Form 12.3 **ESTIMATE OF DAMAGES PREPARED BY PROFESSOR WALTER ROGERS, PH.D. ECONOMICS (PLAINTIFF'S RECORD)**

FOR THE ESTATE: William P. Consumer held the rank of Associate Professor with tenure at Middle State University where he had been employed for five years. His annual salary was $35,000, and he normally earned another $2,500 for summer teaching. He could expect annual raises and promotion to the next higher rank at the university. The average salaries of Associate Professors is $43,000 and for full Professors it is $51,000.

Professor Consumer was 48 years of age, in remarkably good health, and could expect to continue in university employment. His life expectancy is estimated at 27.04 years. (T.C.A. Tables 1998 Supplement)

Assuming an average annual salary increase with promotions of 9%, fringe benefits of 27.5%, a present value discount rate of 8%, and an estimated savings rate of 30%, Professor Consumer's net economic value to the estate, according to Middle State law, would be:

Base: $37,500 X 27 Years Plus Expected Increases and Promotion
Calculated at 9% Compounded = $3,852,117

Fringe benefits of university employment, including group medical insurance and other benefits, are estimated to amount to an additional 27.5%. This would increase the base amount to $4,911,500. This base amount must be discounted by 8% (the average earnings on U.S. Treasury certificates) to estimate what investment would produce this amount in 27 years.

Base Amount Plus Fringe Benefits Discounted for Present Value:

$614,900 (An Investment of This Amount of Money at Present Could Be Expected to Earn the Above Base Amount of $4,911,500 in 27 Years at 8% Interest Compounded)

Middle State law allows an estimate of the decedent's contribution to the household services (14 hours per week at $5 per hour), and we must deduct probable living expenses for the deceased had he lived. *Wallace v. Couch*, 642 S.W.2d 141 (Tenn. 1982). Using an estimated savings rate of 30%, we arrive at the final amount of present economic value in legal damages, and then we add hospital and burial expenses to arrive at the final estate value of the claim.

Present Value Taken from above ($614,900) Plus Household Services	=	$ 713,200	
Minus Probable Living Expenses for the Deceased	–	$ 214,000	= $ 499,200
Plus Medical Expenses	+	$ 1,000	→
Plus Funeral Expenses	+	$ 7,000	→
Grand Total for Deceased	=	$ 507,200	→

FOR WIFE INJURED IN ACCIDENT: Medical expenses for Jane Consumer are evidenced by the hospital and doctor bills amounting to $15,000. Pain and suffering sustained by Jane Consumer from her injuries caused by the defendant is estimated to be five times that of the medical expenses for Jane amounting to $75,000.

Medical Expenses	=	$ 15,000
Plus Pain and Suffering	=	$ 75,000
Grand Total for Damage to Jane Consumer	=	$ 90,000

Total Damage to Both Deceased's Estate and Jane Consumer is Equal to $507,200 Plus $90,000 = $597,200.

Farmer then introduced, without difficulty, the company report on the testing done by the factory (see Form 12.4).

After handing the report to Mr. Tester, she asked. "Is this a true and accurate copy of your report?"

"Yes, it is," he replied.

"What equipment did you use for your testing?" asked Farmer.

Mr. Tester answered, "The mechanical equipment used to test the coils are individual simulators made by *Scientific Teck, Inc.*, the recognized leader in the field on mechanical simulators. This simulator was certified by the Board of Scientific Advisers to be 'state of the art' equipment using the most advanced technology available."

"How did you set up the equipment?" the attorney asked.

"We were able to simulate the effect of these two dissimilar coils on an actual vehicle," Mr. Tester explained, "by mounting randomly selected coils from each type on the three available machines. This enabled us to test them under the condition of uneven distribution of the weight of the vehicle due to the shorter coil on the left side."

"And what was your conclusion?" Farmer asked.

Mr. Tester replied, "Based on this scientific evidence we concluded that the mistakenly assembled coils did not pose a safety risk and that they would hold up for the normal life of the vehicle. We based this decision on the fact that none of the coils broke before having simulated 150,000 miles of normal stress. The mistaken coils were only slightly lower in quality when compared to the originally designed equipment."

Farmer then asked, "What are the government safety standards concerning suspension coils?"

"There are no specific governmental standards for these coils," Mr. Tester answered, "because the suspension coils are not considered essential to the safety of the vehicle. They are installed primarily for passenger comfort. Therefore these coils met governmental safety standards."

"Why did the factory decide to have these coils replaced?" the attorney inquired.

"Because there were complaints about the appearance of the vehicles in question," Mr. Tester explained, "not because they posed a safety hazard. There have been no other complaints about safety or handling problems."

"What would happen if one of these coils broke under normal driving conditions, Mr. Tester?" questioned Farmer.

"The vehicle would drop no more than three inches because the shock absorbers would prevent any further movement," Mr. Tester answered. "The displacement of the weight of the vehicle could cause some handling difficulty, but this automobile is equipped with power steering and the displacement of weight would not prevent the driver from maintaining control of the vehicle even under these adverse conditions."

Form 12.4 **FACTORY MOTOR COMPANY MEMORANDUM REPORT ON TESTING OF COILS MISTAKENLY MOUNTED ON VEHICLE INVOLVED IN THE ACCIDENT**

(DEFENSE EXHIBIT 1)

TESTING DIVISION
FACTORY MOTOR COMPANY, INC., USA

M E M O R A N D U M

TO: Mr. A. B. Johnson, Production Director

DATE: March 15, 2010

SUBJECT: **REPORT ON TESTING OF SUSPENSION COILS SUPPLIED BY ACE SUPPLIERS, INC., BY MISTAKE AND USED IN THE PRODUCTION OF 250 SUPREME BROUGHAM EXECUTIVE PASSENGER VEHICLES IN THE 2009 PRODUCTION RUN (AUG. 20, 2009)**

TESTING WORK ORDER: Simulate normal driving conditions using a random selection of suspension coils from those shipped by the supplier by mistake to determine if they will meet our standard 150,000 mile endurance test.

TEST RESULTS: We used our three simulators mounted with a normal coil on the right side and a randomly selected mistaken coil on the left side. The simulators ran for more than 1,700 hours (or 150,000 miles) without any recorded damage to either types of coils. The first coil broke at 1,700 hours (or 150,000 miles) without any recorded damage to either type of coils. The first coil broke at 1,726 hours, and it was one of the mistaken coils. The second coil to break was a normal coil, which broke at 1,824 hours. The third simulator continued to run until another mistaken coil broke at 1,891 hours. We then stopped our testing.

RECOMMENDATION: We conclude from this test that the mistaken coils will withstand normal wear at our 150,000 mile standard and do not pose a safety hazard.

_____
Superior Tester
Director of Testing

Cross-Examination

John Gaither assumed his position at the lawyer's podium and began his cross by saying, "Good morning, Mr. Tester. Did you have a good plane trip down here from Big City?"

"Yes, thank you," Mr. Tester replied.

"Does your simulator account for the amount of traction on the front tires?" the attorney asked.

"Yes, it does," Mr. Tester confirmed. "The reduced traction was recorded and determined to be within limits set by industry standards."

"Who sets these industry standards?" asked the attorney.

"The Automobile Manufacturer's Association," Mr. Tester replied.

"Is that a government agency?" Gaither asked.

"No," answered Mr. Tester.

"In the absence of a government regulation concerning a particular part," Gaither continued, "does that mean you are free to use anything you want to and say it meets government standards?"

"No," Mr. Tester said.

"The shock absorbers did not prevent the vehicle from dropping the length of the coil on Bill Consumer's car," the lawyer pointed out. "Can you explain that, Mr. Tester?"

"A collision with an impact equivalent to 120 miles an hour would account for that," said Mr. Tester.

"Who pays your salary, Mr. Tester?" Gaither asked.

"The Factory Motor Company," replied the witness.

Maria Farmer saw no need for re-direct examination of this witness.

Direct and Cross-Examination

Bill Green then called Jackie Lifesaver, who added little to his deposition statement. The witness confirmed that the consumer had not been wearing a seat belt, that Jackie had smelled alcohol on the driver's breath, and that Jackie had seen a beer can in the floorboard of the vehicle. Cora Smith declined to cross examine the witness, and Judge Stern declared a recess for lunch.

After lunch, the defense called Jan Intern to the stand. Bill Green carefully laid the foundation for the medical questions he would ask this witness by establishing her credentials and identifying the witness as the attending emergency physician who had initially treated the Consumers at the hospital on the night of the accident. The defense attorney asked for the death certificate that had been produced by the plaintiff earlier and handed it to the witness as he asked, "Who signed the death certificate?"

"I did, as the physician in charge of the patient," Jan replied.

"What was the specific cause of William P. Consumer's death?" Green asked.

"Internal bleeding from severe chest wounds," answered the physician.

"Was the patient alive when he arrived at the hospital?" questioned Green.

"That is a difficult question to answer," Jan said. "He had no pulse, which meant that his heart had stopped beating. However, we are able to revive many such patients today because of improvements in technology."

Green asked, "Why were you unable to revive this patient?"

"We made every effort," Jan assured him, "but the chest wound and internal bleeding caused intense pressure on the heart, preventing it from responding."

"Would this patient have died if he had been wearing a seat belt?" Green inquired.

Smith rose to object. "Objection; your honor, leading question."

"Sustained. Rephrase your question," the judge stated.

"What causes such massive chest wounds in automobile accidents?" Green asked.

Jan answered, "This kind of chest wound could only have been caused by impact against the steering column and a seat belt or driver-side airbag could have prevented it."

"What tests were made on the body during your examination?" the attorney asked.

"I smelled alcohol on the patient's breath," Jan replied. "The distinct odor of alcohol was present, but I took no blood sample for testing. The results would have been inconclusive because his blood had been supplemented by whole blood administered by the medics on the way to the hospital."

Attorney Green asked several more questions that added little to the deposition statement and then ended his direct examination. Cora Smith had no questions of this witness on cross-examination.

Direct and Cross-Examination

Maria Farmer then called Professor Drivesafe to testify as the principal expert witness for the defense. At Farmer's prompting, the professor carefully established his credentials as a nationally prominent expert on the causes of automobile accidents, and he recounted his extensive educational and professional standing as a leading publicist in the field of automotive safety engineering. Farmer asked that he be accepted as an expert witness. The judge granted this request without an objection from the plaintiff. The attorney's direct examination began with the question, "What did you find at the scene of the accident, Professor Drivesafe?"

"The accident report described the location of the accident," the professor responded, "and I was able to verify that location by the deep ruts in the median caused by the accident vehicle. I took measurements of the slope and elevation of the roadbed with surveying equipment. There was a one-inch depression in the roadbed at a point determined to be where the car left the southbound asphalt roadbed. It extended for 20 yards to the north and would have resulted in standing water in the roadbed under heavy rain conditions."

"How deep would the water have been in this depression?" Farmer asked.

"It would vary from half an inch to an inch and one-half in some spots," he replied, "but there would be some standing water along this poorly drained portion of the highway for 20 yards in the area where the driver lost control of his vehicle."

Farmer then introduced an official weather report from the U.S. government weather station at Capital City airport. There were no objections. She asked Professor Drivesafe, "Would you identify this document for us?"

"It is the official U.S. weather report for the Capital City area," the professor stated.

"What amount of rainfall is recorded for September 9, 2009?" the attorney asked.

"Almost one inch in the three-hour reporting period from 9:00 P.M. to 12:00 midnight—98/100 of an inch," replied the witness.

"Where was the record made?" Farmer asked.

"Thirty miles from the accident scene, at the Capital City airport," the professor stated.

"What conclusions can you draw from this evidence about weather conditions at the accident scene?" questioned the attorney.

"Rainfall can vary considerably," the professor answered, "particularly in thundershowers, as reported here, but this would be considered a heavy rain and would be sufficient to create the conditions conducive to hydroplaning under the poor drainage conditions I observed at the accident scene."

Farmer then said, "Now let us go back to your inspection of the vehicle at the garage after the accident. What did your investigation reveal about the cause of the broken coil?"

The witness stated, "Taking into consideration the diagram prepared by the officer, the speeds indicated in the deposition statements of the witnesses and the condition of the vehicle after the accident, I concluded that the coil broke because of the impact and spinning of the vehicle after the crash. The tractor-trailer, traveling at a faster speed, pulled the passenger vehicle along with it, evidenced by the fact that it made a complete circle on the highway after the collision. This twisting force would be sufficient to cause the broken coil."

Cross-Examination

John Gaither approached the podium and asked, "Professor is it possible that the coil could have broken before the accident? Yes or no please."

"Yes, it is possible, but unlikely," he replied.

"Would hydroplaning be more likely to occur if the weight of the vehicle was unevenly distributed?" Gaither asked.

"Yes," confirmed the professor.

"How many times have you testified for the Factory Motor Company in court?" asked Gaither.

"I have not kept count, but I have testified on many occasions," the professor replied.

"What do you get paid for your services?" Gaither asked.

"Objection, your honor, argumentative," Farmer declared.

"Overruled," the judge stated. He told the professor, "You may answer."

The professor said, "Expenses and $200 per hour. What is your fee, counselor?"

Redirect Examination

Farmer took the podium to rehabilitate her witness and asked, "How many times have you testified for the plaintiff in liability suits, Professor?"

"More frequently than for manufacturers," he replied. "Much of my work is done for consumers."

There were no further questions for this witness, and the defense called the next witness to the stand.

Direct Examination

Farmer carefully established the credentials for Professor Alex Smith as an economist specializing in damage estimates. There was no objection to his testimony since he had been called many times before to testify as an expert witness and his credentials were impressive. Farmer asked that Professor Smith's report be read into the record (see Form 12.5), and the judge ordered that this be done.

Farmer asked the witness, "Is the method you used to calculate present value the standard method accepted by most economists?"

"Yes," confirmed Professor Smith. "Damages in the future must be discounted by what they could be expected to yield at standard interest rates, and this is the method I have used."

"Why do you estimate that William P. Consumer would have worked to age 65?" the attorney asked.

"This is the standard calculation in damages of this nature," replied the professor.

Form 12.5 **ESTIMATE OF DAMAGES PREPARED BY PROFESSOR ALEX SMITH, PH.D. ECONOMICS (DEFENSE RECORD)**

FOR THE ESTATE: William P. Consumer held the rank of Associate Professor with tenure at Middle State University where he had been employed for five years. His annual salary was $35,000, and he normally earned another $2,500 for summer teaching. He could expect annual raises and promotion to the next higher rank at the university. The average salaries of Associate Professors is $43,000 and for full Professors it is $51,000.

Professor Consumer was 48 years of age, in remarkably good health, and could expect to continue in university employment. His work expectancy is estimated at 17 years. He could only have expected to work until age 65.

Assuming an average annual salary increase with promotions of 7%, fringe benefits of 27.5%, a present value discount rate of 8%, and an estimated savings rate of 30%, Professor Consumer's net economic value to the estate, according to Middle State law, would be:

Base: $37,500 X 17 Years Plus Expected Increases and Promotion
Calculated at 7% Compounded = $1,156,500

Fringe benefits of university employment, including group medical insurance and other benefits, are estimated to amount to an additional 27.5%. This would increase the base amount to $1,474,500. This base amount must be discounted by 8% (the average earnings on U.S. Treasury certificates) to estimate what investment would produce this amount in 17 years.

Base Amount Plus Fringe Benefits Discounted for Present Value:

$369,000 (An Investment of This Amount of Money at Present Could Be Expected to Earn the Above Base Amount of $1,474,500 in 17 Years at 8% Interest Compounded)

Middle State law allows an estimate of the decedent's contribution to the household services (14 hours per week at $5 per hour), and we must deduct probable living expenses for the deceased had he lived. *Wallace v. Couch*, 642 S.W.2d 141 (Tenn. 1982). Using an estimated savings rate of 30%, we arrive at the final amount of present economic value in legal damages, and then we add hospital and burial expenses to arrive at the final estate value of the claim.

Present Value Taken from above ($369,000)			
Plus Household Services	=	$ 430,900	
Minus Probable Living Expenses for			
the Deceased	−	$ 129,300	= $ 301,600
Plus Medical Expenses	+	$ 1,000	⟶
Plus Funeral Expenses	+	$ 7,000	⟶
Grand Total for Deceased	=	$ 309,600	⟶

FOR WIFE INJURED IN ACCIDENT: Medical expenses for Jane Consumer are evidenced by the hospital and doctor bills amounting to $15,000. Pain and suffering sustained by Jane Consumer from her injuries caused by the defendant is estimated to be three times that of the medical expenses for Jane amounting to $45,000.

Medical Expenses	=	$ 15,000
Plus Pain and Suffering	=	$ 45,000
Grand Total for Damage to Jane Consumer	=	$ 60,000

Total Damage to Both Deceased's Estate and Jane Consumer is Equal to $309,600 Plus $60,000 = $369,600.

Cross-Examination

John Gaither attempted to cast doubt on the expert's testimony by asking whether there were other methods of estimating damages. However, the professor maintained that his estimate was the accepted standard in the professional field of damage estimates.

The defense did not redirect the witness, and Maria Farmer stated that the defense rests its case.

Conclusion of the Defendant's Case in Chief

Now the plaintiff's attorney, John Gaither, moved for a directed verdict in favor of the plaintiff. Judge Stern could have stopped the trial at this point if he believed that a reasonable person could not rule any way other than for the plaintiff, which would mean that the defendant had failed to produce any admissible evidence to refute the plaintiff's claim. Since this was obviously not the case here, the judge overruled the motion and declared a recess until the next day.

CLOSING ARGUMENTS

Judge Stern now called for closing arguments in the *Consumer* case. Each attorney is given an opportunity to review the important evidence and to restate the arguments and contentions in support of their client's case. Like opening statements, closing arguments do not constitute evidence and are offered for summary and clarification purposes. The plaintiff would go first and then the defense, as in the opening statements. Cora Smith gave the closing statement for the plaintiff.

Plaintiff's Closing Arguments

"Ladies and gentlemen of the jury, the defense asked you, in their opening statement, not to be fooled by sympathy or prejudice. We are confident that likewise you will not be fooled by so-called 'scientific evidence.'

"This fatal accident produced irreparable damage to the Consumer family, and it was caused by a defective set of coils installed in the Consumer's automobile by mistake. The Factory Motor Company could have, and should have, corrected this mistake by an immediate recall. Had they done so, Mr. Consumer would be alive today, and we would not have to be here trying this case.

"The factory recall letter came two years and 22,000 miles after the wrong coils were installed. It said merely that the car should be taken in for recall repairs. Bill Consumer got this letter the day before the accident, which took place on a Wednesday, and he fully intended to take the car in on the following morning. A reasonable person could not have known from this letter that he ran the risk of an accident if he did not take the car in immediately.

"Jane Consumer testified, under oath, that her husband had only one glass of beer with his meal on the evening of the accident. That amount of alcohol could not have adversely affected his driving capabilities, nor was there any evidence that his driving was at fault. Jane heard a loud 'popping noise' that sounded like 'a spring breaking under tension' just before the car went out of control. Bill reacted by trying to right the vehicle, but the tires would not respond to the steering wheel because the weight of the vehicle had shifted to the rear when the coil broke. He applied the breaks in time to leave skid marks on the asphalt pavement, as Officer Goodcop testified.

"The defense has produced highly paid experts to try to convince you that this accident was caused by an 'act of God'—the weather did it! Seriously folks, you can't believe that. This accident was caused by their mistakenly assembled coil that broke just before the accident on that fateful night. Had the vehicle been properly balanced by two identical coils, and had the left coil not broken, there would have been no accident.

"Mack Racer is an expert mechanic who does not get $200 an hour to say what his employers want to hear. He gets his normal mechanic's fee, and he told you the truth. The coil broke before the accident, causing the front tires to lose traction, and this, in turn, caused the vehicle to hydroplane on the wet pavement.

"The legal standard in this case requires merely that you find that a defect existed that was not altered before it reached the user and that the defect was a proximate cause of the damages sustained.

"Ladies and gentlemen, we have proved those elements by a preponderance of the evidence. Proximate cause does not require absolute proof but merely that, in the chain of events, the accident would not have happened had the defect not existed. The reduced traction on the front tires caused by defectively mounted coils was a proximate cause of this accident. That condition existed whether you conclude the coil broke before or after the accident, and the accident would not have occurred had the manufacturer installed the proper identical coils on both sides of the vehicle."

Defendant's Closing Arguments

"Ladies and gentlemen of the jury, my able co-counsel, Maria Farmer, said in her opening statement, 'the tragic accident involved in this case was caused by unavoidable weather conditions and driver error, not by any alleged defective condition of the automobile in question.' The witnesses and evidence you have heard at this trial proved those facts. The suspension coils in question were not defective, unsafe, or dangerous. They were tested using 'state of the art' simulation technology as testified to, under oath, by a highly qualified engineer. His report concerning this extensive testing concluded that the coils were safe and would hold up for the 150,000-mile potential life of the vehicle. Mr. Tester also testified that even if the coil broke under expected driving conditions, the power steering mechanism would prevent the vehicle from going out of control.

"The medic who attended the accident victims and the hospital physician testified to the presence of alcohol on the driver's breath. Ladies and gentlemen, we do not have to prove that Bill Consumer was drunk on the evening of the accident. We have proven, however, that he had been drinking and that this affected his driving capabilities, lowering his reaction time, and causing him to be less cautious than he should have been under the adverse weather conditions he encountered.

"Bill Consumer had received a letter from the factory telling him to bring the car in for recall repairs. This he failed to do, and he therefore voluntarily assumed the risk of driving that vehicle after he had been warned of the risk.

"Finally, Professor Drivesafe, a nationally recognized authority on the causes of accidents, has testified that there was a measurable depression in the roadbed that created a drainage problem at the particular spot where Bill Consumer lost control of his vehicle. Officer Goodcop confirmed this finding by documenting two previous accidents and complaints about poor drainage in that same area. All the eyewitnesses to the scene of the accident testified to the heavy downpour that flooded the highway that night prior to the accident.

"The professor testified that the force of the crash and the twisting of the vehicle as it spun around in the highway caused the coil to break.

"Ladies and gentlemen of the jury, the defendant cannot be held liable for the damages resulting from this tragic accident because it was caused by the weather, road conditions, and driver error. These are conditions that are beyond the control of the manufacturer."

JUDGE'S CHARGE TO THE JURY

Judge Stern's instructions for the jury's deliberation were carefully prepared after the lawyers were given an opportunity to submit requested instructions to the judge in writing. Some courts have pattern instructions, which are model statements prepared by committees of judges and lawyers, and their use may be required in some jurisdictions.

Judge Stern took both of the lawyers' suggestions into consideration in preparing his **charge to the jury** in the *Consumer* case. He realized that the way he explained the law to the jury in his charge would be one of the most carefully reviewed aspects of the trial if an appeal were made. Therefore, he

Charge to the jury: Final address by the judge to the jury before the verdict; instructs the jury on the rules of law it must follow.

approached this task cautiously; taking care to explain the language of the law clearly so that the jury could understand the legal standards they would have to apply to the facts in this case.

He began by repeating his initial jury instructions given before the facts were presented. Reminding them that they would be the sole judges of the facts, the judge explained that the jury must consider the credibility of the witnesses, that they should not be influenced by any sympathy or prejudice they might feel regarding the parties, and that they must base their verdict entirely on the evidence presented in the form of testimony of witnesses and documents and exhibits admitted into testimony.

The judge then reviewed some of the facts in the case. He said there was no dispute about the fact that the manufacturer had assembled the automobile in question with rear suspension coils that varied in size and quality, that the vehicle was properly serviced and maintained, and that an accident had occurred involving the same vehicle that had been manufactured and sold by the defendant and was in substantially the same condition as when sold. Judge Stern then explained the law to be applied to the facts in dispute.

Judge Stern said, "Under the law of this state, one who sells a product in defective condition is subject to liability for physical harm thereby caused to the ultimate user or consumer if: (1) the seller is engaged in the business of selling such a product, (2) it is expected to and does reach the user or consumer without substantial change in the condition in which it was sold, and (3) the defective condition was the proximate cause of the injury to the plaintiff.

"All these elements must be present for you to find in favor of the plaintiff. Therefore, the elements in dispute in this case relate primarily to (1) whether the varied size and quality of the suspension coils constituted a defective product and (2) whether the condition of the coils was a proximate cause of the injuries sustained.

"An absolute defense in law is known as 'voluntary assumption of the risk.' That means that the plaintiff knew of the defective condition and assumed the risk with knowledge of the consequences. If you find that under the particular circumstances a reasonable person of ordinary prudence would have used the product despite knowledge of the defect or condition, you may still find for the plaintiff.

"The words 'defective condition' means a condition of a product that renders it unsafe for normal or reasonably anticipated handling and consumption.

"A defective condition proximately causes an injury if the defect directly and in natural and continuous sequence produces or contributes substantially to producing the injury, so that it reasonably can be said that except for the defective condition, the injury complained of would not have occurred.

"This does not mean that the law recognizes only one proximate cause of an injury or damage, consisting of only one factor or thing, or the conduct of only one person. On the contrary, many factors or things, or the conduct of two or more persons, may operate at the same time, either independently or together to cause injury or damage; and in such a case, each may be a proximate cause.

"The burden is on the plaintiff in a civil case, such as this, to prove every essential element of his claim by a preponderance of the evidence. If the proof should fail to establish any essential element of the plaintiff's claim by a preponderance of the evidence in the case, the jury should find for the defendant as to that claim.

"To 'establish by a preponderance of the evidence' means to prove that something is more likely so than not so. In other words, a preponderance of the evidence in this case means such evidence as, when considered and compared with that opposed to it, has more convincing force and produces in your minds belief that what is sought to be proved is more likely true than not true. This rule does not, of course, require proof to an absolute certainty since proof to an absolute certainty is seldom possible in any case.

"In determining whether any fact in issue has been proved by a preponderance of the evidence in the case, you the jury may consider the testimony of all witnesses, regardless of who may have called them, and all exhibits received and admitted into evidence, regardless of who may have produced them.

"I am charging you, the jury, with a special verdict that you must all agree to before your deliberation is complete. You will first elect your own chairperson to aid you in organizing your deliberation. Then you must answer the questions submitted to you *unanimously* (see Form 12.6). You are not finished until you all agree. Only if you find for the plaintiff will you proceed to answer the final questions concerning damages."

The judge then dismissed the alternate juror, and he told the remaining official jurors that he had concluded his charge and that it was time for them to assume their deliberation.

Verdicts

Judge Stern gave the jury a combined special and general **verdict** charge in this case. In federal courts, the judge has discretion to request either a general or a special verdict. A general verdict would require the jury to decide simply for one of the parties and, if damages were sought, to indicate the sum to be awarded. The judge also has the discretion under the federal rules to request a combined special and general verdict, as Judge Stern did in this case. This type of verdict gives the judge more information about the jury's reasoning and understanding involved. If inconsistency is evident, the judge may recharge the jury or order a new trial.

Verdict:
Formal decision or finding made by a jury concerning the matters of fact submitted to them.

Form 12.6 **QUESTIONS SUBMITTED TO THE JURY**

1. Was the condition of the two rear coils at the time of the accident a "defective condition" as defined in law?

   Answer unanimously, YES or NO _____

2. Was that defective condition a "proximate cause" of the injuries sustained in the accident?

   Answer unanimously, YES or NO _____

3. Did William P. Consumer use the automobile in question knowing the risks involved and voluntarily assume those risks?

   Answer unanimously, YES or NO _____

4. Do you find in favor of the plaintiff or the defendant?

   Answer unanimously, plaintiff or defendant _____

(Only if you find for the plaintiff will you proceed to answer the final questions concerning damages.)

5. What were the damages sustained by the estate of William P. Consumer?

   $_____

6. What were the damages sustained by Jane Consumer?

   $_____

The federal rules provide that the parties may stipulate that the finding of a stated majority shall be taken as the verdict. However, Maria Farmer stated in her written request for suggested jury charge that she demanded a unanimous verdict, and a Judge Stern was required to honor that request. Some states provide for less than a unanimous verdict in their rules of procedure.

THE VERDICT AND JUDGMENT OF THE COURT

The jury deliberated for several hours discussing this case. How would you have voted and why? How much would you award, if anything, to the plaintiff?

ASSIGNMENT: If a complete mock trial is not used, at least six students should play the roles of jurors and debate the verdict in class where all listen to the deliberation.

Judge Stern asked the jury to make sure the decision was unanimous and then asked the attorneys whether they wished to enter motions or objections. The judge found that the jury had discharged its function properly, and he entered **judgment** consistent with the jury finding.

Objections could have been raised about the procedure followed in this case, and they would have been entered into the record before the judge's decision. The judge could have ordered a **judgment as a matter of law (n.o.v.)**, which would have allowed the final judgment to differ from the jury's verdict, if he had agreed that a prejudicial (as opposed to harmless) error had taken place at trial. He also could have ordered a new trial or altered the jury's finding, but he would have needed to state a reason founded in law for such a decision.

Either party in a case may appeal the final judgment of the trial court (generally within 30 days). The next chapter discusses the appeal process.

Judgment:
The official decision of the court upon the respective rights and claims of the parties.

Judgment as a matter of law:
The judge overrules the jury verdict, in whole or in part, and enters a judgment as a matter of law (FRCP). State courts may still use the older term judgment n.o.v.

CHAPTER SUMMARY

1. This chapter illustrates the trial procedure that begins with the voir dire (or jury selection) process. This process is an important aspect of the jury trial because the persons selected to serve on the jury may affect the outcome. Opposing lawyers are careful to take advantage of every opportunity to prevent a potentially biased juror from being selected. It is the judge's responsibility to see that jury bias is eliminated to the extent possible.

2. The judge has wide discretionary authority to either conduct the voir dire alone or allow the lawyers to ask questions of the jurors. Some jurisdictions allow extensive leeway to lawyers in conducting the process. The judge, however, must decide all challenges for cause and rule on the qualifications of potential jurors.

3. The lawyers for each party in the dispute have a limited number of peremptory challenges that do not require a showing of cause to

disqualify a potential juror. In civil cases, the number of such challenges for each party is usually limited by statute to three, but this number may vary by jurisdiction and the particular circumstances of the case.

4. Trial arguments begin after the judge is satisfied that an impartial jury has been selected. The judge may provide preliminary jury instructions before the opening statements, but the detailed jury charge cannot be given properly until the evidence has been presented and the jury is ready for deliberation. The opening statements, first by the plaintiff and then by the defendant, are not evidence but provide the court with a brief overview of the subject matter of the case and the major areas of contention.

5. The plaintiff's case in chief follows the opening statements. It includes testimony of all witnesses for the plaintiff and presentation of material or documentary evidence. The opposing attorney may cross-examine each witness after the direct examination by the plaintiff's lawyer. There may be a second examination by the plaintiff's attorney, called the *redirect examination*, and a second examination by the opposing attorney, called the *recross-examination*.

6. The rules of evidence are detailed procedural rules that regulate the admission of evidence at trial. The rule that prohibits the use of leading questions on direct examination but permits such questions on cross-examination is a good example. "Relevancy," "asked and answered," and "argumentative" are typical objections to attempts to elicit testimony or admit evidence at trial.

7. An expert witness is permitted to answer opinion questions within the expert's area of expertise if the expert has been qualified or a proper foundation has first been established for the expertise of that witness. Otherwise, witnesses are restricted to firsthand knowledge of events they have personally observed that are relevant to the case.

8. The best evidence rule and the hearsay rule restrict evidence to that which is clearly authenticated; that is, there must be an opportunity to question the validity of statements or documentary evidence. The rules are quite complex and have many exceptions, but their purpose is to prevent unfair testimony that cannot be verified.

9. After the plaintiff's case in chief, the defense has an opportunity to present its case in chief to refute the claims made against them. After the defense has rested (ended) its case in chief, the judge calls for closing arguments.

10. The judge's charge to the jury is important: It instructs the jury about, and carefully explains, the principles of law the jurors are to use in arriving at their verdict. This charge will be carefully examined by

the appeals court if there is an appeal. The judge must explain the law clearly and make sure that the instructions are understood.

11. A directed verdict may be handed down by the judge at the end of the plaintiff's case in chief if the judge believes that the plaintiff has failed to present admissible evidence to support a valid claim. After the defendant's case in chief, the judge, again, can stop the trial if the judge believes no evidence has been offered to refute the plaintiff's claim.

12. The jury's verdict is not the final judgment in the case. Judgment is made by the court. The judge may set aside the jury's verdict if the judge is convinced that there was prejudicial error in the trial procedure.

REVIEW EXERCISES

Match the following terms with their appropriate meaning.

TERMS	MEANING
1. Voir dire	____ final address by the judge to the jury of their function and explanation of the law
2. Challenges for cause	
3. Peremptory challenges	____ court action that is the result of failure to present a prima facie case during case in chief of the plaintiff
4. Opening statements	____ rule prohibiting statements made out of court and offered to show the truth of matters asserted
5. Closing arguments	
6. Direct examination	____ questioning done by opposing counsel of the party who called the witness
7. Cross-examination	____ fixed number of challenges allowed each party
8. Rules of evidence	____ when the judge overrules the jury's verdict and enters a judgment as a matter of law
9. Leading questions	
10. Hearsay rule	____ presentation of facts that meet burden of proof and will prevail until contradicted by other evidence
11. Best evidence rule	
12. Expert witness	____ requires primary evidence, as opposed to secondary evidence
13. Directed verdict	____ initial questioning by the attorney who calls the witness
14. Burden of proof	____ challenges that are unlimited and made by the judge
15. Prima facie case	____ official decision of the court on respective rights and claims of the parties
16. Charge to the jury	____ required degree of evidence necessary to prove the contention of a party in a contested case
17. Verdict	
18. Judgment	____ questions that instruct witness or put words into the witness's mouth
19. Judgment as a matter of law (n.o.v.)	____ opposing attorneys' summaries of the evidence presented in the trial
	____ examination of jurors or witnesses to determine their qualifications to serve in these capacities
	____ formal decision of finding by a jury concerning the facts in dispute submitted to them
	____ one who is qualified to answer opinion questions relevant to that witness's field of knowledge
	____ detailed rules governing the admissibility of evidence at trials
	____ opposing lawyers' formulations of the nature of the case at the beginning of trial

DISCUSSION QUESTIONS

1. What are the characteristics of the jury selection process, and how can this process affect the outcome at trial?

2. How are challenges for cause and peremptory challenges decided during the voir dire process?

3. What is the basic procedure used for presentation of arguments and evidence at trial?

4. Why are opening and closing arguments by the lawyers not considered evidence?

5. When and how is documentary and material evidence presented to the court and jury at trial?

6. What are the basic purposes and rules concerning direct examination and cross-examination of witnesses?

7. What are some of the basic rules of evidence that regulate the admission of evidence at trial?

8. What is the reason for excluding hearsay evidence, and why are there many exceptions to this rule?

9. What are the assumptions underlying the adversarial roles of the opposing lawyers?

10. Why is the judge's charge to the jury the most carefully examined aspect of the trial by the appeals courts?

11. What is the function of the jury in the trial process, and how is it distinguished from the role of the judge?

12. What is the legal importance of the court's judgment as opposed to the jury's verdict?

ASSIGNMENT

ASSIGNMENT: Students should have been assigned roles as trial participants and/or jurors for the Mock Trial or jury duty in class. Assign matching exercises at end of the chapter.

SOURCES AND SUGGESTED READING

Blanchard, Roderick D. 1990. *Litigation and Trial Practice for the Legal Assistant.* 3d ed. St. Paul: West Publishing.

Devitt, Edward J., Charles B. Blackmar, and Michael A. Wolf. 1987. *Federal Jury Practice and Instructions (Civil).* Vol. 3. 4th ed. St. Paul: West Publishing.

Federal Rules of Civil Procedure. 2010. Available at federalrulesofcivil procedure.net. (See latest edition.)

Imwinkelried, Edward J. 1980. *Evidentiary Foundations.* Charlottesville, Va.: Michie Law Publishers.

Landsman, Stephan. 1988. *Readings on Adversarial Justice: The American Approach to Adjudication.* St. Paul: West Publishing.

Lewis, Alfred J. 1985. *Using American Law Books.* 2d ed. Dubuque, Iowa: Kendall/Hunt.

Tennessee Practice Series. (See latest edition.) *Tennessee Pattern Jury Instructions (Civil).* Vol. 8. St. Paul: West Publishing. (The reader's state may have a similar series of practice volumes that should be consulted for local practice.)

Evaluation of the Civil Process

The hypothetical *Consumer* case in products liability was developed in the last three chapters to illustrate what is involved behind the scenes in the preparation for trial in contested cases. However, this fictitious case was a simplification in order to make it a manageable demonstration of the stages of the civil trial process.

This chapter discusses the appeals procedure for both federal and state civil cases. It then continues to describe the functions of the appellate courts. The rest of this chapter is devoted to explaining the major problems of the appeals process in the area of civil litigation. Alternative dispute resolution (ADR) in civil cases is explained and illustrated, demonstrating that these programs have helped reduce the increasing caseload problem in civil litigation.

The general features of the appeals process are explained in this chapter, along with the manner in which civil legal actions are terminated. The court system is designed to provide a means of individual case evaluation for error correction as well as law development purposes. The intermediate appeals courts are concerned mainly with correcting errors and entertaining disputed issues of law arising from the trial courts.

This chapter also discusses some of the basic problems of our legal system in litigation. Many critics argue that major reforms are needed to improve the system. The most critical problems relate to the extensive caseload burden faced by the court system and the costs of modern civil litigation. These problems are explained, and some of the efforts being made to deal with them are discussed.

THE APPEALS PROCESS

A century ago, the only opportunity to reverse a final judgment was by "writ of error"; this reversal was difficult to accomplish and required an entirely new legal action. Since the 1950s, there has been an enormous expansion of the right of appeal granted through statutory and case law developments.

Contrary to popular belief, there is no automatic right of appeal granted by the U.S. Constitution. In the early history of the United States, appeals were limited by stringent rules. The federal circuit court was not established as a true appellate court until 1891, when the Evarts Act created three-judge panels that included a circuit-riding U.S. Supreme Court Justice to hear initial appeals from district courts.

In 1891 the basic structure of the federal appeals system was created, and in 1925 the jurisdiction of the Supreme Court was made almost entirely discretionary. The effect of this change was to make the decisions of the courts of appeal final in all but a very small percentage of cases (Martineau 1985, 13-14).

The Right of Appeal

Today, the federal appeals court has jurisdiction to review **final judgments** of the district courts as a matter of right in most cases. It also may hear certain interlocutory appeals from lower court judgments, such as injunctions or certifications of questions of law by trial judges to the appellate court.

There are only two states in which there is no right of at least one appeal from a final judgment (Virginia and West Virginia), even though the U.S. Supreme Court has refused to find that due process requires appellate review (Martineau 1985, 9).

There is no absolute **right of appeal** for all decisions rendered by a lower court or administrative agency. Federal and state constitutions and statutory provision create appellate courts and prescribe the types of cases that are within their jurisdictions. An appeal may be granted as a matter of right, such as from a trial court to an intermediate appellate court or only at the discretion of a superior appellate court, for example, by a grant of certiorari by the Supreme Court. If the decision presented does not meet the statutory requirements for review, the appellate court is powerless to hear the appeal and review is denied.

The right to appeal a decision is limited to those parties to the proceeding who are aggrieved by the decision because it has a direct and adverse effect upon their persons or property. In addition, an actual case or controversy must exist at the time of review. Issues that have become moot while the appeal is pending, and cases that have been settled during that time, are not reviewable.

The expansion of the right of appeal has been one of the important contributing factors to the tremendous increase in the workload of the courts. Seventh U.S. Circuit Court of Appeals Judge Richard A. Posner asserted that in the two decades of the 1960s and 1970s (1960-1983), the federal appeals courts increased their caseload by nearly 700 percent, and the district court caseload grew by only 250 percent (Posner 1985, 82).

Final judgment:
One that finally disposes of rights of parties, either upon the entire controversy or upon some definite and separate branch thereof. Trial court final judgment may then be appealed.

Right of appeal:
There is no absolute right of appeal. There is a right to appeal a decision that is limited to the parties who are adversely affected by a lower court decision, and there must be a case or controversy at the time of review.

Since then, the caseload of the federal appeals courts has declined to more reasonable increases. In the ten-year period from 2000 to 2009, the percentage increase in the cases filed in U.S. appeals courts has been reduced to 9.1 percent as opposed to the average annual increase reported by Posner of 29 percent (Judicial Caseload Indicators, 1).

Appeals Court Actions

The appeals court may affirm the lower court's decision, reverse that decision, or remand the case back to the trial court with directions for further action, such as a new trial. The court of appeals does not try the case again, but a panel of at least three judges conducts a review of the record, considering the arguments of both parties concerning the issues of law in dispute.

The **appellant** (party bringing the appeal, who now has the burden of proof) must convince a majority of the appeals court panel that the lower court committed legal or factual error sufficient to mandate a reversal. There are different types of error in the legal system. One is **prejudicial error** (as opposed to, harmless error) that results in a miscarriage of justice. An appellate court will reverse a lower court on a factual error if it finds that the lower court decision was "clearly erroneous." But, the appellate court looks more searchingly for legal error, and it usually reviews these errors under a *de novo* (or fresh look) standard of review. The concern of the appeals court is with issues of law in dispute that are related to the facts (evidence) presented. New facts are not entertained by the appeals court and must be presented to the trial court either by reopening the case (which is very difficult) or by securing an order from the appeals court requiring that a new fact-finding procedure be conducted.

Appellant: Party bringing the appeal, which has the burden of proof on appeal.

Prejudicial error: One that affects the final results of the trial, as opposed to harmless error.

Ability to Appeal

Although the right of appeal has been extended in modern times, the appellant must raise appropriate objections at the trial level and be able to demonstrate a cause of action founded in law for the appeal. Mere dissatisfaction with the trial outcome is not sufficient reason for appeal.

The discussion of the appeals process so far in this chapter applies to cases decided both in federal courts and in state courts in civil cases. However, our hypothetical case illustrates the use of the jurisdiction of the federal courts in cases where the parties are citizens of two different states. In such cases the substantive law of the state where the case is filed must be applied by the federal district court, but federal rules of procedure are applied in such cases.

In a hypothetical appeal of *Consumer v Factory Motor Company*, the appropriate appeals court would be the Federal Circuit Court of Appeals;

therefore, the Federal Rules of Appellate Procedure (FRAP) would apply. The following discussion will focus on the details of these federal rules; however, the state appellate courts have tended to follow these federal rules of procedure fairly closely. For detailed provisions of the rules of a state, consult that state's rules of appellate procedure. Both state and federal procedural rules are kept current on the Internet and must be consulted.

In federal district courts, the appellant must initiate an appeal at the trial court level by filing a notice of appeal with the district clerk within 30 days after the final judgment in civil cases. The district clerk must serve notice of the filing to the parties in the case by mailing a copy of the notice of appeal to each party's counsel of record—excluding the appellant's. (See FRAP Rules 3 and 4 for further details.)

The appellant is required to pay the initial cost of all required fees but may recover these costs after a favorable decision. The appellant must order a transcript of the necessary trial proceedings from the court reporter within 14 days after filing the notice of appeal. The appellant must comply with Rule 10(b) and must do whatever else is necessary to enable the clerk to assemble and forward the record. (See FRAP Rules 10 and 11 for details.)

The Appellate Briefs

The appellant's brief (written arguments) must be filed and served within 40 days after the trial record has been filed with the appeals court. The clerk usually notifies the parties of the date the record was filed, but failure of the clerk to give such notice does not excuse the late filing of the appellant's brief, which can result in dismissal of the appeal. Within 14 days after being served with the appellee's brief, and in any event not less than 7 days before argument, the appellant must serve and file the reply brief, if any (Rule 31, FRAP).

The **appellate brief** is a crucial part of the appeal process. Extreme care should be taken to prepare the brief in a manner that will be useful to the overloaded appeals court judges; in fact, successful appellate lawyers exercise extensive care in preparation of this document. Specific form and organization are required, and simplicity in substance and style is considered an absolute necessity for any litigant who wishes to receive the full attention of either state or federal appellate courts. These courts often adhere to very strict page limits on the appellate briefs.

Appellate brief: Written argument that must be filed on appeal by the party bringing the appeal.

Time elements vary for state appeals courts, but the majority of the state courts allow time periods similar to those of the federal courts. Strict requirements for length, for specific parts of the brief, and for the overall brief are imposed. For federal appellate courts, the initial brief of each party may not exceed 30 pages, and the appellee's reply brief may not exceed 15 pages. Length requirements vary for state appeals courts but average about the same as those for federal courts.

Rule 28 of the Federal Rules of Appellate Procedure (FRAP 28), which defines the contents of the appeal briefs, is the model for most state as well as federal courts. It provides that the appellant's brief include the following:

- A table of contents, with page references
- A table of authorities—cases (alphabetically arranged), statutes, and other authorities—with reference to the pages of the brief where they are cited
- A statement of court's jurisdiction
- A statement of the issues presented for review
- A statement of the case briefly indicating the nature of the case, the course of proceedings, and a statement of the facts relevant to the issues submitted for review with appropriate references to the record (FRAP Rule 28e)
- A summary of the argument, which must contain a succinct, clear, and accurate statement of the arguments made in the body of the brief and which must not merely repeat the argument headings
- The argument, which must contain appellant's contentions and reasons for them, as well as a concise statement of the applicable standard of review
- A short conclusion stating the precise relief sought

(See FRAP Rule 28 for more details.)

The **appellee** is the party against whom the appeal is filed. This party must be notified. An appeal stays payment of the trial damage award, which must not be paid until all opportunities for appeal have been exhausted. The appellee is given an opportunity to respond in writing to the appellant's brief.

Appellee:
Party against whom the appeal is filed. It may have been either the plaintiff or the defendant in the trial court.

The appellee's brief is due within 30 days after service of the appellant's brief. The appellee's brief must conform to the requirements of FRAP Rule 28 except that none of the following need to be included unless the appellee is dissatisfied with the appellant's statement:

1. The jurisdictional statement
2. The statement of issues
3. The statement of the case
4. The statement of the facts
5. The statement of the standard of review

ASSIGNMENT: Look up the Federal Rules of Appellate Procedure using the Internet. These rules change frequently, and one must consult the most recent version of these rules to be accurate in all details. Look up "appeal as a matter of right" and any other matters discussed in this chapter. State rules of appellate procedure may also be found by including the name of your state and rules of appellate procedure. The *Consumer* case was filed in federal district court, which uses federal procedural rules.

Appellate Court Functions

The appeals court has two basic functions: error correction and law development. The successful appellant must keep these functions in mind while preparing the brief. In jury trial cases, the general doctrine is that the jury finding must be upheld if there is sufficient evidence to support the verdict. Sufficiency of evidence at the appeals level means that there is adequate evidence in the record of facts from which the ultimate fact found by the jury can reasonably be inferred. The appellate court may not grant a directed verdict (or a judgment n.o.v.) absent an appropriate motion at the trial court level. The appellate court may not substitute its judgment for that of the jury. The appellant must show that the inferences drawn by the trial jury in favor of the appellee were unreasonable (Martineau 1985, 137).

At the appeals court level, the court may issue majority opinions, dissenting opinions, and concurring opinions, as do courts of final authority. This is, of course, possible since all appeals courts decide by majority vote. Dissenting and concurring opinions add to the understanding of the decision.

Oral Arguments

An important part of our Anglo-American heritage is the role played by oral arguments in the appeals process, but the increase in the caseload has substantially reduced the opportunity for oral presentation.

In English practice, appellate argument was exclusively oral once the record had been filed. The decision was announced at the conclusion of oral argument, with each judge stating that judge's opinion and reasoning. This tradition was extended to the United States and continued until recent years. "Gradually as the courts became busier they began to impose limitations of the length of oral argument. At first each side was allowed several hours, then one hour, then 30 minutes or even less." (Martineau 1985,101)

As of 2010, Rule 34 of the FRAP states that any party may file, or a court may require by local rule, a statement explaining why oral argument should, or need not, be permitted. Oral argument must be allowed in every case unless a panel of three judges who have examined the briefs and record unanimously agrees that oral argument is unnecessary for any of the following reasons:

1. The appeal is frivolous.
2. The dispositive issue or issues have been authoritatively decided.
3. The facts and legal arguments are adequately presented in the briefs and record, and the decisional process would not be significantly aided by oral argument.

The shortened time for oral argument has caused greater emphasis to be placed on the briefs. The general practice, in fact, is to allow oral arguments only when deemed necessary by the appeals panel.

MODIFICATIONS BY STATES TO STRICT LIABILITY

Several states have modified the concept of strict liability as used in the *Restatement of Torts* (second). Therefore, one must consult state statutes to find these modifications.

ASSIGNMENT: Look up your state's code on the Internet by using your state's name and code annotated. Search for the term "products liability," and you will find any new statutes that have been enacted in your state altering the common-law concept of strict liability. Find out what exceptions apply to the law of your state.

In the state of Tennessee, the Products Liability Act of 1978 added a positive legal set of provisions to the previously developed common law of strict liability (*402A Restatement of Torts* [Second]). The act made two important concessions to the manufacturers and sellers of products. Business and insurance interests had contended that traditional strict liability was unfair to producers. The legislature provided new requirements that call for jury instructions concerning "compliance with governmental standards" and "state of the art testing." Similar concessions have been made in many states in recent years.

The following language defines these concepts in Tennessee statutory law.

Tennessee Products Liability Act of 1978

Compliance With Governmental Standards

Compliance by manufacturer or seller with any federal or state statute of administrative regulation existing at the time a product was manufactured and prescribing standards for design, inspection, testing, manufacture, labeling, warning or instructions for use of a product, shall raise a rebuttable presumption that the product is not in an unreasonably dangerous condition in regard to matters covered by these standards. [Acts 1978 (Adj. S.), ch. 703, §4; T.C.A. §23-3704.]

---

continued >

> **State of the Art Testing**
>   (a) A manufacturer or seller of a product shall not be liable for any injury to person or property caused by the product unless the product is determined to be in a defective condition or unreasonably dangerous at the time it left the control of the manufacturer or seller. (b) In making this determination, the state of the scientific and technological knowledge available to the manufacturer or seller at the time the product was placed on the market, rather than at the time of injury, is applicable. Consideration is given also to the customary designs, methods, standards and techniques of manufacturing, inspecting and testing by other manufacturers or sellers of similar products. [Acts 1978 (Adj. S.) 703, §5, 8; T.C.A.§23-3705.]

Ending Civil Legal Actions

There must be some point of finality in civil legal actions, and on issues of state law, the state supreme court is the court of last resort. At this point of finality, the case is referred to as *res judicata.*

Res judicata means that the case is finally decided and cannot be the subject of a future suit involving the same parties. At this point, **satisfaction of judgment** (payment of the award for damages) is required. Further court action can be taken to impose satisfaction by attaching property owned by the defendant if voluntary compliance does not take place.

When all opportunity for appeal has been exhausted and the case is said to be res judicata (ended), this closure of the case is a form of estoppel known as *estoppel by judgment* (further legal action is barred). **Estoppel** refers to a legal procedure barring a variety of evidence, testimony, or legal actions.

Res judicata:
Finally decided; an action that is conclusive with regard to the same issues and parties.

Satisfaction of judgment:
Payment of the court award for damages.

Estoppel:
Legal procedure barring a variety of evidence, testimony, or legal actions.

PROBLEMS OF CIVIL LITIGATION

Many people believe that we have too many lawyers, that our laws are too complex, and that our procedures of adjudication are too cumbersome, causing excessive litigation and imposing excessive costs that benefit lawyers and litigants at the expense of society as a whole. These criticisms are serious and deserve consideration, even in an introductory text.

In comparison with most modern democratic societies, there are about four to five times as many lawyers in the United States (per 100,000 population) than in other modern societies. Our laws are complex and not easily understood by the general public. The litigation explosion of the past three decades is clearly evident in the enormous number of cases that have been filed, flooding our courts and tripling the caseload. The amount of litigation in state and federal courts is clearly larger than in other modern industrial societies, and the costs of the U.S. tort system are undoubtedly higher than those in comparable modern democracies.

The Caseload Problem

Recent statistics gathered by the National Center for State Courts indicate that the overwhelming method of disposition of civil legal actions in state courts is by out-of-court settlement. If dismissal and default cases are excluded, some three-fourths of the cases are normally settled out of court. Only about 10 percent of civil cases go to trial, and more than three-fourths of these cases are conducted as bench trials as opposed to jury trials.

The 2001 *Civil Justice Survey of State Courts: Supplemental Survey of Civil Appeals* tracked appeals from civil trials held during 2001 in 46 of the nation's 75 most populous counties. This study provides some useful conclusions as to the process of appeal. "Case types typically involving more severe injuries, complex medical or scientific evidence, or expert testimony; for example, product liability claims, were appealed most frequently. On the other hand, the most prevalent types of tort claims, such as premises liability and automobile torts, were least likely to be appealed, putting the medical malpractice appeal rate just below the median among tort case types."(Lee and Waters, 2009, 1)

This study also found that product liability cases, not related to asbestos cases, were the most frequently appealed. Of these cases, 33 percent involved an appeal. Medical malpractice was below the median with an appeal rate of 18 percent. Motor vehicle torts had an even lower appeal rate of 6 percent.

Evidence indicates that the appeals explosion has been subsiding. The rising caseloads, particularly at the appeals level of the 1980s and 1990s, have prompted a shift in resources in many civil courts. Data gathered by the National Center for State Courts indicate that dismissals and defaults constitute a large percentage of the civil dispositions in most states.

Negotiated settlements often occur at the end of the discovery process. The use of pretrial conferences to encourage settlement has become a principal tool of civil case management in many states and individual trial courts. However, the shift in emphasis from trial to settlement may raise new questions about the importance of nontrial methods of disposition in civil cases. For example, some critics contend that many suits are initiated for minor damage claims that are settled out of court mainly because the defendant finds it less costly to pay the settlement than to incur the expense of litigation.

ALTERNATIVE DISPUTE RESOLUTION

James J. Alfini, editor of a special issue of *Judicature* in 1986, declared, "[T]he alternative dispute resolution (ADR) movement has taken hold in the United States and is now an established fact." Alfini describes the ADR movement as the second major wave of judicial reform in this country. The first wave emphasized the need for structural and administrative changes in the nation's judicial system, whereas this wave emphasizes the alternative dispute resolution techniques explained below (Alfini 1986, 252).

ADR refers to the multiplicity of procedures used to assist the parties in civil disputes to settle these disputes through mutual agreement. While there are other techniques used, the essential methods are mediation, conciliation, and arbitration. In **mediation**, a third party assists the disputing parties in identifying the points of agreement and disagreement and in finding bases of compromise and possible agreement. In **conciliation**, a third party finds possible solutions in the areas of disagreement and proposes these solutions to the disputants. **Arbitration** is a method by which the parties agree in advance to abide by the decision of a third party.

Mediation:
In which a third party assists in the negotiation of a dispute.

Conciliation:
In which a third party proposes compromise solutions to a dispute.

Arbitration:
In which parties agree in advance to abide by the decision of a third party to avoid litigation.

Court-Annexed Arbitration

One of the most important developments in the ADR movement has been the extensive degree to which mandatory court-annexed arbitration has been adopted by state and federal courts. In 1986 there were an estimated 200 court-administered mandatory arbitration programs in the country's trial courts (Alfini 1986, 271). The first arbitration statute appeared in New York in 1920, and it provided a basis for the Uniform Arbitration Act of 1955, a model law that was adopted by most states and the federal government. The federal government has long encouraged arbitration in labor management disputes and more recently in the area of claims disputes. Court-mandated arbitration, however, is a new concept that is expanding rapidly as a means by which to efficiently handle many types of disputes.

Today, most states and the federal government have promoted the expansion of alternative dispute resolution programs, which have substantially reduced the expansion of litigation in our society. Like many state supreme courts and the federal government, the Tennessee Supreme Court created a commission in 1992 to study alternative dispute resolution in its state. This study was to proceed "with a view toward the use and implementation of procedures to expedite and enhance the efforts of the courts to secure the just, speedy, and inexpensive determination of disputes."

The recommendations of the 1992 commission resulted in the enactment of Supreme Court Rule 31 in January 1996, to establish court-based ADR on a statewide basis. Rule 31 created a system in which litigants, courts, and attorneys can locate qualified alternative dispute resolution mediators and other neutral parties and enlist their assistance in resolving matters pending before courts of record.

Rule 31 does not affect private dispute resolution programs in individual cases that are resolved outside the Rule 31 system. Any case may go to mediation, arbitration, or other form of dispute resolution without having to go through the Rule 31 process. The rule was set up to assist the court in obtaining a mediator or other neutral party when the court or the parties want one.

Rule 31 also established a new alternative dispute resolution commission, which spent over a year devising a way that ADR neutral parties could be trained and approved for use by the courts. During this time, the rule was amended to include more detail regarding the credentials and training required for mediators. The current rule was filed in December 1996 and amended in July 1997.

ASSIGNMENT: Look up the term "alternative dispute settlement" for your state on the Internet and find out what private and public services are available. The list of Rule 31 mediators in Tennessee can be found on the home page of the Administrative Office of the Courts Web site at www.tsc.state.tn.us (select "Programs" and "ADR/Rule 31"). This Web site will provide further information about how to qualify for civil and family mediator courses and how to become listed as a Supreme Court Rule 31 mediator.

Most civil mediators are lawyers, but a considerable number have social work or psychology backgrounds, particularly family mediators. There are also family mediators specifically trained in domestic violence. To become qualified as a mediator there are specific training requirements, such as completing a 40-hour civil course to qualify as a general civil mediator, a 46-hour family course to qualify as a family mediator, and a 12-hour domestic violence course to qualify for designation as a specially trained domestic violence mediator.

Government-sponsored programs offering dispute settlement services are not the only agencies involved. There are also many private groups that offer ADR programs. The major advantage of both types of these programs is to provide an alternative means of settling disputes in a fraction of the time and expense of hiring the traditional attorney. However, other advantages include reduced caseloads and less demand on court resources.

In many of these procedures, the participants are more pleased with the outcome than they would be had they gone through court proceedings because they were allowed to contribute their own input to effect a solution to the conflict. ADR procedures have produced a number of important solutions to the problems of the courts. These results have not only reduced the overcrowded courts but they have also done the following:

- reduced overall costs to litigants
- led to quicker resolution of cases
- improved communication between parties
- facilitated better situations for children in divorces
- generated higher satisfaction levels with the legal system

Respondents to the Tennessee evaluation of the overall impact of the Rule 31 program also noted that at the systems level mediation is helping to "humanize" the legal system.

Arbitration is distinguished from mediation in that in arbitration the parties contract to abide by the arbitrator's decision. The parties select an arbitrator from a specified list of neutral third parties. A mediator, on the other hand, is essentially a third-party facilitator of a negotiated settlement between the disputing parties. Mediation has long been used in marriage counseling and other forms of personality conflicts in which a disinterested third party can facilitate communication and amicable settlement of difficult issues more effectively than can a court.

Court-annexed arbitration is a process in which the judges refer civil suits to arbitrators to render prompt, nonbinding decisions. If a particular decision is not accepted by a losing party, a trial *de novo* (anew) may be held in the court system. Variations of arbitration methods are being widely experimented with, and some of these methods have been thoroughly institutionalized, such as the Philadelphia court-administered arbitration program initiated in 1952, which was the first of its kind.

Labor-management contracts have commonly used binding arbitration clauses that provide particular rules of arbitration procedure and stipulate in advance the agreed-on method for settling various types of disputes. This method of providing for arbitration in advance has been extended to many business interests, and arbitration is becoming widely used to settle intercompany disputes. Many of these arbitration programs use retired judges as arbitrators, and costs are held to a minimum. Binding arbitration contracts are used in many industries, including textile, construction, life and casualty insurance, canning, livestock, air transportation, grain and feed, and securities.

The Tennessee Supreme Court Rule 31 program is relatively new, and its 2005 report finds that mediation was the most commonly used ADR process. The second most commonly used ADR process was the judicial settlement conference. Although arbitration was reportedly used, it most often was described as binding arbitration that was contractually required and thus not Rule 31 arbitration, which is voluntary and more associated with private resource services. Summary jury trials and minitrials were reported but rarely used. Case evaluation was reported as the least-frequently occurring ADR process, and in many counties did not occur at all.

ADR procedures were most often used by circuit courts and very rarely used by general sessions courts in Tennessee (see Table 13.1). General session judges also reported that they made referrals to victim offender reconciliation programs (VORPs), community-based mediation programs, and private mediators, some of which are Rule 31 listed (Nixon 2005, 4).

ADR programs vary widely in procedure and variety of alternative methods of conflict resolution. While they cannot be applied to solve all civil disputes, they have been effective in providing out-of-court solutions in many situations. Private dispute settlement programs have long served insurance companies and other industry and business concerns to hold costs down and speed up the legal process. Today, the ADR concept is in widespread use throughout the country. It is recognized as a way to reduce delay, reduce cost, and increase consumer satisfaction in the outcome of certain types of disputes. With the advent of court-annexed ADR programs in most states, the use of these procedures has been greatly expanded.

Still much must be done to overcome the many barriers to further expansion of ADR procedures. The most frequently cited barriers to ADR programs are cost, negative attitudes of attorneys, lack of public awareness, unrealistic expectations of litigants, and lack of preparation by attorneys. Other common themes include "not mediating in good faith" and/or not having persons of authority "at the table" during mediation attempts. Studies indicate that respondents also mentioned turf issues, for example, competition between attorneys and mediators for billable hours. Lack of education about and experience with "quality" mediation was highlighted as a barrier (Nixon 2005, 9).

Urban areas are more widely aware of ADR programs, and such areas have more extensive court rules that encourage or require mediation or other ADR procedures. They also have more access to trained neutral mediators and conciliators of better quality than those in rural areas. In Tennessee only about 3 percent of the mediations were conducted *pro bono* (as a public service from the mediator), and most of these were conducted through VORPs or community-based mediation programs. Cost was most often seen as a barrier in family mediation. One judge saw mediation as an added expense: "Most people can't afford to get divorced, let alone the cost of mediation." Further, it was more often perceived as an issue when mediation started later in the litigation process, thus adding to the perception that mediation was an extra step when attorneys negatively "couched" mediation as simply a requirement (Nixon 2005, 9).

In Tennessee, efforts are being made to expand the availability of *pro bono* or reduced-fee mediation services, particularly for low-income, *pro se* litigants (in his/her own behalf) and/or litigants living in rural areas who

Table 13.1 **LOCAL COURT RULES IN TENNESSEE RELATED TO ADR**

Civil	Family	Other
Construction contract disputes ". . . shall first be submitted to mediation before being set for trial." (Some counties) Circuit Court and Chancery Court: "In order to facilitate the expeditious hearing of the case, to limit the expense of litigation, and to enhance the goals of the judiciary all litigants are encouraged to seek mediation of cases." (Includes family disputes) Circuit Court: A questionnaire concerning ADR will be sent to each filing party or served with the complaint. Each party will send the form back indicating whether they wish to engage in an ADR procedure. This response form will then be routed to the individual judge. (Some counties) Circuit Court and Chancery Court: "Upon agreement of the parties or upon order of the court any matter may be referred to a Mediator. . . ." (Also includes family disputes; some counties)	Domestic cases involving minor children: All parents are required to attend parenting education and mediation seminars. (Some counties) It is the duty of clerks to disseminate Parent Plan packets. It is also the duty of attorneys to furnish copy of Parent Plan packets to clients, assist clients, and submit order to mediate or waiver request if no agreement within 120 days. (Some counties) Circuit Court: Defendants who dispute temporary Parent Plans may contact agency to begin ADR. In postdivorce filings, the previous plan will continue until education seminar and ADR is completed or waived. (Some counties) Chancery Court: Contested divorces, alimony, child support cases not set for trial until mediation and at least one pretrial conference with chancellor takes place. Mediation waived only in extraordinary circumstances. If mediation is unsuccessful, cases will go to settlement conference, if pretrial conference is unsuccessful, ". . . proceed in good faith, to mediation. . . ." "The mediator is to file a report, and if the mediation was unsuccessful, the mediator	General Sessions Court: For all civil and selected criminal cases, persons will be informed of mediation option. (Some courts) Probate Courts: In contested cases, the court encourages parties to attempt to resolve their differences through mediation. (Some counties) Chancery Court: "In contested divorces at least 15 days prior to the hearing attorneys shall exchange settlement offers." (Some counties)

continued >

Civil	Family	Other
	is to indicate if a party did not cooperate and did not participate adequately in the proceedings." (Some counties) Role of Attorneys in ADR: "Attorneys are expected to act as advisors and counselors and not as litigators."	

do not have access to mediation resources. More attention needs to be devoted to ensure equal access to mediation services for those in poverty situations and among the minority population, particularly within the Hispanic population. Those with issues of culture and language barriers require written materials and bilingual mediators (Nixon 2005, 16).

ADR programs need to increase measurement and reporting of the use and outcomes of ADR experiences. Many acknowledge that they currently have no idea of how often ADR/mediation is used. Mediators also acknowledge the need for more information about the use and outcomes of mediation. Some courts have attempted local measurement, as have some victim offender reconciliation programs. As more judges and attorneys become involved with ADR programs, they are increasing their support for these procedures. However, there is a frequently cited need for additional training and education for judges and attorneys related to ADR benefits. There is also a need for increased training for nonattorney mediators related to legal issues. Finally, a major barrier to use of ADR procedures is the lack of general public knowledge and understanding of these methods and their benefits.

THE LIABILITY PROBLEM

Civil legal actions cover a wide range of types of disputes, including domestic relations, contract, and real property disputes as well as torts. However, the major areas of controversy in civil disputes relate to torts. There are many types of torts, including not only products liability but also medical malpractice and other forms of professional malpractice. Worker's compensation is another major controversial area of law. These controversial areas have received much publicity and are the subjects of heated debate. Insurance providers argue that huge increases in insurance premiums are caused by increased litigation and excessive awards in these areas.

The hypothetical *Consumer* case involving a products liability tort was used in this text because it illustrates a major area of controversy. The example demonstrates a number of legal issues, including the full range of possible judicial procedures. Tort claims, however, represent only a small percentage of the total number of civil cases filed—less than 10 percent in most states, according to the National Center for State Courts.

Contract disputes are more numerous than tort claims and account for a larger portion of the court caseload. Generally, two or three times as many contract cases are filed annually than tort cases in the nation's courts. Together, contract, real property, and domestic disputes constitute the overwhelming majority of civil cases filed in the courts of general jurisdiction. There is insufficient data on the question of whether tort filings have been increasing or declining in relationship to contract and real property cases.

TORT REFORM

The **tort reform** movement began as a general reaction on the part of insurance companies and producers who were forced to shoulder the burden of new liability risks. Peter Schuck (1991) refers to this development as the "politicization" of tort law. This development is illustrated in Tennessee by the alteration of the traditional strict liability common law by statutory enactment. Many states have intervened in this traditional area of common law to enact statutory changes. Nearly every state legislature has enacted tort reform statutes. These reforms were the consequence of the two general waves of tort reform activity, first in the late 1970s and then in the latter part of the 1980s. There is still much controversy over tort reform in the second decade of the twenty-first century.

Congress has been embroiled for more than two decades in disputes over new proposals designed to alter or supplant common-law rules. It has been reluctant to enter this traditional state sphere of authority, but the state changes have been quite far-reaching. Almost all have been in the direction of limiting liability, most commonly by imposing caps on pain and suffering awards and by cutting back on doctrines such as joint liability punitive damage awards that the courts had fashioned.

Tort reform:
Movement to modify tort concepts through legislative enactment.

EXCEPTIONS TO STRICT LIABILITY

The *Consumer* case assumed that the law of Middle State applied the traditional concept of *strict liability* defined in section 402A of the *Restatement of Torts* (Second). However, many states have added new exceptions to this traditional concept, making actual cases more complex.

High-visibility tort actions in modern times have increased the contro-versy over tort reform. Mass society has produced mass action lawsuits. A **class action lawsuit** is one in which one or more persons sue or are sued as representatives of larger groups similarly situated. Although class action suits have been possible for many years, their number has increased sub-stantially since the 1940s as they have become vehicles for issues involving civil rights, legislative reapportionment, welfare, consumer protection, and environmental matters.

The courts generally have favored class action suits because they con-solidate litigation and reduce the caseload when compared with numerous individual actions. Class action suits, however, reduce the chances of out-of-court settlement since compromise has to involve all litigants and cannot be made without the court's permission. The class action suit also diminishes the possibility that a case will be dismissed as moot because the original plaintiff has died. A deceased plaintiff's counsel, to continue the suit, need only substitute another member of the class as the plaintiff.

Congress authorized state attorneys general to bring class action anti-trust suits on behalf of state citizens in 1976. And in 1984, a federal judge in Philadelphia approved a suit against 55 asbestos manufacturers on behalf of the nation's primary and secondary schools, which was reportedly the first nationwide class action for property damage arising out of a products liability question. Federal courts have attempted to reduce the number of class action suits by ruling that each litigant in diversity cases must meet the $75,000 access limit and that all parties in some cases must be notified, but state courts are also frequently involved in class action suits.

Tort reform advocates point to the excessive economic costs of the American tort system and frequently attempt to use comparative data from other modern democratic societies to bolster their argument that the excessive costs of our tort system already does, or will eventually, harm our ability to compete in the international economic arena. Oppo-nents of tort reform claim there is little evidence connecting the workings of the tort system and skyrocketing liability insurance premiums.

There is considerable disagreement concerning the costs of our tort system and no conclusive method of measuring the costs. There is also little evidence of an agreed-on classification scheme by which to ascertain how much of the cost is attributable to the peculiar characteristics of our tort system.

Class action lawsuit: Legal action involving like-situated parties who may collectively sue or be sued.

CHAPTER SUMMARY

1. The appeal process is characterized by a review of the record of the trial court proceeding and concerns the appellate court's error correction and law development functions. The intermediate appeals courts are

involved mainly in error correction and are most concerned about the trial judge's conduct of the due process of law.

2. There is no absolute right of appeal, but there has been an extension of appeals granted as a matter of right in modern times. Appeal from a final judgment is given at least one opportunity for appeal in federal cases and most state cases.

3. The appeals process in federal district court can be initiated by either party raising objections at the trial level concerning questions of law and then filing a notice of appeal with the district clerk. The district clerk then serves notice of the appeal to the opposing parties.

4. The appellant is the party bringing the appeal and is required to pay the initial fees, but fees may be recovered later. Within 14 days after filing notice, the appellant must order a transcript of the necessary proceedings.

5. The appellant is required to file a brief within 40 days after the trial record has been filed with the appeals court. The appellee's brief must be filed within 14 days of receiving appellant's brief and not less than 7 days before argument.

6. The appeal briefs must conform to specific rules concerning length and content. They are now limited in federal court to no more than 30 pages for the appellant and 15 pages for the appellee. Oral arguments have been reduced in general practice to those deemed necessary by the appeals panel.

7. A finding of prejudicial error or legal error may result in reversal of the trial judgment or a remand of the case back to the trial court for further fact-finding procedures. These decisions are made by a majority of a panel of at least three judges.

8. The law development function is usually reserved to the court of last resort, which is usually the state supreme court in questions of state law. When all opportunity for appeal is exhausted, the case is res judicata, or brought to a final conclusion.

9. The traditional concept of strict liability in tort has been altered by statutory exceptions that seek to accommodate new demands for change. Actual cases in modern times are complex and demand consideration of many legal issues related to the public interest.

10. Modern class action law suits have increased public awareness of a growing litigation and liability crisis in our legal system. Not only the number of cases but also the increased costs of our tort system are major problems affecting the civil process.

11. Recent trends indicate a slowing of the growth rate in number of cases filed and appealed. The overwhelming majority of cases filed are dropped, dismissed, or settled out of court; less than 10 percent are contested, and most of these are handled by bench trials. Only about 1 percent of the total cases filed in civil courts are handled by jury trials.

12. Alternative dispute resolution (ADR) techniques involving mediation, conciliation, and arbitration are becoming widely used as a means of

dispute settlement that does not involve the full range of judicial process.

13. The liability problem is related mainly to the area of civil law known as torts. However, torts are only a small percentage of the civil caseload of the courts. Cases concerning contracts, domestic relations, and real property far outweigh the tort cases. Tort disputes constitute only about 10 percent of the civil cases filed.

14. The modern tort reform movement has raised major issues in the area of torts, and this area of law is the most controversial one involving the civil law process.

15. Highly publicized class action law suits and press reports of problems associated with insurance premiums and tort damage awards have increased public awareness of the problems in this area of law.

REVIEW EXERCISES

Match the following terms with their appropriate meaning.

TERMS	MEANING
1. Final judgment	____ movement to modify tort concepts through legislative enactment
2. Right of appeal	____ legal action involving like-situated parties who may collectively sue or be sued
3. Appellant	____ finally decided; ending the legal action
4. Prejudicial error	____ one that affects the final results of the trial, as opposed to harmless error
5. Appellate brief	____ party bringing the appeal
6. Appellee	____ parties agree in advance to abide by decision of third party to avoid litigation
7. *Res judicata*	____ legal procedure barring evidence, testimony, or legal action
8. Satisfaction of judgment	____ party against whom the appeal is filed
9. Estoppel	____ one that ends the trial on the merits of the case, but can be appealed
10. Class action lawsuit	____ where a third party proposes compromise solutions to a dispute
11. Mediation	____ payment of the court award for damages
12. Conciliation	____ written argument filed with the appeals court by the party bringing the appeal
13. Arbitration	____ where a third party assists in the negotiation of a dispute settlement
14. Tort reform	____ there is no absolute right, but there is appeal as a matter of right

DISCUSSION QUESTIONS

1. What are the most important functions of the appellate courts?

2. How are decisions made by the panel of appeals court judges?

3. How is a civil legal action finally terminated, and what are the consequences of this final termination?

4. How important was the law in determining the outcome in the hypothetical *Consumer* case?
5. Would "government standards" and "state of the art testing" exceptions have made a difference?
6. What are some of the most important issues in the area of civil litigation in the United States?
7. What alternative dispute resolution (ADR) techniques are available to reduce the caseload of the courts?
8. Is there a liability crisis concerning the costs and benefits of the U.S. tort system?

ASSIGNMENTS

ASSIGNMENT: Look up the Federal Rules of Appellate Procedure using the Internet. These rules change frequently, and one must consult the most recent edition of these rules to be accurate in all details. Look up "appeal as a matter of right" and any other matters discussed in this chapter. State rules of appellate procedure may also be found by including the name of your state and rules of appellate procedure. The *Consumer* case was filed in federal district court, which uses federal procedural rules and is obligated to use state substantive rules.

ASSIGNMENT: Look up your state's code on the Internet by using your state's name and code annotated. Search for the term "products liability," and you will find any new statutes that have

been enacted in your state altering the common-law concept of strict liability. Find out what exceptions apply to the law of your state.

ASSIGNMENT: Look up the term "alternative dispute settlement" for your state on the Internet and find out what private and public services are available in your state. The list of Rule 31 mediators in Tennessee can be found on the home page of the Administrative Office of the Courts web site at www.tsc.state.tn.us (select "Programs" and "ADR/Rule 31"). This Web site will provide further information about how to qualify for civil and family mediator courses and how to become listed as a Supreme Court, Rule 31 mediator.

SOURCES AND SUGGESTED READING

Alfini, James J., ed. 1986. "Alternative dispute resolution and the courts: An introduction." 69 *Judicature* (February-March).

Judicial Caseload Indicators, Administrative Office of the U.S. Courts, 2009.

Lee, Cynthia G., and Nicole L. Waters. 2009. "Medical Malpractice on Appeal." 16 *Caseload Highlights* 4. (Data from the 2001 Civil Justice Survey of State Courts: Supplemental Survey of Civil Appeals.)

Martineau, Robert J. 1985. *Fundamentals of Modern Appellate Advocacy*. Law Student and Moot Court ed. Rochester, N.Y.: Lawyers Co-operative Publishing.

Murphy, Walter F., and C. Herman Pritchett. 1986. *Courts, Judges, and Politics: An Introduction to*

the Judicial Process. 4th ed. New York: Random House.

National Center for State Courts. 2009. *State Court Caseload Statistics: Annual Report 2009*. Williamsburg, Va.: National Center for State Courts. (See also www.ncsconline.org.)

Nixon, Carol T. 2005. "Evaluation of Supreme Court Rule 31: A Qualitative Assessment of Mediation in Twelve Counties: Final Report Approved by the Tennessee Supreme Court Alternative Dispute Resolution Commission, January 31, 2005." Nashville, Tenn.: Tennessee Supreme Court Alternative Dispute Resolution Commission.

Ostrom, B., and N. Kauder, eds. 1997. *Examining the Work of State Courts, 1996: A National Perspective from the Court Statistics Project*. Williamsburg, Va.: National Center for State Courts.

Posner, Richard A. 1985. *The Federal Courts: Crisis and Reform*. Cambridge, Mass.: Harvard University Press.

Schuck, Peter H., ed. 1991. *Tort Law and the Public Interest: Competition, Innovation and Consumer Welfare*. New York: W.W. Norton.

UNDERSTANDING CRIMINAL LEGAL PROCEDURES

The next four chapters of this text illustrate the major procedural stages of a felony criminal case. Both state and federal governments must adhere to an extensive set of U.S. constitutional guarantees of "due process of law" in the exercise of the government's fundamental responsibility to see that the laws are faithfully executed.

The first chapter in this section introduces a hypothetical criminal case and provides an overview of the constitutional developments regarding criminal due process. The case is followed through the pretrial, trial, and appeal stages and illustrates the functional responsibilities of the control, court, and corrections subsystems of the criminal justice system.

Introduction to Criminal Legal Process

CHAPTER 14

Capital City Banner August 12, 2010
Critical Shooting in Market Robbery

The Jiffy Stop convenience market (at State and Fifth streets) was the scene of an armed robbery last night. The owner, Samuel J. Stone, is reported to be unconscious and in critical condition at Central Hospital after receiving a gunshot wound to the head.

Capital City Police indicate the shooting occurred just before midnight. They were called to the scene by a customer who saw an automobile speed out of the service area of the market and who later discovered the victim and an empty cash register. Police were able to apprehend a prime suspect within hours because of the alert customer's observations.

The suspect is being held for questioning, and police are checking out his story before making official charges.

The newspaper account of an armed robbery involving a convenience store describes an all too familiar occurrence in modern urban centers. However, this incident and subsequent events, as described in the next four chapters, demonstrate the basic concepts of criminal procedure. Note that citations for cases referred to by name and date in each chapter can be found in the Sources and Suggested Reading section at the end of each chapter.

Frank Builder had reported the robbery to the police shortly before midnight on August 11. He had seen two young men jump into their car and speed away as he drove into the convenience store parking lot. Suspecting that something was wrong, he made a note of the car's license plate number. Inside the store, Mr. Builder found the store owner unconscious behind the counter—blood was streaming from his face, and he was clutching a pistol in his right hand.

Builder immediately called 911 and reported the emergency situation, then assisted the officers and paramedics in their efforts to save the victim. Three plainclothes officers from the robbery detail arrived at the scene shortly thereafter to begin their investigation.

383

INITIAL INVESTIGATION AND ARREST

The three officers from the robbery detail were briefed about what had been learned by the officers at the scene and were told the license number of the vehicle. One of the officers radioed in for a "make" on the license number. The detectives then asked Frank Builder to describe exactly what he saw when he arrived at the scene. The customer had calmed down, and the officers let him take his time to think of every detail.

He said he saw a young male with a dark complexion at a gas pump drop the hose and run to the passenger side of the car. He saw another figure run around the front of the car but did not get a good look at him. "He jumped into the driver's side, and the car shot out of there like they were in a big hurry," the witness explained.

He described the vehicle as a dark green passenger car, "pretty old, with several scrapes and dents in the fenders." He was unsure about the "make" of the car: "It wasn't an American car, some type of foreign compact, I think," he explained.

The police officers then cordoned off the gas pump area of the filling station and surrounding the store. They found one of the pump hoses on the concrete pedestal beside the pump and dusted it for fingerprints. They also found an automobile gas cap on the asphalt area near the pump. In the store they found the cash register empty, and they took photographs of the crime scene. By this time, the police dispatcher had been able to identify the owner of the vehicle. It was registered to one Jesse Williams, 367 Elm Street, Apartment 4, in Capital City.

Initial Arrest

The robbery detail had a suspect; the officers wrapped up their preliminary investigation quickly in order to follow this significant lead. A cooperative and observant witness had provided them with something concrete to pursue. Two of the plainclothes officers from the robbery detail were dispatched to the suspect's address while the third remained at the scene to finish the investigation.

Officer Jim Cox and Sergeant Mike Develon located Jesse Williams's address, which belonged to a small, four-unit apartment house on the west side of town. It was after 1:30 A.M.: There were no lights on in the apartment, and there was no car in the front parking lot or on the street that matched the description of the vehicle they were seeking. They decided to "stake out" the place and wait for the occupant to return. As they watched from a convenient vantage point, they called for a records check on the suspect. The department reported that they had no prior arrest or conviction record on this individual.

At 2:21 A.M., a dark gray, four-door Toyota Corolla pulled into the parking lot. It had the suspect's license number. The police officers immediately stopped the individual as he got out of the car and placed him under arrest. They identified themselves as police officers and told the suspect to keep his hands raised and to place them on the top of the car. Mike patted down the suspect to search for concealed weapons, and Jim Cox placed the handcuffs on him. No weapon was found on his person, so they looked inside the vehicle for a weapon.

The officers opened the glove compartment, looked under the seats, and thoroughly examined the passenger area of the vehicle. They found no weapon or other evidence connected with the robbery in the vehicle. They then examined the outside of the vehicle and noted several scratches and dents that corroborated the witness's description of the car, and they also noted the absence of a cap on the vehicle's gasoline tank. The vehicle was locked and sealed with police tape.

The suspect, Jesse Williams, was placed in the officers' vehicle, and while Jim drove to the police station, Mike explained to Jesse, "You have the right to remain silent, anything you say can and will be used against you in a court of law, and you have the right to an attorney to represent you." Jesse said that he understood his rights but that he did not know what this was all about.

Jail and Booking Procedure

At the police station, Jesse was strip-searched by the jailers while police officers Jim and Mike consulted with their partner on the robbery detail. The officers learned that the convenience store victim was in critical condition and was not expected to live. "That means we have a potential murder charge on this one," said the partner. "Let's get the eyewitness down here to make a positive ID," Mike commented. The third partner thought that could wait until the next day. Frank Builder had been a very cooperative witness, and he had been up most of the night. Mr. Builder had been told to come to the police station at 1:00 P.M. the next day.

Jesse was being processed for "booking." This procedure involves fingerprints and "mug shots" to identify and secure the prisoner. These forms of identification enable the police to check their records and national FBI files for possible aliases or other identification the suspect might have used to commit crimes in other areas. The suspect's body cavities and clothing were thoroughly searched, but no concealed weapons, contraband, or further evidence concerning the crime were found. A wrecker was sent to Jesse's apartment to tow his vehicle into the police impoundment lot since it was the most important evidence they had uncovered thus far.

Custodial Interrogation

The robbery squad called Jesse into an interrogation room for questioning. They again informed him of his right to remain silent and his right to a lawyer. He indicated that he understood his rights and wanted to know why he had been arrested. They asked him where he had been until 2:30 in the morning on a Tuesday night. He answered that he had been to see his girlfriend and gave them her name, address, and phone number. Jesse told the police he had been at his girlfriend's house all the time from 10:00 P.M. to 2:00 A.M. Mike asked, "Is that all you want to tell us?"

"Yes," Jesse replied, "but why are you holding me?"

They told him he was being detained on suspicion in connection with a robbery that took place at the Jiffy Stop convenience store. He denied any connection with the robbery.

Further Investigation

The police officers checked the suspect's story by going to his girlfriend's apartment. They checked the police records before they left and found that she had been convicted on charges of prostitution and drug possession. When they arrived, the sun was just coming up, and they were scheduled to go off duty in two hours. After knocking several times, they finally got her to the door. They asked whether she knew Jesse Williams. She answered that she did and that he was with her until 2:00 in the morning. They asked if she would let them come in, and she agreed.

The girlfriend said she had known Jesse for about six months and had gone out with him several times. They did not go out last night, but he came to her apartment.

"When did he arrive?" asked Mike Develon.

"I don't know exactly, but he left about 2:00," she replied.

"Could he have gotten here after midnight?" Develon asked.

"I don't know exactly, it was late and I was asleep on the couch," she said.

"Did he leave anything in the apartment?" asked Jim Cox.

"I don't think so, he brought a six-pack of beer with him, but that's all," she said.

The robbery squad found four beer cans in her trash and two full cans in the refrigerator. The girlfriend gave them permission to take them. The beer cans were carefully placed in plastic bags, and the officers left.

The robbery squad agreed to draft a report and leave a copy for the homicide department so that a detective could continue the investigation when the officers went off duty. They put a "hold order" on Jesse to prevent any possible release on bail. The homicide detective assigned to the case would coordinate a lineup procedure for the witness who would arrive at 1:00. The detective would go over the facts of the case and follow up on a requested FBI check on the suspect.

BASIC CRIMINAL CONCEPTS

Our federal system places primary responsibility for the maintenance of public order and domestic crime control in the state and local units of government. The federal government has no expressly delegated constitutional mandate to make or enforce uniform criminal justice standards for the United States.

This legal concept of state responsibility for the maintenance of public order is generally referred to as the state "police power." The state police power therefore is a reserved power of the states to enact and enforce laws that protect the health, safety, and morals of the people. The independent and decentralized police power is jealously guarded by the states. It is also interpreted by the courts to be one of the most fundamental characteristics of our form of federal government.

Crimes

What is a crime? The fundamental legal concept of crimes, as opposed to torts, is found in the public nature of this substantive area of the law. Crimes are acts or omissions prohibited by law that constitute wrongs against the state (or society as a whole) and must be prosecuted by a designated agent of the government. The concept of the "guilt" of the individual who is accused of having committed a crime is another fundamental characteristic that distinguishes crimes from torts.

An individual's guilt in connection with a crime becomes relevant only after it has been established that a crime has been committed, that is, only after a **prima facie case** has been established. Those elements that the prosecutor must plead and prove to show that a particular crime has been committed are referred to as the **corpus delicti** (or body of the crime). The two most fundamental elements of all serious crimes are:

1. *Actus reus*, the commission of some prohibited act; and
2. *Mens rea*, a criminal state of mind.

These concepts were introduced in Chapter 3 and the illustrative cases (*People v. Moore* and *People v. Braly*) in Appendix B. These ideas are expanded in the next few chapters to facilitate a deeper appreciation of how these basic principles affect the enforcement of criminal law. Each particular crime has its own distinctive elements; generally, the more serious the crime, the more elements it requires. If one or more of these elements is missing, the particular crime could not have been committed.

Prima facie case:
A case that will prevail until contradicted and overcome by other evidence.

Corpus delicti:
The body or substance of the crime, which ordinarily includes two basic elements: *actus reus* and *mens rea*.

Actus reus:
A wrongful act or deed that renders the actor criminally liable if combined with mens rea.

Mens rea:
A guilty mind or criminal intent; guilty knowledge and willfulness.

Development of Various Types of Crime

The development of our common law still influences the criminal law even though most substantive criminal offenses now are defined by statute. As the common law of crimes emerged in England during the twelfth century, one of the primary distinctions was between offenses considered *mala in se* and those that were *mala prohibita*. "Ordinary crimes" (i.e., murder, rape, theft, arson) were considered acts that were "bad in themselves" (*mala in se*). They were considered felonies that could be prosecuted in the central criminal courts. Crimes that were *mala prohibita*, on the other hand, were prohibited by legislation and were considered to be misdemeanors to be enforced by justices of the peace. These offences (rioting, poaching, vagrancy, drunkenness) were crimes because they were prohibited by the positive law (*mala prohibita*).

Modern legislative authorities have become the dominant lawmakers, and today almost all crimes are statutory in nature. The statutory elements of each crime can be found in modern criminal codes. However, these provisions are, in part, codifications of the ancient common-law crimes, and in some states certain aspects of common-law crimes continue to be enforced. Common-law definitions of the legal meanings of the words and phrases typically found in statutes continue our common-law heritage. Many of the classifications of types of crimes are heavily laced with court interpretations based on the common-law origin of these concepts.

Basically, the types of crimes classified as *mala in se* have remained fairly static, and all are considered felonies today. But those crimes known as *mala prohibita* have been greatly expanded. Modern legislatures have added two major groups to the traditional offenses: so-called victimless crimes and regulatory offenses. Victimless crimes (i.e., drug offenses, gambling, prostitution, and regulatory offenses) are the most prevalent types of crime today.

We will discuss **inchoate crimes** later in this illustrative chapter; however, it is important to provide a definition here. These crimes are defined as incipient crimes that generally lead to another crime. An assault has been referred to as an inchoate battery, though the assault is a crime in and of itself. The *Model Penal Code* classifies attempts, solicitation, and conspiracy as inchoate crimes.

Inchoate crimes: Incipient crimes such as attempts, solicitation, and conspiracy to commit crimes.

Treason, Felonies, and Misdemeanors

The common law divided crimes into three major groups according to the gravity of the offense: treason, felonies, and misdemeanors. This division has important legal consequences. In most states, misdemeanors are processed in different court jurisdictions from those of felonies, and convictions carry less severe punishments. The general dividing line between misdemeanors and felonies is one year imprisonment. Petty offenses (speeding, parking violations) are a fourth category of crimes that are treated as summary offenses. Such petty offenses are usually left to the discretion of a local magistrate who has the authority to dispose of them summarily (without trial); however, trials can be demanded, but they are rarely pursued.

Treason is a crime under federal law and some state laws. The U.S. Constitution Article 3, Section 3 states;

> *Treason against the United States, shall consist only in levying War against them, or in adhering to their Enemies, giving them Aid and Comfort. No Person shall be convicted of Treason unless on the Testimony of two Witnesses to the same overt Act, or on confession in open Court.*
>
> *The Congress shall have power to declare the Punishment of Treason, but no Attainder of Treason shall work Corruption of Blood, or Forfeiture except during the Life of the Person attained.*

U.S. Constitution

This is the only crime defined by the U.S. Constitution, and its limitations seem to reflect the experience of the Framers of the Constitution who were all accused of treason against British authority during the Revolutionary War. The majority of the states outlaw treason in their constitutions or statutes similar to that in the U.S. Constitution. There have been only two successful prosecutions for treason on the state level, that of Thomas Dorr in Rhode Island and that of John Brown in Virginia.

Treason:
Defined by the U.S. Constitution, Article 3, Section 3, as levying war against the United States by adhering to its enemies or giving them aid and comfort. Conviction requires two witnesses or confession in open court.

Felonies and Misdemeanors

The distinction between felonies and misdemeanors is the least understood concept in the classification of crimes. Both the state and the federal governments use this distinction, but each of the 51 jurisdictions has a somewhat different definition in statutory law of exactly what constitutes a felony and what constitutes a misdemeanor.

In general, a **misdemeanor** is a less serious crime. It usually is punishable by fines and short terms of incarceration in local jails or county workhouses. Misdemeanors are usually handled by somewhat different procedures from those used in felony cases, and they are disposed of in the local courts. Federal misdemeanors are offences for which the penalty is imprisonment for less than one year. In some states, however, a misdemeanor conviction can result in a maximum fine of $10,000 and imprisonment up to five years. The lack of a uniform standard has caused the U.S. Supreme Court to rule that in "right to counsel" issues, the accused has a right to counsel when the crime carries a potential jail sentence.

Felonies are the type of crimes discussed in the next four chapters. They are subject to the full range of "due process" procedures guaranteed

Misdemeanor:
Offenses lower than felonies, generally punishable by fine or imprisonment in a facility other than a penitentiary.

Felony:
Offense more serious than misdemeanor involving imprisonment for more than one year in most states.

by the U.S. Constitution. The states do not have uniform criminal justice procedures, but decisions of the Supreme Court in recent times have produced a uniform set of minimal standards that can be described as a "national criminal procedure" that is fairly uniform in character.

ASSIGNMENT: Find your state's criminal code by using the library or the Internet and look up the definition of particular crimes that are of interest to you. You can enter your state's name and criminal code, and it should be available on the Internet. You will need to have a term in mind, but you will be able to find the statutory provisions. Crimes within the District of Columbia are found in the D.C. Criminal Code.

CRIMINAL DUE PROCESS

The Bill of Rights in the U.S. Constitution was ratified in 1791 as a result of state concerns over the potential abuse of authority by the national government. Many of these ten amendments (especially the Fourth, Fifth, Sixth, and Eighth) are directly concerned with criminal due process of law.

The amendments originally were interpreted to limit only the federal government in its exercise of the authority given to it by the U.S. Constitution. State criminal procedures were regulated only by state constitutions and were subject to the limitations of their own bills of rights. The various bills of rights were derived from our common-law heritage and had many similarities, but there were substantial differences in both wording and interpretation.

The Fourteenth Amendment

The American Civil War (1861-1865) produced substantial constitutional changes that ultimately led to a set of uniform standards of criminal justice procedure throughout the United States. The Fourteenth Amendment (ratified in 1868) specifically states:

> *No State shall make or enforce any law which shall abridge the privileges or immunities of citizens of the United States; nor shall any State deprive any person of life, liberty, or property, without due process of law; nor deny to any person within its jurisdiction the equal protection of the laws.*

> Fourteenth Amendment to U.S. Constitution

The U.S. Supreme Court has struggled with the precise meaning of the "due process" clause of the Fourteenth Amendment since its ratification. Several individual Supreme Court Justices have argued that the intended meaning of the framers of the Fourteenth Amendment was to incorporate the Bill of Rights and apply those amendments to state criminal actions.

A majority of the Supreme Court Justices has never expressed this total incorporation view of the meaning of the Amendment's provisions. Instead, most Supreme Court Justices have held the common-law view that the Fourteenth Amendment protects "traditional notions" of due process. For example, Justice Benjamin Cardozo's majority opinion in *Palko v. Connecticut* (1937) expresses the philosophy that the Fourteenth Amendment refers to those principles "implicit in the concept of ordered liberty."

What Has Not Been Incorporated?

Several Supreme Court Justices have insisted that the due process clause neither imposes on the states all the requirements of the Bill of Rights nor restricts the reach of the Fourteenth Amendment to only those rights enumerated in the first eight amendments. Fundamental fairness, not mere compliance with the Bill of Rights, is the touchstone. Consequently, under the fundamental rights interpretation, a state may violate due process even though its procedure is not contrary to any specific guarantee in the first eight amendments.

Nonetheless, the Supreme Court has adopted a **selective incorporation doctrine** that combines aspects of both the fundamental rights and the total incorporation theories. This contemporary theory incorporates nearly all the provisions of the Fourth, Fifth, Sixth, and Eighth Amendments into the Fourteenth Amendment Due Process Clause and enforces them against the states in nearly every case, according to the same standards applied to the federal government.

Selective incorporation doctrine: Combines the fundamental rights concept with selected provisions of the federal Bill of Rights to define criminal due process of law required in the Fourteenth Amendment.

Most of this development has occurred since the 1960s and is associated with the Warren Court (the name given to the Supreme Court when Chief Justice Earl Warren presided) era that seemed intent on fashioning a clear set of minimal procedural guarantees in all criminal cases, whether prosecuted in the federal or state courts. There are only a few minor exceptions to these statements. The major exception concerns the Fifth Amendment requirement of grand jury indictment in criminal cases. In the case of *Hurtado v. California*, 110 U.S. 516 (1884), the U.S. Supreme Court majority opinion stated that "the 14th Amendment was not intended to guarantee the right of a grand jury indictment because it would have been specifically referenced." This precedent has never been overruled by the U.S. Supreme Court.

It has been on the basis of this decision that many states have abandoned the requirement for grand juries, usually replacing them with a process known as *information*. The **information** is a procedure that is used in most states instead of a grand jury indictment.

Information: In most states, the information is used in place of a grand jury indictment to bring a person to trial.

The Eighth Amendment prohibition against excessive fines and bails has, remarkably, never been ruled on by the Supreme Court since the issue has never been squarely presented in a specific case (Rossum and Tarr 1987, 427-29)

The specific words of the Constitution in the Fourth, Fifth, Sixth, and Eighth Amendments are of central concern to criminal justice procedure throughout the United States (for the specific wording of these amendments, see Appendix A). The relevant clauses and the Supreme Court cases that have established precedent for the incorporation of those particular clauses into the interpretation of the Fourteenth Amendment Due Process Clause are listed in Table 14.1.

Although there are numerous court decisions that must be consulted to appreciate fully the complexity of the constitutional limitations in the area of criminal due process, this text discusses only the most basic principles and the manner in which U.S. courts have developed the philosophy currently employed to enforce these constitutional limitations.

Table 14.1 **SELECTIVE INCORPORATION OF CRIMINAL PROCEDURAL RIGHTS AND YEAR OF APPLICATION TO THE STATES**

Rights	Case and Year
FOURTH AMENDMENT	
Unreasonable Search and Seizure	*Wolf v. Colorado* (1949)
Exclusionary rule (*Implied)	*Mapp v. Ohio* (1961)
FIFTH AMENDMENT	
Grand Jury Clause	Not incorporated
Double Jeopardy Clause	*Benton v. Maryland* (1969)
Self-Incrimination Clause	*Malloy v. Hogan* (1964)
SIXTH AMENDMENT	
Speedy Trial Clause	*Klopfer v. North Carolina* (1967)
Public Trial Clause	*In re Oliver* (1948)
Impartial Jury Clause	*Parker v. Gladden* (1966)
Jury Trial Clause	*Duncan v. Louisiana* (1968)
Notice Clause	*Cole v. Arkansas* (1948)
Confrontation Clause	*Pointer v. Texas* (1965)
Compulsory Process Clause	*Washington v. Texas* (1967)
Right to Counsel Clause	*Gideon v. Wainwright* (1963)
EIGHTH AMENDMENT	
Excessive Fines and Bails Clause	Not incorporated
Cruel and Unusual Punishment Clause	*Robinson v. California* (1962) (The complete citations for these cases above are provided in the following discussion and at the end of the chapter.)

The Exclusionary Rule

The U.S. Supreme Court has developed a unique remedy for implementing the constitutional guarantees in the area of criminal due process. That remedy is often referred to as the "exclusionary rule" because it invokes a rule that prohibits the use of evidence obtained in violation of the U.S. Constitution. Most democratic societies, including the United Kingdom, allow evidence to be introduced that is relevant to the guilt or innocence of a person no matter how it was obtained. After the case is settled in these countries, the police officers who have violated the constitution may be punished for their own violations of the law in a separate tort action (Wilson 1989, 505).

The American evidence principle is sometimes referred to as the "poisoned fruit doctrine." The doctrine argues that if the tree is poisoned, so is its fruit; therefore, even evidence that proves a defendant's guilt beyond a reasonable doubt cannot be entered into evidence at trial if it was secured in an unconstitutional manner.

The basic philosophy of the Supreme Court was clearly established with regard to federal criminal prosecutions in 1914, when the Court held for the first time that in federal prosecutions the Fourth Amendment bars the use of evidence secured through an illegal search and seizure (*Weeks v. United States* 232 U.S. 383 [1914]). The Court's interpretation of the Fourth Amendment meant, quite simply, that "conviction by means of unlawful seizures and enforced confessions . . . should find no sanction in the judgments of the courts."

However, in *Wolf v. Colorado*, 338 U.S. 25 (1949), the Court discussed for the first time the effect of the Fourteenth Amendment on the states through the operation of the Due Process Clause of the Fourteenth Amendment. Although the Court held "that in prosecution in a State court for a State crime the Fourteenth Amendment does not forbid the admission of evidence obtained by an unreasonable search and seizure," it also concluded that only where "a State affirmatively sanction[ed] such police incursion into privacy [would] it . . . run counter to the guaranty of the Fourteenth Amendment." This decision created a situation of inconsistent application of a fundamental principle of justice that the court ultimately attempted to rectify in its landmark decision unifying the exclusionary rule in 1961."

The Supreme Court, in *Mapp v. Ohio*, 367 U.S. 643 (1961), specifically overruled its previous decision in *Wolf v. Colorado* and created one universal standard by applying the principle expressed in *Weeks v. United States* to state as well as federal prosecutions. The majority opinion was to hold that "all evidence obtained by searches and seizures in violation of the Constitution is, by that same authority, inadmissible in a state court."

Justice Tom Clark, in his majority opinion, explained the logical consistency of this decision by declaring that previous decisions had recognized the purpose of the exclusionary rule, which "is to deter—to compel respect for the constitutional guaranty in the only effectively available way—by removing the incentive to disregard it. To hold otherwise would make the Constitution merely a form of words, granting a right but in reality withholding its privilege and enjoyment." (*Mapp v. Ohio*, 1961)

This logic seems impeccable, but a great deal of criticism has been leveled at the exclusionary rule, especially by persons in law enforcement and political conservatives. The critics have argued that the proper remedy for unconstitutional activity by the police is a tort action, not the suppression of evidence. Why should the criminal go free because the police blundered? Supporters of the exclusionary rule argue that a tort action is an awkward mechanism for controlling police behavior; a rule requiring such an action would be based on the assumption that victims of police misconduct would be able to secure adequate counsel, which is rarely the case.

The *Mapp* decision continues to be controlling precedent, but it has been under heavy attack since 1961. Chief Justice Warren Burger proposed an elaborate plan to eliminate the exclusionary rule in a dissenting opinion in *Bivens v. Six-Unknown Named Agents* (1971). The plan would have involved congressional legislation to establish a claims system for the punishment of constitutional offenders through civil tort actions. However, Congress has never passed such a law, and the Court has never accepted this argument.

The Rehnquist Court has modified the exclusionary rule somewhat through a number of exceptions. In *United States v. Leon*, 468 U.S. 897 (1984) and *Massachusetts v. Sheppard*, 468 U.S. 981 (1984), the Court held that the exclusionary rule should not be applied so as to suppress the introduction of evidence at a criminal trial obtained in the reasonable belief that the search and seizure at issue was consistent with the Fourth Amendment. This "good faith" exception has been supplemented with an "inevitable discovery" exception in *Nix v. Williams*, 467 U.S. 431 (1984), in which the Court held that evidence obtained in violation of due process of law need not be suppressed if it would have been inevitably discovered by lawful means.

The court also has recognized a "public safety exception" to the exclusionary rule that allows police officers to question suspects concerning the whereabouts of dangerous weapons concealed in public places. The Rehnquist Court, for example, held that school officials may search student belongings or lockers for prescribed articles, such as guns and drugs, on reasonable suspicion alone (*New Jersey v. T.L.O.*, 469 U.S. 325 [1985]).

In more recent decisions, the Court has held that introduction of evidence that was seized in violation of the Fourth Amendment is not sufficient ground for reversal of a conviction if there was enough lawfully seized evidence to uphold a conviction. The Rehnquist Court has filled in additional details concerning search and seizure rules, which will be discussed in connection with the hypothetical case initiated in this chapter.

The Right to Counsel

The Sixth Amendment right to counsel was initially interpreted to mean that an individual accused of crime had the right to choose which lawyer to employ. It was not until the twentieth century that the Court began to examine the question of right to counsel for indigent persons accused of crimes who cannot afford to hire counsel to defend them.

In 1932, the Supreme Court began this process by examining the effect of poverty on persons accused of crimes that carried the death penalty. In *Powell v. Alabama, 287 U.S. 45* (1932), the Court held that in capital felony cases the right to appointed counsel at state expense was secured by the Due Process Clause of the Fourteenth Amendment.

Then, in 1938, the right to appointed counsel was broadened to include counsel for indigent defendants in all federal criminal proceedings of a felony nature. In the case of *Johnson v. Zerbst*, 304 U.S. 458 (1938), the Court held, "The Sixth Amendment withholds from federal courts, in all criminal proceedings, the power and authority to deprive an accused of his life or liberty unless he has or waived the assistance of counsel."

With the exception of capital felony cases, the state courts were not required to provide counsel in cases in which the defendant was unable to hire a lawyer. The Court considered the fundamental rights issue in *Betts v. Brady*, 316 U.S. 455 (1942) and concluded that the states had historically considered the appointment of counsel to be a matter of legislative policy and "not a fundamental right essential to a fair trial." Justice Hugo Black dissented, emphasizing that, "whether a man is innocent cannot be determined from a trial in which, as here, denial of counsel has made it impossible to conclude, with any satisfactory degree of certainty, that the defendant's case was adequately presented."

In the celebrated case of *Gideon v. Wainwright*, 372 U.S. 335 (1963), the court specifically overruled *Betts* and unanimously concluded that an indigent defendant's right to court-appointed counsel is fundamental and essential to a fair trial in state as well as federal prosecutions. Justice Black drafted the majority opinion of the Court, declaring that precedent, reason, and reflection "require us to recognize that any person hauled into court, who is too poor to hire a lawyer, cannot be assured a fair trial unless counsel is provided for him."

The principle of the right to counsel was extended to all criminal cases carrying a potential jail sentence in *Argersinger v. Hamlin*, 407 U.S. 25 (1972) and to all "critical stages" of the process, beginning with custodial interrogation by the police, in other decisions. These "critical stages" are explained more fully later in this and subsequent chapters.

Police Procedure

The Fifth Amendment provides that no person "shall be compelled in any criminal case to be a witness against himself." Although this right was applied in federal cases, it was not until *Malloy v. Hogan*, 378 U.S. 1 (1964) that the Fifth Amendment right to remain silent was considered "[a] fundamental right necessary to a system of ordered liberty." The Court earlier, in *Brown v. Mississippi*, 297 U.S. 278 (1936), had overturned convictions of three defendants whom police had physically tortured in order to extort confessions. But the Malloy decision sought to establish uniform minimal standards by incorporating the Fifth Amendment right to remain silent—that is, by applying the federal rules and precedents to state criminal procedure through the Fourteenth Amendment's Due Process Clause.

The *Malloy* decision, however, did not provide adequate guidelines to law enforcement officers regarding the practices that would or would not pass constitutional muster. As a consequence, the Court was confronted with a barrage of "coerced confessions" cases. Practices by police such as attempts to coerce the defendant through a childhood friend on the police force, threats to bring a defendant's wife into custody for questioning, threats to place the defendant's children in the custody of welfare officials, and interrogations of wounded defendants under the influence of so-called truth serums were some of the issues confronting the courts (Rossum and Tarr 1987, 435).

In 1966, the Supreme Court finally broke completely with past cases and established a set of administrative guidelines in *Miranda v. Arizona*. It announced specific procedures that would have to be followed by the police to ensure that confessions were "knowingly, freely, and voluntarily" given. Any statements elicited in violation of these procedures would be inadmissible. A person accused of a crime must be informed of his or her basic right to remain silent, warned that any statements can and will be held against him or her in court, that the person has a right to counsel, and that counsel must be made available to the person at the time of custodial interrogation.

Subsequent court decisions have upheld the **Miranda warnings**, but there have been modifications. For example, the prosecution has been allowed to use evidence suppressed as being in violation of *Miranda* to impeach the credibility of defendants who testify in their own behalf and, in so doing, contradict their earlier statements. In *Harris v. New York*, 401 U.S. 222 (1971), the Court declared that the privilege against self-incrimination does not include the right to commit perjury.

Miranda warnings: Requirement that the accused be informed of basic rights to ensure admissibility of evidence obtained by confessions.

THE PRETRIAL PROCESS

In general, the police function is referred to as the **control subsystem** of the overall criminal justice system. The police officers in our illustrative criminal case acted swiftly and efficiently in pursuit of that function by arresting a potentially dangerous suspect when an eyewitness to an armed robbery and potential murder provided them with evidence. An **arrest** occurs when a person is taken into custody.

Most arrests are made by law enforcement officers, but private individuals are also authorized, under certain conditions, to make interim arrests. Citizens have a duty to report crimes and to assist authorities in the process of law enforcement. Therefore, the control subsystem includes citizen participation and cooperation with law enforcement authorities. However, both private individuals and the police risk considerable danger in this process and can incur civil liability for false arrest or for the use of excessive force in making an arrest.

An arrest without a warrant was made in our illustrative criminal case. Law enforcement officers are generally permitted to arrest any person without a warrant if the crime was committed in the officer's presence or for a felony committed out of the officer's presence when there are reasonable grounds to believe that the individual has committed the felony.

Police officers are given considerable discretionary authority to issue citations for petty offences, to "stop and frisk" persons suspected of criminal activity, and to make arrests. A **stop and frisk** refers to the use of police authority to stop individuals in public places and to "pat them down" for the possession of concealed weapons when the circumstances or actions of the individuals appear suspicious to the trained police officer. As the Supreme Court noted in a frequently quoted case upholding the validity of an arrest made after such a stop and frisk procedure, "[I]t would appear completely unreasonable to deny the officer power to take necessary measures to determine whether the person is in fact carrying a weapon and to neutralize the threat of physical harm." (*Terry v. Ohio*, 392 U.S. 1 [1968]

Exigent circumstances provide another area of reasonable discretionary authority to police officers when emergency-like situations exist. This rule permits police to make warrantless entry to effect an arrest when exigencies of the situation make that course imperative. This is an exception to the rule requiring a search warrant and applies in a wide range of situations, such as when there is eminent danger or the police officer is in hot pursuit of a person who has committed a crime witnessed by the officer. However, this "reasonable" discretionary authority is limited by the due process rules of both federal and state authorities. The arresting officer must file a complaint before a magistrate without unreasonable delay when a person is arrested without a warrant in most jurisdictions. The

Control subsystem:
Refers to the police function of maintaining order and protecting the public safety.

Arrest:
To deprive a person of liberty by legal authority.

Stop and frisk:
The temporary seizure and pat-down search of a person who behaves suspiciously and appears to be armed.

Exigent circumstances:
Presence of emergency-like circumstances when the situation makes this course of action imperative, for example, when there is a "pat-down" for concealed weapons and illegal drugs are found.

Federal Rules of Criminal Procedure and the rules of most states specifically require this "initial appearance" as a check on police discretionary arrests.

An **arrest warrant** is a court order that commands that the individual named by it be taken into custody and brought before the court. A complaint must be filed as an application for an arrest warrant. The complaint must provide facts; mere conjecture or suspicion is not sufficient. The facts must be given under oath or by affirmation by a reliable and trustworthy source. Private persons as well as police officers are authorized to file such an application for an arrest warrant. It is the responsibility of the magistrate (usually a lower-court judge) to determine whether probable cause is sufficient to issue such a court order.

In many jurisdictions and various types of cases, the prosecutor (usually the district attorney) is authorized to seek indictment through a grand jury investigation of suspected criminal activity. If indictment is obtained, an arrest warrant is issued. Arrest is followed by the final pretrial stage generally known as the arraignment.

Arrest warrant:
A written order made on behalf of the state, based on a complaint issued pursuant to statute or court rule, commanding that the person be brought before a magistrate.

Probable Cause

The concept of "probable cause" is central to understanding the entire pretrial process in criminal legal actions. The concept is necessarily vague to allow for reasonable discretionary authority to protect individual rights against arbitrary and unreasonable use of authority. **Probable cause** is defined as more than mere suspicion. Some specific facts attested to by a trustworthy and reliable source are generally required, but probable cause does not require the degree of certainty that is necessary to justify a conviction.

This general definition must be tempered with the realization that different degrees of probable cause are required as the accused moves through the pretrial process, although all individuals accused of crime do not necessarily go through all of these stages. The basic stages in the pretrial process are included in Table 14.2.

Probable cause:
Reasonable cause requiring more than mere suspicion; some evidence and reasonable grounds for belief in the existence of facts warranting the complaint.

Table 14.2 **PRETRIAL PATH OF INCREASING EVIDENCE OF PROBABLE CAUSE AS STAGES INCREASE**

Pretrial Stages	Evidence Needed to Proceed
1. Arrest	Some evidence, officer's discretion
2. Initial appearance	Checked by magistrate's review
3. Preliminary hearing	Judge requires enough evidence to bind over to grand jury or information
4. Grand jury indictment (or information)	Indictment requires enough evidence to warrant putting individual through trial
5. Arraignment	Where the accused is required to enter a plea

A somewhat elevated form of probable cause is required at each stage to warrant movement of the accused to the next stage. The officer's discretionary authority to make an arrest is checked by the magistrate's review at the initial appearance stage. Another judge presides over the preliminary hearing, at which an elevated degree of probable cause is required to "bind the case over" to the grand jury. A grand jury indictment requires still more evidence to warrant putting the individual through the trial process. The final pretrial arraignment stage is where the accused is required to enter a plea. More than 90 percent of criminal cases end in sentencing decisions based on guilty pleas.

Filing a Criminal Complaint

The day following the Jiffy Stop robbery (August 12), the eyewitness, Frank Builder, was asked to make an identification of the suspect from a lineup that included Jesse Williams and several other jail inmates. Frank was unable to make a positive identification of the suspect. He said he was uncertain because he did not get a good look at both suspects.

Frank was taken to the impoundment lot where several rows of cars were parked, including Jesse's. He was asked to identify the vehicle he had seen leaving the crime scene. Frank looked them over carefully from the rear and correctly identified the suspect's car. "That's the car I saw leaving the scene of the crime last night; I'm certain of it. It looks different in the daylight, but it has the same beat-up fenders and broken taillight. I thought it was dark green last night, but that must have been because of the yellow lights at the convenience store," he explained.

Frank Builder dictated a statement to the police legal secretary that was drafted as an affidavit, and he signed it under oath. The secretary was also a notary public and certified that the statement was made and affirmed under oath.

The police officers reviewed all the evidence they had assembled on the case. A check with the hospital revealed that the victim was still in critical condition. He had been identified as the owner of the convenience store in which he was shot. His family had authorized a delicate brain operation to remove the bullet lodged in his skull. A surgeon had removed the bullet, and a police officer was dispatched to retrieve it. The bullet and various sets of fingerprints were sent to the crime laboratory for identification. It would be several days before this information would be adequately processed. However, the police believed they had enough probable cause to charge the suspect, Jesse Williams.

Jesse's alibi was not conclusive. Even if he had been at his girlfriend's apartment, he could have arrived there after the robbery, which took place before midnight. The police were concerned about the accomplice, as the witness had seen two persons in the getaway car. No weapon or other evidence from the holdup had been found, but the eyewitness had placed Jesse's car at the scene of the crime, and Jesse had given no explanation for this. The police decided to charge Jesse with armed robbery involving serious injury to the victim.

Middle State Criminal code defined robbery in two sections of the code as follows:

Section 39-13-401. Robbery.—(a) Robbery is the intentional or knowing theft of property from the person of another by violence or putting the person in fear.

Section 39-13-403. Especially Aggravated Robbery.—(a) Especially aggravated robbery is robbery as defined in §39-13-401:

(1) Accomplished with a deadly weapon; and
(2) Where the victim suffers serious bodily injury.

(b) Especially aggravated robbery is a Class A felony. [Acts 1989, ch. 591, §1.]

The potential penalty for a Class A felony ranged from 15 to 60 years in prison. If the victim were to die, the charge would be first degree murder, which carried the death penalty in Middle State.

Initial Appearance

Jesse Williams was taken before the local magistrate authorized to handle preliminary matters, such as **initial appearance**, bail, and issuance of search and arrest warrants. The magistrate's courtroom was located in another wing of the police headquarters where Jesse was being held. It is often referred to as "night court," but during the day it is also occupied by a magistrate of limited jurisdiction authorized to handle preliminary matters.

Initial appearance: Where a magistrate determines probable cause after arrest, advises defendant of charges, informs defendant of rights, and decides on bail.

Detective Mike Develon filed the complaint (Form 14.1) with the magistrate and took an oath regarding the truth of the contents of his statement. The "judge" turned to the defendant, handed him a copy of the charge, and informed him of his rights. Jesse said that he did not understand the charge; he was at his girlfriend's house last night. The judge asked the arresting officer whether this claim had been checked. The officer assured him that they had talked with Jesse's girlfriend and that she could not swear to his whereabouts at the exact time of the robbery. The judge informed Jesse that the initial appearance would not involve hearing evidence from the defendant and that he had a right to a preliminary hearing, which would be conducted by the general sessions judge on August 19, 2010, at 9:00 A.M. At that time, Jesse would have a right to have his lawyer present and could prepare evidence in his behalf.

"If you cannot obtain funds to hire a lawyer, you will need to make application for securing legal counsel," the magistrate told Jesse. "Do you want the court to appoint counsel for you?"

"Yes, I guess so," replied Jesse. "My mother is on welfare, and I don't have any money to hire a lawyer."

The magistrate gave Jesse an application form (see Form 14.1) and told him to complete it. "This is a very serious charge. If the victim dies, you may be charged under Middle State law with first degree murder, which carries the death penalty," explained the magistrate.

The police officer appealed to the magistrate, asking that Jesse not be released on **bail** because of the potential first degree murder charge that may be pending. The magistrate asked whether Jesse had any prior convictions or whether he was wanted on any outstanding warrants. The officer indicated that they had found no such record, but they had requested a thorough records check through the FBI using Jesse's fingerprints and mug shot as identification.

The magistrate set the bail amount at $100,000. Magistrates are given considerable discretion in setting bail, but most states have general guidelines. In Middle State, the authorities could release the defendant on his own recognizance if the offence was minor and the defendant could assure the court that he would meet court appearances. A bail amount of $1,000 might be sufficient for a misdemeanor, $10,000 for a felony not involving a crime against a person, $50,000 for a felony involving a crime against a person, or $100,000 for some form of homicide.

The judge indicated that he could not deny bail until there was a charge of first degree murder, but he agreed with the officer that the pending potential death of the victim was sufficient to warrant the maximum bail. Bail would be reviewed by the general session judge at the preliminary hearing, which the magistrate had set for August 19. The magistrate thanked Officer Develon for providing the victim's address on the complaint and indicated that notification would be sent in the next day's mail.

Detective Develon then gave the judge an application for a **search warrant** (see Form 14.2). The judge signed it and then signed the actual search warrant (see Form 14.3).

Jesse had completed the application for appointment of counsel by this time, and he handed it back to the judge. The judge checked it and told Jesse that a public defender would be appointed to serve as his legal counsel.

After returning Jesse to his cell, the police officers conducted a thorough search of Jesse's apartment and of the impounded automobile. They did not find a gun or any evidence of goods stolen during the robbery.

Bail:
To procure release of one charged with an offense by ensuring his future attendance in court and compelling him to remain within jurisdiction of the court.

Search warrant:
Written order issued by judicial authority directing law enforcement officers to search and seize any property that constitutes evidence of a crime.

Form 14.1 **CRIMINAL COMPLAINT**

STATE OF MIDDLE STATE v. Jesse Williams
Defendant

Capital City, Middle State   Address: 367 Elm Street, Apt. 4
Magisterial District 1   Capital City, Middle State

I, the undersigned, do hereby state under oath (affirmation):

(1) My name is Detective Sgt. Michael Develon and I live at 1407 Parklawn Drive, Capital City, Middle State;

(2) I accuse Jesse Williams who lives at 367 Elm Street, Apt. 4, Capital City with violating the penal laws of the State of Middle State;

(3) The date when the accused committed the offense was on Tuesday, August 11, 2010; and at about 11:50 P.M.;

(4) The place where the offense was committed was in the County of Local; Capital City, Middle State

(5) The acts committed by the accused were:

Especially Aggravated Robbery. On August 11, 2010, at about 11:50 P.M., defendant did intentionally take the contents from the cash register of the Jiffy Stop Market on the corner of State and Fifth Streets, Capital City, from the owner and operator of said filling station-convenience store at gun point and did cause serious bodily harm to the victim by inflicting a gunshot wound to the head of said victim. All of the above in violation of sections 39-13-401 and 39-13-404 of the Middle State Criminal Code.

The victim's name is Samuel J. Stone. The victim is the owner of the Jiffy Stop Market. His residence is 1405 Main Street, Capital City. He remains in critical condition at Central Hospital at the time of filing this complaint.

(6) I ask that the accused be required to answer the charges I have made; and

(7) I swear to (or affirm) this complaint upon my knowledge, information, and belief, and sign it on August 12, 2010 before _____, whose office is that of magistrate.

_____
Signature of Affiant

SEAL OF MIDDLE STATE   )
LOCAL COUNTY   )
)

Personally appeared before me on _____, 20_____, the affiant above named who, being duly sworn (affirmed) according to law, signed the complaint in by presence and deposed and said that the facts set forth herein are true and correct to the best of _____ knowledge, information and belief.

_____(SEAL)
Issuing Authority

Form 14.2 **APPLICATION FOR APPOINTMENT OF LEGAL COUNSEL**

THE PEOPLE OF MIDDLE STATE Charge _____

              V.

_____ No. _____ Term _____

APPLICATION FORM FOR THE ASSIGNMENT OF COUNSEL

The applicant _____ residing at _____ shows that:

1. I am a defendant in the above-entitled criminal cause of action alleging that I did not commit the crime of _____ in the County of _____ and State of Middle State, on the _____ day of _____, 20_____.

2. I am unable to obtain funds from anyone, including my family and associates, by way of compensation for counsel and represent that the answers to the following question are true to the best of my information and belief;

3. (a) How much money do you have in your possession (on person, in bank, at home, in custody of warden, or elsewhere? State amount _____ location _____

    (b) Do you own an automobile? _____ State estimated value _____ Amount owed on automobile _____ Lien holder _____

    (c) Do you own any real estate? _____ If so, give location:_____
    _____

    (d) Do you own any other property or do you have any other assets? _____
    If yes, furnish description thereof and specify its present location: _____
    _____

    (e) What is your social security number? _____
    Where did you last work? _____
    What was the total amount of your income during the past 12 months? _____
    What is your current employment status? _____

WHEREFORE, petitioner prays:

that this Honorable Court assign counsel to represent the defendant in the above-entitled criminal cause of action without fee or cost to the defendant.

                                                   _____

STATE OF MIDDLE STATE   )

County of_____   )   SS

)

_____ being duly sworn according to law upon oath (or: affirmation)

Deposes and says:

1. I am the petitioner in the above-entitled action.

2. I have read the foregoing petition and know the contents thereof and the same are true to my own knowledge, except regarding matters therein stated to be alleged as to persons other than myself, and as to those matters, I believe them to be true.

3. This affidavit is made to inform the court about my status of indigency and to induce the court to assign counsel to me as an indigent defendant for my defense against the criminal charges that have been made against me.

4. In making this affidavit, I am aware that perjury is a felony and that the punishment is a fine of not more than $3,000 or imprisonment for not more than seven years or both.

Form 14.3 **APPLICATION FOR SEARCH WARRANT**

STATE OF MIDDLE STATE   )
)   SS
County of_____   )

APPLICATION FOR SEARCH WARRANT

_____ OF _____

Being duly sworn (or affirmed) according to law, deposes and says that he has probable cause that certain property is evidence of or the fruit of a crime or is contraband or is unlawfully possessed or is otherwise subject to seizure, and is located at particular premises, as described below:

IDENTIFY ITEMS TO BE SEARCHED FOR AND SEIZED (Be as specific as possible)

Gun and goods stolen from robbery of convenience store

DESCRIPTION OF PREMISES TO BE SEARCHED (e.g., street or other address, including apartment number, or specific description of vehicle, safe deposit box, etc.):

Apartment 4, at 367 Elm Street, Capital City, Middle State, and vehicle owned by defendant and identified as being involved in armed robbery

NAME OF OWNER, OCCUPANT, OR POSSESSOR OF SAID PREMISES (give alias or description if name unknown):

Occupant of apartment is Jesse Williams, defendant in custody; defendant's automobile is impounded in police lot.

CRIME THAT HAS BEEN OR IS BEING COMMITTED (describe conduct by specific statute):

Especially aggravated robbery in violation of Middle State Criminal Code section 39-13-403

PROBABLE CAUSE BELIEF IS BASED ON THE FOLLOWING FACTS AND CIRCUMSTANCES.

Special instructions:

(1) If information was obtained from another person, e.g., an informant, a private citizen, or a fellow officer, state specifically what information was received, and how and when such information was obtained. State also the factual basis for believing such other person to be reliable.

(2) If surveillance was made, state what information was obtained by such surveillance, by whom it was obtained, and date, time, and place of such surveillance.

continued >

(3) State other pertinent facts within personal knowledge of affiant.

(4) If nighttime search is requested (i.e., 11:00 p.m. to 6:00 a.m.), state reasonable cause for seeking permission to search in nighttime.

(5) State reasons for believing that the items are located at the premises specified above.

(6) State reasons for believing that the items are subject to seizure.

(7) State any additional information considered pertinent to justify this application:

On August 12, 2010, Capital City detectives James Cox and Michael Develon arrested Jesse Williams whose address is Apartment 4, at 367 Elm Street, Capital City, charging him with especially aggravated robbery. His automobile was identified by Frank Builder, an eyewitness at the scene of the crime, and was impounded in the police lot. The victim, convenience store owner and operator, was shot with a firearm in the head, and the contents of the cash register are missing. Both the weapon used and the goods stolen are likely to be in the locations specified in this application. We request thorough daytime search of the outside and inside of Jesse William's apartment and his automobile.

_____

Signature of Affiant

SEAL:

_____

Badge Number   District/Unit

Magisterial District
Office Address:
1 State Street
Capital City, Middle State

Sworn to and subscribed before me this
12th day of August, 2010.

Date commission Expires:
December 31, 2015

_____

Signature of Issuing Authority

Form 14.4   SEARCH WARRANT

STATE OF MIDDLE STATE   )
)
County of Local   )

SEARCH WARRANT

TO LAW ENFORCEMENT OFFICER

WHEREAS, facts have been sworn to or affirmed before me by written affidavit(s) attached hereto from which I have found probable cause, I do authorize you to search the following described premises or person:

Apartment house dwelling at 367 Elm Street, Apartment 4, Capital City, Middle State, including area surrounding said dwelling place and the vehicle belonging to Jesse Williams located in the police impoundment lot._____

_____

And to seize, secure, inventory, and make return according to the Middle State rules of Criminal Procedure the following items:
Firearms and goods missing in robbery_____

_____

As soon as practicable but in any event no later than August 13, 2010, and only during the daytime hours of 6:00 a.m. to 11:00 p.m.

SEAL   Issued under my authority on this
                                                12th day of August 2010,
                                                At 2:00 p.m. (Time of issuance must be specified.)

Office Address:
1 State Street
Capital City, Middle State

Date Commission Expires:
December 31, 2015

                                                _____
                                                Signature of Issuing Authority

Defense Counsel

During the week of Jesse's incarceration, Jesse was told that his lawyer wanted to see him. He was taken into an interrogation room and introduced to his **public defender**, Jill Adams. Jill asked him how he was being treated in jail. He replied that nobody would talk to him: "They won't tell me anything. I didn't do nothing."

Public defender:
Lawyer employed by a government agency assigned to defend indigents in criminal cases.

Attorney Jill Adams told him he was charged with a very serious crime and that she would need his full cooperation to help him as his defense counsel. Even though she was appointed by the judge, she had a legal obligation to defend him to the best of her ability. "You have to level with me, Jesse," Jill said.

"If you tell me the truth, I can help you. But if you lie to me, it will only make things worse for you. The lawyer-client privilege is an aspect of the law that tries to ensure that what you tell me in confidence will not be used against you in court. Do you understand my role or have any questions about who I am?"

"Yeah, I understand that you're the lawyer they appointed for me," Jesse answered, "but the inmates tell me you got so many cases to handle you won't find out nothin'."

"Give me a chance, Jesse. If you'll level with me, I can help, believe me!" Adams replied.

Attorney Adams asked a number of background questions, including requests for Jesse's parents' address, school record, and employment history and especially whether Jesse had any prior criminal record. Jesse said he was born in Florida but went to high school in Capital City. He dropped out of high school and joined the army at age 18. He served three years in the military and came back to Capital City two years ago. He had been employed at several fast food restaurants as a short-order cook, but he had lost his last job because he could not get along with the boss. He said he had no prior arrest or conviction record with the police.

Adams said, "Now I want you to tell me everything you did on the night of August 11—I mean every person you met or talked with who could give us a positive time of your exact whereabouts."

Jesse said he was in his apartment until 10:00 P.M. watching television and then decided to go to his girlfriend's house. He said he stayed there until 2:00 A.M., and when he got home, the police arrested him.

"I'll talk to your girlfriend about this and get back to you. Is there anything else you want to tell me about your situation?" asked the attorney.

"Try to find out when this robbery was supposed to go down and what the police know about it. Why they tryin' to pin this on me," Jesse responded.

"Do you own a gun, Jesse?" asked the attorney.

"No, I don't have no gun," he said.

Attorney Jill Adams was not favorably impressed with her new client, but she had seen many like him. She would check his story and see whether she could do anything at the preliminary hearing set for next Wednesday. In the meantime, she had many other clients with whom to consult, and she had a big case going to trial the next day involving child abuse.

Monday morning Adams checked with the police department and found out that Jesse had a prior violent crime record with the military. The FBI check had found a conviction for aggravated assault involving Jesse who had stabbed another soldier in a barracks brawl in 2007. Jesse had a dishonorable discharge. His girlfriend had prior convictions for prostitution and drug possession.

When Adams called the girlfriend to check Jesse's story, the girlfriend said she could not remember when Jesse arrived at her apartment. She knew only that it was late, maybe around midnight. She told Adams that the police had already asked her about this and that they had come into her apartment and had taken some beer cans Jesse brought in that night. Adams set up an interview with the girlfriend for the next day so that they could be prepared for the preliminary hearing on Wednesday. She got a commitment from the girlfriend that she would attend the hearing at 9:00 A.M. in General Sessions Court.

Then the attorney met with Jesse again. She looked him straight in the eye and said, "You lied to me, Jesse. Why didn't you tell me about the conviction for aggravated assault in the military?"

"That was a long time ago, and in the military. I didn't think that counted," Jesse replied.

"You're in more trouble now. Your girlfriend will verify that you were there, but only from about midnight to 2:00 A.M. The police say the robbery occurred before that, and you don't have a real alibi," explained the attorney.

Preliminary Hearing

The purpose of the **preliminary hearing** is to determine whether probable cause exists to believe that a crime has been committed and that the accused committed it. This determination is not the same as the determination of guilt beyond a reasonable doubt, which is the trial standard. The object of the preliminary hearing is to determine whether reasonable grounds exist for holding the accused and binding the defendant over to the grand jury. The grand jury is the next stage in most jurisdictions when a serious felony is involved. At the preliminary hearing, the judge has to decide to either dismiss the case or "bind it over."

Jesse's attorney explained what would be involved in the preliminary hearing, which would be held the following morning. "This won't be a trial, Jesse," Adams said. "But you do have a right to have your lawyer present. I can cross-examine the witnesses they call, and we can call witnesses to refute their evidence. They probably have an eyewitness to the robbery. So you had better start telling me the truth," the attorney explained.

Preliminary hearing: Critical stage in pretrial process where the accused has a right to present evidence. Defendant has right to counsel.

"My girlfriend'll help me out," replied Jesse.

"Don't count on it, Jesse," the attorney warned. "She's got a record, and they will get it out on cross. Besides, she won't even provide an alibi for the time of the robbery. The police say it took place around 11:50. Where were you at 11:50, Jesse?"

"I know I got to her apartment before that," Jesse answered. "Can't you talk to her about it?"

"If you mean that I should coach her to lie for you—no way, Jesse," declared Adams. "But I will let her know how important it is for her to tell the truth and try to think of something that would fix the time of your arrival at her apartment."

Adams then asked whether anyone else could verify Jesse's alibi, but Jesse just shook his head and muttered something under his breath.

The next day at General Sessions Court there were a number of cases, and Jesse's case was not called until 11:15. Most of the other matters were handled very quickly; these were mainly charges of driving while intoxicated and bad-check cases, and all the defendants pleaded guilty and were sentenced. Felony cases are handled in the same court as misdemeanors but cannot be disposed of at this stage unless no probable cause is found.

When the clerk called the case of *People v. Jesse Williams*, the judge explained that this was a felony charge of especially aggravated robbery and checked to see that the defendant and his counsel were present. The judge then turned to the police officers who had been involved in the robbery investigation and Jesse's arrest. The police officer who first arrived at the scene of the crime was placed under oath and was asked to state his observations on his arrival at the scene of the robbery. His testimony clearly established that a crime had taken place and that a witness had identified a vehicle leaving the scene of the crime. Detective Mike Develon was placed under oath and asked to explain how the arrest was made. He explained the eyewitness identification of the license number and description of the vehicle, the arrest, and the subsequent verification of the vehicle in the impoundment lot lineup.

Public Defender, Jill Adams, had an opportunity to cross-examine the officers but declined to do so. She had brought a tape recorder and recorded everything the officers said. This was her first opportunity to learn about the basic facts of the robbery and the eyewitness report. The officers did not produce the eyewitness at this hearing because they did not have to prove anything at the preliminary hearing. The testimony of the police officers was enough to demonstrate probable cause.

The judge recognized Jill Adams as counsel for the defense. She addressed the judge respectfully and requested that the police officers who had appeared as witnesses be excused from the courtroom to allow her to call a witness on behalf of the defendant. She explained that under Middle State case law, either party has the right to exclude opposing witnesses from the courtroom during testimony.

"You are quite right, counselor," the judge agreed. The officers were dismissed from the courtroom. "Please wait outside until you are called," the judge told them.

The defendant's attorney then called Nancy Jones to the stand, and the judge placed her under oath. Attorney Adams established her identity, where she lived, and where she worked. She said she was a waitress at the City Café. The defense attorney asked whether she knew the defendant and how long she had known the defendant. The attorney asked the witness whether she had seen Jesse Williams on the night of August 11, 2010. She said that he was at her apartment until 2:00 in the morning on that night.

"Can you tell the court exactly when he arrived at your apartment?" asked the lawyer.

"It was before midnight; I'm sure because *M.A.S.H.* was on the TV and it comes on at 11:00," replied the witness.

The judge proceeded to cross-examine the witness. He reminded her that she was under oath and explained the penalty for perjury. He asked her whether she was certain of the time. She replied that she had fallen asleep on the couch while watching a *M.A.S.H.* rerun that she had already seen. She said Jesse came in with a six-pack of beer and woke her up, and they had several beers together.

The judge asked Nancy whether she had ever been convicted of a crime. Nancy looked at the public defender and asked whether she had to answer that question. The judge told her, "Yes, Miss Jones, you are under oath and have sworn to tell the truth, the whole truth, and nothing but the truth." Nancy admitted that she had previous convictions for prostitution and drug possession. "But that was five years ago, and I'm straight now," she added.

"Is this the only witness you have, Counselor?" asked the judge. Jill Adams answered affirmatively, and the judge called the officers back into the court.

The judge asked the officers whether they were aware of the defendant's alibi. Mike Develon informed the judge that they had questioned Nancy Jones about that evening and that she could not remember exactly when the defendant arrived at her apartment.

The judge then stated, "I'll have to bind this case over to the grand jury; the police officers' testimony and the eyewitness identification are sufficient to establish probable cause. We are not going to try this case here. The district attorney and the grand jury will have to deal with any conflicting testimony, and ultimately the case will be decided by a trial in criminal court."

The defense attorney asked that the bail be reduced, indicating that the defendant lived in the community and had no record of skipping bail and no outstanding warrants. The judge denied the request, stating that the potential for a first degree murder charge was sufficient to warrant the $100,000 bail set by the initial appearance judge. He also asked whether any relative of the victim was present in the audience. The wife of the victim identified herself. The judge asked about her husband, and she said he was still in critical condition.

Under Middle State law, a person accused of a felony had a right to have the case presented to a grand jury for indictment. This stage is discussed in the next chapter. However, the Supreme Court does not consider this to be a fundamental right. The Fifth Amendment requirement of a grand jury in cases involving a "capital or otherwise infamous crime" allows an information procedure to be used as an alternative charging procedure in cases involving lesser federal offenses. Many states use the information method in criminal cases, especially with regard to less serious crimes. The Middle State constitution required a grand jury indictment.

The **information** process differs from the procedure illustrated above in that the district attorney general reviews the charges made by the police at the initial appearance and makes a decision to draft a charging instrument known as an "information." The document is then heard before a judge at the preliminary hearing. The preliminary hearing is conducted in much the same manner as the one described above; however, an assistant district attorney usually is present to cross-examine defense witnesses. The judge then decides, in open court, whether the information demonstrates probable cause to warrant putting the accused through a trial process. When the information process is used, there is no grand jury review (involving independent citizens).

Information: Accusation by public prosecutor made in open court before a magistrate in a preliminary hearing where the accused may defend himself or herself, as opposed to grand jury indictment.

In both procedures, the criminal case moves out of the control subsystem after the preliminary hearing and into the court subsystem for adjudication if probable cause is found. In many jurisdictions, the district attorney's office becomes involved in the case during the preliminary hearing stage. The police are still involved in the cases that have moved on into the court subsystem, and they assist the district attorney's office; but decisions involving further progress of the cases are in the hands of the district attorney.

CHAPTER SUMMARY

1. State and local governments have primary responsibility for maintaining public order and domestic crime control. Although both federal and state governments may prosecute various forms of criminal activity, the basic "police power" is given to the states.

2. The fundamental elements of serious crimes include both an act prohibited by law (*actus reus*) and the required mental intent (*mens rea*). These elements constitute the body of the crime (*corpus delicti*) and are

generally defined for each specific crime in modern state and federal criminal codes.

3. Crimes were originally classified in English common law as those that were bad in themselves (*mala in se*) and those that were legislatively prohibited (*mala prohibita*). The classification known as *mala in se* (e.g., murder, rape, theft, arson) has remained fairly consistent, and these crimes generally are considered felonies today. Modern legislatures, however, have added victimless crimes and regulatory offenses to the category of crimes that are *mala prohibita*.

4. Both federal and state governments have codified almost all crimes into statutory provisions. Treason, felonies, and misdemeanors are the major classifications of crime today. The federal government has a U.S. constitutional definition of treason, but states may have their own provisions. Felonies are serious crimes, as distinguished from misdemeanors. State and federal definitions of misdemeanors vary, but these crimes carry less severe penalties (usually less than one year of incarceration). Petty offenses (traffic violations) are the least serious violations. They generally involve fines and are called summary offenses.

5. Minimal uniform standards of criminal procedure in both state and federal jurisdictions have been established through selective incorporation of most of the rights expressed in the Fourth, Fifth, Sixth, and Eighth Amendments to the U.S. Constitution and applied against the states through the Fourteenth Amendment's Due Process Clause. Exceptions include the Fourth Amendment Grand Jury Clause and the Eighth Amendment Excessive Fines and Bails Clause.

6. The federal exclusionary rule was applied to the states in 1961 through the Supreme Court's decision in *Mapp v. Ohio*. This rule requires that evidence obtained in violation of the U.S. Constitution be declared inadmissible in criminal trials.

7. The federal right to counsel, including the right to appointed counsel in indigent cases, was applied to the states in *Gideon v. Wainwright* in 1963.

8. In the case of *Miranda v. Arizona* (1966), the Supreme Court established specific procedures that have to be followed by the police to ensure that confessions are "knowingly, freely, and voluntarily" given. The Miranda warning informs the defendant of his or her rights. The police must refrain from using techniques that may coerce confessions in violation of the Fifth Amendment provision prohibiting such confessions.

9. Law enforcement officers have considerable discretionary authority to determine probable cause when making arrests to "stop and frisk" and to conduct "plain view" searches. This discretionary authority, however, is subject to constitutional limitations and is checked by independent judicial authorities.

10. Probable cause is defined as more than mere suspicion but does not require the same degree of certainty necessary to convict a person of a crime. A police officer's determination of probable cause is checked by the local magistrate at initial appearance. Bail is set by the magistrate on the basis of factors involving risk to the community.

11. The accused has a right to a preliminary hearing at which defense counsel must be provided if demanded by the accused. At the preliminary hearing, the defendant may provide evidence to refute the charges. The judge determines whether there is sufficient reason to bind the case over to the grand jury or whether the case should be dismissed. In many states, the information process is used to determine probable cause to send the case to the arraignment stage, and a grand jury is not involved.

12. An individual accused of crime has a right to counsel when the crime involved carries a potential jail sentence. If the accused cannot afford counsel, the state must appoint counsel to advise the defendant. The Supreme Court has held that counsel must be provided at the time of custodial interrogation and at all stages of the criminal process if demanded by the accused. Critical stages include the preliminary hearing, arraignment, trial, and appeal.

REVIEW EXERCISES

Match the following terms with their appropriate meaning.

TERMS
1. Prima facie case
2. *Corpus delicti*
3. *Actus reus*
4. *Mens rea*
5. Inchoate crimes
6. Treason
7. Misdemeanor
8. Felony
9. Selective incorporation doctrine
10. Information
11. *Miranda* warnings
12. Arrest
13. Arrest warrant
14. Control subsystem
15. Stop and frisk rule
16. Exigent circumstances
17. Probable cause

MEANING
____ presence of emergency-like circumstances
____ case that will prevail until contradicted by other evidence
____ incipient crimes such as attempts, solicitation, and conspiracy to commit crimes
____ magistrate determines probable cause for arrest, sets bail, and informs defendant of rights
____ to deprive a person of liberty by legal authority
____ defined by the U.S. Constitution and requires two witnesses or confession in open court to convict
____ the body of the crime including actus reus and mens rea
____ criminal accusation by public prosecutor where preliminary hearing may be demanded by defendant
____ reasonable cause; more than mere suspicion; some evidence from credible source
____ requirement that the accused be informed of basic rights to ensure admissibility of evidence
____ a critical stage in the pretrial process where accused has right to present evidence

18. Initial appearance
19. Bail
20. Search warrant
21. Public defender
22. Preliminary hearing

____ written order by judge that a person be brought before the magistrate to answer to criminal charges

____ doctrine of including selected provisions of Bill of Rights in the Fourteenth Amendment's due process clause

____ lawyer appointed by court or employed by the government to defend indigents accused of crime

____ temporary police pat-down search of a person who behaves suspiciously and appears to be armed

____ crime of a serious nature, punishable by longer prison sentences

____ a guilty mind or criminal intent

____ written court order based on probable cause naming the place to be searched and the things to be seized

____ refers to the police function of maintaining order and protecting public safety

____ lesser criminal offenses punishable by fines or short jail sentences

____ a wrongful act making the actor criminally liable when combined with the required intent

____ to procure release of one charged with an offense by insuring his future attendance in court

DISCUSSION QUESTIONS

1. Why are the states considered responsible for the maintenance of public order in their jurisdiction?
2. What are the basic differences between felonies, misdemeanors, and petty offenses?
3. How important is citizen involvement in effective law enforcement and crime control?
4. Do you agree with the Supreme Court's selective incorporation doctrine?
5. Is the U.S. exclusionary rule the only available way to compel effectively respect for U.S. Constitutional guarantees?
6. Do you agree with the Supreme Court that the right of indigent persons to appointed counsel is necessary to protect fundamental rights? Why, or Why not?
7. Does the prohibition against coerced confessions require the imposition of the *Miranda* guidelines for proper enforcement?
8. Are there any constitutional violations in the illustrative case involving Jesse Williams so far? If so, explain why they are violations.

ASSIGNMENTS

ASSIGNMENT: This criminal case could also be reenacted as a mock trial in the classroom; however, this may be too much for the available class time. A more practical suggestion is to appoint 12 of the students to deliberate before the class as jurors in this case so that everyone can hear the debate involved in the jury deliberation.

ASSIGNMENT: Find your state's criminal code by using the library or the Internet and look up the

definition of particular crimes that are of interest to you. You can enter your state's name and criminal code, and it should be available on the Internet. You will need to have a term in mind, but you will be able to find the statutory provisions. Crimes within the District of Columbia are found in the D.C. Criminal Code.

SOURCES AND SUGGESTED READING ⎯⎯⎯⎯⎯⎯⎯⎯⎯⎯⎯⎯⎯

Abadinsky, Howard. 1991. *Law and Justice: An Introduction to the American Legal System*. 2d ed. Chicago: Nelson-Hall Publishers.

Cole, George F., ed. 1993. *Criminal Justice: Law and Politics*. 6th ed. Belmont, Calif.: Wadsworth Publishing.

Hall, Kermit L., 1992. *The Oxford Companion to the Supreme Court of the United States*. New York: Oxford University Press.

O'Brien, David M. 1991. *Constitutional Law and Politics: Civil Rights and Civil Liberties*. Vol. 2. New York: W.W. Norton.

Rossum, Ralph A., and G. Alan Tarr. 1987. *American Constitutional Law*. 2nd ed. New York: St. Martin's Press.

Wilson, James Q. 1989. *American Government*. 4th ed. Lexington, Mass.: D.C. Heath.

COURT CASES

Argersinger v. Hamlin, 407 U.S. 25, 92 S.Ct. 2006, 32l.Ed.2d 530 (1972)

Benton v. Maryland, 395 U.S. 784, 89 S.Ct. 2056, 32 L.Ed.2d 707(1969)

Betts v. Brady, 316 U.S. 455, 62 S.Ct. 1252, 86 L.Ed. 1595 (1942)

Bivens v. Six-Unknown Named Agents, 403 U.S. 388. 91 S.Ct. 1999, 29 L.Ed. 2d 619 (1971)

Brown v. Mississippi, 297 U.S. 278, 56 S.Ct. 461, 80 L.Ed. 682 (1936)

Cole v. Arkansas, 33 U.S. 196, 68 S.Ct. 514, 92 L.Ed. 644 (1948)

Duncan v. Louisiana, 391 U.S. 145, 88 S.Ct. 1444, 20 L.Ed.2d 491 (1968)

Gideon v. Wainwright, 372 U.S. 335, 83 S.Ct. 792, 9 L.Ed.2d 799 (1963)

Harris v. New York, 401 U.S. 222, 91 S.Ct. 643, 289 L.Ed.2d 1 (1971)

Hertado v. California, 110 U.S. 516, 4 S.Ct. 111, 28 L.Ed 232 (1884)

Illinois v. Krull, 480 U.S. 340, 107 S.Ct. 1160, 94 L.Ed.2d 364 (1987)

Johnson v. Zerbst, 304 U.S. 458, 58 S.Ct. 1019, 82 L.Ed 1461 (1938)

Klopfer v. North Carolina, 386 U.S. 213, 87 S.Ct. 988, 18 L.Ed.2d 1 (1968)

Malloy v. Hogan, 378 U.S. 1, 84 S.Ct. 489, 12 L.Ed.2d 653 (1964)

Mapp v. Ohio, 367 U.S. 643, 81 S.Ct. 3424, 82 L.Ed.2d 737 (1961)

Massachusetts v. Sheppard, 468 U.S. 981 (1984)

Miranda v. Arizona, 384 U.S. 436, 86 S.Ct. 1602, 16 L.Ed.2d 694 (1966)

New Jersey v. T.L.O., 469 U.S. 325, 105 S.Ct. 733, 83 L.Ed.2d 720 (1985)

Nix v. Williams, 467 U.S. 431, 104 S.Ct. 2501, 81 L.Ed.2d 377 (1984)

Oliver, In re, 333 U.S. 257, 68 S.Ct. 499, 92 L.Ed. 684 (1948)

Palko v. Connecticut, 302 U.S. 363, 87 S.Ct. 468, 17 L.Ed. 288 (1937)

Parker v. Gladden, 385 U.S. 363, 87 S.Ct. 468, 17 L.Ed.2d 420 (1966)

Pointer v. Texas, 380 U.S. 400, 85 S.Ct. 1065, 13 L.Ed.2d 923 (1965)

Powell v. Alabama, 287 U.S. 45, 53 S.Ct. 55, 77 L.Ed. 158 (1932)

Robinson v. California, 370 U.S. 660, 82 S.Ct. 1417, 8 L.Ed.2d 758 (1962)

Terry v. Ohio, 392 U.S. 1, 88 S.Ct. 1868, 20 L.Ed.2d 889 (1968)

United States v. Leon, 468 U.S. 897, 104 S.Ct. 3405, 82 L.Ed.2d 677 (1984)

Washington v. Texas, 388 U.S. 14, 87 S.Ct. 1920, 18 L.Ed.2d 1019 (1967)

Weeks v. United States, 232 U.S. 383, 34 S.Ct. 341, 58 L.Ed. 652 (1914)

Wolf v. Colorado, 338 U.S. 25, 69 S.Ct. 1359, 93 L.Ed. 1782 (1949)

The Pretrial Process in Criminal Cases

This chapter explains the court subsystem phase of the pretrial process in criminal cases. The basic stages of the pretrial process and the roles played by the police in the control subsystem were discussed in the previous chapter. An important change takes place when the prosecutor becomes involved in the case. In our illustrative case, this transformation takes place in Middle State after the preliminary hearing; in many states, it takes place before the preliminary hearing, especially when the information process is used. In all jurisdictions, the prosecutor may initiate criminal proceedings and seek indictment by the grand jury prior to arrest.

THE PROSECUTOR

The pretrial phase of the criminal justice system is largely controlled by the public **prosecutor**. The official prosecutor is either appointed or elected to manage the functions of the prosecutor's office for that particular jurisdiction. In rural areas, the official prosecutor may handle all the cases, but in most jurisdictions the official prosecutor manages a small bureaucracy. The district attorney general (DA) is the administrator in charge and hires assistant or deputy district attorneys to perform specific prosecutorial functions. Whether appointed, as in the federal system, or elected, as in most states, the lawyers who seek the office of district attorney frequently have higher political ambitions in mind.

Prosecutor:
One who, in the name of the government, prosecutes another for a crime.

The district attorney in Middle State is an elected public official selected by the voters from the local judicial district for an eight-year term. This elected official has the duty and responsibility to see that the laws are faithfully enforced. Although there is a statewide attorney general's office, the local district attorney is responsible for initiating prosecution in almost all cases. The statewide office handles mainly the state's cases on appeal and advises the governor and the legislature.

Nolle Prosequi

The most important discretionary power given to public prosecutors is the authority not to prosecute **nolle prosequi**. The decision to prosecute an individual is ultimately checked by the courts, but the district attorney's decision not to prosecute is nearly absolute. There are few checks of the prosecutor's *nolle prosequi* or simply, "nol-pros" decision. The decision takes the form of a formal entry on the record by the prosecutor that the state will not prosecute the case any further and is, in effect, a dismissal of the charges.

> **Nolle prosequi:**
> A formal entry on the record by the prosecuting officer declaring that the officer will not prosecute the case further.

The police have discretion in deciding whether to arrest a suspect, but the prosecutor has the responsibility of determining whether the cause of justice will be best served by continuing prosecution of that individual. As an officer of the court, the prosecutor must try to avoid prosecution of a person who is innocent or a person against whom the evidence is not sufficient to justify a verdict of guilty. The prosecutor needs a higher level of evidence to get a conviction than a police officer needs to make an arrest. The prosecutor's standard of evidence is "beyond a reasonable doubt."

Plea Bargaining

The modern American practice of **plea bargaining**, which has become almost routine, is derived from the prosecutor's combined charging function and power not to prosecute. The prosecutor ultimately must fix the official charges brought against the individual and be prepared to go to trial and seek conviction on those charges.

> **Plea bargaining:**
> Process whereby the accused and the prosecutor in a criminal case work out a mutually satisfactory disposition of the case subject to court approval.

The caseload and political pressures of the district attorney's office have grown enormously in most districts in modern times, and these pressures have led to the procedures and practices that characterize the pretrial aspects of the court subsystem. The vast majority of cases never go to trial and are disposed of during the pretrial process. Of the criminal convictions obtained in the United States, more than 90 percent plead guilty and are sentenced at the arraignment stage.

The prosecutor is the dominant figure in this process. Although judges have a responsibility to check abuses of prosecutorial discretion, they depend on the public prosecutor to screen cases and minimize court congestion. The prosecutor has become the most powerful figure in the criminal justice system, and in most state districts that officer has to answer only to the electorate.

Initial Screening and Case Assignment

The district attorney's office in Capital City had set up a screening system in the main office to receive incoming complaints and records. A young lawyer who just graduated from law school was one of those assigned to initially review the files coming into the office and assign them to appropriate units within the department. Bob Clark had been instructed to screen cases on the basis of designated criteria. The Capital City district attorney's office had a horizontally organized system for handling routine cases; misdemeanor, grand jury, and felony trial units existed. There was also a specialized crime unit that handled priority cases vertically after intake. Jesse William's case fit the criteria for assignment to the specialized unit. The charge involved a violent crime and a potential murder charge.

An experienced trial lawyer directed the specialized crime unit and generally assigned cases to one of six experienced trial lawyers who handled cases assigned to the six criminal court judges in Capital City. Jesse Williams's case had been assigned to Judge Otis Mann's court, which meant that Rusty Kovaks would be the attorney on the case. This process of assignment and Kovak's review of the file took a couple of weeks.

Prosecutorial Investigation

When Assistant District Attorney Kovaks reviewed Jesse's file, he became concerned as he realized that the eyewitness had identified two individuals suspected of committing the armed robbery and shooting at the convenience store. He called the arresting officer, Mike Develon, to get a progress report on the police investigation. Develon assured him that the department was making every effort to follow all leads in the search for the second suspect, the weapon used in the crime, and the missing contents of the cash register.

"Jesse's alibi is no good," said the officer. "The beer cans we lifted from his girlfriend's apartment had a Jiffy Stop price label on one of them. Jesse was there all right. He must have picked up that six-pack during the robbery. We haven't questioned him since right after the arrest. We were waiting for the case to be assigned to the DA's office."

Attorney Kovaks asked what progress was being made in locating the other guy involved in the robbery. The police officer explained that they had developed a list of all of Jesse's known friends and were checking on them. The eyewitness had looked at mug shots and had given the artist a description of the suspect's features. They had a "likeness," but no positive identification had been made.

"We have clear thumb and index fingerprints that were found on the gas hose nozzle and the gasoline cap. They did not match Jesse's prints, so we think they are the second suspect's. The lab has given us a positive match on the gasoline cap and Jesse's car," reported Develon.

"Where's the gun and the loot?" asked Kovaks.

The police officer said they were doing all they could. The lab had identified the bullet as one from a .38 "police special," he told Kovaks. "We know what we're looking for—we just haven't found it yet."

"How much money was missing?" Kovaks asked.

"Not more than $300, according to the cash register. We don't know if anything else was taken, except maybe that six-pack that Jesse took to his girl's apartment," explained Develon.

Kovaks also learned from Develon that the victim was still in a coma and on life support systems at the hospital. "The doctors don't know about his chances for recovery," said Develon.

Kovaks told the police officer to keep him informed and to send over the laboratory reports. He would talk to the eyewitness and make an assessment about seeking grand jury indictment. "I don't think we'll get anything out of Jesse until he's ready—let him stew awhile, he'll come around," said Kovaks.

After talking with the eyewitness and checking on his background, Kovaks concluded that he was a good witness who could convince a grand jury. The laboratory reports added corroborating evidence, but he knew that he would need more evidence to convince a trial jury to convict. Kovaks thought to himself, "After a few more weeks and a grand jury indictment, Jesse will be looking for a deal." So he decided to proceed to the grand jury with Jesse's case.

THE GRAND JURY FUNCTION

The grand jury was originally a part of our English common-law heritage and has no counterpart on the continent of Europe or in the civil law systems. In England, it was designed as a charging, or accusatory, instrument before public prosecutors were used.

In the American colonies, both grand juries and petit (trial) juries achieved an enhanced reputation as protectors of the individual against abuses of British colonial authority. Sympathetic grand juries refused to indict opponents of the Stamp Act, and other local juries refused to convict persons accused of violation of laws they considered to be unjust. The U.S. constitutional provisions concerning grand juries and right to jury trials in criminal cases are products of these developments.

England abolished the use of grand juries in 1933 and now confines the use of jury trials only to the most serious offenses. In the United States, this type of citizen involvement in the criminal justice process retains much of its vigor. The grand jury has been expanded to serve as an investigative body that is usually impaneled for a fixed term; however, there are special investigative grand juries that sit until the investigation is completed.

The **grand jury** has a function that is very different from that of the trial (or petit) jury. The grand jury does not determine guilt but rather decides whether there are enough facts to warrant putting the individual through

Grand jury:
Used in some states as charging or investigative juries of lay persons who decide if there is enough evidence to warrant a trial in some states.

the trial process. This is another form of the concept of probable cause and a further test of its existence.

Grand juries continue to exist in about half of the states and in the federal jurisdiction. But even in the federal courts, information procedures are used in lesser offences. However, the defendant can waive a grand jury **indictment** in those states where it is a right.

The Alternate Information Process

The charging instrument that is an alternative to grand jury indictment is known as the **information**. This process was explained in the previous chapter. U.S. Supreme Court decisions have established a right of the accused to demand a preliminary hearing at which the accused can present evidence in defense during this pretrial stage. Where the information is used, the prosecutor must file a "bill of information" with the court in which the trial will be held. The bill of information serves as the official charge that may be challenged in open court if a preliminary hearing is demanded.

In states in which both charging instruments—grand jury indictment and information—are allowed, the prosecutor may have a choice. These choices are usually restricted by the severity of the charges. Prosecutors find the grand jury useful, even in states where it is optional. When the defendant cannot be located or when the statute of limitations is about to expire, the incentives for a prosecutor to seek an indictment are obvious. In addition, the secrecy of the grand jury allows the prosecutor to present all the evidence without fear that the defendant will use this evidence later at trial. Finally, "the need to protect undercover agents, the ability to test a witness before a jury, or the opportunity to involve the community in case screening may be contributing factors." (Emerson, 1983, 13)

In the federal system, the grand jury consists of 23 citizens drawn from voter registration lists in the community served by the court. A quorum (number needed to conduct business) of 16 is required, and 12 votes are needed for an indictment. Charges involving "capital or infamous crimes" under federal jurisdiction must be presented to a grand jury under the Fifth Amendment of the U.S. Constitution. This has been interpreted to allow the grand jury to be bypassed for misdemeanor offenses, which can instead be charged by the prosecutor's information procedure. Some plea agreements also stipulate that the defendant waives prosecution by indictment. However, the defendant must make this waiver in open court and after being advised of the nature of the charge and of his or her rights.

The states have no uniform grand jury practices. The state grand juries vary considerably in size from 12 to 23 members, and the number needed to indict ranges from 4 to 9 in some states, although most states follow the federal standard and require 12 to indict.

Indictment:
Term used to indicate that the grand jury has found enough evidence to warrant putting defendant through the trial process, as opposed to an information.

Information:
An accusation in writing made by a public prosecutor without the intervention of a grand jury where the accused may demand a preliminary hearing.

In Middle State, the grand jury consists of 13 members, including the foreperson. The foreperson has a vote, and 12 votes are required to bring a "true bill" of indictment. This means that only 2 votes are needed to deliver a "no true bill." Middle State is one of the few states in which there is a right to both a preliminary hearing and a grand jury indictment in all felony cases.

Grand Jury Procedure Illustrated

In Capital City, each criminal court judge has a grand jury that sits throughout the year. Individual jurors serve for three-month terms. The judge chooses the foreperson, and that individual is responsible for selecting the grand jury members. These grand juries handle all cases assigned to that judge during the term. On September 7, 2010, they were scheduled to hear Jesse Williams's case as well as five other cases.

Assistant District Attorney Rusty Kovaks requested that the foreperson issue subpoenas to ensure the appearance of Mr. Frank Builder, Officer Bill Sells (who first arrived at the crime scene), Detective Sergeant Michael Develon, and Mrs. Samuel J. Stone (the wife of the victim). The subpoenas used in criminal cases are essentially the same as those used in civil cases to require personal appearances and production of documents. Mike Develon was issued a *subpoena duces tecum* to bring the laboratory reports with him. All witnesses were required to appear on September 7 at 9:30 A.M. on the third floor of the Judicial Building in Capital City for a grand jury hearing in the case of *State v. Jesse Williams*.

The foreperson sent Jesse Williams a notice of the grand jury hearing ten days prior to the scheduled meeting. Jesse talked to his public defender, Jill Adams, about the notice, and she informed him that it was not an invitation—he would not be called, and the defense attorney would not be allowed to be present.

"You mean I can't defend myself at this grand jury?" asked Jesse.

"About all we can do is to petition the foreperson to call your girlfriend and any other witnesses in your behalf," said Adams. "I'll call your girlfriend and see if she will testify, if you want me to."

Jesse agreed, and Jill Adams petitioned the foreperson to allow Nancy Jones to testify before the grand jury. The foreperson agreed to issue her an invitation, and she could appear on a voluntary basis.

On September 7, after the grand jury had completed deliberation on the previously scheduled case, the bailiff called the first witness in Jesse Williams's case, Frank Builder, into the jury room. Frank was ushered into a small room by the bailiff, who administered the oath to tell the truth, the whole truth, and nothing but the truth.

Fourteen people were seated at one large table. Frank took a seat at the head of the table. The foreperson and assistant district attorney were seated at the far end of the table, and they introduced themselves to the witness.

The assistant district attorney, Rusty Kovaks, began questioning the witness by asking about his background and what he had done on the night of the robbery. Frank explained that he was a private building contractor and had been working late on a job. He was on his way home when he pulled into the Jiffy Stop Market to get some gas. He explained what he had observed at the market and the way in which he had identified the car he had seen leaving the scene of the crime at the police impoundment lot.

One of the grand jury members asked Frank how he could be so certain about the car, and he explained that the dented fenders and broken taillight convinced him that it was the same car, and besides, he had written down the license number, and it was the same.

After several other questions, Frank Builder was asked to wait outside the jury room so that other witnesses could be called. The foreperson called the officer who had arrived on the crime scene in response to the 911 call. The officer explained what he had observed and done at the scene: the condition of the victim, the open cash register, and his action in removing the gun from the victim's hand. This testimony did not take long, and Detective Mike Develon was then called to explain his observations at the crime scene as well as the method of identification and arrest of the suspect. Kovaks prompted Officer Develon from time to time with additional questions, and several grand jury members asked questions about the lineup and vehicle identification of the witness.

The store owner's wife was called to provide testimony concerning the condition of the victim and the inventory of stolen property. The victim was still in a coma, and the doctors did not know the extent of the brain damage. She reported that about $300 was missing from the cash register.

Kovaks asked that Sergeant Develon return to add testimony concerning his interview with Jesse's girlfriend, Nancy Jones. Mike Develon explained that Nancy did not know when Jesse arrived at her apartment that night, and he confirmed that the police had taken beer cans with Jiffy Stop price labels on them from her apartment as evidence.

Nancy Jones was then called into the jury room. She gave the grand jury the same testimony that she gave at the preliminary hearing—that she knew Jesse arrived before midnight because *M.A.S.H.* was still on the television. Kovaks reminded her that she was under oath and could be prosecuted for perjury if she was not telling the truth. "The truth is that you don't know for certain when Jesse arrived at your apartment. Isn't that right, Miss Jones?" asked Kovaks.

Nancy repeated her testimony that she was certain that the television program that she was watching was still on when he arrived, and it does not end until 12:00.

"Could the program have been delayed on that evening, Miss Jones?" asked Kovaks.

Nancy could not answer that question.

"Did Jesse have a gun, to your knowledge, Miss Jones?" asked Kovaks.
"No," Nancy replied.
"Did he give you any money that night?" asked the attorney.
"No," she said.

After the witnesses were dismissed, the assistant district attorney was given an opportunity to address the grand jury. He summarized the evidence and challenged the credibility of the defense witness by adding the evidence of her past arrest and conviction records.

Grand Jury Deliberation

Middle State law requires that the district attorney be removed from the grand jury while the jurors deliberated. This gave Rusty Kovaks an opportunity to talk informally with the witnesses who remained outside. Nancy Jones left immediately, but Mike Develon and the victim's wife were still there. This was a good opportunity for Kovaks to get to know his witnesses and formulate a better idea of how to prepare his case for trial. Kovaks knew he had a definite advantage over the defense at this stage. There were no rules of evidence and no judge to supervise the manner of questioning. It would be more difficult to convict on this evidence at trial.

In the jury room, one member said he agreed that the police had found the right car, but had they found the right man? Another member wanted to know about the missing gun and the missing money. The eyewitness had identified two persons who jumped into the car. "Where is the other suspect?" another member asked. The foreperson explained that the grand jury function was not to try the case on the standard of "beyond a reasonable doubt" but to decide whether there was enough evidence to warrant putting the suspect through a trial. Most of the jurors agreed that there was enough evidence to send the case to trial. When they voted, only one jury member cast a "no" vote. The 12 "yes" votes were sufficient to allow the foreperson to sign the true bill of indictment (see Form 15.1).

RIGHT TO A SPEEDY TRIAL

The Sixth Amendment right to a **speedy trial** was incorporated and applied against state actions through the Fourteenth Amendment's Due Process Clause in the case of *Klopfer v. North Carolina*, 386 U.S. 213 (1967). However, the Supreme Court did not establish a "fixed time rule" for either federal or state criminal prosecutions. In *Barker v. Wingo*, 407 U.S. 514 (1972), the Court identified the following factors to be considered in determining whether the speedy trial requirements have been met: (1) the length of delay, (2) the reason for the delay, (3) the defendant's claim of the right to a speedy trial, and (4) prejudice toward the defendant. The most

Speedy trial:
Guaranteed in the Sixth Amendment and interpreted to mean "without unreasonable delay." As applied to the states, it does not necessarily have fixed time elements.

Form 15.1 **BILL OF INDICTMENT**

MIDDLE STATE CRIMINAL COURT
LOCAL COUNTY

STATE OF MIDDLE STATE   )
)   Criminal Action
        V.   )   No. 1386 of 2010
)
Jesse Williams   )

The Grand Jury of Local County by this indictment charges that, on or about August 11, 2010, in said county, Jesse Williams did intentionally take the contents from the cash register of the Jiffy Stop Market on the corner of State and Fifth Streets, Capital City, from the owner and operator of said filling station–convenience store at gun point and did cause serious bodily harm to said victim by inflicting a gunshot wound to the head of said victim. All of the above in violation of sections 39-13-401 and 39-13-403 of the Middle State Criminal Code.

TRUE BILL DELIVERED_____   _____
                                                  Foreperson
By VOTE 12 YEAS TO ONE NO

WITNESSES:

_____

_____

_____

_____

Note: Notice of time, date, and place of arraignment on the reverse side.

important of these four factors is prejudice. In the *Barker* case, the court held that the defendant was not deprived of his right to a speedy trial even though his trial was delayed for over five years. The defendant did not assert that his right to a speedy trial had been violated until three years after his arrest.

Federal Speedy Trial Act

Congress passed the **Speedy Trial Act in 1974** to add the statutory require-ment of a "fixed time rule" in federal criminal prosecutions. This legislation sets the following limits:

1. An information or indictment charging a person with a crime must be filed within 30 days from the time of arrest.
2. The arraignment must be held within 10 days from the time of the information or indictment.
3. The trial must be held within 60 days after the arraignment.

These time limits mean that the accused must be brought to trial within 100 days after arrest in the federal system.

Speedy Trial Act in 1974:
Federal Statute requiring a fixed time rule in federal criminal prosecu-tions of 100 days.

State Speedy Trial Acts

Although most states have enacted speedy trial statutes, their provisions vary considerably. Many states do not have specific time limitations, and some set limits only to prevent prosecution delay. In current practice, most states are taking some form of action to implement the American Bar Asso-ciation's recommendations for effecting speedy trials and prompt disposi-tions of criminal cases. These standards include the following: "(a) the trial of criminal cases should be given preference over civil cases; and (b) the trial of defendants in custody and defendants whose pretrial liberty is rea-sonably believed to present unusual risks should be given preference over other criminal cases."

In Middle State, there was no speedy trial act setting time limitations, but the federal guidelines provided a good indication of the normal practice in most states. Jesse Williams was arrested on August 12 and was indicted on September 7. His arraignment was scheduled for September 17. At the arraignment, the prosecutor makes the formal and specific charges against the defendant, and the defendant is required to make a formal plea.

DEFENSE CONSIDERATIONS

Jill Adams, the defendant's attorney, met with Jesse after receiving notifi-cation of the grand jury indictment. Jesse was nervous and visibly shaken by the news that the grand jury had brought an indictment against him. He was told that he had ten days to decide how he would plead. Adams told him that if he pleaded "guilty," he would probably be able to make a deal with the prosecutor. However, if he pleaded "not guilty," he would face a trial and would risk a more severe penalty. She reviewed the potential penalties for the crime that had been brought in the indictment.

Sentencing Alternatives

Middle State had recently enacted comprehensive penal and sentencing reform legislation. These reform measures were enacted in 1989 when the entire criminal code was rewritten to create a unified approach to the relationship between the definition of an offense and the sentence for that offense. All felony offenses were divided into five classes based on the severity of the offense, with letter designations ranging from the most serious offenses, labeled class A, to the least serious offenses, labeled class E. The purpose of this classification system was to provide like punishment for the same offenses. All theft and theft-related offenses were graded according to the amount of the property taken.

A Modern Sentencing Grid

The classification of offenses permits construction of a **sentencing grid** so that the potential sentence for each offender can be rapidly ascertained. Each felony class carries a maximum and minimum sentence. In Middle State, a class A felony could be punished by incarceration for 15–60 years. This span is divided into three ranges called range I, range II, and range III. The range determination is based on the number of prior convictions, which in turn determines the potential span for the particular offender. Therefore, for a class A felony, a range I sentence is 15–25 years, a range II sentence is 25–40 years, and a range III sentence is 40–60 years.

Sentencing grid: Modern sentencing plan that restricts judicial sentencing by classification of offenses and provides a narrow range of sentencing guidelines.

The sample sentencing grid (see Figure 15.1) shows the five felony classes, A, B, C, D, and E. The numbers below each classification letter indicate the absolute minimum sentence for that class. The release eligibility date, or RED percentages, show the percentage of time that each offender must serve prior to parole eligibility. The RED years translate those percentages into numbers of years.

The second column displays the sentence spans for a defendant classified as an "especially mitigated offender." Where the judge finds mitigating factors but no enhancement factors, the judge may depart from the normal range determination and impose a sentence under the absolute minimum. The trial judge also has the option of decreasing the parole date.

The third column shows the sentence spans for offenders designated as "standard offenders" (range I). A standard offender is a defendant who does not fall into one of the other sentencing ranges (not more than one prior felony conviction).

The next column lists the sentence spans for "multiple offenders" (range II). A multiple offender is one who has several prior convictions (at least two but not more than four). The presence of these convictions enhances the potential length of sentence, depending on the felony class of the prior convictions.

The next column of the sentencing grid lists the ranges for "persistent offenders" (range III), who basically are defined as those having any combination of five or more prior felony convictions.

The final column lists the ranges for the defendant who is designated as a "career offender." A career offender is one who has any combination of six or more class A, B, or C prior felony convictions. A defendant with such a designation must be sentenced to the maximum penalty imposed for range III, with a substantially higher parole eligibility date.

Under Middle State's reform program, all sentences are determinate in nature, and the judge has to fix a specific length of sentence within the appropriate range for that particular offender. The presumptive sentence is the minimum in the range. The judge also has to consider the various mitigating and enhancing factors stipulated in the code when establishing the specific sentence. The judge fixes the specific length of the sentence and also determines how that sentence would be satisfied within the options depicted in the sentencing grid (see Figure 15.1). Note that the blocks shaded the darkest represent higher felony classifications in which the person convicted must serve mandatory continuous confinement with the department of corrections (state penitentiary). In other cases, the trial judge has the discretion to impose a wide range of sentencing alternatives.

Jesse Williams had been indicted for a class A felony and had one prior felony conviction. He fell into the first sentencing block on the second column labeled "Standard Range I," so his sentence would be from 15–25 years in the state penitentiary. After serving 30 percent of that time, he might be eligible for parole if he had a clean record and could convince the parole board that he was no longer a danger to the community.

Jill Adams explained that Jesse could, at the very least, expect a sentence of close to 25 years if he pleaded not guilty, went to trial, and was convicted. His record and the seriousness of the injury to the victim would be considered enhancement factors. "If the victim dies, you could be facing a penalty of death or life imprisonment," said Adams.

"Can't I 'cop a plea' and make a deal with the DA?" asked Jesse.

Plea Bargaining Illustrated

The defense attorney told Jesse, "I'm sure the DA wants to know who your accomplice is and where the gun and the stolen money are located. If you

Sentence Ranges
Release Eligibility Dates

Felony Class	Mitigated	Standard Range I	Multiple Range II	Persistent Range III	Career
A 15–60 yrs. RED % RED yrs.	(13.5 years) (20%) (2.7 years)	(15–25 years) (30%) (4.5–7.5 years)	(25–40 years) (35%) (8.8–14 years)	(40–60 years) (45%) (18–27 years)	(60 years) (60%) (36 years)
B 8–30 yrs. RED % RED yrs.	(7.2 years) (20%) (1.4 years)	(8–12 years) (30%) (2.4–3.6 years)	(12–20 years) (35%) (4.2–7 years)	(13.5 years) (20%) (2.7 years)	(30 years) (60%) (18 years)
C 3–15 yrs. RED % RED yrs.	(2.7 years) (20%) (.5 years)	(3–6 years) (30%) (.9–1.8 years)	(6–10 years) (35%) (2.1–3.5 years)	(13.5 years) (20%) (2.7 years)	(15 years) (60%) (9 years)
D 2–12 yrs. RED % RED yrs.	(1.8 years) (20%) (.4 years)	(2–4 years) (30%) (.6–1.2 years)	(4–8 years) (35%) (1.4–2.8 years)	(13.5 years) (20%) (2.7 years)	(12 years) (60%) (7.2 years)
E 1–6 yrs. RED % RED yrs.	(.9 years) (20%) (.2 years)	(1–2 years) (30%) (.3–.6 years)	(2–4 years) (35%) (2.7 years)	(13.5 years) (20%) (.7–1.4 years)	(6 years) (60%) (36 years)

Presumptive Sentence minimum sentence in range
R.E.D. Release Eligibility Date

Mandatory Continuous Confinement with the Department of Correction.

Alternative Forms of Punishment Encouraged.

Confinement with DOC available; alternative sentencing available if sentence 8 years or less.

Local Incarceration Required if County Contract.

Figure 15.1
Sentencing Grid

can provide this information, the DA will possibly reduce the charges. Assisting the authorities in locating or recovering any property or person involved in the crime is a mitigating factor. However, if the victim dies, they will charge you with first degree murder, and that carries the death penalty or life imprisonment."

"What if I didn't do the shootin'?" Jesse asked.

"In that case you may be able to get a substantially reduced sentence, but as an accomplice you are subject to the same criminal responsibility," explained Adams. "If you 'aided and abetted' and were ready to offer assistance, you are just as guilty as if you had pulled the trigger."

"What happens if I plead 'not guilty'?" Jesse asked.

"Then you will go to trial. We will have about 60 days to prepare for your defense. We will have the court's authority to subpoena witnesses and evidence in your behalf. The DA will have to prove that you are guilty beyond a reasonable doubt. You would have a right to demand a jury trial, and in this state you would get a jury of 12," explained the attorney.

"How many did it take to pass that grand jury indictment?" asked Jesse.

"Twelve people had to agree that there was enough evidence to warrant putting you through a trial, Jesse. But they don't use the 'beyond a reasonable doubt' standard, and we did not have a chance to put up a defense," replied the public defender.

"I've been in here a month now, and my girlfriend won't even talk to me no more. I thought she'd get me out of this, but now I don't know. Do you think they'll convict me?" asked Jesse.

"They have an eyewitness that puts you and your car at the scene of the crime, and they probably have a lot more we don't know about. You are in bad trouble, and you had better start telling me the truth if you expect me to help you," answered Adams.

"I can't tell you no more," Jesse said.

"Do you want me to talk with the DA about a deal in exchange for your coming clean with everything that happened?" the attorney asked.

"That means I'd have to plead guilty to some lesser charge, don't it?" Jesse asked.

"Yes, maybe if you did not do the shooting you could try for the class B felony of aggravated robbery as an accomplice, that would reduce your sentence to 8–12 years and make you eligible for parole in about two and a half years," explained the public defender.

"Okay, see what kind of a deal you can make," said Jesse.

The Agreement

Jill Adams made an appointment with the assistant district attorney assigned to Jesse's case. Assistant District Attorney Rusty Kovaks greeted Jill politely and asked, "What can I do for you, Counselor?"

"My client wants to make a deal. He'll tell you about the crime if you will reduce the charge," Adams replied.

"We've got an eyewitness, Counselor, and the victim may die," said the prosecutor. "I don't think I can help your client with the reduced sentence."

"He might be able to identify the other suspect and enable you to recover the gun and the money taken," said the public defender. "He says he was not the one who fired the shot."

"Do you believe him, Counselor?" asked Kovaks.

"I don't know. You can talk to him and see what you think," said Adams.

"Okay, if you think he's ready to talk, we could set up a meeting," replied Kovaks.

The attorneys went to the jail and met with the defendant. Jesse looked scared but said he was ready to talk if he could get a good deal. Detective

Sergeant Mike Develon set up an interrogation room that was wired for sound. Public Defender Jill Adams, Assistant District Attorney Rusty Kovaks, and Sergeant Develon entered the room with Jesse. First, Jesse was told his rights: that he had a right to remain silent, that what he told the district attorney would be held against him in court, that he had a right to an attorney, and that his attorney was present. "If you or your lawyer want this questioning to stop, all you have to do is tell us, Jesse. Do you understand?" asked Sergeant Develon.

Jesse indicated that he understood and agreed. "What kind of a deal are you going to give me if I tell you what I know?" asked Jesse.

"If you give us information leading to an arrest and you were not the principal instigator, or person doing the shooting, I will recommend that the charge be reduced to aggravated robbery, which carries an 8–12 year sentence," said Kovaks.

"Okay, but how do I know I can trust you to keep your word?" asked Jesse.

"The Supreme Court has held that our promises must be fulfilled," said the assistant DA.

Adams added, "That's right, Jesse; but the judge must accept this plea. If that happens, we could get the confession excluded from the jury if they don't live up to the agreement."

The Confession

Jesse decided to confess. The assistant district attorney then repeated the required Miranda warnings to the accused Jesse Williams. "You have the right to remain silent, anything you tell us can and will be used against you in a court of law, you have the right to have your lawyer present, and your court appointed lawyer is present; do you understand your rights?" asked attorney Kovaks.

"Robert Jackson was the one who did the shooting. He has the gun and the money," said Jesse.

"Where does he live, Jesse?" asked Kovaks.

"He lives on Maple Street, on the west side of town," Jesse answered. "It's about three blocks from the Jiffy Stop Market. You turn right off State Street, and it's the third house on the right. I don't know the number."

Kovaks asked Sergeant Develon to get a map from the police office in order to ascertain the house number. They confirmed the address on the map by checking the telephone book and identified the house number as 12 Maple Street.

"He lives there with his mother," commented Jesse.

"Now tell us everything you know about the robbery," said Kovaks.

Jesse gave the following account of the events of that evening: "I met Robert at a bar, the Pub, on the west side of town. There wasn't much going on there, so we talked about doing some drugs. But neither one of us had any money to make a buy. So we drove around awhile, talking about how we could get some money, Robert had a gun, and we decided to hold up the Jiffy Stop Market. It was late, and there wasn't nobody around.

"Robert went in with me, and I got a six-pack of beer while he checked the place out. When I went up to the counter, Robert pulled his gun. Then the man behind the counter grabbed his gun from under the counter, and Robert shot him. Robert grabbed the money out of the cash register, and we went out to the car. I told him somebody was coming, so we jumped in the car and left.

"We was both scared somebody had spotted us; so we went to his house first. He jumped out and went inside. All I got was a six-pack of beer that I took to my girl's house. He's got the gun and the money."

They went over the story again, and Kovaks asked more questions. Jesse stuck to his story, and the assistant district attorney asked the police department's secretary to type Jesse's confession as an affidavit for Jesse to sign. After Jesse read the typewritten confession, he signed it in front of the secretary, who was also a notary public. The affidavit was witnessed by Jill Adams, Jesse's attorney, and by Rusty Kovaks, the assistant district attorney. Jesse was then escorted back to his cell.

Sergeant Develon immediately filled out a complaint and an arrest warrant application for Robert Jackson and delivered it to the city magistrate on duty along with the affidavit that Jesse had signed. The magistrate signed an arrest warrant, and Sergeant Develon was assigned to pick up the second suspect in the convenience store robbery.

Arrest of the Second Suspect

Sergeant Develon and two uniformed officers went to the address Jesse had given them to make the arrest. They expected the suspect to be armed and dangerous, so they planned their arrest procedure on the way. Develon had the artist's drawing of the suspect, which Jesse had identified as a good likeness of Robert Jackson, and he passed it around to the two uniformed officers.

Develon went to the door of the dwelling at 12 Maple Street with one of the uniformed officers. The other officer went around to the back of the house to block that avenue of escape. An older woman came to the door, and Mike asked whether Robert Jackson lived there.

"Yes, I'm his mother," the elderly woman replied.

Then the officers heard a door slam inside the dwelling and entered with their guns drawn. The officer outside also heard the noise and drew his weapon, shouting, "Stop, police!" as he saw a person run out of the house. The suspect did not stop, but kept running. The officer could see something in the suspect's hand that could have been a handgun.

Should he shoot? The officer ran after the suspect as he turned the corner of another building. When the pursuing officer rounded the corner, he saw the suspect drop something into a neighbor's trash can. The suspect then entered the neighbor's backdoor.

The other two officers had now caught up with the officer chasing the suspect, and they all barged into the neighbor's house and apprehended the suspect. He was forced to the floor, where one of the officers put the handcuffs on him. He was frisked for weapons and identified as Robert Jackson. The occupant of the dwelling demanded an explanation, and Sergeant Develon showed the young woman the arrest warrant. Then Robert Jackson was told that he had a right to remain silent, that anything he told the officers could be used against him, that he had a right to a lawyer, and that a lawyer would be provided for him if he could not afford one.

The officer who had given chase and witnessed the suspect putting something into the neighbor's trash can opened the lid of the can and found a .38 "police special" on top of the garbage. "Is this what we're looking for, Develon?" he asked.

"It sure is," said Develon.

The suspect was taken to the police station, strip-searched, and booked. His fingerprints were taken and sent to the laboratory immediately to see whether they matched the prints found at the scene of the crime. The .38 "police special" was also sent to the laboratory to be matched with the bullet recovered from the victim's head. Within two hours, the police had a laboratory report that provided a positive identification. The assistant district attorney, Rusty Kovaks, was notified of these developments and said that he would come to the station to take Robert before the magistrate.

Robert Jackson was asked how old he was and given an application for appointment of counsel. He was only 18 and said he could not afford a lawyer. He was so scared he could hardly talk. The officers tried to assure him that they were not going to harm him and helped him fill out the application. They gave him a copy of the arrest warrant. Robert just hung his head and remained silent.

When Rusty Kovaks arrived, Sergeant Develon escorted the prisoner to the magistrate, who again informed Robert of his rights. Since Robert had already filled out an application for appointment of counsel, the magistrate accepted the application and said he would see that counsel was promptly appointed. After questioning the arresting officer and learning of the defendant's action to evade arrest, the magistrate decided to refuse to grant bail and ordered the defendant held without bail. He set the preliminary hearing for September 30 at 9:30 A.M.

After Robert had been returned to his cell, the magistrate recognized that the public defender's office was representing the other defendant, Jesse Williams, in the same robbery. Another lawyer from the public defender's office could not be appointed since such an appointment would be a **conflict of interest**. The judge, therefore, would have to appoint counsel from a list of private criminal lawyers. The appointed attorney would be paid a fixed fee of about half what the attorney would normally charge. The judge appointed the next lawyer on the list, who happened to be Attorney Alvin Sharp. Attorney Sharp's office was notified of the appointment.

Conflict of interest:
Ethical conflict involving violation of trust in matters of private interest and gain. A lawyer may not serve two clients with opposing interests.

THE ARRAIGNMENT

The assistant district attorney, Rusty Kovaks, had promised Jesse Williams a reduction in the charge listed in the indictment handed down by the grand jury. Kovaks now had to prepare for the **arraignment**, where he would be required to enter the formal charges against the defendant. He was able to promise Jesse a reduced charge because of the concept of **lesser included offenses**, which means that the crime stipulated in the indictment includes several other offenses. In a trial situation, the judge must charge the jury to consider lesser included offenses as alternative possible convictions.

Arraignment:
Criminal procedural stage where defendant is required to enter a plea.

Lesser included offenses:
Composed of some but not all of the elements of the greater crime.

Plea Alternatives

The basic pleas at the arraignment stage are **guilty** and not guilty, but there are several variations in the plea process that need to be understood. In our example, Jesse pleaded guilty, and the judge had to be satisfied that the accused not only voluntarily but also knowingly and willingly waived his rights. In addition, the judge had to accept the conditions of any plea bargain agreement between the prosecutor and the accused. Failure to accept a plea bargain would allow the defendant to withdraw the plea and exercise his right to a jury trial. The evidence then would be suppressed and would not be given to the jury.

Guilty plea:
Formal admission in court as to guilt of a crime.

Nolo contendere is another form of guilty plea that in effect says, "I will not contest it." This plea has the same effect as a guilty plea and results in a sentencing decision at the arraignment stage. The plea admits, for the purposes of the case, all facts that are well pleaded, but it is not to be used as an admission elsewhere. In a later civil action against the defendant, such a plea cannot be used as evidence.

The plea of **not guilty** indicates a willingness to contest the charges against the defendant, and the judge is required to either dismiss the charges or set a trial date. The defendant has the right to demand a jury trial. A defendant who refuses to make a plea is said to "stand mute before the court." In this situation, the judge is required to send the case to trial, and the defendant is given a jury trial unless that right is waived.

Not guilty plea:
Plea entered by the accused at arraignment that indicates desire to contest the charge at trial.

Not guilty by reason of insanity is essentially the same as a not-guilty plea, and the case goes to trial. The **insanity defense** is a trial consideration, and generally the prosecutor has to prove sanity at trial. The defense must give notice that the insanity defense will be invoked. The prosecution must prove sanity in order to meet the general standards of *mens rea* (mental intent) required by law to convict.

One fairly recent type of plea is now accepted by most states and the federal courts. The *Alford plea* arose out of the 1970 case before the U.S. Supreme Court styled, *North Carolina v. Alford*, 400 U.S. 25 (1970). In that case, the Supreme Court ruled that the defendant could enter a plea of guilty while still asserting his innocence. The ruling of the Court stated that the defendant "may voluntarily, knowingly, and understandingly consent to the imposition of a prison sentence even if he is unwilling or unable to admit his participation in the acts that constitute the crime." This form of guilty plea has been used in local and state courts in the United States; although it constitutes only a small percentage of all pleas in the United States.

Most state courts hold that an Alford plea is the "functional equivalent" of a regular plea of guilty. Only Indiana, Michigan, and New Jersey forbid the usage of Alford pleas within their state court systems (Bibas, 2003, 6).

Insanity defense: The defense is considered in the trial and is the same as not guilty, but sanity must be proved at trial before it becomes effective as a verdict. The prosecutor must be informed of the intent to use this defense before trial.

Plea Day Illustrated

On September 21, Criminal Court Judge Otis Mann conducted what is often referred to as "plea day" in his court. Plea day is a day set aside on the court calendar to hear arraignments. The defendant, Jesse Williams, and his attorney, Jill Adams, were present, as was Assistant District Attorney Rusty Kovaks. The session was held in open court; interested parties, including the press, attended. The assistant district attorney was asked to read the charge against Jesse Williams, and Jesse was given a written copy of the charge, which was for aggravated robbery.

Jesse was told to rise, and the judge asked him, "How do you plead to this charge, Mr. Williams?"

Jesse answered, "Guilty, your honor."

"Do you understand the nature of the charge of aggravated robbery, Mr. Williams?" the judge asked.

"Yes, sir, it's armed robbery and a class B felony," Jesse replied.

"What in fact did you do that makes you guilty of this crime?" asked the judge.

"I participated in the robbery of the Jiffy Stop Market on August 11, 2010," said Jesse.

The judge asked Jesse to tell the court what happened, and Jesse repeated the same story he had given in his confession.

"Do you understand that you have a right to a jury trial?" the judge continued.

"Yes," said Jesse.

"Have you made a plea bargain with the district attorney's office?" asked the judge.

"Yes," Jesse answered. "The DA promised to reduce the charge if I would tell him all I knew about the crime. Robert Jackson was with me, and I told the DA where to find him and the gun used in the robbery."

The judge asked Jesse whether he knew the range of the sentences for the offense of aggravated robbery to which he had pleaded guilty. Jesse said that he understood the range was from 8–12 years imprisonment with a chance of parole after 30 percent of his time had been served.

The judge then turned to Assistant District Attorney Rusty Kovacs and asked, "What specifically has been offered by the district attorney?"

Rusty Kovacs replied, "I offered to recommend the lesser included offense of aggregated robbery if he was not the instigator or the shooter in this crime."

"Have you discovered the accomplice in this crime?" the judge asked.

"Yes, your honor we have apprehended the accomplice and also charged him with aggravated robbery."

Judge Otis Mann addressed Jesse Williams again and made the following statement, "Jesse Williams, I will not accept your guilty plea to this court at this time. There are several reasons why I cannot accept your plea bargain with the assistant district attorney. First of all, I have the mandatory requirement under the Middle State *Rules of Criminal Procedure*, Rule 8, *Joinder of Offenses and Defendants* to require the district attorney to join these two offenses in the same indictment with each offense stated in a separate count, or the offenses consolidated pursuant to Rule 13, if the offenses are based on the same conduct or arise from the same criminal episode.

"Secondly, this set of criminal charges for both of the accused defendants includes a potential death of the victim, which will change the charge involving both defendants.

"Jesse Williams, you have the opportunity to withdraw your plea of guilty; your confession in this court and with the district attorney may not be used as evidence against you. If the plea is not withdrawn, the court may dispose of the case less favorably toward you than provided in the plea agreement."

"Yes, sir; I withdraw my plea of guilty, your honor," replied Jesse.

"It is so ordered," declared Judge Mann.

The judge then called the next case, and Jesse was returned to his cell.

ASSIGNMENT: Look up the rules of criminal procedure in your state. You should be able to find it by entering the name of your state and "rules of criminal procedure." Find out what the rules provide for joining individuals in one consolidated case and how they may be separated. (See also recent rules adopted by the State of Tennessee in their *Tennessee Rules of Criminal Procedure*.)

Rule 8 of the Middle State Rules of Court require a *mandatory joinder* of offenses, which states:

> Two or more offenses shall be joined in the same indictment with each offense stated in a separate count, or the offenses consolidated pursuant to Rule 13, if the offenses are:
>
> (A) Based on the same conduct or arising from the same criminal episode;
>
> (B) Within the jurisdiction of a single court; and
>
> (C) Known to the appropriate prosecuting official at the time of the return of the indictments.

Consolidation of Actions

Consolidation of actions, or joinder of claims, refers to both civil and criminal cases: When actions involving a common question of law or fact are pending before the court, it may order a joint hearing or trial of any or all the matters at issue in the action; it may order all actions consolidated; and it may make such orders concerning proceedings therein as may tend to avoid unnecessary costs or delay (Fed.R. Civil P. 42 (a); New York C.P.L.R. §602; see also Joinder or Joinder of claims in state rules of civil procedure).

Consolidation of actions: Act of uniting several actions into one trial and judgment, by order of a court, where all actions are between the same parties pending in the same court.

The second suspect in the Jiffy Stop robbery, Robert Jackson, had been arrested just before Jesse Williams was scheduled for arraignment. Robert Jackson's arrest, initial appearance, and court appointment of private counsel was described in this chapter. Attorney Alvin Sharp was appointed to represent Robert Jackson.

Jackson was being held without bail in the Capital City jail when Attorney Sharp visited him for an initial interview. This meeting revealed a frightened 18-year-old defendant who had a different story to tell about the robbery from that told by Jesse Williams. Robert Jackson said that he had no knowledge of the robbery before the incident took place. He claimed that he did not shoot the victim and was not in the store at the time of the shooting. He claimed that Jesse Williams shot the victim and robbed the store while he was putting gas into the car. He further claimed that he had no prior knowledge of Jesse Williams's intent to rob the store or even that Jesse had a gun.

Attorney Sharp was impressed by the young man's story, but he was highly skeptical about his ability to defend his client on the basis of such a story. He knew from the police charges that Robert had been charged with a class A felony, **armed robbery** that he had resisted arrest, and that he was caught in possession of the firearm used in the robbery and shooting of the store owner.

Armed robbery: Aggravated robbery; the taking of property by use of force while armed with a dangerous weapon.

The attorney's preliminary investigation tended to verify the defendant's story, but there was no specific evidence available that would convince a judge to dismiss the charges against Robert Jackson. Attorney Sharp advised his client to waive his preliminary hearing set for September 30, and the judge bound the case over to the grand jury without a hearing.

Defense Considerations

Attorney Sharp began the investigation into Robert's background. The police confirmed that they had no record on Robert. The lawyer was given a copy of the laboratory report that matched Robert's fingerprints with those obtained from the crime scene. That report also showed that the markings on the bullet recovered from the victim's head matched a sample fired from the handgun Robert was carrying when arrested.

Robert's mother was a hardworking, respected person in the neighborhood. She was shocked about her son's involvement in criminal activity. She described him as a good boy. She said he had a lot of trouble growing up without a father, but he made good grades in high school and had graduated in May of 2009 in the upper half of his class. She was proud of him and had encouraged him to go to college and do something useful with his life. Robert's mother did not know Jesse Williams, but she had warned her son to stay away from drugs and to be independent.

The neighborhood friends and acquaintances confirmed the impression left by his mother. Robert had never been violent or even in trouble to their knowledge. All of them described him as a good kid. Robert and his mother lived in a poor neighborhood, and his mother worked as a housekeeper in a big hotel downtown. She put in long hours and was very dependable, according to her employer. She had never missed work in the 15 years she had been employed there.

Robert's science teacher confirmed the background information gathered about Robert. She said Robert was a dependable student whom she had advised to go to college. She found it hard to believe that he would be involved in an armed robbery. "All these kids try drugs and get a little wild when they get out of high school, but Robert was just not the type to shoot somebody. He wanted to be an astronaut and was interested in science. He respected his teachers and even did extra work to keep his grades up," said the teacher.

Attorney Sharp was beginning to seriously consider his client's story, but none of the information he had gathered could be used to prevent Robert from being convicted. He was at the scene of the crime and was found with the weapon used in the crime. His fleeing from the police implied guilt and intent. The defense attorney knew he would need some evidence to support the story Robert had told him in order to defend him.

Prosecutor's Decision

At the district attorney's office, Robert Jackson's case had been ordered by the judge to be consolidated with Jesse Williams's case for trial. Since Robert Jackson was not yet brought before the grand jury, it made sense to consolidate the indictment during this procedure. Both defendants were now in custody, and they were basically charged with the same offense. The victim's condition was of major concern because his condition had been getting worse. Assistant District Attorney Rusty Kovaks decided to call the hospital and check on Samuel P. Stone's condition.

The hospital told the district attorney's office that Samuel P. Stone had died at 1:35 A.M. on Monday, September 27, 2010. Rusty Kovaks then contacted the physician and made arrangements to obtain the death certificate for his records. Rusty Kovaks knew he now had to go back to the grand jury for new indictments for both of the defendants in the case involving Jesse Williams and Robert Jackson. There would now be additional charges of first-degree murder that would be added to the offences.

He discussed this development with his boss, the district attorney general. The attorney general reviewed all the preliminary events and processes for both defendants and agreed with Assistant District Attorney Kovaks that both defendants should be charged with first-degree murder and aggravated robbery involving all lesser included offences. "The truth will have to be brought out in the trial processes. But are you sure you have enough evidence to convict?" asked the attorney general.

The assistant district attorney said, "I need more help with this case, since each of these defendants will have his own case to argue, and we need two prosecutors. Each of the defendants already has an appointed attorney working for him."

The DA agreed. "I will appoint Glen Hawkins to be your co-counsel in this case."

"I'll start with Frank Builder and use him to identify Robert Jackson in a lineup. He got a good look at this defendant, and he may be able to help us with more evidence about who the shooter could have been. He will also be called for the combined grand jury investigation."

Once the preliminary hearing involving Robert Jackson was waived and the case was bound over to the grand jury, Criminal Court Judge L.B. Long was assigned to the case. Rusty Kovaks and Glen Hawkins would consolidate the charges against both of the defendants before the grand jury at its next session on October 19. Glen's office was close to Rusty's office, and they had briefly discussed the two cases. Like Rusty, Glen was an experienced assistant district attorney assigned to the special criminal unit.

Glen Hawkins went back to his office and read the file on Robert Jackson thoroughly. He noticed that Robert was only 18 years old and had no prior record. However, Robert had resisted arrest, and he had the gun used in the robbery to kill the victim, all of which tended to confirm Jesse's story that Robert did the shooting. The next step was to go to the grand jury for an indictment. He noted that the eyewitness, Frank Builder, had said he got a good look at one of the robbers at the convenience store on the night of the robbery.

He called Sergeant Develon at the police station and had him set up an identification lineup to see whether the witness could make a positive identification of Robert Jackson. "Does Jackson have a lawyer assigned to his case?" Glen asked Mike Develon.

"Yeah, Al Sharp's been in here to see Jackson," answered Develon.

"Give him a call and invite him to the lineup. I want to make sure we don't lose any evidence in this case," the attorney said.

Right to Counsel at Lineup Identification

In *United States v. Wade*, 388 U.S. 218 (1967), the Supreme Court held that the accused has the right to have counsel present to witness a **pretrial lineup** if a complaint or indictment has been issued. The presence of counsel might not be necessary when a complaint has not yet been filed, but the assistant district attorney was taking no chances that might cause evidence to be suppressed. When the right to counsel is violated at a "critical stage," identification may be excluded at trial.

Pretrial lineup: A postindictment arrest or lineup is a "critical stage" in a criminal proceeding, so the accused has a constitutional right to have counsel present.

The Lineup Procedure

At the lineup, which took place on October 12, Frank Builder identified Robert Jackson in a line of seven inmates. "That's the one I saw running around the car and getting into the passenger side. He's the third one from the left," said Frank Builder.

The identification was witnessed by Assistant District Attorney Glen Hawkins, Alvin Sharp (Robert Jackson's lawyer), and by Sergeant Develon. A supplemental statement was drafted, and it was signed by Frank Builder, the witness, as a true and accurate copy of the identification. Al Sharp raised no objections to the procedure, during which the assistant district attorney informed the defense attorney that the victim had died. Al Sharp had anticipated this development and knew that his client was in more trouble than before. Now he would be charged with first-degree murder.

"My client admits he was there when the robbery took place," Al told the assistant district attorney, "but he did not do the shooting. That was Jesse Williams's gun you caught him with. He's got a clean record, and I believe the kid."

"Come on, Counselor," Glen responded. "You can't be serious. We got this guy cold. You just saw the positive witness ID. We are going to charge your guy with first degree murder."

CHAPTER SUMMARY

1. This chapter explains the transition from the control subsystem to the court subsystem in the criminal justice process. The pretrial phase in the court subsystem is dominated by the public prosecutor, who has extensive discretionary authority.

2. Most state prosecutors are elected by popular vote, whereas federal prosecutors are appointed. The position of prosecutor is a political office of high visibility. These posts are often used as stepping-stones for persons seeking higher public office. The extraordinary discretionary power of those serving as prosecutors subjects them to a high degree of public trust and responsibility.

3. The official prosecutor (district attorney general) in most urban jurisdictions heads a small bureaucracy that is responsible for managing large numbers of assistant prosecutors who handle the daily tasks of the office. Generally, these assistant prosecutors have wide individual discretionary authority; however, there is pressure to adhere to departmental policy concerning priorities, and the entire process is influenced by the caseload and available resources.

4. The most important discretionary power given to prosecutors is the power not to prosecute (*nolle prosequi*). The decision to prosecute an individual is ultimately checked by the courts, but the district attorney's decision not to prosecute is nearly absolute.

5. The Supreme Court has held that a person accused of any crime that carries a potential jail sentence has the right to counsel. In 1967, the Court held that a pretrial lineup after a complaint or indictment has been issued is a "critical stage" in the trial process and that the defendant, therefore, has the right to have counsel present.

6. Plea bargaining has become almost routine and is derived from the prosecutor's combined charging function and power not to prosecute. The heavy caseload and pressures to handle cases more efficiently

have made plea bargaining the characteristic feature of the American system of justice. More than 90 percent of the convictions obtained in the criminal justice system are obtained through guilty pleas, and these cases never go to trial.

7. Prosecutors frequently use their plea bargaining authority to get confessions from defendants, promising more lenient treatment for those who provide information about other criminal activities.

8. The grand jury indictment process involves a probable cause hearing at which a group of private citizens decide whether there is enough evidence to warrant putting the individual through a trial. Grand juries are used in almost all states, but they are discretionary in about half of the states. The number of members ranges from 12 to 23, and it usually takes 12 votes to deliver a true bill of indictment. Grand juries are supposed to check the abuse of authority by prosecutors, but the prosecutor often dominates these lay bodies since that officer is the most authoritative person present.

9. Grand juries have extensive latent power to initiate indictments, subpoena witnesses, and investigate local corruption. The foreperson is selected by the judge. Most grand juries serve for fixed terms and are selected by the foreperson. These juries consider all cases submitted to them by the local prosecutor. There are also special grand juries that sit until an investigation is completed.

10. The grand jury essentially hears the evidence against the accused. The proceeding is not adversarial but rather investigative. The defendant is not heard by the grand jury, and the defendant's attorney is not allowed to be present.

11. The courts generally have used four factors to determine compliance with the Sixth Amendment right to a speedy trial. These four factors are (1) the length of delay, (2) the reason for the delay, (3) the defendant's claim of the right to a speedy trial, and (4) prejudice toward the defendant. However, in 1974 the U.S. Congress enacted a "fixed time rule" for the federal jurisdiction that requires that the defendant be brought to trial within 100 days from the time of arrest. Most states have instituted similar rules, often with longer periods and more discretion. Priority is given to criminal cases over civil cases.

12. The sentencing grid system described in this chapter is similar to those of several other states and the federal jurisdiction. This system is part of comprehensive reforms that are new to criminal justice practice, and the ultimate effect of these reforms is not known. However, the basic features of sentencing grid systems facilitate certainty and predictability in a system that has been severely criticized as lacking in these qualities.

13. The overwhelming majority of cases exit the court subsystem at the arraignment stage of the pretrial process. These cases are moved into

the corrections subsystem for the punishment phase of the criminal justice system.

14. The arraignment proceeding is conducted by a superior (trial) judge, who calls on the prosecutor to enter the formal charges and on the defendant to enter a plea. These judges will generally try the case if it goes to trial and have considerable authority over this procedure. As illustrated in this case, they may overrule plea bargains and order the consolidation of cases against individuals involved in the same crime.

15. The basic pleas are guilty and not guilty. A not-guilty plea (or silence) sends the case to trial; a guilty plea results in sentencing without a trial. A plea of *nolo contendere* results in sentencing at this stage but cannot be used in a civil proceeding against the defendant. A "plea of guilty while asserting innocence" may be accepted as a guilty plea allowing the sentence to follow at this stage in most states and the federal courts (called *Alford pleas*).

16. The U.S. Supreme Court has held that the accused has the right to have counsel present to witness a pretrial lineup if a complaint or indictment has been issued.

REVIEW EXERCISE

Match the following terms with their most appropriate meaning.

Terms
1. Prosecutor
2. Nolle prosequi (nol-pros)
3. Plea bargaining
4. Grand jury
5. Indictment
6. Information
7. Speedy trial
8. Speedy Trial Act of 1974
9. Sentencing grid
10. Conflict of interest
11. Arraignment
12. Lesser included offense
13. Guilty plea
14. Not guilty plea
15. Insanity defense
16. Consolidation of actions
17. Armed robbery

Meaning
____ when the accused is brought before the court to enter a plea after indictment or information
____ government official who has authority to bring criminal actions
____ plea indicating person accused wants to contest the charges at trial
____ restricts judicial sentencing by classification of offenses and sentencing guidelines
____ post-complaint or indictment identification which includes the right to have counsel for the defense present
____ process of uniting several actions into one trial and judgment of several defendants
____ body of citizens who decide probable cause to bind over to arraignment
____ sanity must be proved at trial before the defense becomes effective
____ federal law requiring fixed time limits of 100 days from arrest to trial that apply to federal criminal cases
____ formal admission in court as to guilt of a crime
____ guaranteed in the Sixth Amendment but interpreted by most states as "without unreasonable delay"
____ taking of property of another by use of threat or use of force while armed with a deadly weapon
____ process whereby the accused and the prosecutor agree to a plea of guilty in exchange for a more favorable charge with the consent of the judge

18. Pretrial lineup

_____ written accusation made by the district attorney and subject to review at a preliminary hearing

_____ prosecutor refuses to prosecute the case

_____ composed of some but not all of the elements of the greater crime

_____ ethical standard that lawyers cannot serve clients with opposing interests

_____ action taken by the Grand jury when they find probable cause to bind over to the trial court

DISCUSSION QUESTIONS

1. What are the most important duties and responsibilities of the public prosecutor?

2. Does the prosecutor have too much discretionary power?

3. Should prosecutors be elected or appointed?

4. What charging methods are used in your state? How are the grand jury and information systems used? What are their comparative differences?

5. How many votes does it take to deliver a true bill of indictment in your state if the grand jury is used? What effect does the number of votes have on the process?

6. Does your state employ a sentencing grid system like that used in Middle State? Would your state benefit from the comprehensive reform measures described in this chapter?

7. Is plea bargaining overused and abused in our system of justice? What are the alternatives to the characteristic plea bargaining process described in this chapter?

ASSIGNMENTS

ASSIGNMENT: Find your state's criminal code by using the library or the Internet and look up the definition of particular crimes that are of interest to you. You can enter your state's name and criminal code, and it should be available on the Internet. You will need to have a term in mind, but you will be able to find the statutory provisions. Crimes within the District of Columbia are found in the _D.C. Criminal Code._

ASSIGNMENT: Look up the rules of criminal procedure in your state. You should be able to find it by entering the name of your state and "rules of criminal procedure." Find out what the rules provide for joining individuals in one consolidated case and how they may be separated. (See also recent rules adopted by the State of Tennessee in their _Tennessee Rules of Criminal Procedure._)

SOURCES AND SUGGESTED READING

Bibas, Stephanos. 2003. "Harmonizing Substantive Criminal Law Values and Criminal Procedures: The Case of Alford and Nolo Contendere Pleas." 88 _Cornell Law Review_ (6).

Boland, Barbara, Catherine H. Conly, Lynn Warner, Ronald Sones, and William Martin. 1988. _The Prosecution of Felony Arrests_. Washington, D.C.: U.S. Government Printing Office.

Carp, Robert A., and Ronald Stidham. 1990. *Judicial Process in America*. Washington, D.C.: Congressional Quarterly Press.

Cole, George F., ed. 1993. *Criminal Justice: Law and Politics*. 6th ed. Belmont, Calif.: Wadsworth Publishing.

Emerson, Deborah D. 1984. *The Role of the Grand Jury and the Preliminary Hearing in Pretrial Screening*. Washington, D.C.: U.S. Government Printing Office.

_____. 1983. *Grand Jury Reform: A Review of the Key Issues*. Washington D.C.: U.S. Government Printing Office.

Freeley, Malcom. 1984. "Legal Realism." In the *Guide to American Law: Everyone's Legal Encyclopedia*, 129–131. St. Paul, Minn.: West Publishing.

Gardner, Thomas J. and Terry M. Anderson. 2010. *Criminal Evidence: Principles and Cases*. 7th ed. Belmont, Calif.: Wadsworth/Cengage Learning.

Scheb, John M. and John M. Scheb II. 2009. *Criminal Procedure*. 5th ed. Belmont, Calif.: Wadsworth/Cengage Learning.

Senna, Joseph J., and Larry J. Siegel. 1987. *Introduction to Criminal Justice*. 4th ed. St. Paul, Minn.: West Publishing.

COURT CASES

Barker v. Wingo, 407 U.S. 514, 92 S.Ct. 2182, 33 L.Ed. 2d 101 (1972)

Klopfer v. North Carolina, 386 U.S. 213, 87 S.Ct. 988, 18 L.Ed.2d 1 (1967)

North Carolina v. Alford, 400 U.S. 25 (1970)

The Trial Process in Criminal Cases

This chapter illustrates the basic elements of a criminal trial involving a potential capital offense. In the last chapter, we left our hypothetical case with an order by the trial judge to consolidate the actions concerning the defendants Jesse Williams and Robert Jackson. The circumstances of the crime involving these two defendants have now become more complicated since the victim has died and additional charges are possible. The consolidated case involving Williams and Jackson now goes back to the grand jury for determination of the probable cause involving the additional charge of murder in the first degree.

THE DEATH PENALTY

The most severe penalty for crime is the most controversial. **Capital punishment** has been extensively applied throughout U.S. history and usually has been reserved for the most serious offenses of murder and rape. Between 1930 and 1967, there were 3,859 convicted criminals executed in the United States, and 53.5 percent of those executed were black (Bowers 1974).

Capital punishment: Punishment by death.

During the twentieth century and currently, the death penalty has been criticized as being racially discriminatory in application, lacking in provable deterrent qualities, and inhumane. Critics have pointed to the finality and brutality of the act and the possibility of executing innocent persons by mistake. Most modern industrial societies have abolished the death penalty, as have several states in the United States. However, the death penalty is supported by a majority of U.S. citizens, and public pressure to carry out this form of punishment is mounting.

Constitutional Status of the Death Penalty

The constitutionality of the death penalty has been a major issue before the U.S. Supreme Court for many years. In 1972, the Supreme Court finally confronted the issue in the famous case of *Furman v. Georgia*, 408 U.S.

238 (1972). A brief **per curiam** (by the court) opinion, supported by five justices, effectively invalidated every state death penalty statute then in existence. The five-member majority agreed that "the imposition and carrying out of the death penalty in these cases (several were considered) constituted **cruel and unusual punishment** in violation of the Eighth and Fourteenth Amendments."

The justices, however, agreed on little else, evidenced by each member of the majority writing a separate opinion in an attempt to explain why the death penalty constituted such a violation. Most of the arguments centered on the arbitrary nature of implementation of the death penalty, but three justices, William Douglas, William Brennan, and Thurgood Marshall, held that the death penalty was unconstitutional *per se* (in itself).

Four years later, in *Gregg v. Georgia*, 428 U.S. 153 (1976), the Supreme Court upheld a new Georgia death penalty statute that instituted a two-stage (bifurcated) trial process and state supreme court review comparing the application of the death penalty in similar cases. This new process required that first the defendant be convicted of first degree murder and then that a second trial be held concerning the sentencing, at which statutorily defined aggravating and mitigating circumstances could be argued. Only if there were a finding of at least one aggravating factor using the standard of "beyond a reasonable doubt" could the death penalty be imposed. An example of an aggravating factor would be that the murder was especially heinous, while a mitigating factor might be that the person had no prior criminal history.

The Supreme Court, in *Gregg*, held that the death penalty was constitutional if the procedure included adequate safeguards against it being inflicted in an arbitrary and capricious manner. The concerns expressed in *Furman* could be met by a carefully drafted statute that ensured that the sentencing authority would be given adequate information and guidance. Since *Gregg*, a solid majority of the Court has refused to reconsider the general constitutionality of capital punishment. Nearly 35 states and the federal government have enacted new death penalty statutes, and the number of actual executions is increasing.

As of November 15, 2011, the death penalty was authorized by 34 states, the federal government, and the U.S. military. Those jurisdictions without the death penalty include 16 states (Alaska, Hawaii, Illinois, Iowa, Maine, Massachusetts, Michigan, Minnesota, New Jersey, New Mexico, New York, North Dakota, Rhode Island, Vermont, West Virginia, Wisconsin, plus the District of Columbia). In 2008, the Nebraska Supreme Court ruled that the use of the electric chair as a method of execution violated the Nebraska Constitution. With no alternative method of execution on the books, Nebraska is practically without a death penalty. In *Coker v. Georgia*, 433 U.S. 584 (1977), the Court held the **death penalty for rape** of an adult woman, assuming the victim is not killed, unconstitutional as cruel and

Per curiam:
By the court; a phrase used to distinguish an opinion of the whole court from an opinion written by any one judge.

Cruel and unusual punishment:
Prohibited by the Eighth Amendment to the U.S. Constitution.

Death penalty for rape:
Prohibited as cruel and unusual punishment by court decision when the victim is not killed.

unusual punishment. The new death penalty statutes generally are imposed in connection with premeditated murder, but the Court in *Coker* left unanswered the issue of imposing the death penalty to prevent and deter other types of crime. The *Coker* decision has put a stop to executions for rape, in which the ratio of those executed under earlier laws demonstrated the most pronounced racial bias.

In 2002 the Supreme Court banned the execution of mentally retarded defendants in *Atkins v. Virginia*, 536 U.S. 304, and in 2005 the Court banned capital punishment for people who committed crimes before they were 18 in *Roper v. Simmons*, 543 U.S. 551. The Supreme Court's most recent action was to hold that sentencing someone to death for raping a child is unconstitutional. In *Kennedy v. Louisiana*, 554 U.S. 407 (2008), Justice Anthony M. Kennedy wrote for the majority of five, "[t]he death penalty is not a proportional punishment for the rape of a child," and thus violates the Eighth Amendment's ban on cruel and unusual punishment.

A CONSOLIDATED GRAND JURY INDICTMENT

In this stage of our hypothetical case, we have both defendants bound over to the grand jury for consideration as to whether there is enough evidence to warrant putting these individuals through the trial process.

On October 19, 2010, the grand jury convened to consider all of the evidence available to the prosecution and the new charges. The range of charges involved in the actions of the two defendants now extends from the most severe crime of **first degree murder** to the lesser included offenses of **second degree murder**, especially aggravated robbery, aggravated robbery, robbery, conspiracy to commit robbery, and **accessory after the fact**.

The two assistant district attorneys considered whether to ask for an indictment of both of these persons accused in this combined action on the charge of first degree murder. They needed to define all lesser included offenses for this analysis and consider the consequences if they did not get a conviction on first degree murder charges.

First degree murder: Premeditated and intentional killing of another.

Second degree murder: Knowingly killing of another person.

Accessory after the fact: One who, knowing a felony was committed by another, receives, relieves, comforts, or assists the felon.

This crime is defined in Middle State's *Criminal Code* 39-13-202 as
(a) First degree murder is:
(1) A premeditated and intentional killing of another;
(2) A killing of another committed in the perpetration of or attempt to perpetrate any first degree murder, act of terrorism, arson, rape, robbery, burglary, theft, kidnapping, aggravated child abuse, aggravated child neglect, rape of a child, aggravated rape of a child or aircraft piracy; or

---

continued >

(3) A killing of another committed as the result of the unlawful throwing, placing or discharging of a destructive device or bomb.

(b) No culpable mental state is required for conviction under subdivision (a)(2) or (a)(3), except the intent to commit the enumerated offenses or acts in those subdivisions.

(c) A person convicted of first degree murder shall be punished by:

(1) Death;

(2) Imprisonment for life without possibility of parole; or

(3) Imprisonment for life.

(d) As used in this subdivision (a) (1), "premeditation" is an act done after exercise of reflection and judgment. "Premeditation" means that the intent to kill must have been formed prior to the act itself. It is not necessary that the purpose to kill preexist in the mind of the accused for any definite period of time. The mental state of the accused at the time the accused allegedly decided to kill must be carefully considered in order to determine whether the accused was sufficiently free from excitement and passion as to be capable of premeditation.

39-13-210. Second degree murder

(a) Second degree murder is;

(1) A knowing killing of another,

(b) Second degree murder is a Class A felony

39-13-403. Especially aggravated robbery

(a) Especially aggravated robbery is robbery as defined in §39-13-401:

(1) Accomplished with a deadly weapon; and

(2) Where the victim suffers serious bodily injury.

(b) Especially aggravated robbery is a Class A felony.

39-13-402. Aggravated robbery

(a) Aggravated robbery is robbery as defined in §39-13-401:

(1) Accomplished with a deadly weapon or by display of any article used or fashioned to lead the victim to reasonably believe it to be a deadly weapon; or

(2) Where the victim suffers serious bodily injury.

(b) Aggravated robbery is a Class B felony.

39-13-401. Robbery

(a) Robbery is the intentional or knowing theft of property from the person of another by violence or putting the person in fear.

(b) Robbery is a Class C felony.

Accomplice:
One who knowingly, voluntarily, and with common intent unites with the principal offender in the commission of a crime.

An **accomplice** is defined as a person who knowingly, voluntarily, and with common intent, unites with the principal offender in the commission of a crime. The underlying charges associated with murder in the second degree, especially aggravated robbery, aggravated robbery, robbery, and accessory after the fact, would also be considered lesser included offenses. These crimes are defined as follows:

39-11-411. Accessory after the fact

(a) A person is an accessory after the fact who, after the commission of a felony, with knowledge or reasonable ground to believe that the offender has committed the felony, and with the intent to hinder arrest, trial, conviction or punishment of the offender:

(1) Harbors or conceals the offender;

(2) Provides or aids in providing the offender with any means of avoiding arrest, trial, conviction or punishment; or

(3) Warns the offender of impending apprehension or discovery.

(b) This section shall have no application to an attorney providing legal services as required or authorized by law.

(c) Accessory after the fact is a Class E felony.

All of these charges could come into play against either of these defendants since there was no direct evidence as to who the instigator of this crime was and who actually fired the shot, ultimately killing the victim, Samuel P. Stone. The death certificate obtained from the attending physician designated the cause of death as, "a bullet wound to the cranium causing brain damage that ultimately led to his death, on September 27, 2010, at 1:35 A.M."

The grand jury deliberation of this case was scheduled for October 12, 2010, at the Judicial Building in Capital City, 9:30 A.M. The two prosecuting attorneys agreed to the wording of the joint indictment charges as the following:

> The Grand Jury of Local County by this indictment charges that, on or about August 11, 2010, in said county, Jesse Williams and Robert Jackson did intentionally take the contents from the cash register of the Jiffy Stop Market on the corner of State and Fifth Streets, Capital City, from the owner and operator of said filling station–convenience store at gun point and did cause a gunshot wound to the head of the store owner Samuel P. Stone ultimately killing him on September 27, 2010. All of the above in violation of sections 39-13-202, 39-13-403, and 39-13-402 of the Middle State Criminal Code.

The Grand Jury Indictment

On the morning of October 12, 2010, the foreperson convened the county grand jury with 12 jurors present. The assistant district attorneys, Rusty Kovaks and Glen Hawkins, were present, but neither Jesse Williams nor

Robert Jackson was allowed to attend. Several witnesses were scheduled to be called to testify before this body of lay jurors to decide if there was enough evidence constituting probable cause to put these defendants through the trial process. After the jurors were sworn by the sheriff's deputy the inquiry began.

The first witness called was Frank Builder, a building contractor, who had arrived at the scene of the crime at approximately 11:59 P.M., on the evening of August 11, 2010. The witness saw two individuals who jumped into a car parked beside a gasoline pump at the Jiffy Stop convenience store. He later identified one of these individuals at a police lineup. This individual was Robert Jackson. He could not identify the other participant because he did not get a good look at him that night. However, he identified the automobile he saw that evening as belonging to Jesse Williams. This identification took place at the police impoundment lot in a lineup of impounded vehicles. He made a positive identification, describing the dented fenders and broken taillight and the vehicle license number correctly.

Frank Builder also identified Robert Jackson as the individual who had dropped the gas pump nozzle and jumped into the passenger side of the vehicle he had seen drive away in a hurry.

This witness proceeded into the Jiffy Stop store and found the victim lying on the floor with blood streaming from his head and a pistol in his hand. He immediately called 911, reported a violent crime, and asked for emergency help. When the police arrived about the same time as the ambulance, he assisted the medics attending the victim. He then pointed out the empty cash register, which he had not disturbed, and assisted the police in relating what he had observed. He had also taken down the license number of the vehicle, which led to the quick identification of the vehicle's owner.

Sergeant Michael Develon was the second witness called. He related that he was one of the officers to arrive at the scene of the crime about 10 minutes after the 911 call was received. The police officers found out from Frank Builder that he had written down the license number of the vehicle seen speeding away from the scene of the crime. He got a "make" on the vehicle's owner through the police identification system and proceeded with one other officer to attempt to locate the owner. The third police officer was left to complete the investigation at the scene.

The three police officers gathered fingerprint evidence at the gas pump and on the cash register and other locations at the scene of the crime. This evidence was properly identified and preserved for laboratory analysis. Photographs were made of the scene and a thorough investigation revealed a gas cap near where the witness said he saw the car before it sped off. This object was dusted for fingerprints and carefully preserved for laboratory analysis.

Sergeant Michael Develon and one other police officer located the residence of Jesse Williams and waited for him to return. Jesse Williams arrived at his home address driving the vehicle described by Frank Builder around 2:21 A.M. on August 12, 2010. The two police officers then arrested Jesse Williams but found no proceeds from the robbery and no gun in his possession or in a quick search of the vehicle. They also found nothing in his vehicle after a more thorough search of his residence and vehicle with a search warrant obtained after the arrest.

Michael Develon also described the arrest of Robert Jackson after he was located at his home, 12 Maple Street, Capital City. He told the grand jury that Robert Jackson was identified by a drawing of the suspect made with the assistance of Frank Builder. Robert ran from the police through the back door of his home while two police officers were knocking at the front door. He was apprehended and arrested.

A third police officer, Jim Cox, had waited at the back door for such an attempted escape. He followed the individual fleeing from the house and saw him drop something in a neighbor's trash can before following him into the neighbor's house where he and the other two officers made the arrest. The object Robert Jackson deposited in the trash can was witnessed by all of the police officers and it turned out to be the murder weapon.

The third witness called was Kate Wissenschaftler, the police laboratory director. She gave testimony that the gun obtained from Robert Jackson was tested for evidence of a match with the bullet removed from the victim of this crime, Samuel P. Stone. The bullet had been removed from the victim's skull. It was tested with a bullet fired from the weapon found with Robert Jackson for markings and there was a good match. This evidence identifying the weapon as the same as that used in the robbery was conclusive.

The assistant district attorneys also provided the grand jury with the death certificate of the victim Samuel P. Stone. It was officially signed by the attending physician, with a date of September 27, 2010, at 1:35 A.M.

This information was conveyed to the grand jury by these witnesses with opportunities for considerable individual questioning by the jurors. There were no other witnesses who asked to participate in this proceeding on behalf of the accused. Many jurors also asked questions of the two assistant district attorneys.

One of the basic questions asked was about what evidence is available as to who pulled the trigger in this crime. If this becomes a murder trial, which defendant will be charged with the crime of murder? They will be tried together, and the judge and jury will have to decide that issue. To begin with, both will be tried for the same crime.

When the jury voted after the assistant district attorneys had left the room, all 13 voted for a "true bill" of indictment for both Jesse Williams and Robert Jackson. The court clerk presented the two defendants with copies of the grand jury bill of indictment, which was identical for both of them.

Then he notified them that they were scheduled for arraignment on October 21, 2010, before Judge L.B. Long.

Both defendants then met with their attorneys separately to discuss these important developments. Jesse Williams's attorney Jill Adams had continued to work on his case and was also notified of the grand jury indictment. She arrived at the county jail to confer with her client the day after she was notified of the grand jury action.

Jesse was furious about this news. He did not understand what happened at his first arraignment where he attempted to plead not guilty. "Why did my plea bargain with the DA not get recognized?" he asked Jill.

Adams replied, "I did my best to tell you that the judge could refuse the plea bargain with the DA. They can't use anything you told them against you in court. But now you will have to confront your accomplice at trial. If your story is true you now have a chance to provide it in open court. But Robert Jackson will also have his opportunity to tell his story in open court."

"Can I still plead guilty to a lesser included offense?" Jesse asked.

"You can try it again, but they already have used what you have told them to arrest Robert Jackson, and surely he will testify that you did it," Adams replied. "You now face a murder charge, Jesse."

"What happens if I plead not guilty?" Jesse asked.

"You will get a chance to tell your story at trial. You can take the stand in your behalf and explain what happened," Adams suggested. "You could also tell me the truth and maybe I can help you."

"What if I plead *nolo contendere*," Jesse asked.

"A plea *nolo contendere* is the same as a guilty plea, except the conviction cannot be used against you in a civil trial. It is only granted with the consent of the court," Adams answered.

"What can I do then when I get to the arraignment and the judge asks how do I plea?" Jesse asked.

"You have to answer that for yourself, Jesse," the attorney replied.

Robert Jackson was asking similar questions of his attorney, Sharp who had been busy trying to run down leads to gather evidence to defend Robert. He tried to calm him down about the charges of first degree murder, which had disturbed Robert. He indicated that after the arraignment they could petition for discovery powers, and with a consolidated case they would have access to all information discovered by the prosecution for each codefendant. "That should work in our favor, if you are telling me the truth," Sharp told Robert.

The Arraignment and Pretrial

On October 21, the two defendants, Jesse Williams and Robert Jackson, were brought before Judge L.B. Long and asked how they would plea to the charges included in the indictment. Defendants who are jointly charged may be arraigned separately or together at the court's discretion.

Judge Long elected to arraign them together and asked Jesse Williams first how he intended to plea to the charges filed against him. He answered with a not-guilty plea. Robert Jackson also answered "not guilty." The judge then set a trial date and noted that they both demanded a jury trial.

The two lawyers for the defendants knew they had to prepare for trial and that Middle State, like many other states, had recently revised its criminal procedures to bring it more in line with the Federal **Rules of Criminal Procedure**. Several important recent revisions to these rules have been made in the last decade. These rules now require mandatory **joinder of offenses** and defendants (or consolidation of cases) involving two or more defendants who are being charged with the same crimes. These relevant provisions are as follows:

Rules of criminal procedure:
Rules of criminal procedure in each state. Many states have adopted similar rules that track the federal rules.

Joinder of offenses:
When two or more persons are joined in the same indictment, if they are charged with the same crimes and in the same jurisdiction.

Rule 8. Joinder of Offenses and Defendants

(a) **Mandatory Joinder of Offenses.**

(1) **Criteria for Mandatory Joinder.** Two or more offenses shall be joined in the same indictment, presentment, or information, with each offense stated in a separate count, or the offenses consolidated pursuant to Rule 13, if the offenses are:

(A) Based on the same conduct or arise from the same criminal episode;

(B) Within the jurisdiction of a single court; and

(C) Known to the appropriate prosecuting official at the time of the return of the indictment(s), presentation(s), or information(s).

(2) Failure to join such offenses. A defendant shall not be subject to separate trials for multiple offenses falling within Rule 8 (a)(1) unless they are severed pursuant to Rule 14.

These rules of court also allow for a special motion applying to co-defendants on trial jointly. Rule 12 (D) labeled *codefendants* states:

> *Upon a defendant's request, when the state decides to place codefendants on trial jointly, the state shall promptly furnish each defendant who has moved for discovery under this subdivision with all information discoverable under Rule 16(a) (1) (A), (B), and (C) as to each codefendant.*

Both lawyers submitted requests to the judge in behalf of their defendants for all documents, including recorded oral statements of both defendants, access to all documents and objects within the state's possession, custody, or control when the item is "material to preparing the defense or the state intends to use the item in its case-in-chief."

Table 16.1 **MOTIONS THAT MAY OR MUST BE MADE BEFORE TRIAL**

---

(1) Motions That May Be Made Before Trial. A party may raise by pretrial motion any defense, objection, or request that the court can determine without a trial of the general issue.

(2) Motions That Must Be Made Before Trial. The following must be raised before trial:

   (A) a motion alleging a defect in the institution of the prosecution;

   (B) a motion alleging a defect in the indictment, presentment, or information—but at any time while the case is pending, the court may hear a claim that the indictment, presentment, or information fails to show jurisdiction in the court or to charge an offense;

   (C) a motion to suppress evidence;

   (D) a Rule 16 request for discovery; and

   (E) a Rule 14 motion to sever or consolidate charges or defendants.

Criminal discovery in such cases does not include the district attorney's work papers or law enforcement officer's notes. Nor does this rule authorize discovery of statements made by state witnesses or prospective state witnesses.

After the arraignment all parties would have about 60 days to prepare for trial (see Table 16.1). Judge Long set the trial date for January 5, 2011.

CRIMINAL DISCOVERY PROCESS

The **criminal discovery** process differs considerably from that described in connection with the civil process in earlier chapters. In general, the criminal discovery process is more restrictive. The prosecutor must give the defendant access to all material evidence and allow for independent testing of such evidence.

Criminal discovery:
Differs from civil discovery in that it is more restrictive; depositions are taken only under unusual circumstances, and defendant does not have to testify.

The defense can subpoena witnesses and require relevant evidence to be produced. Physical and mental examinations can be required if relevant. The names of witnesses against the accused may be required and produced, but the prosecution's witnesses are not subject to cross-examination prior to trial, and their statements may be withheld until trial.

The defendant's right to remain silent ensures that the prosecution will not be able to cross-examine the witness before trial unless this right is waived. If the defendant takes the stand voluntarily in his or her own defense, the prosecutor may have a chance to cross-examine the defendant. In jury trials, the defendant's past criminal record can be suppressed— a **motion to suppress** (*in limine*) may prevent any mention of such a record. The Supreme Court has held that the prosecutor must share any

Motion to supress
(*in limine*):
A written motion that is usually made before or after the beginning of the trial for a protective order against prejudicial questions and statements.

exculpatory evidence (that which tends to relieve the accused of guilt) with the defense whether it is requested or not. (See *Brady v. Maryland*, 373 U.S. 83 (1963).)

Exculpatory evidence: That which tends to indicate defendant's innocence or mitigate defendant's criminality.

Pretrial Planning (for the Prosecution)

Glen Hawkins, the assistant district attorney, pulled his file on Robert Jackson and reviewed the case again. He made a list of the witnesses and the laboratory evidence. After rereading the confession Jesse had given to Sergeant Develon and Rusty Kovaks, he asked Kovaks to review the evidence with him.

"Al Sharp is the defense attorney for Robert Jackson," said Hawkins. "Sharp implied at the lineup, where Robert was identified, that Jesse Williams might be lying about Robert doing the shooting. We found the gun in Robert's possession, but do you think he can crack Jesse's story?"

Kovaks said, "It is possible. Jesse made a pretty good deal with me. He lied first about his alibi, maybe he was lying in his confession that the judge refused to accept. However, his confession is suppressed and can't be used against him."

When the indictment charges a capital offense and the district attorney general intends to ask for the death penalty, the Rules of Court require the district attorney general to file notice of intention to ask for the death penalty not less than 30 days before trial. This amount of time is required to allow the defendants' counsel to prepare for trail. The notice must specify that the state intends to seek the death penalty and shall specify the aggravating circumstances the state intends to rely on at the sentence hearing. This notice must be in writing, filed with the court, and served on counsel for the defendants. If the notice refers to a prior conviction or other sensitive matters, the court may permit the notice to be filed under seal.

The district attorney general, in the case involving Jesse Williams and Robert Jackson, filed notice before the court asking for the death penalty. This notice was filed in a timely manner, and the following aggregating circumstances were specified:

1. The defendant was convicted previously of one or more felonies, other than the present charge, that involved the use or threat of violence to a person.
2. The murder was committed while the defendant was engaged in committing, or was an accomplice in the commission of, or was attempting to commit, or was fleeing after committing or attempting to commit, any first degree murder, arson, rape, robbery, burglary, larceny, kidnapping, aircraft piracy, or unlawful throwing, placing, or discharging of a destructive device or bomb.

The district attorney general also requested that the judge place the aggravating circumstances under seal since the previous conviction cannot be revealed during the trial.

The court notified the two attorneys for the defendants that the state intended to seek the death penalty.

Pretrial Planning (for Defendant Williams)

Jill Adams met with her client, Jesse Williams, to go over the information she had received from the DA's office. There was not much that this defendant did not already know. He had made a confession that had been rejected when the plea bargain fell through.

Attorney Jill Adams asked Jesse, "Are you willing to take the stand in the court room at the trial?"

"Would it do me any good to take the witness stand?" Jesse asked.

"If you tell the truth, it could possibly save your life if you were not the instigator of the robbery and did not shoot the victim. Even if you did and you defended yourself against premeditation being involved in the shooting, you could get a lesser sentence," Adams answered.

"I'll think about it," Jesse said.

Pretrial Planning (for Defendant Jackson)

Attorney Al Sharp and his assistant met to discuss their preparation for trial. They had received all the information requested from the prosecutor's office about both defendants. They had interviewed character witnesses that would testify in court, and they could use some of the prosecution witnesses to corroborate Robert's story.

A friend of Jesse Williams told Mark, Al Sharp's assistant, that Jesse had bought a gun from Jake Jones who lived in one of the apartments where Jesse lived—but this person could not be found. He had moved out of the apartment, and there was no record of his whereabouts. This secondhand information would be useless in court, as it would be suppressed as hearsay. Serial number checks indicated that the gun was not registered with the police.

Mark said he would keep looking for Jake Jones, but he did not have much information on him. Sharp told Mark to check the jail and prison records for Jake Jones to see whether he could be located in that manner.

"We've got one break," said the attorney. "I talked with Robert and asked him what he did with the $100 Jesse had given him from the robbery. He said he didn't want the money and had put it into an envelope and mailed it to Mrs. Stone, the victim's wife."

"Has she confirmed that?" Mark asked.

"Yes," Sharp replied. "She told me over the phone that she had received $100 in cash in an envelope with no return address. She thought it was from someone who felt sorry for her."

"When did she receive it?" Mark asked.

"She says it was about two weeks after her husband was shot and therefore before Robert was arrested," answered Sharp. "She destroyed the envelope, unfortunately. We will want to call her as a witness. Her testimony will be a big advantage for Robert."

Now Mark had a lead on Jake Jones and had located him in the neighboring town of Centerville. He was willing to testify that he sold Jesse Williams a .38 "police special" pistol in 2009. He would be subpoenaed for deposition-taking next week and agreed to be present.

Mark continued the report of his preliminary work. "I've gone over the two statements we have and basically it's Robert's word against Jesse's. That means Robert's character witnesses will help us, but we'll just have to hope that we can catch Jesse in some inconsistencies."

Al Sharp then met with Robert Jackson at the jail and let him know what possibilities they had at trial in his case. He indicated that there was some hope for a favorable outcome in his situation, but it would require his willingness to take the witness stand and tell his story to the jury.

"I don't know if I can do that," Robert said.

"All you need to do is tell the truth, Robert," replied the attorney. "But, you will need to prepare yourself for the cross-examination by the prosecuting attorneys."

Attorney Sharp told Mark he could find nothing in the record or the account Robert had given him that indicated the need for any pretrial motions. "We could have asked for a **continuance** if we had not found Jake Jones, but other than that any delay is just going to work against our client," Sharp said.

Continuance: Postponement of a session, hearing, trial, or other proceeding to a subsequent day or time.

Possible pretrial motions include the following:

1. A motion to suppress, requiring a pretrial hearing to exclude evidence illegally obtained
2. A *nolle proseque* motion made by the prosecutor
3. A motion to disqualify the judge
4. A motion to request a psychological examination of the accused
5. A request for a pretrial conference, change of venue (place of trial), to quash the indictment, or for a bill of particulars

None of these motions seemed applicable in the case against Robert Jackson.

Pretrial Judge's Conference

The pretrial judge's conference discussed questions of procedure at trial and agreed upon how the trial would proceed. The judge, the two assistant

Table 16.2 **PRETRIAL JUDGE'S CONFERENCE**

WITNESSES

Prosecution Witnesses
1. Frank Builder
2. Sergeant Michael Develon
3. Kate Wissenschaftler (police laboratory director)

Defense Witnesses
1. Jesse Williams
2. Alexandria Poole
3. Jake Jones
4. Mrs. Samuel Stone
5. Robert Jackson

DOCUMENTS

1. Pictures of crime scene and victim's injuries
2. Laboratory report of fingerprints found at the crime scene
3. Laboratory report of test firing of the gun found in possession of the defendant and matching of the bullets used in the test
4. Bullet taken from victim's head
5. Bullet fired from the weapon recovered from defendant
6. Gun found in possession of defendant
7. Death certificate showing cause of victim's death

---

district attorneys, and the two defendants' attorneys agreed that the trial procedure would allow the two defense attorneys to call their witnesses during the defense case in chief as in a normal single defendant trial. Each witness may be cross-examined by the opposing defendant's attorney or the prosecuting attorneys, if they elected to do so. Otherwise, the trial would proceed in the normal single defendant trial manner.

After the exchange of evidence, a list of witnesses and other forms of evidence was made available to both parties and the judge (see Table 16.2).

THE TRIAL: JURY SELECTION AND OPENING STATEMENTS

On January 5, 2011, Jesse Williams's and Robert Jackson's case was announced by the bailiff in Capital City's Criminal Court, presided over by Judge L.B. Long. Judge Long noted that a jury trial had been demanded and that there was a first degree murder charge involving a potential death sentence. He explained that the *voir dire* process would involve the selection of a single jury whose members would serve as the deciders of facts in dispute in a **bifurcated trial process**.

Bifurcated trial process: Trial of issues, such as guilt and punishment, or guilt and sanity, separately in criminal trial.

In Middle State, the death penalty statute required that there first be a unanimous conviction for first degree murder, which is defined as "A killing of another committed in the perpetration of any first degree murder, act of terrorism, arson, rape, robbery, burglary, theft, kidnapping, aggravated child abuse, aggravated child neglect, rape of a child, aggravated rape of a child or aircraft piracy . . . ."

If the defendant is found guilty beyond a reasonable doubt of first degree murder, the same jury would have to be reconvened to determine whether the accused would have to be punished by death or by life imprisonment. These alternatives were the only sentences for a person convicted of first degree murder. The jury had to find the existence of one or more of the statutory aggravating circumstances beyond a reasonable doubt to impose the death penalty. Table 16.3 lists 12 **aggravating circumstances** provided in Middle State's Criminal Code.

The state law provided that in arriving at the punishment, the jury had to consider any **mitigating circumstances**. The mitigating circumstances included, but were not limited to, the criteria given in Table 16.4.

If the jury decided that the death penalty was warranted, the jurors would be required to use a verdict form (see Form 16.1), on which they would list the aggravating circumstances that outweigh the mitigating circumstances. The jurors would have to sign their names to the appropriate sections of this document.

Aggravating circumstances: Circumstances attending the commission of a crime that increase defendant's guilt or add to injurious consequences of the crime.

Mitigating circumstances: That which reduces the degree or moral culpability but does not justify or excuse the offense in question.

Criminal Voir Dire

Both defendants had demanded a jury trial in this case, and they will be tried together before this same jury. Jury selection is one of the most crucial aspects of any trial, but in this case the seriousness of the charges and the consolidated nature of the proceeding with two defendants being tried at one time requires more elaborate explanation.

Judge Long had received a request from the parties concerning the number of alternate jurors to be involved. Twelve jurors would need to be impaneled, with four alternates chosen in case the lengthy process resulted in unforeseen circumstances that would require replacements.

The voir dire and trial process in criminal cases follow the same general outlines described earlier in the civil trial process. However, the detailed rules of criminal procedure are applied. In criminal trials, more peremptory challenges are allowed than in civil cases. The number of peremptory challenges varies with the severity of the potential punishment. In death penalty cases, Middle State allows the defense 15 peremptory challenges and the prosecution 8. Each side would get 1 additional peremptory challenge for each alternate juror selected. The two defense attorneys in this case would both get 1 additional peremptory challenge for each alternate juror.

Table 16.3 **STATE CODE LIST OF AGGRAVATING CIRCUMSTANCES**

Middle State code provides that no death penalty shall be imposed by a jury but on a unanimous finding of the existence of one or more of the statutory aggravating circumstances, which shall be limited to the following:

1. The murder was committed against a person less than 12 years of age, and the defendant was 18 years of age or older.
2. The defendant was previously convicted of one or more felonies, other than the present charge, that involved the use or threat of violence to a person.
3. The defendant knowingly created a great risk of death to two or more persons, other than the victim murdered, during the act of murder.
4. The defendant committed the murder for remuneration or the promise of remuneration or employed another to commit the murder for remuneration or employed another to commit the murder for remuneration or the promise of remuneration.
5. The murder was especially heinous, atrocious, or cruel in that it involved torture or depravity of mind.
6. The murder was committed for the purpose of avoiding, interfering with, or preventing a lawful arrest or prosecution of the defendant or another.
7. The murder was committed while the defendant was engaged in committing, or was an accomplice in the commission of, or was attempting to commit, or was fleeing after committing or attempting to commit, any first degree murder, arson, rape, robbery, burglary, larceny, kidnapping, aircraft piracy, or unlawful throwing, placing, or discharging of a destructive device or bomb.
8. The murder was committed by the defendant while the defendant was in lawful custody or in a place of lawful confinement or during the defendant's escape from lawful custody or from a place of lawful confinement.
9. The murder was committed against any peace officer, corrections official, corrections employee, or firefighter who was engaged in the performance of his or her duties, and the defendant knew or reasonably should have known that the victim was a peace officer, corrections official, corrections employee, or firefighter engaged in the performance of his or her duties.
10. The murder was committed against any present or former judge, district or state attorney general, or assistant district or assistant state attorney general due to or because of that person's official duty or status, and the defendant knew that the victim occupies or occupied said office.
11. The murder was committed against a national, state, or local popularly elected official due to or because of the official's lawful duties or status, and the defendant knew that the victim was such an official.
12. The defendant committed "mass murder," which is defined as the murder of three or more persons within the state of Middle State within a period of 48 months, and perpetrated in a similar fashion in a common scheme or plan.

Table 16.4 **STATE CODE LIST OF MITIGATING CIRCUMSTANCES**

Middle State Code provides that in arriving at the punishment, the jury shall consider any mitigating circumstances, which shall include, but are not limited to, the following:

1. The defendant has no significant history of prior criminal activity.
2. The murder was committed while the defendant was under the influence of extreme mental or emotional disturbance.
3. The victim was a participant in the defendant's conduct or consented to the act.
4. The murder was committed under circumstances that the defendant reasonably believed to provide a moral justification for his or her conduct.
5. The defendant was an accomplice in the murder committed by another person, and the defendant's participation was relatively minor.
6. The defendant acted under extreme duress or under the substantial domination of another person.
7. The defendant was very young or advanced in age at the time of the crime.
8. The capacity of the defendant to appreciate the wrongfulness of the conduct or to conform his or her conduct to the requirements of the law was substantially impaired as a result of mental disease or defect or intoxication that was insufficient to establish a defense to the crime but that substantially affected the defendant's judgment.
9. Any aspect of the defendant's character or record or any aspect of the circumstances of the offense favorable to the defendant that is supported by the evidence.

The voir dire process is quite lengthy and time consuming in criminal trials: at least three days of the court's time is consumed with jury selection alone in such cases. The skills of the lawyers are severely tested in making the extensive number of decisions required. In many cases, if adequate resources are available, private research consultants are hired to advise the lawyers in their selections. Neither Jesse Williams nor Robert Jackson had such resources, so Jill Adams and Al Sharp had to rely on their own judgment. Al Sharp's law firm would lose money on this case, and he had no interest in delaying the trial process.

Judge's Charge at Jury Selection

Judge L.B. Long addressed the panel of prospective jurors in the case of *Middle State v. Jesse Williams and Robert Jackson* with the following words.

"There will be two defendants in this case and the state has charged these individuals with murder in the first degree. Murder in the first degree is punishable by imprisonment for life without possibility of parole; or imprisonment for life or death.

Form 16.1 **JURY VERDICT FORM FOR DEATH SENTENCING**

PUNISHMENT OF DEATH

(1) We, the jury, unanimously find the following listed statutory aggravating circumstance or circumstances:

(Here list the statutory aggravating circumstance or circumstances so found, which shall be limited to those enumerated by the Court for your consideration.)

_____

_____

_____

_____

_____

_____

(2) We, the jury, unanimously find that the statutory aggravating circumstance or circumstances so listed above outweigh the mitigating circumstance or circumstances.

(3) Therefore, we, the jury, unanimously find that the punishment for the defendant shall be death.

Jury Foreman	Juror
Juror	Juror
Juror	Juror
Juror	Juror
Juror	Juror
Juror	Juror

[A similar form would be provided for Punishment of Life Imprisonment, which was the only other alternative once the defendant was convicted of first-degree murder.]

"Now because the death penalty may become an issue in this case I want to tell you how it is tried.

"The death penalty only becomes possible under certain circumstances. Let me explain.

"If, and only if, the jury returns a verdict of guilty of murder in the first degree in this case, the jury will reconvene for purpose of rendering an advisory recommendation as to which sentence, death or life imprisonment, should be imposed.

"At this hearing, evidence of aggravating and mitigating circumstances will be presented for you to consider. Then both the state and the defendants will have an opportunity to present argument for and against the death penalty. Following those arguments I will give you written instructions on the law that you are to apply in weighing those circumstances and making your recommendation.

"The final determination of which sentence should be imposed is my responsibility. However, under the law I must give your recommendations 'great weight.'

"Many people have strong feelings about the death penalty, both for it and against it. The fact that you may have such feelings does not disqualify you to serve as a juror as long as you are able to put those feelings aside and apply the law as I instruct you. In other words, you must be willing to be bound by your oath as a juror to obey the laws of this state in making your recommendation.

"Now, with that explanation, I must ask you a few questions.

"Are any of you unalterably opposed to the death penalty such that you could not consider it as a penalty under any circumstances?

"Are any of you of the opinion that death is the only appropriate penalty for murder in the first degree and that opinion is so strong that you could not consider life imprisonment as a penalty under any circumstances?

"If the jury returns a verdict of murder in the first degree in this case, will you *weigh* the aggravating and mitigating circumstances presented, *listen* to the arguments of the attorneys, apply the law as I instruct you, and *fairly consider both possible penalties* before making your penalty recommendation?"

All potential jurors raised their hands in positive response.

Peremptory Challenge Issues

Until 1986, both sides could use any criteria whatsoever to exclude potential jurors with their peremptory challenges. The Supreme Court in *Swain v. Alabama* 380 U.S. 202 (1965) had ruled that a defendant would have to show a pattern and practice of using peremptory challenges in a racially discriminatory manner to establish a valid claim. This was an insurmountable burden of proof for defendants in an individual case. However, in 1986, the Supreme Court ruled in *Batson v. Kentucky* 476 U.S. 79 that the Equal Protection Clause of the Fourteenth Amendment precludes prosecutors from striking blacks (and other minorities) from the jury simply because the prosecutor thinks that blacks will be partial toward black defendants. An individual defendant now could establish racial discrimination on the use of peremptory challenges in his or her individual case without referring to past cases. This ruling was reaffirmed and broadened in *Powers v. Ohio* 499 U.S. 400 (1991) when the Court ruled that it is unconstitutional to exclude blacks on the basis of race even when defendants are white. Justice Kennedy said, in the majority opinion, "Race cannot be a proxy for determining juror bias or competence."

When prosecutors challenge racial minorities, they may be required to explain their grounds for objection apart from the matter of race. However, "[e]ven after the *Batson* decision, race [has] continued to be used as a basis for peremptory challenges because trial judges have yet to engage in searching probes of the reasons for such challenges." (Levine 1992, 51)

ASSIGNMENT: The instructor should appoint 12 class members to the task of performing the role of jurors. These student jurors should deliberate in class to come up with a verdict and allow the class members to hear and observe.

THE TRIAL: PROSECUTOR'S CASE IN CHIEF

After both sides, including the two defense lawyers, had exercised their peremptory challenges and challenges for cause, the judge impaneled a 12-person jury and an appropriate number of alternates for the trial. After further preliminary procedures, Judge L.B. Long delivered his opening statements before the entire court. He repeated much of what he said to the jury in the voir dire process of jury selection and added the following instructions to the jury.

"Since this trial will involve two defendants and multiple charges to be considered by the jury you may become confused, and to make sure there is sufficient evidence for each separate count against each defendant you will receive written information about these charges. Since you will need an understanding of what to look for during the trial, I have provided a list of the definitions of the potential charges in your packet of information.

"Rule 24.1 of the Middle State Rules of Court requires that you, the jury members, are allowed to take notes during the trial deliberation, and you have been given suitable materials for this purpose. You will have access to these notes during recesses and deliberations. After the jury has rendered a verdict, the notes shall be collected and destroyed. This packet of information for each of you will include my instructions to you and copies of written and other exhibits.

"Jurors may submit written questions. The court may permit a juror to ask a question of a witness. The following procedures apply: the juror shall put the question in writing and submit it to the judge through a court officer at the end of a witness's testimony. A juror's question shall be anonymous, and the juror's name shall not be included in the question. I will review all such questions and, outside the hearing of the jury, shall consult the parties about whether the question should be asked. I may change the question in whole or in part and may change the wording of the question before asking it. I may also allow counsel to ask the question in its original or amended form.

"I must also inform you that the attorneys representing the defendants will both have an opportunity to question any witnesses called by the prosecutor and all witnesses called by the other defendant's lawyer. Please indicate your understanding of this statement by raising your hand and asking for clarification.

"I will now introduce each attorney representing the three parties in this case. The state prosecutors' office is represented by Rusty Kovaks and Glen Hawkins. Please stand so that the jury can make notes as to who you are. These prosecutors will represent the state in bringing charges against these defendants.

"The defendants in this case are Jesse Williams and Robert Jackson. Their attorneys will represent them in this trial.

"Jesse Williams will be represented by Jill Adams, public defender. She has the duty to bring out or present any evidence favoring her client, Jesse Williams. Will Jesse Williams and Jill Adams please stand to allow the jury to make notes as to who you are and which defendant you represent?

"Robert Jackson will be represented by Al Sharp, private defense attorney. He will have the duty to bring out or present any evidence favoring his client, Robert Jackson. Will Robert Jackson and his attorney Al Sharp please stand to allow the jury to make notes as to who you are and which defendant you represent?"

The judge then admonished the jury to be aware that opening statements are not to be considered evidence. They give the opposing sides opportunity to explain what will be presented as evidence by each side and to help the judge and jury organize the facts to look for from the witnesses and evidence that will be presented in their cases in chief.

"We may now begin by hearing the prosecutions opening statements about this case."

Opening Statements for the Prosecution

Assistant District Attorney Rusty Kovaks representing the state rose to provide the prosecution's opening statements about the case of *Middle State v. Jesse Williams and Robert Jackson*.

"Ladies and gentlemen of the jury, the accused Robert Jackson and Jesse Williams killed Samuel P. Stone in the course of an armed robbery on the night of August 11, 2010. The state will bring witnesses and facts to prove these accusations. We will first call Frank Builder. Mr. Builder is a construction contractor who, on the night of August 11, 2010, was driving home from a construction job and decided to stop at the Jiffy Stop Market at the corner of State and Fifth streets in Capital City.

"When he pulled into this convenience store and filling station he saw two figures jump into a vehicle parked at the gas pump in apparent haste to flee from the scene. He had a suspicion that something was wrong and noted the license number of the vehicle.

"He then entered the store and found Samuel P. Stone lying on the floor with blood streaming out of his head and a pistol in his hand. Mr. Builder immediately called for emergency medical and police help. He found the cash register empty and cleaned out. He assisted in attending the victim before transport to the hospital, and provided the police officers with his recorded license plate number of the suspicious vehicle. He will provide additional evidence about this vehicle and its owner as well as identification of the defendants and their positions relevant to the escape vehicle.

"Police Sergeant Michael Develon will describe his investigation of the crime scene and the fingerprints that he found at the scene of the crime. He will also tell you about how he apprehended Jesse Williams and Robert Jackson. Jesse Williams was apprehended at his residence after a license check on the defendant's automobile and later confirmed by Frank Builder's identification of Jesse Williams's vehicle in a lineup at the police impoundment lot. Robert Jackson was arrested after an arrest warrant was issued for his arrest, and Michael Develon was one of the officers involved in that arrest.

"The police laboratory director, Kate Wissenschaftler, who is an acknowledged fingerprint and ballistic expert, will testify that the fingerprints found at the scene of the crime matched those of Robert Jackson. She will also explain how she matched the markings on the bullet removed from the victim Samuel P. Stone with those test fired from the gun Robert Jackson was carrying when he was apprehended.

"These facts will be testified to by our witnesses, and there will be ample opportunity for them to go into detail about their findings and positive identification of these two defendants accused of first degree murder and all lesser included offences involved in this crime.

"They prove beyond a reasonable doubt that the two accused defendants committed these crimes and should be punished to the limit of the law for their killing of the owner of the Jiffy Stop Market, Samuel P. Stone."

The judge then called upon Attorneys Jill Adams and Al Sharp to provide opening statements for the defense. He explained that both attorneys will have an opportunity to explain what will be presented on behalf of each of the two defendants.

Opening Statements for Jesse Williams

Jill Adams began her opening statements for her client Jesse Williams.

"Ladies and gentlemen of the jury, Jesse Williams did not commit first degree murder against Samuel P. Stone. He attempted a confession to the assistant district attorney in which he identified Robert Jackson as the perpetrator of this crime and helped law enforcement officers to apprehend him. His confession was not accepted by Judge Mann and he now presents himself before the court as a witness in his own behalf. He will tell you who committed this crime and all that he knows about the Jiffy Stop robbery on the night of August 11, 2010.

"When he explains his relationship to this crime he will convince you that he did not kill Samuel P. Stone."

Opening Statements for Robert Jackson

The judge then called upon Al Sharp to provide the opening statements for his client Robert Jackson.

"Ladies and gentlemen of the jury, I represent Robert Jackson in this trial. He is not guilty of first degree murder or even robbery in this case. He will tell you that he first met Jesse Williams on the evening of the Jiffy Stop robbery. The two defendants met at a bar in Capital City and went out cruising in Jesse's car on the night of August 11, 2010.

"When Robert testifies, he will tell you that Jesse pulled into the Jiffy Stop Market to get gas and Jesse told him to pump the gas while he went in to pay for it and get some beer. Robert heard a gunshot while he was pumping gas and then Jesse came out of the store with a six-pack of beer and yelled *jump into the car*!

"He did not know what happened in the store, but he followed Jesse's orders to get into the car. Only then did he find out what had happened from Jesse, who said the store clerk had pulled a gun and he had to shoot him.

"Jesse then asked him where he lived. Robert was anxious to get home and away from Jesse. When they got to Robert's house Jesse pushed the gun and $100 into his hands and said you keep these. Robert did not know what to do, so he ran into his house. Robert will tell you about these events in his own words. He was very frightened by all that he had witnessed and only wanted to get away from Jesse.

"We will call Alexandria Poole, a high school teacher who knew Robert as a student. She will tell you about Robert and his behavior in high school. She will provide character evidence about Robert that will support the fact that he had never been involved with illegal activities and was an honest and diligent student who had great promise. Her testimony is from a person of great respect in this community and will convince you that Robert could not have killed another person in a premeditated robbery.

"Jake Jones will be our next witness. He was a neighbor of Jesse Williams two years ago and sold Jesse the .38 caliber 'police special' handgun that will later be identified as the gun used in this robbery. This evidence will establish that the pistol used to kill Samuel P. Stone belonged to Jesse Williams not Robert Jackson.

"Finally, we will call Mrs. Samuel P. Stone, the wife of the deceased. She will testify that she received a letter about two weeks after her husband was shot with $100 in it. There was no note or return address, but she had not received any other notes like this. Robert Jackson will also tell you that he sent the money Jesse had given him from the robbery to Mrs. Stone because he believed that she should have it. He will tell you about this in his own words.

"Ladies and gentlemen of the jury, when you have finished hearing these witnesses you will agree that Robert Jackson is not guilty of murder or even robbery. He was the unfortunate victim of a reckless person with criminal intent on the night of August 11, 2010."

Prosecution's Case in Chief

Judge L.B. Long now called upon the prosecution to present their case in chief.

Attorney Kovaks called Frank Builder to the stand, and the judge administered the oath to tell the truth, the whole truth, and nothing but the truth.

"State your name and occupation for the court," Kovaks stated.

"I am Frank Builder, 37 years old, and a building contractor," answered the witness.

Would you tell the court what you witnessed on the evening of September 11, 2010," prompted the attorney.

"I was driving home from working late on a construction job and drove into the Jiffy Stop Market to get some gas when I saw two figures running toward the car parked at the gas pumps. They were in a big hurry and took off at a fast pace. I got suspicious and quickly recorded the license number of this vehicle on the pad on my dashboard in the truck I was driving."

"What happened then?" asked the attorney.

"I went into the market and found Mr. Stone on the floor with blood flowing from his head and a pistol in his hand. I immediately called 911 for medical assistance and the police. I noticed the cash register drawer was open, and it was empty. The ambulance came pretty quickly, and the police were not far behind. I showed them what I had discovered and helped with the victim," Frank Builder stated.

"Did you talk to the police officers?" asked the attorney.

"Yes, I showed them the license plate number that I had written down and told them about seeing the getaway car leave the scene of the crime," Frank replied.

"Did you describe the getaway car," asked attorney Kovaks.

"Yes, I did, it was a light green foreign car with beat-up fenders and a broken taillight," replied Mr. Builder.

"Thank you Mr. Builder," replied the attorney.

"Were you able to identify that vehicle at the police impoundment lot sometime later?" asked the assistant district attorney.

"Yes, I was," answered Frank Builder. "It looked a little different in the lineup. Probably because of the yellow lights at the Jiffy Stop Market at night, but it was dark gray in the daylight. It had the same beat-up fenders and broken taillight. Finally, I looked at the license plate, and it had the same numbers as I had recorded the night before.

"Thank you Mr. Builder," stated the DA.

Cross-examination

The judge asked which attorney would like to cross-examine this witness.

Al Sharp came to his feet slowly and took his place at the podium, obviously engrossed in thought and taking his time to select his first question.

"Mr. Builder, you identified Robert Jackson in a police lineup did you not?" asked the attorney.

"Yes, I did," answered Frank Builder.

"You also assisted an artist in drawing a likeness of Robert so that he could be identified, didn't you?" asked the defendant's attorney.

"Yes, I did," answered the witness.

"Could you tell the court where, in relationship to the car and the gas pumps, you first saw Robert Jackson at the scene of the crime?" the attorney asked.

Frank Builder paused and thought about the question carefully before he answered. "He was dropping the gas hose and then ran to the passenger's side of the getaway vehicle and jumped into the car," replied Mr. Builder.

"Thank you, no further questions your honor," stated the attorney.

"Are there any questions from the jury?" asked the judge. Having seen no indication of questions from the jury, he called for the next witness for the prosecution.

Direct Examination

Sergeant Michael Develon was called, and the judge administered the oath to tell the truth.

Assistant district attorney Glen Hawkins then asked the police officer to state his name and occupation for the court.

He replied that his name was Michael Develon and that he was a detective sergeant for the Capital City Police Department, with 10 years of service.

"Were you one of the officers arriving at the Jiffy Stop Market on August 11, 2010?" asked attorney Hawkins.

"Yes, I was. I arrived on the scene at about 12:05 and talked with the eyewitness, Frank Builder. We first examined the scene and assisted the victim Samuel P. Stone to be transported by the medics. Frank Builder told me he had recorded the license number of a suspicious vehicle that left the scene of the crime in a hurry just before he arrived," the detective stated.

"What happened then, Sergeant?" asked the DA.

"There were two other officers on the scene by this time, and we marked off the crime scene to prevent destruction of evidence. We then proceeded to gather evidence from a gasoline hose left on the concrete at a gas pump. We also found a vehicular gas tank cap on the concrete in front of a gas pump. This gas cap was identified by Frank Builder as in the proper location of the getaway car he had seen. We carefully preserved the gas tank cap for examination at the police laboratory," stated the police officer.

"What happened next?" the assistant district attorney asked.

"I decided to attempt to identify the vehicle by the license number Frank Builder had given me. We got a prompt reply and the address of Jesse Williams at 367 Elm Street, Apartment 4, in Capital City. One of my colleagues and I went to that address in hopes of making an arrest. The other officer was left to complete the investigation," the Sergeant replied.

"What happened at this location, officer?" Glen Hawkins prompted.

"We decided to wait until the occupant of this apartment returned home, having first checked to see if he was there. Finally, he arrived at about 2:30 in the morning of August 12, 2010, in the same vehicle identified by Frank Builder. We stopped and frisked this individual because we had probable cause that he was armed. We did not find a gun on him or in his vehicle in plain view, but we had probable cause to arrest him and bring him down to the station for booking. We filed a complaint against him for the Jiffy Stop Market robbery and gunshot wound to the victim," stated the witness.

"Were you also involved in the arrest of Robert Jackson?" the DA asked?

"Yes, I was," replied Develon. "Jesse Williams' attorney approached us about a possible plea bargain concerning the charge involving shooting of the victim. We were willing to recommend a reduced sentence if he was not the instigator or the shooter at the scene of the crime. Jesse then told us where we could find Robert Jackson. On the basis of this probable cause, we filed for an arrest warrant for Robert Jackson. We also had a drawing made by a police artist from Frank Builder's description of an individual he had seen at the scene of the crime and used it to identify him at his home," continued Sergeant Devalon.

"Objection, your honor," stated Jill Adams, counsel for Jesse Williams.

"Please state your objection, counselor," the judge replied.

"This information was obtained in a plea bargain confession overruled by the arraignment judge prior to arraignment, your honor. It cannot be used as evidence against my client," the attorney asserted.

"Attorney Hawkins, how do you respond to this accusation raised by the defendant's attorney?" the judge asked.

Glen Hawkins responded that Judge Mann refused to accept this plea bargain and ordered this case consolidated to be tried now before this court. "We accept the prohibition against using this information to prosecute Jesse Williams. However, the apprehension of the second accomplice in this crime is not being used as evidence against Jesse Williams. If anything, it provides evidence against Robert Jackson."

"Objection overruled," stated the judge. "You may continue your direct examination."

"You may continue with your testimony concerning the apprehension of Robert Jackson, Sergeant," stated the assistant DA.

"We had probable cause to believe that Robert Jackson was armed. There were three armed police officers with a warrant for the arrest of Robert Jackson. One of my colleagues and I approached the front door of his home, and his mother answered. The third police officer was stationed near the back door of the dwelling. We heard a door slam and entered the dwelling from the front door to pursue the suspect. The officer at the rear of the building saw a person fleeing from the back door and followed him in hot pursuit. After seeing him with what appeared to be a weapon and ordering him to halt, he continued pursuit around the corner of a building and observed him depositing something into the neighbor's trash can," continued the police officer.

"And then what happened?" asked the prosecutor.

"Within less than a minute, all three of us had apprehended the suspect in the neighbor's kitchen. Police officer Jim Cox, who had observed the suspect drop something into the neighbor's trash can, then went over to look for what it might have been. There in the trash can on top of the trash he found a .38 'police special' handgun. We carefully bagged the weapon and sent it off to the police laboratory for analysis of fingerprints and to test for a match with a bullet removed from the victim's head," explained the sergeant.

"Thank you very much Sergeant Develon," stated the attorney.

The judge then asked the defendants' lawyers if they intended to cross-examine this witness. Both attorneys declined the opportunity to cross-examine Develon.

"Do any of the jury members have questions they wish to ask of this witness?" the judge asked.

There was no indication from the jury that they had any questions, so the judge called for the next witness.

Direct Examination

The prosecuting attorney, Rusty Kovaks, then called Kate Wissenschaftler to the stand. After being placed under oath to tell the truth by the judge, the attorney began.

"Will you identify yourself and your background for the court Mrs. Wissenschaftler?" asked the district attorney.

"I am Kate Wissenschaftler, director of the Capital City Police Laboratory. I am also a qualified fingerprint and ballistics expert," she replied.

"What did you conclude from your analysis of the fingerprints on the vehicle gas cap that the police recovered from the scene of the crime?" asked Kovaks.

"There were good-quality prints lifted from the gas cap, and they matched the thumb and forefinger prints taken from Robert Jackson during his booking procedure," answered the expert witness.

"Did you test the weapon recovered from the possession of Robert Jackson for a ballistics check against the bullet removed from the victim, Samuel P. Stone?" asked the district attorney.

"Yes, I performed a test firing of the weapon into a plastic gel substance to recover the markings made by the weapon and compared them with the bullet recovered from the victim's body," replied Kate.

"And what was your conclusion?" asked the attorney.

"The markings on the two bullets were identical, indicating that they were fired from the same weapon," replied the expert witness.

Then the assistant district attorney introduced the documents that had been in the possession of the police and carefully stored as evidence:

1. Pictures taken of the crime scene and victim's injuries
2. Laboratory report of test firing and comparison of the bullets fired from the pistol found in possession of the defendant Robert Jackson
3. The bullet fired into plastic gel from the recovered weapon

4. Bullet taken from the victim's head
5. Handgun found in possession of the defendant Robert Jackson
6. Death certificate showing cause of victim's death

There were no objections to the introduction of these items of written and material evidence.

The judge then called a recess until the next morning, when the trial would continue. He instructed the jury not to discuss this case with anyone during this period.

We will continue the trial with the defense case in chief and closing arguments in the next chapter. This next chapter will also continue the discussion through verdict and appeal.

CHAPTER SUMMARY

1. This chapter describes a hypothetical case that was used to illustrate the full criminal trial process. However, fewer than 10 percent of criminal cases are actually tried. The overwhelming majority of convictions result from guilty pleas. Full trial cases are the exception rather than the rule.

2. The Supreme Court has held that a person accused of any crime that carries a potential jail sentence has the right to counsel. In 1967, the Court held that a pretrial lineup after a complaint or indictment has been issued is a "critical stage" in the trial process and that the defendant, therefore, has the right to have counsel present.

3. The state rules of criminal procedure have been amended in most states to bring them more in line with the Federal Rules of Criminal Procedure. Rule 8 requires *joinder* of offenses when two or more defendants are charged with the same crimes and are within the jurisdiction of the same court.

4. Codefendants on trial jointly are entitled to move for discovery of all evidence in the possession of the prosecutor. The state shall promptly furnish each defendant with all information discoverable under Rule 16 of the Federal Rules of Criminal Procedure.

5. In 1976, the U.S. Supreme Court upheld new death penalty statutes requiring a two-stage (bifurcated) trial process. The accused must first be convicted of a death penalty crime and then be sentenced in a second trial in which evidence of aggravating and mitigating circumstances are presented before the same jury.

6. In 1977, the Supreme Court held that the imposition of the death penalty for rape of an adult woman, if she is not killed, is unconstitutional and constitutes cruel and unusual punishment.

7. The Supreme Court decisions regarding the death penalty have reduced the degree of racial bias in the implementation of the death penalty in the United States and have eliminated the practice of executing persons for the crime of rape, which was an area in which racial bias was most pronounced. The Court also has invalided the death penalty for mentally retarded inmates and those who committed murder when they were juveniles.

8. All current death penalty statutes require convictions for first degree murder, although the Court has left open the possibility of imposing the death penalty to prevent and deter other types of crime.

9. The criminal discovery process is more restrictive than the civil discovery process. There is an opportunity to suppress evidence obtained in violation of constitutional guarantees. Exculpatory evidence that may excuse or clear the accused must be shared with the defense by the prosecution.

10. In criminal cases, depositions are generally not exchanged, except in cases in which the witness may be unable to appear in court. Both sides can demand the names of witnesses to be called, but the accused has a right to remain silent, and the prosecutor can withhold witness statements in some cases until the trial. The prosecutor must share any exculpatory evidence with the defense regardless of whether the defense requests it.

11. Both sides have the authority to subpoena witnesses, who are then required by law to appear and answer questions under oath at trial.

12. Continuances and suppression motions for a pretrial hearing are the most frequently used pretrial motions during the discovery period, although there are many opportunities for delay and to request pretrial hearings regarding issues of discovery and trial conditions. Interrogatories and requests to produce evidence also are frequently used.

13. Lists of aggravating and mitigating circumstances are extensive in modern death penalty statutes, and the process of analyzing them is very complex. The lists provided in this chapter are typical of those used in the 37 states that currently impose the death penalty. Most modern societies and several U.S. states have abolished the death penalty.

14. Criminal jury selection is marked by several exceptions that do not usually apply in the civil voir dire process. More extensive peremptory challenges are allowed in criminal cases than in civil cases, and lawyers and judges may not exclude minorities on the basis of race alone, although this rule is difficult to enforce.

15. The criminal trial process follows the general outline of the civil trial process, but the detailed rules of criminal procedure must be applied. These rules of procedure, like those regarding voir dire, are different in some of their specifics and exceptions from those in civil trials.

REVIEW EXERCISES

Match the following terms with their most appropriate meaning.

TERMS

1. Accomplice
2. Capital punishment
3. Cruel and unusual punishment
4. *Per curiam*
5. Death penalty for rape alone
6. Criminal discovery
7. Exculpatory evidence
8. Continuance
9. Motion to suppress
10. Bifurcated trial
11. Aggravating circumstances
12. Mitigating circumstances
13. Rules of criminal procedure
14. Joinder of offenses
15. First degree murder
16. Second degree murder
17. Accessory after the fact

MEANING

____ detailed rules of procedure in criminal cases

____ evidence that may indicate a reduction of the defendant's criminality

____ circumstances reducing the degree of moral culpability but not excusing the offense in question

____ more restrictive than in civil cases in that depositions are rarely taken and the defendant cannot be compelled to testify

____ one who, knowing that a felony has been committed, receives, relieves, comforts, or assists the felon

____ facts that increase a defendant's guilt or add to injurious consequences of the crime

____ prohibited as cruel and unusual punishment by court decision

____ one who knowingly, willingly, and with common intent unites with the principal offender

____ separate consideration of issues, such as guilt and punishment or sanity and guilt, in criminal trial

____ prohibited by the Eighth Amendment

____ motion to exclude evidence because it was unconstitutionally acquired

____ punishment by the death penalty

____ knowingly killing another

____ postponement of a session, hearing, or other proceeding

____ case opinion by the court rather than one judge or justice

____ a premeditated and intentional killing of another

____ when two or more offences are joined in the same indictment and trial

DISCUSSION QUESTIONS

1. What is the purpose of requiring consolidation of the trial of the two defendants in this case?
2. Why are defendants entitled to move for and receive all evidence in possession of the prosecutor?
3. Has the requirement of a bifurcated trial in capital cases reduced the chances of miscarriage of justice?
4. How is the discovery process more restrictive in criminal cases than in civil cases?
5. How does the jury selection process in criminal cases differ from that in civil cases?

ASSIGNMENT

ASSIGNMENT: Your instructor should appoint 12 class members to the task of performing the role of jurors in this criminal case. These student jurors should deliberate in class, come up with a verdict, and allow the class members to hear and observe.

SOURCES AND SUGGESTED READING

Bowers, William. 1974. *Executions in America.* Lexington, Mass.: D.C. Heath.

Carp, Robert A., and Ronald Stidham. 1990. *Judicial Process in America.* Washington, D.C.: Congressional Quarterly Press.

Hudson, David L. Jr. 2004. *Does Capital Punishment Have a Future?* Chicago: American Bar Association.

Kassin, Saul M., and Lawrence S. Wrightsman. 1988. *The American Jury on Trial: Psychological Perspectives.* New York: Hemisphere Publishing.

Levine, James P. 1992. *Juries and Politics.* Pacific Grove, Calif.: Brooks/Cole Publishing.

Tennessee Judicial Conference. 2011. *Tennessee Pattern Jury Instructions: Criminal* (T.P.I.-CRIM.). 15th ed. St Paul, Minn.: West Publishing. (See practice volumes for your state that contain jury instructions.)

Tennessee Rules of Criminal Procedure (cited as Tenn. R. Crim. P.). (See latest edition).

U.S. Census Bureau. 2010. *The 2012 Statistical Abstract.* Washington, D.C.: U.S. Government Printing Office.

COURT CASES

Atkins v. Virginia, 536 U.S. 304 (2002)

Batson v. Kentucky, 476 U.S. 79, 106 S.Ct. 1712, 90 L.Ed.2d 69 (1986)

Coker v. Georgia, 433 U.S. 584, 97 S.Ct. 2861, 53 L.Ed.2d 1982 (1977)

Furman v. Georgia, 408 U.S. 238, 92 S.Ct. 2726, 33 L.Ed.2d 346 (1972)

Gregg v. Georgia, 428 U.S. 153, 96 S.Ct. 2909, 49 L.Ed.2d 859 (1976)

Kennedy v. Louisiana, 554 U.S. 407 (2008)

Lockhart v. McCree, 476 U.S. 162, 106 S.Ct. 1758, 90 L.Ed.2d 137 (1986)

Powers v. Ohio, 499 U.S. 400, 111 S.Ct. 1364, 113 L.Ed.2d 411 (1991)

Pulley v. Harris, 465 U.S. 37, 104 S.Ct. 871, 79 L.Ed2d 29 (1984)

Roper v. Simmons, 543 U.S. 551 (2005)

Swain v. Alabama, 380 U.S. 202 (1965)

Trop v. Dulles, 356 U.S. 86, 78 S.Ct. 590, 2 L.Ed.2d 630 (1958)

United States v. Agurs, 427 U.S. 97, 96 S.Ct. 2392, 49 L.Ed.2d 342 (1976)

United States v. Wade, 388 U.S. 218, 87 S.Ct. 1926, 18 L.Ed.2d 1149 (1967)

Witherspoon v. Ilinois, 391 U.S. 510, 88 S.Ct. 1770, 20 L.Ed.2d 776 (1968)

The Jury's Verdict, Sentencing, and Appeal

This chapter begins with the defense case in chief. We left the trial of *Middle State v. Jesse Williams and Robert Jackson* after the opening statements of both sides and the prosecution's presentation of its case in chief. Now we will finish the trial presentation with the opportunity of the defense to present their case in chief. After conclusion of the trial, we will present the judge's charge to the jury and discuss the verdict and sentencing in this case. This chapter will also explain the appeals process in criminal cases.

TRIAL: DEFENSE CASE IN CHIEF

The next morning the judge called for the defendants' attorneys to present their case in chief. "Call your first witness," the judge stated.

Defense attorney Jill Adams called Jesse Williams to the stand.

The judge then addressed Jesse Williams and asked if he understood that he did not have to testify and that he had the constitutional right to remain silent under the Fifth Amendment of the U.S. Constitution.

Jesse answered that he understood his rights and had voluntarily agreed to testify in his own behalf.

He was duly sworn under oath by the judge to tell the truth, the whole truth, and nothing but the truth. The judge then ordered Robert Jackson from the court room.

Attorney Jill Adams began by asking Jesse to state his name and age before the court. Jesse stated that he was Jesse Williams, age 32.

"Did you shoot Samuel P. Stone on August 11, 2010?" asked the attorney.

"Yes, I did, but I didn't mean to kill him," answered Jesse. "The man pulled a gun on me and I defended myself by using my own pistol."

"Describe what happened on that night for the court," asked attorney Adams.

"I met Robert at The Pub on the west side of town. We talked about doing some drugs, but we had no money, so Robert asked me if I knew how to get some money. I told him I had a gun if he knew how to use it. He said he knew that the Jiffy Stop Market would be an easy target since only an old man was there at night."

"And what happened then Jesse?" Adams prompted.

"Robert and I went in and I got a six-pack of beer while checking out the place. I had my own gun, and the man behind the counter grabbed a gun himself from under the counter. That's when I shot him. I grabbed the money out of the cash register and we went out to the car. I told him somebody was coming, so we jumped into the car and left."

"What happened then?" the attorney asked.

"We was both scared somebody had spotted us; so we went to his house first. He jumped out and went inside. All I got was a six-pack of beer," answered Jesse.

"Where did you go after that?" asked attorney Adams.

"I went to my girlfriend's house and had a few beers before I went home," Jesse replied.

Cross-examination

Al Sharp rose to defend his client Robert Jackson.

"Did you buy the gun you said Robert Jackson used from Jake Jones in 2009?" attorney Sharp asked.

"Yes, I did," Jesse replied.

"Did your girlfriend attempt to provide an alibi for you at the grand jury hearing?" asked Al Sharp.

"I don't know, maybe," answered Jesse.

"Why isn't she being called for this trial?" asked the attorney.

"Because they could not find her," answered Jesse.

"Did Robert put gas into your vehicle when you pulled up to the Jiffy Stop Market on the night of the robbery?" asked Sharp.

"No, he did not. He was in the store," Jesse replied.

"Thank you, no further questions your honor," concluded the attorney.

Redirect Examination

Jill Adams rose to defend her client and asked, "Do you regret being involved in the crime of robbery, Jesse?"

"Yes, I do. I did not know I would have to pull the trigger and kill Mr. Stone. It all happened so fast that I could not stop it," answered Jesse.

"Do you admit to the crime of especially aggravated robbery?" asked Jill Adams.

"Yes I do," Jesse said.

There was no recross examination, and the judge called for any further questions for this witness from opposing counsel or from the jury. "There being none, we will continue. Next witness," the judge concluded.

Direct Examination

Al Sharp then rose to call the next witness, Jake Jones, to the stand.

"Please state your name, age, occupation, and place of residence for the court," prompted the attorney.

"My name is Jake Jones, age 34. I am a carpenter, and I live in Centerville, Middle State, about 30 miles from here," answered the witness.

"How do you know Jesse Williams, Mr. Jones?" asked Al Sharp.

"Two years ago I lived in an apartment next to Jesse Williams," Mr. Jones replied.

"Did you own a handgun, Mr. Jones?" asked the attorney.

"Yes, I did, but I sold it to Jesse Williams for $50 before I moved away in 2009," answered the witness.

Attorney Al Sharp retrieved the murder weapon from the clerk's desk and showed it to the witness. "Is this the weapon you sold to Jesse Williams?" Sharp asked.

"Yes, it is, I remember the markings on it, and I have a record of the serial number in my possession; it is from the bill of sale when I purchased it," replied Jake Jones.

"Your honor, I would like to move this document into evidence with this witness," the attorney stated, as he was showing the opposing attorneys the document.

"Are there any objections to admitting this document?" asked the judge. "There being none, it is so admitted."

"Is there any cross-examination of this witness?" asked the judge. "There being none, call your next witness."

Direct Examination

Attorney Sharp then called Mrs. Samuel P. Stone to the witness stand.

"Would you please tell the court your name and how you are related to this case?" the attorney prompted.

"I am Mrs. Samuel P. Stone, and I am the wife of Samuel P. Stone who was shot during this robbery involving these two defendants," she replied.

"How long was your husband in the hospital after the shooting, Mrs. Stone?" asked Sharp.

"About 86 days; he was unconscious during this entire period and in a coma," answered the witness.

"When did the doctors remove the bullet from his skull?" the attorney asked.

"It was about three weeks after the robbery and shooting," she answered.

"Did you receive a letter in the mail with $100 in it, Mrs. Stone?" asked Sharp.

"Yes, I did. I received it about two weeks after the robbery," she said.

"Did you receive any other similar letters in the mail with money in them?" asked the attorney.

"No, I did not," Mrs. Stone replied.

"Thank you Mrs. Stone," concluded the attorney.

The judge again asked if any of the lawyers wanted to cross-examine the witness and whether any jurors wished to ask a question. "There being none, we may proceed. Call your next witness," stated the judge.

Direct Examination

Attorney Al Sharp then called the defendant Robert Jackson to the witness stand. The judge asked Robert if he understood that he had the right to remain silent. Robert replied that he did and then proceeded to the witness stand. Judge Long then ordered the co-defendant Jesse Williams to be removed from the court.

"Would you state your name, age, and occupation for the court?" attorney Sharp asked.

"I am Robert Jackson, age 19, and I have just graduated from high school. I am not employed," Robert stated.

"Would you tell the court what happened on the evening of August 11, 2010?" asked the attorney.

"That night I went out alone to the Pub, a bar not very far from my home, and met Jesse Williams for the first time. We had some drinks and decided to go out for a cruise around town in his car. He wanted to do some drugs and asked me for some money to make a buy. I told him that I had no money, just a few dollars for beer. Then he decided to stop for gas at the Jiffy Stop Market, and he pulled into the filling station. He asked me to pump gas while he went in to pay for it," stated Robert.

"What did you do then, Robert?" asked attorney Sharp.

"Jesse went into the store, and I got the gasoline hose and waited for him to pay and activate the pump. The pump went on and I started putting gas into the vehicle. Then I heard a loud bang and wondered what happened. Jesse then came running out and shouted 'get in the car!'" Robert replied.

"What happened then?" the attorney prompted.

"We drove off at a fast pace, and Jesse said to me, 'He pulled a gun on me and I had to shoot him.' This caused me to panic; I had no idea that this could happen," replied the witness.

"Objection, your honor, this witness is testifying to hearsay," Jill Adams declared.

The judge asked for a response from the attorney who had called the witness, Al Sharp.

Al Sharp responded, "Exception to the hearsay rule; admission by party opponent."

"Objection overruled," replied the judge. "Continue the direct examination."

"What happened after Jesse made this statement to you?" asked Sharp.

"He asked me where I lived and took me home. When we arrived and I was getting out of his car he pushed the gun and $100 in cash into my hand and took off. I did not have a chance to refuse. I ran into my home as quick as I could, to get away from Jesse Williams," answered the witness Robert Jackson.

"What did you do with the $100 Jesse Williams gave you from the robbery?" asked Al Sharp.

"I did not know what to do with it until I heard over the radio and TV that Mr. Stone had been shot during the robbery. This news made me sick, and about two weeks after the robbery I put the $100 in a plain envelope and mailed it to Mrs. Stone," Robert replied.

"Thank you Robert," responded the attorney.

The judge called for cross-examination of the witness. There were no questions from the other defense attorney or the prosecutors. No jurors attempted to question this witness. The judge called for the next witness.

Direct Examination

Al Sharp then called his last witness, Alexandria Pool.

"Please state your name and occupation for the court," the attorney said.

"My name is Alexandria Pool, and I have taught high school science for 20 years," answered the teacher.

"How long have you known Robert Jackson as a student, Mrs. Pool?" attorney Sharp asked.

"I have known Robert for three years, and he was in my classes for this entire period. I got to know him very well during these three years. He was a very good student," answered the science teacher.

"What was Robert's character as a high school student?" asked Al Sharp.

"He was a dependable student and made good grades in my classes. I advised him to go on to college. I find it hard to believe that he could be involved in armed robbery," she replied.

"Did he respect his teachers?" asked the attorney.

"Yes, he did. He wanted to be an astronaut and was interested in science. He respected his teachers and even did extra work to keep his grades up," she said.

"Is there anything else you would like to say about Robert's character?" Sharp asked.

"Yes, all these kids try drugs and get a little wild when they get out of high school, but Robert is just not the type to shoot somebody," she said.

"Thank you, Mrs. Pool," stated the attorney.

The judge asked if there was any cross-examination or questions that needed to be asked of this witness. "There being none, we have concluded the defendants' case in chief and I order a recess until tomorrow morning. The jury members are admonished to refrain from discussing this case with anyone.

"We will begin with closing arguments when we return," explained the judge.

Closing Arguments

Judge L.B. Long addressed the jury the next morning and called for the prosecution and defense closing arguments. He cautioned the jury that closing arguments are not considered evidence but rather a summation of the relevant evidence presented.

Assistant District Attorney Glen Hawkins approached the podium and began his closing arguments.

"Ladies and gentlemen of the jury; the state is asking for the death penalty in this case because it is the law, and you will find the aggravating circumstances listed in the sealed notice filed with the judge 30 days before this trial began. Whether you decide that Jesse Williams or Robert Jackson perpetrated this crime by shooting and killing Samuel P. Stone, both of these defendants are guilty of the serious crimes of especially aggravated robbery and the killing of an innocent man. They conspired together to commit this crime and both are guilty.

"The judge will charge you with a clear understanding of your responsibilities under the law, but the evidence you have heard concerning intent in this case boils down to how much of the testimony of the two suspects you are willing to accept as the truth. There is no question that both of these culprits, who testified against each other, were involved in the crime. Jesse Williams admits to having shot Samuel P. Stone with his own gun during the robbery. However, both of these defendants conspired to commit robbery. They may even be lying to protect each other. The consistent fact remains that Jesse Williams and Robert Jackson went riding around that night looking for money to buy drugs. They planned to commit that robbery, and Robert picked the Jiffy Stop Market because he knew that it was an easy score.

"The judge will charge you with a description of the lesser included offenses in this case. He will tell you that if you have reasonable doubt concerning first degree murder, you will have to decide whether the defendant is guilty of second degree murder or accessory after the fact. These crimes carry lesser punishments, but this criminal activity on Robert Jackson's part cannot be allowed to go unpunished.

"Robert Jackson knew, or should have known, what was about to happen that night. Regardless of whose story you believe, he was there at the Jiffy Stop Market while the robbery took place. He stood ready to, and did, lend assistance in the perpetration of armed robbery that resulted in the death of an innocent victim.

"This community cannot be made safe unless the good citizens, like you, make the hard choices and will ensure that criminals are punished."

Closing Arguments for Jesse Williams

Jill Adams took the podium in defense of her client, Jesse Williams.

"Ladies and gentlemen of the jury, Jesse Williams took the stand in this trial when he could have remained silent. He told you the truth this time that he did not kill Samuel P. Stone because of malice of forethought. He pulled the trigger because his life was at stake and in response to the deadly weapon that threatened him. He told you and Robert Jackson that he had to shoot the victim because the victim pulled a gun on him. Sergeant Develon removed that gun from the victims hand as he testified in court. Therefore we have confirmation by each of these three witnesses that Jesse is telling the truth about this aspect of the crime.

"He is undoubtedly guilty of especially aggravated robbery and should be punished accordingly, but he is not guilty of first degree murder."

Closing Arguments for Robert Jackson

The judge now called upon attorney Al Sharp to deliver his closing arguments in defense of his client.

"Ladies and gentlemen of the jury, we have heard some incredible statements in this trial by the defendant Jesse Williams. He has attempted to manipulate this case from the very beginning and has told one lie after another to try to lessen the severity of the crime he has committed. He first lied to the district attorney and police officers about an alibi he concocted about being at his girlfriend's house when the robbery was committed; then he tried to implicate Robert Jackson as the one who pulled the trigger on the victim in this crime by attempting a plea bargain with the district attorney. Now he says, yes, he was the shooter of Samuel P. Stone, but only in self-defense. It should be clear to everyone who has heard this evidence that Jesse Williams is an habitual liar. You knew he was lying when he opened his mouth.

"Robert Jackson is not a liar, and he is not a criminal. He told you the truth. He would never lie to the police, or to a judge, or even to his attorney. He told the truth from the beginning. He is a decent young man with a promising future. His youth and immaturity got him into trouble the night of the robbery and the senseless killing of Samuel P. Stone, but Robert Jackson did not kill him. Jesse Williams did, and he admitted it to this court.

"Robert Jackson was outside the store pumping gas into the car when Mr. Stone was shot. You have heard corroborating evidence by the defendant, Robert Jackson, by the eyewitness, Frank Builder, and by the fingerprint expert, that Robert was at the gas pumps when the murderous shot was fired. Jesse Williams even now is not telling the truth about where Robert was when this happened. He is still lying; he told this court under oath that Robert was with him in the store when Mr. Stone was shot. Frank Builder testified to the fact that Robert Jackson was outside pumping gas when he arrived at the scene of the robbery. Jesse has lied so much that he can't even remember his own lies.

"Robert showed remorse and regret when he sent Mrs. Stone the $100 dollars that Jesse had shoved into his hands along with the gun when he left the car that night. This act of integrity and compassion was confirmed by Mrs. Samuel P. Stone when she took the stand in this courtroom.

"There were no objections to the state's witnesses in this case. The evidence presented clearly proves that both of these defendants were guilty of some offence connected to this robbery and murder. But Robert Jackson did not conspire with Jesse Williams to commit this crime. However, he did aid and abet Jesse in concealing the weapon used and not reporting this to the police. Instead he ran from the police and tried to protect the perpetrator of these crimes.

"He should be punished for his going along with Jesse Williams that night and for his youth and innocence that resulted in not knowing who he was associating with. He is young and immature, but deserves a second chance."

Judge L.B. Long stated that the jury had now heard the evidence by the witnesses and facts presented in this case. He declared a recess until the next morning when he will charge the jury in the case of *Middle State v. Jesse Williams and Robert Jackson*. Again, he admonished the jury not to discuss this case with anyone else.

The next morning, Judge Long entered the courtroom as the bailiff called, "Oyez Oyez, all rise; the Circuit Court of Middle State is now in session, the honorable Judge L.B. Long, presiding."

Judge Long took his place at the bench and proceeded to prepare for his instructions to the jury in the case of *Middle State v. Jesse Williams and Robert Jackson*. He first checked to see that all 12 of the jurors and alternates were present and that the defendants and their attorneys were ready. He asked if there were any further motions or petitions by the attorneys before he began his charge to the jury.

TRIAL: JUDGE'S INSTRUCTIONS TO THE JURY

"Ladies and gentlemen of the jury, you are the exclusive judges of the facts in this case. Also, you are the exclusive judges of the law under the direction of the court. You should apply the law to the facts in deciding this case.

You should consider all of the evidence in the light of your own observations and experience in life.

"You should give separate consideration to each defendant in this case. Each is entitled to have his case decided on the evidence and the law that is applicable to that particular defendant. Any evidence that was limited to a particular defendant should not be considered by you as to any other defendant.

"You can acquit both or convict both, or you can acquit one and convict the other, or you can convict each of the defendants on different offenses.

"If you cannot agree upon a verdict as to both of these defendants, but do agree upon a separate verdict for each one of these defendants, you must render a verdict as to one or both upon which you agree. The verdict must be unanimous; all 12 of you must agree. You will be required to remain sequestered until you have arrived at a verdict. When you are sequestered in the jury room, you will have an opportunity to take all exhibits and writings into the jury room with you for examination during your deliberations. Select a foreperson from your number to assist you in organizing your discussion and try to arrive at a unanimous verdict.

"The crimes charged in this case include the following potential verdicts for each of the defendants before you. The defendants Jesse Williams and Robert Jackson are charged in the indictment with first degree murder or other lesser included offenses. The offence necessarily includes the lesser offenses of second degree murder, robbery, criminal conspiracy to commit robbery, and accessory after the fact.

"Any person who commits *first degree murder* is guilty of a crime. For you to find the defendant guilty of this offense, the state must have proven beyond a reasonable doubt the existence of the following elements:

"1. That the defendant unlawfully killed the alleged victim; and
2. That the killing was committed in the perpetration of or the attempt to perpetrate the alleged robbery; and was not a separate, distinct, and independent event; and
3. That the defendant intended to commit the alleged robbery.

"For you to find the defendant guilty of this offense, the state must have proven beyond a reasonable doubt the existence of the following elements:

"1. That the defendant knowingly obtained or exercised control over property owned by Samuel P. Stone; and
2. That the defendant did not have the owner's effective consent: and
3. That the defendant intended to deprive the owner of the property; and
4. That the defendant took such property from the person in fear; and
5. That the defendant took such property intentionally or knowingly.

"The intent to commit the underlying felony must exist prior to or concurrent with the commission of the act causing the death of the victim. Proof that such intent to commit the underlying felony existed before, or concurrent with, the act of killing, is a question of fact to be decided by the jury after consideration of all the facts and circumstances.

"*Intentionally* means that a person acts intentionally with respect to the nature of the conduct or to a result of the conduct when it is the person's conscious objective or desire to engage in the conduct or cause the result.

"If you find from the proof beyond a reasonable doubt that the defendant is guilty of murder in the first degree, you will so report, and your verdict in that event shall be: 'We, the jury, find the defendant guilty of murder in the first degree.'

"If you so find, then it shall be your duty after a separate sentencing hearing to determine whether the defendant will be sentenced to death, life imprisonment without the possibility of parole, or life in prison, but you will not consider punishment for this offense at this time.

"If you do not find unanimously that the defendant is guilty of first degree murder, then you may consider second degree murder, robbery, criminal conspiracy, or accessory after the fact.

"For you to find the defendant guilty of *second degree murder*, the state must have proven beyond a reasonable doubt the existence of the following essential elements:

"1. That the defendant unlawfully killed the alleged victim; and
2. That the defendant acted knowingly.

"*Knowingly* means that a person acts with awareness that his conduct is reasonably certain to cause the death of the alleged victim or that the defendant acted intentionally.

"Any person who conspires to commit an offense is guilty of a crime. For you to find the defendant guilty of *criminal conspiracy*, the state must have proven beyond a reasonable doubt the existence of the following elements:

"1. That the defendant entered into an agreement with one or more people to commit the offense of robbery. It is not necessary that the object of the agreement be attained. And
2. That each of the parties to the conspiracy had the intent to commit the offense of robbery; and
3. That each party acting for the purpose of promoting or facilitating the commission of the offense of robbery, agreed
   a) that one or more of them engage in conduct that constitutes the offense; and
   b) that one of the parties to the conspiracy committed an overt act in furtherance of the conspiracy. (An overt act is an act done by one of the parties to carry out the intent of the conspiracy, and it must be a step toward the execution of the conspiracy.)

"Any person who commits the offense of *accessory after the fact* is guilty of a crime. For you to find the defendant guilty of this offense, the state must have proven beyond a reasonable doubt the existence of the following essential elements:

"1. That the defendant knew or had reasonable grounds to believe that the offender committed a felony; and

2. That the defendant acted with intent to hinder the arrest, trial, conviction, or punishment of the offender; and

    a) that the defendant harbored or concealed the offender; or

    b) that the defendant provided or aided in providing the offender with any means of avoiding arrest, trial, conviction, or punishment; or

    c) that the defendant warned the offender of impending apprehension or discovery.

"*Knowing* means that a person acts knowingly with respect to the conduct or to circumstances surrounding the conduct when the person is aware of the nature of the conduct or that the circumstances exist. A person acts knowingly with respect to a result of the person's conduct when the person is aware that the conduct is reasonably certain to cause the result. This requirement is also established if it is shown that the defendant acted intentionally.

"The jury will now be sequestered in the jury room for your deliberations. If after a reasonable period of time you cannot unanimously agree on a verdict for each of the defendants, you will so inform the court and seek any additional instructions.

"You, the jury, will have copies of this set of instructions with you for guidance and reference during your deliberations. If there are any further questions about it, you may request clarification through the bailiff."

The **bailiff** was then instructed by the judge to **sequester** the jury, and the jurors were given the documentary material and copies of the judge's jury instructions for their deliberations. The bailiff explained that they could not communicate with anyone other than each other. If any difficulties should arise during their deliberations, they may contact the bailiff who will communicate with the judge.

Bailiff:
A court officer who has charge of keeping order in the court, custody of the jury, and prisoners while in the court.

Sequester:
To separate or isolate. To sequester jurors is to isolate them from the public during the course of their deliberations.

ASSIGNMENT: The instructions to the jury can be found on the Internet by typing in your state's name and "patterned jury instructions." You should be able to fine your state's list of these selections for almost any type of crime. You must find the specific crime, and if more than one is involved, you will have to understand how to merge them into the circumstances involved. These lists usually begin with general concepts. Look up another crime that interests you and find out how the jury would be charged.

Jury Deliberations and Verdict

We will let you the readers decide how you would have voted and what arguments you would have made in the jury deliberations. This is a very good opportunity for class discussion and clarification of the process. The rules of criminal procedure provide clarification of some of the situations that may arise during this phase of the procedure, not covered in the judge's instructions.

If there are multiple defendants, the jury may return a verdict at any time during its deliberations as to any defendant about whom it has agreed. If the jury cannot agree on all defendants, the state may try again any defendant on whom the jury was not in agreement by declaring a mistrial with regard to that defendant (Tenn. R. Crim. P, Rule 31. Verdict).

If the court instructs the jury on one or more lesser included offenses and the jury reports that it cannot unanimously agree on a verdict, the court shall address the foreperson and inquire whether there is disagreement as to the charged offense and each lesser offense on which the jury was instructed. The following procedures apply:

(A) The court shall begin with the charged offense and, in descending order, inquire as to each lesser offense until the court determines at what level of the offense the jury has disagreed.

(B) The court shall then inquire if the jury has unanimously voted not guilty to the charged offense.

(i) If so, at the request of either party, the court shall poll the jury as to their verdict on the charged offense.

(ii) If it is determined that the jury found the defendant not guilty of the charged offense, the court shall enter a not guilty verdict for the charged offense.

(C) The court shall then inquire if the jury unanimously voted not guilty as to the next, lesser instructed offense.

(i) If so, at the request of either party, the court shall poll the jury as to their verdict on this offense.

(ii) If it is determined that the jury found the defendant not guilty of the lesser offense, the court shall enter a not guilty verdict for that offense.

(D) The court shall continue this inquiry for each lesser instructed offense, or the court may direct the jury to deliberate further as to that lesser offense, or the court may direct the jury to deliberate further as to that lesser offense as well as any remaining offenses originally instructed to the jury. (Tenn. R. Crim. P., Rule 31)

TRIAL: VERDICT, JUDGMENT, AND SENTENCING

After the verdict is returned but before the verdict is recorded, the court shall—on a party's request or on the court's own initiative—poll the jurors individually. If the poll indicates that there is not unanimous concurrence in the verdict, the court may discharge the jury or direct the jury to retire for further deliberations (Rule 31, Tenn. R. Crim. P.).

A unanimous verdict of guilty of first degree murder on either of these defendants will require another hearing for sentencing, where at least one aggravating circumstance must be present and mitigating circumstances are considered. The jury then can deliver only three verdicts or sentences: death, life imprisonment, or life imprisonment without the possibility of parole.

Sentencing

A verdict of guilty on any of the counts, other than first degree murder, will proceed to the sentencing phase of the trial process. The judge will usually take some time for consideration of a sentencing evaluation and opportunities for additional input to these decisions. In Middle State, after a verdict or plea of guilty, the court shall set the sentence, except to habitual criminal charges or capital cases where notice has previously been given. When the court imposes sentence, the sentence shall be fixed as provided by law.

In case of a verdict of multiple convictions for a single defendant, the trial judge shall determine whether the defendant's sentences shall be served concurrently or consecutively. A **concurrent sentence** is when there are two or more terms of imprisonment, all or part of which is served simultaneously. A **consecutive sentence** is when one sentence must follow the other. The order must specify the reasons for this decision, and it is reviewable on appeal. Unless it affirmatively appears that the sentences are consecutive, they are deemed to be concurrent.

Concurrent sentence: When the sentences are served simultaneously (the person must serve the longest sentence).

Consecutive sentence: When one sentence must follow the other.

The law requires consecutive sentences when the defendant has been convicted of multiple offenses from one trial or when the defendant has additional sentences not yet fully served as the result of convictions in the same or other courts and the law requires consecutive sentences; the sentence shall be consecutive whether the judgment explicitly so orders or not. This rule applies (1) to a sentence for a felony committed while on parole for a felony, (2) to a sentence for escape or for a felony committed while on escape, (3) to a sentence for a felony committed while the defendant was released on bail and the defendant is convicted of both offenses, and (4) for any other ground provided by law.

Victim's Rights

Middle State law required that the victim be informed of the developments in a felony case, including any plea bargain agreements. Rusty Kovaks had called Mrs. Stone, the victim's wife, and asked her to come to his office so that he could tell her about the plea bargain agreement with Jesse Williams. He also informed her of the refusal of the judge to accept the plea bargain and the order to consolidate the two defendants' cases.

Victim Impact Statements

The concept of violent crime victim impact statements originated after the Charles Manson murders in California in 1969. Reaction led by Doris Tate, the mother of actress Sharon Tate, who was one of the Manson cult murder infamous victims, ultimately produced public reaction in California against that state's correction system. This led to amendments to the California criminal law in 1982 allowing crime victims and their families to make victim impact statements during sentencing and at parole hearings. Doris Tate was the first person to make such an impact statement under the new law when she spoke at the parole hearing of one of her daughter's killers, Charles "Tex" Watson. She later said that she believed the changes in the law had afforded her daughter dignity that had been denied her before, and that she had been able to "help transform Sharon's legacy from murder victim to a symbol of victim's rights."

In 1991, the U.S. Supreme Court held that a victim impact statement in the form of testimony was allowed during the sentencing phase of a trial in *Payne v. Tennessee*, 501 U.S. 808 (1991). It ruled that the admission of such statements did not violate the Constitution and that the statements could be ruled as admissible in death penalty cases. By 1997, some 44 states allowed the presentation of victim impact statements during sentencing procedures. The law varies in different states, and while most states allow statements to be made during the sentencing phase of the trial, Indiana and Texas allow for statements also to be made after sentencing.

All 50 states now allow victims to be heard. All states allow some form of impact information at sentencing. Some states even included victims' rights amendments to their state constitutions. Most states allow either oral or written statements, or both, from the victim at the sentencing hearing and require that victim impact information be included in the presentence report, which is given to the judge prior to imposing sentence. In a majority of the states, victim impact statements are also allowed at parole hearings, whereas in others a copy of the original statement is attached to the offender's file to be reviewed by the parole board. Some states allow these statements to be updated by the victims to include any additional impact the original crime has had on their lives.

"A judgment of conviction shall be signed by the judge and entered by the clerk. A judgment of conviction shall include; the plea; the verdict or findings; and the adjudication and sentence." (Tenn. R. Crim. P., Rule 32)

New Trial

On its own initiative or on motion of a defendant, the court may grant a new trial as required by law. If trial was by the court without a jury (a bench trial), the court on motion of a defendant for the new trial may vacate the judgment if entered, take additional testimony, and direct the entry of a new judgment. The **motion for a new trial** must be in writing or, if made orally in open court, be reduced to writing within 30 days of the date the order of sentence is entered. The court shall liberally grant motions to amend the motion for a new trial until the day of the hearing on the motion for a new trial.

> **Motion for a new trial:** A request that the judge set aside the judgment and order a new trial on the basis that the trial was improper or unfair due to specified prejudicial errors that occurred (Tenn. R. Crim. P., Rule 59.02).

It is important to note that a motion for a new trial must be filed within 30 days of the date the order of sentence is entered, without regard for when judgment is entered upon the verdict. This time period applies whether or not any other motion or petition is filed. Some attorneys seek to "reserve the right to amend" a motion for a new trial and subsequently file such amendments without a court order permitting it. This rule is intended to permit timely amendments, and for that reason the rule does not close that time frame until the motion is heard. The trial judge retains the power to deny amendments, and strong consideration should be given to whether the new ground being raised was promptly brought to the court's attention (Tenn. R. Crim. P.; see Advisory Commission comment).

Affidavits provide a method for resolving factual issues, if the trial judge is satisfied that they adequately serve the purpose. The judge is not required to believe an incredible affidavit and may always require an evidentiary hearing with witnesses. Under subdivision (e), neither the filing nor the denial of a motion for a new trial waives the right to make a motion in **arrest of judgment** so long as it is filed within 30 days of verdict.

> **Arrest of judgment:** The act of staying a judgment or refusing to render judgment in an action at law and in criminal cases after the verdict for some matter in error, such as the court not having jurisdiction.

A grant of a new trial must be distinguished from a granted **motion for judgment of acquittal**. In the granting of a new trial, there is no double jeopardy. However, the motion for a judgment of acquittal cannot be tried again because it would violate the constitutional prohibition of the **double jeopardy** rule. Acquittal is the same as not guilty.

In *Tibbs v. Florida*, 457 U.S. 31 (1982), the U.S. Supreme Court held that a reversal based on the weight of the evidence, rather than sufficiency of the evidence, permits the state to initiate a new prosecution.

> **Motion for judgment of acquittal:** Cannot result in a new trial because that would involve double jeopardy.

A motion of acquittal exemplifies the theory of the court being the "thirteenth juror" and can negate the jury's verdict where the judge disagrees with the jury's resolution of conflicting testimony.

> **Double jeopardy:** Fifth Amendment prohibition against a second prosecution for the same offense after a first trial.

> *"Just as a deadlocked jury does not result in an acquittal barring retrial under the Double Jeopardy Clause of the Fifth Amendment, an appellate court's*

disagreement with the jurors' weighing of the evidence does not require the special deference accorded verdicts of acquittal. Moreover, a reversal on the weight of the evidence can occur only after the State has presented sufficient evidence to support conviction and has persuaded the jury to convict. The reversal simply affords the defendant a second opportunity to seek acquittal. Giving him this second chance does not amount to governmental oppression of the sort against which the Double Jeopardy Clause was intended to protect." (Tibbs v. Florida, *457 U.S. 31, 39-44 (1982)*)

The trial court may reduce a sentence upon a motion filed within 120 days after the date the sentence is imposed or probation is revoked. No extensions shall be allowed on the time limitation. No other actions start the running of this time limitation. In Middle State, the trial judge retains jurisdiction to modify any sentence that is to be served in the jail or workhouse. However, the statute deprives the court of authority to modify a sentence to the department of corrections once the judgment is final in the trial court (Tenn. R. Crim. P. Rule 35; see Advisory Commission comment).

THE APPEALS PROCESS

An **appeal** as of right in Middle State is an appeal that does not require permission of the trial or appellate court as a prerequisite to bringing an appeal. There is now officially only one method of appeal to be known as an "appeal as of right." All other appeal motions are abolished. (However, all of the previously used appeal motions that are in the nature of writs of error are consolidated under use of this one form of notification.) Failure to take any step other than the timely filing of a notice of appeal does not affect the validity of the appeal but is ground only for such action as the appellate court deems appropriate, which may include dismissal of the appeal (T.R.A.P., Rule 3 (e), p. 2).

Appeal:
Resort to appellate court to review the decision of an inferior court.

After overruling a motion for a new trial or a motion in arrest of judgment, whichever comes last, the trial judge shall advise the defendant of the right to appeal and determine from the evidence or stipulation for the record whether the defendant is indigent. If the defendant is indigent, the court shall advise the defendant that if he or she has not already retained appellate counsel or if counsel has not previously been appointed, the court will appoint appellate counsel and that a transcript or statement of the evidence will be furnished at the state's expense.

Before the judgment on a guilty verdict becomes final, counsel for the defendant shall file a timely notice of appeal with the trial court clerk. This notice of appeal must be filed within 30 days from the date of judgment to meet the rules of the appeals court. It must contain a certified question of law that is dispositive of the case, and this question of law is stated in the judgment or document so as to identify clearly the scope and limits of the legal issue reserved, and that the judgment document reflects that the defendant, the state, and the trial court are of the opinion that the certified question is dispositive of the case.

This provision permits an appeal in the context of a controlling question that needs answering, such as the constitutionality of a statute upon which a charge is grounded or the validity of the search upon which the state's case must be made. The rules regarding certified questions of law that are dispositive of the case vary depending on whether there is a plea bargain and whether the state agrees to the appeal.

In order for an attorney to perfect an appeal of a certified question, the attorney must be certain that the application fully comports with the requirements for this type of an appeal as set forth by the Tennessee Supreme Court in its decision *State v. Preston*, 759 S.W.2d 647 (Tenn. 1988). The Tennessee high court ruled:

> *Regardless of what has appeared in prior petitions, orders, colloquy in open court or otherwise, the final order or judgment from which the time begins to run to pursue a T.R.A.P. [Tennessee Rules of Appellate Procedure] appeal must contain a statement of the dispositive certified question of law reserved by defendant for appellate review and the question of law must be stated so as to clearly identify the scope and the limits of the legal issue reserved.*

Failure to follow the dictates of the *Preston* decision could result in the dismissal of the appeal.

Rule 37 (e) also requires that the defendant must be advised of pertinent appellate rights. In all cases, if an appeal is to be waived, this must be put on the record. Retained counsel who commences the appellate process is deemed to be fully retained to complete it (Tenn. R. Crim. P.; see Advisory Commission comments at the end of Rule 37 [p. 51–52]).

The trial court clerk shall promptly serve all filed notices of appeal on the clerk of the appellate court designated in the notice of appeal. The clerk of the appellate court shall enter the appeal on the docket immediately upon receipt of the copy of the notice of appeal served upon the clerk of the appellate court by the trial court clerk (T.R.A.P. Rule 5 [b] and [c]).

This shift in the responsibility for serving copies of notices of appeal from the appellant counsel to the trial court clerk was instituted to assist the appellate court system in tracking all cases after trial (T.R.A.P. Rule 5 Advisory Commission comments, 1997).

The Advisory Commission comments in 2007 state in regard to Rule 5 (c) that the amended language requires the trial court clerk to promptly serve either the appeal bond or affidavit of indigence with the notice of appeal upon the appellate court clerk.

This amendment will ensure that appellants timely file their appeal bond or affidavit with the notice of appeal. Failure to do so will result in the trial court clerk notifying the appellate court clerk that no appeal bond or affidavit has been filed so that action can be taken to dismiss the appeal under Rule 6 (a) prior to the filing of the record (T.R.A.P. Rule 5 Advisory Commission comments (2007)).

These changes in appellate procedure are indication of the active nature of these new rules, which are frequently updated to increase the efficiency and perhaps even the simplicity of the appeals process. The Rules of Appellate Procedure in Middle State provide that the rules may be suspended to allow individuals without professional knowledge of the law to attempt an appeal on their own.

An attorney retained by the defendant to represent the defendant for the trial but not for appeal shall timely advise the trial court of this fact at the hearing on the motion for a new trial. Thereupon, such counsel will be permitted to withdraw as counsel of record. If the defendant is indigent at the time counsel is permitted to withdraw, the court shall appoint appellate counsel for the defendant (Tenn. R. Crim. P. Rule 37(e)). The Rules of Appellate Procedure are now applicable after the trial court's final judgment. These rules seem complex; however, the process has been simplified, as the following notice of appeal, Form 17.1, illustrates (see Tennessee Rules of Appellate Procedure).

The copy of the notice of appeal filed with the clerk of the appellate court should include a list of the parties upon whom service of notice of docketing of the appeal is required by Rule 5 of these rules.

So, in our hypothetical criminal case, any party, including the district attorney, Jesse Williams, or Robert Jackson, could have filed a timely notice with the trial court within 30 days after sentencing stating a dispositive certified question of law as a notice of appeal. If this notice had been filed, all that party would have to do is fill out the form (Form 17.1) and file the appeal with the trial court clerk. This simple application would require the trial court clerk to deliver up the entire court record for this case, and the appellant would also have to serve notice of appeal on the district attorney general of the county in which the judgment was entered and on the attorney general in the Nashville office.

The court record on appeal consists of (1) copies, certified by the clerk of the trial court, of all papers filed in the trial court except as hereafter provided; (2) the original of any exhibits filed in the trial court; (3) the transcript or statement of the evidence or proceedings, which shall clearly indicate and identify any exhibits offered in evidence and whether received or rejected; (4) any requests for instructions submitted to the trial judge for consideration, whether expressly acted upon or not; and (5) any other matter designated by a party and properly includable in the record.

Form 17.1 **NOTICE OF APPEAL**

In the _____ Court for _____County, Tennessee

No. _____

A. B., Plaintiff

v.   Notice of Appeal

C. D., Defendant

Notice is hereby given that C. D., defendant above named, hereby appeals to the (Supreme Court of Tennessee or Court of Appeals or Court of Criminal Appeals) from the final judgment entered in this action on

The _____ day of _____, 20_____.

/s/ _____

_____
Counsel for C. D.

The briefs are arguments presented to the appeals court. The *appellant's brief* is that of the party bringing the appeal, which must contain appropriate headings and be in the order indicated here:

1. A table of contents, with references to the pages in the brief
2. A table of authorities, including cases (alphabetically arranged), statutes, and other authorities cited, with references to the pages in the brief where they are cited
3. A jurisdictional statement in cases appealed to the supreme court directly from the trial court, indicating briefly the jurisdictional grounds for the appeal to the supreme court

4. A statement of the issues presented for review
5. A statement of the case, indicating briefly the nature of the case, the course of proceedings, and its disposition in the court below
6. A statement of the facts, setting forth the facts relevant to the issues presented for review with appropriate references to the record
7. An argument, which may be preceded by a summary of argument, setting forth the contentions of the appellant with respect to the issues presented and the reasons therefore, including the reasons why the contentions require appellate relief, with citations to the authorities and appropriate references to the record (which may be quoted verbatim) relied upon
8. A short conclusion, stating the precise relief sought

The brief of the *appellee* and all other parties shall conform to the foregoing requirements, except that items (3), (4), (5), and (6) of this rule need not be included except to the extent that the presentation by the appellant is deemed unsatisfactory. If appellee is also requesting relief from the judgment, the brief of the appellee shall contain the issues and arguments involved in his request for relief as well as the answer to the brief of the appellant.

Page limitations are also imposed for the length of these briefs. Except by order of the appellate court or a judge thereof, arguments in principal briefs shall not exceed 50 pages, and arguments in reply briefs shall not exceed 25 pages. In cases involving multiple parties, including cases consolidated for purposes of the appeal, any number of parties may join in a single brief, and any party may adopt by reference any part of the brief of another party. Parties may similarly join in reply briefs.

A leave or request of the court is needed, but **amicus curiae** (friend of the court) briefs and oral arguments are possible. An *amicus* brief may be conditionally filed with the motion for leave. A motion for leave shall identify the interest of the applicant and shall state how a brief of an interested *amicus* will assist the appellate court. The *amicus curiae* may participate in oral argument only by leave of court granted on motion or at the request of the appellate court.

Oral argument is not usually entertained, except when granted at the request of the appellate court. Such a brief shall follow the form prescribed for the brief of an appellee. The court shall fix the time and conditions for the filing of the amicus curiae brief.

Amicus curiae
("friend of the court"):
A person with strong interest in or views on the subject matter of an action may petition the court for permission to file a brief.

The appeals courts may direct counsel for the parties to appear before the court or a judge thereof for a prehearing conference to consider the simplification of the issues and such other matters as may aid in the disposition of the proceeding by the court. The court or judge shall make an order that recites the action taken at the conference and the agreements made by the parties as to any of the matters considered and that limit the issues to those not disposed of by admissions or agreements of counsel; such order when entered controls the subsequent proceeding on its merits if no prejudice results.

Any party to an appeal who desires oral argument shall so request by stating at the bottom of the cover page of the party's brief that oral argument is requested. If any party to an appeal requests oral argument, it is unnecessary for any other party to do so. No party may argue unless the party has filed a brief as required by these rules. Unless the appellate court otherwise orders, each side requesting the same relief is allowed 30 minutes for argument. Additional time may be requested, and the court may terminate the argument whenever in its judgment further argument is unnecessary.

The state supreme court, court of appeals, and court of criminal appeals shall grant the relief on the law and facts to which the party is entitled or the proceeding otherwise requires and may grant any relief, including the giving of any judgment and making of any order, provided, however, relief may not be granted in contravention of the province of the trier of fact. Nothing in this rule shall be construed as requiring that relief be granted to a party responsible for an error or who failed to take whatever action was reasonably available to prevent or nullify the harmful effect of an error. A party is not entitled to relief if the party invited error, waived an error, or failed to take whatever steps were reasonable to cure an error.

A final judgment from which relief is available and otherwise appropriate shall not be set aside unless, considering the whole record, error involving a substantial right more probably than not affected the judgment or would result in prejudice to the judicial process. When necessary to do substantial justice, an appellate court may consider an error that has affected the substantial rights of a party at any time, even though the error was not raised in the motion for a new trial or assigned as error on appeal

Tennessee Rules of Appellate Procedure, Rule 13

The above wording deals with the difficult question of determining whether an error is harmless or prejudicial. The harmful effect of the error is measured by the effect the error had on the judgment entered. Under this rule, an error is prejudicial if it "more probably than not" affected the judgment. This rule also requires reversal of a judgment when affirming it would be prejudicial to the judicial process. Although the concept cannot be fully defined, it certainly would include situations in which, for example, an accused was denied the effective assistance of counsel, or the decision maker was obviously biased, or there was improper discrimination in jury selection.

The notation of a judgment in the docket constitutes entry of the judgment. The clerk of the appellate court shall prepare and enter the judgment following receipt of the opinion of the appellate court unless the court orders otherwise. The clerk shall, on the day judgment is entered, mail a copy of the opinion and notice of the date of entry of the judgment to the parties. Entry of judgment shall not be delayed for the taxing of costs.

If an appeal is dismissed, costs shall be taxed against the appellant unless otherwise agreed by the parties or ordered by the court; if a judgment is affirmed, costs shall be taxed against the appellant unless otherwise ordered; if a judgment is reversed, costs shall be taxed against the appellee unless otherwise ordered; and if a judgment is affirmed or reversed in part, or is vacated, costs shall be allowed only as ordered by the appellate court.

When a review by the state supreme court is sought, the timely filing of an application for permission to appeal to the supreme court shall stay the issuance of the mandate of the court of criminal appeals. This stay is effective until final disposition by the supreme court. Upon the filing of an order of the supreme court denying the application for permission to appeal, the mandate shall issue immediately.

When review by the Supreme Court of the United States is sought, the appellate court whose decision is sought to be reviewed or a judge thereof, and in any event the Supreme Court of the state or a judge thereof, may stay the mandate.

The state supreme court or the U.S. Supreme Court may decide not to hear the case when the application does not receive sufficient votes on application of **writ of certiorari**. If the court denies the writ, the court refuses to hear the appeal and, in effect, the judgment below stands unchanged. When the writ is granted, then it has the effect of ordering the lower court to certify the record and send it up to the higher court, which has used its discretion to hear the appeal.

Writ of certiorari:
An order by the appellate court that is used when the court has discretion on whether or not to hear an appeal.

When the appellate court dismisses the appeal or affirms the judgment and the mandate is filed in the trial court, execution may issue and other proceedings may be conducted as if no appeal had been taken. Intermediate appeals courts usually hear cases by a panel of at least three judges. However, they may sit en banc (as the whole court) on occasion and make decisions by majority vote.

The general rule concerning denial of certiorari at the U.S. Supreme Court level is that it requires at least four votes out of the nine justices to accept a case on appeal. This is called "the rule of four." State supreme courts (or state courts of final appeal) vary in size from five to nine members (all state high courts are either five, seven, or nine members) and usually require one less than a majority to review the case. All require a majority of the members of the court for approval of a final judgment.

CONSTITUTIONAL ISSUES

Defendants who plead guilty as a result of a plea bargain forfeit several constitutional rights, including, among others, the Fifth Amendment's right to protection against self-incrimination and the Sixth Amendment rights to a public trial, to confront one's accusers, as well as the presumption of innocence. This issue has stimulated considerable debate about the acceptance of certain practices as meeting valid constitutional due process standards.

The U.S. Supreme Court has reviewed the constitutional issues of plea bargaining in a series of court decisions involving mainly the voluntariness of guilty pleas. In *Boykin v. Alabama*, 395 U.S. 238 (1969), the Court held that an affirmative action, such as a verbal statement, indicating that the plea was made voluntarily must exist on the record before a trial judge may accept a guilty plea. In *Brady v. United States*, 397 U.S. 742 (1970), the Court held that a guilty plea is not valid merely because it is entered to avoid the possibility of the death penalty. Justice Byron White, in his opinion for the Court, upheld the constitutionality of plea bargaining as having a "mutuality of advantage." He stated that the state "conserves scarce judicial and prosecutorial resources" and achieves "more promptly imposed punishment"; and at the same time, the defendant's "exposure is reduced, the correctional process can begin immediately, and the practical burdens of a trial are eliminated."

Once a plea bargain has been agreed to by the prosecutor, it must be honored. This legal principle is clearly established in *Santobello v. New York*, 404 U.S. 257 (1971), in which the state prosecutor reneged on a bargain struck with the defendant. The bargain was not fulfilled because of a change in prosecutors, and the defendant was given a maximum sentence contrary to the plea agreement. The Supreme Court reversed the decision.

Critics of plea bargaining question the constitutionality of defendants' forfeiting of their rights no matter how thorough the bargaining process, and the Supreme Court has been willing to consider some of these complaints. In a highly controversial decision that split the Court five to four, the Supreme Court held that a defendant's due process rights are not violated when a prosecutor threatens to reindict the accused on more serious charges if the accused does not plead guilty to the original offense (*Bordenkircher v. Hayes*, 434 U.S. 357 [1978]).

The defendant, Paul Hayes, was indicted by a Kentucky grand jury for forging a check in the amount of $88.30, an offense then punishable by a term of 2–10 years. The prosecutor offered to recommend a sentence of 5 years' imprisonment if Hayes pleaded guilty. The prosecutor also stated that if Hayes did not plead guilty, the prosecutor would return to the grand jury and seek an indictment under the Kentucky Habitual Criminal Act, which would subject Hayes to a mandatory life sentence because of his two prior felony convictions.

Hayes pleaded not guilty, and the prosecutor obtained an indictment charging him under the Habitual Criminal Act. At trial, the jury found

Hayes guilty of the original charge, and under the Habitual Criminal Act, Hayes was sentenced to life imprisonment. The Kentucky Court of Appeals affirmed the sentence. On a writ of habeas corpus, the federal district court dismissed the petition, but the U.S. Court of Appeals for the Sixth Circuit reversed, holding that the prosecutor's conduct had violated Hayes's due process rights. The U.S. Supreme Court then granted certiorari to consider the constitutional question because of its importance to the administration of criminal justice.

On the Fourteenth Amendment issue, the circuit court had held that the substance of the plea offer itself violated the limitations imposed by the Due Process Clause. However, the Supreme Court concluded that the appeals court was mistaken in its ruling. The majority stated that there is no element of punishment or retaliation as long as the accused is free to accept or reject the prosecution's offer. A rigid constitutional rule would prohibit a prosecutor from acting forthrightly in dealing with the defense, which would only invite unhealthy subterfuge that would drive the practice of plea bargaining back into the shadows from which it had so recently emerged. Therefore, in *Bordenkircher v. Hayes*, 434 U.S. 357 (1978), the five-member majority held that a threat to indict on more serious charges was not a violation of the defendant's due process rights.

The *Bordenkircher* case illustrates the extent of prosecutorial discretion. Although the Court recognized the potential for individual and institutional abuse, it concluded that the prosecutor's conduct was not unlawful.

Another constitutional issue regarding plea bargains is whether defendants have a right to effective counsel. In *McMann v. Richardson*, 397 U.S. 759 (1970), three defendants claimed that their confessions were coerced and that their court-appointed attorney had incompetently represented them. The Court, however, held that their attorney was "reasonably competent" and that defendants must assume the risk of "ordinary error" by their attorneys.

However, in *Henderson v. Morgan*, 426 U.S. 637 (1976), the Court set aside a conviction because the defendant pleaded guilty to second degree murder without being informed of the consequences. The Court held that if a person of low mental ability has not been given an explanation of the difference between manslaughter and murder, the person's guilty plea is involuntary.

In *United States v. Cronic*, 466 U.S. 648 (1984), Justice John Paul Stevens explained that the right to counsel includes the right to effective counsel because competent counsel is essential to the accusatory system and "the reliability of the trial process." Public defenders do not enjoy absolute immunity from being sued for incompetent representation. However, the Court has been reluctant to hold that defendants have been denied effective counsel.

In *Strickland v. Washington*, 466 U.S. 668 (1984), Justice Sandra Day O'Connor set forth a difficult test for determining when the right to effective counsel has been denied. To establish an ineffective assistance of counsel claim, the defendant must first show that counsel's performance was deficient to the extent of making errors so serious that they constituted a denial of the Sixth Amendment-based right to counsel. The defendant also must show that the deficient performance created prejudice against the defense to such an extent that it deprived the defendant of a fair trial.

Defendants have a right to effective counsel on their first appeal (*Evitts v. Lucey*, 469 U.S. 387 (1985)), although attorneys may withdraw from cases in which defendants tell their attorneys that they are going to lie on the witness stand without denying the defendants' right to effective counsel. In *Mallard v. United States District Court for the Southern District of California*, 490 U.S. 296, the Court held that a judge could not compel a lawyer to serve as an attorney for several inmates in a civil rights case.

Prisoner's Rights

Prior to the 1960s, it was generally accepted that on conviction for a crime an individual forfeited all rights not expressly granted by statutory law or correctional policy. State and federal court had adopted a "hands off" doctrine of noninterference with corrections authorities unless the case indicted a serious breach of the Eighth Amendment's protection against cruel and unusual punishment.

The Federal Civil Rights Act (1963), 42 U.S.C. §1983, contains the following provision.

> *Every person who, under color of any statute, ordinance, regulation custom, or usage of any State or territory subjects, or causes to be subjected, any citizen of the United States or other person within the jurisdiction thereof to the deprivation of any rights, privileges, or immunities secured by the Constitution and laws shall be liable to the party injured in an action at law, suit in equity, or other proper proceeding for redress.*
>
> Federal Civil Rights Act (1963)

This language, often referred to as the **under color of law doctrine**, allows prisoners to sue for civil rights violations. In *Cooper v. Pate*, 378 U.S. 546 (1964), the Supreme Court ruled that inmates being denied the right to practice their religion are entitled to legal redress under 42 U.S.C. §1983. An earlier decision in 1941, *Ex parte Hull*, declared that access to the courts for an inmate is a basic constitutional right. Subsequent decisions in the 1970s expanded this concept to deal with the problems of lack of access to legal services in prisons and many other aspects of prison life. In the case of *Johnson v. Avery*, 393 U.S. 483 (1969), the Supreme Court held that unless

Under color of law doctrine: Federal statute prohibiting denial of constitutional rights under a disguise or pretext of law.

the state could provide some reasonable alternative to inmates in the preparation of petitions for postconviction relief, a **jailhouse lawyer** must be permitted to aid illiterate inmates in filing *habeas corpus petitions*.

A **habeas corpus petition** involves a court order directing an official who has a person in custody to show cause for the person's detention. Illegal denial of rights can be brought before the courts in this manner. In *Haines v. Kerner*, 404 U.S. 519 (1972), the Court held that prisoners' petitions must be reviewed even if they have only a limited amount of legal merit. Ten years later, the expansion of prisoner's access to the federal courts was somewhat limited by actions of the conservative Burger Court. In *Rose v. Lundy*, 455 U.S. 509 (1982), the Court held that before a federal court can review an inmate's habeas corpus petition, the inmate must exhaust all legal avenues available in the state courts. The Rehnquist Court moved even further in the direction of limiting access to the federal courts through these petitions.

The substantive rights areas of current recognition by the courts include limited prisoners' rights in regard to freedom of the press, freedom of religion, the right to medical treatment, and the right to be free from cruel and unusual punishment.

The courts have consistently held that only when a compelling state interest exists can prisoners' First Amendment rights be modified. Therefore, corrections authorities must justify the limiting of freedom of speech by showing that granting such freedom would threaten institutional security. Recent decisions have upheld prisoners' rights to receive mail from one another, but prison officials can restrict mail to prisoners in temporary disciplinary detention as a means of increasing the deterrent value of the punishment. In 1980, the institutional policy of refusing to deliver mail in a language other than English was held unconstitutional.

The right to send and receive communications with the outside world is a fundamental right of prisoners recognized by the courts. In *Pocunier v. Martinez*, 416 U.S. 396 (1974), the Supreme Court held that censorship is allowable only when justified by prison security needs and when the restrictions are not greater than those demanded by security precautions. However, in *Turner v. Safley*, 482 U.S. 78 (1987) the Court ruled that prison officials could censor inmates' outgoing mail as long as their policy was reasonably related to security, safety, or rehabilitative concerns. In *Saxbe v. Washington Post Co.*, 417 U.S. 843 (1974), the Court held that a federal prison rule forbidding individual press interviews with specific inmates was justified. The Federal Bureau of Prisons successfully argued that interviews enhance the reputation of particular inmates and jeopardize the possibility of achieving equal treatment of prisoners while in prison.

In 1976, after reviewing the legal principles established during the previous 20 years, the Supreme Court, in *Estelle v. Gamble*, 429 U.S. 97 (1976), clearly stated that the inmate's right to medical care is supported by the constitutional guarantee against cruel and unusual punishment. The Court

Jailhouse lawyer: Inmate of a penal institution who spends his or her time reading the law and giving legal assistance and advice to inmates.

Habeas corpus petition: A writ of habeas corpus as a postconviction remedy that extends to all constitutional challenges.

stated, "Deliberate indifference to serious medical needs of prisoners constitutes the 'unnecessary and wanton infliction of pain' . . . proscribed by the Eighth Amendment."

Treatment of prisoners that (1) degrades the dignity of human beings, (2) is more severe than the offense for which it is given, or (3) shocks the general conscience and is fundamentally unfair has been held unconstitutional by the courts. Corporal punishment has been severely limited by court decisions, and even solitary confinement under prolonged and barbaric conditions has been held to be in violation of the Eighth Amendment. Prisoners have a right to adequate personal hygiene, exercise, mattresses, ventilation, and rules specifying how they can earn release from solitary confinement.

Community treatment in corrections has become prominent in the last 20 years. Today, there are hundreds of private and state-administered community programs. Drug and alcohol treatment, community-based group therapy, and educational programs that employ exoffenders are used for lesser offenses and nonviolent crimes. Probationary release under some supervision and inducements to require utilization of these programs are being tried in many communities. The traditional **community-based programs** include juvenile justice systems and have been developed in all jurisdictions, as well as pretrial diversion programs that were instituted in the 1960s.

Today's juvenile court systems embody both rehabilitative and legalistic orientations. The development of separate systems for handling juvenile offenders is a twentieth-century reform that has been severely criticized by many people. Like the adult corrections systems, these systems have witnessed many changes since the 1960s.

The central concept of the juvenile justice systems is the principle of *parens patriae*. This term refers to government authority to treat delinquents as the parent would be expected to treat them when they violate rules. The state is to act on behalf of the parent in the interests of the child.

Prior to the 1960s, juvenile court proceedings were informal and were subject to relaxed procedural rights. After the 1960s, however, the U.S. Supreme Court began to set a series of precedents making it clear that the most fundamental constitutional rights of children have to be respected. These legalistic reforms have produced a reaction consistent with the recent "get tough on criminals" attitude brought on in part by increasingly serious violations of the law by children.

Juvenile justice systems are still characterized by important differences in the procedures followed and the treatment of the accused as compared to adult justice systems; however, court decisions have blurred these differences. The primary purpose of juvenile procedures is protection and treatment of the child according to the principle of *parens patrae*. The aim is not primarily punishment of the guilty. Age determines the jurisdiction of juvenile courts, which is generally available to those younger than 18 years

Community-based programs: Correctional programs that provide rehabilitation or punishment supervision at the community level rather than in prison.

Parens patriae (parent of the country): Refers traditionally to the role of the state as sovereign and guardian of persons under legal disability.

Juvenile justice systems: Juvenile courts and corrections facilities having special jurisdiction, of a paternal nature, over delinquent, dependent, and neglected children.

of age as of 2008. However, juvenile jurisdiction may be waived, particularly for serious crimes. The age limit for this treatment has been changing as states have enacted new legislation reducing the age limits for juvenile courts (see Table 17.1). As of 2008 the cutoff age for Juvenile Courts was typically 17. Children through age 17 must be tried in juvenile court in 39 states and the District of Columbia. The cutoff age is 16 in 9 states and 15 in 2—New York and North Carolina.

In *Roper v. Simmons*, 543 U.S. 551 (2005), the U.S. Supreme Court held the death penalty unconstitutional for those under the age of 18 at the time of their crime. However, some states may still try juveniles as adults under the age of 18 when the offense was committed. Table 17.1 lists those states by age at which suspects can be tried as adults in the United States as of 2008.

Juvenile proceedings are not considered criminal proceedings, and they generally are conducted on an informal basis. Juvenile court records must be kept confidential, and parents are highly involved in the process. However, the standards for arrests of juveniles are less stringent than those for adults. Juveniles usually are released into parental custody as opposed to being released on bail as are adults. Since the proceedings technically are

Table 17.1 **CUTOFF AGE FOR JUVENILE COURTS: 2008**

Age 15 and Above	Age 16 and Above	Age 17 and Above
New York, North Carolina	Georgia, Illinois, Louisiana, Massachusetts, Michigan, Missouri, South Carolina, Texas, Wisconsin	Alabama, Alaska, Arizona, Arkansas, California, Connecticut Colorado, Delaware, Florida, Hawaii, Idaho, Indiana, Iowa, Kansas, Kentucky, Maine, Maryland, Minnesota, Mississippi, Montana, Nebraska, Nevada, New Hampshire, New Jersey, New Mexico, North Dakota, Ohio, Oklahoma, Oregon, Pennsylvania, Rhode Island, South Dakota, Tennessee, Utah, Vermont, Virginia, Washington, West Virginia, Wyoming, plus the District of Columbia

Source: Sarah Hammond. 2008. "Adults or Kids." *State Legislature* (April).

not criminal proceedings, juveniles have no rights to jury trials (unless they are being tried as adults).

Indeterminate terms in correctional facilities for juvenile and youthful offenders are the form of institutional dispositions. The juvenile's procedural rights are based on the concept of fundamental fairness as opposed to the adult rights to due process. A juvenile has the right to rehabilitation treatment, but an adult has no such right. The juvenile's record is sealed until the age of majority is reached, whereas the adult's criminal record is permanent.

For juvenile offenders, search and seizure rules, Miranda warning, protection from prejudicial lineups, the right to counsel, and other safeguards are required to protect juveniles when they make confessions. Pretrial motions, rules concerning plea negotiation, and the right to trial based on the "beyond a reasonable doubt" standard of proof are also similar to adult standards.

CHAPTER SUMMARY

1. This chapter began with the defendants' case in chief, which allowed both defendants to take the stand as witnesses in a consolidated trial involving multiple charges and multiple defendants in the same trial. This is now mandatory when they are charged with the same offense in the same court jurisdiction.

2. The detailed jury instructions are one of the most important responsibilities of the trial judge. Patterned jury instructions can be found through the Internet when your state is entered first and then "patterned jury instructions." They specifically define each term that must be clarified for the jury.

3. The state Rules of Criminal Procedure will provide detailed rules of procedure for criminal cases and these also may be found through the Internet. These rules concerning issues such as polling the jurors and the specific requirements of rendering a valid jury verdict, as well as motions for a new trial, will be explained.

4. Capital punishment, in states that provide for the death penalty, first require a jury verdict on first degree murder and then a hearing by the same jury to determine whether the sentence will be death or imprisonment for life with or without parole. The sentencing hearing will involve aggravating and mitigating circumstances.

5. Sentences other than the death penalty are the responsibility of the trial judge, and multiple counts of guilty in the same trial require serving consecutive sentences. The judge may decide in most cases whether sentences are to be served concurrently or consecutively.

6. Victim impact statements are now allowed in all 50 states. They allow victims of serious crimes to make statements during the sentencing process that will appear in the court record. Most states also allow oral or written statements before parole hearings.

7. A motion for a new trial and a motion for acquittal are very different and have different consequences. If granted a new trial, the defendant may be tried again because the judge can declare a mistrial; this does not involve double jeopardy. Granting a motion for acquittal allows the defendant to go free because double jeopardy prohibits another trial.

8. The appeal process starts with the trial court where a notice of appeal must be entered within 30 days after the judgment and sentencing and must include a question of law that defines the basis of appeal. An appeal as of right means that the trial court does not have to agree to the appeal.

9. The appeal is then activated by filing the simple motion provided by the appeals court. The defendant or defendant's attorney does not have to serve process papers on the necessary parties. This task is the responsibility of the trial court clerk, who notifies all necessary parties and is responsible for producing the trial court record for the appeals court.

10. Indigent counsel may be appointed by the trial court or extended from the trial process. The trial court must have informed the defendant of his or her right to counsel.

11. The appeals court requires briefs of the appellant that are no more that 50 pages in length and must cover a specified set of requirements as headings in the brief arguing for relief from the court. The appellee is the opposing party who is also given leave to submit arguments limited to 25 pages.

12. The appeals court judges must then determine the difference between harmless and prejudicial error. A grant of relief must be based upon a prejudicial error that could have affected the outcome of the case. A party is not entitled to relief if they invited error, failed to take available actions to prevent it, or contributed to the error themselves.

13. There is further opportunity to appeal to the state's highest court or to the U.S. Supreme Court upon writ of certiorari, which can be denied in most cases.

14. Appeals court judges sit usually in panels of three and may hear oral arguments when a party petitions for them. Their time is limited to 30 minutes, and opposing parties as well as friends of the court may participate with permission from the court.

15. The state supreme court and the U.S. Supreme Court include from 6 to 12 judges and decide questions of law by majority vote. They have their own rules, which are discussed in Chapter 3 of this text.

16. Habeas corpus petitions may be used by jailhouse lawyers to petition the courts for further relief while in prison. Community-based programs and juvenile justice systems are additional processes available in all states for special defendants who may be very young, first-time offenders, or those under the age of 18.

REVIEW EXERCISES

Match the following terms with their most appropriate meaning.

TERMS
1. Bailiff
2. Sequester
3. Concurrent sentence
4. Consecutive sentence
5. Motion for a new trial
6. Arrest of judgment
7. Motion for acquittal for judgment
8. Double jeopardy
9. Appeal
10. Writ of certiorari
11. Amicus curiae
12. Under color of law doctrine
13. Jailhouse lawyer
14. Habeas corpus petition
15. Community-based program
16. *Parens patriae*
17. Juvenile justice system

MEANING
____ courts and corrections facilities with jurisdiction over delinquent, dependent, and neglected children
____ inmate of a penal institution who provides legal assistance and advice to inmates
____ traditional role of the state as sovereign guardian of persons under legal disability
____ federal statute prohibiting denial of constitutional rights under a disguise or pretext of law
____ court officer in charge of keeping order in the court and custody of the jury
____ prohibition against second prosecution in criminal cases
____ order by appellate court used when court has discretion on whether or not to hear an appeal
____ "friend of the court" may petition court to file brief in appeal process
____ to isolate jury from the public during course of their deliberations
____ when one sentence must follow the other
____ request that the judge set aside the judgment and order a new trial
____ when sentences are to be served simultaneously
____ stay of judgment after verdict for prejudicial error
____ cannot result in a new trial because it would involve double jeopardy
____ resort to a superior court to review the decision of a lower court
____ (you have the body) writ to deliver prisoner to test the legality of detention
____ correctional programs that provide rehabilitation or punishment supervision at the community level

DISCUSSION QUESTIONS

1. Is the consolidated trial of two or more individuals at once a fair method of conducting a trial?
2. Why are the judge's final jury instructions most important to the trial process?
3. How would you have decided the hypothetical case illustrated in this chapter?
4. What opportunities are there for the trial judge to reconsider his or her actions at the trial level and correct his or her own errors?
5. What is meant by the appeal as a matter of right that is illustrated in our hypothetical case?

6. Do the recent changes in the appeals procedure simplify or complicate the process (in Tennessee)?

7. What is meant by prejudicial error as opposed to harmless error?

8. What potential actions are available to the appeals court to correct errors at the trial level?

ASSIGNMENTS

ASSIGNMENT: The instructions to the jury can be found on the Internet by typing in your state's name and "patterned jury instructions." You should be able to find your state's list of these selections for almost any type of crime. You must select the specific crime, and if more than one is involved, you will have to understand how to merge them into the circumstances involved. These lists usually begin with general concepts. Look up another crime that interests you and find out how the jury would be charged.

SOURCES AND SUGGESTED READING

Abadinsky, Howard. 1991. *Law and Justice: An Introduction to the American Legal System*. Chicago: Nelson-Hall Publishers.

Abraham, Henry J. 1986. *The Judicial Process*. 5th ed. New York: Oxford University Press.

Alschuler, Albert. 1968. "The Prosecutor's Role in Plea Bargaining." *Yale Law Review* 84:1175.

Boland, Barbara, Catherine H. Conly, Lynn Warner, Ronald Sones, and William Martin. 1988. *The Prosecution of Felony Arrests, 1986*. Washington, D.C.: U.S. Government Printing Office.

Cole, George F., ed. 1988. *Criminal Justice; Law and Politics*. 5th ed. Pacific Grove, Calif: Brooks/Cole Publishing.

Hammond, Sarah. 2008. "Adults or Kids." *State Legislature* (April).

Heumann, Milton. 1978. *Plea Bargaining*. Chicago: University of Chicago Press.

McDonald, William. 1985. *Plea Bargaining: Critical Issues and Common Practices*. Washington, D.C.: U.S. Government Printing Office.

Tennessee Rules of Appellate Procedure. 2008.(See latest edition.) www.tncourts.gov/courts/court-rules/rules-procedure

Tennessee Rules of Criminal Procedure. 2008. (See latest edition.) www.tncourts.gov/courts/court-rules/rules-criminal-procedure

COURT CASES

Bordenkircher v. Hayes, 434 U.S. 357, 98 S.Ct. 663, 54 L.Ed.2d 604 (1978)

Boykin v. Alabama, 395 U.S. 238, 89 S.Ct. 1709, 23 L.Ed.2d 427 (1969)

Brady v. United States, 397 U.S. 742, 90 S.Ct. 1463, 25 L.Ed.2d 747 (1970)

Breed v. Jones, 421 U.S. 519, 95 S.Ct. 1779, 44 L.Ed.2d 346 (1975)

Cooper v. Pate, 378 U.S. 546, 84 S.Ct. 1733, 12 L.Ed.2d 1030 (1964)

Douglas v. California, 372 U.S. 353, 83 S.Ct. 814, 9 L.Ed.2d 811 (1963)

Estelle v. Gamble, 429 U.S. 97, 97 S.Ct. 285, 50 L.Ed.2d 25 (1976)

Evitts v. Lucey, 469 U.S. 387, 105 S.Ct. 830, 83 L.Ed.2d 821 (1985)

Gault, In re, 387 U.S. 1, 87 S.Ct. 1428, 18 L.Ed.2d (1967)

Haines v. Kerner, 404 U.S. 519 (1972)

Henderson v. Morgan, 426 U.S. 637, 96 L.Ed.2d 108 (1976)

Hull, Ex parte, 312 U.S. 546, 61 S.Ct. 640, 85 L.Ed. 1034 (1941)

Johnson v. Avery, 393 U.S. 483, 89 S.Ct. 747, 21 L.Ed.2d 718 (1969)

Kent v. United States, 383 U.S. 541, 86 S.Ct. 1045, 16 L.Ed.2d 84 (1966)

McMann v. Richardson, 397 U.S. 759 (1970)

Payne v. Tennessee, 501 U.S. 808 (1991)

Procunier v. Martinez, 416 U.S. 396, 94 S.Ct. 1800, 40 L.Ed.2d 224 (1974)

Roper v. Simmons, 543 U.S. 551 (2005)

Rose v. Lundy, 455 U.S. 509, 102 S.Ct. 1198, 71 L.Ed.2d 379 (1982)

Santobello v. New York, 404 U.S. 257, 92 S.Ct. 495, 30 L.Ed.2d 427 (1971)

Saxbe v. Washington Post Co., 417 U.S. 843, 94 S.Ct. 2811, 41 L.Ed.2d 514 (1974)

State v. Preston, 759 S.W.2d 647 (Tenn. 1988)

Strickland v. Washington, 466 U.S. 668, 104 S.Ct. 2052, 80 L.Ed.2d 674 (1984)

Tibbs v. Florida, 457 U.S. 31 (1982)

United States v. Cronic, 466 U.S. 648, 104 S.Ct. 2039, 80 L.Ed.2d 657 (1984)

Winship, In re, 397 U.S. 358, 90 S.Ct. 1068, 25 L.Ed.2d 368 (1970)

UNDERSTANDING ADMINISTRATIVE DUE PROCESS

The next chapter of this text discusses the basic concepts of administrative due process, or fundamental due process of law, guaranteed by the Fifth and Fourteenth Amendments to the U.S. Constitution. This text provides only an introduction to the vast field of administrative law that is of great concern in modern society. More advanced courses in administrative law or business law are recommended for students interested in law-related professional careers. Most undergraduate programs provide more advanced courses in political science or business administration.

Administrative Due Process

Administrative law includes the entire range of action by government with respect to the citizen and by the citizen with respect to the government, except for those matters dealt with by the criminal law and those left to private litigation. . . .

Federal Appeals Court Judge Henry Friendly, who sat on the Second U.S. Circuit Court of Appeals from 1959 until 1986.

The third grand division of legal procedures is generally referred to as administrative law. It is one of the least understood and most controversial areas of law. Nonetheless, it is also the most dynamic and rapidly expanding area of legal activity in our increasingly regulated society.

Although the field of administrative law is exceptionally broad, as indicated by Judge Friendly above, administrative legal actions are another form of due process of law. Administrative due process is the subject of this chapter. This overview of the basic areas of administrative legal procedure is not intended to explain thoroughly the vast field of administrative law; that would require a separate course. The objective of this chapter is to provide a description of the basic concepts of administrative due process.

Modern governments, including both the federal and state governments in the United States, exercise extensive regulatory authority. This authority includes "rule making" powers to determine the detailed rules and regulations that implement specific legislation. It also includes authority to investigate and impose penalties for noncompliance with administrative regulations. The rule-making, investigative, and adjudicative functions of administrative agencies are discussed in this chapter, as are the oversight functions of the courts and the power of judicial review.

Other countries, especially those on the continent of Europe, have had more experience with the problems of modern bureaucracies that administer the welfare state. The procedures of some of these countries are discussed in this chapter because they illustrate interesting institutional developments that address such problems. The office of *ombudsman*, for example, which originated in Sweden, provides assistance to individuals who must defend their interests and rights against powerful bureaucracies.

In France and Germany, separate and independent administrative law courts provide the average person with access to the courts to address the problems of powerful bureaucracies.

GENERAL ADMINISTRATIVE LAW CONCEPTS

Government has always been associated with regulatory activity and the development of common standards of behavior that promote the health, safety, and morals of the people. When our federal system was established, the states were generally thought to have this basic authority, and only limited powers of regulation were given to the national government. The increasingly interdependent nature of modern society has led to the recognition that national standards are required in many areas of activity.

Federal Regulation

The U.S. Constitution provides a limited role for the national government in the area of regulatory activity, but constitutional amendments and court interpretations have significantly altered this role. The vagueness of some language in the Constitution leaves considerable room for interpretation regarding what powers are to be surrendered to the national government.

Regulation of money, patents and copyrights, weights and measures, Indian affairs, and foreign policy were clearly recognized in the earliest days of the Republic as areas subject to federal regulation. Congress created administrative agencies to issue patents in 1790 and to manage Native American affairs in 1896; however, the primary growth in federal regulatory agencies has occurred since 1900.

The antitrust movement of the Progressive Era met with strong court opposition to the expansion of federal regulatory authority, which did not occur until the New Deal period in the late 1930s. At that time, regulation of the nation's economic and social affairs was left to state and local governments.

We now have more than 40 federal regulatory agencies, the overwhelming majority of which were created during and after the decade of the 1930s, when the Supreme Court began to broaden its view of the original constitutional grant of national authority to regulate commerce "among the several states." Therefore, federal regulatory agencies are relatively new, but they have become extensive and important in many areas of business, economic, and social policy. The supremacy clause of the Constitution gave the national government power to preempt state authority if that is the intent of Congress in the area of regulation of commerce.

State Regulation

Many regulatory bodies exist at the state and local levels of government. State administrative agencies monitor environmental pollution, license drivers, determine automobile insurance requirements, oversee public utilities, and regulate a wide range of professions and occupations, including hairdressers, barbers, teachers, doctors, lawyers, and psychologists (just to mention a few). Local administrative agencies operate zoning boards, housing authorities, water and sewer commissions, and historical commissions.

The extent of modern government regulatory activity is so pervasive that hardly any area of human endeavor is spared some form of regulatory restriction. The First Amendment freedoms—religion, speech, press, assembly, and petition—are the most obvious areas that are relatively free from government regulations. But even in these areas, when a "compelling state interest" has been demonstrated, the courts have allowed exceptions. Today, it is easier to construct a list of those areas that are not regulated than those that are regulated. Both Congress and the states have responded to increasing demands that the government use its authority to regulate abusive business practices and to protect the health and safety of the people.

The corresponding increase in government bureaucracies at both the federal and state levels has resulted in the development of numerous departments of government. These departments represent the major divisions of government activity, but they are complex organizations that have been divided into specialized agencies. Relatively few of these agencies are regulatory in character.

The states have less clearly defined specialization of agencies within departments than does the federal government. A simple classification of federal agencies according to the mission of each agency, as defined by law, includes (1) clientele agencies, (2) agencies for maintenance of the Union, (3) regulatory agencies, and (4) redistributive agencies (Lowi and Ginsberg 1992, 319–323). These types of agencies, other than regulatory agencies, are essentially service functions that do not have the authority to impose regulatory rules.

REGULATORY AGENCIES

A **regulatory agency** is defined as an agency or commission that has been delegated relatively broad powers and is authorized by the legislative body to make detailed rules governing the conduct of individuals and business activity within broad legislative guidelines. Some regulatory agencies, such as the Environmental Protection Agency (EPA), have departmental status; most of these agencies, however, are bureaus within departments, such as the Food and Drug Administration (FDA) in the Department

Regulatory agency: An agency or commission that has been delegated rule-making authority by an act of law.

of Health and Human Services, the Occupational Safety and Health Administration (OSHA) in the Department of Labor, and the Agricultural Stabilization and Conservation Service (ASCS) in the Department of Agriculture.

Other regulatory agencies are independent regulatory commissions that are somewhat isolated from presidential control. Examples of these independent commissions include the Interstate Commerce Commission (ICC), which dates back to 1883, and the Federal Trade Commission (FTC), created in 1914. As Lowi and Ginsberg explain, "Whether departmental or independent, an agency is regulatory if Congress delegates relatively broad powers over a sector of the economy or a type of commercial activity and authorizes it to make rules governing the conduct of people and businesses within that jurisdiction." (Lowi and Ginsberg 1992, 337–338)

Rules made by regulatory agencies have the effect of legislation as long as they are made within the bounds of the authorizing or enabling act and meet constitutional standards. This delegation of governmental authority generally has been upheld by the courts and allows specific agencies to exercise quasi-legislative and quasi-judicial powers in addition to their obvious executive function.

Rule-making Functions

Regulatory agencies came into existence because legislative bodies recognized that they could not achieve desired regulatory goals within the existing governmental structure. Although legislative bodies could provide general policy direction, they possessed limited subject matter expertise and could not devote attention to the multitude of problems that are involved in the development of detailed regulatory rules and their enforcement. Regulatory agencies placed within existing governmental departments or created expressly for this purpose can assemble the necessary factual data and expertise to draft detailed rules and work toward achieving the objectives stipulated in the legislation.

Regulatory agencies are created by legislative enactments referred to as **enabling acts**. These acts create agencies or authorize the chief executive to create agencies. The enabling act determines the agency's organizational structure, defines its functions and powers, and establishes basic operational standards and guidelines. These standards and guidelines help reviewing courts control the abuse of discretion. Courts also use the agency's own written directives (rules) to assess whether an agency is operating according to the legislative intent.

Enabling act: Statutory authority defining the functions and powers of governmental agencies.

Government agencies perform a variety of functions. For example, they monitor businesses and professions in order to prevent the use of unfair methods of competition. They prevent the use of fraud and deceptive practices, and they help ensure that drug manufacturers produce pure medications or monitor food products to ensure that they are safe to consume. They also function to protect society from environmental pollution and insider trading practices in the stock market. The regulatory agencies are those units specifically authorized to draft the detailed rules necessary to carry out the will of the legislative act that grants them authority (see Table 18.1).

Table 18.1 **FEDERAL REGULATORY AGENCIES**

Dept. of Agriculture: Animal and Plant Health Inspection Service Food Safety and Inspection Service USDA Procurement Policy and Regulations **Dept. of Commerce:** Office of the Assistant General Counsel for Legislation and Regulations Federal Acquisition Regulations (FAR) Bureau of Industry and Security Economic Development Administration International Trade Administration **Dept. of Defense:** Defense Federal Acquisition Regulations Supplement (DFARS) Travel Regulations **Dept. of Energy:** Office of Civilian Radioactive Waste Management Office of Energy Efficiency and Renewable Energy: Building Technologies Program (includes Yucca Mountain Project) **Dept. of Education:** Proposed Regulations, Priorities, and Other Rules	Final Regulations, Priorities, and Other Rules Announcements (grant competitions, requests for comment, etc.) **Dept. of Health and Human Services:** Centers for Disease Control and Prevention, NIOSH: Office of Compensation Analysis and Support, Public Docket Centers for Disease Control and Prevention, NIOSH: Federal Register Notices Centers for Medicare & Medicaid Services; Regulations and Guidance Food and Drug Administration, Division of Dockets Management Food and Drug Administration, Center for Devices and Radiological Health Inspector General, Federal Register Documents Office of Civil Rights, National Standards to Protect the Privacy of Personal Health Information **Dept. of Homeland Security:** Laws and Regulations Transportation Security Administration, Security Regulations U.S. Coast Guard, Commercial Regulations and Standards Directorate U.S. Immigration and Customs Enforcement, Federal Register	**Dept. of Housing and Urban Development:** Client Information and Policy System **Dept. of Justice:** Bureau of Alcohol, Tobacco, Firearms, and Explosives Department of Justice Legal Documents Drug Enforcement Administration, Office of Diversion Control, Federal Register **Dept. of Labor:** Federal Register Documents Occupational Safety and Health Administration, Docket Office **Dept. of Transportation:** Dockets Information Office of Drug and Alcohol Policy and Compliance, Regulations Federal Aviation Administration, Regulations Federal Highway Administration, Legislation, Regulations, and Guidance National Highway, Traffic Safety Administration, Regulations Office of Pipeline Safety, Regulations and Rulemaking Pipeline and Hazardous Materials Administration, Rules and Regulations

The term **rule making** is often used to describe the **quasi-legislative powers** of regulatory agencies. Agencies that have been granted rule-making functions are authorized to make, alter, or repeal rules and regulations to the extent permitted by the terms of their enabling statutes. These statutes set the general standards, authorize the agencies to determine the content of the regulations, and provide general sanctions for noncompliance with administrative directives.

The body of substantive federal administrative law can be found in the extensive volumes of the *Code of Federal Regulations* (C.F.R.). These volumes of detailed rules now exceed the volumes of legislation found in the *United States Code* (U.S.C.). For example, four pages in the U.S.C. explaining an act of Congress amending the Clean Air Act may eventually turn into over 400 pages in the C.F.R. rules and regulations that have the force of law for the regulated industry.

> **ASSIGNMENT:** Use the list of federal regulatory agencies in Table 18.1 to find an agency that you are particularly interested in and type into the Internet search box the agency's name. Go to that agency's home page and read the description of the agency. Then read further to find out what is currently underway in that agency to improve or develop new rules in the areas of their legislative responsibility. Then go to the *Code of Federal Regulations* and look up a regulation of interest. This code is organized like the *U.S. Code* or the *Tennessee Code*. You will need a specific topic for which to search.

The Web site, Regulations.gov, provides assistance in making public comments to these federal agencies that issue nearly 8,000 regulations per year. Each day, public users may submit comments on these regulations using the e-mail address listed at the site.

The states create formative bodies of administrative law as well, but they are somewhat less defined than those of federal law. Many states publish separate administrative codes similar to the C.F.R. The entire body of substantive administrative law may be more difficult to find in states that do not publish such indexed codes, but administrative rules in these states can be found in separate administrative publications.

At the federal level, the **Administrative Procedures Act** of 1946 and its amendments provide detailed procedural rules for drafting and promulgating administrative regulations and define the rights of persons and corporations affected by these regulations. This legislation has become the major source of law governing the procedures of regulatory agencies and provides for judicial review of administrative determinations. The states have enacted legislation in recent years that closely resembles the federal requirements in the area of administrative procedure.

Rule making:
The process of developing detailed rules or regulations having the force of law and issued by executive authority.

Quasi-legislative powers:
Delegated rule-making authority.

Administrative Procedures Act:
Laws enacted by federal and many state jurisdictions governing practices and procedures before administrative agencies.

The Investigative Function

Governmental administrative agencies cannot develop the necessary facts and knowledge to perform their regulatory functions without extensive investigative powers. Therefore, as regulation has expanded and intensified, legislative and judicial authorities have conferred broad investigative powers to practically all administrative agencies.

Statutes usually grant an agency the power to use a variety of methods in carrying out its fact-finding functions. These methods include requirements of reports from regulated businesses, the conducting of inspections, and the use of judicially enforced subpoenas. Failure to comply with agency requests for information is usually dealt with swiftly by easily obtained court orders requiring compliance.

The power to investigate is one of the functions that distinguish the administrative law process from the traditional civil law process. The administrative law process is more like the criminal law process in that the investigative power gives governmental agencies a standing right to monitor and detect violations of rules.

In regard to administrative agencies, this power extends to the development of information necessary to create or alter existing rules. Modern administrative agencies have become specialized, and attempts have been made to employ the idea of "separation of powers" within particular departments or bureaus. Therefore, some agencies have been created mainly to perform the fact-finding or investigative function.

Administrative agencies are limited by constitutionally protected rights. Corporations are vested with a certain element of public interest in that they are licensed by government authority, so the extent of the administrative agencies' authority to investigate them is considerably greater than that which is granted to agencies in their investigation of individuals. Warrants are usually granted to agencies in their investigation of individuals, and they are required, especially in detailed administrative investigations.

The Adjudicative Function

When a regulatory agency's actions involve enforcement of the rule-making function, the agency does not have to make use of the ordinary courts used in civil and criminal cases. The quasi-judicial powers of the administrative agencies are extensive. The internal procedures that have been developed through statutory enactment and court interpretation to prevent abuse of authority involve the determination of legal rights, duties, and obligations as well as fact-finding procedures involving adjudicatory hearings that resemble a court's decision-making process.

Judicial Oversight

In cases involving the rule-making function and the imposition of regulatory fines, the affected individual or corporation must pursue all administrative remedies before filing a lawsuit in court to overturn an administrative ruling. After the agency has made its final judgment in such disputed cases, the affected party must file an appeal at the appellate court level and successfully argue that the agency exceeded the limitations of its legislative authority or that the legislative enabling act violates some constitutional provision. This appeal action to the regular courts that have appellate jurisdiction is referred to as *judicial review*. The term *judicial review* is used in the same sense here as in Chapter 2—the power of the courts to hold acts of all government agencies unconstitutional and, therefore, nonenforceable.

Administrative regulatory agencies, therefore, have internal functions that resemble the trial level courts in civil and criminal cases. Judicial review by appellate courts act as a check on potential abuse, but the agency performs the fact-finding functions. Even in cases in which the courts find administrative abuse, the issue is remanded back to the administrative agency with instructions for proper procedure.

Actions of government administrative agencies may involve the filing of both civil and criminal suits against alleged violators of the law. Such suits are subject to the same procedures previously described in this textbook. However, the administrative due process, which is the focus of this chapter, is distinctly different from ordinary civil and criminal process.

Before administrative sanctions can be imposed, an alleged violator is entitled to (1) **due notification** of the actions of the agency adversely affecting the legal interests of the individual or corporation and (2) a **fair hearing** before an impartial and competent tribunal that affords the affected party the opportunity to be heard and allows confrontation of witnesses. These basic rules are explained in detail in the Federal Administrative Procedure Act and various state administrative procedures acts. Such procedural rules are supplemented by the enabling acts that create the administrative agencies involved. The type of procedure required varies from agency to agency.

Due notification:
To be informed of the action taken against an individual, corporation, or agency.

Fair hearing:
Opportunity to be heard. Where authority is fairly exercised consistent with fundamental principles of justice; to present evidence, cross-examine, and have findings supported by evidence.

Quasi-judicial Procedure

The Administrative Procedure Act (APA) of 1946 (P.L. 79-404) is the federal law that governs the way in which administrative agencies of the federal government propose and establish regulations. It also sets up a process for the federal courts to directly review agency decisions. It is one of the most important aspects of administrative law. The text of the APA can be found under Title 5 of the *United States Code*, beginning at Section 500.

There is a similar Model State Administrative Procedure Act (Model State APA), which was drafted by the National Conference of Commissioners on Uniform State laws for oversight of state agencies. Not all states have adopted the model law wholesale as of 2007.

Congress and the New Deal administration of President Franklin D. Roosevelt, beginning in 1933, enacted several statutes that created new federal agencies as a part of the New Deal legislative plan, which was designed to deliver the nation from the social and economic hardships of the Great Depression. However, Congress became concerned about the expanding powers of the federal agencies and enacted the APA to regulate the regulators. The House of Representatives report discusses the ten-year period of "painstaking and detailed study and drafting" that went into the Administrative Procedures Act of 1941.

The final report defined a federal agency as a governmental unit with "the power to determine . . . private rights and obligations" by rule making or adjudication. The final report applied that definition to the largest units of the federal government and identified "19 executive departments and 18 independent agencies." If various subdivisions of the larger units were considered, the total number of federal agencies in 1946 increased to 51.

To provide constitutional safeguards, the APA creates a framework for regulating agencies and their unique role. The *Attorney General's Manual on the Administrative Procedure Act* states that the basic purposes of the APA are (1) to require agencies to keep the public informed of their organization, procedure, and rules; (2) to provide for public participation in the rule-making process; (3) to establish uniform standards for the conduct of formal rule making and adjudication; and (4) to define the scope of judicial review.

The APA defines an "agency" as "each authority of the Government of the United States, whether or not it is within or subject to review by another agency," with the exception of the various enumerated authorities, including the Congress, federal courts, and governments of territories or possessions of the United States. Courts have held that the U.S. president is not an agency under the APA (*Franklin v. Mass.*, 505 U.S. 788 (1992)).

Formal adjudication involves a trial-like hearing with witness testimony, a written record, and a final decision. Under informal adjudication, however, agency decisions are made without formal trial-like procedures, using inspections, conferences, and negotiations instead. Because formal adjudication produces a record of proceedings and a final decision, it may be subject to judicial review. As for rule making resulting in agency rules and regulations, the final report noted that many agencies provided due process through hearings and investigations, but there was a need for well-defined, uniform standards for agency adjudication and rule-making procedures.

Since 2005, the House Judiciary Committee has been undertaking the Administrative Law, Process and Procedure Project to determine what, if any, changes should be made in the APA. The study has revealed one interesting preliminary finding: approximately 50 percent of the court challenges to agency rule makings are successful. Further study is needed to confirm this finding.

The Administrative Law, Process and Procedure Project is a bipartisan undertaking of the Committee on the Judiciary of the House of Representatives of the U.S. Congress. One of the principle goals of the project is to further substantiate the need to reactivate the Administrative Conference of the United States (ACUS), a nonpartisan private-public "think tank" that proposed valuable recommendations that improved administration aspects of regulatory law and practice. ACUS (which was reactivated in 2004) served as an independent agency charged with studying "the efficiency, adequacy, and fairness of the administrative procedure used by administrative agencies in carrying out administrative programs." (5 U.S.C. Section 594 (1))

During its previous 28 years of existence, ACUS has helped to focus attention on the need for the federal government to be made more efficient, smaller, and more accountable. It was viewed as one of the leading federal proponents of encouraging practical ways to reduce administrative litigation. In this regard, it has actively promoted information technology initiatives, such as developing methods by which the public could actively participate electronically in agency rule-making proceedings to increase public access to government information and foster greater openness in government operations.

U.S. Supreme Court Justice Antonin Scalia, a former ACUS chair, described ACUS as "a worthwhile organization" that offered "a unique combination of talents from the academic world, from within the executive branch . . . and, thirdly, from the private bar, especially lawyers particularly familiar with administrative law." He observed, "I did not know another organization that so effectively combined the best talent from each of those areas." Both Justice Scalia and Supreme Court Justice Stephen Breyer cited the huge savings to the fellow public as a result of ACUS recommendations. (See *Reauthorization of the Administrative Conference of the United States before the Subcommittee on Commercial and Administrative Law of the House Committee on the Judiciary*, 108th Cong., 2004, pp. 15–38.)

Fundamental Due Process Illustrated

The APA requires that in order to set aside agency action, the court must conclude that the regulation is "arbitrary and capricious, and abusive of discretion, or otherwise not in accordance with the law." However, Congress may further limit the scope of judicial review of agency actions by including such language in the organic statute.

The Supreme Court has held that the fundamental constitutional guarantee of due process of law applies to both state and federal actions. The principles of due process require at least rudimentary procedural fairness. Even the actions of local school boards in suspending students for disciplinary infractions of school rules require some degree of procedural fairness. In *Goss v. Lopez*, 419 U.S. 565 (1975), the U.S. Supreme Court held that a public school must give notice and conduct a hearing before subjecting a student to a long-term suspension. The Court held that a suspension without a hearing violated the Due Process Clause of the Fourteenth Amendment to the U.S. Constitution. This decision applies to the states as well as the public schools in the District of Columbia.

The majority opinion in this case illustrates the minimal requirements of **administrative due process**; however, the extent of procedural rights that must be complied with by government agencies is by no means uniform. These rights, beyond the minimal requirements, depend on the specific provisions of the statutory enabling act and the agency's own procedural rules. Various boards or commissions may conduct the required fair hearings, but many agencies now require that administrative law judges conduct these hearings.

Administrative due process:
Notice, fair hearing, and conformity with established rules are minimal requirements of due process.

ADMINISTRATIVE LAW JUDGES

The **administrative law judge (ALJ)** is an official who conducts trial-like hearings to resolve disputes between a government agency and someone affected by a decision. These individuals were called "hearing examiners" before the 1978 amendments to the ADA, which renamed them *administrative law judges* and strengthened their independence. Federal ALJs are appointed under civil service rules and are protected against arbitrary dismissal and loss of salary. There are approximately 1,200 of these judges who serve in 30 federal departments and agencies.

The APA requires that federal ALJs be appointed based on scores achieved in a comprehensive testing procedure, including a four-hour written examination and an oral examination before a panel that includes an Office of Personnel Management representative, American Bar Association representative, and a sitting federal ALJ. Federal ALJs are the only merit-based judicial corps in the United States.

Administrative law judge (ALJ):
The official who presides at an administrative trial-type hearing to resolve a dispute between a government agency and someone affected by a decision.

In U.S. administrative law, ALJs are Article I judges, and are not Article III judges under the U.S. Constitution. Unlike Article III judges, Article I judges are not confirmed by the Senate. (See Table 18.2 for list of Article I, II, III, and IV courts.)

Table 18.2 **LIST OF ARTICLE I, II, III, and IV TRIBUNALS**

Article I Tribunals	Article II Tribunals	Article III Tribunals	Article IV Tribunals
Administrative law adjudicative entities, e.g.: Social Security Office of Disability Adjudication and Review Armed Services Board of Contract Appeals Board of Patent Appeals and Interferences Civilian Board of Contract Appeals The District of Columbia Judiciary D.C. Court of Appeals Superior Court of the District of Columbia Trademark Trial and Appeal Board U.S. Court of Appeals for Veterans Claims U.S. Court of Appeals for the Armed Services U.S. Court of Federal Claims U.S. Merit Systems Protection Board U.S. Postal Service Board of Contract Appeals U.S. Tax Court U.S. Armed Forces courts-martial	Guantanamo Military Commission High Court of American Samoa	Supreme Court of the United States U.S. courts of appeals U.S. district courts U.S. Court of International Trade	U.S. Territorial Court

The APA is designed to guarantee the decisional independence of ALJs. They have absolute immunity from liability for their judicial acts and are triers of fact "insulated from political influence." Federal ALJs are not responsible to or subject to the supervision or direction of employees or agents of the federal agency engaged in the performance of investigative or prosecution functions for the agency. **Ex parte** (on one side only) communications are prohibited. ALJs are exempt from performance ratings, evaluation, and bonuses. Agency officials may not interfere with their decision making. ALJs may be discharged only for good cause based upon a complaint filed by the agency with the Merit Systems Protections Board established and determined after an APA hearing on the record before a Merit System Protection Board ALJ. Only ALJs receive these statutory protections; "hearing officers" or "trial examiners," with delegated hearing functions, are not similarly protected by the APA.

Ex parte:
By or for one party; done for, in behalf of, or on the application of, one party only.

The U.S. Supreme Court has recognized that the role of a federal ALJ is "functionally comparable" to that of an Article II judge. An ALJ's powers are often, if not generally, comparable to those of a trial judge: The ALJ must issue subpoenas, rule on proffers of evidence, regulate the course of the hearing, and make or recommend decisions. The process of agency adjudication is currently structured so as to assure that the hearing examiners exercise independent judgment on the evidence before them, free from pressures by the parties or other officials within the agency (*Butz v. Economou*, 438 U.S. 478 (1978)).

Table 18.3 provides a list of the federal agencies with administrative law judges.

The procedure for reviewing an ALJ's decision varies depending upon the agency. Agencies generally have an internal appellate body, with some agencies having a cabinet secretary deciding the final internal appeals. Moreover, after the internal agency appeals have been exhausted, a party may have the right to file an appeal in the state or federal courts. Relevant statutes usually require a party to exhaust all administrative appeals before they are allowed to sue an agency in court.

Most U.S. states have a statute modeled after the APA or somewhat similar to it. In some states, such as New Jersey, the state law is also known as the Administrative Procedure Act.

Unlike the federal ALJs, whose powers are guaranteed by the APA federal statute, state ALJs have widely varying powers and prestige. In some state law contexts, ALJs have almost no power; their decisions are accorded practically no deference and become, in effect, recommendations. In some cities, notably New York City, ALJs are

Table 18.3 **LIST OF FEDERAL AGENCIES WITH ADMINISTRATIVE LAW JUDGES**

Coast Guard	Federal Labor Relations Authority
Commodity Futures Trading Commission	Federal Maritime Commission
Department of Agriculture	Federal Mine Safety and Health Review
Department of Health and Human Services/	Commission
Department Appeals Board	Federal Trade Commission
Department of Health and Human Services/	Food and Drug Administration
Office of Medicare Hearings and Appeals	International Trade Commission
Department of Housing and Urban	Merit Systems Protection Board
Development	National Labor Relations Board
Department of the Interior	National Transportation Safety Board
Department of Justice/Executive Office for	Nuclear Regulatory Commission
Immigration Review	Occupational Safety and Health Review
Department of Labor	Commission
Department of Transportation	Office of Financial Institution Adjudication
Department of Veterans Affairs	Patent and Trademark Office
Drug Enforcement Administration	Postal Service
Federal Aviation Administration	Securities and Exchange Commission
Federal Communications Commission	Small Business Administration
Federal Energy Regulation Commission	Social Security Administration

really employees of the agency, making their decisional independence potentially questionable. In some agencies, ALJs dress like lawyers in business suits, share offices, and hold hearings in ordinary conference rooms. In other agencies (particularly the Division of Workers' Compensation of the California Department of Industrial Relations), ALJs wear robes like Article III judges, are referred to as "Honorable" and "Your Honor," work in private chambers, hold hearings in special "hearing rooms" that look like small courtrooms, and have court clerks who swear in witnesses.

Other federal agencies may request the U.S. Office of Personnel Management to lend them ALJs from other federal agencies for a period of up to six months.

Some states, such as California, follow the federal model of having a separate corps of ALJs attached to each agency that uses them. Others, like New Jersey, have consolidated all ALJs together into a single agency that holds hearings on behalf of all other state agencies. This type of state adjudicatory agency is called a "central panel agency." Many states have a central panel agency, but the agency does not handle all the hearings for every agency. Table 18.4 provides a list of state-level departments and agencies with ALJs.

Table 18.4 **LIST OF STATE DEPARTMENTS AND AGENCIES WITH ADMINISTRATIVE LAW JUDGES**

Alabama Department of Revenue	New Jersey Office of Administrative Law (does hearings for all state agencies)
California Department of Consumer Affairs	New York City Office of Administrative Trials and Hearings (does hearings for all city agencies)
California Department of Health Services	
California Department of Industrial Relations	
California Department of Social Services	New York City Taxi and Limousine Commission Taxicabs of the United States
California Employment Development Department	
California Public Utilities Commission	New York State Department of Environmental Conservation
Florida Division of Administrative Hearings	
Illinois Human Rights Commission	New York State Department of Labor
Industrial Commission of Arizona	Pennsylvania Department of Insurance
Iowa Department of Inspections and Appeals- Division of Administrative Hearings (does hearings for some but not all state agencies)	Pennsylvania Department of Labor and Industry, Bureau of Workers' Compensation
	Pennsylvania Liquor Control Board
Iowa Workforce Development Department	Pennsylvania Public Utility Commission
Louisiana Division of Administrative Law	South Carolina Administrative Law Court (does hearings for all state agencies)
Maryland Office of Administrative Hearings	
Maryland Public Service Commission (hearings for public utility cases)	Texas Department of Banking
	Texas Finance Commission
Massachusetts Executive Office of Transportation	Texas Health and Human Services Commission
Massachusetts Department of Environmental Protection	Texas State Office of Administrative Hearings (does hearings for only some state agencies)
Michigan State Office of Administrative Hearings and Rules	Traffic Violations Bureau of New York State DMV
Minnesota Office of Administrative Hearings (does hearings for some but not all state agencies)	Washington Office of Administrative Hearings (does hearings for all state agencies plus some local ones)

THE OSHA PROCEDURE ILLUSTRATED

A typical example of the quasi-judicial fact-finding process involving administrative fines imposed by the Occupational Safety and Health Administration (OSHA) is the use of ALJs who conduct hearings in disputed cases.

An employee who suspects that there are safety violations in the workplace can contact the local OSHA office and file a complaint. The OSHA agency is authorized to make an unannounced inspection of the premises, and it has broad powers to investigate alleged violations of agency standards. If the inspection reveals violations, the government inspector may issue either civil or criminal citations.

For civil citations, OSHA may impose fines of up to $70,000 for each willful and repeated violation and $7,000 for less serious violations.

These limits are subject to change by legislative enactment to provide reasonable inducement to enforce the agency's policies.

In 2010, Congress enacted the new Severe Violator Enforcement Program intended to focus OSHA enforcement resources on recalcitrant employers who endanger workers by demonstrating indifference to their responsibilities under the law. This supplemental enforcement tool includes increased OSHA inspections in these worksites, including mandatory OSHA follow-up inspections, and inspections of other worksites of the same employer where similar hazards and deficiencies may be present.

The average penalty for a serious violation will increase from about $1,000 to an average of $3,000–$4,000. Monetary penalties for violations of the OSHA Act will raise these penalties from the previous maximums to $12,000 for serious violations and $250,000 for willful violations. Future penalty increases will also be tied to inflation.

An employer against whom a fine is levied may contest the citation by filing an appeal with the OSHA agency within a limited period of time. The employer is then given a hearing at a specified date before an ALJ. The judge allows both the inspector and the employer to present evidence regarding the factual nature of the findings alleged by the agency. If the agency citation is found to be in error, the judge may dismiss or alter the citation in much the same way that local courts of limited jurisdiction handle traffic citations.

The judge's decision is not the final decision of the agency, and even if the judge finds against the employer, the adversely affected party has another opportunity to appeal to the three-member Occupational Health Review Commission. This commission is appointed by the president and has final administrative authority to overrule the judge's decision. If no member of the commission is willing to place the matter on the commission's agenda, the ALJ's decision becomes the final action of the agency after 30 days.

Administrative agencies are authorized to issue criminal citations in certain cases, although they do so infrequently. When a criminal citation is warranted, the case is handed over to the Justice Department for criminal prosecution.

JUDICIAL REVIEW

In the area of enforcement of administrative rules and regulations, where government agencies have the authority to impose civil penalties and fines or withhold licenses, the courts have regarded these agencies as collaborators in the task of safeguarding the public interest. Therefore, unless exceptional circumstances exist, the courts are reluctant to interfere with the operation of a program administered by a government agency. This policy of judicial self-restraint usually results in the court's deference to the government agency in the performance of its constitutionally recognized functions.

Parties against whom administrative actions are taken must first seek administrative remedies for their complaints. They must **exhaust administrative remedies** before the courts consider the issue "ripe" for judicial intervention. There are exceptions to this rule, but the complaining party must meet the heavy burden of providing proof that the court's failure to interrupt the administrative process would be unfair. To determine this standard of fairness, the court considers (1) the possibility of injury if the case is not heard, (2) the degree of doubt of the agency's jurisdiction, and (3) the requirement of the agency's specialized knowledge (Grilliot and Schubert 1992, 490).

> **Exhaust administrative remedies:**
> Courts must be satisfied that an individual seeking court action has first pursued all available administrative remedies.

Reviewing courts often acknowledge that the fact situations and agency standards are complex and technical, and the courts rely on the agency's expertise. The courts uphold the administrative findings if they are satisfied that the agency examined the issues, reached its decision within appropriate standards, and followed the required procedures. Since the court action is essentially a review function, the complaint before the court must be filed at the appeals court level. As in other appellate jurisdiction cases, the court hears only questions of law in dispute.

Questions of fact are left to the agency's procedures and are given the same deference given to jury decisions when all applicable due process procedures are followed. Even when the court rules against the agency on legal issues, the matter is usually remanded to the administrative agency for further fact finding.

The regulatory authority of the federal government appears to be extensive, but the states share this authority. The state powers may be even more pervasive in their impact on individuals. In areas in which the federal government has not precluded state regulation, the state courts are the final authority.

OTHER SPECIALIZED COURTS

State and federal governments have created many specialized courts with limited jurisdiction to handle various types of cases. Among those at the federal level are the U.S. Tax Court and the U.S. Court of Claims. These **specialized federal courts** were created by Congress under the authority granted in Article I of the Constitution for the express purpose of helping to administer specific congressional statutes. They often possess administrative and quasi-legislative as well as judicial duties.

> **Specialized federal courts:**
> Created by Congress under authority granted in Article I as opposed to Article III of the Constitution. They often possess administrative and quasi-legislative as well as judicial duties.

State legislatures have created many similar quasi-judicial bodies, often called **commissions**. State public service commissions and worker's compensation commissions (or boards) are some of the more prominent administrative bodies that perform many court functions. These bodies are administrative in character and are not properly said to have the inherent powers of a court, but nonetheless they perform significant judicial functions. Increasingly, states have attempted to relieve the overloaded civil courts and reduce costs by the institution of such quasi-judicial administrative agencies.

Commissions:
Term often used in regard to state quasi-judicial bodies; also called boards

The Anglo-American concept of sovereign immunity is very confusing and goes back to the ancient Anglo-Saxon principle "that the king can do no wrong" (Abraham 1986, 273). This principle forms a fundamental rule of law known as sovereign immunity. The basic principle of **sovereign immunity** in Anglo-American law is that the state cannot be sued without its express consent.

Sovereign immunity:
Doctrine precludes litigant from asserting an otherwise meritorious cause of action against a sovereign or a party with sovereign attributes unless the sovereign consents to the suit.

Many law enforcement officers are weighted down with heavy burdens of civil cases filed against them personally for alleged civil wrongs. Corrections officials, school administrators, teachers, and other civil servants are perplexed; why, in performing a government duty, should a civil servant be personally responsible for civil liability. Modern governments in the United Kingdom and the United States require many of these public officials to be bonded (insured) against such liability suits, and state agencies assist in their defense. But the time, inconvenience, and expense of such a system is a major problem that demoralizes many civil servants.

The United States has enacted modern statutes to allow civil suits (claims) against the government itself. These laws make the government responsible for the actions of their servants under certain circumstances. Most of these statutes have loopholes and exceptions and generally exclude law enforcement agencies such as the police, military services, and foreign affairs.

U.S. Claims Courts

In 1982 Congress consolidated all of the historical functions of the former U.S. Claims Court and its predecessors into what is now known as the **U.S. Court of Federal Claims**. This court handles all claims against the U.S. government that have been authorized by Congress. These are exceptions to the rule of sovereign immunity. The justices are all title III judges under the U.S. Constitution. This court is located in Washington, D.C., and may hear a broad range of contractual and tort claims. The Court of Federal Claims hears all monetary claims based upon a law, and prepares bills for payments to claimants whose petitions were approved by the court.

U.S. Court of Federal Claims:
Unique court that has jurisdiction over all claims against the United States where Congress has given authority to sue for claims, including contracts with the United States.

A unique aspect of the court's jurisdiction throughout its history has been the authority to act on congressional references of legislative proposals for compensation of individual claims. As eventually codified in 28 U.S.C. §1492, either house of Congress may refer a bill to the chief judge of the court for an investigation and a report to Congress. A judge of the court is assigned to act as the "hearing officer" and presides over the judicial proceedings. Then a three-judge review panel submits a report to Congress for its consideration and disposition of such claims for compensation. Appellate jurisdiction over the court's action is vested in the U.S. Court of Appeals for the Federal Circuit.

The various states have similar **courts of claims**, which should not be confused with **small claims courts**. Small claims courts handle minor disputes between individuals, whereas courts of claims are courts that allow the state to be sued in certain circumstances. All states have enacted some statutory authority to bring suit against the state in certain circumstances. Because of the concept of sovereign immunity, these circumstances are limited by statutory authority. For example, the State of New York has jurisdiction over actions allowed against the State of New York, as well as certain authorities who are sued under their own names.

The court does not have jurisdiction over any individuals, including state employees, although claims may be maintained against the state based on allegedly wrongful conduct of employees for which the state is responsible under the legal principle of *respondeat superior*. Generally, state agencies do not have a legal existence separate from that of the state, and thus where a claim is based on alleged improper conduct of, for example, the New York Department of Transportation or the New York Department of Correctional Services, the named defendant should be "The State of New York."

In New York, certain authorities who are considered to have a distinct legal existence are sued in the court of claims under their own names. These include the New York State Thruway Authority, the City University of New York, and the Power Authority of the State of New York (for appropriate claims only).

It is important to note that the statutory authority for handling these claims must be checked to determine which court has authority to handle the claims allowed. In New York, the Court of Claims Act governs the procedure in the court of claims. The court of claims has no jurisdiction over lawsuits involving county, town, city, or village governments, agencies, or employees. These governmental entities are all distinct from the state, and litigation against them is governed by the provisions of the General Municipal Law.

A growing number of states now have some form of claims courts, but these functions may not have a court specifically organized for this purpose.

Courts of claims: Courts that are authorized to handle claims against state and federal authorities where statutory authority allows such actions.

Small claims courts: A special court (sometimes called "conciliation court") that provides expeditious, informal, and inexpensive adjudication.

Respondeat superior: Legal doctrine that holds the employer (master) is responsible for the actions of employees performed within the course of their employment.

U.S. Bankruptcy Court

The federal bankruptcy court is perhaps the most widely used unit of courts attached to the federal district courts. These courts are legislative courts created under Article I of the U.S. Constitution and have subject matter jurisdiction over almost all bankruptcy cases in the United States. The federal district courts have original and exclusive jurisdiction over all cases arising under the bankruptcy code (see 28 U.S.C. §1334(a)); bankruptcy cases cannot be filed in state courts. Each of the 94 federal judicial districts handles bankruptcy matters. The current system of bankruptcy courts was created by the U.S. Congress in 1979.

The bankruptcy judges in each judicial district in regular active service constitute a "unit" of the applicable U.S. district court. The bankruptcy judge is appointed for a term of 14 years by the U.S. court of appeals for the circuit in which the applicable district is located (see U.S.C. §152).

Technically, the U.S. district courts have subject matter jurisdiction over bankruptcy matters. However, each such district court may, by order, "refer" bankruptcy matters to the bankruptcy court. As a practical matter, most district courts have a standing "reference" order to that effect so that all bankruptcy cases in that district are handled, at least initially, by the bankruptcy court. In unusual circumstances, a district court may in a particular case withdraw the reference (i.e., take the case or a particular proceeding within the case away from the bankruptcy court and decide the matter itself) under 28 U.S.C. §157(d).

The overwhelming majority of all proceedings in bankruptcy are held before a U.S. bankruptcy judge, whose decision in all matters is final, subject to appeals to the district court. In some judicial circuits, appeals may be taken to a Bankruptcy Appellate Panel. Federal Rules of Bankruptcy Procedure (FRBP) govern procedure in the U.S. bankruptcy courts. Decisions of the bankruptcy courts are not collected and published in an official reporter produced by the government. Instead, the de facto official source for opinions of the bankruptcy courts is *West's Bankruptcy Reporter*, published privately by Thomson/West Publishers.

Bankruptcy courts appoint a trustee to represent the interests of the creditors and administer the cases. The U.S. trustee appoints Chapter 7 trustees for a renewable period of one year. Chapter 13 trustees are "standing trustees" who administer cases in a specific geographic region.

U.S. Tax Court

The U.S. Tax Court has jurisdiction over those matters where the federal government has given its consent in advance to be sued. The tax court was transformed into a legislative court in 1969. This court still has some characteristics of a quasi-administrative agency, but it is independent of the

Internal Revenue Service (IRS) in many respects and, therefore, is the clos-est relative of the independent continental European administrative courts. Its jurisdiction includes disputes over tax assessments made by the IRS. The commissioner of the IRS is always the defendant party and a "repeat player" with certain advantages. The tax court may conduct trials anywhere in the United States, and its caseload is quite large.

Because the tax court is a court of record, a record is made of all its proceedings. It is an independent judicial forum. It is not controlled by or connected with the IRS. Congress created the tax court as an independent, judicial authority for taxpayers disputing certain IRS determinations. The tax court's authority to resolve these disputes is called its jurisdiction. Generally, a taxpayer may file a petition in the tax court in response to certain IRS determinations. A taxpayer who begins such a proceeding is known as the "petitioner," and the Commissioner of Internal Revenue is the "respondent."

In 1998, Congress conducted extensive hearings exposing significant abuse of authority by the IRS. Much to the surprise of both Congress and the public, it was revealed that the tax court's procedures placed the burden of proof on the taxpayer rather than the IRS in these disputes. Significant changes were put into effect July 31, 1998, to shift the burden of proof away from individual taxpayers in cases in which disputes move from audits through internal IRS appeals and into civil tax court. The new law leaves intact the requirement that taxpayers prove their case during an audit, but once the relevant documents are turned over, the new law places the burden of proof on the IRS. The new law also makes it easier for citizens to recover legal fees and provides higher reimbursement rates in cases where judges rule against the IRS. Additionally the new rule requires that the taxpayer need only show the IRS to be "negligent," rather than "recklessly or intentionally" disregarding the law, to prevail.

In *Butz v. Economou*, 438 U.S. 478 (1978), the Court permitted suits against federal officials who were or should have been aware that they were violating constitutional rights except when it has been demonstrated that absolute immunity is essential for conducting the public business. In subsequent court decisions, local governments have been made subject to damage suits for civil rights violations (*Monell v. City of New York Department of Social Services*, 436 U.S. 658 (1978)); municipalities have not been allowed to assert the good faith of their officials as a defense (*Owen v. City of Independence, Missouri*, 445 U.S. 622 (1980)); and private parties have been held entitled to sue their own states whenever state policy allegedly violates any federal law (*Maine v. Thiboutot*, 448 U.S. 1 (1980)).

Despite these significant decisions, the principle of sovereign immunity still leaves many areas of governmental responsibility immune from ordinary liability that would have allowed recovery of damages if the acts had been done by private parties.

THE OMBUDSMAN

An **ombudsman** is a person who acts as a trusted intermediary between an organization or agency and some internal or external constituency while representing the broad scope of constituent interests. This concept originated in Scandinavian countries and means something like "the peoples representative." This office has become widespread in modern industrial societies to serve as a means of assisting the general public in making complaints against governmental regulatory and other agencies or governmental offices.

Usually appointed by the organization, but sometimes elected by the constituency, the ombudsman may, for example, investigate constituent complaints relating to the organization and attempt to resolve them, usually through recommendations (binding or not) or mediation. Ombudsmen sometimes identify organizational roadblocks running counter to constituent interests.

While these agencies are very widespread in European countries today, the United States has instituted only a modest variety of these agencies. The U.S. Department of Homeland Security (DHS) Citizenship and Immigration Services (CIS) ombudsmen provide recommendations for resolving individual and employer problems with the U.S. Citizenship and Immigration Services (USCIS). As mandated by the Homeland Security Act of 2002 §452, the Office of the CIS Ombudsman (CISOMB) is not a part of USCIS; it is an independent Department of Homeland Security office that reports directly to the DHS Deputy Secretary. The DHS Citizen and Immigration Service ombudsman does the following:

1. Assists individuals and employers in resolving problems with the USCIS;
2. Identifies areas in which individuals and employers have problems in dealing with USCIS; and
3. Proposes changes to mitigate problems.

This agency submits an annual report to the House and Senate Committees on the Judiciary without any prior comment or amendment from any administrative agency official, including the secretary, deputy secretary, or director of U.S. Citizenship and Immigration Services.

The ombudsman also submits an annual report identifying systematic issues that cause delay in granting immigration benefits as well as pervasive and serious problems faced by individuals and employers in their interactions with the immigration services.

The U.S. Navy implemented an ombudsman program in 1970 under the direction of Admiral Elmo Zumwalt. Through the Navy Ombudsman Program, communications between the spouses of active duty personnel

Ombudsman:
An official to whom people may come with grievances connected with the government. The ombudsman stands between, and represents, the citizen before the government.

and the command is kept open, thereby improving the quality of life for everyone involved. The Navy command ombudsman is a volunteer position, with no special favors bestowed upon him or her.

The U.S. Equal Employment Opportunity Commission (EEOC) has authority to investigate charges of discrimination against employers who are covered by the law. Its role in an investigation is to fairly and accurately assess the allegations in the charge and then make a finding. If the EEOC finds that discrimination has occurred, it will try to settle the charge. If the EEOC is not successful, it has the authority to file a lawsuit to protect the rights of individuals and the interests of the public. The EEOC does not file lawsuits in all cases where they find discrimination but rather seeks mediation and other functions, similar to the ombudsman concept.

There are also several states and local governments in the United State that have ombudsman programs. King County Ombudsman's Office was created by the voters of King County, Washington, in the Home Rule Charter of 1968, and it operates as an independent office within the legislative branch of King County government. The office investigates complaints regarding the administrative conduct of King County agencies and alleged violations of county codes dealing with employee ethics, whistleblower protection, and lobbyist disclosure. The King County Ombudsman is appointed to a renewable five-year term by the King County Council and is removable midterm only for cause.

The Los Angeles County Department of Ombudsman was created by the approval of an ordinance in 1993 by the Los Angeles County Board of Supervisors. This department was first of its kind in the state of California and the first nationally involved in law enforcement oversight.

The New York City Public Advocate has an ombudsman team that investigates and responds to telephone and written complaints and queries regarding city agency services, providing information and referrals.

Every state in the United States has a long-term health care ombudsman, and many states have supplemental programs developed to protect long-term residents' rights.

These agencies are very modest compared with the Western European countries, which have very extensive use of the ombudsman concept in most areas of governmental regulation. Such ombudsmen are needed in the complex areas of regulation, where it is difficult for the public to know how to defend their rights.

However, in most cases involving a governmental agency, even a public school principle, a hearing may be requested, and if denied, there may be opportunity through various boards and commissions for assurance of fundamental due process procedures to be obtained.

CHAPTER SUMMARY

1. Administrative law is the most dynamic and rapidly expanding area of law today. It includes both state and federal regulatory authority, the rules of which have the force of law. Administrative agencies exercise quasi-legislative, quasi-judicial, and executive functions.

2. Federal regulatory agencies have become extensive and important in many areas of business, economic, environmental, and social policy since the 1930s, but state regulatory activity also has expanded in modern times. State and federal authorities now regulate almost all areas of human activity.

3. Regulatory agencies have broad powers to make detailed rules and regulations governing the conduct of individuals and business activity. These agencies are given rule-making and enforcement powers by legislative enabling acts that are upheld by the courts as long as they do not violate constitutional limitations.

4. The powers of administrative agencies are defined as quasi-legislative and quasi-judicial functions. The decisions of these agencies have the force of law. The detailed administrative rules and regulations are found in the *Code of Federal Regulations* and similar publications by state agencies.

5. The Federal Administrative Procedures Act of 1946 and similar state statutory authority provide detailed procedures and rights of persons and corporations affected by administrative regulations. Agencies have broad investigative powers that enable them to perform their government functions.

6. Regulatory agencies may take enforcement actions without using the ordinary courts regularly used for civil and criminal cases. They may impose civil fines and penalties, which can be appealed through the agency's own internal procedures for a fair hearing and review of lower-agency decisions.

7. A party affected by administrative actions has a right to due notification, to a fair hearing, and to an opportunity to challenge the decision in appeals court after all administrative remedies have been exhausted. These are the minimal requirements of administrative due process.

8. Administrative law judges, who conduct fair hearings, have been strengthened in their independence from agency influence at the federal level, but generally their decisions can be overruled by the highest administrative authority in the agency.

9. Judicial review of agency decisions usually must be filed at the appeals court level. The basic criterion for overruling an administrative decision is an agency's failure to provide the required constitutional administrative due process. Agency rules may not exceed legislative

authority, and the underlying legislative authority may be challenged. Fact-finding procedures usually are left to the administrative agency.

10. Specialized courts have been established at the federal level, but internal agency fact-finding procedures are used extensively to deal with administrative disputes.

11. The Anglo-American concept of sovereign immunity makes it difficult to hold government agencies responsible for their actions. Governments in the United States have passed legislation making it possible to sue the government for claims in ordinary civil liability, but the process is limited to what the legislative authority allows and is administrated by separate claims courts.

12. The United States has instituted a number of ombudsman programs at both the national and local levels of government that assist in the process of making complaints and securing individual rights. These programs are much more widely available to citizens in Western European nations.

REVIEW EXERCISES

Match the following terms with their most appropriate meaning.

TERMS

1. Regulatory agency
2. Enabling act
3. Rule making
4. Quasi-legislative powers
5. Due notification
6. Fair hearing
7. Administrative Procedures Act
8. Administrative due process
9. Administrative law judge
10. Ex parte
11. Exhaust administrative remedies
12. Specialized federal courts
13. Commissions
14. Sovereign immunity
15. U.S. Court of Federal Claims

MEANING

____ courts must be satisfied that all available administrative remedies have been pursued

____ procedures involving fact-finding hearings that resemble a court's decision-making process

____ a special court that provides expeditious, informal, and inexpensive adjudication in minor cases

____ agency that has been delegated rule-making authority by the legislature

____ legal doctrine that requires employers to be responsible for the actions of employees in certain circumstances

____ separate and independent administrative courts providing protection against government abuse

____ presides over administrative hearings with power to make agency determinations of factual matters

____ by or for one party

____ delegated rule-making authority

____ process of developing detailed rules and regulations having the force of law

____ notice, fair hearing, and conformity with established rules are minimal requirements

____ unique court that has jurisdiction over all claims against the United States authorized by Congress

16. Courts of claims
17. Small claims courts
18. *Respondeat superior*
19. Ombudsman

_____ office to which people may come with grievances connected with the government; stands between, and represents, the citizen before the government

_____ legal doctrine that does not allow the government to be sued without its consent

_____ opportunity to be heard and where authority is fairly exercised

_____ statutory authority defining functions and powers of governmental agencies

_____ term used for state quasi-judicial bodies; sometimes called boards

_____ to be informed of the government action taken against an individual, corporation, or agency

_____ statutory authority defining functions and powers of governmental agencies

DISCUSSION QUESTIONS

1. What is administrative law, and how important is this area of law in modern society?
2. How extensive is federal and state regulatory activity in the United States today?
3. What are the basic investigative, rule-making, and enforcement powers given to regulatory agencies by the enabling acts of legislative authority?
4. Where can the detailed rules and regulations of administrative agencies, which have the force of law, be found?
5. What is meant by fundamental due process of law, and how have modern state and federal administrative procedures acts attempted to codify and extend procedural rules?
6. What basic procedural rights are involved in the minimal requirements of administrative due process?
7. What is involved in the process of administrative hearings and judicial review by the courts?
8. How has sovereign immunity been changed to allow some claims against government?
9. Would the extension of the Scandinavian ombudsman system in the United States strengthen the citizen's ability to prevent administrative abuse of authority?

ASSIGNMENTS

ASSIGNMENT: Use the list of federal regulatory agencies in Table 18.1 to find an agency that you are particularly interested in and type into the Internet search box the agency's name. Then go to that agency's home page and read their description of the agency. Read further to find out what is currently underway in that agency to improve or develop new rules in the areas of their legislative responsibility.

Then go to the *Code of Federal Regulations* and look up a regulation of interest. This code is organized like the *U.S. Code* or the *Tennessee Code*. You will need a specific topic for which to search.

SOURCES AND SUGGESTED READING

Abraham, Henry J. 1986. *The Judicial Process.*
5th ed. New York: Oxford University Press.

Grilliot, Harold J., and Frank A. Schubert. 1992.
Introduction to Law and the Legal System. 5th ed.
Boston: Houghton Mifflin.

Lowi, Theodore J., and Benjamin Ginsberg. 1992.
American Government: Freedom and Power.
2d ed. New York: W.W. Norton.

Neubauer, David W. 1991. *Judicial Process: Law,
Courts and Politics in the United States.* Pacific
Grove, Calif.: Brooks/Cole Publishing.

*Reauthorization of the Administrative Conference
of the United States Before the Subcommittee on
Commercial and Administrative Law of the House
Committee on the Judiciary,* 108th Cong. (2004),
pp. 15–38. www.ombwatch.org/node/3739.

Wilson, James Q. 1989. *Bureaucracy: What
Government Agencies Do and Why They Do It.*
New York: Basic Books.

COURT CASES

Arndt v. Department of Licensing, 147 Mich. App.
97, 383 N.W.2d 136 (1986)

Butz v. Economou, 438 U.S. 478, 98 S.Ct. 2894,
57 L.Ed.2d 895 (1978)

Dow Chemical Co. v. United States, 476 U.S. 227
(1986)

Franklin v. Mass., 505 U.S. 788 (1992)

Goss v. Lopez, 419 U.S. 565, 106 S.Ct. 1819, 90
L.Ed.2d 226 (1975)

Maine v. Thiboutot, 448 U.S. 1, 100 S.Ct. 2502, 65
L.Ed.2d 555 (1980)

*Monell v. City of New York Department of Social
Services,* 436 U.S. 658, 98 S.Ct. 2018, 56 L.Ed.2d
611 (1978)

Owen v. City of Independence, Missouri, 445 U.S.
622, 100 S.Ct. 1398, 63 L.Ed.2d 673 (1980)

The Constitution of the United States of America

We the People of the United States, in Order to form a more perfect Union, establish Justice, insure domestic Tranquility, provide for the common defence, promote the general Welfare, and secure the Blessings of Liberty to ourselves and our Posterity, do ordain and establish this CONSTITUTION for the United States of America.

ARTICLE I

Section 1.

All legislative Powers herein granted shall be vested in a Congress of the United States, which shall consist of a Senate and House of Representatives.

Section 2.

[1] The House of Representatives shall be composed of Members chosen every second Year by the People of the several States, and the Electors in each State shall have the Qualifications requisite for Electors of the most numerous Branch of the State Legislature.

[2] No person shall be a Representative who shall not have attained to the Age of twenty-five Years, and been seven Years a Citizen of the United States, and who shall not, when elected, be an Inhabitant of that State in which he shall be chosen.

[3] Representatives and direct Taxes shall be apportioned among the several States which may be included within this Union, according to their respective Numbers, which shall be determined by adding to the whole Number of free Persons, including those bound to Service for a Term of Years, and excluding Indians not taxed, three fifths of all other Persons. The actual Enumeration shall be made within three Years after the first Meeting of the Congress of the United States, and within every subsequent Term of ten Years, in such Manner as they shall by Law direct. The Number of Representatives shall not exceed one for every thirty Thousand, but each State shall have at Least one Representative; and until such enumeration shall be made, the State of New Hampshire shall be entitled to chuse three, Massachusetts eight, Rhode-Island and Providence Plantations one, Connecticut five, New York six, New Jersey four, Pennsylvania eight, Delaware one, Maryland six, Virginia ten, North Carolina five, South Carolina five, and Georgia three.

[4] When vacancies happen in the Representation from any State, the Executive Authority thereof shall issue Writs of Election to fill such Vacancies.

[5] The House of Representatives shall chuse their Speaker and other Officers; and shall have the sole Power of Impeachment.

Section 3.

[1] The Senate of the United States shall be composed of two Senators from each State, chosen by the Legislature thereof, for six Years; and each Senator shall have one Vote.

[2] Immediately after they shall be assembled in Consequence of the first Election, they shall be divided as equally as may be into three Classes. The Seats of the Senators of the first Class shall be vacated at the Expiration of the Second Year, of the second Class at the Expiration of the fourth Year, and of the third Class at the Expiration of the sixth Year, so that one-third may be chosen every second Year; and if Vacancies happen by Resignation, or otherwise, during the Recess of the Legislature of any State, the Executive thereof may make temporary Appointments until the next Meeting of the Legislature, which shall then fill such Vacancies.

[3] No person shall be a Senator who shall not have attained to the Age of thirty Years, and been nine Years a Citizen of the United States, and who shall not, when elected, be an Inhabitant of that State for which he shall be chosen.

[4] The Vice President of the United States shall be President of the Senate, but shall have no Vote, unless they be equally divided.

[5] The Senate shall chuse their Officers, and also a President pro tempore, in the absence of the Vice President, or when he shall exercise the Office of President of the United States.

[6] The Senate shall have the sole Power to try all Impeachments. When sitting for that Purpose, they shall be on Oath or Affirmation. When the President of the United States is tried, the Chief Justice shall preside: And no Person shall be convicted without the Concurrence of two-thirds of the Members present.

[7] Judgment in Cases of Impeachment shall not extend further than to removal from Office, and disqualification to hold and enjoy any Office of honor, Trust, or Profit under the United States: but the Party convicted shall nevertheless be liable and subject to Indictment, Trial, Judgment, and Punishment, according to Law.

Section 4.

[1] The Times, Places and Manner of holding Elections for Senators and Representatives, shall be prescribed in each State by the Legislature thereof; but the Congress may at any time by Law make or alter such Regulations, except as to the Places of chusing Senators.

[2] The Congress shall assemble at least once in every Year, and such Meeting shall be on the first Monday in December, unless they shall by Law appoint a different Day.

Section 5.

[1] Each House shall be the Judge of the Elections, Returns, and Qualifications of its own Members, and a Majority of each shall constitute a Quorum to do Business; but a smaller Number may adjourn from day to day, and may be authorized to compel the Attendance of absent Members, in such Manner, and under such Penalties as each House may provide.

[2] Each House may determine the Rules of its Proceedings, punish its Members for disorderly Behavior, and with the Concurrence of two thirds, expel a Member.

[3] Each House shall keep a Journal of its Proceedings, and from time to time publish the same, excepting such Parts as may in their Judgment require Secrecy; and the Yeas and Nays of the Members of either House on any question shall, at the Desire of one fifth of those Present, be entered on the Journal.

[4] Neither House, during the Session of Congress, shall, without the Consent of the other, adjourn for more than three days, nor to any other Place than that in which the Two Houses shall be sitting.

Section 6.

[1] The Senators and Representatives shall receive a Compensation for their Services, to be ascertained by Law, and paid out of the Treasury of the United States. They shall in all Cases, except Treason, Felony and Breach of the Peace, be privileged from Arrest during their Attendance at the Session of their respective Houses, and in going to and returning from the same; and for any Speech or Debate in either House, they shall not be questioned in any other Place.

[2] No Senator or Representative shall, during the Time for which he was elected, be appointed to any civil Office under the Authority of the United States, which shall have been created, or the Emoluments whereof shall have been increased during such time; and no Person holding any Office under the United States, shall be a Member of either House during his Continuance in Office.

Section 7.

[1] All Bills for raising Revenue shall originate in the House of Representatives; but the Senate may propose or concur with Amendments as on other Bills.

[2] Every Bill shall have passed the House of Representatives and the Senate, shall, before it become a Law, be presented to the President of the United States; if he approve he shall sign it, but if not he shall return it, with his Objections to that House in which it shall have originated, who shall enter the Objections at large on their Journal, and proceed to reconsider it.

If after such Reconsideration two thirds of that House shall agree to pass the Bill, it shall be sent, together with the Objections, to the other House, by which it shall likewise be reconsidered, and if approved by two thirds of that House, it shall become a Law. But in all such Cases, the Votes of both Houses shall be determined by Yeas and Nays, and the Names of the Persons voting for and against the Bill shall be entered on the Journal of each House respectively. If any Bill shall not be returned by the President within ten Days (Sundays excepted) after it shall have been presented to him, the Same shall be a Law, in like Manner as if he had signed it, unless the Congress by their Adjournment prevent its Return, in which Case it shall not be a Law.

[3] Every Order, Resolution, or Vote to which the Concurrence of the Senate and House of Representatives may be necessary (except on a question of Adjournment) shall be presented to the President of the United States; and before the Same shall take Effect, shall be approved by him, or being disapproved by him shall be repassed by two thirds of the Senate and House of Representatives, according to the Rules and Limitations prescribed in the Case of a Bill.

Section 8.

The Congress shall have Power

[1] To lay and collect Taxes, Duties, Imposts and Excises, to pay the Debts and provide for the common Defence and general Welfare of the United States; but all Duties, Imposts and Excises shall be uniform throughout the United States;

[2] To borrow money on the credit of the United States;

[3] To regulate Commerce with foreign Nations, and among the several States, and with the Indian Tribes;

[4] To establish an uniform Rule of Naturalization, and uniform Laws on the subject of Bankruptcies throughout the United States;

[5] To coin Money, regulate the Value thereof, and of foreign Coin, and fix the Standard of Weights and Measures;

[6] To provide for the Punishment of counterfeiting the Securities and current Coin of the United States;

[7] To Establish Post Offices and post Roads;

[8] To promote the Progress of Science and useful Arts, by securing for limited Times to Authors and Inventors the exclusive Right to their respective Writings and Discoveries;

[9] To constitute Tribunals inferior to the Supreme Court;

[10] To define and punish Piracies and Felonies committed on the high Seas, and Offenses against the Law of Nations;

[11] To declare War, grant Letters of Marque and Reprisal, and make Rules concerning Captures on Land and Water;

[12] To raise and support Armies, but no Appropriation of Money to that Use shall be for a longer Term than two Years;

[13] To provide and maintain a Navy;

[14] To make Rules for the Government and Regulation of the land and naval Forces;

[15] To provide for calling forth the Militia to execute the Laws of the Union, suppress Insurrections and repel Invasions;

[16] To provide for organizing, arming, and disciplining the Militia, and for governing such Part of them as may be employed in the Service of the United States, reserving to the States respectively, the Appointment of the Officers, and the Authority of training the Militia according to the discipline prescribed by Congress;

[17] To exercise exclusive Legislation in all Cases whatsoever, over such District (not exceeding ten Miles square) as may, by Cession of particular States, and the acceptance of Congress, become the Seat of the Government of the United States, and to exercise like Authority over all Places purchased by the Consent of the Legislature of the State in which the Same shall be, for the Erection of Forts, Magazines, Arsenals, dock-Yards, and other needful Buildings;—And

[18] To make all Laws which shall be necessary and proper for carrying into Execution the foregoing Powers, and all other Powers vested by this Constitution in the Government of the United States, or in any Department or Officer thereof.

Section 9.

[1] The Migration or Importation of Such Persons as any of the States now existing shall think proper

to admit, shall not be prohibited by the Congress prior to the Year one thousand eight hundred and eight, but a tax or duty may be imposed on such Importation, not exceeding ten dollars for each Person.

[2] The privilege of the Writ of Habeas Corpus shall not be suspended, unless when in Cases of Rebellion or Invasion the public Safety may require it.

[3] No Bill of Attainder or ex post facto Law shall be passed.

[4] No capitation, or other direct, Tax shall be laid, unless in Proportion to the Census or Enumeration herein before directed to be taken.

[5] No Tax or Duty shall be laid on Articles exported from any State.

[6] No preference shall be given by any Regulation of Commerce or Revenue to the Ports of one State over those of another; nor shall Vessels bound to, or from, one State be obliged to enter, clear, or pay Duties in another.

[7] No money shall be drawn from the Treasury, but in Consequence of Appropriations made by Law; and a regular Statement and Account of the Receipts and Expenditures of all public Money shall be published from time to time.

[8] No Title of Nobility shall be granted by the United States: And no Person holding any Office of Profit or Trust under them, shall, without the Consent of the Congress, accept of any present, Emolument, Office, or Title, of any kind whatever, from any King, Prince, or foreign State.

Section 10.

[1] No State shall enter into any Treaty, Alliance, or Confederation; grant Letters of Marque and Reprisal; coin Money; emit Bills of Credit; make any Thing but gold and silver Coin a Tender in Payment of Debts; pass any bill of Attainder, ex post facto Law, or Law impairing the Obligation of Contracts, or grant any Title of Nobility.

[2] No State shall, without the Consent of the Congress, lay any Imposts or Duties on Imports or Exports, except what may be absolutely necessary for executing its inspection Laws: and the net Produce of all Duties and Imposts, laid by any State on Imports or Exports, shall be for the Use of the Treasury of the United States; and all such Laws shall be subject to the Revision and Control of the Congress.

[3] No State shall, without the Consent of Congress, lay any duty of Tonnage, keep Troops, or Ships of War in time of Peace, enter into any Agreement or Compact with another State, or with a foreign Power, or engage in War, unless actually invaded, or in such imminent Danger as will not admit of delay.

ARTICLE II

Section 1.

[1] The executive Power shall be vested in a President of the United States of America. He shall hold his Office during the Term of four Years, and together with the Vice President, chosen for the same Term, be elected, as follows:

[2] Each State shall appoint, in such Manner as the Legislature thereof may direct, a Number of Electors, equal to the whole Number of Senators and Representatives to which the State may be entitled in the Congress: but no Senator or Representative, or Person holding an Office of Trust or Profit under the United States, shall be appointed an Elector.

[3] The Electors shall meet in their respective States, and vote by Ballot for two persons, of whom one at least shall not be an Inhabitant of the same State with themselves. And they shall make a List of all the Persons voted for, and of the Number of Votes for each; which List they shall sign and certify, and transmit sealed to the Seat of the Government of the United States, directed to the President of the Senate. The President of the Senate shall, in the Presence of the Senate and House of Representatives, open all the Certificates, and the Votes shall then be counted. The Person having the greatest Number of Votes shall be the President, if such Number be a Majority of the whole Number of Electors appointed; and if there be more than one who have such Majority, and have an equal Number of Votes, then the House of Representatives shall immediately chuse by Ballot one of them for President; and if no Person have a Majority, then from the five highest on the List the said House shall in like Manner chuse the President. But in chusing the President, the Votes shall be taken by States, the Representation from each State having one Vote; A quorum for this Purpose shall consist of a Member or Members from two-thirds of the States, and a

Majority of all the States shall be necessary to a Choice. In every Case, after the Choice of the President, the Person having the greatest Number of Votes of the Electors shall be the Vice President. But if there should remain two or more who have equal Votes, the Senate shall chuse from them by Ballot the Vice President.

[4] The Congress may determine the Time of chusing the Electors, and the Day on which they shall give their Votes; which Day shall be the same throughout the United States.

[5] No person except a natural born Citizen, or a Citizen of the United States, at the time of the Adoption of this Constitution, shall be eligible to the Office of President; neither shall any Person be eligible to that Office who shall not have attained to the Age of thirty-five Years, and been fourteen Years a Resident within the United States.

[6] In case of the removal of the President from Office, or of his Death, Resignation, or Inability to discharge the Powers and Duties of the said Office, the same shall devolve on the Vice President, and the Congress may by Law provide for the Case of Removal, Death, Resignation or Inability, both of the President and Vice President, declaring what Officer shall then act as President, and such Officer shall act accordingly, until the Disability be removed, or a President shall be elected.

[7] The President shall, at stated Times, receive for his Services, a Compensation, which shall neither be increased nor diminished during the Period for which he shall have been elected, and he shall not receive within that Period any other Emolument from the United States, or any of them.

[8] Before he enter on the Execution of his Office, he shall take the following Oath or Affirmation:—"I do solemnly swear (or affirm) that I will faithfully execute the Office of President of the United States, and will to the best of my Ability, preserve, protect and defend the Constitution of the United States."

Section 2.

[1] The President shall be Commander in Chief of the Army and Navy of the United States, and of the Militia of the several States, when called into the actual Service of the United States; he may require the Opinion, in writing, of the principal Officer in each of the executive Departments, upon any subject relating to the Duties of their respective Offices, and he shall have Power to grant Reprieves and Pardons for Offenses against the United States, except in Cases of Impeachment.

[2] He shall have Power, by and with the Advice and Consent of the Senate, to make Treaties, provided two-thirds of the Senators present concur; and he shall nominate, and by and with the Advice and Consent of the Senate, shall appoint Ambassadors, other public Ministers and Consuls, Judges of the Supreme Court, and all other Officers of the United States, whose Appointments are not herein otherwise provided for, and shall be established by Law; but the Congress may by Law vest the Appointment of such inferior Officers, as they think proper, in the President alone, in the Courts of Law, or in the Heads of Departments.

[3] The President shall have Power to fill up all Vacancies that may happen during the Recess of the Senate, by granting Commissions which shall expire at the End of their next Session.

Section 3.

He shall from time to time give to the Congress Information of the State of the Union, and recommend to their Consideration such Measures as he shall judge necessary and expedient; he may, on extraordinary Occasions, convene both Houses, or either of them, and in Case of Disagreement between them, with Respect to the Time of Adjournment, he may adjourn them to such Time as he shall think proper; he shall receive Ambassadors and other public Ministers; he shall take Care that the Laws be faithfully executed, and shall Commission all the Officers of the United States.

Section 4.

The President, Vice President and all civil Officers of the United States, shall be removed from Office on Impeachment for, and Conviction of, Treason, Bribery, or other high Crimes and misdemeanors.

ARTICLE III

Section 1.

The judicial Power of the United States, shall be vested in one supreme Court, and in such inferior Courts as the Congress may from time to time ordain and establish. The Judges, both of the supreme and inferior Courts, shall hold their Offices during good Behaviour, and shall, at stated Times, receive for their Services a Compensation which shall not be diminished during their Continuance in Office.

Section 2.

[1] The judicial Power shall extend to all Cases, in Law and Equity, arising under this Constitution, the Laws of the United States, and Treaties made, or which shall be made under their Authority;—to all Cases affecting Ambassadors, other public Ministers and Consuls;—to all Cases of admiralty and maritime Jurisdiction;—to Controversies to which the United States shall be a Party;—to Controversies between two or more States;—between a State and Citizens of another State;—between Citizens of the same State claiming Lands under Grants of different States, and between a State, or the Citizens thereof, and foreign States, Citizens or Subjects.

[2] In all Cases affecting Ambassadors, other public Ministers and Consuls, and those in which a State shall be Party, the supreme Court shall have original Jurisdiction. In all the other Cases before mentioned, the supreme Court shall have appellate Jurisdiction, both as to Law and Fact, with such Exceptions, and under such Regulations as the Congress shall make.

[3] The trial of all Crimes, except in Cases of Impeachment, shall be by Jury; and such Trial shall be held in the State where the same Crimes shall have been committed; but when not committed within any State, the Trial shall be at such Place or Places as the Congress may by Law have directed.

Section 3.

[1] Treason against the United States, shall consist only in levying War against them, or, in adhering to their Enemies, giving them Aid and Comfort. No Person shall be convicted of Treason unless on the Testimony of two Witnesses to the same overt Act, or on Confession in open Court.

[2] The Congress shall have power to declare the Punishment of Treason, but no Attainder of Treason shall work Corruption of Blood, or Forfeiture except during the Life of the Person attainted.

ARTICLE IV

Section 1.

Full Faith and Credit shall be given in each State to the public Acts, Records, and judicial Proceedings of every other State. And the Congress may by general Laws prescribe the Manner in which such Acts, Records and Proceedings shall be proved, and the Effect thereof.

Section 2.

[1] The Citizens of each State shall be entitled to all Privileges and Immunities of Citizens in the several States.

[2] A Person charged in any State with Treason, Felony, or other Crime, who shall flee from Justice, and be found in another State, shall on demand of the executive Authority of the State from which he fled, be delivered up, to be removed to the State having Jurisdiction of the Crime.

[3] No Person held to Service or Labour in one State, under the Laws thereof, escaping into another, shall, in Consequence of any Law or Regulation therein, be discharged from such Service or Labour, but shall be delivered up on Claim of the Party to whom such Service or Labour may be due.

Section 3.

[1] New States may be admitted by the Congress into this Union; but no new State shall be formed or erected within the Jurisdiction of any other State; nor any State be formed by the Junction of two or more States, or parts of States, without the Consent of the Legislatures of the States concerned as well as of the Congress.

[2] The Congress shall have Power to dispose of and make all needful Rules and Regulations respecting the Territory or other Property belonging to the United States; and nothing in this Constitution shall be so construed as to Prejudice any Claims of the United States, or of any particular State.

Section 4.

The United States shall guarantee to every State in this Union a Republican Form of Government, and shall protect each of them against Invasion; and on Application of the Legislature, or of the Executive (when the Legislature cannot be convened) against domestic Violence.

ARTICLE V

The Congress, whenever two-thirds of both Houses shall deem it necessary, shall propose Amendments to this Constitution, or, on the Application of the Legislatures of two-thirds of the several States, shall call a Convention for proposing Amendments, which, in either Case, shall be valid to all Intents and Purposes, as part of this Constitution, when ratified by the Legislatures of three-fourths of the several States, or by Conventions in three-fourths thereof, as the one or the other Mode of Ratification may be proposed by the Congress; Provided that no Amendment which may be made prior to the Year One thousand eight hundred and eight shall in any Manner affect the first and fourth Clauses in the Ninth Section of the first Article; and that no State, without its Consent, shall be deprived of its equal Suffrage in the Senate.

ARTICLE VI

[1] All Debts contracted and Engagements entered into, before the Adoption of this Constitution shall be valid against the United States under this Constitution, as under the Confederation.

[2] This Constitution, and the Laws of the United States which shall be made in Pursuance thereof; and all Treaties made, or which shall be made, under the Authority of the United States, shall be the supreme Law of the Land; and the Judges in every State shall be bound thereby, any Thing in the Constitution or Laws of any State to the Contrary notwithstanding.

[3] The Senators and Representatives before mentioned, and the Members of the several State Legislatures, and all executive and judicial Officers, both of the United States and of the several States, shall be bound by Oath or Affirmation, to support this Constitution; but no religious Test shall ever be required as a Qualification to any Office or public Trust under the United States.

ARTICLE VII

The Ratification of the Conventions of nine States shall be sufficient for the Establishment of this Constitution between the States so ratifying the Same.

ARTICLES IN ADDITION TO, AND AMENDMENT OF, THE CONSTITUTION OF THE UNITED STATES OF AMERICA, PROPOSED BY CONGRESS, AND RATIFIED BY THE LEGISLATURES OF THE SEVERAL STATES, PURSUANT TO THE FIFTH ARTICLE OF THE ORIGINAL CONSTITUTION.

AMENDMENT I [1791]

Congress shall make no law respecting an establishment of religion, or prohibiting the free exercise thereof; or abridging the freedom of speech, or of the press; or the right of the people peaceably to assemble and to petition the Government for a redress of grievances.

AMENDMENT II [1791]

A well regulated Militia, being necessary to the security of a free State, the right of the people to keep and bear Arms, shall not be infringed.

AMENDMENT III [1791]

No Soldier shall, in time of peace be quartered in any house, without the consent of the Owner, nor in time of war, but in a manner to be prescribed by Law.

AMENDMENT IV [1791]

The right of the people to be secure in their persons, houses, papers, and effects, against unreasonable searches and seizures, shall not be violated, and no Warrants shall issue, but upon probable cause, supported by Oath or affirmation, and particularly describing the place to be searched, and the persons or things to be seized.

AMENDMENT V [1791]

No person shall be held to answer for a capital, or otherwise infamous crime, unless on a presentment or indictment of a Grand Jury, except in cases arising in the land or naval forces, or in the Militia, when in actual service in time of War or public danger; nor shall any person be subject for the same offence to be twice put in jeopardy of life or limb; nor shall be compelled in any criminal case to be a witness against himself, nor be deprived of life, liberty, or property, without due process of law; nor shall private property be taken for public use, without just compensation.

AMENDMENT VI [1791]

In all criminal prosecutions, the accused shall enjoy the right to a speedy and public trial, by an impartial jury of the State and district wherein the crime shall have been committed, which district shall have been previously ascertained by law, and to be informed of the nature and cause of the accusation; to be confronted with the witnesses against him; to have compulsory process for obtaining witnesses in his favor, and to have the Assistance of Counsel for his defence.

AMENDMENT VII [1791]

In suits at common law, where the value in controversy shall exceed twenty dollars, the right of trial by jury shall be preserved, and no fact tried by jury, shall be otherwise reexamined in any Court of the United States, than according to the rules of the common law.

AMENDMENT VIII [1791]

Excessive bail shall not be required, nor excessive fines imposed, nor cruel and unusual punishments inflicted.

AMENDMENT IX [1791]

The enumeration in the Constitution, of certain rights, shall not be construed to deny or disparage others retained by the people.

AMENDMENT X [1791]

The powers not delegated to the United States by the Constitution, nor prohibited by it to the States, are reserved to the States respectively, or to the people.

AMENDMENT XI [1798]

The Judicial power of the United States shall not be construed to extend to any suit in law or equity, commenced or prosecuted against one of the United States by Citizens of another State, or by Citizens or Subjects of any Foreign State.

AMENDMENT XII [1804]

The electors shall meet in their respective states and vote by ballot for President and Vice-President, one of whom, at least, shall not be an inhabitant of the same state with themselves; they shall name in their ballots the person voted for as President, and in distinct ballots the person voted for as Vice-President, and they shall make distinct lists of all persons voted for as President, and of all persons voted for as Vice-President, and of the number of votes for each, which lists they shall sign and certify, and transmit sealed to the seat of the government of the United States, directed to the President of the Senate;—The President of the Senate shall, in presence of the Senate and House of Representatives, open all the certificates and the votes shall then be counted;—The person having the greatest number of votes for President, shall be the President, if such number be a majority of the whole number of Electors appointed; and if no person have such majority, then from the persons having the highest numbers not exceeding three on the list of those voted for as President, the House of Representatives shall choose immediately, by ballot, the President. But in choosing the President, the votes shall be taken by states, the representation from each state having one vote; a quorum for this purpose shall consist of a member or members from two-thirds of the states, and a majority of all the states shall be necessary to a choice. And if the House of Representatives shall not choose a President whenever the right of choice shall devolve upon them, before the fourth day of March next following, then the Vice-President shall act as President, as in the case of the death or other constitutional disability of the President.—The person having the greatest number of votes as Vice-President, shall be the Vice-President, if such number be a majority of the whole number of Electors appointed, and if no person have a majority, then from the two highest numbers on the list, the Senate shall choose the Vice-President; a quorum for the purpose shall consist of two-thirds of the whole number of Senators, and a majority of the whole number shall be necessary to a choice. But no person constitutionally ineligible to the office of President shall be eligible to that of Vice-President of the United States.

AMENDMENT XIII [1865]

Section 1.

Neither slavery nor involuntary servitude, except as a punishment for crime whereof the party shall have been duly convicted, shall exist within the United States, or any place subject to their jurisdiction.

Section 2.

Congress shall have power to enforce this article by appropriate legislation.

AMENDMENT XIV [1868]

Section 1.

All persons born or naturalized in the United States, and subject to the jurisdiction thereof, are citizens of the United States and of the State wherein they reside. No State shall make or enforce any law which shall abridge the privileges or immunities of citizens of the United States; nor shall any State deprive any person of life, liberty, or property, without due process of law; nor deny to any person within its jurisdiction the equal protection of the laws.

Section 2.

Representatives shall be apportioned among the several States according to their respective numbers, counting the whole number of persons in each State, excluding Indians not taxed. But when the right to vote at any election for the choice of electors for President and Vice-President of the United States, Representatives in Congress, the Executive and Judicial officers of a State, or the members of the Legislature thereof, is denied to any of the male inhabitants of such State, being twenty-one years of age, and citizens of the United States, or in any way abridged, except for participation in rebellion, or other crime, the basis of representation therein shall be reduced in the proportion which the number of such male citizens shall bear to the whole number of male citizens twenty-one years of age in such State.

Section 3.

No person shall be a Senator or Representative in Congress, or elector of President and Vice-President, or hold any office, civil or military, under the United States, or under any State, who, having previously taken an oath, as a member of Congress, or as an officer of the United States, or as a member of

any State legislature, or as an executive or judicial officer of any State, to support the Constitution of the United States, shall have engaged in insurrection or rebellion against the same, or given aid or comfort to the enemies thereof. But Congress may by a vote of two-thirds of each House, remove such disability.

Section 4.

The validity of the public debt of the United States, authorized by law, including debts incurred for payment of pensions and bounties for services in suppressing insurrection or rebellion, shall not be questioned. But neither the United States nor any State shall assume or pay any debt or obligation incurred in aid of insurrection or rebellion against the United States, or any claim for the loss or emancipation of any slave; but all such debts, obligations and claims shall be held illegal and void.

Section 5.

The Congress shall have power to enforce, by appropriate legislation, the provisions of this article.

AMENDMENT XV [1870]

Section 1.

The right of citizens of the United States to vote shall not be denied or abridged by the United States or by any State on account of race, color, or previous condition of servitude.

Section 2.

The Congress shall have power to enforce this article by appropriate legislation.

AMENDMENT XVI [1913]

The Congress shall have power to lay and collect taxes on incomes, from whatever source derived, without apportionment among the several States, and without regard to any census or enumeration.

AMENDMENT XVII [1913]

The Senate of the United States shall be composed of two Senators from each State, elected by the people thereof, for six years; and each Senator shall have one vote. The electors in each State shall have the qualifications requisite for electors of the most numerous branch of the State legislatures.

When vacancies happen in the representation of any State in the Senate, the executive authority of such State shall issue writs of election to fill such vacancies: Provided, That the legislature of any State may empower the executive thereof to make temporary appointments until the people fill the vacancies by election as the legislature may direct.

This amendment shall not be so construed as to affect the election or term of any Senator chosen before it becomes valid as part of the Constitution.

AMENDMENT XVIII [1919]

Section 1.
After one year from the ratification of this article the manufacture, sale, or transportation of intoxicating liquors within, the importation thereof into, or the exportation thereof from the United States and all territory subject to the jurisdiction thereof for beverage purposes is hereby prohibited.

Section 2.
The Congress and the several States shall have concurrent power to enforce this article by appropriate legislation.

Section 3.
This article shall be inoperative unless it shall have been ratified as an amendment to the Constitution by the legislatures of the several States, as provided in the Constitution, within seven years from the date of submission hereof to the States by the Congress.

AMENDMENT XIX [1920]

The right of citizens of the United States to vote shall not be denied or abridged by the United States or by any State on account of sex.

Congress shall have the power to enforce this article by appropriate legislation.

AMENDMENT XX [1933]

Section 1.
The terms of the President and Vice President shall end at noon on the 20th day of January, and the terms of Senators and Representatives at noon on the 3d day of January, of the years in which such terms would have ended if this article had not been ratified; and the terms of their successors shall then begin.

Section 2.
The Congress shall assemble at least once in every year, and such meeting shall begin at noon on the 3d day of January, unless they shall by law appoint a different day.

Section 3.
If, at the time fixed for the beginning of the term of the President, the President elect shall have died, the Vice President elect shall become President. If a President shall not have been chosen before the time fixed for the beginning of his term, or if the President elect shall have failed to qualify, then the Vice President elect shall act as President until a President shall have qualified; and the Congress may by law provide for the case wherein neither a President elect nor a Vice President elect shall have qualified, declaring who shall then act as President, or the manner in which one who is to act shall be selected, and such person shall act accordingly until a President or Vice President shall have qualified.

Section 4.
The Congress may by law provide for the case of the death of any of the persons from whom the House of Representative may choose a President whenever the right of choice shall have devolved upon them, and for the case of the death of any of the persons from whom the Senate may choose a Vice President whenever the right of choice shall have devolved upon them.

Section 5.
Sections 1 and 2 shall take effect on the 15th day of October following the ratification of this article.

Section 6.
This article shall be inoperative unless it shall have been ratified as an amendment to the Constitution by the legislatures of three-fourths of the several States within seven years from the date of its submission.

AMENDMENT XXI [1933]

Section 1.
The eighteenth article of amendment to the Constitution of the United States is hereby repealed.

Section 2.

The transportation or importation into any State, Territory, or possession of the United States for delivery or use therein of intoxicating liquors, in violation of the laws thereof, is hereby prohibited.

Section 3.

This article shall be inoperative unless it shall have been ratified as an amendment to the Constitution by conventions in the several States, as provided in the Constitution, within seven years from the date of the submission hereof to the States by the Congress.

AMENDMENT XXII [1951]

Section 1.

No person shall be elected to the office of the President more than twice, and no person who has held the office of President, or acted as President, for more than two years of a term to which some other person was elected President shall be elected to the office of the President more than once. But this Article shall not apply to any person holding the office of President when this Article was proposed by the Congress, and shall not prevent any person who may be holding the office of President, or acting as President, during the term within which the Article becomes operative from holding the office of President or acting as President during the remainder of such term.

Section 2.

This article shall be inoperative unless it shall have been ratified as an amendment to the Constitution by the legislatures of three-fourths of the several States within seven years from the date of its submission to the States by the Congress.

AMENDMENT XXIII [1961]

Section 1.

The District constituting the seat of Government of the United States shall appoint in such manner as the Congress may direct:

A number of electors of President and Vice President equal to the whole number of Senators and Representatives in Congress to which the District would be entitled if it were a State, but in no event more than the least populous State; they shall be in addition to those appointed by the States, but they shall be considered, for the purposes of the election of President and Vice President, to be electors appointed by a State; and they shall meet in the District and perform such duties as provided by the twelfth article of amendment.

Section 2.

The Congress shall have power to enforce this article by appropriate legislation.

AMENDMENT XXIV [1964]

Section 1.

The right of citizens of the United States to vote in any primary or other election for President or Vice President, for electors for President or Vice President, or for Senator or Representative in Congress, shall not be denied or abridged by the United States or any State by reason of failure to pay any poll tax or other tax.

Section 2.

The Congress shall have power to enforce this article by appropriate legislation.

AMENDMENT XXV [1967]

Section 1.

In case of the removal of the President from office or his death or resignation, the Vice President shall become President.

Section 2.

Whenever there is a vacancy in the office of the Vice President, the President shall nominate a Vice President who shall take the Office upon confirmation by a majority vote of both houses of Congress.

Section 3.

Whenever the President transmits to the President pro tempore of the Senate and the Speaker of the House of Representatives his written declaration that he is unable to discharge the powers and duties of his office, and until he transmits to them a written declaration to the contrary, such powers and duties shall be discharged by the Vice President as Acting President.

Section 4.

Whenever the Vice President and a majority of either the principal officers of the executive departments, or of such other body as Congress may by law provide, transmit to the President pro tempore of the Senate and the Speaker of the House of Representatives their written declaration that the President is unable to discharge the powers and duties of his office, the Vice President shall immediately assume the powers and duties of the office as Acting President.

Thereafter, when the President transmits to the President pro tempore of the Senate and the Speaker of the House of Representatives his written declaration that no inability exists, he shall resume the powers and duties of his office unless the Vice President and a majority of either the principal officers of the executive department, or of such other body as Congress may by law provide, transmit within four days to the President pro tempore of the Senate and the Speaker of the House of Representatives their written declaration that the President is unable to discharge the powers and duties of his office. Thereupon Congress shall decide the issue, assembling within 48 hours for that purpose if not in session. If the Congress, within 21 days after receipt of the latter written declaration, or, if Congress is not in session, within 21 days after Congress is required to assemble, determines by two-thirds vote of both houses that the President is unable to discharge the powers and duties of his office, the Vice President shall continue to discharge the same as Acting President; otherwise, the President shall resume the powers and duties of his office.

AMENDMENT XXVI [1971]

Section 1.

The right of citizens of the United States, who are eighteen years of age, or older, to vote shall not be denied or abridged by the United States or by any state on account of age.

Section 2.

The Congress shall have the power to enforce this article by appropriate legislation.

AMENDMENT XXVII [1992]

No law, varying the compensation for the services of the Senators and Representatives, shall take effect, until an election of Representatives shall have intervened.

Illustrative Cases in Law

The following cases will give beginning students practice in reading and briefing cases of general interest. These cases illustrate many of the fundamental concepts introduced in Part I of this text and demonstrate the use of these concepts in practice.

COMMON LAW DEVELOPMENT

The *Du Pont* case illustrates the manner in which judges decide questions concerning justiciability of disputes and ways in which the common law remains alive today. This civil case involves diversity of citizenship of the two parties and, therefore, illustrates an area of overlapping jurisdiction between state and federal courts. Since Du Pont had the initial choice of trial courts, the Christophers have the same choice on appeal. The federal court, however, is bound by the *Erie doctrine* to decide the issue using Texas substantive law.

The *Restatement of Torts* is a general formulation of the principles of common law that have evolved from case law development.

These principles have been reformulated by the American Law Institute to resemble the form of statutory law. The *Restatement* does not have the specific force of law until recognized by the courts of appropriate jurisdiction. An interlocutory appeal is an appeal to review a preliminary trial court judgment prior to trial on the merits of the case. The Federal Interlocutory Appeals Act grants discretion to the courts of appeals to review any interlocutory order whatever in a civil case if the trial judge, in making the order, has stated in writing that the order involves a controlling question of law regarding which there is substantial ground for difference of opinion and for which an immediate appeal from the order may materially advance the ultimate termination of litigation (28 U.S.C.A. §1292(b)).

The abbreviation "F.2d" in the citation for this case denotes the case reporter series entitled *Federal Reporter* (2nd edition). All federal appeals court cases are found in this series of volumes.

E. I. Du Pont de Nemours & Company, Inc. v. Christopher

431 F.2d 1012
United States Court of Appeals, Fifth Circuit
August 25, 1970

GOLDBERG, JUSTICE. This is a case of industrial espionage in which an airplane is the cloak and a camera the dagger. The defendants-appellants, Rolfe and Gary Christopher, are photographers in Beaumont, Texas. The Christophers were hired by an unknown third party to take aerial photographs of new construction at the Beaumont plant of E. I. du Pont de Nemours & Company, Inc. Sixteen photographs of the Du Pont facility were taken from the air on March 19, 1969, and these photographs were later developed and delivered to the third party.

Du Pont employees apparently noticed the airplane on March 19 and immediately began an investigation to determine why the craft was circling over the plant. By that afternoon the investigation had disclosed that the craft was involved in a photographic expedition and that the Christophers were the photographers. Du Pont contacted the Christophers that same afternoon and asked them to reveal the name of the person or corporation requesting the photographs. The Christophers refused to disclose this information, giving as their reason the client's desire to remain anonymous.

Having reached a dead end in the investigation, Du Pont subsequently filed suit against the Christophers, alleging that the Christophers had wrongfully obtained photographs revealing Du Pont's trade secrets which they then sold to the undisclosed third party. Du Pont contended that it had developed a highly secret but unpatented process for producing methanol, a process which gave Du Pont a competitive advantage over other producers. This process, Du Pont alleged, was a trade secret developed after much expensive and time-consuming research, and a secret which the company had taken special precautions to safeguard. The area photographed by the Christophers was the plant designed to produce methanol by this secret process, and because the plant was still under construction parts of the process were exposed to view from directly above the construction area. Photographs of that area, Du Pont alleged, would enable a skilled person to deduce the secret process for making methanol. Du Pont thus contended that the Christophers had wrongfully appropriated Du Pont trade secrets by taking the photographs and delivering them to the undisclosed third party. In its suit Du Pont asked for damages to cover the loss it had already sustained as a result of the wrongful disclosure of the trade secret and sought temporary and permanent injunctions prohibiting any further circulation of the photographs already taken and prohibiting any additional photographing of the methanol plant.

The Christophers answered with motions to dismiss for lack of jurisdiction and failure to state a claim upon which relief could be granted. Depositions were taken during which the Christophers again refused to disclose the name of the person to whom they had delivered the photographs. Du Pont then filed a motion to compel an answer to this question and all related questions.

On June 5, 1969, the trial court held a hearing on the pending motions. The court denied the Christophers' motions to dismiss for want of jurisdiction and failure to state a claim. The court granted Du Pont's motion to compel the Christophers to divulge the name of their client. Agreeing with the trial court's determination that Du Pont had stated a valid claim, we affirm the decision of that court.

This is a case of first impression, for the Texas courts have not faced this precise factual issue, and sitting as a diversity court we must sensitize our Erie antennae to decide what the Texas courts would do if such a situation were presented to them. The only question involved in this interlocutory appeal is whether Du Pont has asserted a claim upon which relief can be granted. The Christophers argued both at trial and before this court that they committed no "actionable wrong" in photographing the Du Pont facility and passing these photographs on to their client because they conducted all of their activities in public airspace, violated no government aviation standard, did not breach any confidential relation, and did not engage in any fraudulent or illegal conduct. In short, the Christophers argue that for an appropriation of trade secrets to be wrong there must be a trespass, other illegal conduct, or breach of a confidential relationship. We disagree.

It is true, as the Christophers assert, that the previous trade secret cases have contained one or more of these elements. However, we do not think that the Texas courts would limit the trade secret protection exclusively to these elements. On the contrary, in *Hyde Corporation v. Huffines*, 1958, 158 Tex. 566, 314 S.W.2d 763, the Texas Supreme Court specifically adopted the rule found in the Restatement of Torts which provides:

> One who discloses or uses another's trade secret, without a privilege to do so, is liable to the other if (a) he discovered the secret by improper means, or (b) his disclosure or use constitutes a breach of confidence reposed in him by the other in disclosing the secret to him. . . .

Thus, although the previous cases have dealt with a breach of confidential relationship, a trespass or other illegal conduct, the rule is much broader than the cases heretofore encountered. Not limiting itself to specific wrongs, Texas adopted subsection (a) of the Restatement which recognizes a cause of action for the discovery of a trade secret by any "improper" means.

The question remaining, therefore, is whether aerial photography of plant construction is an improper means of obtaining another's trade secret.

We conclude that it is and that the Texas courts would so hold. The supreme court of that state has declared that "the undoubted tendency of the law has been to recognize and enforce higher standards of commercial morality in the business world." *Hyde Corporation v. Huffines, supra* 314 S.W.2nd at 773. That court has quoted with approval articles indicating that the proper means of gaining possession of a competitor's secret process is "through inspection and analysis" of the product in order to create a duplicate. Later another Texas court explained:

> The means by which the discovery is made may be obvious, and the experimentation leading from known factors to presently unknown results may be simple and lying in the public domain. But these facts do not destroy the value of the discovery and will not advantage a competitor who by unfair means obtains the knowledge without paying the price expended by the discoverer. (*Brown v. Fowler*, Tex. Civ. App. 1958, 316 S.W.2d 111.)

We think, therefore, that the Texas rule is clear. One may use his competitor's secret process if he discovers the process by reverse engineering applied to the finished product; one may use a competitor's process if he discovers it by his own independent research; but one may not avoid these labors by taking the process from the discoverer without his permission at a time when he is taking reasonable precautions to maintain its secrecy. To obtain knowledge of a process without spending the time and money to discover it independently is improper unless the holder voluntarily discloses it or fails to take reasonable precautions to ensure its secrecy.

In the instant case the Christophers deliberately flew over the Du Pont plant to get pictures of a process which Du Pont had attempted to keep secret. The Christophers delivered their pictures to a third party who was certainly aware of the means by which they had been acquired and who may be planning to use the information contained therein to manufacture methanol by the Du Pont process. The third party has a right to use this process only if he obtains this knowledge through his own research efforts, but thus far all information indicates that the third party has gained this knowledge solely by taking it from Du Pont at a time when Du Pont was making reasonable efforts to preserve its secrecy. In such a situation Du Pont has a valid cause of action to prohibit the Christophers from improperly discovering its trade secret and to prohibit the undisclosed third party from using the improperly obtained information.

We note that this view is in perfect accord with the position taken by the authors of the restatement. In commenting on improper means of discovery the savants of the Restatement of Torts said:

> *f. Improper Means of Discovery.* The discovery of another's trade secret by improper means subjects the actor to liability independently of the harm to the interest in the secret. Thus, if one uses physical force to take a secret formula from another's pocket, or breaks into another's office to steal the formula, his conduct is wrongful and subjects him to liability apart from the rule stated in this section. Such conduct is also an improper means of procuring the secret under this rule. But means may be improper under this rule even though they do not cause any other harm than that to the interest in the trade secret. Examples of such means are fraudulent misrepresentations to induce disclosure, tapping of telephone wires, eavesdropping or other espionage. A complete catalogue of improper means is not possible. In general they are means which fall below the generally accepted standards of commercial morality and reasonable conduct.

In taking this position we realize that industrial espionage of the sort here perpetrated has become a popular sport in some segments of our industrial community. However, our devotion to freewheeling industrial competition must not force us into accepting the law of the jungle as the standard of morality expected in our commercial relations. Our tolerance of the espionage game must cease when the protections required to prevent another's spying cost so much that the spirit of inventiveness is dampened. Commercial privacy must be protected from espionage which could not have been reasonably anticipated or prevented. We do not mean to imply, however, that everything not in the plain view is within the protected vale, nor that all information obtained through every extra optical extension is forbidden. Indeed, for our industrial competition to remain healthy there must be breathing room for observing a competing industrialist. A competitor can and must shop his competition for pricing and examine his products for quality, components, and methods of manufacture. Perhaps ordinary fences and roofs must be built to shut out incursive eyes, but we need not require the discoverer of a trade secret to guard against the unanticipated, the undetectable, or the unpreventable methods of espionage now available.

In the instant case Du Pont was in the midst of constructing a plant. Although after construction the finished plant would have protected much of the process from view, during the period of construction the trade secret was exposed to view from the air. To require Du Pont to put a roof over the unfinished plant to guard its secret would impose an enormous expense to prevent nothing more than a school boy's trick. We introduce here no new or radical ethic since our ethos has never given moral sanction to piracy. The market place must not deviate far from our mores. We should not require a person or corporation to take unreasonable precautions to prevent another from doing that which he ought not to do in the first place. Reasonable precautions against predatory eyes we may require, but an impenetrable fortress is an unreasonable requirement, and we are not disposed to burden industrial inventors with such a duty in order to protect the fruits of their efforts. "Improper" will always be a word of many nuances, determined by time, place, and circumstances. We therefore need not proclaim a catalogue of commercial improprieties. Clearly however, one of its commandments does say "thou shall not appropriate a trade secret through deviousness under circumstances in which countervailing defenses are not reasonably available."

Having concluded that aerial photography, from whatever altitude, is an improper method of discovering the trade secrets exposed during construction of the Du Pont plant, we need not worry about whether the flight pattern chosen by the Christophers violated any federal aviation regulations. Regardless of whether the flight was legal or illegal in that sense, the espionage was an improper means of discovering Du Pont's trade secret.

The decision of the trial court is affirmed and the case remanded to that court for proceedings on the merits.

CASE QUESTIONS

1. Can you state the holding of this case in clear, concise terms, including the important facts that would be required to be similar if this decision is used as precedent in like cases in the future?
2. What methods of legal reasoning are used to arrive at the court's conclusion?
3. Was Du Pont really interested in suing the Christophers or somebody else for damages?
4. When does a rule of social morality become law?
5. Would a lawyer have been able to predict the result of the Du Pont case with a high degree of certainty?
6. Has the spirit of the law or the letter of the law been applied in this case?
7. If the court had ruled in favor of the Christophers, how would the functioning of the law have been affected by changing technology?

FUNDAMENTAL DUE PROCESS

The *Ryan* case illustrates a form of procedural due process that courts have applied even against private universities. This case is a civil action but contains many of the fundamental ideas of fairness used in administrative actions regarding government agencies. The common-law method of accretion of law is illustrated in this case. The question of whether the facts in this case are on point (alike) or whether there are important differences in regard to the precedent cited should be examined.

Ryan v. Hofstra University
67 Misc. 2d 651, 324 N.Y.S.2d 964
Supreme Court, Nassau County
October 14, 1971

HARNETT, JUSTICE. Hofstra University, though termed a "private" university, cannot expel, bar and fine a student without following fair and reasonable procedures. It cannot be arbitrary. It must abide by constitutional principles of fair conduct implicit in our society.

Issues surrounding the conduct of college students and their treatment by college officials tend to be emotionally charged. When campus unrest marches apace with an older generation's discontentment with it, difficulties arise in sifting out legal substance and retaining the long view necessary for social continuance. Many changes have come in legal implication as society has grown and institutions altered, producing overlaps and perspectives unimagined earlier. More narrowly to the point, university character has changed over the years, as have the relationships of people of all ages and kinds to the state and the numerous activities of mixed public and private nature which continually insinuate themselves into our lives.

Here we have Robert Ryan, Jr., accused of throwing rocks through the book store window at Hofstra. It is the case of a young man accused of vandalism of college property. If he is guilty, he should be punished and the university should have broad discretion to punish him. It would be the university's duty for the protection of its people and facilities to address itself firmly to his discipline. However, the university too is a creature of the law. The university must abide by legal procedures and respect private rights. If the university is to break the law by violating private rights, it has no superior legal or moral position to one whose law breaking consists of breaking windows.

Nineteen-year-old Robert Ryan, Jr., was a Hofstra freshman last semester, and a mover in student protests against tuition increases. He was suspected by the administration of previous violent conduct, although no charges were made and no disciplinary proceedings were had.

On June 10, 1971, Robert was apprehended on campus by security police and accused of throwing a rock through the plate glass display window of the university bookstore that evening. He was taken to the campus security office where, under disputed circumstances, in the sole presence of the campus security chief and the dean of students, he wrote out a confession in which he admitted guilt to three separate rock-throwing incidents.

On June 11, 1971, he was called to face a disciplinary committee of three staff members appointed by the dean. According to the testimony of a committee member, he repeated there his guilt to the rock-throwing incidents, although later in court he recanted his admissions. The committee later also spoke with a school psychologist, and the chief security officer, and apparently considered the statement of a security policeman who claimed to be an eyewitness. It then reported to the dean.

On June 22, 1971, the dean expelled Robert from Hofstra, severing him from the University "completely and permanently." He barred Robert from any part of the campus without his express prior permission under pain of arrest as a trespasser. Finally, he fined Robert and his family $1,011.61 for the ostensible cost of replacing the windows.

At no time prior to his expulsion, barring and fining, was Robert given a choice of procedure, was he represented by any counsel, nor did he have an opportunity to confront any witnesses, nor was he interviewed by any school psychologist or medical personnel.

The dean claims that Robert was guilty of the rock-throwing charges, and that in light of these and the other uncharged incidents he was troublesome and emotionally disturbed. Robert claims he is innocent, that his confession was pressured from him, and that the university is and has been harassing him because of his tuition protest activities.

The Hofstra Disciplinary Regulations for Nonacademic Conduct provide that when the dean of students is advised of an incident possibly requiring disciplinary action he may either interview the student himself or refer the matter to a member of his staff. Upon determining that disciplinary hearing is appropriate, the student is given a choice of appearing before either a student judiciary board or members of the dean of student's staff.

The dean specified in his testimony that Robert was not given a choice of the student judiciary board, based on that portion of the Hofstra rules which provide that a student "whose records suggest significant emotional or psychological disturbances which may be relevant" will be heard only by the dean's staff. The dean did not consult any psychologist or psychiatrist before making the disciplinary reference to his staff committee. The testimony was that the staff committee concerned itself with emotional disturbance upon talking with a university psychologist.

There are no rules as to the procedures of the dean's staff committee except that its members present their recommendations to the dean. The dean must then interview the student and give his decision. Hofstra's rules do provide an "appeal" procedure for non-academic disciplinary situations. If the student believes that the dean's punishment is inappropriate, he may have a hearing by a review committee of five university staff and faculty members and two students upon his petition submitted to the vice president for student affairs within ten days after penalty. The vice president is then supposed to advise the student of his right to call witnesses on his behalf and to confront and cross-examine those who appear against him and of his right to seek counsel, which counsel is limited, however, only to a university staff or faculty member.

The review committee is charged with examining the evidence, hearing witnesses as to the facts and the student's character, and weighing extenuating circumstances. The administration, but not the student, has a further right of appeal to the university board of trustees.

During June, Robert orally requested of the dean and the Hofstra vice president of student affairs a hearing, but was told that he had to petition in writing. A lawyer representing Robert requested an appeal hearing by letter dated July 9, 1971, to the dean. This letter was returned to the lawyer suggesting that the request be directed to the university vice president for student affairs. Thereupon, the attorney mailed a similar letter to that official on July 23, 1971, requesting that the review be held prior to the fall semester, but the administration took no action on this.

On August 4, 1971, Robert requested that because of family illness the hearing be delayed until the fall and that he be permitted to attend classes pending the completion of the appeal. This request was turned down by the vice president for student affairs on August 9, 1971, who volunteered that Robert's right to petition for a hearing was extended to September 1, 1971. On August 26, 1971, Robert wrote personally to the vice president for student

affairs requesting an appeal. On September 9, 1971, Robert received a letter (dated September 1st) from an assistant president stating that there was no more vice president for student affairs, advising Robert that he would be notified of a hearing date "as soon as practicable," and directing communication to him.

On September 14, 1971, without any further word from the administration as to review, Robert commenced this proceeding to compel Hofstra to readmit him to classes. On September 16, 1971, classes reopened at Hofstra for the fall season. Sometime after the hearing of this judicial proceeding on September 23, 1971, a review proceeding was first scheduled for October 5, 1971.

Essentially, Robert's contention is that the university's action was improper and arbitrary and that the proceedings deprived him of due process of law. In reply, Hofstra asserts that the university acted properly and that Hofstra, as a private institution, was not legally obliged to afford fair process to its students. Hofstra argues that since it is a private university it suffers no restriction at all in its disciplining of its students. However one gauges the contemporaneous sensitivity of this attitude, it is plainly not the law. Whatever the application to this case, there are some limits.

The dean testified that he gave Robert no choice of appearing before the student judiciary board because of that provision of the rules requiring staff referral only for "students whose records suggest significant emotional or psychological disturbance." Even though Robert was sent to the staff committee and given no student judiciary board choice because of an assumed record of emotional or psychological disturbance, Robert was at no time interviewed by any medical or psychological personnel, nor were any records produced suggesting the offending disturbance.

Under the adopted rules, Robert was entitled to a student judiciary board choice unless the record suggested significant emotional disturbance on his part. There was no proof of any such record prior to his referral to the dean's committee. It was indeed the reverse. It was the staff committee which raised the emotional concern after the student judiciary board choice had already been withheld.

Accordingly, in the absence of a foundation for his conduct, the dean acted arbitrarily and in abuse of discretion in not giving Robert the choice of appearing before a student judiciary board as required by the Hofstra rules.

Implicit in the rules must be a requirement for the university to act with reasonable promptness on review applications. The testimony reflects without doubt that the Hofstra administration delayed materially in scheduling a review hearing. Where after oral notification, it had a written notice on July 9, 1971, and subsequent written requests on July 23rd and August 26th, it first scheduled an appeal hearing on October 5, 1971, three weeks after school reopened. And this scheduling came only after the court hearing in this proceeding.

Given the time necessary to conduct an appeal and reach a reasoned decision, it is apparent that the procedure adopted will necessarily deprive Robert of a semester's attendance in class, or at best put him under an onerous make-up schedule, if possible, even if he is totally successful on appeal.

This delay works the imposition of a significant penalty which entirely bypasses the review procedure, and must be termed arbitrary and capricious, and abusive of discretion, on the part of the Hofstra administration.

The university's insistence on a written petition in Robert's personal hand to the vice president for student affairs as an excuse for delay is hypertechnical and not legitimate justification. After oral notice from Robert, it rejected the first written communication from his lawyer because it was addressed to the moving and visible dean and not to a certain vice president, and then rejected the lawyer's written request to the officer to which it directed him on the ground that Robert personally, not a lawyer, had to write out the request. The administration was fully and fairly informed by the lawyer's letters of July 9, 1971, to the dean of students and of July 23, 1971, to the vice president of student affairs. A lawyer acts as a personal representative of his client and for him. The administration's treatment of this simple request for review smacks of a "runaround." Moreover, if technicality is the order of the day, nothing in the rules precludes petition by a lawyer writing on behalf of a student, unlike the review procedures which specifically limit right to counsel. Amusingly enough, even the administration departed from its insistence on communication with one indispensable officer as the touchstone for its procedure, for in August Hofstra dispensed with its position of vice president for student affairs altogether. After Robert had personally petitioned that requisite officer, it turned out the office no longer existed, and the university itself requested Robert to communicate with some assistant president. Even then it delayed for six more weeks until October 5, 1971.

Finally, the hasty imposition on Robert and his family of a money fine in excess of $1000 for three separate incidents, of which only one had a claimed eyewitness, without even submitted proof of damage, was precipitous. The family was not heard at all and in no way signed for any responsibility. A particularly unreasonable part of the skimpy procedure here is that the expelled student cannot get a transcript to enable transfer admission to another school until he pays the fine to the university. Accordingly, a student is put into the position of being required to pay or prosecute a successful appeal, no matter the time delay, before he can transfer to another school. This financial obligation springs into existence without benefit of counsel or fair hearing.

In *Dixon v. Alabama Board of Education*, 294 F.2d 150, the court held a student could not be expelled from a tax supported university without notice and some opportunity to be heard. In defining "due process," the court emphasized that the nature of the hearing depended on the circumstances of the particular case. It said that "full dress judicial hearings" are not required, because they are not appropriate to college context, but that the requirements of due process are fulfilled by having "the rudimentary elements of fair play." There must be "every semblance of fairness" in school disciplinary procedure. Due process is then a variable thing. Something different is called for by a criminal trial than a college disciplinary proceeding. But, the constant factor is that the procedure afforded must be traditionally fair and conscionable in the context taken.

Bearing in mind that this is a college disciplinary matter, and not a criminal trial (although the acts charged are crimes and admissions taken damaging), it must be observed that Robert's treatment fell short of the rudimentary requirements of fair play.

In the collegiate context, the initial nonacademic discipline procedure at Hofstra is not unreasonable, provided it is followed. Since the subsequent appeal or review procedure contemplates an open hearing with witnesses and confrontation, the juxtaposition is not inconsistent with the need to keep order. But when the prescribed procedure is not followed, when punitive delay is set in, and when excessive punishment is summarily dealt, the administration violates the necessary rudiments of fair play.

Based on the findings and principles set forth above, the action of the Hofstra University dean in expelling Robert Ryan, Jr., barring him from the campus, and fining him and his family will be nullified.

CASE QUESTIONS

1. Do you agree with the Court's ruling in this case? Why or why not?
2. If you were the lawyer for Hofstra University, would you appeal this decision? Why or why not?
3. Would the judge have ruled the same way if Hofstra had merely expelled the student? Why or why not?
4. What is meant by a fair hearing?
5. What procedural rules exist on your campus?
6. Is the court creating law in this case or merely following stare decisis?

VAGUENESS AND SUBSTANTIVE DUE PROCESS

The *Moore* case involves use of the basic principle of conflict of laws to render part of a statutory law unconstitutional. The concepts of vagueness and substantive due process are illustrated in this case. Substantive due process limits the legislative authority and requires that the enactment provide a standard that can be applied by the court. Note that this is a trial level court making a decision in a criminal case about the applicability of a state statute. Judges at all levels take an oath to uphold the Constitution. Intent is a significant element in criminal cases where guilt must be established beyond a reasonable doubt.

People v. Moore
377 N.Y.S.2d 1005
Fulton County Court
December 12, 1975

MARIO M. ALBANESE, JUDGE. These defendants, all municipal officials of the City of Gloversville, New York, were indicted, charging them with violating Article 18, Section 805-a subdivision (1) of the General Municipal Law of the State of New York.

All three defendants move for the dismissal of this particular charge on the grounds the same is unconstitutional claiming it fails to adequately and sufficiently set a standard by which reasonable men could reach a determination as to what are "circumstances in which it could reasonably be inferred that the gift was intended to influence the defendants or could reasonably be expected to influence them in the performance of their respective official duties"; the statute, so it is further claimed, is so vague and unspecific that a reasonable man would be compelled to speculate at his peril whether the statute permits or prohibits the act he contemplates committing and as such, is repugnant to the due process clause of the Constitutions of the United States and New York, as well as violative of the protection afforded an individual thereunder.

The District Attorney, on the other hand, directly opposes the contentions of the three defendants, claiming instead that the entire act is constitutional without any vagueness, uncertainty or ambiguity and all that is required to identify the nature of the conduct prohibited is the exercise of common sense.

The pertinent portion of Section 805-a of the General Municipal Law reads as follows:

No municipal officer or employee shall: a. directly or indirectly, solicit any gift, or accept or receive any gift having a value of twenty-five dollars or more, whether in the form of money, service, loan, travel, entertainment, hospitality, thing or promise, or in any other form, under circumstances in which it could reasonably be inferred that the gift was intended to influence him, or could reasonably be expected to influence him, in the performance of his official duties or was intended as a reward for any official action on his part.

To ascertain the legislative background, its intents and purposes the Court referred to the "Report of the Governor's Special Commission on Ethical Standards in Public Service," dated December 12, 1969, with Malcolm Wilson, then Lieutenant Governor, as its Chairman. This report sets forth the intended and express proscription of two distinct and separate types of conduct, the first of which forbids the *solicitation*, directly or indirectly, *of any gift of any value* (italics added for emphasis) under all circumstances; the second forbids the *acceptance or receipt* (italics added for emphasis) of any gift of Twenty-Five Dollars ($25.00) or more, even if unsolicited, whether in the form of money or in any other form, under circumstances intended or expected to influence the official in his official duties.

A municipal officer or employee, under the first prohibition, is forbidden to: "directly or indirectly, solicit any gift." This particular prohibition and language is clear, definite and unequivocal, so much so that no rational argument can be levied against its intent and meaning. This being so, the Court will dispose of this portion of the statute before us without further discussion thereon by declaring the first prohibition to be constitutional.

With respect to the second prohibition, a municipal officer or employee is forbidden to:

> accept or receive any gift having a value of twenty-five dollars or more, whether in the form of money, service, loan, travel, entertainment, hospitality, thing or promise, or in any other form, under circumstances in which it could reasonably be inferred that the gift was intended to influence him, or could reasonably be expected to influence him, in the performance of his official duties or was intended as a reward for any official action on his part.

The wording and language of this second proscription presents a different and difficult situation more specifically that portion thereof which reads: *"under circumstances in which it could reasonably be inferred that the gift was intended to influence him, or could reasonably be expected to influence him."*

(Italics added for emphasis.) The Court holds such language to be vague and without any standard or guidelines whatsoever; accordingly, is unconstitutional as violative of the due process and equal protection clauses of the Constitutions of the State of New York and the United States.

The wording being examined hereunder is lacking in specificity. It should clearly indicate what it is a man's duty to avoid. It must be so "clear and positive" as to give "unequivocal warning" to citizens of the rule to be obeyed. Furthermore, it has no well-defined or agreed upon meaning. *Tozer v. United States*, 8 Cir., 52 F. 917, states in part that a person should be "able to know in advance whether his act is criminal or not." In short, this language also suffers from vagueness. The test of due process is met by a statute whose language is sufficiently definite to establish a standard of conduct ascertainable by persons familiar with the field in which the statute is operative.

In the opinion of this Court, these are serious deficiencies that result in a denial of due process. *Connally v. General Construction Co.*, 269 U.S. 385, 46 S.Ct. 126, 70 L.Ed. 322 holds: "A statute which either forbids or requires the doing of an act in terms so vague that men of common intelligence must necessarily guess at its meaning and differ as to its application violates the first essential of due process of law." The test in matters of this kind as to whether or not a statute may be upheld as constitutional seems to be whether the phrases used have "a technical or other special meaning . . . or a well-settled common law meaning" or whether the text of the statute involved or the subject with which it dealt sets up some kind of standard.

The additional language ("under circumstances, etc.") in our particular case does not condemn any act, omission or clearly defined set of circumstances but, in fact leaves it to the discretion if not the whim of the police or enforcement official to determine or ascribe criminality or wrongdoing. More disturbing still, it is the intent of the donor and not that of the municipal official that controls—a contention with which the District Attorney fully concurs. Admittedly, then, one intending no wrong can nevertheless be victimized by accepting or receiving a gift by the malintent of the giver alone. That this is unfair and repugnant is self-evident. These are serious deficiencies which also deny to one the equal protection of the law as guaranteed by the Constitution.

In conclusion, the Court interprets the statute to be read in the disjunctive delineating as aforementioned, the distinction between the two conducts so prohibited and as such, is severable. Also: "A statute may be constitutional in part and unconstitutional in part, and the invalid part may be severed from the remainder, if after the severance the remaining portions are sufficient to effect the legislative purposes deducible from the entire act, construed in the light of contemporary events." The first prohibition, being constitutional, is retained, while the second prohibition, being unconstitutional, is to be severed from Section 805-a, of the General Municipal Law of the State of New York, and of no force and effect.

CASE QUESTIONS

1. How does the Court define vagueness in this decision?
2. Is it clear whether the defendants were charged with the first or second part of the state statutory provision in question?
3. Could the defendants be tried on the basis of the first part of the statute? Why or why not?
4. How could the legislature change the statute to make it enforceable through the courts?

CRIMINAL STANDARDS OF DUE PROCESS

In the *Braly* case, the exacting standards of due process in criminal cases are illustrated. A crime is a very serious offense, and this case involves two convictions for felonies (serious crimes) as opposed to misdemeanors (minor criminal offenses). Conviction for a serious crime requires proof of culpability (guilt), which includes mental intent (mens rea). This element of crime is usually specified in the statute defining the crime. Conspiracy is an inchoate (or vague) crime requiring proof of deliberate planning to commit a crime. Sufficiency of evidence refers to at least some admissible evidence. The rules of evidence are extensive, but all courts are required to prohibit the use of hearsay (secondhand) evidence in criminal and civil trials. The standard of proof in criminal cases is beyond a reasonable doubt.

People vs. Braly
532 P.2d 325
Supreme Court of Colorado
January 20, 1975

GROVES, JUSTICE. Defendant Terrell Braly was tried by a jury and convicted of conspiracy to sell narcotic drugs and assault with a deadly weapon. On appeal, defendant challenges the sufficiency of the evidence on both counts and assigns further prejudicial errors at trial. We reverse both convictions.

The circumstances surrounding the charges against the defendant are as follows. Two undercover police officers, agent Carter and O'Dell, attempted to arrange a purchase of fifty pounds of marijuana from one Stahl. Carter contacted Stahl by telephone. Stahl told him that he could sell fifty pounds of marijuana, and that the price would be $4,200. Stahl told Carter to come to his house in Boulder at about 5:30 or 6 that afternoon. Upon the arrival of agents Carter and O'Dell, Mr. Stahl asked to see the money and officer O'Dell showed it to him. Stahl told the officers to return in about a half hour; they then left, and did return at about 6:30.

On their return, the agents went into the Stahl residence. Stahl made a phone call and then told them that he wanted to talk further about the purchase, but not in the house, suggesting the use of the agents' vehicle. There the three talked further about the proposed buy and at about 7 p.m. the agents dropped Stahl off at the hill area in Boulder. They picked him up again at about 8 and returned to Stahl's house. That evening, at about 8:30, there was a knock at the door. Stahl asked the agents to go to the basement bedroom and to wait for him. The agents heard voices upstairs, and then Stahl returned to the basement and gave them a Winston cigarette pack containing two marijuana cigarettes, explaining that this was a sample of the marijuana that was the subject of the purchase. Stahl told the agents that he had the marijuana but wanted to have the money before they could see the narcotics. Stahl made several trips up and down the stairs. Finally, he took the agents up with him and asked them to remain inside a bedroom upstairs. Stahl, acting as a go-between for the agents and the people in the other bedroom, was given the money which he showed to the others, who questioned whether it was marked. Agent Carter asked if he could see the marijuana. Shortly thereafter, the deal fell through. Except for an earlier visit, when the agents saw Stahl's mother and sister, no one was seen by the agents in the Stahl house. There was testimony by a surveillant officer that the defendant was in the house while the agents were last there; and the defendant's counsel stipulated that he was there at the time in question.

The events that followed are confusing. When the defendant and his companion left the Stahl house that night, surveillance cars attempted to follow the car that defendant was driving and a car of a companion of Braly. It becomes unclear who was following—or who was trying to elude—whom but the record reflects a classic "cops and robbers" chase through the streets of Boulder, complete with squealing tires and U-turns. Six cars were involved, four of which were police vehicles. At one point, however, the car which defendant was driving came alongside a surveillance car and swerved toward it about three times, and the surveillance car took evasive action, swerving toward the right curb. The testimony of the defendant, and of the police, indicates that there were two lanes of travel in that direction, and that defendant's car never left his lane of traffic, nor did it hit the agents' car. Further the testimony indicates that the defendant could have hit the agents' car if he had so desired, and that the agents' car never left the roadway, though its tires squealed and at one point bumped the curb.

Shortly thereafter, defendant was stopped and arrested. The assault charge stems from the interlude in the automobiles. No marijuana, other than the two cigarettes, was recovered. The prosecution's case was established through the testimony of the narcotics and surveillance officers, and through the testimony of Stahl's mother as to what she had overheard and what her son had told her. Stahl never testified, though his statements composed a major portion of the prosecution's evidence.

The defendant, testifying in his own behalf, stated that he had gone to the Stahl house in an attempt to take the agents' money and leave, after having been told that the men at Stahl's house were narcotics agents. A Dan Conley testified that he had contacted

the defendant on the afternoon of the 6th, and had told him not to go to the Stahl house that night because the people there would be narcotics agents.

[The court reversed the conspiracy to sell narcotics conviction because of insufficient evidence.] Defendant was charged with assault under C.R.S. 1963, 40-2-34 which reads in pertinent part:

> An assault with a deadly weapon, instrument or other thing, with an intent to commit upon the person of another a bodily injury where no considerable provocation appears or where the circumstances of the assault show an abandoned or malignant heart, shall be adjudged to be a felony. . . .

Assault is defined under C.R.S. 1963, 40-2-33 to be an "unlawful attempt coupled with a present ability to commit a violent injury on the person of another."

The intent with which the act is committed is the gist of the offense.

Where a crime consists of an act combined with a specific intent, the intent is just as much an element of the crime as is the act. In such cases, mere general malice or criminal intent is insufficient, and the requisite specific intent must be shown as a matter of fact, either by direct or circumstantial evidence. The rule is especially applicable where a statutory offense, consisting of an act and a specific intent, constitutes substantially an attempt to commit some higher offense than that which the accused succeeded in accomplishing. The general rule that a criminal intention will be presumed from the commission of the unlawful act does not apply; and proof of the commission of the act does not warrant the presumption that accused had the requisite specific intent. Although it is settled that even specific intent may be inferred from the circumstances, it is argued that the circumstances in this case seem to negate such specific intent. We agree. The testimony of the officers, and of the defendant, showed that the car defendant was driving never left his lane of traffic; that there were two lanes traveling in the direction of the two cars; that there was adequate room in both lanes; and that although defendant could have made contact if he had wanted to, no contact was made.

The court in *Shreeves v. People*, 126 Colo. 413, 249 P.2d 1020 (1952), stated:

> The term "abandoned and malignant heart" as the same is used in the statute here under consideration, is evidenced by the use of some instrumentality likely to produce great bodily harm, and by the brutal and unrestrained use of such instrumentality in the commission of the crime charged.

In viewing the facts in the light most favorable to the prosecution, we think that there was not sufficient evidence to establish criminal assault.

Judgment reversed and cause remanded with directions to grant defendant's motion for acquittal as to both counts.

LEE, JUSTICE (concurring in part and dissenting in part). The evidence presented by the People, together with the reasonable inferences there from, concerning the manner in which the defendant drove his vehicle during the "cops and robbers" chase, in my view, was sufficient to sustain the verdict of guilty of assault with a deadly weapon.

Viewing the chase in the context of the events of the evening, as described in the majority opinion, it becomes clear that the swerving of defendant's vehicle was not the innocent act of one who was lawfully operating his vehicle on the streets of Boulder and who unfortunately became the victim of a mechanical brake or steering malfunction, as the defendant suggested in his testimony. The swerving was not an isolated occurrence but happened, according to the police officers, three times during the high-speed chase which lasted for a period of approximately twenty minutes.

The jury could reasonably conclude under all the circumstances that the defendant three times deliberately swerved his car toward the surveillance car during the chase, thus forcing the surveillance car to take evasive action to avoid a collision and potentially grievous personal injuries; that the defendant's conduct in driving his car toward the police car was motivated by an abandoned and malignant heart, as evidenced by the unrestrained manner in which the car was being driven at the time; and that defendant's intention was to cause bodily injury upon the officers in the other car.

That the defendant's car did not cross the lane dividing the two driving lanes or make actual contact with the police car would not, in my view, lessen the criminal culpability demonstrated by the defendant in the operation of his car under the circumstances then existing.

I would affirm the judgment of conviction of assault with a deadly weapon.

CASE QUESTIONS

1. Was Braly found to be innocent of these crimes?
2. Do you agree with the majority of the court or with the dissenter?
3. What would have been the most appropriate criminal charge in this case, given the facts presented?
4. Should the court be able to override the jury in cases like this one? Why or why not?

CIVIL DUE PROCESS

The *Katko* case illustrates that criminal and civil actions are completely independent of each other. They are separate forms of legal action. In criminal cases, only the prosecutor can file suit, but in a civil action, the injured party is allowed to initiate legal process to recover damages. This case also illustrates the distinctive functions of the trial courts and the appeals courts. Appeals courts do not include juries and do not conduct fact-finding procedures. They must rely on trial courts to develop the facts and to decide on issues of fact in dispute. Juries often are used in both civil and criminal cases to decide questions of fact in dispute. Appeals courts decide questions of law in dispute, and these issues must be raised at the trial court level in order to be reviewed by appeals courts.

Katko v. Briney
183 N.W.2d 657
Supreme Court of Iowa
February 9, 1971

MOORE, CHIEF JUSTICE. The primary issue presented here is whether an owner may protect personal property in an unoccupied boarded-up farm house against trespassers and thieves by a spring gun capable of inflicting death or serious injury.

We are not here concerned with a man's right to protect his home and members of his family. Defendants' home was several miles from the scene of the incident to which we refer *infra*.

Plaintiff's action is for damages resulting from serious injury caused by a shot from a 20-gauge spring shotgun set by defendants in a bedroom of an old farm house which had been uninhabited for several years. Plaintiff and his companion, Marvin McDonough, had broken and entered the house to find and steal old bottles and dated fruit jars which they considered antiques.

At defendants' request plaintiff's action was tried to a jury consisting of residents of the community where defendants' property was located. The jury returned a verdict for plaintiff and against defendants for $20,000 actual and $10,000 punitive damages.

After careful consideration of defendants' motions for judgment notwithstanding the verdict and for new trial, the experienced and capable trial judge overruled them and entered judgment on the verdict. Thus we have this appeal by defendants.

Most of the facts are not disputed. In 1957 defendant Bertha L. Briney inherited her parents' farm land in Mahaska and Monroe Counties. Included was an eighty-acre tract in southwest Mahaska County where her grandparents and parents had lived. No one occupied the house thereafter. Her husband, Edward, attempted to care for the land. He kept no farm machinery thereon. The outbuildings became dilapidated.

For about ten years, 1957 to 1967, there occurred a series of trespassing and housebreaking events with loss of some household items, the breaking of windows and "messing up of the property in general." The latest occurred June 8, 1967, prior to the event on July 16, 1967, herein involved.

Defendants through the years boarded up the windows and doors in an attempt to stop the intrusions. They had posted "no trespass" signs on the land several years before 1967. The nearest one was thirty-five feet from the house. On June 11, 1967, defendants set a "shotgun trap" in the north bedroom. After Mr. Briney cleaned and oiled his 20-gauge shotgun, the power of which he was well aware, defendants took it to the old house where they secured it to an iron bed with the barrel pointed at the bedroom door. It was rigged with wire from the doorknob to the gun's trigger so it would fire when the door was opened. Briney first pointed the gun so an intruder would be hit in the stomach but at Mrs. Briney's suggestion it was lowered to hit the legs. He admitted he did so "because I was mad and tired of being tormented" but "he did not intend to injure anyone." He gave no explanation of why he used a loaded shell and set it to hit a person already in the house. Tin was nailed over the bedroom window. The spring gun could not be seen from the outside. No warning of its presence was posted.

Plaintiff lived with his wife and worked regularly as a gasoline station attendant in Eddyville, seven miles from the old house. He had observed it for several years while hunting in the area and considered it as being abandoned. He knew it had long been uninhabited. In 1967 the area around the house was covered with high weeds. Prior to July 16, 1967, plaintiff and McDonough had been to the premises and found several old bottles and fruit jars which they took and added to their collection of antiques. On the latter day about 9:30 P.M. they made a second trip to the Briney property. They entered the old house by removing a board from a porch window which was without glass. While McDonough was looking around the kitchen area plaintiff went to another part of the house. As he started to open the north bedroom door the shotgun went off striking him in the right leg above the ankle bone. Much of his leg, including part of the tibia, was blown away. Only by McDonough's assistance was plaintiff able to get out of the house and after crawling some distance was put in his vehicle and rushed to a doctor and then to a hospital. He remained in the hospital forty days.

Plaintiff's doctor testified he seriously considered amputation but eventually the healing process was successful. Some weeks after his release from the hospital plaintiff returned to work on crutches. He was required to keep the injured leg in a cast for approximately a year and wear a special brace for another year. He continued to suffer pain during this period.

There was undenied medical testimony plaintiff had a permanent deformity, a loss of tissue, and a shortening of the leg.

The record discloses plaintiff to trial time had incurred $710 medical expense, $2056.85 for hospital service, $61.80 for orthopedic service and $750 as a loss of earnings. In addition thereto the trial court submitted to the jury the question of damages for pain and suffering and for future disability.

Plaintiff testified he knew he had no right to break and enter the house with intent to steal bottles and fruit jars therefrom. He further testified he had entered a plea of guilty to larceny in the nighttime of property of less than $20 value from a private building. He stated he had been fined $50 and costs and paroled during good behavior from a sixty-day jail sentence. Other than minor traffic charges this was plaintiff's first brush with the law. On this civil case appeal it is not our prerogative to review the disposition made of the criminal charge against him.

The main thrust of defendants' defense in the trial court and on this appeal is that "the law permits use of a spring gun in a dwelling or warehouse for the purpose of preventing the unlawful entry of a burglar or thief." They repeated this contention in their exceptions to the trial court's instructions 2, 5, and 6. They took no exception to the trial court's statement of the issues or to other instructions.

In the statement of issues the trial court stated plaintiff and his companion committed a felony when they broke and entered defendants' house. In instruction 2 the court referred to the early case history of the use of spring guns and stated under the law their use was prohibited except to prevent the commission of felonies of violence and where human life is in danger. The instruction included a statement breaking and entering is not a felony of violence.

Instruction 5 stated: "You are hereby instructed that one may use reasonable force in the protection of his property, but such right is subject to the qualification that one may not use such means of force as will take human life or inflict great bodily injury. Such is the rule even though the injured party is a trespasser and is in violation of the law himself."

Instruction 6 stated: "An owner of premises is prohibited from willfully or intentionally injuring a trespasser by means of force that either takes life or inflicts great bodily injury; and therefore a person owning a premise is prohibited from setting out 'spring guns' and like dangerous devices which will likely take life or inflict great bodily injury, for the purpose of harming trespassers. The fact that the trespasser may be acting in violation of the law does not change the rule. The only time when such conduct of setting a 'spring gun' or like dangerous device is justified would be when the trespasser was committing a felony of violence or a felony punishable by death, or where the trespasser was endangering human life by his act."

Instruction 7, to which defendants made no objection or exception, stated: "To entitle the plaintiff to recover for compensatory damages, the burden of proof is upon him to establish by a preponderance of the evidence each and all of the following propositions:

"1. That defendants erected a shotgun trap in a vacant house on land owned by defendant, Bertha L. Briney, on or about June 11, 1967, which fact was known only by them, to protect household goods from trespassers and thieves.

"2. That the force used by defendants was in excess of that force reasonably necessary and which persons are entitled to use in the protection of their property.

"3. That plaintiff was injured and damaged and the amount thereof.

"4. That plaintiff's injuries and damages resulted directly from the discharge of the shotgun trap which was set and used by defendants."

The overwhelming weight of authority, both textbook and case law, supports the trial court's statement of the applicable principles of law.

Prosser on Torts, third edition, pages 116–18, states: the law has always placed a higher value upon human safety than upon mere rights in property, it is the accepted rule that there is no privilege to use any force calculated to cause death or serious bodily injury to repel the threat to land or chattels, unless there is also such a threat to the defendant's personal safety as to justify a self-defense. . . . Spring guns and other man-killing devices are not justifiable against a mere trespasser, or even a petty thief. They are privileged only against those upon whom the landowner, if he were present in person would be free to inflict injury of the same kind.

Restatement of Torts, section 85, page 180, states: The value of human life and limbs, not only to the Individual concerned but also to society, so outweighs the interest of a possessor of land in excluding from it those whom he is not willing to admit thereto that a possessor of land has, as is stated in §79, no privilege to use force intended or likely to cause death or serious harm against another whom the possessor sees about to enter his premises or meddle with his chattel, unless the intrusion threatens death or serious bodily harm to the occupiers or users of the premises. . . . A possessor of land cannot do indirectly and by a mechanical device that which, were he present, he could not do immediately and in person. Therefore, he cannot gain a privilege to install, for the purpose of protecting his land from intrusions harmless to the lives and limbs of the occupiers or users of it, a mechanical device whose only purpose is to inflict death or serious harm upon such as may intrude, by giving notice of his intention to inflict, by mechanical means and indirectly, harm which he could not, even after request, inflict directly were he present.

In *Hooker v. Miller*, 37 Iowa 613, we held defendant vineyard owner liable for damages resulting from a spring gun shot although plaintiff was a trespasser and there to steal grapes. At pages 614, 615, this statement is made: "This court has held that a mere trespass against property other than a dwelling is not a sufficient justification to authorize the use of a deadly weapon by the owner in its defense; and that if death results in such a case it will be murder, though the killing be actually necessary to prevent the trespass. *State v. Vance*, 17 Iowa 138." At page 617 this court said: "[T]respassers and other inconsiderable violators of the law are not to be visited by barbarous punishments or prevented by inhuman inflictions of bodily injuries."

The facts in *Allison v. Fiscus*, 156 Ohio 120, 100 N.E.2d 237, 44 A.L.R.2d 369, decided in 1951, are very similar to the case at bar. There plaintiff's right to damages was recognized for injuries received when he feloniously broke a door latch and started to enter defendant's warehouse with intent to steal. As he entered a trap of two sticks of dynamite buried under the doorway by defendant owner was set off and plaintiff seriously injured. The court held the question whether a particular trap was justified as a use of reasonable and necessary force against a trespasser engaged in the commission of a felony should have been submitted to the jury. The Ohio Supreme Court recognized plaintiff's right to recover punitive or exemplar damages in addition to compensatory damages.

In *United Zinc & Chemical Co. v. Britt*. 258 U.S. 268, 275, 42 S.Ct. 299, page 299, 66 L.Ed. 615, 617, the Court states: "The liability for spring guns and mantraps arises from the fact that the defendant has . . . expected the trespasser and prepared an injury that is no more justified than if he had held the gun and fired it."

In addition to civil liability many jurisdictions hold a land owner criminally liable for serious injuries or homicide caused by spring guns or other set devices. See *State v. Childers*, 133 Ohio 508, 14 N.E.2d 767 (melon thief shot by spring gun); *Pierce v. Commonwealth*, 135 Va. 635, 115 S.E. 686 (policeman killed by spring gun when he opened unlocked front door of defendant's shoe repair shop); *State v. Marfaudille*, 48 Wash. 117, 92 P. 939 (murder conviction for death from spring gun set in a trunk); *State v. Beckham*, 306 Mo. 566, 267 S.W. 817 (boy killed by spring gun attached to window of defendant's chili stand); *State v. Green*, 118 S.C. 279, 110 S.E. 145, 19 A.L.R. 1431 (intruder shot by spring gun when he broke and entered vacant house).

In Wisconsin, Oregon, and England the use of spring guns and similar devices is specifically made unlawful by statute. 44 A.L.R., section 3, pages 386, 388.

The legal principles stated by the trial court in instructions 2, 5, and 6 are well established and supported by the authorities cited and quoted supra. There is no merit in defendants' objections and exceptions thereto. Defendants' various motions based on the same reasons stated in exceptions to instructions were properly overruled.

Plaintiff's claim and the jury's allowance of punitive damages, under the trial court's instructions relating thereto, were not at any time or in any manner challenged by defendants in the trial court as not allowable. We therefore are not presented with the problem of whether the $10,000 award should be allowed to stand.

We express no opinion as to whether punitive damages are allowable in this type of case. If defendants' attorneys wanted that issue decided it was their duty to raise it in the trial court.

The rule is well established that we will not consider a contention not raised in the trial court. In other words we are a court of review and will not consider a contention raised for the first time in this court.

Under our law punitive damages are not allowed as a matter of right. When malice is shown or when a defendant acted with wanton and reckless disregard of the rights of others, punitive damages may be allowed as punishment to the defendant and as a deterrent to others. Although not meant to compensate a plaintiff, the result is to increase his recovery. He is the fortuitous beneficiary of such an award simply because there is no one else to receive it.

The jury's findings of fact including a finding defendants acted with malice and with wanton and reckless disregard, as required for an allowance of punitive or exemplary damages, are supported by substantial evidence. We are bound thereby.

This opinion is not to be taken or construed as authority that the allowance of punitive damages is or is not proper under circumstances such as exist here. We hold only that question of law not having been properly raised cannot in this case be resolved.

Study and careful consideration of defendants' contentions on appeal reveal no reversible error.

Affirmed.

LARSON, JUSTICE (dissenting). I respectfully dissent, first, because the majority wrongfully assumes that by installing a spring gun in the bedroom of their unoccupied house the defendants intended to shoot any intruder who attempted to enter the room. Under the record presented here, that was a fact question. Unless it is held that these property owners are liable for injury to an intruder from such a device regardless of the intent with which it is installed, liability under these pleadings must rest upon two definite issues of fact, i.e., did the defendants intend to shoot the invader, and if so, did they employ unnecessary and unreasonable force against him?

It is my feeling that the majority oversimplifies the impact of this case on the law, not only in this but other jurisdictions, and that it has not thought through all the ramifications of this holding.

There being no statutory provisions governing the right of an owner to defend his property by the use of a spring gun or other like device, or of a criminal invader to recover punitive damages when injured by such an instrumentality while breaking into the building of another, our interest and attention are directed to what should be the court determination of public policy in these matters. On both issues we are faced with a case of first impression. We should accept the task and clearly establish the law in this jurisdiction hereafter. I would hold there is no absolute liability for injury to a criminal intruder by setting up such a device on his property, and unless done with an intent to kill or seriously injure the intruder, I would absolve the owner from liability other than for negligence. I would also hold the court had no jurisdiction to allow punitive damages when the intruder was engaged in a serious criminal offense such as breaking and entering with intent to steal.

CASE QUESTIONS

1. Do you agree with the majority opinion of the court or with the dissenter?
2. Should this case have been treated as one of first impression considering the public policy issues involved?
3. Could the state legislature overrule the supreme court and change the law?
4. Is there a conflict of law involved in this case?

CONTRACTS

In the *Marvin* case, the court's decision illustrates that even oral promises may create legal obligations for the parties involved. The plaintiff in this case filed the suit in contract and did not attempt to rely on the concept of common-law marriage that is recognized in some states. Contracts must be made under conditions required by law in order to be enforced by the courts: The contracting parties must be of legal age, there must be an exchange of some consideration of value between the two parties, and the contract cannot involve a promise to do an illegal act.

Marvin v. Marvin

134 Cal. Rptr. 815, 557 P.2d 106
Supreme Court of California
December 27, 1976

TOBRINER, JUSTICE. During the past 15 years, there has been a substantial increase in the number of couples living together without marrying. Such nonmarital relationships lead to legal controversy when one partner dies or the couple separates. We take this opportunity to declare the principles which should govern distribution of property acquired in a nonmarital relationship.

We conclude that the courts should enforce express contracts between nonmarital partners except to the extent that the contract is explicitly founded on the consideration of meretricious sexual services.

In the instant case plaintiff, Michelle Marvin, and defendant, Lee Marvin, lived together for seven years without marrying; all property acquired during this period was taken in defendant's name. When plaintiff sued to enforce a contract under which she was entitled to half the property and to support payments, the trial court granted judgment on the pleadings for defendant, thus leaving him with all property accumulated by the couple during their relationship.

Plaintiff avers that in October of 1964 she and defendant "entered into an oral agreement" that while "the parties lived together they would combine their efforts and earnings and would share equally any and all property accumulated as a result of their efforts whether individual or combined." Furthermore, they agreed to "hold themselves out to the general public as husband and wife" and that "plaintiff would further render her services as a companion, homemaker, houseckeeper and cook to. . . . defendant."

Shortly thereafter plaintiff agreed to "give up her lucrative career as an entertainer and singer" in order to "devote her full time to defendant as a companion, homemaker, housekeeper and cook;" in return defendant agreed to "provide for all of plaintiff's financial support and needs for the rest of her life."

Plaintiff alleges that she lived with defendant from October of 1964 through May of 1970 and fulfilled her obligations under the agreement. During this period the parties as a result of their efforts and earnings acquired in defendant's name substantial real and personal property, including motion picture rights worth over $1 million. In May of 1970, however, defendant compelled plaintiff to leave his household. He continued to support plaintiff until November of 1971, but thereafter refused to provide further support.

On the basis of these allegations plaintiff asserts two causes of action. The first, for declaratory relief, asks the court to determine her contract and property rights; the second seeks to impose a constructive trust upon one half of the property acquired during the course of the relationship.

In *Trutalli v. Meraviglia* (1932) 215 Cal. 698, 12 P.2d 430 we established the principle that nonmarital partners may lawfully contract concerning the ownership of property acquired during the relationship. We reaffirmed this principle in *Vallera v. Vallera* (1943) 21 Cal.2d 681, 685, 134 P.2d 761, 763, stating that "If a man and woman [who are not married] live together as husband and wife under an agreement to pool their earnings and share equally in their joint accumulations, equity will protect the interests of each in such property."

In the case before us plaintiff, basing her cause of action in contract upon these precedents, maintains that the trial court erred in denying her a trial on the merits of her contention. Although that court did not specify the ground for its conclusion that plaintiff's contractual allegations stated no cause of action, defendant offers some four theories to sustain the ruling; we proceed to examine them.

Defendant first and principally relies on the contention that the alleged contract is so closely related to the supposed "immoral" character of the relationship between plaintiff and himself that the enforcement of the contract would violate public policy. He points to cases asserting that a contract between nonmarital partners is unenforceable if it is "involved in" an illicit relationship. A review of the numerous California decisions concerning contracts between nonmarital partners, however, reveals that the courts have not employed such broad and uncertain standards to strike down contracts. The decisions instead disclose a narrower and more precise standard: a contract between nonmarital partners is unenforceable only to the extent that it explicitly rests upon the immoral and illicit consideration of meretricious sexual services.

Although the past decisions hover over the issue in the somewhat wispy form of the figures of a Chagall painting, we can abstract from those decisions a clear and simple rule. The fact that a man and woman live together without marriage, and engage in a sexual relationship, does not in itself invalidate agreements between them relating to their earnings, property, or expenses. Neither is such an agreement invalid merely because the parties may have contemplated the creation or continuation of a nonmarital relationship when they entered into it. Agreements between nonmarital partners fail only to the extent that they rest upon a consideration of meretricious sexual services. Thus the rule asserted by defendant, that a contract fails if it is "involved in" or made "in contemplation" of a nonmarital relationship, cannot be reconciled with the decisions.

Defendant secondly relies upon the ground suggested by the trial court: that the 1964 contract violated public policy because it impaired the community property rights of Betty Marvin, defendant's lawful wife. Defendant points out that his earnings while living apart from his wife before rendition of the interlocutory decree were community property under 1964 statutory law and that defendant's agreement with plaintiff purported to transfer to her a half interest in that community property. But whether or not defendant's contract with plaintiff exceeded his authority as manager of the community property defendant's argument fails for the reason that an improper transfer of community property

is not void *ab initio*, but merely voidable at the instance of the aggrieved spouse.

In the present case Betty Marvin, the aggrieved spouse, had the opportunity to assert her community property rights in the divorce action. The interlocutory and final decrees in that action fix and limit her interest. Enforcement of the contract between plaintiff and defendant against property awarded to defendant by the divorce decree will not impair any right of Betty's, and thus is not on that account violative of public policy.

Defendant's third contention is noteworthy for the lack of authority advanced in its support. He contends that enforcement of the oral agreement between plaintiff and himself is barred by Civil Code section 5134, which provides that "All contracts for marriage settlements must be in writing. . . ." A marriage settlement, however, is an agreement in contemplation of marriage in which each party agrees to release or modify the property rights which would otherwise arise from the marriage. The contract at issue here does not conceivably fall within that definition, and thus is beyond the compass of section 5134.

Defendant finally argues that enforcement of the contract is barred by Civil Code section 43.5, subdivision (d), which provides that "No cause of action arises for. . . . [b]reach of a promise of marriage." This rather strained contention proceeds from the premise that a promise of marriage impliedly includes a promise to support and to pool property acquired after marriage to the conclusion that pooling and support agreements not part of or accompanied by promise of marriage are barred by the section. We conclude that section 43.5 is not reasonably susceptible to the interpretation advanced by defendant, a conclusion demonstrated by the fact that since section 43.5 was enacted in 1939, numerous cases have enforced pooling agreements between nonmarital partners, and in none did court or counsel refer to section 43.5.

In summary, we base our opinion on the principle that adults who voluntarily live together and engage in sexual relations are nonetheless as competent as any other persons to contract respecting their earnings and property rights. Of course, they cannot lawfully contract to pay for the performance of sexual services, for such a contract is, in essence, an agreement for prostitution and unlawful for that reason. But they may agree to pool their earnings and to hold all property acquired during the relationship in accord with the law governing community property; conversely they may agree that each partner's earnings and the property acquired from those earnings remain the separate property of the earning partner. So long as the agreement does not rest upon illicit meretricious consideration, the parties may order their economic affairs as they choose, and no policy precludes the courts from enforcing such agreements.

In the present instance, plaintiff alleges that the parties agreed to pool their earnings, that they contracted to share equally in all property acquired, and that defendant agreed to support plaintiff. The terms of the contract as alleged do not rest upon any unlawful consideration. We therefore conclude that the complaint furnishes a suitable basis upon which the trial court can render declaratory relief. The trial court consequently erred in granting defendant's motion for judgment on the pleadings.

CASE QUESTIONS

1. Has the court decided that the plaintiff has a valid contract in this case? Why or why not?
2. Is the court making new law in the case or merely relying on stare decisis?
3. What considerations of morality are involved in the Marvin case?
4. How is the concept of equity illustrated in the case?

Witness Statements

Witness Statement 1 **JANE CONSUMER**

This statement was given by Jane Consumer on September 10, 2011, during a deposition attended by attorneys Bill Green and Maria Farmer, and before a notary public.

1   My name is Jane Consumer. I am forty-six years old and am the wife of the
2 deceased, William P. Consumer. I am a housewife, married to the deceased for the
3 past twenty years, and mother of three children, ages 19, 15, and 7, at the time of
4 the accident that killed my husband.
5   On the evening of the accident, my husband and I were returning home
6 from shopping and dinner in Capital City, thirty miles from our home. My husband,
7 Bill, was driving our family car, a 2009 Supreme Brougham Executive. We were
8 nearly home when a rain shower began to fall. I noticed that Bill was going
9 about 65, and he slowed down to about 60 as he turned the windshield wipers
10 on. We came upon a van traveling in the right lane of the interstate highway at a
11 slower speed. Bill turned the wheel to pass the van and I heard a loud noise, like
12 something popped under the car. Bill screamed in panic, as he tried to get back into
13 the left traffic lane. "My God, the wheel won't turn!" he shouted. By this time the car
14 was going across the grassy part of the median and seemed to speed up. I could see
15 a truck in front of us on the opposite side of the interstate and I closed my eyes and
16 tried to brace myself. That's all I remember about the crash.
17   I remember an officer asking me if I could move my limbs. He may have
18 prevented me from injuring my spinal cord by keeping me calm until the ambulance
19 arrived. They put a brace on me and lifted me into the ambulance. Bill was
20 unconscious and bleeding on the driver's side. The emergency crew went back to
21 help him. It seemed like forever before they brought him back in a stretcher into the
22 ambulance with me. He never regained consciousness while the ambulance
23 attendant worked over him trying to give him blood. They did their best to save him.

continued >

24   They kept me in the hospital for two weeks. The doctors put me under
25 sedation and reset my back. When I regained consciousness, I was in traction
26 and was kept that way for a week and a half. Even after they released me from
27 the hospital, I had to go back for therapy three times a week. Luckily, everything
28 was healed.

29   The car we were driving at the time of the accident was purchased from the
30 City Auto Company on October 20, 2008. It was a 2009 model, and we took it in for
31 regular maintenance. Last winter we had some trouble with it on snow and ice. It
32 was always getting stuck, even on a slight hill, and Bill got mad when we had to get
33 someone to help us. He also noticed that the car leaned to the left when it was
34 standing on the flat surface of our driveway. He told me he had complained to the
35 service department at the City Auto Company, but they indicated that there was
36 nothing wrong with it.

37   We had driven the car for two years, and it only had 22,000 miles on it when
38 the accident occurred. Bill had received a recall letter from the factory just before
39 the accident. He planned to take it into the garage to get the needed repairs when
40 the accident took place. He received the letter on Thursday and the accident
41 occurred the next day, on September 8, 2010.

Jane Consumer

SEAL OF NOTARY PUBLIC

Witness Statement 2 **JIM TRUCKER**

This statement was given by Jim Trucker on September 11, 2011, at a deposition attended by attorneys Bill Green and Maria Farmer, and before a notary public.

1   My name is Jim Trucker. I am thirty-six years old and have been employed by
2   Big City Haulers, Inc., for the last five years. I live in Capital City, Middle State. I was
3   driving an eighteen-wheel, tractor-trailer rig from River City to Capital City on the
4   night of September 8, 2010, when an automobile driven by the deceased, William
5   P. Consumer, collided with the rear corner of my trailer.
6   I was going about 65 on Interstate 24, traveling north toward Capital City.
7   A rainstorm set in just before the accident. It was dark, about 10:30 at night, and I
8   had just come under an overpass when I saw lights coming at me from the opposite
9   side of the interstate. They were coming right at me, so I "put the pedal to the
10   metal" and sped up as much as possible to try to get past before the other vehicle
11   collided with my truck. It was the only thing I could think of to do at the time. I could
12   see the car missed my tractor, but I felt the crash that caused the rig to begin to
13   sway. I knew it had hit my trailer, so I pulled over as soon as possible. I put on my
14   hazard lights and went back to check on the wreck. I could see it was bad and that
15   the passengers needed help right away. So I got back in the cab and used my CB
16   radio to call for help.
17   Then I went to the wreck. I could see that the driver's side was collapsed,
18   and I didn't even try to open it. The passenger side was free, and I opened the door.
19   Jane Consumer was unconscious in the passenger seat. She had taken a bad crash,
20   and I didn't think I should try to move her. The highway patrol car arrived in a few
21   minutes, and I was glad to let the officer take over.
22   The police officer and I helped the ambulance emergency crew to free the
23   driver, and they took the two passengers off to the hospital. By this time it had
24   stopped raining, and I went back to check on my rig. The left rear corner of my trailer
25   was smashed and the tail gate was bent back toward the right side, but I was able to
26   move it. I recorded the license number of the vehicle that hit me, and talked with
27   the patrolman while he filled out the accident report.

Jim Trucker

SEAL OF NOTARY PUBLIC

Witness Statement 3 **GEORGE GOODCOP**

This statement was given by Patrolman George Goodcop on September 14, 2011, at a deposition attended by attorneys Bill Green and Maria Farmer, and before a notary public.

1   My name is Patrolman George Goodcop. I am thirty years old and have been
2   a highway patrolman for the past four years. I was on duty driving patrol on Inter-
3   state 24 when the accident involving the death of William P. Consumer took place
4   on September 8, 2010. I received a call from the dispatcher at about 10:40 P.M.
5   informing me of an accident about three miles from Centerville on I-24 north.
6   Since I was very close to this location, it only took me about five minutes to arrive
7   on the scene. Jim Trucker was already on the scene, and there was no immediate
8   danger to other vehicles. The wrecked passenger car was off of the highway on the
9   right side of the northbound portion of the interstate, and the trucker assured me
10   that his vehicle was well off the highway and marked with hazard lights.
11   The trucker had opened the passenger door of the crashed automobile and
12   a female passenger was strapped in a forward position, her head leaning against the
13   dash. She was regaining consciousness, and I asked her to see if she could move her
14   legs and arms. She indicated that she could and attempted to right herself in the
15   seat. This obviously caused her pain, and I cautioned her to stay in her original
16   position. Her back was more than likely injured, and I wanted the medics to remove
17   her with their equipment. I used my flashlight to try to examine the driver, but could
18   conclude very little about his condition. His face was smashed up against the win-
19   dow and he was wrapped around the steering wheel. Blood was everywhere, and I
20   knew he was in very bad condition. The driver's side of the vehicle was crushed, and
21   the driver could not be accessed through the driver's door.
22   The ambulance arrived in about ten minutes, by this time it was nearly
23   11:00. The emergency crew removed the passenger, and then we all helped to
24   pry the driver's door open to remove the driver. As I stated in my accident report,
25   the passenger was wearing her seat belt, but the driver was not wearing a seat belt.
26   The automobile involved was resting with the front facing west and was located on
27   the right far side of the interstate north bound lanes. From the condition of the
28   vehicle, it had obviously taken the impact of the crash on the driver's side.
29   After inspecting the condition of the tractor-trailer rig and the skid marks
30   across the median, it was clear that the driver of the passenger car had lost control
31   while driving south on the interstate and had proceeded across the median, col-
32   liding with the trailer of the trucker's rig on the rear corner. The motor and hood of
33   the passenger car had hit the trucker's tailgate, and the driver's side had received
34   the full impact of the corner of the trailer. I made the following sketch of the col-
35   lision in my report.

George Goodcop

SEAL OF NOTARY PUBLIC

Witness Statement 4 **MACK RACER**

This statement was given by Mack Racer on September 15, 2011, at a deposition attended by attorneys Bill Green and Maria Farmer, and before a notary public.

1   My name is Mack Racer. I'm forty years old and am self-employed as the
2 owner of Speed Shop in Centerville, Middle State. I trained as a mechanic, obtaining
3 a certificate of qualification from the Factory Motor Company in 2008. I also have
4 twenty years of experience working on Factory Motor Company vehicles as well as
5 those of other manufacturers. I have worked for several nationally famous race car
6 drivers as a mechanic and engineering consultant regarding safety features of rac-
7 ing stock cars.
8   I was asked to inspect the 2009 Supreme Brougham Executive owned by
9 William P. Consumer. It had been towed to a garage in Centerville where I examined
10 the wreckage carefully. I jacked up the vehicle and removed the suspension coils
11 from both sides of the undercarriage. The left coil spring was broken in half and was
12 obviously made of thinner metal than the coil spring removed from the right side.
13 These springs hold the passenger vehicle about six inches above the axle to ensure
14 a smooth ride. If one of them breaks at the base, as in this case, the car would drop
15 about six inches to the left. This would account for the driver's inability to right the
16 vehicle in a turn.
17   The coils that I removed are in the possession of the plaintiff, and I can attest
18 to the fact that they do not belong on the same vehicle. They were obviously made
19 for two different vehicles having different weights and suspension requirements. I
20 don't know how they got on this vehicle, but they should not have been used
21 together. Both of these coils should have been identical. Their differences would
22 account for the leaning to the left complained of by the plaintiff. I measured them,
23 and the left coil (complete) is about one inch shorter than the right coil.
24   A reasonably alert mechanic trained by the Factory Motor Company should
25 have detected the difference from a visual inspection and the vehicle's appearance,
26 since the complaint noted the leaning to the left. An inspection of the vehicle after
27 the accident indicates that it was unlikely that the left coil was damaged by the
28 impact of the collision. The stress from the impact would have been on the right
29 coil, since it would have had to absorb the impact to the left driver's side. At any
30 rate, I don't think the collision broke the coil. It must have happened before the
31 accident.

Mack Racer

SEAL OF NOTARY PUBLIC

Witness Statement 5 **SUPERIOR TESTER**

This statement was given by Superior Tester on August 6, 2011, at a deposition attended by attorneys John Gaither and Cora Smith, and before a notary public.

1   My name is Superior Tester. I am forty-six years old and have been employed
2 by the Factory Motor Company for the past eight years as a laboratory technician
3 and safety engineer. I was promoted two years ago to director of testing for the
4 company. I have a master's degree in mechanical engineering from the Massachu-
5 setts Institute of Technology.
6   In January of 2010, my lab was asked to test coils manufactured by our
7 supplier, Ace Suppliers, Inc. The Factory Motor Company production director indi-
8 cated on the work order that there had been a mix-up and these coils were
9 mounted on 250 of our 2009 Supreme Brougham Executive model autos by
10 mistake. The order required that we test the coils that were mistakenly mounted
11 on these passenger cars. We have three simulation machines that replicate the wear
12 and stress on such coils; so we set up the test on all three machines with a mistaken
13 coil and a normal coil mounted on each machine.
14   After the machines had been running for a simulation equivalent of more
15 than 200,000 miles, the coils we were testing began to break. The first coil to break
16 was one of the mistakenly mounted coils. It broke at 1,726 hours, or the equivalent
17 of 207,120 miles. The second coil to break was one of the normal coils that broke at
18 1,824 hours. Another mistaken coil broke at 1,891 hours, when we stopped our
19 testing. Our normal wear standard is 1,700, or the equivalent of 204,400 miles.
20 Since the mistaken coils met this standard, we concluded that the coils were
21 safe under normal driving conditions for the expected life of the vehicle.
22   The coils in question were about one inch shorter than the normal coil and
23 would have caused some tilting of the vehicle. The suspension coils are primarily to
24 ensure a smooth ride, and even if one broke, it would not cause the vehicle to go
25 out of control. The vehicle would be supported by the shock absorbers and would
26 not drop more than three inches. It would cause some noise and discomfort, but
27 would not cause an accident under normal driving conditions.
28   At a conference with the production director in May of 2010, we discussed
29 this problem, and he concluded that it would not be necessary to recall the vehicles
30 in question based on our lab report. Later in August of 2010, we had a second
31 conference on this subject. He told me they had been getting a number of com-
32 plaints about the appearance of the automobiles while standing on a flat surface. At
33 this time, we decided to recall them and have the coils replaced, primarily to satisfy
34 customer complaints. We did not believe these coils posed a safety hazard. We have
35 no reports of accidents in our records concerning this problem, with the exception
36 of the case in question here.

Superior Tester

SEAL OF NOTARY PUBLIC

Witness Statement 6 **JACKIE LIFESAVER**

This statement was given by Jackie Lifesaver on September 18, 2011, at a deposition attended by attorneys John Gaither and Cora Smith, and before a notary public.

1   My name is Jackie Lifesaver. I am thirty-five years old and have been
2   employed by the Rural County Emergency Squad for the past six years. I am a
3   licensed emergency medical attendant and was in charge of the emergency
4   team that assisted Mrs. Consumer and her husband on the night of the accident.
5   My assistant, Ron Helper, and I received an emergency call to a location
6   about three miles from Centerville on I-24 north at about 10:40 P.M. on September
7   8, 2010. When we arrived on the scene, the highway patrol officer was already there.
8   We were able to remove the female passenger after applying a back brace and
9   carefully placing her on the stretcher. The driver was in worse shape. His side of
10   the vehicle was crushed, and we had to use special prying equipment we carry to
11   open the door on his side. I crawled in from the opposite side across the passenger's
12   seat and tried to stop the bleeding. I got a faint pulse, but there was no way to stop
13   the bleeding. His head was smashed partly through the windshield, but his more
14   serious injuries were in the chest area.
15   He was not wearing a seat belt, and the impact of the crash had thrust him
16   against the steering column. I knew this meant internal bleeding and chest wounds.
17   An air bag or seat belts could have saved him, but neither were employed. I smelled
18   alcohol on his breath and observed an empty beer can on the floorboard next to the
19   driver's seat.
20   By this time, my assistant and the patrol officer had managed to free the
21   driver's door, and we were able to remove him from the vehicle. We set up a blood
22   transfusion before leaving for the hospital. I was driving and my assistant was
23   attending the victims in the rear of the emergency vehicle. When we arrived at
24   the hospital, the emergency doctor on duty checked the driver's vital signs and
25   could get no pulse.

Jackie Lifesaver

SEAL OF NOTARY PUBLIC

Witness Statement 7 **PROFESSOR DRIVESAFE**

This statement was given by Professor Drivesafe on August 8, 2011, at a deposition attended by attorneys John Gaither and Cora Smith, and before a notary public.

1   My name is Professor Drivesafe. I am fifty-two years old and am employed as
2 professsor of safety engineering at Lake State University. I have a master's degree
3 from Lake State University in engineering and a Ph.D. from the California Institute of
4 Technology. My particular field of expertise is in automobile safety, and I have
5 served as a consultant in numerous automobile accidents where I have been called
6 upon to assess the causes of these accidents. I have also authored several
7 professional papers on the causes of automobile accidents and safety engineering.
8   I was asked to examine the automobile involved in the accident that took
9 place on I-24 on September 8, 2010, and to assess the causes of this accident. After
10 thorough investigation of the automobile, the two coils removed from the vehicle,
11 and the scene of the crash, it is my scientific judgment that the accident was caused
12 by hydroplaning due to the rainstorm that was occurring at the time of the
13 accident.
14   The scene of the accident presents a classic example of the type of gentle
15 slope that produces the conditions for vehicle hydroplaning when there is a heavy
16 rain. That area recorded one inch of rain in less than half an hour on the night of the
17 accident. This amount of rainfall would produce enough water flowing down the
18 slope in question to raise the front wheels above the surface of the pavement. This
19 would account for the driver's inability to steer the vehicle.
20   The broken coil was most likely a result of the impact and spinning of the
21 vehicle after the crash. The vehicle struck the rear corner of the truck and was pulled
22 around by the tractor-trailer's forward motion, so that it made a complete turn,
23 ending up facing in the opposite direction from that of initial impact.
24   The Department of Transportation safety standards were not violated by
25 the coils used in the production of the vehicle in question. There are no suspension
26 coil standards imposed by federal authority. The coil suspension on this vehicle is a
27 comfort feature and not a vital engineering component. Even if the coil did break at
28 a crucial moment, the shock absorbers would have prevented it from affecting the
29 steering capabilities of the vehicle. I cannot conclude from these facts that the
30 suspension coil in question was the cause of the accident.

Professor Drivesafe

SEAL OF NOTARY PUBLIC

Witness Statement 8 **JAN INTERN**

This statement was given by Dr. Jan Intern on September 18, 2011, at a deposition attended by attorneys John Gaither and Cora Smith, and before a notary public.

1   My name is Jan Intern. I am forty-two years old and I am presently self-
2   employed in my own private practice as a physician specializing in internal
3   medicine. I graduated from Vanderbilt Medical School in 2009 and was employed
4   as emergency intern at Mid-State Hospital in Centerville from October 1, 2009, to
5   November 10, 2010.
6   On the evening of September 8, 2010, I was serving as emergency medical
7   physician at Mid-State Hospital. We received a call from the medics at about 11:15
8   P.M. indicating that two severely injured patients were in route to the hospital. When
9   they arrived at about 11:25 P.M., I examined the two patients as quickly as possible.
10   The male patient was the most severely injured and was suffering from internal
11   bleeding caused by severe chest wounds. We could not get a pulse and attempted
12   to revive his heart function. This procedure was unsuccessful, and I concluded that
13   any further attempt to revive him would be futile. The female patient suffered
14   severe back injury but had been carefully handled by the medics and was properly
15   transported, preventing further injury. We stabilized her condition and x-rayed the
16   extent of the damage to the spine.
17   Later, I reexamined the body of the male patient to determine the cause of
18   death and to file a death certificate. X-rays revealed that the impact to his chest had
19   crushed his heart and severed internal arteries, causing massive bleeding that filled
20   the chest cavity. We could have saved him if he had been wearing a seat belt or if
21   the car had been equipped with a driver's side air bag. This kind of injury could only
22   have been caused by impact against the steering wheel. His head injuries were
23   minor and would not have caused death.
24   I did smell alcohol on his breath, so I took some blood samples, but because
25   he had been given two pints of whole blood by the medics, the sample would be of
26   no value in determining how much alcohol he had consumed.

Jan Intern

SEAL OF NOTARY PUBLIC

Glossary

ABA Model Rules of Professional Conduct   Model statements of ethical standards drafted by the American Bar Association.

Abandonment   Recognized ground for divorce when a spouse leaves the family for a certain period of time.

Accessory after the fact   One who, knowing a felony was committed by another, receives, relieves, comforts, or assists the felon.

Accomplice   One who knowingly, voluntarily, and with common intent unites with the principal offender in the commission of a crime.

Actual (or express) malice   Acting with knowing or deliberate falsity or reckless disregard of the truth.

Actus reus   A wrongful act or deed that renders the actor criminally liable if combined with mens rea.

Administrative courts   Those courts created under the grant of legislative authority in Article I, Section 8, of the U.S. Constitution. They perform administrative and quasi-legislative roles as well as serve as quasi-judicial bodies.

Administrative due process   Notice, fair hearing, and conformity with established rules are minimal requirements of due process.

Administrative law judge (ALJ)   The official who presides at an administrative trial-type hearing to resolve a dispute between a government agency and someone affected by a decision.

Administrative Procedures Act   Laws enacted by federal and many state jurisdictions governing practices and procedures before administrative agencies.

Adoption   Legal process in which persons become the legal parents or guardians of a child who is not their birth child.

Affidavit   Written statement of facts made voluntarily under oath.

Affirmative action   Policies designed to create greater diversity for historically underrepresented groups.

Affirmative defense   In pleading it raises new matter that constitutes a defense. It must be raised in the answer in response to the pleading (Rule 8(c), FRCP).

Age Discrimination in Employment Act of 1967 (ADEA):   Provides that employers may not discharge or otherwise discriminate against employees who are 40 years of age or older.

Agency adoptions   Either a public or private adoption that is licensed by the state.

Aggravating circumstances   Circumstances attending the commission of a crime that increase defendant's guilt or add to injurious consequences of the crime.

Alimony   Support of one spouse by the other while the parties are going through divorce proceedings or for a defined period.

American Bar Association (ABA)   Voluntary national association of lawyers and judges that represents the legal profession in the United States.

American Law Reports (A.L.R.)   Contain detailed overview articles called annotations that cite cases all across the United States.

Americans with Disabilities Act of 1990 (ADA)   Prohibits discrimination against qualified individuals with a disability in the workplace.

Amicus curiae ("friend of the court")   A person with strong interest in or views on the subject matter of an action may petition the court for permission to file a brief.

Analogistic form of reasoning   By analogy; analysis of comparative likeness and differences.

Annotated codes   Statutory law placed topically into the official code or collection of statutory law.

Answer   Formal written statement setting forth the grounds of defense.

Appeal   Resort to appellate court to review the decision of an inferior court.

Appellant   Party bringing the appeal, which has the burden of proof on appeal.

Appellate brief   Written argument that must be filed on appeal by the party bringing the appeal.

Appellate courts   Courts that do not conduct fact-finding procedures as trial courts do. They consider only questions of law in dispute and exercise review over trial courts performing the functions of error correction and law development. There are both intermediate appellate courts and courts of last resort.

Appellee   Party against whom the appeal is filed. It may have been either the plaintiff or the defendant in the trial court.

Appropriation or misappropriation   Using another's name, likeness, or personality for advertising, a commercial purpose, or similar use without the permission of the person.

Arbitration   In which parties agree in advance to abide by the decision of a third party to avoid litigation.

Armed robbery   Aggravated robbery; the taking of property by use of force while armed with a dangerous weapon.

Arraignment: Criminal procedural stage where defendant is required to enter a plea.

Arrearages   Significant amounts of child support owed to the custodial parent by the noncustodial parent.

Arrest   To deprive a person of liberty by legal authority.

Arrest of judgment   The act of staying a judgment or refusing to render judgment in an action at law and in criminal cases after the verdict for some matter in error, such as the court not having jurisdiction.

Arrest warrant   A written order made on behalf of the state, based on a complaint issued pursuant to statute or court rule, commanding that the person be brought before a magistrate.

Assault   Intentional causing of an apprehension or appretiation of harmful contact.

Attorneys' conference   Meeting of lawyers for both sides in a civil legal action to discuss the results of the discovery process and reach settlement or prepare for trial.

Bail   To procure release of one charged with an offense by ensuring his future attendance in court and compelling him to remain within jurisdiction of the court.

Bailiff   A court officer who has charge of keeping order in the court, custody of the jury, and prisoners while in the court.

Bailment   A delivery of goods or personal property by one person to another in trust for the execution of a special service beneficial either to the *bailor* or to the *bailee* or both. Includes express or implied contractual obligation.

Bar examination   A test of proficiency required to obtain license to practice law, give legal advice, and represent clients.

Battery   Consummation of an unlawful assault by making contact with the other person or the causing of a harmful or offensive contact upon another. (You can have a battery without an assault or contact without apprehension.)

Bench trial   Trial conducted without a jury in which the judge decides issues of both fact and law in dispute.

Best evidence rule   Requires primary evidence as opposed to secondary evidence, in other words, the best evidence available.

Best interest of the child   A flexible, multifactor test to determine custody for the parties' children.

Bifurcated trial process   Trial of issues, such as guilt and punishment, or guilt and sanity, separately in criminal trial.

Bigamy   Having multiple spouses, which is prohibited in all U.S. jurisdictions.

Breach of duty of care   Failure on the part of the tortfeasor to adhere to a reasonable standard of care.

Burden of proof   Obligation of a party to establish by evidence a requisite degree of belief concerning a fact in the mind of the court.

Capital punishment   Punishment by death.

Case of first impression   A dispute involving a new factual situation never previously before the courts that adds new precedent when decided.

Cause of action   The fact or facts that give a person a right to judicial relief.

Certification   A request from a U.S. court of appeals asking the Supreme Court for instructions.

Challenges for cause   Requests from parties to the judge to remove potential jurors for specified reasons.

Charge of discrimination   Complaint filed with EEOC that an employee has suffered some type of discrimination in the workplace.

Charge to the jury   Final address by the judge to the jury before the verdict; instructs the jury on the rules of law it must follow.

Child custody   Legal process of determining what parent or legal guardian assumes custody over a minor.

Child support   Money provided by the noncustodial parent to the custodial parent to provide economic help in that support.

Citation   Shorthand reference to legal authority.

Civil union   Relationship between two persons providing many of the benefits of marriage (recognized in a few states).

Class action lawsuit   Legal action involving like-situated parties who may collectively sue or be sued.

Closing arguments   Opposing lawyers' summaries of the evidence they think has been established or refutations of opposing evidence.

Collective bargaining agreement (CBA)   Contract between management and employee's union that regulates terms and conditions of employment.

Commissions   Term often used in regard to state quasi-judicial bodies; also called boards

Common-law marriage   Some states recognize that couples living together for a period of years (usually seven) and that hold themselves out as married are regarded as having marriage rights and duties.

Common law   The body of judge-made law that has no source other than judicial decisions. It originated in medieval England.

Community-based programs   Correctional programs that provide rehabilitation or punishment supervision at the community level rather than in prison.

Comparative negligence   Measures in terms of percentages of fault on each side so that the trier of fact compares the negligence of the plaintiff and defendant to determine the appropriate degree of fault.

Compensatory damages or actual damages   Those damages that compensate the plaintiff for the harm suffered as a result of the defendant's negligent conduct, as opposed to punitive damages.

Complaint   Initial pleading by which a legal action is commenced.

Conciliation   In which a third party proposes compromise solutions to a dispute.

Concurrent jurisdiction   Areas where both state and federal courts have jurisdiction to hear the same types of disputes.

Concurrent powers   Shared powers, or those powers given to the national government but *not* denied to the states (i.e., taxing power, creation of courts, laws, and regulations to promote public health and safety are a few of these shared powers).

Concurrent sentence   When the sentences are served simultaneously (the person must serve the longest sentence).

Conflict of interest   Ethical conflict involving violation of trust in matters of private interest and gain. A lawyer may not serve two clients with opposing interests.

Conflict of laws   When different sources of law come into conflict with each other, the courts must decide which law prevails. The general principle of determination is that the more fundamental law prevails. (See *Restatement of the Law.*)

Consecutive sentence   When one sentence must follow the other.

Consolidation of actions   Act of uniting several actions into one trial and judgment, by order of a court, where all actions are between the same parties pending in the same court.

Contingency fee contract   Agreement to pay for attorney services contingent on recovery in damage suit.

Continuance   Postponement of a session, hearing, trial, or other proceeding to a subsequent day or time.

Contract   The area of law involving agreements between two or more parties that create, modify, or destroy a legal relationship.

Contract action   Legal action to recover damages or to enforce legal obligations resulting from a contract.

Contributory negligence Act or omission amounting to lack of ordinary care on the part of the complaining party that, along with defendant's negligence, is the proximate cause of injury.

Control subsystem Refers to the police function of maintaining order and protecting the public safety.

Conversion When one receives possession of personal property belonging to another and permanently deprives the owner of the rightful use of the property.

Copyright Exclusive statutory rights to exercise control over copying and other exploitation of works for a specific period of time.

Corpus delicti The body or substance of the crime, which ordinarily includes two basic elements: *actus reus* and *mens rea*.

Court reporter A person who transcribes by shorthand or stenographically takes down testimony during court proceedings.

Courts of claims Courts that are authorized to handle claims against state and federal authorities where statutory authority allows such actions.

Covenant An agreement, convention, or promise of two or more parties, by deed in writing, signed, and delivered, by which either of the parties pledges himself or herself to do something or not do something or stipulates as the truth of certain facts concerning the estate.

Covenant marriage A couple freely enters into authorized premarital counseling and agrees that grounds for divorce will be more limiting for them.

Criminal discovery Differs from civil discovery in that it is more restrictive; depositions are taken only under unusual circumstances, and defendant does not have to testify.

Cross-examination Questioning done by opposing counsel of the party who called the witness.

Cruel and unusual punishment Prohibited by the Eighth Amendment to the U.S. Constitution.

Death penalty for rape Prohibited as cruel and unusual punishment by court decision when the victim is not killed.

Defamation Communication of a false statement of fact that harms someone's reputation.

Delegated powers Those powers given to the national government in Article I, Section 8, of the U.S. Constitution (and in several amendments).

Deposition Testimony of a witness taken outside of court, where both parties may question the witness and a transcript of the statement is made.

Descriptive word indexes Indexes that enable a researcher to find the appropriate terms used by the publication.

Dicta (or obiter dicta) Statements in opinions that go beyond the facts and specific legal issues before the court. Generalizations that may not accurately reflect the narrow kernel of law decided in the case.

Digests The entire body of published case law is indexed in these publications.

Direct examination Initial questioning by the attorney who calls the witness.

Directed verdict When the party with the burden of proof has failed to present a prima facie case for jury consideration, the trial judge may enter a verdict as a matter of law.

Discovery The legal process in which each party to a lawsuit has access to the court's power to compel testimony and factual materials relevant to the case (FRCP Rules 26-37).

Disparate impact claims Apparently neutral employment practices that have an adverse impact on a particular group of individuals based on race or sex.

Disparate treatment When an employer intentionally treats an employee substantially worse than other similarly situated employees not in the protected class or category.

Diversity jurisdiction Civil legal actions involving disputes between citizens of different states where the sum in question is greater than $75,000.

Divorce Process of formally ending a marriage.

Divorce decree The formal legal document in which a marriage is dissolved and the parties' legal responsibilities are explained.

Docket List of important acts done in court in the process of each case; sometimes used to refer to the calendar of cases set to be tried in a specific term.

Double jeopardy Fifth Amendment prohibition against a second prosecution for the same offense after a first trial.

Due care That degree of care that persons of ordinary prudence would exercise under similar circumstances with respect to their own property or the property of others placed in their custody.

Due notification To be informed of the action taken against an individual, corporation, or agency.

Duty of good faith and fair dealing Courts in a few states apply an exception to the employment-at-will doctrine based on this standard of good faith, but most states do not allow this exception.

Easement A right to use over the property of another, including rights of way, rights concerning flowing waters, and other interests.

Eminent domain The power to take private property for public use by a government entity; authorized to exercise functions of a public character.

Employee handbooks or manuals Documents that may create a legally binding contract if the employer agrees to be bound by its provisions.

Employee Polygraph Protection Act of 1988 Places restrictions on employer's use of lie detector tests on employees but allows some testing when employer is engaged in ongoing investigation of theft.

Employment-at-will doctrine Either the employer or the employee can terminate the employment relationship at will.

Enabling act Statutory authority defining the functions and powers of governmental agencies.

Equal Employment Opportunity Commission (EEOC) The federal agency that enforces Title VII and other antidiscrimination laws.

Equity Refers to a remedy seeking a specific performance order of the court such as an injunction or cease and desist order.

Erie doctrine Federal practice of civil diversity cases applying the substantive law in the state where the case is filed.

Estate The degree, quantity, nature, and extent of interest a person has in real and personal property.

Estate in fee simple Maximum real property rights to which an owner is entitled, including all rights to sell, transfer, and pass on to heirs.

Estoppel Legal procedure barring a variety of evidence, testimony, or legal actions.

Ethical standards Professional standards, usually set by state bar associations, that are often legally binding and the violation of which can result in suspension or loss of license to practice law.

Ex parte By or for one party; done for, in behalf of, or on the application of one party only.

Exclusive jurisdiction Areas of federal court jurisdiction that are denied to the states.

Exclusive national powers Those powers given to the national government but denied to the states (e.g., foreign policy, coining money, and regulation of interstate and foreign commerce).

Exculpatory evidence That which tends to indicate defendant's innocence or mitigate defendant's criminality.

Exhaust administrative remedies Courts must be satisfied that an individual seeking court action has first pursued all available administrative remedies.

Exigent circumstances Presence of emergency-like circumstances when the situation makes this course of action imperative, for example, when there is a "pat-down" for concealed weapons and illegal drugs are found.

Expert witness One who has specialized knowledge in a particular field, obtained from either education or personal experience, that qualifies the person to answer opinion questions.

Fact pleading Common-law emphasis on detail in pleadings that was rigid and cumbersome.

Fair hearing Opportunity to be heard. Where authority is fairly exercised consistent with fundamental principles of justice; to present evidence, cross-examine, and have findings supported by evidence.

Fair use Defense for the reproduction of particular works such as criticism, news reporting, teaching, scholarship, and research.

False imprisonment Unjustifiable intentional confinement of another against his or her will.

Fault divorce Petition for divorce alleging fault on a spouse.

Federal district courts The basic trial courts in the federal system.

Federal question jurisdiction The basic jurisdiction of the federal courts to hear and decide all cases in law and equity arising under the U.S. Constitution, the laws of the United States, and treaties.

Federal Rules of Civil Procedure (FRCP) Detailed rules of federal civil procedure that must be followed in federal court litigation. Most states have similar statutory rules.

Federalism Divided sovereignty, or division of authority of government between the national and state governments.

Felony More serious than misdemeanor involving imprisonment for more than one year in most jurisdictions.

Final judgment Action of the trial court concluding the trial process and ending the litigation on the merits, where nothing more remains to do but to execute the judgment.

Finder of lost property One who has good title against everyone except the true owner. The finder has a duty to make reasonable efforts to locate the true owner.

First degree murder Premeditated and intentional killing of another.

Fixture An object in the nature of personal property that has been so annexed to the realty that it is regarded as a part of the land.

Form books Sources that provide model forms in various legal fields such as *American Jurisprudence Legal Forms* (or *AmJur Legal Forms*).

Fraud Intentional false representation, which is a serious crime.

General jurisdiction Authority to decide questions of both state and federal law in the course of litigation and not limited to a restricted list of delegated authority. The state courts are restricted only by the very narrow range of cases that fall within the exclusive jurisdiction of the federal courts.

Gifts A voluntary transfer of property to another made gratuitously and without consideration, requiring capacity, intention, and completed delivery by donor and acceptance by donee.

Good Samaritan statute Law that generally provides some protection for rescuers who attempt to help people in harm except for instances of extreme negligence.

Grand jury Body of citizens whose duty it is to determine whether probable cause exists in a criminal case to warrant an indictment, as opposed to a petit (or trial) jury.

Grandparent visitation statutes Many states have statutes that recognize grandparent visitation rights, but parents have the ultimate power to determine the level of visitation by nonparents.

Guilty plea Formal admission in court as to guilt of a crime.

Habeas corpus (Latin for "you have the body") This is the most common form of the habeas corpus writ, the purpose of which is to test the legality of the detention or imprisonment; not whether the accused is guilty or innocent. This writ is guaranteed by the U.S. Constitution Article I, Section 9, and by state constitutions.

Habeas corpus petition A writ of habeas corpus as a postconviction remedy that extends to all constitutional challenges.

Headnotes The main points of law found in the body of the judicial opinion.

Hearsay rule Testimony in court of a statement made out of court, offered to show the truth of matters asserted, is not permitted.

Holding Legal precedent drawn from the opinion of the court on a specific legal question.

Hostile workplace environment claims Situations in which an employee has to endure severe and pervasive sexual harassment that negatively impacts the employee's working environment.

Incest Marrying a family member who is too closely related in blood line.

Inchoate crimes Incipient crimes such as attempts, solicitation, and conspiracy to commit crimes.

Information An accusation in writing made by a public prosecutor without the intervention of a grand jury where the accused may demand a preliminary hearing.

Information process Accusation by public prosecutor made in open court before a magistrate in a preliminary hearing where the accused may defend himself or herself, as opposed to grand jury indictment.

Inheritance Property that is distributed according to a will or by the court intestate.

Initial appearance   Where a magistrate determines probable cause after arrest, advises defendant of charges, informs defendant of rights, and decides on bail.

Insanity defense   The defense is considered in the trial and is the same as not guilty, but sanity must be proved at trial before it becomes effective as a verdict. The prosecutor must be informed of the intent to use this defense before trial.

Intentional torts   Tortfeasor intends a certain result or acts with substantial certainty that his or her conduct will result in harm.

Interlocutory appeal   From interlocutory (pre-liminary) orders of a trial court before a trial takes place.

Intermediate scrutiny   A government regulation must advance a substantial government interest.

International law   The law of nations that consists of customary practices, regarded by them as legally binding, and treaty obligations.

Interrogatories   Written questions about the case submitted by one party to the other party.

Invitee   Person who enters another's property by invitation, expressed or implied, or in connection with business invitation where there is benefit to the owner.

Irreconcilable differences   When parties agree that the marriage has broken down and they cannot live in harmony.

Jailhouse lawyer   Inmate of a penal institution who spends his or her time reading the law and giving legal assistance and advice to inmates.

Jim Crow laws   Laws that segregate the races.

Joinder of offenses   When two or more persons are joined in the same indictment, if they are charged with the same crimes and in the same jurisdiction.

Joint custody   The parents share in legal custody of the child.

Judge's role   One of impartiality and neutrality toward the parties.

Judgment   The official decision of the court upon the respective rights and claims of the parties.

Judgment as a matter of law   The judge overrules the jury verdict, in whole or in part, and enters a judgment as a matter of law (FRCP). State courts may still use the older term judgment n.o.v.

Judicial review   The power of the courts to hold acts of all branches and levels of government unconstitutional, null and void, and non-enforceable.

Jurisprudence   Philosophy or study of law.

Jury trial   Trial of issues of fact in dispute by an impartial and qualified jury.

Just-cause clause   An employee may only be terminated for good reason.

Justiciable controversy   A controversy that the court may properly entertain. It must be between bona fide adversaries and assert a claim of legal right by one who has a personal interest at stake.

Juvenile justice systems   Juvenile courts and corrections facilities having special jurisdiction, of a paternal nature, over delinquent, dependent, and neglected children.

KeyCiting   Validating legal case authority by the Westlaw process.

Law review or law journal articles   Secondary sources that provide researchers with citations to primary authority.

Law School Admission Test (LSAT)   A test almost universally used in the United States as a criterion for admission to law schools; an aptitude test of logic and critical thinking.

Law-related education   Programs developed to promote integration of legal concepts into the K-12 curriculum.

Lawyer's role   Acts to advocate for the client, who is entitled to vigorous and competent representation.

Leading questions   Questions framed in such a way that they instruct the witness how to answer or put words into the witness's mouth to be echoed back.

Leasehold   An estate in *realty* held under lease. Rights and privileges that the lessor of property has by virtue of the nature of his or her lease.

Legal assistant   A person with legal skills who works under the supervision of a lawyer.

Legal encyclopedias   Secondary sources that provide short overviews on legal topics, such as *Corpus Juris Secundum* (C.J.S.) and *American Jurisprudence* (AmJur).

Legal representation and advice Only a lawyer admitted to the bar may represent a person in court, advise a client about legal rights and duties, and especially advise the proper course of action as it relates to the law.

Legal research Answering questions about application of legal rules governing particular situations.

Legislative process The law-making process defined in the U.S. Constitution, which has become similar in most of the states.

Legitimate nondiscriminatory reason A legally acceptable employer defense where there is evidence of discharge for reasonable cause.

Lesser included offenses: Composed of some but not all of the elements of the greater crime.

LEXIS and Westlaw Subscription-based online legal research databases.

License A temporary grant of authority, such as when a landowner grants permission to hunt or fish on the land.

Limited jurisdiction Authority to decide subject matter disputes in a limited number of types of cases.

Litigation A general term used to refer to matters brought before a court of law.

Magistrates Lower court judicial authorities, including justices of the peace.

Malpractice Negligence committed by professionals.

Mandatory authority Legal precedent that a court must follow.

Marital property Generally property acquired during the course of a party's marriage subject to equitable division by the court.

Marriage Civil contract between a man and a woman (in most jurisdictions) to live together and share their lives.

Material change in circumstances Usually means that the noncustodial parent must show that the custodial parent has committed some wrongdoing or has put the child at risk.

Mediation In which a third party assists in the negotiation of a dispute.

Mens rea A guilty mind or criminal intent; guilty knowledge and willfulness.

Miranda warnings Requirement that the accused be informed of basic rights to ensure admissibility of evidence obtained by confessions.

Misdemeanor Offenses lower than felonies, generally punishable by fine or imprisonment in a facility other than a penitentiary.

Mislaid property Items of value that are intentionally left in a place and later forgotten. Mislaid property belongs to the owner of the premises where it is located if unclaimed by the true owner.

Missouri Plan (or merit plan) Appointment of judges by the governor from a list of qualified applicants. The appointee must be accepted by the voters and is subject to periodic retention approval by the voters.

Mitigating circumstances That which reduces the degree or moral culpability but does not justify or excuse the offense in question.

Motion for a new trial A request that the judge set aside the judgment and order a new trial on the basis that the trial was improper or unfair due to specified prejudicial errors that occurred (Tenn. R. Crim. P., Rule 59.02).

Motion for judgment of acquittal Cannot result in a new trial because that would involve double jeopardy.

Motion to dismiss A motion that is generally filed before trial to attack the action on the basis of insufficiency of the pleading, of process, venue, etc. (Rule12(b), FRCP).

Motion to supress (*in limine*) A written motion that is usually made before or after the beginning of the trial for a protective order against prejudicial questions and statements.

Natural language search Search using natural language terms to find judicial opinions.

Negligence Failure to exercise due care or acting carelessly or recklessly in a way that causes harm to others.

Negligence per se The unexcused violation of a law or regulation by a defendant that leads to harm suffered by the victim.

No-fault divorce Petition for divorce without alleging fault, such as irreconcilable differences.

Nolle prosequi A formal entry on the record by the prosecuting officer declaring that the officer will not prosecute the case further.

Not guilty plea Plea entered by the accused at arraignment that indicates desire to contest the charge at trial.

Notice pleading   Simplified rules of modern pleading that emphasize notification and response and leave the narrowing of facts to discovery.

Nuisance   Activity that arises from unreasonable, unwarranted, or unlawful use of a person's own property, working obstruction, or injury to the right of another, or to the public producing such material annoyance, inconvenience, and discomfort that the law will presume resulting damage.

Ombudsman   An official to whom people may come with grievances connected with the government. The ombudsman stands between, and represents, the citizen before the government.

On point   Directly related to the legal question at issue in the case and analogous with the basic facts of the case.

Opening statements   Opposing lawyers' formulations of the nature of the case and anticipated proof to be presented.

Paralegal   A person formally trained and experienced as a legal assistant to lawyers or an administrative agency.

Paralegal administrator   A person employed by large law firms for skills in recruitment, training, and management of office paralegals.

Parens patriae **(parent of the country)**   Refers traditionally to the role of the state as sovereign and guardian of persons under legal disability.

Patent   An exclusive right granted to anyone who invents a new, useful, and nonobvious process, machine, article of manufacture, or composition of matter, or any new and useful improvement thereof, and claims that right in a formal patent application.

Paternity   When the actual father of the child is established, then the court can award child support.

Pendent jurisdiction   Discretionary authority allowing an exclusive state matter to be decided in federal courts.

Per curiam   By the court; a phrase used to distinguish an opinion of the whole court from an opinion written by any one judge.

Peremptory challenges   In jury selection, the parties may be given a limited number of challenges to eliminate jurors without cause.

Permanent alimony   A party will receive alimony for the rest of that person's life.

Personalty   Personal property; movable property; chattels. Things that are movable and not attached to land or real property interests. Also includes intangible property, such as intellectual property interests, money, and other paper substitutes for ownership rights.

Persuasive authority   Legal authority that a court may, but does not have to, follow.

Pinpoint citation   A point of law found on a specific page of a case.

Plea bargaining   Process whereby the accused and the prosecutor in a criminal case work out a mutually satisfactory disposition of the case subject to court approval.

Pocket part   The method of validation of case law authority when using the traditional book method whereby annual paper inserts are found in the back of the volume used.

Political question doctrine   In court practice, matters left to the discretionary authority of the political branches of government and therefore non-justiciable.

Pregnancy Discrimination Act of 1978 (PDA)   Prohibits employers from not hiring or firing employees because they are pregnant.

Prejudicial error   One that affects the final results of the trial, as opposed to harmless error.

Preliminary hearing   Critical stage in pretrial process where the accused has a right to present evidence. Defendant has right to counsel.

Prenuptial agreements   Enforceable contracts that the parties enter into to protect their individual assets before marriage.

Present value   Adjustment to account for investment earnings of a specific sum of money over time.

Pretext stage   When burden of proof shifts back to the plaintiff after employer asserts a legitimate nondiscriminatory reason.

Pretrial lineup   A postindictment arrest or lineup is a "critical stage" in a criminal proceeding, so the accused has a constitutional right to have counsel present.

Preventative law   The practice of preventing legal actions against clients. Since a major function of the practice of law is to give legal advice, competent legal advice prevents adverse legal action against the client.

Prima facie case   A case that will prevail until contradicted and overcome by other evidence.

Private adoptions   The parties themselves handle the adoption process.

Probable cause   Reasonable cause requiring more than mere suspicion; some evidence and reasonable grounds for belief in the existence of facts warranting the complaint.

Probate   The court procedure by which a will is proved. The term includes all matters and proceedings concerning administration of estates of deceased persons.

Procedural due process   Protection of notice and hearing to contest adverse action by a governmental agency pursuant to a fair process or procedure.

Procedural law   Rules that restrict governmental authorities in administering the substantive law (e.g., fair trial, jury procedure in criminal cases, fair hearing in administrative cases).

Products liability   Legal liability of manufacturers and sellers to compensate buyers, users, and even bystanders for damages or injuries suffered because of defects in goods purchased.

Prosecution   A criminal legal action filed by a designated government official known as a prosecutor.

Prosecutor   One who, in the name of the government, prosecutes another for a crime.

Proximate (or legal) cause   That which, in a natural and continuous sequence, unbroken by any superseding cause, produces injury and without which the result would not have occurred.

Public defender   Lawyer employed by a government agency assigned to defend indigents in criminal cases.

Punitive damages   Those damages designed to punish the tortfeasor as opposed to compensate the plaintiff.

Quasi-legislative powers   Delegated rule-making authority.

Quid pro quo claims   When an employer or supervisor engages in conduct seeking sexual favors in exchange for job benefits.

Ratio decendendi   The grounds for or reasoning behind the decision; the point in the case that determines the judgment.

Rational basis   Government must only show that it has a legitimate reason that is not arbitrary.

Real estate transaction   Conveyances of title to real property by sale that must be in writing under the Statute of Frauds. Such transactions usually involve the services of a lawyer, broker, mortgagor, financier, and others who assist in the transaction process.

Realty   Brief term for real property or real estate; also anything that partakes of the nature of real property, including land and anything fixed to the land as well as interests attached to the land. Also includes easements and tenant rights.

Reasonable accommodation   Employers must offer such accommodation to an employee who is a qualified individual with a disability unless granting such an accommodation would work an undue hardship.

Regulatory agency   An agency or commission that has been delegated rule-making authority by an act of law.

Rehabilitative alimony   Form of financial support for a set period of time after divorce.

Replevin   An equitable remedy that results only in the return of the property or a specific performance order.

Request to produce   Discovery method used to secure relevant documents or material evidence.

Res ipsa loquitur   Common law principle that the defendant's negligence can be inferred through circumstantial evidence.

Res judicata   Finally decided; an action that is conclusive with regard to the same issues and parties.

Reservation-of-rights clause   Gives employers discretion to modify the terms and conditions in the handbook.

Respondeat superior   Legal doctrine that holds the employer (master) is responsible for the actions of employees performed within the course of their employment.

Restatements of the Law   Scholarly treatises that restate the common law in a form that expresses clearly the basic concepts of that body of law. They are authored by panels of judges, professors, and leading attorneys in different areas of law.

Right of appeal   There is no absolute right of appeal. There is a right to appeal a decision that is limited to the parties who are adversely affected by a lower court decision, and there must be a case or controversy at the time of review.

Right to sue letter   EEOC informs the individual of the right to sue and must file suit in court within 90 days.

Rule making   The process of developing detailed rules or regulations having the force of law and issued by executive authority.

Rules of criminal procedure   Rules of criminal procedure in each state. Many states have adopted similar rules that track the federal rules.

Rules of evidence   Detailed rules that govern the admissibility of evidence at trials and hearings.

Satisfaction of judgment   Payment of the court award for damages.

Search warrant   Written order issued by judicial authority directing law enforcement officers to search and seize any property that constitutes evidence of a crime.

Second degree murder   Knowingly killing of another person.

Secondary authority   Legal materials that help to explain, clarify, or inform about the law, but are not law.

Selective incorporation doctrine   Combines the fundamental rights concept with selected provisions of the federal Bill of Rights to define criminal due process of law required in the Fourteenth Amendment.

Selective prosecution   Allegation that the government has selectively singled out a particular group for criminal prosecution.

Sentencing grid   Modern sentencing plan that restricts judicial sentencing by classification of offenses and provides a narrow range of sentencing guidelines.

Separate but equal doctrine   Early Court reasoning that as long as each race had substantially equal facilities there was no violation of the Equal Protection Clause.

Separate property   Belonging to the individual spouse and does not have to be divided in the divorce.

Separation of powers   The division of authority within a governmental structure to prevent abuse of power by a system of checks and balances between the legislative, executive, and judicial branches.

Sequester   To separate or isolate. To sequester jurors is to isolate them from the public during the course of their deliberations.

Service of process   Reasonable notice to the defendant of legal proceedings to afford the defendant an opportunity to appear and be heard.

Sexual harassment   Discrimination in the form of severe and pervasive harassment based on sex.

Shepardizing   Validating legal case authority by the LEXIS process.

Small claims courts   A special court (sometimes called "conciliation court") that provides expeditious, informal, and inexpensive adjudication.

Socratic method   Typical method of teaching in law schools that involves engaging students in direct questioning and relies on uncertainty about answers to develop critical thinking skills.

Sole custody   One parent has legal custody of the child.

Sovereign immunity   Doctrine precludes litigant from asserting an otherwise meritorious cause of action against a sovereign or a party with sovereign attributes unless the sovereign consents to the suit.

Sovereignty   Supreme and independent political authority of the nation-state within its own territory.

Specialized federal courts   Created by Congress under authority granted in Article I as opposed to Article III of the Constitution. They often possess administrative and quasi-legislative as well as judicial duties.

Speedy trial   Guaranteed in the Sixth Amendment and interpreted to mean "without unreasonable delay." As applied to the states, it does not necessarily have fixed time elements.

Speedy Trial Act in 1974:   Federal Statute requiring a fixed time rule in federal criminal prosecutions of 100 days.

Standard elements of an enforceable contract   Offer and acceptance, competent parties, agreement, consideration, and not in violation of law or public policy.

Standing to sue Requirement that is satisfied if plaintiff has a legally protected and tangible interest in the litigation.

Standing to sue doctrine A jurisdictional requirement that the person bringing suit must have a personal stake in the litigation.

Stare decisis The doctrine of following judicial precedent.

Statute of Frauds Provides for certain contracts to be in writing, which in modern times has been enacted in some form by every jurisdiction.

Statute of limitations Statutes that prescribe the periods within which actions may be brought on certain claims or within which certain rights may be enforced.

Statutory law Legislative enactments, written sources of law in the form of statutes.

Stipulation Agreement, admission, or confession made in a judicial proceeding by the parties or their attorneys.

Stop and frisk The temporary seizure and patdown search of a person who behaves suspiciously and appears to be armed.

Strict liability Concept applied by the courts in product liability cases in which a seller or manufacturer is liable for any and all defective or hazardous products that are the cause of injury or damage.

Strict scrutiny Requires that the government show that its policy or regulation advances a compelling or extremely strong interest in a very narrowly tailored manner.

Subpoena A command by a judge to appear at a certain time and place to give testimony on a certain matter.

Subpoena duces tecum Adds to the personal subpoena a command that the person bring along relevant documents or materials in their possession.

Substantive due process Term used to describe the power of the courts to hold acts of the legislative authority non-enforceable when in violation of constitutional powers granted to the legislature.

Substantive law Rules of law that restrict individual behavior (e.g., crimes and torts).

Summary judgment A dispositive motion filed by a party that argues the judge should dismiss the case before trial because there are no genuine issues of material fact and the moving party is entitled to prevail as a matter of law.

Summons Instrument used as a means of acquiring jurisdiction over a party and to commence a civil action.

Supervised visitation A person may have visitation, but it must be supervised by someone appointed by the court to ensure the child's safety.

Supremacy clause Defines the U.S. Constitution, acts of Congress, and all treaties as the supreme law of the land, making them superior to all other forms of law (Art. VI, para. 2).

Suspect class A class that historically has been saddled with inequities or injustices.

Syllogism The full logical form of a single argument in deductive logic.

Tenant One who has minimal property rights, whereas an owner has maximal property rights.

Termination clause Provision in contract for termination of the employee.

Terms and connectors search Search using certain user-supplied words that should be found in the judicial opinions.

Title VII of the Civil Rights Act of 1964 Makes it unlawful to discriminate against employees on the basis of race, color, religion, sex, or national origin.

Tort law The area of civil law involving personal injury or property damages, excluding contracts.

Tort reform Movement to modify tort concepts through legislative enactment.

Tortfeasor Person who allegedly committed a tort or engaged in socially unreasonable conduct that harmed another.

Treason Defined by the U.S. Constitution, Article 3, Section 3, as levying war against the United States by adhering to its enemies or giving them aid and comfort. Conviction requires two witnesses or confession in open court.

Trespasser One who without permission enters on the property of another without any right, lawful authority, or an express or implied invitation or license.

Trial courts   Decide cases or controversies involving facts in dispute or questions of law in dispute. Juries are frequently given the capacity to decide questions of fact in dispute. The judge decides all questions of law in dispute.

U.S. Court of Federal Claims   Unique court that has jurisdiction over all claims against the United States where Congress has given authority to sue for claims, including contracts with the United States.

U.S. courts of appeals   The intermediate appeals courts in the federal system.

U.S. Supreme Court   The court of last resort in all cases involving federal law.

Under color of law doctrine   Federal statute prohibiting denial of constitutional rights under a disguise or pretext of law.

Uniform Commercial Code   An attempt to codify the common law of commercial transactions that is now adopted in some form by all states in the United States.

Uniform Electronic Transaction Act (UETA)   Model legislation adopted by most states to validate commercial electronic transactions concerning records and signatures.

Verdict   Formal decision or finding made by a jury concerning the matters of fact submitted to them.

Visitation rights   The parent who does not receive legal or primary custody usually will receive reasonable opportunity to these rights.

Voir dire   Preliminary examination of jurors, or witnesses, to challenge their qualifications to serve in such capacities.

Voluntary assumption of a known risk   In which the plaintiff voluntarily assumed a know risk.

Writ of certiorari   Order by the appellate court that is used when the court has discretion regarding whether or not to hear the appeal. An order to have lower court records sent to higher court for review. It requires the approval of four Justices to be reviewed by the U.S. Supreme Court.

Writ of error   Issued from a court of appellate jurisdiction, directed to the judge of the court of record requiring the court to remit to the appellate court the record of an action before them in which the final judgment has been entered.

Wrongful death and survival statutes   A cause of action in favor of decedent's personal representative for the benefit of certain beneficiaries.

Index